EU and UK Competition Law

PEARSON

At Pearson, we take learning personally. Our courses and resources are available as books, online and via multi-lingual packages, helping people learn whatever, wherever and however they choose.

We work with leading authors to develop the strongest learning experiences, bringing cutting-edge thinking and best learning practice to a global market. We craft our print and digital resources to do more to help learners not only understand their content, but to see it in action and apply what they learn, whether studying or at work.

Pearson is the world's leading learning company. Our portfolio includes Penguin, Dorling Kindersley, the Financial Times and our educational business, Pearson International. We are also a leading provider of electronic learning programmes and of test development, processing and scoring services to educational institutions, corporations and professional bodies around the world.

Every day our work helps learning flourish, and wherever learning flourishes, so do people.

To learn more please visit us at: www.pearson.com/uk

EU and UK Competition Law

Second Edition

Cosmo Graham

University of Leicester

PEARSON

Harlow, England • London • New York • Boston • San Francisco • Toronto • Sydney
Auckland • Singapore • Hong Kong • Tokyo • Seoul • Taipei • New Delhi
Cape Town • São Paulo • Mexico City • Madrid • Amsterdam • Munich • Paris • Milan

PEARSON EDUCATION LIMITED
Edinburgh Gate
Harlow CM20 2JE
United Kingdom
Tel: +44 (0)1279 623623
Fax: +44 (0)1279 431059
Web: www.pearson.com/uk

First published 2010 (print)
Second Edition published 2013 (print and electronic)

Contains public sector information licensed under the Open Government Licence (OGL) v1.0.
www.nationalarchives.gov.uk/doc/open-government-licence.

Pearson Education is not responsible for the content of third-party internet sites.

ISBN: 978-1-4479-0444-1 (print)
       978-1-4479-0445-8 (PDF)
       978-1-292-00341-2 (eText)

British Library Cataloguing-in-Publication Data
A catalogue record for the print edition is available from the British Library

Library of Congress Cataloging-in-Publication Data
Graham, Cosmo.
  EU and UK competition law / Cosmo Graham. -- Second Edition.
    pages cm
  ISBN 978-1-4479-0444-1 (pbk.)
  1. Antitrust law -- Great Britain. 2. Antitrust law -- European Union countries. 3. Antitrust law -- United States.
I. Title. II. Title: European Union and United Kingdom competition law.
  KD2218.G73 2013
  343.4107'24--dc23

                                                                              2013002364

10 9 8 7 6 5 4 3 2 1
16 15 14 13 12

Print edition typeset in 9/12.5pt ITC Giovanni by 35
Print edition printed and bound in Great Britain by Ashford Colour Press Ltd, Gosport, Hampshire

NOTE THAT ANY PAGE CROSS-REFERENCES REFER TO THE PRINT EDITION

Brief contents

Contents

Companion Website

For open-access **student resources** specifically written to complement this textbook and support your learning, please visit **www.pearsoned.co.uk/legalupdates**

Preface

There have been some significant changes to this second edition. The order of the chapters has been changed and they have also undergone some re-structuring. I have also added some material which gives an indication of how American antitrust law approaches certain problems.

The book is still aimed primarily at undergraduate competition law students in the UK, although I hope it will be helpful to anyone approaching the subject for the first time. Like all textbooks it is just a starting point; there is no substitute for reading the primary sources and the secondary journal literature.

Competition law is a topic that is constantly changing. Sometimes these changes are incremental, for example, the changes to the block exemptions and associated guidelines that have occurred since the first edition. Sometimes they are more radical, for example, the UK Government's proposed merger of the Office of Fair Trading and the Competition Commission, or the European Commission's response to the financial crisis which began in 2008. I have attempted to incorporate all these changes up until 1st September 2012.

I would like to thank again my editors at Pearson, Cheryl Cheasley, Donna Goddard and Tim Parker, for their assistance and, again, patience. My sons managed to stop playing and watching DOTA on the main computer at home sufficiently for me to work on the book. Above all, Tina managed to put up with me writing it and has been, as ever, a constant source of support and encouragement.

Tables of equivalences

Treaty on European Union (TEU) as amended by the Treaty of Lisbon: from 1 December 2009	Treaty on European Union (TEU) or European Communities Treaty (EC): from 1 May 1999 to 30 November 2009	Treaty of Rome: from 1 January 1958 to 30 April 1999
Article 3 TEU	Article 2 EC	Article 2
Article 4, para 3	Article 10 EC	Article 5
Article 6 TEU	Article 6 TEU	No equivalent
Article 19, para 1 TEU	Article 220 EC	Article 164
Article 19, paragraph 2, first subparagraph	Article 221, para 1 EC	Article 165
Article 19, paragraph 2, second subparagraph	Article 224 EC The first sentence of the first subparagraph	Article 168a

Treaty on the Functioning of the European Union (TFEU): from 1 December 2009	European Communities Treaty: from 1 May 1999 to 30 November 2009	Treaty of Rome: from 1 January 1958 to 30 April 1999
Articles 3–6 TFEU and Article 8 (para 2). Note also Protocol 27 on the internal market and competition	Article 3	Article 3
Article 14	Article 16	No equivalent
Article 18	Article 12	Article 6
Article 37	Article 31	Article 37
Article 93	Article 73	Article 77
Article 101	Article 81	Article 85
Article 102	Article 82	Article 86
Article 103	Article 83	Article 87
Article 104	Article 84	Article 88
Article 105	Article 85	Article 89
Article 106	Article 86	Article 90
Article 107	Article 87	Article 92
Article 108	Article 88	Article 93
Article 109	Article 89	Article 94
Article 119	Article 4	Article 3a
Article 246	Article 215	
Article 251 now contains paras 2 and 3	Article 221, paras 2 and 3	Article 165
Article 254	Article 224 (except first sentence of first subparagraph)	Article 168a
Article 258	Article 226	Article 169
Article 259	Article 227	Article 170
Article 263	Article 230	Article 173
Article 265	Article 232	Article 175
Article 267	Article 234	Article 177
Article 268	Article 235	Article 178
Article 296	Article 253	Article 190
Article 340	Article 288	Article 215
Article 346	Article 296	Article 223
Article 352	Article 308	Article 235

Guided tour

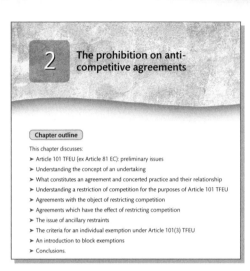

Chapter outline

This chapter discusses:

➤ Article 101 TFEU (ex Article 81 EC): preliminary issues
➤ Understanding the concept of an undertaking
➤ What constitutes an agreement and concerted practice and their relationship
➤ Understanding a restriction of competition for the purposes of Article 101 TFEU
➤ Agreements with the object of restricting competition
➤ Agreements which have the effect of restricting competition
➤ The issue of ancillary restraints
➤ The criteria for an individual exemption under Article 101(3) TFEU
➤ An introduction to block exemptions
➤ Conclusions.

Summary

➤ The subject of competition law is the regulation of markets in order to ensure that they remain competitive. There are three main areas of concern: anti-competitive agreements, abuse of dominant position and merger control. EU law is also concerned with controlling state activities to prevent the distortion of competition.

➤ Historically, the objectives of systems of competition law have varied including both economic and non-economic objectives.

➤ A fundamental objective of EU competition law has been to ensure that private undertakings are not allowed to partition the European market into national segments and this goal explains much of the past case law.

➤ There is a widespread consensus today that the purpose of competition law is to protect consumer welfare and that non-economic goals do not have a place within competition law. This is most clear within UK competition law but is also seen within EU competition law.

➤ The benefits of competitive markets, as opposed to monopolies, are that they bring about allocative and productive efficiency.

➤ The definition of a market is a key part of any competition law inquiry. The product market is determined by looking, first, at demand-side substitution and then at supply-side substitution.

➤ Competition law is enforced through public agencies or private litigation. In the UK and EU, historically public enforcement has taken priority.

Look at the **chapter outlines** at the beginning of each chapter, outlining the main topics you will be covering. You can use these, during the course of your reading, as a checklist of the concepts with which you should be familiar.

End of chapter **summaries** draw together the key points you will particularly need to be aware of following your reading of any chapter.

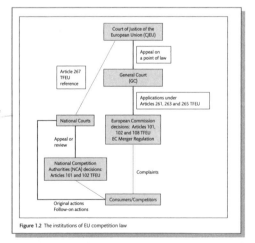

Figure 1.2 The institutions of EU competition law

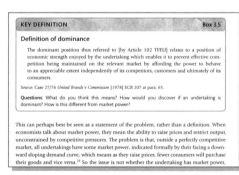

Diagrams and **flowcharts** are used throughout to highlight complex legal processes and models within the EU and UK legal systems.

Key definitions feature throughout to assist you with complex economic terms and legal jargon.

A full **Glossary** of key economic terms located at the back of the book can be used throughout your reading to clarify unfamiliar vocabulary.

Glossary of economic terms

Note: Glossary terms followed by '(OECD)' are taken or adapted from the OECD website at *http://stats.oecd.org/glossary/index.htm* and are from the original source publication *Glossary of Industrial Organisation Economics and Competition Law*, compiled by R.S. Khemani and D.M. Shapiro, commissioned by the Directorate for Financial, Fiscal and Enterprise Affairs, OECD, 1993. Copyright OECD. Glossary terms followed by '(CC)' are taken or adapted from *Merger references: Competition Commission Guidelines*, June 2003. Copyright Competition Commission 2003.

Allocative efficiency This state occurs when resources are so allocated that it is not possible to make anyone better off without making someone else worse off. (OECD)

Anti-competitive agreements Agreement refers to an explicit or implicit arrangement between firms normally in competition with each other to their mutual benefit. Agreements to restrict competition may cover such matters as prices, production, markets and customers. (OECD)

Competition Law in Practice boxes in every chapter provide you with relevant examples of the law in action, to help you identify legal issues, analysis and application in context.

COMPETITION LAW IN PRACTICE

Recent examples

British Airways/Virgin and fuel surcharges
Between 2004 and 2006 British Airways and Virgin Atlantic colluded over the price of fuel surcharges for long-haul flights, mainly from the UK to New York. Over that period, the surcharges rose from £5 to £60 per ticket for a typical BA or Virgin Atlantic long-haul return flight. In other words, the companies concerned agreed between themselves what they would charge for these surcharges, rather than setting the price independently. British Airways was fined a record £121.5 million by the Office of Fair Trading (OFT), although Virgin Atlantic was not fined because it had given information to the OFT about the arrangement. In addition to this corporate liability, four executives of BA were charged by the OFT with criminal offences[2] flowing from these actions. The case was heard in mid 2010 and collapsed when it became apparent that a significant number of emails had not been disclosed to the defence (they were in files that were thought to be corrupted but were later recovered).[3] This investigation was undertaken in parallel with a similar case brought by the US Department of Justice which involved British Airways and Korean Airlines, as well as Virgin Atlantic and Lufthansa, and covered cargo flights, as well as passenger flights. Under US law, this was a criminal investigation and British Airways and Korean Airlines admitted breaching competition law and agreed to pay separate US $300 million fines.[4] In addition, as part of a settlement of a court case brought against them in the US, the airlines concerned set up a website which provided refunds to passengers who had paid the fuel surcharges with a potential liability of up to around £73 million.[5] Furthermore, BA was unsuccessfully sued in the UK courts by an importer of cut flowers, which claimed that it was damaged by the arrangements in relation to cargo flights.[6]

Supermarkets and dairy products
The OFT has also conducted an investigation into the allegation that large supermarkets and dairy processors colluded to increase the prices of dairy products, which the OFT estimated led to a cost to consumers of around £270 million. This case involved Asda, Safeway (prior to its acquisition by Morrisons), Sainsbury and Tesco, as well as dairy processors Arla, Dairy Crest, Lactalis McLelland, The Cheese Company and Wiseman. The OFT issued a Statement of Objections in September 2007 which provisionally found that these supermarkets and dairy processors engaged in fixing the retail prices for milk, butter and cheese, in breach of the Competition Act 1998, by sharing highly commer-

KEY CASE EXTRACT   Box 1.13

Definition of the geographic market

Source: Case T-219/99 *British Airways v Commission* [2004] 4 CMLR 1008 at para. 108:

... the geographic market ... may be defined as the territory in which all traders operate in the same or sufficiently homogeneous conditions of competition in so far as concerns specifically the relevant products or services, without it being necessary for those conditions to be perfectly homogeneous.

Questions: Think of examples of geographic markets. Is the market for recorded music local, regional, national or worldwide? What about supermarkets?

Key legal provisions, Key case extracts and **Key official extracts** are highlighted throughout the text to provide you with up to date case examples and interesting points for discussion. These are accompanied by questions from the author to stretch you further.

KEY LEGAL PROVISION   Box 2.10

Agreements with no appreciable effect on competition

No appreciable restriction for:

– *Horizontal agreements*: if the combined market share of the parties does not exceed 10%

– *Vertical agreements*: if the combined market share of the parties does not exceed 15%

– *Networks of agreements*: if the combined market share is less than 5% and the networks cover less than 30% of the relevant market.

This does not apply:
● in the case of an agreement between *competing undertakings* if there is a provision which:

– directly or indirectly fixes prices, shares markets or limits production, or
● in the case of an agreement between *non-competing undertakings* containing a provision which:

Tables and **graphs** of key statistics illustrate past and emerging trends to show you how competition law operates in practice.

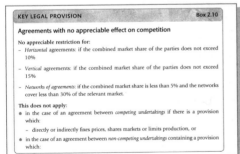

Table 10.1 The prisoner's dilemma

	Confess	Don't confess	
Prisoner A	5, 5	0, 10	Confess
Prisoner B	10, 0	0, 0	Don't confess

Table 10.2 Profit and the prisoner's dilemma

	High Price	Low Price	
Company A	6, 6	2, 10	High Price
Company B	10, 2	2, 2	Low Price

uncertainty, the best move for either prisoner to make is to confess because that provides the least worst outcome, no matter what the other prisoner does. This idea can be adapted for an oligopolistic market with the outcomes being measured in profit, which would produce Table 10.2.

customer groups, for instance to reach customers in one's own territory, are considered passive sales. General advertising or promotion is considered a reasonable way to reach such customers if it would be attractive for the buyer to undertake those investments also if they would not reach customers in other distributors' (exclusive) territories or customer groups.

Source: European Commission, *Guidelines on Vertical Restraints* (n. 5) at para. 51.

Question: How useful is this distinction in the age of Internet selling?

Questions tied to key features throughout ask you to think further on sources within the book, encouraging you to develop your analytical skills and reflect on the implications of what you have read.

➤ The benefit of the block exemption may be withdrawn from particular agreements by the Commission or a national competition authority. The Commission may decide that the BER does not apply to certain categories of vertical agreements.

Further reading

Official publications

European Commission Regulation (EC) No. 330/2010 on the application of Article 101(3) TFEU to categories of vertical agreements and concerted practices, L102/1, 23.04.2010. *The core rules on how vertical agreements are to be treated.*

European Commission, Guidelines on Vertical Restraints, OJ C130/01, 19.05.2010. *Exposition of Commission's approach to vertical agreements in general, as well as its interpretation of the BER.*

Other

Dethmers, F. and de Boer, P.P., 'Ten Years On: Vertical agreements under Article 81' (2009) 30 European Competition Law Review 424. *Critical assessment of the Guidelines and the BER, pointing out what the authors see as certain problems that need a solution.*

Dobson, P. and Waterson, M., Vertical Restraints and Competition Policy (OFT, London, 1996). *Although dated, excellent and accessible introduction to the economic issues involved.*

Goyder, J., EU Distribution Law (6th edn, Hart Publishing, 2011). *Comprehensive discussion of the law.*

Hawk, B., 'System Failure: Vertical restraints and EC Competition Law' (1995) 32 Common Market Law Review 973. *The classic criticism of the Commission's previous approach to vertical agreements.*

Trade and Industry Select Committee, Pub Companies (2004) HC 128-I. *Official investigation of a controversial area dominated by vertical agreements. Chapters 6–9 in particular.*

Each chapter ends with a **Further Reading** section to direct you to further resources available, allowing you to delve deeper into the subject.

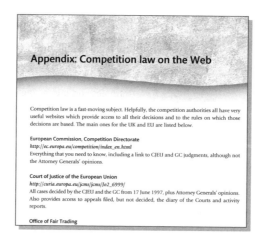

Appendix: Competition law on the Web

Competition law is a fast-moving subject. Helpfully, the competition authorities all have very useful websites which provide access to all their decisions and to the rules on which those decisions are based. The main ones for the UK and EU are listed below.

European Commission, Competition Directorate
http://ec.europa.eu/competition/index_en.html
Everything that you need to know, including a link to CJEU and GC judgments, although not the Attorney Generals' opinions.

Court of Justice of the European Union
http://curia.europa.eu/jcms/jcms/Jo2_6999/
All cases decided by the CJEU and the GC from 17 June 1997, plus Attorney Generals' opinions. Also provides access to appeals filed, but not decided, the diary of the Courts and activity reports.

Office of Fair Trading

You can also use the **Competition Law on the Web** section at the back of the book to find out what sources and relevant further reading is available online.

Acknowledgements

We are grateful to the following for permission to reproduce copyright material:

Tables

Table 4.1 from *The Economics of EC Competition Law*, 2nd ed., Sweet and Maxwell (Bishop, S. and Walker, M. 2002) p. 209.

Text

Box 3.10 from *EU Competition Law*, 4th ed. Oxford University Press (Jones, A. and Sufrin, B. 2011) pp. 389–90. By permission of Oxford University Press.

In some instances we have been unable to trace the owners of copyright material, and we would appreciate any information that would enable us to do so.

Table of cases

Table of European legislation

Directives

Table of UK legislation

Table of US legislation

Table of international agreements

1 Introduction to competition law and policy

Introduction

Everyone reading this book will have had experience of buying and selling goods and services on a market. Everyday life, certainly in western industrialised countries, is dominated by market transactions; we buy food, clothing, entertainment, transport and many other things through markets. We assume that these markets give us choices, and we complain when we think that this is not the case. What we do not do is to think about how or why the markets are competitive and what keeps them so, although we recognise that sometimes markets are not competitive; there may only be one supplier or all the firms within the market may have agreed to offer the same product at the same price. The aim of competition law is to try and prevent agreements between or conduct by companies with substantial market power[1] which unreasonably restricts the operation of competition on a market. Some recent examples of anti-competitive action are illustrated below. The examples indicate that large sums of money are at stake in competition law, both in terms of possible penalties and estimates of the damage to consumers, and that a wide range of everyday products and services may be covered by competition law.

---

[1] In other words, companies which have a major presence on a market, up to a monopoly. At what point a company has such market power is a highly controversial issue.

COMPETITION LAW IN PRACTICE

Recent examples

British Airways/Virgin and fuel surcharges

Between 2004 and 2006 British Airways and Virgin Atlantic colluded over the price of fuel surcharges for long-haul flights, mainly from the UK to New York. Over that period, the surcharges rose from £5 to £60 per ticket for a typical BA or Virgin Atlantic long-haul return flight. In other words, the companies concerned agreed between themselves what they would charge for these surcharges, rather than setting the price independently. British Airways was fined a record £121.5 million by the Office of Fair Trading (OFT), although Virgin Atlantic was not fined because it had given information to the OFT about the arrangement. In addition to this corporate liability, four executives of BA were charged by the OFT with criminal offences[2] flowing from these actions. The case was heard in mid 2010 and collapsed when it became apparent that a signficant number of emails had not been disclosed to the defence (they were in files that were thought to be corrupted but were later recovered).[3] This investigation was undertaken in parallel with a similar case brought by the US Department of Justice which involved British Airways and Korean Airlines, as well as Virgin Atlantic and Lufthansa, and covered cargo flights, as well as passenger flights. Under US law, this was a criminal investigation and British Airways and Korean Airlines admitted breaching competition law and agreed to pay separate US $300 million fines.[4] In addition, as part of a settlement of a court case brought against them in the US, the airlines concerned set up a website which provided refunds to passengers who had paid the fuel surcharges with a potential liability of up to around £73 million.[5] Furthermore, BA was unsuccessfully sued in the UK courts by an importer of cut flowers, which claimed that it was damaged by the arrangements in relation to cargo flights.[6]

Supermarkets and dairy products

The OFT has also conducted an investigation into the allegation that large supermarkets and dairy processors colluded to increase the prices of dairy products, which the OFT estimated led to a cost to consumers of around £270 million. This case involved Asda, Safeway (prior to its acquisition by Morrisons), Sainsbury and Tesco, as well as dairy processors Arla, Dairy Crest, Lactalis McLelland, The Cheese Company and Wiseman. The OFT issued a Statement of Objections in September 2007 which provisionally found that these supermarkets and dairy processors engaged in fixing the retail prices for milk, butter and cheese, in breach of the Competition Act 1998, by sharing highly commer- cially sensitive information, including details of the levels of price increases, over a two-year period (2002 and 2003). In response to these allegations, a number of the parties

---

[2] Under s. 188 of the Enterprise Act 2002, the 'cartel offence'.
[3] See *http://www.oft.gov.uk/OFTwork/competition-act-and-cartels/ca98/closure/fuel-surcharges* (accessed 17/01/12).
[4] See OFT Press Release, 1 August 2007 available at: *http://www.oft.gov.uk/news/press/2007/113-07* and Department of Justice Press Release, 1 August 2007 available at: *http://www.usdoj.gov/atr/public/press_releases/2007/224928.htm* (both accessed 17/01/12).
[5] See *https://www.airpassengerrefund.co.uk/* (accessed 17/01/12).
[6] *Emerald Supplies* v *British Airways* [2009] EWHC 741 (Ch) and [2010] EWCA Civ 1284 (CA).

(Asda, Dairy Crest, Safeway (in relation to conduct prior to its acquisition by Morrisons), Sainsbury, Lactalis McClelland, The Cheese Company and Wiseman) admitted involvement in some of the anti-competitive practices and reached an early resolution agreement with the OFT and will in total pay penalties to a maximum of over £116 million. Arla received complete immunity, as it was the first company to alert the OFT to the possible problem and it applied for leniency. Tesco, however, contested the allegations. In 2011, the OFT formally announced that it had found breaches of competition law and fined the companies concerned around £50 million.[7] Tesco has appealed the decision to the Competition Appeal Tribunal. An interesting sideline to this case was that Morrisons threatened to sue the OFT for libel because of the terms of the first press release. The OFT settled the case with an apology and a payment of £100,000 but not until after a High Court judge had accused them of trying to attract 'sensationalist publicity'.[8]

Replica football kit

In 2003, the OFT fined ten businesses a total of £18.6 million for fixing the prices of Umbro replica football kits, primarily for the England kit, although other teams were involved. These businesses included JJB Sports, Umbro, Manchester United and the FA and the result of the investigation was that the price of replica football kits fell and that consumers were able to shop around for a better deal, unlike before, when all retailers were required to charge the same price.[9] A number of the companies concerned appealed, unsuccessfully, against this decision, first to the Competition Appeal Tribunal and then to the Court of Appeal.[10] In addition, the Consumer's Association (Which) brought an action against JJB Sports as a representative of consumers. This claim was settled when JJB Sports agreed to compensate consumers who bought football shirts at inflated prices contrary to the competition rules. Press reports suggested that there were 600 consumers who had joined the action and that the total cost to JJB would be in the region of £20,000 as opposed to an original fine of £6.7 million.[11] Issues about anti-competitive activity in this sector arose again, when it became public that the OFT was investigating JJB and Sports Direct for suspected price fixing.[12] The OFT closed this investigation, largely on the grounds that the chances of proving an infringement were too low.[13]

Box 1.1 indicates the core issues for competition law and the legal provisions which cover them. As we shall see later, competition law in the European Union (EU) also attempts to control the actions of states that will damage competition, as well as the activities of private parties.

---

[7] See *http://www.oft.gov.uk/OFTwork/competition-act-and-cartels/ca98-current/dairy-products/* (accessed 17/01/12) and the links to the press releases.

[8] *The Daily Telegraph*, 24 April 2008 and see *http://www.oft.gov.uk/news/press/2008/54-08* (accessed 17/01/12).

[9] See OFT Press Release, 1 August 2003 available at: *http://www.oft.gov.uk/news/press/2003/pn_107-03* and OFT 'Football kit price fixing' available at: *http://www.oft.gov.uk/OFTwork/competition-act-and-cartels/ca98/decisions/football-kit* (both accessed 17/01/12).

[10] *Argos, Littlewoods et al.* v *Office of Fair Trading* [2006] EWCA Civ 1318.

[11] The *Financial Times*, 10 January 2008.

[12] *The Guardian*, 10 September 2009.

[13] See OFT Press Release, 17 October 2011 available at: *http://www.oft.gov.uk/OFTwork/competition-act-and-cartels/ca98/closure/sports-goods/* (accessed 17/01/12).

KEY LEGAL PROVISIONS Box 1.1

The core competition law problems and the provisions that deal with them

Anti-competitive agreements: Article 101 TFEU (ex Art. 81 EC) and s. 2 of the Competition Act 1998 (the Chapter I prohibition).

Anti-competitive conduct by companies with a strong market position: Article 102 TFEU (ex Art. 82 EC) and s. 18 of the Competition Act 1998 (the Chapter II prohibition) – generally referred to as abuse of a dominant position.

Mergers which will substantially reduce competition: Council Regulation 139/2004 EC and Part 3 of the Enterprise Act 2002.

Question: Should the regulation of state activity be considered a core part of competition law?

This chapter begins with a brief overview of the history of competition law in the European Union, the United Kingdom and the United States, tracing the evolution of policy objectives from a mix of differing ideas to the present day consensus, among competition agencies, that what is important is consumer welfare. What consumer welfare means is not intuitively obvious (for a definition, see Box 1.2), and the next section of the chapter outlines the insights of economics which underpin this consensus, as well as illustrating the tensions within it that cause problems in its application in practice. Having set out the objectives of competition law, the next stage is a description of the institutions responsible for enforcing the law and their relationships. The chapter ends by discussing the relationship between European Union[14] and United Kingdom competition law, in order that the reader can appreciate where the boundary between the two lies.

KEY DEFINITION Box 1.2

Consumer welfare

Consumer welfare refers to the individual benefits derived from the consumption of goods and services . . . In practice, applied welfare economics uses the notion of consumer surplus to measure consumer welfare . . . In anti-trust applications, some argue that the goal is to maximize consumers' surplus, while others argue that producer benefits should also be counted.

Source: OECD at *http://stats.oecd.org/glossary/detail.asp?ID=3177* (accessed 17/01/12).

Questions: Should competition law be concerned with maximising consumer welfare or the welfare of society? Is this all competition law should be concerned about?

---

[14] From 1958 until 1993 what is now the EU was the European Economic Community. From 1993 until December 2009 this became the European Community.

Objectives of competition law and policy

It is, of course, possible to envisage a system of competition law which has only one major objective. This is the argument of the late Robert Bork, a very influential American competition law professor who served as a federal judge for a period and was nominated, unsuccessfully, for the Supreme Court, when he puts forward the idea that the only legitimate goal of anti-trust, the American term for competition law, in the United States was the maximisation of consumer welfare.[15] What is striking, however, if we look at the history of competition law in the European Union, Britain and the United States is that there have been multiple goals and objectives from the beginning of each of these systems and that views on the appropriate objectives for competition law have changed over time to the point where it is only recently that there seems to be a reasonable consensus on the main objectives of competition law. One way of approaching this issue is to look, briefly, at the history of competition law in these three jurisdictions because the history illustrates the possible objectives and the gradual convergence towards some sort of consensus. In relation to the European Union and deci-sions of its courts, it is important to bear this history in mind.

History of US antitrust law

Modern American antitrust law dates from the Sherman Act 1890, which remains in force today. This Act was passed in the context of major changes to the American economy in the late nineteenth century with the growth of large corporations, or what were then known as 'trusts', which began to have an important influence on significant parts of the American economy. The activities of these large corporations or trusts were politically highly controversial and pressure was placed on Congress to produce a federal law to regulate their activities, following in part the example of some states. The classic example was Standard Oil, which was initially organised as a form of trust. At its peak it controlled around 90% of oil produc-tion in the United States and it was heavily criticised for the practices it used to obtain and maintain this market position. The Sherman Act was produced against this background and its main provisions can be seen in Box 1.3. The Act provides no definition of its key terms, such as 'restraint of trade', and left enforcement up to the federal courts on the basis of actions brought either by the US government or private plaintiffs and a complex and elaborate body of case law has come to be erected on these foundations.

What was Congress intending to accomplish with this statute? Bork has argued that, if the legislative history is examined, then the aim of Congress was to protect consumer welfare.[16] This is a controversial position, not least because modern economics was only just beginning to be developed at the time, and there are alternative, and probably historically more accurate, views that Congress had other objectives in mind at the time of passing this legislation as well as concerns about economic efficiency.

As an alternative, it has been argued that one of the objectives of the Sherman Act was to prevent the large corporations and trusts from attaining private power and, in so doing, to

---

[15] R. Bork, *The Antitrust Paradox* (2nd edn, Free Press, New York, 1993), p. 51.

[16] Bork (n. 15), ch. 2 and R. Bork, 'Legislative Intent and the Policy of the Sherman Act' (1966) 9 *Journal of Law and Economics* 7.

preserve democratic government.[17] In some respects this is a uniquely American argument, stemming in part from the close relationship between large business and politicians at the turn of the twentieth century, which still exists in some form today. Nevertheless, it is worth noting because it is a theme which underpins the intellectual foundations of European Union competition policy, although never articulated very explicitly,[18] and underpinning the economic arguments about the objectives of competition law is the idea that in a perfectly competitive market firms do not have power. Another suggestion has been that the aim of the Sherman Act was to prevent the unfair redistribution of wealth from consumers to producers.[19]

KEY LEGAL PROVISIONS   Box 1.3

Sherman Act, ss. 1 and 2

1   Every contract, combination in the form of trust or otherwise, or conspiracy, in restraint of trade or commerce among several States, or with foreign nations, is hereby declared to be illegal. [Violators] . . . shall be deemed guilty of a felony . . .

2   Every person who shall monopolize, or attempt to monopolize, or combine and conspire with any other person or persons, to monopolize any part of the trade or commerce among the several States, or with foreign nations, shall be deemed guilty of a felony.

Questions: All contracts restrict the freedom of parties to them. Are all contracts therefore in restraint of trade? How would you distinguish unreasonable restraints from normal commercial dealing? How would you distinguish an attempt to monopolise from normal commercial practice?

A second argument in relation to the Sherman Act is that it was passed at the behest of small businesses and the aim of this legislation was to protect their position.[20] This is an important idea and one that has been very influential in the development of competition law, particularly in the United States but also in the European Union. Intuitively, when we think of a competitive market we think of one that has many buyers and sellers in it. To put it another way, commonsense ideas of competitive markets tend to assume that small businesses are an important component of them and that the activities of large businesses which drive out small businesses will make the markets less competitive. We will, however, see that economic analysis cautions us against identifying the interests of small businesses with a competitive market.

The Sherman Act was followed in 1907 by the Clayton Act, which dealt with mergers and set up the Federal Trade Commission, and later on by the Robinson-Patman Act 1936,

---

[17] See D. Millon, 'The Sherman Act and the Balance of Power' (1988) 61 *Southern California Law Review* 1219; R. Hofstadter, 'What Happened to the Antitrust Movement?' in E.T. Sullivan (ed.) *The Political Economy of the Sherman Act* (Oxford University Press, 1991); and E. Fox, 'The Modernisation of Antitrust: A New Equilibrium' (1981) 66 *Cornell Law Review* 1140 at 1153.

[18] See G. Amato, *Antitrust and the Bounds of Power* (Hart Publishing, Oxford, 1997) at pp. 40–1 and 113–14.

[19] R.H. Lande, 'Wealth Transfers as the Original and Primary Concern of Antitrust: The Efficiency Interpretation Challenged' (1982) 34 *Hastings Law Journal* 65.

[20] See T.J. DiLorenzo, 'The Origins of Antitrust: An Interest Group Perspective' (1985) 5 *International Review of Law and Economics* 73; T.W. Hazlett, 'The Legislative history of the Sherman Act Re-examined' (1992) 30 *Economic Inquiry* 263; H. Hovenkamp, *The Antitrust Enterprise* (Harvard University Press, 2005), pp. 39–42.

dealing with price discrimination, and an important amendment of the merger rules in 1950 through what is known as the Cellar-Kefauver Act. Hovenkamp, a distinguished American antitrust scholar, has argued that if you look at the context of these Acts and their legislative history, these statutes are aimed at protecting small businesses.[21] This basic approach to antitrust seems to have been reflected in decisions of the American courts, particularly during the time of the Supreme Court led by Chief Justice Earl Warren (1953–69). Support in economic theory came from a group of economists known as the 'Harvard School' whose work, based primarily on empirical studies of particular industries, emphasised the importance of the structure of particular markets and was sceptical about the claims of efficiency of large corporations going to the point, indeed, of suggesting that government be given power to break up large corporations, even if they had not committed a breach of the antitrust laws.

From the 1960s there was a reaction against this approach to antitrust law, led by a group of scholars referred to as the 'Chicago School' because they were in various ways associated with University of Chicago. Unlike the Harvard School economists of the 1950s and 1960s who focused on industrial structure, Chicago School thinkers started by looking at specific questions and tried to explain business behaviour with the insights of economic theory. This led them to what Posner, a distinguished American antitrust scholar and federal court judge, has called a conclusion of great significance, namely that firms cannot in general obtain or enhance monopoly power by unilateral action. This meant that the focus of antitrust should be on price by fixing agreements between competitors and mergers which would lead to monopoly or make it easier to enter into price-fixing agreements by drastically reducing the number of sellers in the market.[22]

This analysis proved to be very influential in American thinking throughout the 1970s and 1980s, and also crossed to Europe, and reoriented the thrust of antitrust policy towards a focus on consumer welfare and away from a concern with the protection of small businesses and the dispersion of private economic power. In so doing, it helped to bring the case law closer to the insights of economic analysis. It did, however, become apparent that the possibilities for anti-competitive behaviour were wider than the Chicago School or at least some of its adherents recognised, given the imperfections of markets and the strategic behaviour of firms within these markets. This has not led to a return to non-economic values or to protecting small businesses but to a sharpening of the tools of economic analysis. Today the consensus in America is summarised by Hovenkamp: 'Few people dispute that antitrust's core mission is protecting consumers' right to the low prices, innovation, and diverse production that competition promises.'[23]

European Union competition law

The history of the Treaty Articles

Although competition policy has been a part of the European Union since the Coal and Steel Community began (1951) and the founding of the European Economic Community through

---

[21] Hovenkamp (n. 20) at p. 42.

[22] R. Posner, 'The Chicago School of Antitrust Analysis' (1979) 127 *University of Pennsylvania Law Review* 925 at 928.

[23] Hovenkamp (n. 20) at p. 1. See also the Antitrust Modernisation Commission, *Report and Recommendations* (2007) at pp. 2–3 available at: *http://govinfo.library.unt.edu/amc/report_recommendation/toc.htm* (accessed 17/01/12).

the Treaty of Rome in 1957, the historical background and the discussions surrounding it remain shrouded in mystery, in part because the minutes and documents underlying the Treaty of Rome are not in the public domain.[24] The six original members of the Coal and Steel Community and the European Economic Community[25] had no experience of competition law in their history. It was only in 1958 that the Germans passed their law on the control of concentrations, that is, mergers, on the same day that the Treaty of Rome was signed. What then were the original Member States trying to do by including provisions on competition in these two Treaties?

As far as the Coal and Steel Treaty is concerned, there was pressure from the United States to have provisions relating to the control of cartels.[26] Although this explains how two Articles of the Treaty (65 and 66) dealing with anti-competitive agreements, a form of merger control and the problems created by a dominant position, came to be inserted, it does not explain anything about how they took their form. Although apparently some initial drafting work was undertaken by an American, the provisions of the Coal and Steel Treaty do not obviously reflect American legislation or concepts.

The problem of what these provisions were for becomes more mysterious if we look at the Treaty of Rome (Box 1.4 compares the two Treaties). Two provisions survived in the form of Articles devoted to anti-competitive practices and abuse of a dominant position but the text relating to merger control was dropped. There was also no provision for their enforcement, either by private action, as direct applicability had not been foreseen, or by the European Commission (this came about in 1962). In addition, there was a clear provision in Article 85 (which is now Article 101 TFEU [ex Art. 81 EC]) for the exemption of agreements which met certain conditions and the abuse of dominant position provision became a clear prohibition in the Treaty of Rome (and is now Article 102 TFEU [ex Art. 82 EC]), unlike its original incarnation in the Coal and Steel Treaty, which only allowed for recommendations to be made by the High Authority (the equivalent of the European Commission). Furthermore, the Rome Treaty also contained provisions relating to the ability of Member States to intervene in the operation of competitive markets, notably the provisions regulating the use of state aids to industry as well as what was then the rather gnomic Article 90 (and is now Article 106 TFEU [ex Article 86 EC]) dealing with undertakings with special and exclusive rights, public undertakings and revenue producing monopolies, which went further than the Coal and Steel provisions. This part of the story is not touched upon by Gerber, the leading academic authority on the history of European Union competition law, who focuses almost exclusively on the role played by the then Articles 85 and 86 (now Articles 101 and 102 TFEU), in other words, the regulation of the behaviour of private companies and firms.

---

[24] The most comprehensive treatment is D. Gerber, *Law and Competition in Twentieth Century Europe* (Clarendon Press, Oxford, 1998). See also G. Marenco, 'The Birth of Modern Competition Law in Europe' in A. Bogdandy *et al.*, *European Integration and International Co-ordination* (Kluwer, The Hague, 2002).

[25] Belgium, France, Italy, Luxembourg, The Netherlands and West Germany.

[26] A cartel is defined by the OECD as a formal agreement amongst firms in an oligopolistic industry: that is, an industry with few sellers, classically three to six. There may be agreement on such matters as prices, total industry output, market shares, allocation of customers, allocation of territories, bid-rigging, establishment of common sales agencies, and the division of profits or a combination of these. See: *http://stats.oecd.org/glossary/detail.asp?ID=3157* (accessed 17/01/12).

KEY LEGAL PROVISIONS　　　　　　　　　　　　　　　　　　　　**Box 1.4**

Competition provisions of the Coal and Steel Treaty compared to the EEC Treaty

ECSC Treaty	EEC Treaty
Article 60 Prohibition of unfair and discriminatory pricing practices	Article 85 Prohibition of anti-competitive agreements
Article 65 Prohibition of anti-competitive agreements	Article 86 Prohibition of abuse of a dominant position
Article 66 Control of mergers Power to make recommendations to enterprises in a dominant position to prevent use of that position for purposes contrary to the Treaty	

Question: Why are these different?

The text of Articles 101 and 102 TFEU is outlined below.

KEY LEGAL PROVISIONS　　　　　　　　　　　　　　　　　　　　**Box 1.5**

Text of Articles 101 and 102 TFEU

Article 101

1　The following shall be prohibited as incompatible with the internal market: all agreements between undertakings, decisions by associations of undertakings and concerted practices which may affect trade between Member States and which have as their object or effect the prevention, restriction or distortion of competition within the internal market, and in particular those which:

(a)　directly or indirectly fix purchase or selling prices or any other trading conditions;

(b)　limit or control production, markets, technical development, or investment;

(c)　share markets or sources of supply;

(d)　apply dissimilar conditions to equivalent transactions with other trading parties, thereby placing them at a competitive disadvantage;

(e)　make the conclusion of contracts subject to acceptance by the other parties of supplementary obligations which, by their nature or according to commercial usage, have no connection with the subject of such contracts.

2　Any agreements or decisions prohibited pursuant to this article shall be automatically void.

➡

3 The provisions of paragraph 1 may, however, be declared inapplicable in the case of:

- any agreement or category of agreements between undertakings,
- any decision or category of decisions by associations of undertakings,
- any concerted practice or category of concerted practices,

which contributes to improving the production or distribution of goods or to promoting technical or economic progress, while allowing consumers a fair share of the resulting benefit, and which does not:

(a) impose on the undertakings concerned restrictions which are not indispensable to the attainment of these objectives;

(b) afford such undertakings the possibility of eliminating competition in respect of a substantial part of the products in question.

Article 102

Any abuse by one or more undertakings of a dominant position within the internal market or in a substantial part of it shall be prohibited as incompatible with the internal market in so far as it may affect trade between Member States.

Such abuse may, in particular, consist in:

(a) directly or indirectly imposing unfair purchase or selling prices or other unfair trading conditions;

(b) limiting production, markets or technical development to the prejudice of consumers;

(c) applying dissimilar conditions to equivalent transactions with other trading parties, thereby placing them at a competitive disadvantage;

(d) making the conclusion of contracts subject to acceptance by the other parties of supplementary obligations which, by their nature or according to commercial usage, have no connection with the subject of such contracts.

Gerber sees Articles 101 and 102 TFEU (see Box 1.5) as being the outcome of a compromise between the German and the French delegations.[27] Although he is less clear about what the French approach to competition law was, he emphasises that the German approach was strongly influenced by a doctrine called 'ordo-liberalism' and, because a number of commentators have highlighted the influence of these ideas on European Union competition law, it is worth more explanation. Ordo-liberalism[28] was a set of ideas originally developed in Germany from the mid 1930s, which was substantially influenced by its founders' interpretations of the rise of Nazism. It was in essence a view about how to organise a society and its economy and it was one that placed the preservation of the competitive process at the centre of its thought, as a way of restraining both governmental and private power. It has been said

[27] Gerber (n. 24) at pp. 333–4. See also H. Schweitzer, 'The History, Interpretation and Underlying Principles of Section 2 Sherman Act and Article 82 EC' in C. Ehlermann and M. Marquis (eds) *European Competition Law Annual 2007* (Hart Publishing, Oxford, 2008). A different view, as regards Article 82, is taken by P. Akman, 'Searching for the Long-lost Soul of Article 82 EC' (2009) 29 *Oxford Journal of Legal Studies* 267.

[28] There is little material in English on Ordo-liberalism. Gerber (n. 24) is the best source, notably chs 7 and 8. See also C. Ahlborn and C. Grave, 'Walter Eucken and Ordoliberalism: An Introduction from a Consumer Welfare Perspective' (2006) 2 *Competition Policy International* 197.

that: 'The actual goal of the competition policy of Ordo-liberalism lies in the protection of individual economic freedom of action as a value in itself, or vice versa, in the restraint of undue economic power.'[29] Effectively this means a concern with competitors and ensuring that they have access to markets, even if this would not result in the most efficient economic outcome.[30] As we shall see (notably in Chapter 3), it has been argued that European Union competition law has, historically, paid too much attention to the interests of competitors as opposed to those of consumers.

Objectives of the European Union

It must also be remembered that the competition provisions of the Treaty of Rome were only a small part of the entire Treaty, which had the larger and more grandiose aim of creating a common market amongst the founder members, although this was to be an economic organisation with distinctly political overtones. Much of the original Treaty was concerned with regulating the activities of the Member States in order to ensure that they did not take decisions which prevented the creation of a common market. This leads to two points which are key to the understanding of European Union competition policy.

First, the fundamental underlying purpose of the European Union has been to create a single European market where the same conditions apply to economic transactions in Portsmouth, Paris or Prague. Therefore, European Union law has always been very hostile to the activities of states which create barriers to trade between states. Controlling the activities of states is only part of the picture; private entities must not be allowed to erect equivalent barriers to trade between states and one of the fundamental objectives of European Union competition law has always been to prevent this happening. European integration or the creation of a single market is a non-economic objective which means that certain decisions may be contrary to economic logic or theory but are defensible from the point of view of integration. To put it another way, if there is a choice between greater integration and economic efficiency, the Treaties direct that integration is to have priority. This is a foundational principle, which explains many decisions of the European Courts and the European Commission and underpins a number of the doctrines. Whether the integration principle should be enforced with such rigour in today's European Union is a separate question, as is the issue of how it can be isolated in relation to UK competition law, insofar as that depends on European Union doctrines.

The second point is that a key part of European Union competition law has always been, at least in theory, about the control of state actions. In addition to Article 90 (now Article 106 TFEU [ex Article 86 EC]), mentioned above, the Treaty of Rome also contained provisions relating to, and limiting, state aids to industry (such as providing grants to British car manufacturers), on the grounds that these were distortions of competition (currently Articles 107–9 TFEU [ex Articles 87–8 EC]). From an American point of view, this is not part of antitrust law at all, because governments are allowed to act in ways that private companies are not. From the European point of view it is something that is of significant importance, especially since the enlargement of the Union in 2004 bringing in a number of central and eastern European countries with a strong history of state intervention in the economy and weak free market

---

[29] W. Möschel, 'Competition Policy from an Ordo Point of View' in A. Peacock and H. Willerodt (eds) *German Neo-liberals and the Social Market Economy* (Macmillan, London, 1989) at p. 146.

[30] See D. Chalmers *et al.*, *European Union Law* (2nd edn, Cambridge University Press, 2010) at p. 917.

traditions. The financial crisis of 2008 also led to a vast increase in state aid to banks and other financial institutions, which has emphasised the importance of this area of work.

In summary, the starting point for European Union competition law was very different from that of the United States. Although there is uncertainty about its beginnings, the foundational ideas were an overriding concern with market integration, a concern with protecting competition as a process, inherited from the German intellectual background and provisions to deal with state intervention in markets. Consumer welfare, on this account, comes in third place.

Although this is the starting point, European Union competition law has not remained static. Its history can very roughly be divided into four phases: the beginnings up until around 1972, development (1972 to around 1990), the 1990s and, finally, the new model, modernised competition law that exists today.[31]

EU competition law until 1972

One of the first questions in relation to the foundation of EU competition law was the question of how it was to be enforced and a decision was taken that enforcement was to be centralised in the European Commission. This meant that all agreements which might restrict competition had to be notified to the Commission and that the Commission was the only body with the power to decide if an agreement which restricted competition could be exempt from the prohibition in Article 101(1) TFEU on the grounds that its benefits outweighed the detriments, as outlined in Article 101(3) TFEU. This monopoly meant that private litigation on anti-competitive agreements could not really take place as parties to allegedly anti-competitive agreements could defend themselves by applying for an exemption to the Commission. Although a procedural matter, this decision was to have profound implications for the development of EU competition law. The Commission started slowly and focused its enforcement efforts on anti-competitive agreements. Most controversially, as well as assessing horizontal agreements, that is, agreements between competitors, the Commission also assessed vertical agreements, that is, agreements between companies at different stages of the production process. The general view amongst economists is that horizontal agreements between competitors represent a greater threat to competition than vertical agreements not made between competitors, which means that the latter should be treated more leniently. Because at this stage the Commission was concerned with preventing private companies from partitioning the common market into national markets, it focused substantial efforts on assessing vertical agreements because it is common to place territorial restrictions in such agreements: for example, an agreement between a manufacturer and a retailer that the retailer will be the only person who sells that manufacturer's products in that region or country. The Commission took a wide view of the interpretation of Article 101 TFEU and the concept of inter-state trade, in which interpretation it was supported by the European Court of Justice. This meant that a large number of commercial agreements had to be notified to the Commission, who were then required to decide upon their legality. This produced an administrative crisis, as the European Commission was unable to provide sufficient legally binding decisions on all the agreements that were notified to it and it began to develop more general rules to allow businesses to know in advance whether their agreements were legal, referred to as block

---

[31] The periodisation is just meant to help illustrate the argument that follows. The best history is again Gerber (n. 24), ch. 9, although his story finishes in roughly 1997 and this account is partly based on his work.

exemptions. The Commission was heavily criticised on two grounds.[32] First, when examining an agreement to see whether it restricted competition it tended to take the view that restrictions on commercial freedom equaled a restriction on competition, rather than conducting an analysis of the actual effects on competition in the market of the agreement. Secondly, the block exemptions that it developed required agreements to meet certain formal criteria, again without considering the economic effects of the agreement, which significantly limited the flexibility available to businesses.

EU competition law 1972–90

The second period from 1972 was notable for the first cases dealing with abuse of dominant position under Article 102 TFEU (that is, unilateral conduct by companies with arguably substantial market power) reaching the European Courts, some very wide-ranging decisions of the Courts and the Commission continuing to develop its work on anti-competitive agreements, as well as engaging in more vigorous enforcement of the competition rules. From about 1990, there were three major developments:

1　The Court of First Instance (CFI), now known as the General Court (GC), was created in 1989 with a brief to hear competition cases at first instance, among other things.

2　The first Merger Control Regulation came into force in 1991, giving the European Commission jurisdiction to rule on certain cross-border measures for the first time, and filling a hole in the competition law system of the European Union.

3　The European Commission began to concentrate more effort on enforcing the competition rules against Member States as well as becoming an advocate for the liberalisation of economies and markets.

EU competition law post 1990s

The final stage can be dated from around 1999, with the implementation of the block exemption Regulation on vertical agreements (a set of general rules about how to treat vertical agreements for the purposes of competition law).[33] Although this topic is discussed in more detail later in the text (Chapters 2 and 11), here we can simply note that the Commission responded to criticisms of its approach to vertical agreements by taking a more economics-based approach to these agreements. This seems to have heralded a change in attitude within the Commission, perhaps brought about by the planned enlargement of the Union in 2004. As part of this, a radically new approach to enforcement was taken, encompassed in Regulation 1/2003,[34] which abandoned the notification system for agreements and in effect delegated much of the enforcement of Union competition law to national competition authorities and national courts, a major move away from the centralised system that had existed for around forty years. In addition, the European Commission has tried to encourage private litigants

---

[32] See B. Hawk, 'System Failure: Vertical Restraints and EC Competition Law' (1995) 32 *Common Market Law Review* 973 and C. Bright, 'EU Competition Policy: Rules, Objectives and Deregulation' (1996) 16 *Oxford Journal of Legal Studies* 535.

[33] Commission Regulation (EC) No. 2790/1999 of 22 December 1999 on the application of Article 81(3) of the Treaty to categories of vertical agreements and concerted practices, OJ L336, 29.12.1999, pp. 21–5.

[34] Council Regulation (EC) No. 1/2003 of 16 December 2002 on the implementation of the rules on competition laid down in Articles 81 and 82 of the Treaty, OJ L1, 04.01.2003, pp. 1–25.

and opened a discussion on improving their position.[35] The guidance that the Commission gave on how it would exercise its discretion in this new system also reflected a more economics-based approach, as well as a Regulation for technology transfer licensing agreements and its accompanying guidance,[36] although issues of market integration did not disappear entirely. This more economic approach was also seen in the European Commission's proposals for a review of the provisions on the abuse of dominance (Article 102 TFEU [ex Art. 82 EC]), where it was said that the objective was the protection of competition on the market as a means of enhancing consumer welfare.[37]

In summary, there have been major changes in the orientation of Union competition law over its fifty-odd years of existence. Having started as a system with integration as its primary rationale, with a secondary objective the protection of the competitive process, backed up by a centralised enforcement system, it then moved to a system where the stated aim was the protection of consumer welfare (see Box 1.6), although issues of integration remained important, with a much more decentralised system of enforcement. It is, however, important to remember this history, as it is very difficult to wipe the slate clean – decisions taken at one point in the history of the European Union still have value, especially court decisions, at later periods.

The effect of the Lisbon Treaty

This interpretation was based on the EC Treaty, in force until December 2009, and the relevant Articles are set out below (in Box 1.7), with perhaps the most important being Article 3(g), which sets out that one of the objectives of the EC was to have a system which ensures that competition in the internal market is not distorted and this has been referred to regularly in the case law of the European courts, as well as the Commission's mission statement (Box 1.6).

KEY OFFICIAL EXTRACT   **Box 1.6**

The objectives of the European Commission

The mission of the Directorate General for Competition is to enforce the competition rules of the Community [Union] Treaties, in order to ensure that competition in the EU market is not distorted and that markets operate as efficiently as possible, thereby contributing to the welfare of consumers and to the competitiveness of the European economy.

Source: DG Comp 'Management Plan 2007' available at: *http://ec.europa.eu/dgs/competition/index_en.htm* (accessed 24/08/12).

---

[35] European Commission 'Damages actions for breach of the EC antitrust rules' (Green Paper) COM (2005) 672, 19.12.2005 and European Commission 'Damages actions for breach of the EC antitrust rules' (White Paper) COM (2008) 165, 02.04.2008.

[36] European Commission, 'Guidelines on the application of Article 81(3) of the Treaty' [2004] OJ C101/8, Commission Regulation (EC) No. 772/2004 of 27 April 2004 on the application of Article 81(3) of the Treaty to categories of technology transfer agreements, OJ L123, 27.04.2004, pp. 11–17, European Commission 'Guidelines on the application of Article 81 of the EC Treaty to technology transfer agreements' OJ C101 27.04.2004, pp. 2–42.

[37] European Commission, *Discussion Paper on the application of Article 82 of the Treaty to exclusionary abuses* (2005) at para. 4. See now European Commission, *Guidance on the Commission's enforcement priorities in applying Article 82 of the EC Treaty to abusive exclusionary conduct by dominant undertakings*, COM (2009) 864 final (9 February 2009).

Compare, however, the most recent statement:

The mission of the Directorate General for Competition (DG Competition) is to enable the Commission to make markets deliver more benefits to consumers, businesses and the society as a whole, by protecting competition on the market and fostering a competition culture. We do this through the enforcement of competition rules and through actions aimed at ensuring that regulation takes competition duly into account among other public policy interests.

Source: DG Comp 'Management plan for 2012', available at: *http://ec.europa.eu/dgs/competition/index_en.htm* (accessed 24/08/12).

On the same point, read the statement below by Neelie Kroes, Competition Commissioner from 2004 to 2009:

Consumer welfare is now well established as the standard the Commission applies when assessing mergers and infringements of the Treaty rules on cartels and monopolies. Our aim is simple: to protect competition in the market as a means of enhancing consumer welfare and ensuring an efficient allocation of resources.

Source: Neelie Kroes, Commissioner for Competition, speech on 15 September 2005, available at: *http:// ec.europa.eu/competition/speeches/index_2005.html* (accessed 17/01/12).

Now compare it with this statement by Joaquin Almunia, Competition Commissioner from 2010:

Our competition policy is the expression of the model born in Europe after World War II and known as 'social market economy'. Competition policy, contrary to what some think, is not about neo-liberalism or the jungle. Its purpose is completely different and positive. Competition policy in Europe is about encouraging entrepreneurship and innovation, the creation of jobs and the placing in the market of innovative products and services that bring choice and competitive prices for the consumer. The role of competition enforcers is to make sure companies play fair, do not gain excessive power and when they acquire power through organic growth, not to abuse it. Competition policy, therefore, has a regulatory role and this role is essential to preserve a social economy and social fairness . . . competition policy is about 'the market when possible, the state where necessary' . . . competition policy seeks to balance the free functioning of the market and public goals. There are many similar examples in which a market economy approach is combined with instruments to promote social cohesion. And this is a successful model.

Source: Joaquin Almunia, Commissioner for Competition, speech on 14 January 2011, available at: *http:// europa.eu/rapid/pressReleasesAction.do?reference=SPEECH/11/17* (accessed 17/01/12).

Questions: In what ways has the interpretation of the Commission's mission changed? To what extent will these change in emphasis make a difference in terms of how EU competition law is enforced? How do you balance the free functioning of the market against public goals?

There is, however, some question as to whether this will remain the approach in the future as the Lisbon Treaty makes substantial changes to these Articles (see Box 1.7 and Box 1.8).

EC Treaty Articles relevant to competition law

Article 2

The Community shall have as its task, by establishing a common market and an economic and monetary union and by implementing common policies or activities referred to in Articles 3 and 4, to promote throughout the Community a harmonious, balanced and sustainable development of economic activities, a high level of employment and of social protection . . . a high degree of competitiveness and the convergence of economic performance.

Article 3

1   For the purposes set out in Article 2, the activities of the Community shall include, . . . :

(c)   an internal market . . .

(g)   a system ensuring that competition in the internal market is not distorted;

   . . .

(k)   the strengthening of economic and social cohesion;

   . . .

(m) the strengthening of the competitiveness of Community industry;

(n)   the promotion of research and technological development;

   . . .

(t)   (a contribution to the strengthening of consumer protection.

Article 4

. . . the adoption of an economic policy . . . conducted in accordance with the principle of an open market economy with free competition.

Question: Are there tensions between these various objectives?

The EC Treaty and the Lisbon Treaty

Existing provisions of the EC Treaty	*Revisions under the Lisbon Treaty*
Article 2 The Community shall have as its task, by establishing a common market and an economic and monetary union and by implementing common policies or activities referred to in Articles 3 and 4, to promote throughout the Community a harmonious, balanced and sustainable development of economic activities, a high level of employment and of social protection . . . a high degree of competitiveness and the convergence of economic performance.	**Treaty on European Union – new Article 3(3)** The Union shall establish an internal market. It shall work for the sustainable development of Europe based on balanced economic growth and price stability, a highly competitive social market economy, aiming at full employment and social progress, and a high level of protection and improvement of the quality of the environment.

Existing provisions of the EC Treaty	Revisions under the Lisbon Treaty
	PROTOCOL (No. 27) ON THE INTERNAL MARKET AND COMPETITION THE HIGH CONTRACTING PARTIES, CONSIDERING that the internal market as set out in Article 3 of the Treaty on European Union includes a system ensuring that competition is not distorted, HAVE AGREED that:
	To this end, the Union shall, if necessary, take action under the provisions of the Treaties, including under Article 352 of the Treaty on the Functioning of the Union.
Article 3 1. For the purposes set out in Article 2, the activities of the Community shall include, . . . : (c) an internal market . . . (g) a system ensuring that competition in the internal market is not distorted; . . . (k) the strengthening of economic and social cohesion; . . . (m) the strengthening of the competitiveness of Community industry; (n) the promotion of research and technological development; . . . (t) a contribution to the strengthening of consumer protection.	**Article 3(1) – repealed – new Article 3 Treaty on the Functioning of the European Union (TFEU)** 1. The Union shall have exclusive competence in the following areas: (a) customs union; (b) the establishing of the competition rules necessary for the functioning of the internal market; . . .
Article 4 For the purposes set out in Article 2, the activities of the Member States and the Community shall include, . . . the adoption of an economic policy . . . conducted in accordance with the principle of an open market economy with free competition.	**Article 4 – becomes Article 119 TFEU** Wording cited is retained.

Question: What difference do you think that these changes would mean, if any?

Article 3(1) has been repealed and replaced with an Article that simply says, among other things, that the EU shall have exclusive competence in establishing the competition rules necessary for the functioning of the internal market. The objectives of the EC are replaced with a new section relating again to the EU, the relevant part of which says:

The Union shall establish an internal market. It shall work for the sustainable development of Europe based on balanced economic growth and price stability, a highly competitive social market economy, aiming at full employment and social progress, and a high level of protection and improvement of the quality of the environment.

In other words, the reference to ensuring that competition in the internal market is not distorted will be removed under these proposals and be replaced by the notion of a highly competitive social market economy. A key question is what this idea entails and whether it heralds an important change in orientation. Protocol 27 to the Lisbon Treaty, however, sets out the Member States' view that the internal market includes a system ensuring that competition is not distorted and that the EU shall, if necessary, take action under the Treaties. There was major controversy at the time about what these changes meant.[38] The then French President, Nicolas Sarkozy, took the view that, 'we have obtained a major reorientation on the objectives of the Union. Competition is no longer an objective of the Union or an end in itself, but a means to serve the internal market' and that this would support the emergence of firms as European champions and a true industrial policy, whatever that may mean. Certainly this interpretation would suggest a reorientation of competition policy, away from the current emphasis on consumer welfare and economic analysis and towards more non-economic objectives which would affect even the core areas of control of anti-competitive agreements, abuse of a dominant position and merger control. There has not, however, been any evidence in decided cases that such a change has taken place.

The history of UK competition policy

Competition law in the UK up until the year 2000 was accurately described by Sharpe, a leading competition QC:

> Competition law in the United Kingdom . . . seldom serves to regulate behaviour: what takes place is more the selective ad hoc application of public powers, exercised in a non doctrinaire, pragmatic spirit, allowing little opportunity for compensation in favour of those affected by the anti-competitive action of others.[39]

What this means is that, unlike the American and European systems, there were no general prohibitions of conduct and agreements which, if broken, would lead to significant sanctions. Instead, the public authorities would investigate specific situations which they decided were worthy of concern and would, in appropriate circumstances, propose changes which would improve the situation for the future. Although the history of British competition policy is a fascinating study,[40] the passage of the Competition Act 1998, which came into force in 2000, and subsequently the Enterprise Act 2002, represented an enormous change in both the institutions and the values underlying competition policy in the UK, such that very little remains of previous approaches. Prior to this, Wilks, an eminent politics professor, argued that there were five policy goals for British competition policy: efficiency, international competitiveness, policy linkage, regulation and information.[41] One of Wilks' points is that issues of efficiency were linked to other policy areas and issues of international competitiveness and trade-offs ensued which sometimes meant, in the then existing institutional structure, that elected politicians were heavily involved in the decision making. The Competition Act 1998 changed this approach radically by replacing existing British law on anti-competitive

---

[38] See A. Riley, 'The EU Reform Treaty & the Competition Protocol: Undermining EC Competition Law', Centre for European Policy Studies Briefing Paper No. 142, available at: *http://www.ceps.eu/book/eu-reform-treaty-and-competition-protocol-undermining-ec-competition-law* (accessed 24/08/12).

[39] T. Sharpe, 'British Competition Policy in Perspective' (1985) 1 *Oxford Review of Economic Policy* 80 at 81.

[40] See H. Mercer, *Constructing a Competitive Order* (Cambridge University Press, 1995); T. Freyer, *Regulating Big Business* (Cambridge University Press, 1992); S. Wilks, *In the Public Interest: Competition Policy and the Monopolies and Mergers Commission* (Manchester University Press, 1999). Mercer ends in 1964 with the abolition of retail price maintenance and Freyer's detailed consideration ends in 1948.

[41] Wilks, ibid. at pp. 26–33.

agreements and abuse of a dominant position with a United Kingdom version of European Union competition policy (see Box 1.9 for the text). The 1998 Act created domestic versions of the prohibitions in Articles 101 and 102 TFEU, almost word for word, the enforcement of which was given over to an independent agency, the Office of Fair Trading.

KEY LEGAL PROVISIONS Box 1.9

UK law on agreements and conduct: Competition Act 1998, ss. 2 and 18

2 Agreements etc. preventing, restricting or distorting competition

(1) Subject to section 3 [excluded agreements], agreements between undertakings, decisions by associations of undertakings or concerted practices which –

(a) may affect trade within the United Kingdom, and

(b) have as their object or effect the prevention, restriction or distortion of competition within the United Kingdom,

are prohibited unless they are exempt in accordance with the provisions of this Part.

(2) Subsection (1) applies, in particular, to agreements, decisions or practices which –

(a) directly or indirectly fix purchase or selling prices or any other trading conditions;

(b) limit or control production, markets, technical development or investment;

(c) share markets or sources of supply;

(d) apply dissimilar conditions to equivalent transactions with other trading parties, thereby placing them at a competitive disadvantage;

(e) make the conclusion of contracts subject to acceptance by the other parties of supplementary obligations which, by their nature or according to commercial usage, have no connection with the subject of such contracts.

(3) Subsection (1) applies only if the agreement, decision or practice is, or is intended to be, implemented in the United Kingdom.

18 Abuse of dominant position

(1) Subject to section 19 [excluded cases], any conduct on the part of one or more undertakings which amounts to the abuse of a dominant position in a market is prohibited if it may affect trade within the United Kingdom.

(2) Conduct may, in particular, constitute such an abuse if it consists in –

(a) directly or indirectly imposing unfair purchase or selling prices or other unfair trading conditions;

(b) limiting production, markets or technical development to the prejudice of consumers;

(c) applying dissimilar conditions to equivalent transactions with other trading parties, thereby placing them at a competitive disadvantage;

(d) making the conclusion of contracts subject to acceptance by the other parties of supplementary obligations which, by their nature or according to commercial usage, have no connection with the subject of the contracts.

Some four years later the Enterprise Act completed this process by giving responsibility for decisions in merger cases and market investigations to a different independent agency, the Competition Commission (CC), while at the same time limiting the matters that the CC could consider to issues of economic analysis as opposed to broader public interest considerations, which had been part of the old law.

If we look for a general statement of the objective of current UK competition policy, the most guidance is given by the OFT, which says that its objective is to make markets work well for consumers, which seems to be a populist version of consumer welfare.[42] This approach will be formalised under the Enterprise and Regulatory Reform Bill which creates a Competition and Markets Authority which must seek to promote competition, both within and outside the United Kingdom, for the benefit of consumers.[43] Although the substantive law in relation to anti-competitive agreements and abuse of dominant position is modelled on EU provisions, UK law is not concerned with market integration, as it is already a single market. Other non-economic objectives are generally seen as no longer having a place within the enforcement of competition law. Indeed, one of the general objectives of reform under the Enterprise Act 2002 was to reduce the amount of political intervention in individual cases, whilst restricting the independent agency to considering matters of economics.

The economic arguments for competition law[44]

The argument for competition law is made by economists on the basis of explaining what will happen in a perfect market and contrasting that with the outcomes of a monopoly of the same market. The initial argument that follows is stylised and abstract but it makes certain important points, upon which more concrete arguments and issues can be built.[45] A perfect market is a market with many buyers and sellers, where the goods sold are homogeneous (there are no significant price or quality differences), both buyers and sellers have perfect information, there are no costs to switching sellers for the buyers, new producers may enter the market freely and it is possible to exit the market freely.

For economists, the effects of this are typically illustrated in the form of a graphic (see Figure 1.1). In the figure, the horizontal axis represents the quantity of goods that are sold, while the vertical axis represents the price at which the goods are sold. Typically, the higher the price of the goods, the less that are sold, so there is a curve sloping from left to right, which is called the demand curve and represents demand in that particular market. How are prices set in a competitive market? From the point of view of a seller, they will start by wanting to recover the costs of production, which include their fixed costs (the costs that do not vary with output, such as the rent for a factory) and their variable costs (the costs that do vary with output, such as raw material costs). Typically an element would also be included for the costs of financing the business, which would include an element of profit. Setting a price can be done by adding up all the cost elements and dividing by the quantity of the output. So if

---

[42] See *http://www.oft.gov.uk/* (accessed 24/08/12).

[43] HC Bill 61 (2012–13) clause 19.

[44] Generally see: S. Bishop and M. Walker, *The Economics of EC Competition Law* (3rd edn, Sweet & Maxwell, London, 2010), ch. 2; M. Motta, *Competition Policy* (Cambridge University Press, 2004), ch. 2; R. Van den Bergh and P. Camesasca, *European Competition Law and Economics* (2nd edn, Sweet & Maxwell, London, 2006) at pp. 19–38.

[45] It also assumes a static market.

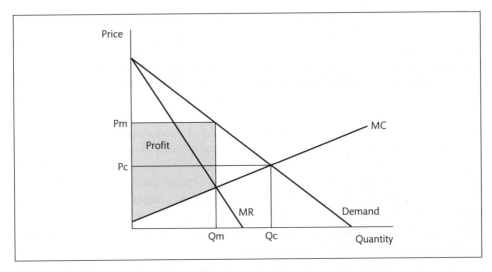

Figure 1.1 Perfect and monopoly markets

all the costs are £100 when 100 items are being made, then a price of £1 per item will cover the costs. At this point, another concept becomes critical, namely that of marginal cost, which is the change in total costs that arises when one extra unit is produced. As long as the price which can be obtained in the market is higher than the marginal cost, it makes sense for the producer to produce the extra item. So, in a perfectly competitive market, the price will equal the marginal cost, that is, the place where the marginal cost curve (MC) meets the demand curve. That in turn leads to two other points on this graph, Pc and Qc, which represent the competitive price and quantity mix.

Different producers may have different production costs but, in a perfectly competitive market, those with higher costs than other producers will not make any sales, because consumers have perfect information and can switch, and so they will have to exit the market. In theory, there will be one competitive market price. Economists consider that the main advantage of this situation is that it is one where there is allocative efficiency. Allocative efficiency is defined, in terms of a market, as where resources are allocated in a way that maximises the net benefit from their use. A perfect market is allocatively efficient because the goods are produced for their cost and sold to consumers who are willing to pay at least the cost of their production, as defined above. If the price of the goods was more than their cost then some consumers, who would be willing to pay for the goods at the competitive price, would not be able to buy the goods and would divert their resources into some other good which would be their second choice. A second advantage of a competitive market is productive efficiency, that is, where production of goods is done at the lowest cost possible because if a firm prices goods above marginal cost, given perfect information and no switching costs, that firm will make no sales.

So, if these are the advantages of a perfect market, what happens when there is a monopoly? If we assume that there is one producer, producing one product, who is unable to price discriminate between consumers, that is, the good must be sold at the same price to everyone, then the following consequences arise. The important issue for a monopolist is marginal revenue (MR), that is, the additional revenue brought in by the sale of an extra good. Since a monopoly does not face competition, it may choose the price at which it sells: the higher the price, the more marginal revenue per good, but the less that are sold. Nevertheless, as long as the marginal revenue is above the marginal cost, it makes sense for the monopoly to sell at that price. The revenue maximising position for the monopoly is when marginal revenue equals marginal cost (see diagram). As compared to a competitive market, fewer goods are sold at a higher price as can be seen by comparing the positions of Pm and Qm with Pc and Qc.

This has a number of consequences. First, there is an overall loss to societal welfare because fewer goods are produced at a higher price, what is called 'dead-weight loss' by economists. This is the area in the diagram represented by the triangle with the points Pm, Qc and the intersection of Pc and Qm. This represents those consumers who would have bought the good at a competitive price but now no longer do so and those who would still buy it, but at a higher price than they would pay in a competitive market. Secondly, the surpluses are distributed differently, away from the consumers and to the monopolist, but for economists, the distributional consequences are not of prime importance, although this has been, in the past, a motivating concern behind competition policy.

This argument explains, in very general terms, why we should favour perfect competition over monopoly. Applying these insights in the real world is not easy because perfect markets do not exist and single firm monopolies are rare. To complicate matters more, what should be the response if the monopolist argues that monopoly production is more productively efficient than what would take place in a competitive market?[46] If we assume a merger to monopoly which reduces the cost of production but raises the prices of the good produced and reduces the quantity produced, this produces the possibility that the gains in productive efficiency may outweigh the dead-weight loss but the surplus created will go to the monopolist. This creates a problem for competition authorities because, on the view favoured by many economists,[47] this is not something that they should take into account. Overall, society is better off and that is all that matters. Competition authorities in the EU and the UK do not take such a purist approach, given that they see their job as the protection of consumer welfare. Instead they look to see that the consumer receives a fair share of the benefits, which means that under Article 101 TFEU (ex Art. 81 EC) the net effect of agreements must at least be neutral[48] or, in mergers, that consumers should not be worse off as a result of the merger.[49] Under the UK legislation both the OFT and the Competition Commission are allowed to take into account any relevant customer benefits when making their decisions in relation to mergers.[50] There are two points here. First, it is possible to accept the argument that there are anti-competitive effects of an agreement or a merger, which are outweighed by its benefits. Secondly, the answer given by competition agencies is not one which necessarily follows from economic analysis.

Further issues arise if we move away from considering a static model and think about the effects on innovation and the development of new products, or what is sometimes called

---

[46] Discussed in more detail by Van den Bergh and Camesasca (n. 44) at pp. 31–5.

[47] For example, Bork (n. 15) at pp. 110–12; Motta (n. 44) at pp. 20–2.

[48] European Commission, *Guidelines on the application of Article 81(3) of the Treaty*, OJ C101/8, 27.04.2004, pp. 97–118 (at para. 85).

[49] European Commission, *Guidelines on the assessment of horizontal mergers under the Council Regulation on the control of concentrations between undertakings*, OJ C31, 05.02.2004, pp. 5–18 (at para. 79).

[50] Ss. 30 and 35 Enterprise Act 2002. See Competition Commission *Merger Remedies* (2008) paras 1.14–1.20; OFT, *Mergers: Exceptions to the duty to refer and undertakings in lieu of reference guidance* (2010) s. 4.

'dynamic efficiency'. First, there is an argument that monopolies are more likely to innovate, or to have been innovative, because of the amount of investment needed to create new products. The underlying idea is that in a perfectly competitive market there are not the resources to innovate; firms concentrate their efforts on the short term. The empirical evidence supporting this proposition is ambiguous, at best, and the better view seems to be that monopolies are less likely to be innovative than firms faced with a competitive market.[51] The second, related, point is that firms are only going to innovate if they decide that the innovation will be profitable and that they will be able to reap the rewards of their investment and the associated risk. Often, what is happening in such circumstances is that firms are competing *for* a market, rather than in a market, they want to be the first, and initially only, firm to provide a good or service and the reward for this would be monopoly profits, at least for a period of time. Examples of this sort of innovation would be Xerox, which produced the first photocopiers, or IBM, which produced the first commercial computers. These markets may also be within industries with high fixed costs and low marginal costs, for example, computer software, which suggests that prices have to be above marginal costs. Such markets may also exhibit network effects, that is, that the products are more valuable to the user when other people are using the same product, such as social networking sites like Facebook and Twitter.[52] What this suggests for competition authorities, to put it crudely, is that big is not necessarily a problem and that it is important not to penalise firms for their success. The difficulty is in trying to work out which side of the line corporate behaviour falls in this situation, a problem illustrated by the Microsoft litigation in Europe and the United States (which is discussed in Chapter 4).

Finally, competition authorities are not often faced with a simple monopolistic market. Typically, they deal with markets that are oligopolistic, that is, where there are only a few producers. The economics of these markets is discussed in more detail later (in part in Chapter 2 and in Chapter 10),[53] but it is worth noting here that a pervasive problem in these markets is that firms act strategically, in other words, their behaviour will depend on what their competitors do, unlike in perfect competition, where no one actor can affect the market, or a monopoly, where there is only one producer. The problem for competition authorities is that behaviour within an oligopoly may be an indication of a competitive industry or it may be the behaviour of an uncompetitive industry and it is not easy to distinguish the two. For example, under perfect competition, all firms charge the same price. If there is a cartel in place within an oligopoly, all the firms participating in the cartel will charge the same price. There is no simple test for distinguishing the two situations.

In summary, we can see that, in principle, there are clear benefits to having competitive markets as opposed to monopolies. Applying this insight to the real world of oligopolistic markets and markets characterised by dynamic competition is, however, not a straightforward proposition for the competition authorities. Before coming to the issue of whether a market is sufficiently competitive or, to put the question another way, whether or not the practices of firms hinder competition, there is a preliminary issue: namely, what is the market under consideration?

---

[51] See Motta (n. 44) at pp. 56–7.
[52] Bishop and Walker (n. 44), paras 2–37 explains these points.
[53] See ibid. at paras 2-020–2-029.

An introduction to market definition

This is a key aspect of any competition inquiry because commercial practices which are acceptable in a competitive context may be viewed with suspicion when a company has significantly more market power than its competitors. To decide the issue of market power requires specifying what market or markets are at stake. For example, if there is a competition inquiry into passenger rail services between Manchester and London, which are provided by only one train company, if the market was defined as rail services, then it would be an obvious conclusion that this company had significant market power, indeed was a monopoly. If the market was defined as transport between Manchester and London, so including cars, buses and airplanes as well as rail, then the train company appears to have much less market power. In the former example, we might be very worried about pricing practices whereas, in the latter, we might not be worried at all because of the degree of competition. As a result of this, exercises in market definition are often fiercely contested in cases by the parties concerned.

The law recognises this point. As the CJEU has put it:

KEY CASE EXTRACT   **Box 1.10**

The importance of market definition

Source: Case 6/72R *Europemballage Corporation* v *Commission* [1973] ECR 215 at para. 32:

> the definition of the relevant market is of essential significance, for the possibilities of competition can only be judged in relation to those characteristics of the products in question by virtue of which those products are particularly apt to satisfy an inelastic need and are only to a limited extent interchangeable with other products.

Question: How do you know when products are interchangeable?

This is equally the case as regards UK law.[54] Due to the importance of this issue, the OFT, the Competition Commission and the European Commission have issued guidelines which indicate how they approach the issue of market definition.[55] There is a reasonable amount of common ground between them, but the European Commission's guidelines are somewhat older than those of the UK authorities and rather less clearly written. As far as the UK is concerned, the focus will be on the OFT guidance, as this is most pertinent to the s. 18 issues that are being discussed.

Markets can be thought of, very generally, as social arrangements within which individuals carry out voluntary exchanges of goods or services, which for convenience will be referred to as products in the ensuing discussion. All markets have two dimensions: the product market, that is, what goods or services are traded, and the geographical market, that is, where the products are traded. For example, if we think of competition between supermarkets we tend

---

[54] See OFT, *Market Definition* (London, 2004); *Chester City Council v Arriva Plc* [2007] EWHC 1373.

[55] European Commission, 'Notice on the definition of the relevant market for the purposes of Community competition law', OJ C372, 09.12.1997, pp. 5–13; OFT, *Market Definition* (London, 2004); Competition Commission and OFT, *Merger Assessment Guidelines* (London, 2010), section 5.2; and Competition Commission, *Market Investigation References* (London, 2003), Part 2.

to focus on groceries, which would bring in Marks & Spencer, local shops and markets, but we might, in another context, focus on non-food items which are a significant part of supermarkets' activities. Geographically, although we might intuitively think of competition between supermarkets as national, the many competition inquiries into this sector have suggested that actually there is a succession of local markets based on a driving time of around 15 minutes. Markets may also have a temporal dimension, for example, seasonal markets, but this tends not to be of primary importance for competition analysis and for our purposes can be subsumed within the discussion of the product market.

Product market

There are two elements within the product market to consider: demand-side substitutability and supply-side substitutability. The former deals with the issue of what products are interchangeable or, to put it another way, which products compete with each other, while the latter addresses the issue of to what extent new producers can, in a short space of time, provide substitute products. The main concern of competition authorities is typically with demand-side substitution, so we will start there.

All the authorities agree that market definition is a tool for identifying the competitive constraints acting on the supplier of a given product or service. This is not to underestimate its importance, however, because the result of an investigation into the definition of the market may effectively determine the outcome of any particular case. How, then, is the job of undertaking market definition done? The European Commission has stated that the relevant product market comprises all those products and/or services which are regarded as interchangeable or substitutable by the consumer, by reason of the products' characteristics, their prices and their intended use.[56] Case law also tends to start by emphasising the interchangeability of products, as can be seen by the quotes in Box 1.11.

KEY CASE EXTRACTS   Box 1.11

Interchangeability of products

Source: Case T-504/93 *Tiercé Ladbroke* v *Commission* [1997] ECR II–923 at para. 81:

> [T]he relevant product or service market includes products or services which are substitutable or sufficiently interchangeable with the product or service in question, not only in terms of their objective characteristics, by virtue of which they are particularly suitable for satisfying the constant needs of consumers, but also in terms of the conditions of competition and/or the structure of supply and demand on the market in question.

Source: *Aberdeen Journals* v *Director General of Fair Trading* [2002] CAT 4 at paras 96–7:

> [T]he relevant product market is to be defined by reference to the facts in any given case, taking into account the whole economic context, which may include notably (i) the objective characteristics of the products; (ii) the degree of substitutability or interchangeability between the products, having regard to their relative prices and intended use; (iii) the

---

[56] European Commission, 'Notice on the definition of the relevant market for the purposes of Community competition law', OJ C372, 09.12.1997, pp. 5–13 (at para. 7).

competitive conditions; (iv) the structure of the supply and demand; and (v) the attitudes of consumers and users. However, this check list is neither fixed, nor exhaustive, nor is every element mentioned in the case law necessarily mandatory in every case. Each case will depend on its own facts, and it is necessary to examine the particular circumstances in order to answer what, at the end of the day, are relatively straightforward questions: do the products concerned sufficiently compete with each other to be sensibly regarded as being in the same market?

Question: Do these extracts provide a workable test?

This suggests that any inquiry begins by looking at products' characteristics and trying to determine what other products, if any, it is competing against. Although this does seem a plausible starting point, it creates a number of problems, which can be illustrated by examining the well-known case of *United Brands*.[57]

In this case, the European Commission had found that United Brands (UB) had infringed Article 102 TFEU by abusing its dominant position in the banana market by preventing its distributors from selling green bananas, imposing dissimilar and unfair prices and refusing to supply certain distributors. In its defence, UB argued that bananas were not a separate market but were part of the fresh fruit market, where bananas were reasonably interchangeable with other types of fresh fruit. The approach taken by the Advocate General and the CJEU was that bananas had certain characteristics, such as appearance, taste, softness, seedlessness, easy handling and constant level of production which meant that they were not interchangeable with other types of fruit and were particularly important for the very young, the old and the sick.[58] The difficulty with this approach to the question of market definition is that it is very subjective and it is unclear whether these differences are, in themselves, important to consumers. So, for example, a red car is different in appearance from a black car, Pepsi Cola tastes differently from Coca-Cola. Does this mean that there are separate product markets for red and black cars and that Pepsi and Coke are in separate product markets?

In order to try and deal with the problem of subjectivity, the competition authorities in the European Union and the UK have adopted what is known as the 'hypothetical monopolist' test as a conceptual framework to try and understand what consumers in the market will do. In the context of the product market and the issue of demand-side substitutability, the test asks: what would consumers do if there was a Small but Significant Non-transitory Increase in the Price (SSNIP) of the relevant products?[59] The question is whether the increase in price would be profitable for the producer of the products. When the price of a product is increased, typically the quantity sold decreases because customers either stop buying or substitute other products. If the price increase is or would be profitable, then the competition authorities have found the relevant market because there are no substitute products which would constrain the producer from raising prices. If the price increase would not be profitable, because enough consumers had switched to competing products, then the test is run again, but this time asking whether a SSNIP for the original plus the competing products would be profitable for a hypothetical monopolist. If the answer is yes, then the market

---

[57] Case 27/76 *United Brands v Commission* [1978] ECR 207.
[58] Ibid., para. 31 and pp. 312–13.
[59] The price increase is normally of a range of 5 to 10%, although the lower boundary tends to be favoured.

is established. If the answer is no, the test is run again, until there is a market reached which can be successfully monopolised. The example given below in Box 1.12 may make this clearer.

EXAMPLE   **Box 1.12**

An example of the hypothetical monopolist test

Suppose that there is an inquiry as to whether Coca-Cola has been engaged in anti-competitive practices in relation to Coke. Assume that there is one product, Coke, which is sold at £0.50 per item, of which £0.05 per item is profit and that the market consists of 1,000 units. The profit on Coke in this market is £50. The hypothetical monopolist test asks what would happen if Coke raised its price to £0.55 per item? If it did this, its profit would be £0.10 per item. If this happened and Coke sold 600 units, it would receive £60 profit and the outcome of the test would indicate that Coke was a monopoly. If, on the other hand, it sold 400 units, because consumers switched to Pepsi and other colas, it would receive £40 profit and the test would indicate that the market was wider than just Coke. The next question could then be: do Coke and Pepsi, between themselves, constitute a market on their own? What would happen if the SSNIP test was run? If Coke and Pepsi together do not constitute a market on their own, then the potential market could be widened to all branded colas and from there to branded and non-branded colas and from there to carbonated soft drinks. At some point the evidence would suggest that there was a group of products worth monopolising, which constituted the relevant market for competition purposes.

Questions: Consider altering the variables in this example. What happens if the market is larger or smaller? What if the market is growing? What evidence could you use to show the likelihood of consumer switching rates?

A number of important points should be raised about the example and the test more generally. The example is very simple and suggests high profitability for the sale of each product. As a result, there can be substantial switching which remains profitable for the supplier. If the profit per item is reduced, the level of switching that can be suffered whilst remaining profitable reduces accordingly. Secondly, *not all consumers have to switch* – the constraint on the producer is provided by the marginal consumers, those who are prepared to switch when there is a small price increase. There will always be some consumers who are not prepared to switch in the face of a price rise. The fact that some are unwilling to switch, assuming that the producer is offering the same prices to all consumers, is not an indication of substantial market power.

What is critical is whether enough consumers are willing to switch to make the small price rise unprofitable. The third point is that there is a potential problem with this test, one that is of particular relevance to Article 102 cases, which is referred to as the 'cellophane fallacy', so-called after a United States case involving this product and which is discussed in detail later in the text (Chapter 3).[60] The basic point is that the test assumes competitive prices and will give misleading answers if the prices are set at a monopoly level.

What sort of evidence is used in practice to determine market definition? The hypothetical monopolist test is a hypothetical test, which relies on indirect evidence from the past of how consumers have behaved. Both the European Commission and the OFT indicate in their guidance the sort of evidence that they will consider and the differences are outlined in Table 1.1.

---

[60] *United States v E I du Pont de Nemours*, 351 US 377 (1956).

Table 1.1 Evidence for product market definition[61]

European Commission	OFT
Product characteristics and intended use	Product characteristics
Views of customers and competitors	Views of customers and competitors
Barriers and costs associated with switching	Substitution costs
Quantitative estimates of own and cross-price elasticities (the responsiveness of demand for a product in response to a change in price of another product)	Evidence of own or cross-price elasticities of demand
Evidence of substitution in the recent past	Evidence from the undertakings
Consumer preferences	Patterns in price changes
Different categories of customers and price discrimination	Critical loss analysis, e.g. the minimum percentage loss in volume of sales required to make a 5% or 10% price increase unprofitable
	Price concentration relationships: how the price of a product in a distinct area varies according to the number of other products sold in the same area

None of the items listed above is very surprising and there is not, in terms of the evidence that they are willing to consider, much apparent difference between the European Commission and the OFT. The differences in the items on the list reflect differences in presentation, rather than anything else. So, for example, the OFT has a section discussing the issue of price discrimination, but this is separate from the list mentioned above. Perhaps a more important difference is that the European Commission's guidance refers to the hypothetical monopolist test as 'one way' of determining the relevant market, whereas the OFT implicitly takes the hypothetical monopolist test as the only way forward.[62]

Supply-side substitutability

This is a more controversial area in terms of market definition. The basic insight here is that a product may not be worth monopolising, even if consumers cannot switch, if other producers are able to react quickly enough to any change in prices. An example of this could be bus services in cities in the UK outside London. Assume that there is more than one bus company in a city. Company A has a profitable route or routes within the city, on which it is currently the sole provider. Assume that it raises its prices on this route(s) and that customers are unable to switch to other forms of transport. It is perfectly possible for bus companies B and C to start operating on those routes, undercutting Company A, either through diverting their buses from less profitable routes or from leasing additional buses. One of the conclusions that could be drawn from this analysis is that, in any one city, there is not a market for individual routes but instead, arguably, a local bus market so that the position of Company A must be looked at in the context of, amongst other things, how it relates to Company B and

---

[61] European Commission, 'Notice on the definition of the relevant market for the purposes of Community competition law', OJ C372, 09.12.1997, pp. 5–13 (at paras 36–43); OFT, *Market Definition* (London, 2004), para. 3.7.

[62] European Commission, 'Notice on the definition of the relevant market for the purposes of Community competition law', OJ C372, 09.12.1997, pp. 5–13 (para. 15).

Company C.[63] There is an alternative way of looking at this example, which is to say that there are markets for local routes but Company A's power is constrained by the ability of Companies B and C to enter the market and compete with it. In one sense it does not matter at what stage these considerations are taken into account, as long as they are. There is certainly a tendency within US antitrust practice to focus on demand-side substitution and there have been arguments that markets should be based solely on demand substitution.[64] This appears to be the preference of the European Commission, as expressed in its guidance, where it is stated that, 'The competitive constraints arising from supply side substitutability . . . are in general less immediate and in any case require an analysis of additional factors. As a result such constraints are taken into account at the assessment stage of the competition analysis.'[65] Bishop and Walker take the view that this is reflected in the European Commission's practice in that the focus is almost completely on demand side issues and the danger is that markets will be too narrowly drawn.[66]

By contrast, more emphasis is placed by the OFT on supply-side substitutability in its guidance. The key question for the OFT is whether, to what extent and how quickly, undertakings would start supplying a market in response to a hypothetical monopolist attempting to sustain supra-competitive prices.[67] Important questions relate to how quickly this entry is possible, how much entry would cost and whether new suppliers have sufficient spare capacity. The OFT also recognises that what is important is taking into account the competitive constraints, not necessarily at which stage they are considered. In other words, for the purpose of assessing these competition constraints it does not matter if they are described as supply-side substitutability, and therefore part of the market, or potential new entry and therefore not part of the current market but serving as effective competitive constraints.

The geographic market

Having established the products involved in a market, then the next stage to consider is its physical location. Case law of the European Courts gives a definition of the geographic market (see Box 1.13).

KEY CASE EXTRACT   **Box 1.13**

Definition of the geographic market

Source: Case T-219/99 *British Airways v Commission* [2004] 4 CMLR 1008 at para. 108:

> . . . the geographic market . . . may be defined as the territory in which all traders operate in the same or sufficiently homogeneous conditions of competition in so far as concerns specifically the relevant products or services, without it being necessary for those conditions to be perfectly homogeneous.

Questions: Think of examples of geographic markets. Is the market for recorded music local, regional, national or worldwide? What about supermarkets?

---

[63] Again, a very simplified example, which ignores the possibility of using other modes of transport as substitutes for buses.

[64] J. Baker, 'Market Definition: An Analytical Overview' (2008) 74 *Antitrust Law Journal* 129.

[65] European Commission, 'Notice on the definition of the relevant market for the purposes of Community competition law', OJ C372, 09.12.1997, pp. 5–13, para. 14.

[66] Bishop and Walker (n. 44), para. 4-015.

[67] OFT, *Market Definition* (London, 2004), para. 3.15.

In principle, the same approach is taken as when defining the product market: first the demand side is examined and then the supply side in order to see whether, within particular areas, the pricing and output decisions of the undertaking being investigated are constrained. In addition to the normal pieces of evidence that will be examined, the European Commission states that it will also take into account evidence of diversion to other areas, the current geographic pattern of purchases, trade flows and the pattern of shipments and, of course, transport costs.[68] Although this is the stated position of the European Commission, it has been criticised for giving too much prominence to regional differences and, in Article 102 cases, for defining the market solely by reference to the area in which the abuse takes place and thus, by adopting a narrow market definition, making it easier to show that there is a problem.[69] The clearest example of this latter tendency came in the first *Michelin* case.[70] Here the European Commission had fined the Dutch subsidiary of Michelin for an abuse of dominant position committed in relation to the market for heavy vehicle new replacement tyres in the Netherlands. It was argued by Michelin that this defined the market too narrowly, but the CJEU rejected this on the grounds that in practice Dutch dealers obtained their supplies only from within the Netherlands.[71] What was not considered was whether the dealer's *customers* could have bought tyres outside the Netherlands, which would have meant that the dealers would not have been able to pass on any higher costs that had been created (although there was no allegation that prices to consumers were higher).[72] In its second *Michelin* decision, by contrast, the European Commission devoted some time to discussing whether the new replacement and retread tyre markets in France were international or simply national before concluding that the relevant geographic market was France.[73] This approach to the market was not challenged by Michelin in front of the General Court (GC).[74]

If in the first *Michelin* case the European Commission was criticised for defining the geographical market too narrowly, in the UK, the OFT has been criticised for defining the geographic market too widely in *M E Burgess* v *Office of Fair Trading*.[75] This was a dispute about access to a crematorium situated in the Stevenage/Knebworth area, which was owned by a firm of funeral directors which had refused to allow a competing firm of funeral directors access to it. Here the OFT decided that the relevant geographic market for crematoria services included all crematoria within a 30-kilometre radius of Stevenage/Knebworth. In its decision, the OFT felt that a key consideration was that if the crematoria had increased prices above the competitive level, funeral directors would quite easily have been able to switch to other crematoria. The Competition Appeal Tribunal (CAT) rejected this contention, holding that there was no evidence to support this in the decision and, after reviewing the evidence before it, in particular evidence on pricing and usage which showed that the crematorium's usage had increased at the same time as its prices, came to the conclusion that there was a distinct

---

[68] European Commission, 'Notice on the definition of the relevant market for the purposes of Community competition law', OJ C372, 09.12.1997, pp. 5–13, paras 44–52.

[69] Bishop and Walker (n. 44), para. 4-036.

[70] Case 322/81 *Michelin* v *Commission* [1983] ECR 3461.

[71] Ibid, para. 26.

[72] See V. Korah, 'The Michelin Decision of the Commission' (1982) 7 *European Law Review* 130 at 131.

[73] *Michelin* [2001] OJ L143/1, paras 119–71.

[74] Case T-203/01 *Michelin* v *Commission* [2003] ECR II-4701 at para. 44.

[75] [2005] CAT 25.

geographic market for crematoria services in the Stevenage/Knebworth area. On the basis of this, the crematorium was found to be in a dominant position and to have breached the s. 18 prohibition. It is worth noting that this case involved a small, discrete local market.

Finally, we need to discuss the issue of chains of substitution, which is best illustrated in terms of the geographic market, although it is also an issue in terms of the product market. Bishop and Walker neatly summarise the argument:

> output from plant A compete with output from plant B because they are relatively close to each other; output from plant B compete with output from plant C because they are relatively close to each other; therefore plant A and plant C are in the same geographic market because the price of the output from plant A constrains the price of the output from plant B, which in turn constrains the price of the output from plant C.[76]

Although this argument is recognised in the guidance from the European Commission and the OFT,[77] it is difficult to think of real examples. It is important to remember that, although there may be a chain of substitution, for the purposes of the competition inquiry, it may not be relevant to look at the entire length of the chain. One part may suffice and this part could be sufficiently isolated from other parts of the chain. It is also possible that there are breaks in the chain, in which case there will be no competition between the parts on different sides of the break.

How market definition is used in particular contexts will be discussed later (in Chapters 2–4 and 13–14), but it is now time to turn to the institutions that are responsible for enforcing competition law in the EU and the UK. Figures 1.2 and 1.3 summarise the complicated enforcement structure that currently exists.

The institutions of competition law in the EU and UK

Figures 1.2 and 1.3 set out, schematically, the institutional arrangements for the enforcement of competition law. The latter sets out the arrangements for both EU and UK law, while the former deals only with EU law. It will be seen, however, that there is a significant amount of overlap.

European Union institutions

The European Commission

The central body for the enforcement of EU competition law is the European Commission. The European Commission has responsibility for policing anti-competitive agreements (Article 101 TFEU), abuses of dominant position (Article 102 TFEU) and mergers (the Merger Regulation 139/2004). All of these are what might be called mainstream competition policy but the Commission also has responsibility for ensuring that the activities of the Member States do not distort competition, most controversially through policing of the Treaty Articles on the provision of state aid (Articles 107–109 TFEU [ex Articles 87–89 EC]).

---

[76] Bishop and Walker (n. 44), para. 4-040.

[77] European Commission, 'Notice on the definition of the relevant market for the purposes of Community competition law' OJ C372, 09.12.1997, pp. 5–13, para. 57; OFT, *Market Definition* (London, 2004), para. 3.11.

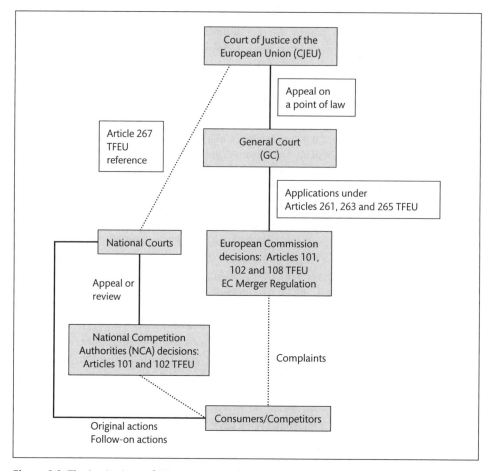

Figure 1.2 The institutions of EU competition law

The Commission is made up of twenty-seven Commissioners, one from each member state, nominated by their Member States for a renewable period of five years and appointed by the Council of the European Union subject to the approval of the European Parliament.[78] The Council of the EU, effectively the governments of the Member States, appoint the President of the Commission, whose nomination is approved by the European Parliament. Decisions by the Commission are made on a majority basis. The Commission is given the responsibility in the Treaty:

● to ensure that the provisions of the Treaty and the decisions of the institutions are applied,

● to formulate recommendations or deliver opinions on matters within the Treaty,

● to have its own power of decision, and

● to participate in the decision-making process of the European Union as set out in the Treaties and to exercise the powers conferred on it by the Council of Ministers for the implementation of the rules laid down by the Council.[79]

---

[78] Article 245 TFEU and Article 17, paras 3 and 7 TEU (ex Articles 213 and 214 EC).
[79] Article 17, para. 1 TEU (ex Article 211 EC).

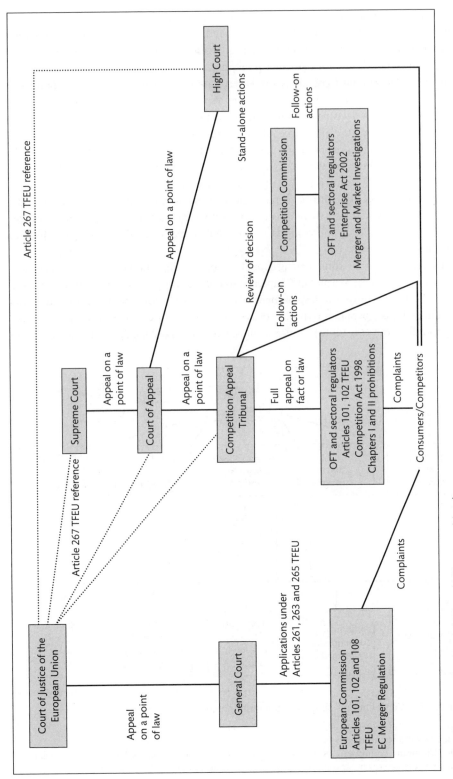

Figure 1.3 The institutions of EU and UK competition law

Note: Arrangements for the cartel offence and directors' disqualification are omitted from this Figure.

Members of the Commission are required, in the general interest of the EU, to be completely independent in the performance of their duties and, in particular, not to take instructions from their governments.[80] The Commission is organised into a number of Directorates General with responsibility for particular policy areas, each headed up by a Commissioner. One of those Directorate Generals is the Directorate General for Competition, familiarly known as 'DG Comp', which has the day-to-day responsibility for the enforcement of competition law, although decisions are taken in the name of the Commission as a whole.

Internally, DG Comp is split between the Cabinet of the Commissioner, currently Joaquin Almunia, and the staff side, which is headed by a Director General, currently Alexander Italianer, beneath whom are three Deputy Director Generals, responsible for mergers, antitrust and state aid. DG Comp is further divided into five sections dealing with specific industries, with subsections for antitrust, mergers and state aid, a cartel enforcement section and a state aid section, as well as two sections dealing with administrative and general issues (see Figure 1.4). Overall, DG Comp comprises about 900 staff as of 2009 and it regards itself as understaffed.[81]

A number of points are worth making about DG Comp as an institution. First, it has extensive powers (discussed in more detail in Chapter 5) to obtain information from companies[82] and others and extensive powers to impose penalties and remedies for breach of the competition rules. It may impose penalties of up to 10% of the annual worldwide turnover of an undertaking and these can constitute significant sums, with the largest single penalty being that of

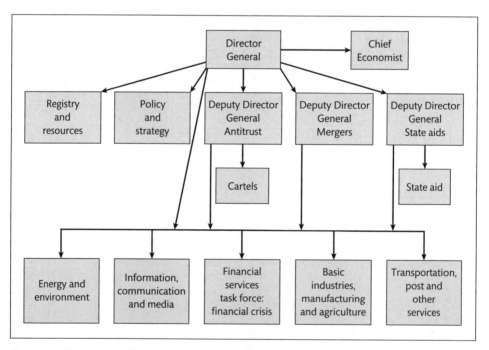

Figure 1.4 DG Competition – simplified organisation chart

[80] Article 245 TFEU (ex Article 213 EC).
[81] See the European Commission, 'DG Competition Annual Management Plan 2009' (Brussels, 2008) at p. 10.
[82] Technically, the subjects of EU competition law are referred to as 'undertakings' (see Chapter 2).

€1.06 billion imposed on Intel in 2009 for abuse of a dominant position. Even more importantly, decisions can require companies to change their business practices quite radically, which may be more costly than a fine, and, as a last resort, the Commission has power to order companies to be broken up, even though it has never exercised this power.[83]

EXAMPLE   Box 1.14

Recent examples of large fines by the European Commission

E.ON and GDF Suez €1,106,000,000 – market sharing in French and German gas markets (2009)

Car glass producers €1,383,896,000 – market sharing (2008)

Lifts and escalators cartels €992,312,200 (2007)

Gas insulated switchgear €750,712,500 (2007)

Intel €1,060,000,000 – excluding competitors from the market for computer chips (2009)

Source: Commission Press Release MEMO/09/323, 8 July 2009.

Question: How would you assess whether these fines deter anti-competitive conduct?

Secondly, in making these decisions, it is DG Comp which decides, outside merger control, which cases are going to be pursued, what evidence is going to be obtained and what the decision is going to be. In other words, DG Comp investigates, prosecutes and decides whether an infraction has taken place and what will be the penalty. This procedure has been heavily criticised over the years, and a number of internal safeguards have been put in place by DG Comp, but the main protection is the right for affected undertakings to appeal to the General Court (GC) and from there to the Court of Justice of the European Union (CJEU). There has been debate in the past about how independent DG Competition is and there have been suggestions, largely from Germany, that what is needed is some form of cartel office which is insulated from political intervention.[84]

Thirdly, because competition policy is only one of a number of policies of the European Commission, and important decisions are taken by the European Commission as a whole, not just by the Competition Commissioner, this has raised concerns about just how much individual decisions on competition cases are divorced from other policy considerations. This has seemed to be more of an issue in state aid cases and certain high-profile merger decisions but it remains an underlying matter of concern.

Court of Justice of the European Union (CJEU) and General Court (GC)

Individual decisions of the European Commission can only be challenged through the European Courts and the courts' interpretation of EU law through these challenges has led to the

---

[83] Council Regulation (EC) 1/2003 of 16 December 2002 on the implementation of the rules on competition laid down in Articles 81 and 82 of the Treaty, OJ L1, 04.01.2003, pp. 1–25 (Art. 7).

[84] For the debate, see S. Wilks and L. McGowan, 'Disarming the Commission: The Debate over a European Cartel Office' (1995) 33 *Journal of Common Market Studies* 259; C. Ehlermann, 'Reflections on a European Cartel Office' (1995) 32 *Common Market Law Review* 471; A. Riley, 'The European Cartel Office: A Guardian without Weapons?' (1997) 18 *European Competition Law Review* 3; M. Nordmann, 'The Case for a European Cartel Office' (1997) 3 *European Public Law* 223.

development of a substantial body of case law. This is not, however, the only role that the courts play, as we shall see below.

Both the CJEU and the GC are based in Luxembourg, with the CJEU being the original court; the GC was established in 1989 (and was known as the Court of First Instance until 1 December 2009) to ease the workload of the CJEU, in particular to take on competition cases because of the complex factual issues involved in them. The role of the CJEU and GC is to ensure that in the interpretation and application of the Treaty the law is observed (Article 19(1) TEU). The CJEU is composed of one judge from each Member State, while the GC has twenty-seven judges, effectively one judge per Member State (Article 19 TEU and Article 48 TEU, Protocol 3). The judges are required to be persons whose independence is beyond doubt and who possess the qualifications required for appointment to the highest judicial offices in their respective countries or who are jurisconsults of recognised competence (for the CJEU) or who possess the ability required for appointment to high judicial office (GC). The responsibility for appointing the judges is stated to be by the agreement of the governments of the Member States but, in practice, each Member State nominates its own judges for a term of six years, with provision for reappointment. There has been some suggestion that the relatively short term of office and the provisions for reappointment may raise issues over independence and the influence of Member States, but there are no obvious examples of this and it has not been relevant in the field of competition law.[85]

The European Courts operate in a different manner from United Kingdom courts. This is most immediately noticeable in relation to their judgments, which are the judgment of the *Court*, rather than individual judges, and dissenting judgments are not allowed in this European context (the European Court of Human Rights is different in this respect). Judgments, therefore, represent the agreed position of those who have decided the case, which can lead to compromises, although this is not expressed in the text. Most of the casework of the CJEU and GC is done by panels of three to five judges, known as Chambers, although there is provision for all the judges of a court to decide particularly important cases, known as a Grand Chamber. The writing style of judgments is also very different from that used by UK courts. The CJEU in particular follows a French style where there is little discursive discussion of the factual and legal issues, but instead a statement of governing principles, followed by a set of conclusions based on those principles. This is also due, in part, to another institutional difference between the CJEU and UK courts, namely the role of the Advocate General.[86] An Advocate General is required to meet the same standards for qualification as a judge of the CJEU but their role is to give, before the case is decided, a reasoned submission to the CJEU in public. These submissions will set out the facts and legal issues in the case, as well as suggesting an answer to the questions that have been posed. The Advocate General's opinion is often easier to follow and it will set out the competing arguments in a case, rather than just the conclusions, and try and find a solution that fits the pattern of previous case law. In that way, it may often give a better idea of the issues at stake in any particular case. The opinion is not, however, binding on the court and the Advocate General takes no part in the deliberations of the judges. So, although as a general rule the court will follow the opinions of the Advocate General, this is by no means a given outcome and there are significant numbers of cases where the court has departed from the Advocate General's suggestions,

---

[85] R. Dehousse, *The European Court of Justice* (Macmillan, London, 1998) at pp. 12–13.
[86] Generally, see N. Burrows, *The Advocate General and EC Law* (Oxford University Press, 2007).

either as to outcome or to the approach to be taken. Because the Advocate General is peculiar to the CJEU, the GC's judgments contain more discussion of the case law involved, as well as detailed discussions of the factual background of each case. The other point to notice is that the procedure in both European Courts is much more dependent on written, rather than oral, submissions, although there is an opportunity for the parties to make oral submissions.

The jurisdiction and work of the European Courts

For our purposes, the European Courts have two main jurisdictions. The first is under Article 263 TFEU (ex Article 230 EC),[87] which allows them to review the legality of acts of the Union institutions on grounds of lack of competence, infringement of an essential procedural requirement, infringement of the EC Treaty or of any rule of law relating to its application, or misuse of powers. The typical case is where the decision of the European Commission on a competition matter, such as the imposition of a fine, is challenged by the undertaking upon whom the fine is imposed. This will be heard in the first instance by the GC, whose decision is subject to appeal, on a point of law only, to the CJEU. The second main jurisdiction is where a national court or tribunal makes a reference to the CJEU, under Article 267 TFEU (ex Article 234 EC)[88] (and only the CJEU can hear these references), asking it to give a preliminary ruling regarding the interpretation of the Treaty and the validity and interpretation of acts of the Union institutions. In terms of competition law, the typical case has been where there has been a contractual dispute between two undertakings and one of them has raised points of EU competition law, often as a defence, and the national court has sought the opinion of CJEU on the point of Union law.

To concentrate on competition law does give a distorted picture of the activities of the CJEU in particular, which does not aid our understanding of the case law. The CJEU is not, never has been and was never intended to be a specialist competition court. For example, 1,854 new cases were lodged with the CJEU from 2009 to 2011, of which 97, or 5%, involved competition issues.[89] It is, instead, the supreme judicial body of the European Union and shares in many respects the attributes of a constitutional court. It has decided important cases relating to the distribution of power between EU institutions as well as establishing fundamental principles of EU law which were not laid out explicitly in the Treaties but were said to follow as a matter of logical implication: the principles of direct effect and the supremacy of EU law over domestic law.[90] The CJEU has been described as having a very integrationist agenda and as having moved the cause of European integration forward at times when the European Union institutions were unable to agree, for political reasons, on the way forward.[91] Even though it has, arguably, recently exercised greater self-restraint, this concern with integration and moving the European project forward has left its mark on EU competition law, notably in the treatment of vertical agreements, recently in relation to private actions for damages and in relation to merger control, prior to the implementation of the merger control regulation.[92]

---

[87] Article 265 TFEU makes provision for actions on the basis of a failure to act.

[88] Generally, see B. Rodger, *Article 234 and Competition Law* (Kluwer, Deventer, 2008).

[89] See CJEU 'Statistics of judicial activity' available at: *http://curia.europa.eu/jcms/jcms/Jo2_7032/* (accessed 24/08/12). There were about the same number of state aid cases.

[90] Case 26/62 *Van Gend en Loos* [1963] ECR 1 and Case 6/64 *Costa* v *ENEL* [1964] ECR 585.

[91] Dehousse (n. 85), ch. 3.

[92] See Case 56/64 *Consten & Grundig* [1966] ECR 299; Case C-453/99 *Courage* v *Crehan* [2001] ECR I-6297; Case 6/72R *Europemballage and Continental Can* v *Commission* [1973] ECR 215; Case C-730/79 *Philip Morris Holland* v *Commission* [1980] ECR 2671.

Within competition law there is often a tension between the demands of integration and the insights of economic analysis and one of our recurring themes will be to examine how this tension is managed.

This takes us on to another point about the methods of interpretation used by the CJEU and the GC. The approach is often described as being teleological, that is, the judge searches for the meaning or the purpose of the provision in front of them, rather than concentrating on the textual meaning. The classic example of this in competition law is the *Continental Can* case.

KEY CASE EXTRACT   **Box 1.15**

Teleological interpretation – *Continental Can*

Source: Case 6/72R *Europemballage and Continental Can* v *Commission* [1973] ECR 215, esp. at paras 18–27:

Here Continental Can had merged with another company and the European Commission had decided, prior to having any specific powers to control mergers, that this constituted a breach of Article [102 TFEU]. The company argued that the Commission had no power to do this, as it was contrary to a literal interpretation of Article [102 TFEU], as well as the intention of its authors. The CJEU rejected this argument, saying that one had to look at the spirit, general scheme and wording of Article [102 TFEU], as well as the aims and objectives of the EC Treaty. Since Article [101 TFEU] prevented restrictive agreements, it should not be permissible to allow companies to merge and render any serious chance of competition impossible. This, the CJEU felt, would make a breach in competition law which would jeopardise the function of the common market.

Questions: Would a UK court have decided this issue in the same way? Is this an appropriate role for a court?

In the context of a European Union where there is not one authentic language for any text, but twenty-three equally authentic official languages, a purely textual approach makes less sense. When combined with the concern with integration and what might be called constitutional issues, this can bring about some wide-ranging judgments, which are based more on general principles than a close look at the factual background to the cases.

However one looks at it, much of competition law is not about issues of constitutional significance to the European Union, even though the cases will be of great importance to the parties. As a result of this, and the number of competition cases and their factual complexity, as well as the growing caseload of the CJEU, the GC was set up in 1989 in order to hear, among other things, competition cases. Competition and state aid cases are currently the second largest part of the GC's caseload, after intellectual property cases, and are almost all taken under Article 263 TFEU, as can be seen from Table 1.2. The GC is closer to a specialist competition court which is exercising a reviewing jurisdiction, even though, over the period 2009–11, only 8% of its caseload was competition cases. This leads to three issues: how intense is the GC's review of European Commission decisions, what is the relationship between the GC and the CJEU, and how long does it take to get a case decided?

Table 1.2 GC – New cases 2007–11 – subject matter of action[93]

	2007	2008	2009	2010	2011
Competition	62	71	42	79	39
State aid	37	55	46	42	67
Intellectual property	168	198	207	207	219
Other	197	178	273	308	397
Total	**464**	**502**	**568**	**636**	**722**

Standard of review of Commission decisions[94]

There are two elements to the jurisdiction of the CJEU and the GC. They have unlimited jurisdiction to hear appeals against penalties imposed on undertakings[95] and, under Article 263 TFEU, they may review the legality of decisions by the European Commission, as mentioned above. The jurisdiction regarding penalties relates simply to the issue of penalties; it does not affect the question of legality, which is separate, although often cases challenging European Commission decisions will challenge both the legality and the penalty. As regards the standard of review that will be applied by the GC, the starting point can be found in a decision of the CJEU, regarding a merger case, although the approach does not appear to be different outside mergers:

> . . . the basic provisions of the Regulation . . . confer on the Commission a certain discretion, especially with respect to assessments of an economic nature. Consequently, review by the Community [Union] judicature of the exercise of that discretion, . . . must take account of the discretionary margin implicit in the provisions of an economic nature which form part of the rules on concentration.[96]

Although this suggests that the GC allows the institutions considerable discretion in carrying out their activities,[97] the GC has always exercised a close scrutiny over European Commission decisions, being concerned with not only whether the law is being correctly applied but also whether there is sufficient factual evidence on which the European Commission can base its decision. This became particularly controversial in 2002 when the GC quashed three merger decisions of the European Commission in relatively quick succession and, in the course of the judgments, was very critical of the factual basis of each decision.[98] The European Commission took the view that the GC was overstepping the boundaries in regard to the intensity of review and appealed the *Tetra Laval* case (involving the merger between two companies which the Commission had prohibited) to the CJEU where it was argued that the GC had failed to take account of the discretion vested in the Commission.[99] The CJEU did

---

[93] Source: CJEU, *Annual Report 2006*. Excludes staff cases and special forms of procedure.
[94] Generally see H. Schweitzer, 'Judicial Review in EU Competition Law', in D. Geradin and I. Lianos (eds) *Research Handbook on EU Antitrust Law* (Cheltenham, Edward Elgar, forthcoming).
[95] Regulation 1/2003, Art. 31.
[96] Cases C-68/94 and C-30/95 *France v Commission* [1998] ECR I-1375 at paras 223–4.
[97] See D. Chalmers *et al.*, *European Union Law* (Cambridge University Press, 2006) at p. 436.
[98] Case T-342/99 *Airtours v Commission* [2002] ECR II-2585; Case T-310/01 *Schneider Electric v Commission* [2002] ECR II-4071; Case T-5/02 *Tetra Laval v Commission* [2002] ECR II-4381.
[99] Case C-12/03P *Commission v Tetra Laval* [2005] ECR I-987 at paras 19 and 25–36. See B. Vesterdorf, 'Standard of Proof in Merger Cases: Reflections in the Light of Recent Case Law of the Community Courts' (2005) 1 *European Competition Journal* 3 making reference to discussions of this issue.

not agree with this argument, as seen in Box 1.16, and this approach has been followed in later cases.[100]

KEY CASE EXTRACT   **Box 1.16**

The standard of review

Source: Case C-12/03P *Commission v Tetra Laval* [2005] ECR I-987 at para. 35:

> Whilst the Court recognises that the Commission has a margin of discretion with regard to economic matters, that does not mean that the Community [Union] Courts must refrain from reviewing the Commission's interpretation of information of an economic nature. Not only must the Community [Union] Courts, inter alia, establish whether the evidence relied on is factually accurate, reliable and consistent but also whether that evidence contains all the information which must be taken into account in order to assess a complex situation and whether it is capable of substantiating the conclusions drawn from it.

Question: How intrusive is this standard of review? How different is it from that operated by the UK courts in judicial review cases?

What this means is that, although the CJEU recognises that there is an element of judgement in Commission decisions ('discretion') with which it should not interfere, it is willing to assess whether there is sufficient evidence to back up the Commission's judgement and whether it is capable of supporting the Commission's conclusions. This may well involve some analysis and assessment of the reasoning of the Commission. How far the Court should go here is a matter of controversy, and the context of an appeal is important. So, for example, in a merger case the Commission has much less time, a maximum of roughly four months, to make a decision than in an Article 102 TFEU case, which may take at least a couple of years, so the Court might have an inclination to look more carefully at the evidence base.

The relationship of the CJEU and the GC

The role of the CJEU in relation to the GC is to hear appeals on a point of law and on the grounds of a lack of competence, a breach of procedure or the infringement of Union law. It seems that the CJEU takes a narrow view of this jurisdiction.[101] The outcomes of appeals in competition cases are set out in Table 1.3, which indicates that appeals in competition cases

Table 1.3 GC – Results of competition appeals to CJEU

	2006	2007	2008	2009	2010	2011
Appeal dismissed	10	13	4	18	8	10
Decision totally or partially set aside	5	2	1	5	3	4
Removed from register	1	0	0	0	0	2
Total	16	15	5	23	11	16

---

[100] See Case T-210/01 *General Electric v Commission* [2005] ECR II-5575 at paras 60–4.
[101] See Cases C-204/00P etc. *Aalborg Portland v Commission* [2004] ECR I-123 at paras 47–51.

are wholly or partially successful in about 23% of the cases. Although this might seem a relatively low strike rate, it contrasts favourably with other areas. For example, in the same period only about 15% of appeals in non-competition cases were successful. These figures suggest that there is significant scope for disagreement between the CJEU and the GC on competition cases.

Currently, at the GC it takes just under four years for a competition case to be heard, assuming that the expedited or fast track procedure is not invoked. Even if the expedited procedure is invoked, which is quite rare, the fastest a case has been dealt with is seven months. It took about sixteen months for preliminary rulings cases to be heard by the CJEU in 2008, which represented a decline from somewhat over two years in 2004, whereas the average time for appeals was a year and a half.[102] The amount of time that it takes for cases to be decided has been a source of some concern for the business community, particularly in relation to mergers, where quick decisions are particularly important and the amount of delay led to the claim that if a business received an unfavourable decision, it had virtually no remedy.[103]

This led the Confederation of British Industry (CBI) to put forward a proposal for a specialist competition court which would resolve all merger cases within six months, as well as hearing other competition cases which were brought by private parties, either against European Commission decisions or by way of private actions. This led to an investigation by the House of Lords Select Committee on the European Union, which acknowledged the problems of delay, attributing them partly to the GC becoming overloaded, especially with intellectual property cases, and issues in relation to the translation of documents. The Select Committee did not support the case for a new court, arguing instead that a number of shorter-term practical reforms could be implemented, which would deal with the problems identified, such as better case management, transferring trademark cases to a judicial panel and a reduction in the number of cartel cases before the GC as a result of changes in the working practices of the European Commission.[104]

UK competition law institutions

The Office of Fair Trading

The Office of Fair Trading (OFT) is the central institution for the enforcement of competition law in the United Kingdom and it states that its mission is to 'make markets work well for consumers'. It is responsible for taking action against anti-competitive agreements and abuse of dominant position under either the Competition Act 1998 or Articles 101 and 102 TFEU; as well as deciding on whether to refer mergers to the Competition Commission for a full investigation. It has powers to conduct market studies of particular sectors of the economy and, if necessary, refer a market to the Competition Commission for investigation. Finally, it is responsible for the investigation and prosecution of criminal cartels under the Enterprise Act 2002, a power which does not exist in EU law. In order to carry out these responsibilities, it has wide powers to investigate and obtain information.

---

[102] CJEU, 'Statistics of judicial activity 2011', available at: *http://curia.europa.eu/jcms/jcms/Jo2_7032/* (accessed 24/08/12).

[103] Select Committee on the European Union, 'An EU Competition Court', HL (2006–07) 75 at para. 24.

[104] Ibid., Foreword. See also T. Cowen, 'Justice Delayed is Justice Denied: The rule of law, economic development and the future of the European Community courts' (2008) 4 *European Competition Journal* 1.

The OFT is not, however, just a competition authority; it also has major responsibilities in the field of consumer protection and one of the organisational issues for it has always been the relationship between these two activities. For our purposes, the overlap is seen most clearly in s. 11 of the Enterprise Act 2002, which allows designated consumer bodies to make what are known as 'super-complaints' to the OFT about the functioning of particular markets in the United Kingdom. Such complaints may or may not raise competition issues and the OFT is allowed to respond in a manner that it feels is appropriate. So, for example, while the super-complaint on personal accounts and banking in Northern Ireland was referred to the Competition Commission in order for it to carry out a market investigation, the super-complaint on private dentistry services led to a market study which was followed up by a consumer information campaign.[105]

The OFT's powers vary depending on whether it is concerned with anti-competitive agreements and abuse of dominant position as opposed to mergers and market investigations. When the OFT is exercising its powers under either Articles 101 and 102 TFEU or Chapters I and II of the Competition Act 1998, it is acting in a manner very similar to the European Commission. It investigates the area, hears the submissions of the parties and others, such as complainants, and then makes a decision: for example, imposing a fine. Any challenges to such a decision must be made to the Competition Appeal Tribunal, whose jurisdiction is discussed below. By contrast, when examining mergers and market cases, the OFT is not the final decision maker; it is deciding whether or not this is an appropriate case to be referred to the Competition Commission, which will take the final decision. So in these areas the preliminary investigation stage is conducted by one body and then the detailed look at the issues in the case, and the decision, is the responsibility of another organisation. Arguably, this division of responsibilities helps to protect against any psychological bias which the original investigators might have but it inevitably creates some coordination problems, given that there are two separate organisations.

From the beginning, the OFT was designed as a regulatory agency which was to operate independently of politicians. The need for independence has become much more important since the OFT gained powers in 1998 under the Competition Act to enforce the prohibitions against anti-competitive agreements and abuse of a dominant position. The OFT is considered a non-ministerial government department, which is led by a Board consisting of a chairman,[106] an executive director and five non-executive members, all of whom are appointed by the Secretary of State. Underneath the Board are a Policy and Strategy section and a Markets and Projects section. This latter section is divided into goods, services, consumer, infrastructure and, in addition, a dedicated merger control team and one devoted to dealing with cartel activity. There is also a preliminary investigation unit which sets down enforcement priorities.

How successful the OFT has been in exercising the new powers it has gained since 1998 is a matter of some controversy. There have been several high-profile, successful cases, notably on price-fixing of replica football kits, which involved a total fine of approximately £18.5 million, and price-fixing in relation to Hasbro toys and games, which resulted in a fine of approximately £22.5 million imposed on three companies. In addition, the OFT has taken action against a number of construction cartels in Britain which, although individually small, may well have had a deterrent effect. On the other hand, it has been the subject of a National

---

[105] See *http://www.oft.gov.uk/advice_and_resources/resource_base/super-complaints/* for details (accessed 24/08/12).
[106] This is the official title.

Audit Office report, which was critical of the OFT's process for deciding on priorities, the amount of time it took in completing investigations, its quality control mechanisms and the level of transparency of its operations.[107] This was followed up by a very critical report from the Public Accounts Committee of the House of Commons,[108] which said that the OFT was too reliant on complaints for starting investigations, had no database of its own to support investigations, took too long over investigating cases, created uncertainty for the companies subject to its investigations and did not use its statutory powers to obtain information. The Committee concluded that, 'The OFT is an organisation in transition, which has yet to demonstrate that it can make effective use of the substantial extra resources it has been given.'[109] This has led to a major change to the structure of the OFT but its record subsequently remained patchy. For example, in 2005 the OFT decided that the domestic 'interchange fee' agreed between the banks in the United Kingdom participating in the MasterCard credit card scheme infringed Article 101(1) TFEU and the Chapter I prohibition imposed by s. 2 of the Competition Act 1998, and did not qualify for exemption from those provisions under Article 101(3) TFEU or s. 9 of that Act, which was the culmination of an investigation started in 2000. The parties appealed to the CAT and, after much procedural wrangling, the OFT decided to withdraw the decision in 2006, a course of action described by the CAT as 'highly regrettable' given that this was a 'flagship' case.[110] Having said this, it has successfully brought some high-profile cartel cases in the last couple of years, as discussed in 'Competition law in practice' (above), as well as bringing the first successful criminal prosecution under the Enterprise Act 2002. Criticisms were raised about the level of enforcement activity by the OFT, its perceived relative lack of success and the speed of its processes. Partly as a result of these criticisms, the government undertook a wide-ranging review of competition policy of which one of the main changes will be to abolish the OFT and the Competition Commission and create a new Competition and Markets Authority (CMA) from April 2014.[111]

Competition Commission

The Competition Commission (CC) has two main roles:[112]

1 it makes decisions on whether mergers, either contemplated or completed, might lead to a substantial lessening of competition and, if it finds that they do, whether the merger should be prohibited or allowed to proceed subject to certain conditions, and

2 conducts investigations into particular markets in order to determine whether there are any features of the market which may distort or restrict competition. Again, if there are problems in markets, the CC is entitled to decide upon the appropriate remedies.

Unlike either the European Commission or the OFT, the CC is not entitled to investigate anything of its own accord. It will only act when a merger or a market is referred to it, usually by the OFT, although certain cases may be referred by the Secretary of State or other

---

[107] National Audit Office, 'The Office of Fair Trading: Enforcing competition in markets', HC (2005–06), 593 at 2–3.

[108] Committee of Public Accounts, 'Enforcing Competition in Markets', HC (2005–06) at para. 841.

[109] Ibid. at p. 5.

[110] See *Mastercard UK Members Forum* v *OFT* [2006] CAT 14 at para. 28.

[111] For the consultation see: *http://www.bis.gov.uk/Consultations/competition-regime-for-growth* (accessed 24/08/12). For the planned legislation see Enterprise and Regulatory Reform Bill, HC Bill 61 2012–13.

[112] For the CC's other roles, see: *http://www.competition-commission.org.uk/about-us* (accessed 24/08/12).

regulators. The Commission is composed of a chairman, three deputies and about fifty part-time members, all of whom are supported by around one hundred and fifty staff, with a mix of economists, accountants, business advisers, lawyers and generalists. Each case is heard by a panel of ideally five members, although sometimes less, supported by a staff team. Members of the CC, including the chairman and deputies, are appointed by the Secretary of State; but the Secretary of State has no power to intervene in the workings of the CC.

The CC has, in one shape or another, been part of the landscape of UK competition policy since 1948 even though its jurisdiction and powers have changed in many ways throughout that time.[113] Its main asset over that period of time has been a reputation for independence and for producing high quality reports analysing the problems that have been referred to it. It is, however, a very unusual public body. On the one hand it is like a court because it is independent and makes judgments on individual cases. On the other hand, these are judgments about economic matters and judgments about what will happen in the future, particularly in relation to mergers, whereas a court is concerned with past conduct. The OFT, by contrast, is often engaged in sanctioning companies for breach of the competition rules, while the CC is doing something different. In terms of merger control, it is preventing problems from arising and in terms of market investigations it is trying to solve problems for the future, which is not the same as punishing companies for their past behaviour. In relation to market inquiries, this represents a different approach to competition law than that taken by the European Union with its prohibition system and harks back to the older days of UK competition policy. As mentioned above, the Competition Commission will be abolished by the Enterprise and Regulatory Reform Bill and its functions will be taken over by the new CMA.

Competition Appeal Tribunal

The Competition Appeal Tribunal (CAT) was set up under the Enterprise Act 2002,[114] although it had existed in a slightly different form as part of the Competition Commission, rather oddly, under the Competition Act 1998. The Enterprise Act creates the CAT as a truly independent judicial body, which is critical as its main role is to hear appeals and review decisions of both the OFT and the CC. The CAT's other main job is to hear actions for damages and monetary claims which might be made under the Competition Act for breaches of either domestic or European competition law. Finally, the CAT may also hear appeals against decisions of the Office of Communications and the Secretary of State under the Communications Act 2003.[115]

In its main activities, the CAT is doing three different things. When it hears appeals against decisions by the OFT, these are appeals on the merits of the decision and the CAT is entitled to take any decision that the OFT has taken. This involves, therefore, potentially very close scrutiny of OFT decisions. When it is dealing with challenges to decisions on mergers and market cases from the Competition Commission, the CAT is meant to apply judicial review principles, that is, it may scrutinise only the legality of the decision, not its merits. This should involve a lower level of scrutiny than in the case of a full appeal of an OFT decision. Finally, when it is dealing with monetary claims, this is in the context of what are known as

---

[113] Wilks, *In the Public Interest* (n. 40) is the definitive study of this institution.
[114] Section 12 and Sch. 2.
[115] Communications Act 2003, s. 192.

'follow-on actions', that is, actions which follow the decision of the OFT or the European Commission that there has been a breach of competition law and the question is whether this has caused damage to the person(s) complaining. This latter is a new jurisdiction and, so far, only sixteen such cases have been brought before the CAT, the first of which was settled on confidential terms before it reached a judgment.[116]

The CAT is a Tribunal in the sense that when it hears cases these are decided by a panel of three people: a legally qualified chairman[117] and two ordinary members who may be, but are not necessarily, legally qualified, as they also have backgrounds in economics, business, accountancy and regulation and are appointed by the Secretary of State. The chairmen are appointed by the Lord Chancellor and are senior lawyers (so far all coming from the Bar). A number of Justices of the High Court are chairmen whilst the remainder are currently either QCs or very experienced competition lawyers. There is a President who is in charge of the CAT and the first one was Sir Christopher Bellamy, who had previously been a member of the GC. If we look at the jurisdiction and composition of the CAT, the fact that appeals from it go direct to the Court of Appeal[118] rather than the High Court, it is apparent that it is a specialist competition court, even though referred to as a Tribunal. Under its first president, the CAT has had the reputation of being an interventionist tribunal, which has not been afraid to overturn the decisions of the bodies whose judgment it is reviewing, principally the OFT and the sector regulators.

The High Court

The ordinary courts, the High Court in England and Wales, are involved in competition matters in three circumstances. First, when a plaintiff may bring a private action for damages in the Chancery Division of the High Court. This may either be a follow-on action, as discussed above, or it may be based on an allegation that there has been a breach of competition law, where the conduct or agreement in question has not been the subject of a decision by either the OFT or the European Commission that the defendant has breached the competition rules. This is referred to as a 'stand-alone' action. The routes for private actions are illustrated in Figure 1.5 below. There have been very few stand-alone actions and no successful reported damages actions.[119] Secondly, competition law issues may arise in the context of other proceedings, when the competition law point is raised as a defence. Thirdly, when proceedings are taken to disqualify directors of companies for certain breaches of competition law, an application has to be made to the High Court by the OFT or the relevant regulator under s. 9A of the Company Directors Disqualification Act 1986. There have, as yet, been no such applications.

---

[116] *Healthcare at Home* v *Genzyme Limited*: see Order of the Tribunal of 11 January 2007. The other notable cases are *Consumers Association* v *JJB Sports* (also settled: see Chapter 5), *Emerson Electric Co and others* v *Morgan Crucible and others* (this is based on the decision of the European Commission in the carbon graphites case) and *Enron Coal Services* v *EWS* [2009] CAT 36.

[117] This is the official term.

[118] Competition Act 1998, s. 49.

[119] Although there have been a number of settled cases: see B. Rodger, 'Private Enforcement of Competition Law, the Hidden Story: competition litigation settlements in the United Kingdom, 2000–2005' (2008) 29 *European Competition Law Review* 96. See also *Purple Parking Ltd* v *Heathrow Airport Ltd* [2011] EWHC 987. There were only four competition law actions issued in the Chancery Division in 2011: see: *http://www.justice.gov.uk/ statistics/courts-and-sentencing/judicial-annual-2011* (accessed 24/08/12), table 5.3.

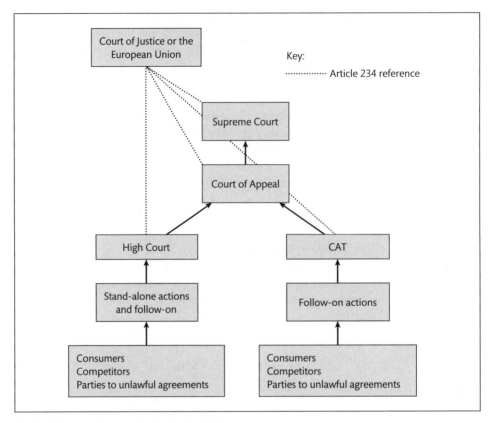

Figure 1.5 Private enforcement in the UK

The relationship between EU and UK competition law

One of the initial aims behind the protracted reform of UK competition law in the 1990s was to produce a system that was consistent with EU competition law, so that businesses, when assessing their own behaviour and agreements, did not have to go through very different assessments, depending on whether they were dealing with UK or EU law. This produced the Competition Act 1998 which based the UK's substantive law on the control of restrictive agreements and abuse of dominant position on Articles 101 and 102 TFEU of the EC Treaty. Shortly after that, merger control and what were previously called monopoly investigations, renamed as market investigations, were reformed under the Enterprise Act 2002 but these changes did not follow the European model. At around the same time as the Enterprise Act was being discussed in the UK, EU debates had moved to discussing a modernisation of competition policy enforcement which led to the drafting and implementation of Regulation 1/2003, which came into force in May 2004. This dismantled the notification system and gave national competition authorities and national courts the power to apply Articles 101 and 102 TFEU in their entirety in the appropriate circumstances. So there are two important introductory points: first, to what extent is it possible for UK competition law to differ from EU competition law and, secondly, in relation to EU law, who is responsible for its enforcement?

First, the UK law on mergers, market investigations and the criminal consequences of cartel activity is separate from EU law and enforced entirely by the relevant UK institutions: the OFT and the CC. Secondly, the UK law on anti-competitive agreements and conduct which is contained in Chapters I and II of the Competition Act 1998 is modelled on Articles 101 and 102 TFEU.

So the starting point is, to what extent can Chapters I and II be applied in a manner different from Articles 101 and 102 TFEU? The answer is provided by s. 60 of the Competition Act 1998[120] (Box 1.17) which has the main aim of ensuring that decisions taken under Chapters I and II are *consistent* with their treatment in EU law, having regard to any relevant differences between the provisions. The section provides guidance to the UK courts, which includes the CAT for these purposes, and the OFT as to the principles to be applied when dealing with questions under the Competition Act, but does not apply to the CC, presumably because, when originally enacted, it was assumed that the CC would not be dealing with questions relating to Articles 101 and 102 TFEU. As we shall see later, the issue is not quite as straightforward as had been hoped.

KEY LEGAL PROVISION   **Box 1.17**

The relationship between UK and EU competition law

Competition Act 1998, s. 60

(1) The purpose of this section is to ensure that so far as is possible (having regard to any relevant differences between the provisions concerned), questions arising under this Part in relation to competition within the United Kingdom are dealt with in a manner which is consistent with the treatment of corresponding questions arising in EU law in relation to competition within the Community [Union].

(2) At any time when the court determines a question arising under this Part, it must act (so far as is compatible with the provisions of this Part and whether it would otherwise be required to do so) with a view to securing that there is no inconsistency between –

(a) the principles applied, and decision reached, by the court in determining that question; and

(b) the principles laid down by the Treaty and the European Court, and any relevant decision of that Court, as applicable at that time in determining any corresponding question arising in EU law.

(3) The court must, in addition, have regard to any relevant decision or statement of the Commission.

(4) Subsections (2) and (3) also apply to –

(a) the OFT; and

(b) any person acting on behalf of the OFT in connection with any matter arising under this Part.

---

[120] Generally, see K. Middleton, 'Harmonisation with Community Law: the Euro Clause' in B. Rodger and A. MacCulloch (eds) *The UK Competition Act* (Hart Publishing, Oxford, 2000).

(5) In subsections (2) and (3), 'court' means any court or tribunal.

(6) In subsections (2)(b) and (3), 'decision' includes a decision as to – (a) the interpretation of any provision of EU law; (b) the civil liability of an undertaking for harm caused by its infringement of EU law.

Questions: What counts as a relevant statement by the Commission? Does consistency of treatment imply consistency of outcome?

The main aim of s. 60 is to ensure that decisions under the Competition Act are taken in a way that is consistent with their treatment in EU competition law, so far as it is possible, having regard to any relevant differences between the provisions. Use of the phrase 'provisions' seems to suggest that an approach which is inconsistent with EU law can only be taken if authorised by different wording within the Competition Act.

If this is the case, it becomes critical to look for differences in wording and the substantive, as opposed to procedural and enforcement, provisions of the Competition Act are very similar to Articles 101 and 102 TFEU with one certain exception and another possible one. First, s. 2 of the Competition Act 1998 applies to restrictive agreements which affect trade within the United Kingdom and, according to s. 2(3), which either are, or are intended to be, implemented within the United Kingdom. This latter provision immediately marks out a difference with EU law, which can apply to restrictive agreements that are implemented outside the EU but have an effect on trade within it.[121] Secondly, s. 18 of the Competition Act 1998 prohibits any conduct which amounts to the abuse of a dominant position, whereas Article 102 TFEU simply prohibits abuse of a dominant position. A leading UK academic has suggested that if the insertion of conduct was deliberate it might have been meant to exclude certain types of behaviour which were an offence under EU law, such as the refusal to supply.[122] This would be a radical interpretation and at odds with one of the fundamental aims of the Competition Act and there is no sign that the OFT, for example, interprets s. 18 in this way.[123]

In order to ensure consistency, subss. (2) and (3) of s. 60 require the competition authorities to act with a view to ensuring that there is no inconsistency between their decisions and the principles laid down by the Treaty and decisions of the European Court. In addition, they must have regard to relevant decisions or statements by the European Commission, which is a lesser obligation. In the OFT's view this is limited to statements or decisions which have the authority of the European Commission as a whole, such as decisions on cases under Articles 101 and 102 TFEU, notices and clear statements about its policy published in the Annual Report on Competition Policy, as opposed to press releases or speeches.[124] So, in summary, UK law on anti-competitive agreements and conduct should be identical in substance to EU law, although there are differences in enforcement and procedure.

While s. 60 sets out the rule of consistency, the Modernisation Regulation[125] sets out the responsibilities of national bodies regarding the enforcement of Articles 101 and 102 TFEU.

---

[121] Case C-306/96 *Javico International* v *Yves Saint Laurent* [1998] ECR I-1983.

[122] Middleton (n. 120) at p. 32.

[123] See also B. Sufrin, 'The Chapter II Prohibition' in B. Rodger and A. MacCulloch (eds), *The UK Competition Act* (Hart Publishing, Oxford, 2000) at p. 121, who regards the difference in language as 'insignificant'.

[124] OFT, *Modernisation* (London, 2004) at para. 4.11.

[125] Council Regulation (EC) No. 1/2003 of 16 December 2002 on the implementation of the rules on competition laid down in Articles 81 and 82 of the Treaty, OJ L1, 04.01.2003, pp. 1–25.

Articles 5 and 6 of the Regulation allow national competition authorities and national courts to apply Articles 101 and 102 TFEU to individual cases. The relationship between national and EU competition is set out in Article 3 (see Box 1.18).

KEY LEGAL PROVISION   **Box 1.18**

Relationship between Articles 101 and 102 TFEU and national competition laws

Regulation 1/2003, Article 3

1 Where the competition authorities of the Member States or national courts apply national competition law to agreements, decisions by associations of undertakings or concerted practices within the meaning of Article [101](1) of the Treaty which may affect trade between Member States within the meaning of that provision, they shall also apply Article [101] of the Treaty to such agreements, decisions or concerted practices. Where the competition authorities of the Member States or national courts apply national competition law to any abuse prohibited by Article [102] of the Treaty, they shall also apply Article [102] of the Treaty.

2 The application of national competition law may not lead to the prohibition of agreements, decisions by associations of undertakings or concerted practices which may affect trade between Member States but which do not restrict competition within the meaning of Article [101](1) of the Treaty, or which fulfil the conditions of Article [101](3) of the Treaty or which are covered by a Regulation for the application of Article [101](3) of the Treaty. Member States shall not under this Regulation be precluded from adopting and applying on their territory stricter national laws which prohibit or sanction unilateral conduct engaged in by undertakings.

3 Without prejudice to general principles and other provisions of Community [Union] law, paragraphs 1 and 2 do not apply when the competition authorities and the courts of the Member States apply national merger control laws nor do they preclude the application of provisions of national law that predominantly pursue an objective different from that pursued by Articles [101] and [102] of the Treaty.

Questions: Why would a Member State want to apply stricter sanctions for unilateral conduct than EU law? What types of law are envisaged by paragraph 3?

Article 3 says:

1 Where national competition authorities or national courts apply national competition law either to agreements or to abuses which are regulated by Articles 101 and 102 TFEU then they *must* also apply Articles 101 and 102 TFEU to such agreements or practices.

2 When national competition law is being applied to agreements which are caught by Article 101 TFEU it may not be used to prohibit agreements which do not restrict competition or which benefit from a block or an individual exemption. In other words, an agreement

which is legitimate under EU competition law cannot be prohibited under a national competition law.

3 However, Member States are allowed to apply stricter national laws which prohibit or sanction unilateral conduct engaged in by undertakings.

4 The provisions of paras 1 and 2 of Article 3 do not apply to national merger control laws nor to provisions of national law that predominantly pursue an objective different from that pursued by Articles 101 and 102 TFEU.

These provisions raise a number of awkward questions in a UK context. The first point is that the competition authorities are the OFT and the sector regulators: the Competition Commission has not been designated as a competition authority for the purposes of this Regulation, which creates some problems in the context of market investigations (see Chapter 10) and generally in relation to remedies.[126]

Although the understanding of the proviso in para. 2, relating to unilateral conduct, at the time was that it would allow the United Kingdom to carry on with its market investigation system, this is not a straightforward matter. Paragraph 2 applies to unilateral conduct only and the problems identified in many market investigations are not simply those relating to unilateral conduct but the problems of common practices by a number of market participants. For example, in the Competition Commission's inquiry into store cards, sparked by concerns over the high rate of interest charged on such cards, the issues revolved around the practices of a number of providers of store cards, not simply one, and the practices were put into effect through contractual agreements between the card providers and the retailers.[127]

As for the exclusions in para. 3, what is covered by merger control is straightforward enough but provisions of national law which pursue an objective different from Articles 101 and 102 TFEU is a different and more complicated idea. Recital 9 of Regulation 1/2003 states that Articles 101 and 102 TFEU have as their objective the protection of competition on the market. The Recital goes on to identify legislation which prohibits or imposes sanctions on unfair trading practices, which may be unilateral or contractual, as the sort of legislation which has a different objective from Articles 101 and 102 TFEU. Another possible example, suggested by Richard Whish, a leading UK competition lawyer, is that regulatory obligations imposed on undertakings other than for reasons of competition, such as obligations in relation to vulnerable customers, would fall within this exception.[128] The caveat is important because one of the general objectives of regulatory systems in the United Kingdom is the promotion of competition where this is practicable or feasible and the regulators have concurrent powers under the Competition Act with the OFT.

Despite these reservations, the basic effect of Article 3 is clear. When the OFT or court is applying national competition law to agreements or practices which fall within Articles 101 and 102 TFEU, it *must* apply those two articles. Effectively, at this point the OFT or the national court is acting as an institution of the EU, rather than as a national

---

[126] See S. Dhana, 'Impact of Modernisation: Have the UK competition authorities seen their power to issue remedies reduced?' (2005) 4 *Competition Law Journal* 33.

[127] Competition Commission, *Store Card Credit Services* (London, 2006).

[128] R. Whish and D. Bailey, *Competition Law* (7th edn, Oxford University Press, 2012) at p. 78.

body.[129] Agreements cannot be prohibited if they are not restrictive of competition under Article 101(1) TFEU or if they benefit from an individual or a block exemption. It is only in the case of unilateral practices that a stricter approach can be taken than is done in EU law and, given the approach taken to unilateral practices under Article 102 TFEU, it is unlikely that a national body would want to be even more strict (see discussion in Chapters 3 and 4). So the next issue will be to understand when a case falls within EU law and when it does not.

The boundary between EU and national competition law: an effect on trade between Member States

Articles 101, 102 and 107 TFEU (state aids) apply to only agreements, conduct or aids which 'affect trade between Member States'. The meaning of these words is not defined in the TFEU and has been the subject of substantial case law and the European Courts have not drawn any distinction between the three Articles as regards this matter. As regards merger control, the means of drawing the distinction between the jurisdiction of the EU and that of Member States is done on a completely different basis, largely relating to the amount of turnover of undertakings and its location (which is discussed in Chapter 13).

The starting point for considering the meaning of these words is a case known as *STM*.[130] In this case a German company, M, had agreed to sell a number of road graders to a French company, STM, who were given the exclusive right to sell the machines in France, subject to certain other obligations, such as maintaining an adequate stock of spare parts and not selling competitors' products without the permission of M. A dispute arose between the two undertakings over the suitability of the machines for sale, which was decided in favour of M at first instance in the French courts. STM appealed and argued that the agreement was void as it breached Article [101 TFEU] and had not been notified to the European Commission. The Cour d'Appel of Paris used Article [267 TFEU] to ask the CJEU what interpretation should be applied to Article [101(1) TFEU] with regard to agreements which contained an exclusive right of sale but did not impose any territorial restrictions on the parties or other distributors of the machines in other parts of the common market? One of the issues that the CJEU addressed was what was meant by the words 'may affect trade between Member States'. The response is set out in Box 1.19.

The first sentence in Box 1.19 demonstrates that underlying the CJEU's statement is a concern to catch all agreements which might impede the creation of a single market. This is, however, only a jurisdictional criterion: it sets out when EU competition law applies; it does not say whether an agreement or conduct is anti-competitive. The assessment of the agreement or conduct is a separate exercise from deciding whether it is subject to EU law. If it is not subject to EU law, the agreement or conduct falls to be assessed, for our purposes, under UK law.

---

[129] To prevent conflicts occurring Regulation 1/2003 sets down procedures for coordinating the work of the national competition authorities and national courts with that of the European Commission: see Articles 11 and 15.

[130] Case 56/65 *Société La Technique Minière Ulm* v *Maschinenbau* [1966] ECR 235.

KEY CASE EXTRACT **Box 1.19**

The meaning of 'affect trade between Member States'

Source: Case 56/65 *Société La Technique Minière Ulm* v *Maschinenbau* [1966] ECR 235 at p. 249:

> This provision, clarified by the introductory words of Article [101 TFEU] which refers to agreements in so far as they are 'incompatible with the Common Market', is directed to determining the field of application of the prohibition by laying down the condition that it may be assumed that there is a possibility that the realization of a single market between Member States might be impeded. It is in fact to the extent that the agreement may affect trade between Member States that the interference with competition caused by that agreement is caught by the prohibitions in Community [Union] law . . . For this requirement to be fulfilled it must be possible to foresee with a sufficient degree of probability on the basis of a set of objective factors of law or fact that the agreement in question may have an influence, direct or indirect, actual or potential, on the pattern of trade between Member States.

Questions: Can an agreement between two or more parties in a Member State have an effect on trade between Member States? Could an agreement between two or more parties in *part* of a Member State have an effect on trade? Does there have to be a negative effect on trade?

The final sentence in Box 1.19 sets out the basic test which is to be applied, and this approach has been confirmed in subsequent cases; the European Commission has attempted to summarise the case law and explain its approach in a notice.[131] The European Commission takes the view that there are three major elements to this test:

1 trade between Member States,

2 the notion of 'may affect', and

3 the idea of appreciability.

Trade between Member States

As regards trade between Member States, the Commission's view is that it is not limited to just exchanges of goods and services across borders, but covers all cross-border economic activity including establishment. Trade also applies to cases where agreements and practices affect the competitive structure of the market. Finally, the implication is that there is an impact on cross-border economic activity in at least two Member States.[132]

May affect trade

The notion of 'may affect' when combined with the reference to a sufficient degree of probability leads to the conclusion that it is not necessary that the agreement or practice has an *actual* effect; it is sufficient that it is capable of having that effect.[133] Whether it is capable of having that effect is determined by looking at objective factors of law or fact, rather than simply the parties' subjective intentions. Nor is it required that the agreement or practice has

---

[131] European Commission, 'Guidelines on the effect on trade concept contained in Articles 81 and 82 of the Treaty', OJ [2004] C101/07.

[132] Ibid., paras 19–22.

[133] This para. summarises paras 23–43 of the Commission Guidelines.

a negative effect on trade; EU jurisdiction can be established even if the agreement has a positive effect and causes an increase in trade. The effect on trade may also be direct or indirect, actual or potential. Direct and actual are reasonably clear notions, but indirect or potential need some more explanation. Indirect effects can occur in relation to products that are related to those covered by the agreement or practice, as well as in relation to the products covered.

EXAMPLE   **Box 1.20**

Indirect effects on trade

The European Commission gives, as an example of an indirect effect on products related to an agreement, an agreement involving the fixing of prices for spirits used in the production of cognac. Although the spirits were not exported, the cognac was, hence there was an effect on trade. An example of the products being affected is where a manufacturer limits warranties to products sold by distributors within their Member States, thus making it less attractive to buy outside the Member State or engage in parallel importing.

Source: European Commission, 'Guidelines on the effect on trade concept contained in Articles 81 and 82 of the Treaty' [2004] OJ C101/07 at paras 38–9.

Finally, potential effects are those that may occur in the future, with a sufficient degree of probability. In other words, even if trade is not being affected at the time of the agreement or practice, if it looks like the agreement or practice would affect it in the future, this falls within EU competition law.

Appreciability

What should be apparent from the discussion so far is that the interpretation of the concept of effect on trade is very wide. In theory, a potential indirect effect on trade which increases trade could be caught by EU competition law. The scope of this doctrine is qualified by the case law and the practice of the European Commission, as set out in the Guidelines.

The European Commission takes the view that subsequent case law has established a threshold of around 5% of the market, although turnover also has to be taken into account.[134] The Guidelines go on to say that there is a presumption that agreements between small and medium-sized enterprises (SMEs) are not capable of affecting trade between Member States. Furthermore, the notice sets out what is called the Non-Appreciable Affect on Trade (NAAT) rule, which is a negative rebuttable presumption applying to agreements within Article 101(1) TFEU, irrespective of the nature of the restrictions contained in the agreement, even if restrictions which are normally considered clearly anti-competitive[135] are included. The two cumulative conditions that have to be met are that the aggregate market share of the parties on any relevant market within the Union affected by the agreement does not exceed 590 and that, for horizontal agreements, the aggregate annual EU turnover of the undertakings concerned in the products covered by the agreement does not exceed €40 million. For vertical agreements, it is the aggregate annual EU turnover of the supplier.[136]

[134] European Commission (n. 131), para. 46.
[135] Typically referred to as 'hard-core' (see Chapters 2 and 11 for discussion).
[136] European Commission (n. 131), para. 52

KEY CASE EXTRACT | Box 1.21

The meaning of appreciability

Source: Case 5/69 *Völk v Vervaecke* [1969] ECR 295.

This case arose out of a contractual dispute between a German manufacturer of washing machines and their Belgian distributor which was referred to the CJEU under Article [267 TFEU]. They had entered into a contract which was taken to give absolute territorial protection to the Belgian distributor and would therefore, in principle, have been contrary to Article [101(1) TFEU]. The German manufacturer had a market share of less than 1% of production in Germany. The CJEU held that agreements fell outside the prohibition when they had only an insignificant effect on the market, taking into account the weak position which the persons have on the market concerned.

Questions: How small is too small? Where should the line or lines be drawn?

In practical terms, what this means is that agreements or conduct which take place over two or more Member States will be taken to fall within Articles 101 and 102 TFEU, subject to the appreciability point. In addition, agreements and conduct which take place wholly within one Member State will fall within Articles 101 and 102 TFEU because, on the tests applied above, they will have an effect on trade between Member States.[137] For example, a cartel which divides up production within one Member State will typically be concerned with preventing imports into the market, which would destabilise the cartel. This would fall within EU competition law even if there was no history of imports, if it could be foreseen that there would be imports in the future, absent the activities of the cartel. Vertical agreements may also have an effect on trade if their consequence is to foreclose the market and make it more difficult for undertakings to enter from outside the Member State. It is also possible that agreements or conduct which covers only part of a Member State may be taken to have an effect on trade. Finally, it is also clear that if the agreements and conduct relate to undertakings located outside the European Union, these may also be considered to have an effect on trade between Member States.[138] So, for example, if a distributor in the European Union enters into an agreement with a non-EU manufacturer, giving them exclusive dealing rights and territorial protection in one Member State, this affects trade between Member States because it would prevent, for example, a distributor in another Member State importing its products into the first Member State.[139]

What should be evident from this discussion is that EU competition law has developed a wide jurisdictional reach, based on a concern for ensuring that a single market cannot be distorted by the actions of private undertakings. It has been argued that, given the development of the EU and the parallel development of national systems of competition law, such a broad approach to jurisdiction is no longer appropriate,[140] although that is not evident from

---

[137] Ibid., paras 77–99.
[138] Ibid., paras 100–9.
[139] See Case 22/71 *Béguelin Import* v *G L Import Export* [1971] ECR 949 at para. 12.
[140] R. Wesseling, *The Modernisation of EC Antitrust Law* (Hart Publishing, Oxford, 2000), ch. 4.

the European Commission's Guidelines on the subject. It appears as if this issue has been dealt with through administrative means, namely the implementation of Regulation 1/2003, which obliges national competition authorities and national courts to apply EU competition law in the appropriate circumstances. Since the Regulation obliges national competition authorities to notify the European Commission of cases in which they are applying Articles 101 and 102 TFEU, and the European Commission may intervene to take over suitable cases,[141] this means that, in principle, cases of EU-wide significance will be dealt with by the European Commission, whilst cases which, although falling under EU law, are primarily focused in one Member State, will be dealt with by the national competition authority. In the context of the United Kingdom, where domestic competition law is modelled on Articles 101 and 102 TFEU, it is difficult to see how there can be a significant difference in the law that is applied.

Summary

➤ The subject of competition law is the regulation of markets in order to ensure that they remain competitive. There are three main areas of concern: anti-competitive agreements, abuse of dominant position and merger control. EU law is also concerned with controlling state activities to prevent the distortion of competition.

➤ Historically, the objectives of systems of competition law have varied including both economic and non-economic objectives.

➤ A fundamental objective of EU competition law has been to ensure that private undertakings are not allowed to partition the European market into national segments and this goal explains much of the past case law.

➤ There is a widespread consensus today that the purpose of competition law is to protect consumer welfare and that non-economic goals do not have a place within competition law. This is most clear within UK competition law but is also seen within EU competition law.

➤ The benefits of competitive markets, as opposed to monopolies, are that they bring about allocative and productive efficiency.

➤ The definition of a market is a key part of any competition law inquiry. The product market is determined by looking, first, at demand-side substitution and then at supply-side substitution.

➤ Competition law is enforced through public agencies or private litigation. In the UK and EU, historically public enforcement has taken priority.

➤ The enforcement agencies, the European Commission and OFT, are to a large extent independent of political influence and combine the functions of investigator, prosecutor and decision maker in their day-to-day activities.

[141] Regulation 1/2003 (n. 125), Art. 11.

➤ The CJEU, GC and CAT play a hugely important role in the development of competition law through their power to review decisions of the European Commission, OFT and CC as well as, in the case of the CJEU, receiving preliminary references from national courts under Article 267 TFEU.

➤ UK competition is modelled on EU competition law as regards control of anti-competitive practices and abuse of dominant position. It is required to be consistent with EU law in these areas. It has different rules for merger control and market investigations as well as criminal sanctions for certain activities.

➤ EU law applies where there is an effect on trade between Member States. This concept has been interpreted very broadly by the European Courts.

➤ National competition authorities and courts are required to apply EU competition law to agreements and conduct which affects trade between Member States when they are applying national competition law.

Further reading

Official texts

Competition Commission, *Market Investigation References* (both London, 2003), Part 2. *The Competition Commission's view on how to do market definition – very clearly written.*

Council Regulation (EC) No. 1/2003 of 16 December 2002 on the implementation of the rules on competition laid down in Articles 81 and 82 of the Treaty, OJ L1, 04.01.2003, pp. 1–25. *Often referred to as the 'Modernisation Regulation'. Key Regulation setting out European Commission's enforcement powers, its relationship with national courts and national competition authorities and their power to enforce EU competition law.*

European Commission, 'Guidelines on the effect on trade concept contained in Articles 81 and 82 of the Treaty' [2004] OJ C101/07. *The Commission's interpretation of the boundary between EU and national competition law.*

European Commission, 'Notice on the definition of the relevant market for the purposes of Community competition law', OJ C372, 09.12.1997, pp. 5–13. *The Commission's view on how to do market definition.*

Office of Fair Trading, *Market Definition* (London, 2004). *The OFT's view on how to do market definition – very clearly written.*

General

Amato, G., *Antitrust and the Bounds of Power* (Hart Publishing, Oxford, 1997). *Short set of reflections on the purpose of competition law by a leading Italian politician and competition lawyer.*

Bork, R.H., *The Antitrust Paradox* (2nd edn, Free Press, New York, 1993). *Classic and very influential text of Chicago School, first published in 1978. Entirely about American system and not balanced but very accessible.*

Hovenkamp, H., *The Antitrust Enterprise* (Harvard University Press, Cambridge Mass., 2005). *Short modern take on American competition law by eminent academic. Nothing on Europe but general reflections very interesting.*

Objectives of competition law and policy

Ehlermann, C. (ed.), *European Competition Law Annual 1997 What are the objectives of competition policy?* (Hart Publishing, Oxford, 1998). *Collection of conference essays on the theme.*

Furse, M., 'The Role of Competition Policy: A Survey' (1996) 4 *European Competition Law Review* 250. *Good overview article.*

Monti, G., *EC Competition Law* (Cambridge University Press, 2007), ch. 2. *Good discussion of differing schools of thought about the objectives of competition law.*

Pitofsky, R., 'The Political Content of Antitrust' (1979) *University of Pennsylvania Law Review* 1051. *Unusual American article by ex-Chairman of the Federal Trade Commission suggesting that objectives of antitrust may be wider than just consumer welfare.*

US antitrust law

Hovenkamp, H., *Federal Antitrust Policy: The Law of Competition and Its Practice* (4th edn, West Publishing, St Paul, Minnesota, 2011). *One volume textbook on US antitrust law by a leading professor.*

Posner, R., 'The Chicago School of Antitrust Analysis' (1979) 127 *University of Pennsylvania Law Review* 925. *Classic overview article by one of its leading protagonists and now a federal judge.*

European Union competition law

Gerber, D., *Law and Competition in Twentieth Century Europe* (Clarendon Press, Oxford, 1998). *The major historical work on European competition policy. Ends in 1997.*

Hawk, B., 'System failure: vertical restraints and EC competition law' (1995) 32 *Common Market Law Review* 973. *The classic, and very influential, critique of the unmodernised enforcement system for Article 101 TFEU.*

Riley, A., 'The EU Reform Treaty & the Competition Protocol: Undermining EC Competition Law', Centre for European Policy Studies Briefing Paper No. 142, available at: *http://shop.ceps.eu/BookDetail. php?item_id=1541. Accurate although polemical description of the changes.*

UK competition law

Sharpe, T., 'British Competition Policy in Perspective' (1985) 1 *Oxford Review of Economic Policy* 80. *One of the few overviews of British competition policy before the major changes in 1998 and 2002, written by a leading QC.*

Wilks, S., *In the Public Interest: Competition Policy and the Monopolies and Mergers Commission* (Manchester University Press, 1999). *Views from a leading political scientist. Although ostensibly about only the CC, in fact it goes much wider to look at competition policy as a whole. Does not cover the period after the Enterprise Act 2002.*

Economics and competition law

Bishop, S. and Walker, M., *The Economics of EC Competition Law* (3rd edn, Sweet & Maxwell, London, 2010). *Excellent discussion of the economic issues involved in competition law by two leading consultants.*

Fishwick, F., *Making Sense of Competition Policy* (Kogan Page, London, 1993). *Now quite dated but the economic discussion is excellent and very clear.*

Motta, M., *Competition Policy: Theory and Practice* (Cambridge University Press, 2004). *Views from a leading Italian competition professor. Some of it is very accessible, some of it is very technical.*

Scherer, F.M. and Ross, D., *Industrial Market Structure and Economic Performance* (3rd edn, Houghton Mifflin, New York, 1990). *American economics textbook. Very clear and a good concentration of antitrust.*

van den Bergh, R. and Camesasca, P., *European Competition Law and Economics* (2nd edn, Sweet & Maxwell, London, 2006). *Two leading practitioners give a critical overview of EU competition law, testing it against economic theory and comparing it to the American experience.*

2 The prohibition on anti-competitive agreements

Introduction

The purpose of this chapter is to provide a general introduction to the rules relating to agreements which are considered, or alleged to be, anti-competitive. As such, it will not say anything in detail about more specific rules relating to horizontal agreements, cartels and distribution agreements which will be dealt with later (Chapters 8 to 11). Instead, this chapter discusses general issues relating to the types of agreement that fall to be controlled by competition law. Three interrelated themes underpin this discussion and it will be seen that the development of the law relating to anti-competitive agreements has been heavily influenced by procedural concerns. The first is a debate over what constitutes a restriction of competition. This will be discussed in more detail shortly. The second theme has been a concern for ensuring that the European Commission is able to enforce the rules effectively and that undertakings engaged in anti-competitive activities are unable to rely on what are perceived as 'technical' defences. The third theme relates to the major procedural changes that have taken place since 1999 and which culminated in the implementation of

Regulation 1/2003 in May 2004.[1] In its early days, European Union competition law was based on a system which required undertakings operating agreements which fell within Article 101(1) TFEU to notify them to the Commission, which would make a decision as to whether they did fall within Article 101(1) TFEU and, if they did, whether they could benefit from the exemption in Article 101(3) TFEU.[2] The Commission took a broad interpretation of Article 101(1) TFEU but it soon became apparent that this broad interpretation encouraged a mass of notifications, which the Commission was unable to process. It responded to this problem by setting up informal procedures to dispose of cases and creating block exemptions, that is, general rules which exempted certain categories of agreements from breach of the prohibition in Article 101(1) TFEU. Under this system, the interpretation of the scope of Article 101(1) TFEU became crucial, particularly because the coverage of the block exemptions was patchy and they were rather rigid. In the light of considerable criticism, the system has now been changed to one where notification to the Commission is no longer required, indeed it can only be done in exceptional circumstances, and a decision on an Article 101(3) TFEU exemption can now be made by national competition authorities and national courts and this is combined with broader block exemptions. The Commission has accompanied this change with a different approach to the interpretation of Article 101(1) TFEU and, in practical terms, most undertakings will be concerned with whether they can benefit from a block exemption. So one of the most critical and difficult questions is to what extent decisions by the courts and the Commission prior to this new approach are useful guides, or precedents, for decisions which have to be taken today. This adds an important element of uncertainty to the entire area.

This chapter is structured around an account of Article 101 TFEU because, as explained previously (Chapter 1), the UK's Competition Act 1998 is modelled on Article 101 TFEU and s. 60 of that Act provides that questions arising in relation to competition are to be dealt with in a manner which is consistent with the treatment of corresponding questions in Union law. Furthermore, Regulation 1/2003 provides that, when a national competition authority applies its competition law to agreements which affect trade between Member States, it is also obliged to apply EU law. Therefore, in order to understand how UK law operates a sound understanding of how Article 101 TFEU functions is necessary. For the purposes of this chapter, it will be assumed that the EU and UK law on anti-competitive agreements is the same, unless specific differences are noted. The enforcement procedures are different, but this is dealt with subsequently (Chapter 5).

This chapter has the following structure: first, we discuss the concept of an undertaking because this determines what types of organisation are subject to competition law. Secondly, we discuss the meaning of 'agreement', 'concerted practice' and 'decisions by associations of undertakings' because Article 101 TFEU can apply to only these sorts of arrangements. Thirdly, we look at the key issue of what it means for an agreement or concerted practice or decision by an association of undertakings to have as its object or effect the prevention, restriction or distortion of competition in the common market. Having done this, we then look at when the prohibition may be considered inapplicable to either categories of agreements or an individual agreement: in other words, the criteria in Article 101(3) TFEU.

---

[1] Council Regulation (EC) No. 1/2003 of 16 December 2002 on the implementation of the rules on competition laid down in Articles 81 and 82 of the Treaty, OJ L1, 04.01.2003 (hereafter 'Regulation 1/2003'). It is sometimes referred to in the literature as the Modernisation Regulation.

[2] Only the Commission could make a decision on Article 101(3) TFEU.

Article 101 TFEU: preliminary issues

Article 101 TFEU, in outline (see Box 2.1 for text), prohibits agreements between undertakings which may affect inter-state trade and which have as their object or effect the prevention, restriction or distortion of competition within the internal market. Agreements which are in breach of this prohibition are declared automatically void under Article 101(2) TFEU but the prohibition may be declared inapplicable under Article 101(3) TFEU if certain conditions are met. Regulation 1/2003 provides that so long as these conditions are met, no prior decision of a competition authority is needed.[3] National competition authorities and national courts have been given the power to make decisions on whether the prohibition is to be declared inapplicable because it meets the conditions in Article 101(3) TFEU and the European Commission retains this power in exceptional circumstances where there is a Union public interest in making such a decision: for example, in relation to a novel form of agreement.[4]

KEY LEGAL PROVISION   **Box 2.1**

Article 101 TFEU (Ex Article 81 EC)

(1) The following shall be prohibited as incompatible with the internal market: all agreements between undertakings, decisions by associations of undertakings and concerted practices which may affect trade between Member States and which have as their object or effect the prevention, restriction or distortion of competition within the internal market, and in particular those which:

(a) directly or indirectly fix purchase or selling prices or any other trading conditions;

(b) limit or control production, markets, technical development, or investment;

(c) share markets or sources of supply;

(d) apply dissimilar conditions to equivalent transactions with other trading parties, thereby placing them at a competitive disadvantage;

(e) make the conclusion of contracts subject to acceptance by the other parties of supplementary obligations which, by their nature or according to commercial usage, have no connection with the subject of such contracts.

2 Any agreements or decisions prohibited pursuant to this article shall be automatically void.

3 The provisions of paragraph 1 may, however, be declared inapplicable in the case of:

– any agreement or category of agreements between undertakings,
– any decision or category of decisions by associations of undertakings,
– any concerted practice or category of concerted practices,

---

[3] Regulation 1/2003 (n. 1), Art. 1(2).

[4] Ibid., Arts 3 and 10. No decisions had been taken under Art. 10 in the first five years of operation: see European Commission, 'Staff Working Paper accompanying the Report on the functioning of Regulation 1/2003' (SEC (2009) 574 final) at paras 112–14.

which contributes to improving the production or distribution of goods or to promoting technical or economic progress, while allowing consumers a fair share of the resulting benefit, and which does not:

(a) impose on the undertakings concerned restrictions which are not indispensable to the attainment of these objectives;

(b) afford such undertakings the possibility of eliminating competition in respect of a substantial part of the products in question.

Questions: What requirements have to be met before an arrangement falls within Article 101 TFEU? How do Article 101(1) and (3) TFEU relate to each other? How should an inquiry under this Article be structured?

As can be seen in Box 2.2, ss. 2 and 9 of the Competition Act 1998 are very similar to Article 101 TFEU, with the main difference being that they apply to only agreements which affect trade within the United Kingdom and are intended to be implemented within the United Kingdom, whereas Article 101 TFEU applies to agreements which affect trade between Member States.

KEY LEGAL PROVISIONS   Box 2.2

Competition Act 1998, ss. 2 and 9

2 Agreements etc. preventing, restricting or distorting competition
1 Subject to section 3, agreements between undertakings, decisions by associations of undertakings or concerted practices which –

(a) may affect trade within the United Kingdom, and

(b) have as their object or effect the prevention, restriction or distortion of competition within the United Kingdom,

are prohibited unless they are exempt in accordance with the provisions of this Part.

(2) Subsection (1) applies, in particular, to agreements, decisions or practices which –

(a) directly or indirectly fix purchase or selling prices or any other trading conditions;

(b) limit or control production, markets, technical development or investment;

(c) share markets or sources of supply;

(d) apply dissimilar conditions to equivalent transactions with other trading parties, thereby placing them at a competitive disadvantage;

(e) make the conclusion of contracts subject to acceptance by the other parties of supplementary obligations which, by their nature or according to commercial usage, have no connection with the subject of such contracts.

(3) Subsection (1) applies only if the agreement, decision or practice is, or is intended to be, implemented in the United Kingdom.

(4) Any agreement or decision which is prohibited by subsection (1) is void.

9 Exempt agreements

(1) An agreement is exempt from the Chapter I prohibition if it –

(a) contributes to –

    (i) improving production or distribution, or

    (ii) promoting technical or economic progress, while allowing consumers a fair share of the resulting benefit; and

(b) does not –

    (i) impose on the undertaking concerned restrictions which are not indispensable to the attainment of those objectives; or

    (ii) afford the undertakings concerned the possibility of eliminating competition in respect of a substantial part of the products in question.

Questions: Can you find any significant differences with Article 101 TFEU? Could there be any justifiable reasons for interpreting these provisions differently from Article 101 TFEU in a UK context?

In order for an agreement to fall within EU competition law, it must meet a number of criteria, all of which need discussion:

- There must be *an agreement or a decision by an association of undertakings or a concerted practice*.
- The agreement, decision or concerted practice must be between *undertakings*.
- The agreement, decision or concerted practice must *affect trade between Member States*.
- The agreement, decision or concerted practice must have as its *object or effect the prevention, restriction or distortion of competition, in an appreciable manner,*[5] *within the internal market*.

Before reaching the substantive question of whether the agreement[6] has the object or effect of restricting[7] competition there are a number of preliminary issues which have to be considered. One of them – what is meant by inter-state trade – we have considered earlier (Chapter 1), because it draws the line between EU and domestic competition law. The others will be discussed in turn. Before doing this, it is worth reflecting on the key substantive issue: what is meant by an agreement having the object or effect of preventing, restricting or distorting competition?

The problem is sometimes said to arise because all agreements between contracting parties restrict their freedom of action (see Box 2.3).

So, for example, if a farmer sells a crop to a supermarket, he cannot sell that crop to another supermarket or a producer of processed food. Although the farmer's freedom of action is limited by the agreement, this is not a competition problem for the other supermarkets if there are other farmers who produce the same or substitute crops. The farmer is not faced

---

[5] Alert readers will note that this phrase does not appear in the text of Article 101 TFEU.

[6] From now on, 'agreement' will be used as shorthand for 'agreement, decision by an association of undertakings or concerted practice' unless otherwise specified.

[7] Similarly, 'restricting' or 'restriction' will be used as shorthand for 'prevention, restriction or distortion' of competition unless otherwise noted.

with a competition problem if there are other buyers for the crop than that one supermarket. By contrast, assume that all the farmers who produce a particular crop agree between themselves that they will sell only at a particular price. Or, alternatively, that all the buyers agree amongst themselves to purchase at a particular price. In both cases, this would be regarded as a competition problem, because the farmers and the buyers have substituted the market power given to them by their agreement for the workings of a competitive market. So the issue is not whether the agreement restrains the freedom of action of the participants, but whether the agreement has an effect which is detrimental to competition or competitive markets.

KEY CASE EXTRACT   Box 2.3

Source: Justice Brandeis in *Chicago Board of Trade v United States*, 246 US 231 (1918) quoted in E. Gellhorn, W. Kovacic and S. Calkins, *Antitrust Law and Economics* (5th edn, West Publishing, St Paul, Minnesota, 2004) at p. 210:

> Every agreement concerning trade, every regulation of trade, restrains. To bind, to restrain, is of their very essence. The true test of legality is whether the restraint imposed is such as merely regulates and perhaps thereby promotes competition or whether it is such as may suppress or even destroy competition.

Question: To what extent is it accurate to describe an agreement freely entered into as a restraint? What sort of questions would you have to ask to apply Justices Brandeis's test?

Modern commercial arrangements do not make it easy to answer this question. Although an agreement to fix prices and output between competitors is clearly an example of substituting an agreement for the working of a competitive market, other arrangements raise more difficult questions for competition policy. How should we react to an agreement between the two biggest producers in a market to pool their research efforts to produce a new product? Is this an exercise of market power, or an efficient use of resources? What about the various arrangements where a manufacturer gives exclusive distribution rights to one company for a period of time? Is this an exercise of market power or simply a sensible commercial arrangement?

The starting point for most economists is to distinguish horizontal and vertical agreements (see Box 2.4). The former are agreements between undertakings which operate at the same level of production, such as manufacturers of the same good. Vertical agreements are agreements between undertakings which operate at different levels of production: for example, an agreement by a clothes manufacturer to supply a retail store with its clothes.

KEY DEFINITION   Box 2.4

Horizontal and vertical agreements

Horizontal agreement: co-operation is of a 'horizontal nature' if an agreement is entered into between actual or potential competitors . . . Two companies are treated as actual competitors if they are active on the same relevant market. A company is treated as a

---

potential competitor of another company if, in the absence of the agreement, in case of a small but permanent increase in relative prices it is likely that the former, within a short period of time, would undertake the necessary additional investments or other necessary switching costs to enter the relevant market on which the latter is active.

Vertical agreement: an agreement between two or more undertakings that operate, for the purposes of the agreement, at different levels of the production or distribution chain.

Sources: European Commission, *Guidelines on the applicability of Article 101 TFEU to horizontal cooperation agreements*, OJ C11, 14.01.2011 at paras 1 and 10; Commission Regulation (EC) No. 330/2010 of 20 April 2010 on the application of Article 101(3) TFEU to categories of vertical agreements and concerted practices, OJ L102, 23.04.2010, Art. 2 (with some textual alterations).

Question: Will commercial arrangements always fall neatly into either of these two categories?

Economists take differing approaches to the competitive effects of these agreements. Horizontal agreements are viewed with more suspicion, as these may obviously be attempts to create market power, for example through price-fixing, although there may be horizontal agreements which are efficiency enhancing (see Chapter 9). Although views have evolved over time, today vertical agreements are, however, viewed more favourably or neutrally, as agreements which are less likely to create or exploit market power. Indeed, some economists would go further than this and view *all* vertical agreements as pro-competitive or efficiency enhancing, although this is perhaps a view at one extreme end of the spectrum.[8] The text of Article 101 TFEU does not draw such a distinction and it has been confirmed by the Court of Justice of the European Union (CJEU) that the Article applies equally to horizontal and vertical agreements, provided they meet the criteria within the Article.[9]

From an economist's point of view, the distinction between horizontal and vertical agreements does not take us very far, as it is important to examine the effects of an agreement on the competitive process and to see whether it is damaging to total societal welfare, or consumer welfare, depending on the standard adopted, or not. In the context of EU competition law such an approach would create at least two important problems. First, as we have seen (Chapter 1), one of the key objectives of the European Union has been the creation of a single internal market. Much of European Union law is about preventing the Member States from erecting barriers to trade between them and an important objective of EU competition law has been to prevent private undertakings from erecting equivalent barriers; that is, dividing markets along national lines.[10] Thus EU competition law is concerned to regulate or prohibit agreements which divide up markets on national lines even though, on an economic analysis, such agreements would have no detrimental effect on societal welfare; they might even be positive. So, historically, EU competition law has taken a much stricter approach to, especially, vertical agreements than economic analysis would suggest, even though the attitude has begun to change in recent years.

---

[8] For example, R. Bork, *The Antitrust Paradox* (2nd edn, Free Press, New York, 1993) at p. 288: 'every vertical restraint should be completely lawful'.
[9] Cases 56 and 58/64 *Consten & Grundig* [1966] ECR 429.
[10] This is not a concern for UK competition law because we already have a single, domestic market.

The second problem for a 'pure' economics approach is a procedural one, because an administrative agency, such as the European Commission, does not have the resources to examine the actual effects of every commercial agreement. As we have seen, Article 101 TFEU makes provision for a procedure whereby the prohibition can be declared inapplicable in certain circumstances, and therefore any undertaking(s) which had doubts about their agreement could apply to the Commission for a decision on the matter. In practice, from the beginning of the EU system of competition law, this proved impossible to work effectively because the Commission was swamped with notifications from undertakings seeking guidance on the legality of their agreements, not least because this gave the notifying undertakings immunity from being fined for breach of the prohibition from the date of notification. It is therefore necessary to develop some general rules, which are reasonably predictable, which will allow the administrative agency to focus its efforts on those agreements which are most damaging to the competitive process, whilst ignoring those which are neutral or even beneficial. Given the structure of Article 101 TFEU, a prohibition followed by an exemption, this could be done either by focusing on the definition of what constitutes a restriction on competition, the Article 101(1) TFEU phase, or by focusing on what criteria constitute an exemption, the Article 101(3) TFEU phase. It is, however, important to see that the two phases of Article 101 TFEU are related; if an expansive interpretation of Article 101(1) TFEU is taken and many agreements fall within it, then there is a greater need for general rules under Article 101(3) TFEU allowing exemptions. If a narrower interpretation of Article 101(1) TFEU is taken, then there is less work to be done under Article 101(3) TFEU. Whichever approach is taken has important consequences for the competition authorities and businesses concerning who has the power to make decisions. If an expansive approach to Article 101(1) TFEU is taken, then the rules on exemptions become more important and these rules are decided by the European Commission, with less scrutiny by the European Courts, and so the Commission is able to have a greater influence on the content of commercial agreements. If a narrower interpretation of Article 101(1) TFEU is taken, then the European Commission has less influence over commercial agreements and its decisions are likely to be subjected to greater scrutiny in the European Courts. Historically, the European Commission has taken an expansive view of the scope of Article 101(1) TFEU, although it has pulled back somewhat more recently, while its critics have argued that a narrower approach to Article 101(1) TFEU should be taken.

It is worthwhile explaining, very briefly, how the problem of categorising agreements as anti-competitive or not has been dealt with in the United States, because this has influenced critics of the Commission's policy and the terminology has been imported into European debates. Section 1 of the Sherman Act 1898 provides that 'every contract, combination . . . or conspiracy in restraint of trade or commerce . . . is hereby declared to be illegal' and, unlike EU competition law, there is no provision for an exemption. Enforcement of American antitrust law is done through the ordinary courts either by public agencies or by third parties bringing a case against those involved in the allegedly anti-competitive cartel or agreement. Within the American system a fundamental problem has been to define what is meant by the words 'restraint of trade' and how the courts should approach agreements. This was solved initially by deciding that the Sherman Act applied to unreasonable restraints of trade only, which was the foundation for the rule of reason approach. Exactly what this meant and how it should be applied has always been a matter of some controversy within US law: indeed, one commentator said, 'No one knows what the Rule of Reason means.'[11] The original, and very influential statement of it said:

> The true test of legality is whether the restraint imposed is such as merely regulates and perhaps therby promotes competition or whether it is such as may suppress or even destroy competition. To determine that question the court must ordinarily consider the facts peculiar to the business to which the restraint is applied; its condition before and after the restraint was imposed; the nature of the restraint and its effect, actual and probable.[12]

Whish and Sufrin, two of the leading academic commentators in the UK on competition law, describe this as a wide-ranging inquiry, which includes analysis of the product market and sensitivity to economic theory and weighing the pro- and anti-competitive effects of an agreement against one another. If the former outweigh the latter, then no infringement is found.[13] More critically, a leading American commentator has said that Justice Brandeis' statement is one of the most damaging in the history of antitrust because it has suggested to many courts that, under rule of reason analysis, nearly everything is relevant and does not allow for a focus on the important issues.[14] Within the American system there is also a category of agreements which are considered *per se*, that is, conclusively presumed to be, in breach of the Sherman Act and where no elaborate inquiry into the context of the agreement is required.[15] The idea here is that there are classes of agreements which, on the basis of judicial experience are considered to be clearly damaging the competitive process so that they can be condemned without the full scale inquiry needed for a rule of reason analysis and, critically, without having to submit this question to a jury.

So, in American practice, there are agreements which are *per se* unlawful, that is conclusively presumed to be unlawful, where no major inquiry is needed by the courts, and agreements which are subject to some form of rule of reason approach, which may involve a wide ranging inquiry into the agreement and, ultimately, balancing the pro- and anti-competitive effects of it. Often, under the rule of reason approach, the agreement will be found not to violate the Sherman Act. It is important, however, to understand that the American approach is not so much a question of two categories, but has become in recent years more nuanced. In particular, the American courts have begun to develop a variety of approaches to rule of reason cases, which are sometimes referred to as the 'quick look' approach, the idea being that something shorter than a full rule of reason inquiry is used. However, the Supreme Court has said: 'The truth is that our categories of analysis of anticompetitive effect are less fixed than terms like *"per se"*, *"quick look,"* and *"rule of reason"* tend to make them appear.'[16] The Court went onto say that what was required was an opinion fit for the case; in some circumstances less inquiry was needed, in others more would be needed and this does not depend on the label given to the inquiry. Furthermore, because the approach to be taken depends on the experience of the courts, in the light of the evidence before them, the approach taken may

---

[11] R. Posner and F. Easterbrook, *Antitrust* (2nd edn, West Publishing, St Paul, Minnesota, 1981) at p. 597; and see O. Black, 'Per se Rules and Rules of Reason: What are They?' [1997] 3 *European Competition Law Review* 145, who identifies thirteen varieties of the rule of reason, as well as J. Peeters, 'The Rule of Reason Revisited' (1989) 37 *American Journal of Comparative Law* 521.

[12] *Chicago Board of Trade* v *United States*, 246 US 231 (1918) at 238 per Justice Brandeis.

[13] R. Whish and B. Sufrin, 'Art 85 and the Rule of Reason' (1987) 7 *Yearbook of European Law* 1 at 6.

[14] H. Hovenkamp, *Federal Antitrust Policy* (11th edn, West Publishing, St Paul, Minnesota, 2011) at 275.

[15] See *Northern Pacific Railway* v *US* 356 US 1, 5 (1958).

[16] *California Dental Association* v *Federal Trade Commission*, 526 US 756 (1999) per Souter, J.

change over time. Thus, for example, minimum resale price maintenance had been considered as a *per se* antitrust violation since a decision in 1911,[17] which was changed in 2007 when the Supreme Court ruled that minimum resale price maintenance should be assessed under a rule of reason standard.[18]

EU competition law is not, however, structured in this way. According to Article 101(1) TFEU there are agreements, or, more precisely, clauses within agreements, which have the 'object' of restricting competition and these fall foul of the prohibition in Article 101(1) TFEU without much inquiry being needed.[19] They may, however, still benefit from the exemption in Article 101(3) TFEU if they meet its conditions. There are also agreements which have the 'effect' of restricting competition and here there needs to be greater inquiry into the economic context of the agreement but, and this is the crucial point, it is not a full-scale economic analysis but concentrates on whether there are negative effects on competition. If there are, that agreement falls within the prohibition in Article 101(1) TFEU and the inquiry then moves to whether it can benefit from the exemption in Article 101(3) TFEU, which is where consideration of the pro- and anti-competitive effects of the agreement will take place. EU law draws a clear distinction between agreements with the 'object' and 'effect' of restricting competition in the initial phase of deciding whether they constitute a restriction of competition. Both 'object' and 'effect' agreements may benefit from the exemption in Article 101(3) TFEU if they meet its conditions in contrast to the American system where an agreement which is *per se* unlawful will not, by definition, create sufficient countervailing benefits. The result of this structure, when combined with an approach which takes a broad interpretation of Article 101(1) TFEU because of the objective of market integration and perhaps the Ordo-liberal philosophy behind some of EU competition law, means that a wide range of commercial agreements fall to be regulated by EU competition law, even though, on a pure economic analysis, they do not cause competition problems. Much of the history of recent EU competition law involves an attempt, as we shall see, to focus enforcement activity on agreements which are of concern to the competition authorities while providing clear rules to ensure that neutral or beneficial agreements are not prevented.

The concept of an undertaking

European Union competition law only applies to 'undertakings', a word used not only in Article 101 TFEU but also in Articles 102 TFEU (ex Article 82 EC) and 106 TFEU (ex Article 86 EC), although there is no definition of the term in the Treaties. This is therefore a question relating to the scope of competition law, that is, to what extent are particular activities to be regulated by the rules on competition as opposed to other considerations? The question of whether or not an entity is or is not an undertaking is therefore an absolutely critical one for deciding whether there is a competition issue to discuss. Underlying this technical question is a much wider policy issue about how far we are prepared to see decisions in particular areas of social life determined by market forces and how far we want other considerations to

---

[17] *Dr Miles Medical Co* v *John D. Park*, 220 US 373 (1911).

[18] *Leegin Creative Leather Products* v *PSKS*, 551 US 877 (2007).

[19] See European Commission, *Guidelines on the application of Article 81(3) of the Treaty*, OJ C101, 27.04.2004 at para. 20, citing Case C-49/92P, *Commission v Anic Partecipazioni SpA* [1999] ECR I-4125 at para. 99. See recently Case C-209/07, *Competition Authority* v *Beef Industry Development Society* [2008] ECR I-8637 at para. 16.

predominate. For example, how far should arrangements relating to health care, welfare benefits, the regulation of professions and the regulation of sport be subject to the rules on competition law and how far should they be decided on other grounds? This is an issue that the European Courts have struggled with.

The basic definition of an undertaking was given by the European Court of Justice in the *Höfner* case (see Box 2.5).

KEY DEFINITIONS   Box 2.5

Definition of an undertaking

in the context of competition law, . . . the concept of an undertaking encompasses every entity engaged in an economic activity, regardless of the legal status of the entity and the way in which it is financed.

Source: Case C-41/90 *Höfner and Elser v Macrotron* [1991] ECR I-1979 at para. 21.

any activity consisting in offering goods and services on a given market is an economic activity.

Source: Cases C-180 to 184/98 *Pavlov and others* [2000] ECR I-6451, para. 74.

The first point to notice about this definition is that the legal status of the entity is not relevant. Thus individuals may be undertakings,[20] as may partnerships, cooperatives and other forms of private sector business organisations. The entity does not have to be profit-making[21] and nor does it have to be part of the private sector: entities which are part of the state may be undertakings, provided that they engage in economic activity.[22] The case law is also clear that an entity does not have to be an undertaking for all of its activities; it may be subject to competition law in relation to some of its activities but not in relation to others.[23] This is typically an issue in relation to public sector organisations and may not always be a straightforward question to answer. Thus, for example, Eurocontrol, a body which carries out a variety of services in relation to air traffic control, was held by the GC to be an undertaking in relation to its provision of assistance to national administrations, but not in relation to its activities relating to technical standardisation. The ruling on the provision of assistance to national administrations was reversed by the CJEU.[24]

So the critical question is whether an entity is engaged in economic activity. Economic activity would seem to mean engaging in transactions on a market, that is, buying and selling goods and services, where the price is determined by the market.[25] We should note first that

---

[20] European Commission Decision 76/29, *AOIP v Beyrard* [1976] 1 CMLR D14 (opera singers).

[21] Case C-49/07 *Motosykletistiki Omospondia Ellados NPID (MOTOE) v Elliniko Dimosio* [2008] ECR I-4863 at para. 27.

[22] European Commission, *Spanish Courier Services* [1990] OJ L233/19; Case C-41/90 *Höfner and Elser v Macrotron* [1991] ECR I-1979, Case C-138/11 *Compass-Datenbank GmbH v Republik of Austria* decision of 12 July 2012 (GC).

[23] See Case C-113/07P *SELEX Sistemi Integrati v Commission* [2009] ECR I-2207 and Case C-138/11 *Compass-Datenbank GmbH v Republik of Austria* decision of 12 July 2012 (GC).

[24] Case T-155/04 *SELEX Sistemi Integrati v Commission* [2006] ECR II-4797; Case C-113/07P *SELEX Sistemi Integrati v Commission* [2009] ECR I-2207 at paras 66–85.

[25] See, for example, Case C-35/96 *Commission v Italy* [1998] ECR I-3851 at para. 36.

simply paying money is not an indicator of a market transaction.[26] When we pay taxes, we are paying money to an organisation but it is not a market transaction: there is no choice about whether to pay the tax and there is no direct reciprocity – we do not receive anything directly once the tax has been paid (although we do receive public services that have been financed out of taxation). Having made this point, it is clear that public bodies quite often finance their activities by levying charges on the consumers of their goods or services. Thus when we go to a local authority leisure centre to use the swimming pool we pay money; when local authority pest control officers are called in, they charge for their services. In the same way, charges may be made for the issue of licences and for the grant of planning permission. Intuitively, some of these charges look more like market transactions than others do. A charge for a licence or planning permission is determined by the public authority, on a variety of possible bases, but is not determined by the market, by the play of supply and demand. A charge for entry to a swimming pool or museum looks closer to a price: the local authority may have considered competing attractions and set the price to maximise income, although it may also have taken other matters into account – for example, the social effects of its charges. So we can see that, although the distinction in principle between market and non-market transactions can be clearly stated, in practice it might be difficult to assign a charge to one side of the line or another.

The problem has been exacerbated by the growing move towards liberalisation, privatisation and generally market oriented means of governance that have grown up in Western Europe since around the late 1970s. For our purposes, two trends can be discerned. The first is the growing tendency for states to entrust the provision of public services to private sector organisations, whether for profit or not for profit. Thus, for example, in the United Kingdom there are now a number of private providers of prisons and the Health and Social Care Act 2012 allows for the provision of health services by private providers.[27] Secondly, there has also been a tendency to introduce market mechanisms into the provision of public services and a reluctance to finance these services out of direct taxation but rather through contributions from users or beneficiaries. This has created a number of problems in relation to the application of competition law in what might loosely be called the social services area.

The exercise of public powers or official authority

Before looking at those cases, there is a general principle to be outlined: that the competition rules are not applicable to activities in the exercise of official authority, whether these are carried out by public bodies. Such an activity is:

> a task in the public interest which forms part of the essential functions of the State' and where that activity 'is connected by its nature, its aim and the rules to which it is subject with the exercise of powers . . . which are typically those of a public authority.[28]

This principle can be illustrated by two cases. In *SAT* v *Eurocontrol*,[29] Eurocontrol, an international organisation, was responsible for air traffic control in Northern Europe and levied

---

[26] On this point, see the AG's opinion in Case C-138/11 *Compass-Datenbank GmbH* v *Republik* v *Austria* decision of 12 July 2012 (GC) at para. 52.

[27] And also introduces a system of competition regulation: Health and Social Care Act 2012, ss. 72–80.

[28] AG Jacobs in Case C-67/96 *Albany International* v *Stichting Bedrijfspensioenfonds textielindustrie* [1999] ECR I-5751 at para. 314, quoting *SAT Fluggesellschaft* v *Eurocontrol* at para. 30.

[29] Case C-364/92 *SAT Fluggesellschaft* v *Eurocontrol* [1994] ECR I-43.

route charges on its users. SAT challenged the scale of those route charges under Article 102 TFEU and the question arose as to whether Eurocontrol was an undertaking. The CJEU held that Eurocontrol's activities were connected to the exercise of powers relating to the control and supervision of air space which were typically those of a public authority and were not of an economic nature justifying control by competition law.[30] It is worth noting that in a subsequent case in relation to Eurocontrol there was a dispute as to whether all of its activities fell within the category of the exercise of public powers, although it was ultimately held that they all did.[31] In the *Diego Cali* case,[32] a private limited company (SEPG) carried out anti-pollution surveillance activities for which it charged the users of the port. The charges levied by it were challenged by one of the users as an abuse of a dominant position. The CJEU decided that the tasks that SEPG was responsible for were tasks of the public interest which formed one of the essential functions of the state. The point, which comes out clearly in the Advocate General's opinion, was that such surveillance activities could not be undertaken by private companies on a market basis. The charges in this case were not levied as a result of SEPG clearing up any pollution caused, which might well have been seen differently, but simply for the monitoring function that it was carrying out.[33]

Health and social services

More problematic over recent years has been a number of cases arising in the area of social security schemes and the provision of health care and associated activities. In relation to the first two categories, the European Courts have developed the notion of 'solidarity' in order to indicate what sort of operations should be excluded from the rules on competition. The starting point for discussion is the case of *Poucet and Pistre*,[34] where two people challenged the requirement to make compulsory payments to a sickness and maternity scheme and an old-age pension scheme. The question in the case was whether these schemes were undertakings, that is, engaged in an economic activity. The CJEU held that they were not, as they fulfilled an exclusively social function and were based on the principle of solidarity. The indicators of solidarity were that, in the sickness and maternity scheme, the scheme was financed by contributions proportional to the income of the persons making them, and there was some provision for exemption from payments, whereas the benefits were identical to all those who received them. In other words, there was an element of redistribution in the scheme. In the old-age scheme, the indicator of solidarity was that the contributions paid by active workers financed the pensions of the retired workers. Finally, those social security schemes with a surplus contributed to financing those with structural financial difficulties. This can usefully be contrasted with another French case, *FFSA*,[35] which involved a challenge by insurance companies to the working of an optional insurance scheme for farmers. On a preliminary reference from the French Conseil d'État, the CJEU held that this was an undertaking. First,

---

[30] Ibid. at para. 30.

[31] Case T-155/04 *SELEX Sistemi Integrati v Commission* [2006] ECR II-4797 (GC); Case C-113/07P *SELEX Sistemi Integrati v Commission* [2009] ECR I-2207 at paras 66–85.

[32] Case C-343/95 *Diego Cali v SEPG* [1997] ECR I-1547. See also Case C-138/11 *Compass-Datenbank GmbH v Republik v Austria* decision of 12 July 2012 (GC).

[33] Diego Cali at para. 20 of the judgment and para. 43 of the AG's opinion.

[34] Cases C-159–160/91 *Poucet and Pistre v AGF and Cancava* [1993] ECR I-637.

[35] Case C-244/94 *Fédération Française des Sociétés d'Assurance v Ministère de l'Agriculture* [1995] ECR I-4013.

the scheme was financed on the basis of capitalisation, that is, the payments made were collected together (capitalised) and invested in financial products and therefore the amount of benefits paid out depended on both the contributions which were made and the success or otherwise of the investments. The fund therefore carried out an economic activity in competition with life assurance companies.[36] Secondly, although there were elements of solidarity and social purpose in this fund, they were limited and did not prevent the fund from being an undertaking for the purposes of Article 101 TFEU.

How difficult it is to decide whether an operation is characterised by solidarity or not can be seen by looking at the *Albany* case,[37] which involved the question of the status of supplementary Dutch pension funds, which had been set up by collective bargaining between the employers and the trade unions and affiliation to them was made compulsory by a decision of the Minister of State. Here it was argued that the compulsory affiliation to the scheme for particular sectors rendered it a public social security service, that it was non-profit-making and that it was based on solidarity, as all workers had to be accepted, pension rights could accrue even if workers were incapacitated and there was no link between the level of contributions and the benefits which would be received. The CJEU rejected this argument, pointing out that the funds worked on the basis of capitalisation and therefore the benefits depended on the financial results of investments. In addition, there were various possibilities for exempting undertakings that had provided equivalent pension schemes for their employees. So again, although there were elements of solidarity in the running of the scheme, this did not take it entirely outside Article 101 TFEU, although the elements of solidarity were relevant to the question of whether they might justify the exclusive right to manage supplementary pension schemes; that is, could they benefit from the derogation in Article 106(2) TFEU, a point which is discussed later (Chapter 7).

Equally difficult was the case of *AG2R Prévoyance* v *Beaudout Père et Fils SARL*.[38] This case involved the payment of health care costs in the French social security system. Under this system, some of the costs are paid by the basic social security system while the remainder may be paid, in part, by supplementary health care insurance schemes, which cover around 93% of the French population. Within the traditional bakery sector, the employers' and the employees' representatives (the social partners) agreed to set up such a supplementary scheme. Under their collective agreement, French law provided that such a scheme could only be administered by insurance companies, provident societies or mutual insurance associations. AG2R Prévoyance (AG2R), a non-profit-making provident society, was chosen to administer the scheme. Flat rate contributions of €40 per month per employee were laid down and half of those contributions were paid by the employer. The relevant French Minister issued a decree which made affiliation to this scheme compulsory and there was no possibility for exemption. The dispute arose because Beaudout had made its own supplementary health care insurance arrangements and AG2R brought a case in the French courts, seeking to make it affiliate to the agreed scheme. The case was referred to the CJEU and one of the questions was whether AG2R was an undertaking for the purposes of Article 102 TFEU.

---

[36] Ibid., para. 17.

[37] Case C-67/96 *Albany International* v *Stichting Bedrijfspensioenfonds textielindustrie* [1999] ECR I-5751. See also Cases C-180–184/98 *Pavel Pavlov* v *Stichting Pensioenfonds Medische Specialisten* [2000] ECR I-6451 for a similar decision in relation to supplementary funds organised on a professional basis.

[38] Case C-437/09 *AG2R Prévoyance* v *Beaudout Père et Fils SARL* [2011] 4 CMLR 19.

In order to decide whether AG2R was an undertaking, the Court asked two questions: did the scheme apply the principle of solidarity and to what extent was it under supervision by the state, as these factors would tend to suggest that the activity was not economic. On the solidarity point, the Court found that there were sufficient indicators because of the flat fees paid, which meant that the services and scope of cover provided were not proportional to the contributions. In addition, in certain circumstances, the services were provided even if the contributions had not been paid. On the state control point, however, the Court pointed out that the employers and employees had chosen this form of a supplementary scheme and that the law also allowed them to choose among different types of providers. So there was no obligation to appoint AG2R to manage the scheme or for AG2R to take it up. So, depending on the circumstances of AG2R's appointment and the room for negotiation it might have on the terms and conditions under which it operated, it would be possible to see it as an undertaking engaged in economic activity which was chosen by the social partners, on the basis of financial and economic considerations, from among other undertakings with which it is in competition on the market in the provident services which it offers. The ultimate conclusion was, however, up to the referring court.

Controversy in this area came about in the United Kingdom through the judgment of the Competition Appeal Tribunal (CAT) in the *Bettercare* case.[39] In this case the appellant provided nursing home and residential care in Northern Ireland under contract to the North and West Belfast Health and Social Service Trust and the Trust also provided its own residential care through directly owned care homes. The appellant complained to the Office of Fair Trading that the Trust had been in breach of the Chapter II prohibition in the Competition Act 1998, the equivalent to Article 102 TFEU, basically through favouring its own operations. The initial question was whether the Trust was an undertaking for the purposes of competition law and the Director General of Fair Trading decided that it was not. Bettercare then appealed to the CAT, trying to get this decision reversed. The CAT held that the Trust was an undertaking because it was engaged in an economic activity on a market. First, there was a market for contracting out of residential provision; secondly the Trust was also active itself in providing residential accommodation through its own homes; and, thirdly, it received remuneration for the provision of its services.[40] As a 'cross-check' on its approach, the CAT took the view that the allegations of anti-competitive conduct were the sorts of things that competition law was trying to prevent.[41] The decision was thus remitted to the OFT for a second decision. The OFT subsequently decided that the Trust had not engaged in any abuse and that it did not have the jurisdiction to investigate the other public authorities engaged in the running of the NHS in Northern Ireland, which were responsible for the pricing policy of the Trust, as they were not undertakings.[42]

What this case did do, however, was to suggest that a broader approach to the concept of an undertaking than had previously been applied in CJEU cases might be possible. Subsequently, the CJEU has taken a different direction to the CAT and it would seem to be the case that *Bettercare* should not be regarded as an accurate statement of the law.[43] This

[39] *Bettercare Group Ltd* v *Office of Fair Trading* [2002] CAT 7.
[40] Ibid. at paras 196–201.
[41] Ibid. at para. 202.
[42] OFT, 'BetterCare Group Ltd/North & West Belfast Health & Social Services Trust (Remitted case)' (2003).
[43] See OFT, 'The Competition Act 1998 and public bodies', Policy note 1/2004 (2004) which comes to a similar conclusion.

comes out clearly in the *FENIN* case.[44] Here an association which marketed medical equipment complained to the Commission that the Spanish Health Service had abused their dominant position by delaying payment for medical goods. The Commission rejected the complaint on the grounds that the body running the Spanish health system was not acting as an undertaking. FENIN appealed this decision unsuccessfully to the GC and from there onto the CJEU. The GC took the view that purchasing goods, even in great quantities, did not, in itself, constitute activity on the market. In order to determine this, one had to look at the use to which the goods were put. In this case, the Spanish health service operated on the principle of solidarity because it was funded by social security contributions and provided free of charge.[45] Despite the fact that such an entity could wield considerable economic power, even resulting in a monopsony, it could not be categorised as an undertaking.[46] The CJEU supported the GC's view that the activity of purchasing could not be disassociated from the use to which the goods were put.[47]

A similar approach can be seen in a slightly earlier case which involved the question of whether German sickness funds which, under German legislation, determined the maximum amount payable by those funds for the costs of certain medicines constituted undertakings.[48] The CJEU took the view that such funds fulfilled a purely social function and operated on the basis of solidarity. In particular, they were obliged to offer essentially identical benefits which did not depend on contributions from members, there was an equalisation of costs and risks between them and they were not in competition with private sector entities. Although there was some limited competition between them, this did not change the nature of their activities. However, the CJEU accepted that in principle the funds could also engage in economic activities and looked to see if this was the case in setting the maximum amounts but decided that this was not an economic activity.[49]

Conclusions on the concept of an undertaking

What conclusions can we draw on the basis of this case law? The test is whether an entity is engaged in an economic activity. In many cases, the answer to this question will be straight-forward but the difficult cases involved those areas where the provision of public services is done using a mixture of public and private sector techniques, not falling clearly within the scope of official authority. The question to ask is not whether the effects of the activity are those that competition law is meant to protect against, as this was effectively rejected in *FENIN* and *AOK*, nor whether in principle the activity could be carried out by private bodies, as almost any activity could be carried out by private bodies. The question is whether the activity is dominated by concerns of solidarity and, in deciding this, there are a number of indicators of solidarity. First, the question of whether a scheme is compulsory is important, but perhaps most important is, secondly, the issue of capitalisation and the relationship of benefits to contributions. If there is an arrangement whereby contributions are invested and this funds the benefits received, this looks much more like an economic

---

[44] Case C-205/03 *Federación Española de Empresas de Tecnologia Sanitaria (FENIN)* v *Commission* [2003] ECR II-357 (GC), [2006] ECR I-6295 (CJEU).

[45] Although there was a question about charging non-Spanish nationals for services.

[46] Ibid. at paras 37–40.

[47] Ibid. at para. 26.

[48] Case C-264/01 *AOK Bundesverband* v *Icthyol Gesellschaft Cordes* [2004] ECR I-2493.

[49] Ibid. at paras 51–65. And compare the Advocate General's opinion.

Table 2.1 Indicators of solidarity and economic activity

Indicators of solidarity	Indicators of economic activity
Whether affiliation with the scheme is compulsory	Optional membership
Whether the scheme pursues an exclusively social purpose	The principle of capitalisation (dependency of entitlements on the contributions paid and the financial results of the scheme)
Whether the scheme is non-profit	Their profit-making nature
Whether the benefits are independent of the contributions made	The provision of entitlements which are supplementary to those under a basic scheme
Whether the benefits paid are not necessarily proportionate to the earnings of the person insured	
Whether the scheme is supervised by the State	

Source: European Commission 'Communication on the application of the European Union State aid rules to compensation granted for the provision of services of general economic interest', OJ C8, 11.1.2012, pp. 4–14, paras 18–19.

activity than one relying on solidarity because of the competition on the financial markets with other insurance companies. Conversely, if the benefits received are not tied to contribution rates – in other words, if those who are better off in some sense subsidise the worse off – this is an indicator of solidarity. Thirdly, if schemes with a surplus transfer resources to schemes in deficit, this is also an indicator of solidarity. Finally, the case law indicates an unwillingness of the European Courts to extend the boundaries of competition law too widely and to allow other considerations to predominate in the area of health care, social provision and collective agreements between unions and employers.[50] The European Commission has summarised the indicators of solidarity and economic activity and these are presented in Table 2.1 above.

Undertakings as separate entities

We have seen how the definition of an undertaking is a difficult matter. In this section we examine the issue of when undertakings can be considered to be separate entities for the purposes of Article 101 TFEU, which applies to only agreements *between* undertakings. Why this needs some discussion can be illustrated as follows. Companies these days organise themselves as corporate groups; there will be a parent company and the parent will have various subsidiaries. Company law within the United Kingdom says that each company is a separate legal entity from every other company in the group. Could agreements between them, therefore, be caught under Article 101 TFEU if all the other requirements were met?

Within Union competition law, the answer that has been given is that it depends on whether the companies concerned form one economic entity or two, or more, separate economic entities. This was established in the *Viho* case.[51] This involved Parker Pens, an English company, which made writing equipment which it distributed throughout Europe through a mixture of independent distributors and its own, wholly owned subsidiaries. Parker's distribution system prohibited exports between Member States and also did not allow the sale of Parker products to people outside the distribution system on the same terms

---

[50] For trade unions and employees, see: Case C-22/98 *Jean Claude Becu* [1999] ECR I-5665 (employees are part of an undertaking); Case C-67/96 *Albany International* v *Stichting Bedrijfspensioenfonds textielindustrie* [1999] ECR I-5751 (collective employment agreements fall outside Article 101 TFEU).

[51] Case C-73/95P *Viho Europe BV* v *Commission* [1996] ECR I-5457.

as Parker's subsidiaries and independent distributors. Viho was a Dutch firm that marketed office equipment and complained to the Commission that it was unable to receive the same terms as Parker's subsidiaries and that it was forced to deal with the subsidiary established in the Netherlands, rather than being able to deal with the one that offered the best terms. Viho brought two complaints: one aimed at the independent distributors, the other at Parker's subsidiaries, and it is only the second that we are concerned with here. The Commission rejected the complaint on the grounds that Parker and its subsidiaries formed one economic entity and that the subsidiaries had no freedom of action; not only were they wholly owned, but their marketing decisions were controlled by an area team of directors. Viho appealed to the GC and then to the CJEU, both courts rejecting the appeal. The CJEU pointed out that Parker owned 100% of its subsidiaries and controlled their marketing and sales activities tightly. In those circumstances, the CJEU concluded that Parker and its subsidiaries formed 'a single economic unit within which the subsidiaries do not enjoy real autonomy in determining their course of action in the market, but carry out the instructions issued to them by the parent company controlling them'.[52] This was the case even though Parker's policy, which consisted in dividing national markets between its subsidiaries, was capable of affecting the competitive position of third parties. The GC made this point more clearly, saying that although the division of national markets might thwart the fundamental objective of the Common Market,[53] nevertheless, this did not fall within the scope of Article 101 TFEU.

Several comments can be made about this case. First, in principle, it is a correct decision as a parent company and a wholly owned subsidiary would not be competing against each other on the market so, in the absence of this arrangement, the market would not be more competitive. If there is a competition problem here, it should be addressed under Article 102 TFEU. Insofar as these arrangements involved the independent distributors, the Commission decided that these did, indeed, breach Article 101 TFEU and led to the parties being fined.[54] Secondly, this was an easy case because the subsidiaries were wholly owned, as have been other cases where this issue was raised, and tightly controlled. Indeed, the most recent decision of the CJEU has said that in the case of wholly owned subsidiaries there is a rebuttable presumption that the parent company exercises decisive influence over the subsidiary.[55] What is not clear is at what point a subsidiary, which is not wholly owned, becomes an independent entity. The key question is whether it has real autonomy in its decision making and this would seem to depend on the factual circumstances of the case. As Whish and Bailey point out,[56] the European Merger Control Regulation recognises the possibility in Article 3(2) that a minority shareholder may have the possibility of exercising decisive influence over the affairs of another undertaking, such as to constitute a concentration. It is, however, not clear that this is the same concept as the single economic entity idea. The GC has, however, held that a shareholding of just over 25% did not justify the conclusion that the two undertakings formed one economic unit;[57] and the Commission has held in two cases that holdings of around 50% in a joint venture meant that the two undertakings were separate from each other.[58]

[52] Ibid. at para. 16.
[53] Case T-102/92 [1995] ECR II-17 at para. 52.
[54] See Commission Decision, *Viho/Parker Pen* [1992] OJ L233/27; Case T-66/92 *Herlitz v Commission* [1994] ECR II-531; and Case T-77/92 *Parker Pen v Commission* [1994] ECR II-549.
[55] Case C-97/08P *Akzo Nobel v Commission* [2009] ECR I-8237 at para. 60.
[56] *Competition Law* (7th edn, Oxford University Press, 2012) at p. 94.
[57] Case T-145/89 *Bauhstahlgewehr v Commission* [1995] ECR II-0987 at para. 107.
[58] Commission Decisions, *Gosmé/Martell-DMP* [1991] OJ L185/23 and *Eirpage* [1991] OJ L306/22.

The issue is an important one in practice because it affects the liability of companies for breach of EU competition rules. Companies tend to operate as corporate groups, often relatively complex, and this means that, under the single entity doctrine, if a subsidiary company commits a breach of competition law, then its parent company may be held liable for the breach. This is possible even if there is an intermediate company between the parent and the subsidiary.[59] Because the presumption that a parent company exercises decisive influence over the activities of its subsidiary is rebuttable, there have been a large number of cases where companies have tried to rebut this presumption, generally unsuccessfully.[60] One example of such an argument being successful was in *FLSmidth & Co A/S and FLS Plast* v *Commission*[61] where the GC held that the Commission was unable to rely on the presumption for a year in which the parent company held only 60% of the shares of the subsidiary.

Finally, the single economic entity doctrine is not confined to groups of companies. It may encompass the relationship between an individual and the companies he or she controls;[62] this may also cover relationships between a principal and an agent[63] and between a contractor and a subcontractor.[64]

Agreements, decisions by associations of undertakings and concerted practices

Article 101 TFEU only applies to agreements between undertakings, decisions by associations of undertakings and concerted practices between undertakings. Each of these concepts requires some explanation and, in particular, the relationship between agreements and concerted practices needs exploration.

The idea of an 'agreement' is central to the enforcement of Article 101 TFEU. At the beginning of any enforcement proceedings, the burden of proof is on the Commission to show that the undertakings accused have done particular actions.[65] Given that undertakings will dispute findings of anti-competitive behaviour vigorously, it is important that the notion of an agreement is defined in a broad manner, which does not allow for technical defences to succeed. This is indeed the way that the case law has developed. There is thus no need for the agreement to be legally binding, nor for it to be in written form; it can be a verbal agreement between the parties.[66] The point has been put in general terms by the GC (Box 2.6).

---

[59] For example, Case C-90/09P *General Quimica SA* v *Commission* [2011] 4 CMLR 13.

[60] For example Case T-77/08 *Dow Chemical Company* v *Commission* [2012] 4 CMLR 19; Case T-76/08 *EI Du Pont de Nemours* v *Commission* [2012] 4 CMLR 18; Case T-349/08 *Uralita SA* v *Commission* [2012] 4 CMLR 4; *Alliance One International Inc* v *Commission* [2011] 5 CMLR 35.

[61] Cases T-64-5/06 judgments of 6 March 2012 (GC).

[62] Case 170/83 *Hydrotherm* v *Compact* [1984] ECR 2999.

[63] See European Commission, *Guidelines on vertical restraints* [2010] OJ C130 19.05.2010, paras 12–21. Most recently Case T-325/01 *DaimlerChrysler AG* v *Commission* [2005] ECR II-3319 (GC).

[64] This will depend on whether the agreement is vertical, in which case it falls under the block exemption for vertical restraints or horizontal, in which case see European Commission, *Guidelines on the applicability of Article 101TFEU to horizontal cooperation agreements*, OJ C11, 14.01.2011 at paras 150–4. In addition, also see the European Commission, 'Notice concerning its assessment of certain subcontracting agreements in relation to Article 8[1](1) of the EEC Treaty' [1979] OJ C1/2.

[65] Regulation 1/2003, Art. 2.

[66] Case 41/69 *ACF Chemiefarma* v *Commission* [1970] ECR 661 at para. 112; Cases 209–215 and 218/78 *Van Landewyck* v *Commission* [1980] ECR 3125 at paras 85–6.

KEY DEFINITION   **Box 2.6**

Agreement

The concept of an agreement within the meaning of Article 85(1) [101(1) TFEU] of the Treaty, as interpreted by the case-law, centres around the existence of a concurrence of wills between at least two parties, the form in which it is manifested being unimportant so long as it constitutes the faithful expression of the parties' intention.

Source: See Case T-41/96 *Bayer AG* v *Commission* [2000] ECR II-3383, para. 69; upheld on appeal, Cases C-2 and 3/01P *Bundesverband der Arzneimittel-Importeure* v *Bayer* [2004] ECR I-23.

Nor does it matter if one of the parties has entered into the agreement reluctantly or with reservations. The case law makes it clear that an undertaking may escape liability only if it makes it publicly clear that it is not taking part in an anti-competitive agreement.[67] The undertaking cannot argue that although it participated in the meeting it did not give its express approval because failure to distance itself publicly constitutes tacit approval. Nor is it an excuse if the undertaking does not act on the agreement or has not taken part in all aspects of the agreement, or only a relatively minor part of it. Although this might affect the level of the penalty imposed, it does not affect liability.[68]

The second issue arises from the fact that cartels may be complex arrangements, existing over a number of years, where the participants have had to make a number of decisions about how the cartel will be run, and the identity of the participants may fluctuate. Undertakings have argued that such arrangements should be considered as a series of agreements and that the Commission should therefore be obliged to prove the existence of each one, a formidable practical obstacle. The Commission's response has been to refuse to draw a clear dividing line between the notion of an agreement and that of a concerted practice (discussed below) and to talk in terms of a continuing infringement, that is, interpreting the cartel as one overarching set of agreements or concerted practices for the period of its continuation (see Box 2.7). This approach has been endorsed by the European Courts, where it has been said:

> in the context of a complex infringement which involves many producers seeking over a number of years to regulate the market between them, the Commission cannot be expected to classify the infringement precisely, for each undertaking and for any given moment, as in any event, both those forms of infringements are covered by Article 85 of the Treaty [101 TFEU].[69]

---

[67] Case C-49/92P *Commission* v *Anic Partecipazioni SpA* [1999] ECR I-4125 at para. 96.

[68] This sentence, and the preceding two, summarises Cases C-204–205, 211, 213, 217 and 219/00P *Aalborg Portland A/s* v *Commission* [2004] ECR I-123 at paras 81–6. See also Case T-83/08 *Denki Kagaku Kogyo Kabushiki Kaisha* v *Commission* judgment of 2 February 2012 (GC) at paras 51–4.

[69] Joined Cases T-305/94 etc. *Limburgse Vinyl Maatschappij and others* v *Commission (PVC II)* [1999] ECR II 931, para. 696. And see also Cases C-204–205, 211, 213, 217 and 219/00P *Aalborg Portland A/s* v *Commission* [2004] ECR I-123 at paras 258–61.

KEY CASE EXTRACT   Box 2.7

Relationship between agreement and concerted practice

Source: Electrical and Mechanical Graphite Products, Commission Decision of 3 December 2003, Case C.38.359, para. 221:

> However, it is not necessary for the Commission, particularly in the case of a complex infringement of long duration, to characterise conduct as exclusively one or other of these forms of illegal behaviour. The concepts of agreement and concerted practice are fluid and may overlap. The anti-competitive behaviour may well be varied from time to time, or its mechanisms adapted or strengthened to take account of new developments. Indeed, it may not even be possible to make such a distinction, as an infringement may present simultaneously the characteristics of each form of prohibited conduct, while when considered in isolation some of its manifestations could accurately be described as one rather than the other. It would however be artificial analytically to sub-divide what is clearly a continuing common enterprise having one and the same overall objective into several different forms of infringement.

Concerted practices

Whereas the central idea behind an agreement is of a mutual concurrence of wills, the idea of a concerted practice goes wider. It is convenient to start with the CJEU's definition in Box 2.8.

KEY DEFINITION   Box 2.8

Concerted practice

> A form of coordination between undertakings which, without having reached the stage where an agreement properly so-called has been concluded, knowingly substitutes a practical cooperation between them for the risks of competition.

Source: Cases 48, 49 and 51–57/69 *ICI* v *Commission (Dyestuffs)* [1972] ECR 619 at para. 64.

Questions: What does practical cooperation mean? How do you prove it?

One way of looking at this idea is that it aims to catch those situations where undertakings have been in contact with each other but there is insufficient evidence to prove the existence of an agreement. In other words, the idea is to catch a situation, for example, where undertakings signalled their future prices to each other and depended on their competitors to react to this information. This type of situation is more likely to arise in certain types of markets than others and can be labelled the 'oligopoly problem' (see Box 2.9). This is confirmed by the case law of the courts which, whilst accepting that economic undertakers have the right to react intelligently to market conditions, this right of independent action:

> does, however, strictly preclude any direct or indirect contact between such operators the object or effect whereof is either to influence the conduct on the market of an actual or potential

competitor or to disclose to such a competitor the course of conduct which they themselves have decided to adopt or contemplate adopting on the market.[70]

EXAMPLE   Box 2.9

The oligopoly problem

Imagine a market where there are three manufacturers who produce homogeneous goods, using the same technology, the market is not expanding and there is no possibility of entry. Assume that consumers have perfect information about the price of the goods and that there are no costs to switch from one producer to another. Assume as our starting point that each good is priced at 1.0 and that the total market of 300 is divided equally amongst the three manufacturers (i.e. 100 each), producing a profit of 50, that is, 0.5 per sale. If one of the manufacturers reduces the price to 0.5, thus only making 0.25 profit per sale, they will gain all the market and boost their profit. However, we can also assume that the other manufacturers will match this price cut and the market will return to an equal distribution of market shares but with everyone having a lower profit level. (This is illustrated in the tables below.) From the point of view of the manufacturers, there is no incentive in this market to compete, as it just leads to lower profits. Agreeing to divide the market is, of course, contrary to competition law, but reacting intelligently to what your competitors do is not. A key issue therefore become transparency of pricing; if you know what your competitors are going to charge, you can align your prices on them. In some markets transparent pricing may be the norm – for example, supermarket shelf prices – in others it is not. The idea of concerted practices is to catch those situations where competitors are signalling or communicating their intentions to each other short of reaching an agreement but in a way that is not just normal commercial practice.

Period 1

	Price	Sales	Profit
A	1.0	100	50
B	1.0	100	50
C	1.0	100	50

Period 2

	Price	Sales	Profit
A	0.5	300	75
B	1.0	0	0
C	1.0	0	0

Period 3

	Price	Sales	Profit
A	0.5	100	25
B	0.5	100	25
C	0.5	100	25

---

[70] Case T-7/89P *Hercules* v *Commission* [1991] ECR II-1711 at para. 258 (GC).

We will see later (Chapter 10, which also discusses the case law in more detail) that the oligopoly problem is a very difficult one for competition policy to deal with, but we should note here that most of the concerted practices cases involve situations where there has been contact between undertakings and the issue for the Commission has been one of proof, rather than the question of how to deal with an oligopolistic market. For example, in the *Dyestuffs* case[71] there were three price increases in 1964, 1965 and 1967 by the producers. The 1964 increase took place in January 1964 in Italy, the Netherlands, Belgium and Luxembourg and was extended to Germany on 1 January 1965, whilst on the same day an additional 10% increase was introduced on dyes and pigments in those countries not covered by the first increase. On 16 October 1967 there was an increase of 8% announced on all dyes by almost all the producers in Germany, the Netherlands, Belgium and Luxembourg. The French increase was 12%, but there was no increase in Italy. In its appeal against the Commission decision, ICI argued, in effect, that this was simply the behaviour that could be expected in an oligopolistic market. The CJEU rejected this argument, saying that the three price increases revealed progressive cooperation and that the behaviour of two undertakings which announced their intention to execute a price rise in advance allowed the other undertakings to observe the various responses and adapt themselves accordingly and these advance announcements allowed them to eliminate uncertainty.[72] In this context, it is worth noting that the undertakings had met in Switzerland in 1967 in August and then announced a price rise in September, taking effect in October. The Advocate General's opinion contains suggestions, notably in relation to the 1964 price increase, that there must have been contact before the increase was announced due to the similarity of instructions and the rapidity of action.[73] The decision in the case has been criticised for too easily finding that there was cooperation between the parties and not studying the market sufficiently but this seems to ignore or play down the evidence of contact between the undertakings concerned.[74]

There is a useful contrast with a case that was decided almost 20 years later, known familiarly as *Wood Pulp II*.[75] In this case the Commission had levied fines on 43 wood pulp producers, alleging breaches of Article 101 TFEU. The Commission objected to a system of quarterly price announcements made to consumers which, it argued, was evidence of concertation that had taken place at an earlier stage. Although the Commission had evidence of meetings and contacts between the parties, this evidence was excluded from consideration by the CJEU as the Commission was unable to specify which undertakings were affected by this evidence.[76] So, insofar as the CJEU was concerned, the issue came down to whether the system of pre-announced quarterly prices was sufficient to constitute a concerted practice. The CJEU, on the basis of a specially commissioned experts' report, took the opposite view to the Commission, finding that the parallelism of prices and the simultaneous announcements of prices were due to the market conditions, rather than coordination between the producers. The CJEU made the point that 'parallel conduct cannot be regarded as furnishing proof of concertation unless concertation constitutes the only plausible explanation for such conduct'.[77] And in this case the market conditions provided such a plausible explanation.

[71] Cases 48, 49 and 51–57/69 *ICI v Commission (Dyestuffs)* [1972] ECR 619.
[72] Ibid. at paras 99–101.
[73] Ibid. at p. 681.
[74] V. Korah, 'Concerted Practices' (1973) 36 *Modern Law Review* 260; R. Joliet, 'La notion de partique concertée et l'arrêt ICI dans une perspective comparative' [1974] CDE 251.
[75] Cases C-89, 104, 114, 116–117 and 125–129/85 *Ahlström Oy v Commission* [1993] ECR I-1307.
[76] Ibid. at para. 69.
[77] Ibid. at para. 71.

The two cases can usefully be contrasted because in both of them are found parallel price announcements, an argument that the behaviour of the producers is due to the market conditions, rather than coordination, and yet contrasting decisions of the CJEU. In part this is because of contrasting views of the market: in the *Dyestuffs* case the CJEU rejected the argument that the market was an oligopoly, whereas they accepted this, on the basis of independent reports, in the *Wood Pulp* cases. The other significant differences were that the Commission had evidence of contact in *Dyestuffs* but not in *Wood Pulp* and the differences in the price announcement procedures in the two cases, the latter coming down to the differences in the markets, as in *Wood Pulp* the system of price announcements had grown up at the request of the purchasers, which tended to be large undertakings in contact with a number of producers and had long-term contracts. The upshot of this case law is that it is very hard for the Commission to tackle oligopolistic markets via Article 101 TFEU, although not in theory impossible.

Although the phrase 'concerted practices' suggests that there should be a pattern of conduct, the *T-Mobile* case[78] makes it clear that one event, on its own, can constitute a concerted practice. This case involved a meeting between five mobile phone operators in the Netherlands where they discussed the reduction of remuneration to dealers for signing up what were called post-paid mobile subscriptions, what would in the UK be referred to as contracts. The Dutch competition authority decided that this was a breach of, among other things, Article 101(1) TFEU and imposed a fine on the operators who challenged this before a Dutch court. The Dutch court made a preliminary reference to the CJEU asking whether this meeting constituted a concerted practice. The CJEU replied:

> a concerted practice pursues an anti-competitive object for the purpose of Article 81(1) EC [Article 101 TFEU] where, according to its content and objectives and having regard to its legal and economic context, it is capable in an individual case of resulting in the prevention, restriction or distortion of competition within the common market. It is not necessary for there to be actual prevention, restriction or distortion of competition or a direct link between the concerted practice and consumer prices. An exchange of information between competitors is tainted with an anti-competitive object if the exchange is capable of removing uncertainties concerning the intended conduct of the participating undertakings.[79]

This makes it clear that there can be an individual case of a concerted practice.

We should note another aspect of the interrelationship between the idea of an agreement and that of concerted practices. Once an agreement has been proved, there is no need for the Commission to show that any undertaking which is party to the agreement has taken any action in consequence of the agreement. As regards a concerted practice, logically it might be suggested that, since there is no agreement, it would be necessary for the Commission to show that the undertakings concerned have changed their behaviour in the light of the concerted practice. This would add another hurdle to the Commission's task and, therefore, the European Courts have avoided the logical outcome by stating that, although in principle there should be subsequent conduct on the market caused by the concerted practice, once the Commission has produced evidence of concertation it is for the undertaking to establish that this did *not* cause it to behave in the particular way in question.[80]

---

[78] Case C-8/08 *T-Mobile Netherlands v Raad van Bestur* [2009] ECR I-4529.

[79] Ibid., para. 43.

[80] Case C-199/92P *Hüls AG v Commission* [1999] ECR I-4287 at paras 158–167 and also Case C-8/08 *T-Mobile Netherlands v Raad van Bestur* [2009] ECR I-4529.

The effect of the case law is that what becomes important is not distinguishing between an agreement and a concerted practice but in trying to distinguish between collusive behaviour and parallel independent behaviour which can be explained by market conditions. The difficulty raised by the oligopoly problem, as discussed in Box 2.9 above, is that, in theory, the outcomes of collusive behaviour and oligopolistic behaviour may be similar. Although the theory of an oligopolistic market suggests that this type of behaviour can happen without more, in practice it would be in undertakings' interests to put in place mechanisms to ensure that they behaved in a non-competitive way, if they felt that they could escape detection and sanction. There is thus an incentive in these situations to, for example, share information or arrange meetings.

Unilateral agreements

It is worth explaining the so-called concept of unilateral agreements. Obviously, this concept is a contradiction in terms, as we have seen that an agreement requires a mutual concurrence of wills, that is, it cannot be unilateral (see Box 2.6 above). Nevertheless, this concept has been used to refer to a particular policy issue, which has been worked out in the context of the definition of an agreement. The issue has arisen in the context of a manufacturer's arrangements with its distributors, which may take the form of a distribution agreement (as, for example, with new motor cars) or may be a series of individual contracts, although the relationship may last over a number of years. These are, of course, vertical agreements. In the context of a European-wide market, where the conditions of trading are different between Member States, it is possible that the manufacturer may be able to charge different prices for its goods in different Member States or to ensure that its distributors charge different prices. This, however, provides an incentive for those distributors in the cheaper Member States to resell the manufacturer's goods in the more expensive states because they will be able to make an additional profit. From the manufacturer's point of view this is undesirable, because it reduces their profit overall and the distributors in the more expensive states will complain at being undercut by other distributors. Economic analysis tells us that, as long as the market for the manufacturer's goods in each Member State is competitive, that is, there is sufficient inter-brand competition, we should not be concerned about the manufacturer's effort to divide the market up along national lines; indeed, there may be good commercial reasons for doing this and society as a whole would not be worse off. EU competition law tells us the opposite, however, as one of the overriding policy objectives is to bring about the creation of a single market, which means that trading conditions should be the same across Europe. It has been established, therefore, that agreements which provide for absolute territorial protection are unlawful under EU competition law.[81] Manufacturers have sought to prevent parallel trading through means which do not fall within the prohibitions of competition law, while the Commission has sought to prevent them pushing this too far.

A good example of the issue came in the *Ford* case.[82] Here Ford had an agreement with its distributors of new cars in Germany and the United Kingdom, amongst other countries. At the time, prices for British cars were cheaper in Germany than in Britain and so a growing number of British buyers bought their cars in Germany. Being concerned about the effect on

---

[81] Cases 56 and 58/64 *Consten & Grundig* [1966] ECR 429.
[82] Cases 25–6/84 *Ford v Commission* [1985] ECR 2725.

its British sales and distributors, Ford notified its German dealers by a circular that it would no longer accept orders for right hand drive cars from them. The Commission took the view that Ford's decision was a breach of Article 101 TFEU because it reduced intra-brand competition and erected barriers between national markets. Ford argued that this was a unilateral act on its behalf, which therefore did not fall within Article 101 TFEU. The CJEU did not accept this argument, noting that these sorts of distribution agreements were normally concluded in order to govern their distribution over a number of years and, because not all technological developments are foreseeable, the agreements necessarily had to leave certain matters to be decided later by the manufacturers, which included the models to be delivered. Such a decision on the part of the manufacturer did not constitute a unilateral act; on the contrary, it was part of the contractual relations between the manufacturer and its dealers and therefore a breach of Article 101 TFEU.[83]

This decision led to further court cases, and a line of Commission decisions, which were aimed at stopping manufacturers from erecting barriers to parallel trade, even though it was argued that the decisions were unilateral.[84] A change in this area has been brought about, however, starting with the decision in the *Bayer* case.[85] Bayer manufactured a drug, Adalat, used for the treatment of certain heart diseases, which it exported to France, Spain and the United Kingdom, among other countries. As a result of the particular policies adopted by the NHS, prices for Adalat were some 40% higher in the UK than in France and Spain, and so the French and Spanish distributors[86] took advantage of this by reselling Adalat in the UK. Bayer wished to stop or discourage this practice, so it instituted a system whereby it accepted orders from the distributors only on the basis of their orders in the previous year, plus a 10% margin of increase. The Commission took the view that this action constituted an export ban and that it had been put into effect with the tacit acquiescence of the distributors, who aligned their purchasing practices to comply with Bayer's ban. The Commission had no documentary evidence of an agreement and based its findings on the conduct of the distributors. The GC disagreed with this analysis, and could not find any evidence of tacit acquiescence by the distributors and therefore was able to distinguish previous case law. The Commission appealed this decision to the CJEU, which upheld the GC's ruling, stating as follows:

> it is true that the existence of an agreement within the meaning of [Article 101 TFEU] can be deduced from the conduct of the parties concerned. However, such an agreement cannot be based on what is only the expression of a unilateral policy of one of the contracting parties, which can be put into effect without the assistance of others. To hold that an agreement prohibited by Article 85(1) of the Treaty [Article 101 TFEU] may be established simply on the basis of the expression of a unilateral policy aimed at preventing parallel imports would have the effect of confusing the scope of that provision with that of Article 86 of the Treaty [Article 102 TFEU]. For an agreement within the meaning of Article 85(1) of the Treaty [Article 101 TFEU] to be capable of being regarded as having been concluded by tacit acceptance, it is necessary that the manifestation of the wish of one of the contracting parties to achieve an anti-competitive goal constitute an invitation to the other party, whether express or implied, to fulfil that goal

---

[83] Ibid. at paras 20–1.

[84] See, in particular, Case C 277/87 *Sandoz v Commission* [1990] ECR I-45 and the decisions cited in Whish and Bailey (n. 56) at pp. 106–7.

[85] Cases C-2 and 3/01 *Bundesverband der Arzneimittel-Importeure v Bayer* [2004] ECR I-23.

[86] Referred to as wholesalers in the judgments and decisions.

jointly, and that applies all the more where, as in this case, such an agreement is not at first sight in the interests of the other party, namely the wholesalers.[87]

This case represents an important change in attitude by the European Courts, which was confirmed in the later *Volkswagen* decision.[88] In this case, the motor car manufacturer had issued a set of circulars exhorting its dealers in Germany to maintain price discipline, that is, not to advertise or sell them below the recommended retail price, over the price of Passats. The Commission took the view that these circulars should be read within the context of the distribution agreements and were therefore to be taken as an agreement, rather than a unilateral action. The problem here was not so much market partitioning, but resale price maintenance, which would also clearly be a breach of competition law. The GC rejected the Commission's argument, pointing out that the distribution agreement was a lawful agreement, whereas, in principle, the circulars were unlawful. It could not therefore be assumed, without more, that the distributors had agreed with an unlawful change in the contract. Since the Commission had no evidence as to whether the distributors had changed their conduct, this could not be considered to be an unlawful agreement. The CJEU did not agree with the GC that the distribution agreement could not, in principle, allow action contrary to competition law. It did accept, however, that because the GC had found that the distribution agreement only provided for non-binding price recommendations, and that there was no evidence of acquiescence by the distributors, the Commission had not established that there was an agreement.

A useful contrast is *Automobiles Peugeot SA* v *Commission*.[89] At issue here was a remuneration system operated by Peugeot in the Netherlands for its dealers which discouraged them from exporting cars outside the Netherlands. The European Commission decided that these arrangements had the object of restricting competition and imposed a fine of around €49 million, which was appealed to the General Court. One of the issues was whether the arrangements amounted to an agreement, as Peugeot argued that the system was imposed unilaterally and that the Commission had not proven that the dealers had agreed to it. Simply continuing to order cars did not constitute agreement or tacit acquiescence. The GC pointed out that here the Commission had actively sought evidence of agreement or tacit acquiescence, unlike in the previous *Volkswagen* case. Looking at the facts of the case, the GC said that the Commission was entitled to infer the dealers' acquiescence from their continuing to purchase cars from Peugeot.

What we can see in these recent cases is the European Courts limiting the Commission's ability to use Article 101 TFEU to deal with issues relating to parallel trading in particular. This seems partly driven by a concern to protect the integrity of Article 101 TFEU and to suggest that parallel trading should be dealt with by other routes.

Decisions by associations of undertakings

It is quite common for undertakings to come together in trade associations for a variety of legitimate reasons, such as presenting the industry case to government, establishing common

---

[87] Cases C-2 and 3/01 *Bundesverband der Arzneimittel-Importeure* v *Bayer* [2004] ECR I-23 at paras 100–2.

[88] Case T-208/01 *Volkswagen* v *Commission* [2003] ECR II-5141 (GC); upheld on appeal in Case C-74/04P *Volkswagen* v *Commission* [2006] ECR I-6585.

[89] Case T-450/05 *Automobiles Peugeot SA* v *Commission* [2009] ECR II-2533 (GC). See also Case T-18/03 *CD-Contact Data Gmbh* v *Commission* [2009] ECR II-1021, upheld on appeal Case C-260/09P *Activision Blizzard Germany GmbH* v *Commission* [2011] 4 CMLR 17.

standards, discussing specialist issues, promulgating best practice, etc. Some of these issues may have nothing to do with competition in the market, but others may have such an effect. For example, establishing common standards in an industry can be seen as a means of equalising the quality of goods or services amongst competing undertakings and thus possibly limiting competition. Alternatively, it has been the case that certain trade associations have served as covers for price-fixing cartels.[90] There is, therefore, a need for competition law to cover these sorts of arrangements, which are pretty common throughout the developed world.

There are two issues to discuss in this context: first, to what extent does the status of the trade association matter; and, secondly, what constitutes a decision for these purposes? As regards the first issue, the association does not itself have to carry out an economic activity, that is, it does not have to be an undertaking. It is sufficient that its membership is composed of undertakings.[91] Nor is it relevant that the association may have a public law status of some sort, provided that it is the undertakings that are in control of the activities of the association, rather than the state. The borderline between whether a decision of an association is required by the state, and so outside Article 101(1) TFEU, and whether the state simply allows such decisions, albeit subject to a measure of supervision, can produce some difficult problems in practice. In particular, professional associations, such as the Council of the Bar or the Law Society may be associations of undertakings for the purposes of the competition rules and therefore decisions taken by them may be subject to competition law scrutiny.[92]

As regards what constitutes a decision for these purposes, it has been clearly established by the courts that the decision does not have to be binding according to the rules of the association; a non-binding recommendation can fall within Article 101(1) TFEU, provided that it is implemented by members of the association.[93] Other expressions of policy by associations may also fall under Article 101(1) TFEU. Thus, the Commission has held that the rules of an association may constitute a decision and that a certification scheme for cranes in the Netherlands equally constituted a decision by an association of undertakings.[94]

An appreciable effect on competition

Although Article 101(1) TFEU simply talks about a 'restriction on competition', it has become clear from the case law that this restriction must have an appreciable effect on competition. The point is made clearly in *Völk v Vervaecke*[95] which involved an exclusive distribution agreement between a German manufacturer of washing machines and a distributor in Belgium and Luxembourg. The German company had less than 0.1% of the Union market and under 1% of the market in Germany, Belgium and Luxembourg. On a preliminary reference, the Court held that an exclusive dealing agreement, even with absolute territorial protection, could fall outside Article 101(1) TFEU for the following reason:

---

[90] H. Mercer, *Constructing a Competitive Order* (Cambridge University Press, 1995) in ch. 2 explains their working in Britain in the 1930s.

[91] Cases T-25/95, etc. *Cimenteries CBR SA v Commission* [2000] ECR II-491 at para. 1320.

[92] See, e.g., Case C 309/99 *Wouters v Algemene Raad van de Nederlandse Orde van Advocaten* [2002] ECR I-1577 where the CJEU held that the General Council of the Dutch bar was an association of undertakings.

[93] Case 218/78 *Van Landewyck* [1980] ECR 3125.

[94] Commission Decision, *National Sulphuric Acid* [1980] OJ L260/24; Cases T-213/95 and T-18/96 *Stichting Certificatie Kraanverhuurbedrijf v Commission* [1997] ECR II-1739.

[95] Case 5/69 *Völk v Vervaecke* [1969] ECR 295.

> An agreement falls outside the prohibition in Article 85 [Article 101 TFEU] when it has only an insignificant effect on the markets, taking into account the weak position which the persons concerned have on the market of the product in question.[96]

Having established the principle, the problem arises as to where one can draw the line and how can this be done in a clear manner? The Commission has dealt with this through a series of Notices on minor agreements, generally called the *de minimis* notices. The most recent Notice is summarised in Box 2.10.

The Commission does, however, say that if agreements contain certain restraints, such as price-fixing, limiting output or sales or allocating markets or customers, then it will not take the view that these agreements escape Article 101(1) TFEU.[97] This does seem contrary to the view taken by the Court in *Völk* but the best explanation seems to be that the Commission takes the view that the Court's decisions allow for a sliding-scale approach, that is, the more serious the restriction of competition, the lower the market share the undertakings have to have.[98] Although this is potentially a sensible approach, it is not clear that it is one the Courts have taken, preferring to see the question as a binary one: either the agreement has an appreciable effect or it does not.[99] It is important to note as well that, even if the aggregate market shares exceed those stated in the Notice, this does *not* automatically imply an appreciable restriction on competition, as the Commission acknowledges in para. 2 of the Notice and has been decided in case law.[100]

KEY LEGAL PROVISION   Box 2.10

Agreements with no appreciable effect on competition

No appreciable restriction for:

- *Horizontal* agreements: if the combined market share of the parties does not exceed 10%

- *Vertical* agreements: if the combined market share of the parties does not exceed 15%

- *Networks of agreements*: if the combined market share is less than 5% and the networks cover less than 30% of the relevant market.

This does not apply:

- in the case of an agreement between *competing undertakings* if there is a provision which:

  - directly or indirectly fixes prices, shares markets or limits production, or

- in the case of an agreement between *non-competing undertakings* containing a provision which:

---

[96] Ibid., para. 5/7.
[97] Ibid., para. 11, which is more detailed than the text.
[98] See A. Jones and B. Sufrin, *EC Competition Law* (4th edn, Oxford University Press, 2011) at p. 176.
[99] See Case 19/77 *Miller* v *Commission* [1978] ECR I-131 at para. 10.
[100] Cases T-374–375, 384 and 388/94 *European Night Services* v *Commission* [1998] ECR II-3141 at para. 103.

- limits a buyer's ability to determine its resale price, or
- restricts a buyer operating at a retail level from selling to any end user in response to an unsolicited order (passive selling), or
- restricts active or passive selling by the authorised distributors to end-users or other authorised distributors in a selective distribution network, or
- restricts, by agreement between a supplier of components and a buyer who incorporates those components in its products, the supplier's ability to sell the components as spare parts to end users or independent repairers not entrusted by the buyer with the repair or servicing of its products.

Source: European Commission, 'Notice on agreements of minor importance which do not appreciably restrict competition under Article 81(1)' [2001] OJ C368/13.

Perhaps the best way to view the Notice is as a statement of the enforcement priorities of the Commission and to see it within the new context of enforcement post Regulation 1/2003. The Commission's view is that it should concentrate on the most serious offences or matters of general policy. Agreements which are around the thresholds of the *de minimis* Notice would not seem to fall into either of these categories and should be left to enforcement by national competition authorities, which will have their own enforcement priorities. For example, the OFT's administrative priorities suggest that before taking action the relevant potential consumer benefit needs to be assessed, its strategic significance, the use of resources and the likelihood of success.[101] It is worth discussing, in this context, a series of decisions that the OFT took in relation to collusive tendering for flat roofs in 2004 to 2006. Although not strictly Article 101 TFEU cases, as they were decided under the Chapter I prohibition of the Competition Act 1998, they provide a useful indication of the OFT's approach. Here there was a relatively large market for contract roofing, of which flat felt roofing was a subsection, but the market was very fragmented, being composed of numerous small firms. The OFT took action against a number of regionally based collusive tendering arrangements, even though they fell below the 10% threshold in the *de minimis* Notice. Given the type of practices, collusive tendering, they were considered to have an appreciable effect on competition, whether they fell below the 10% threshold.[102]

Restrictions on competition

This is really the core question as regards the application of Article 101 TFEU – what constitutes a restriction on competition? The text of Article 101(1) TFEU does not give many signposts; it talks simply about agreements, draws a distinction between those with the object of restricting competition and those that have the effect of restricting competition and gives

---

[101] OFT, *Prioritisation Principles* (2008).

[102] OFT, 'Collusive tendering in relation to contracts for flat-roofing services in the West Midlands' (2004) at paras 368–70; 'Collusive tendering for felt and single ply flat-roofing contracts in the North East of England' (2005) at paras 236–8; 'Collusive tendering for felt and single ply roofing contracts in Western-Central Scotland' (2005) at paras 253–5; 'Collusive tendering for flat roof and car park surfacing contracts in England and Scotland' (2006) at paras 687–90.

five examples of agreements which it sees as restricting competition. Agreements which restrict competition under Article 101(1) TFEU are prohibited and void under Article 101(2) TFEU unless they qualify for an exemption under Article 101(3) TFEU which involves, roughly, a weighing of the pro- and anti-competitive effects of the agreement. Therefore the interpretation given to Article 101(1) TFEU affects the operation of the entire Article. If Article 101(1) TFEU is interpreted widely and catches many agreements, then there must be a high amount of decisions taken under Article 101(3) TFEU. If it is interpreted narrowly, so few agreements are caught, then there will be correspondingly less activity under Article 101(3) TFEU. What is felt to be the correct answer depends on one's judgement of two, related, matters. The first is whether the danger is in catching too many agreements that are either neutral or pro-competitive (a false positive or Type 1 error) and hence discouraging their formation, or in missing out too many agreements that are anti-competitive (a false negative or Type 2 error) (see Box 2.11 for a definition). The second issue is whether the person or body making decision under Article 101(3) TFEU can take those decisions efficiently and accurately. If the problem is false negatives, then a wide interpretation of Article 101(1) TFEU will be preferred but if the problem is seen as one of false positives, then a narrow interpretation will be preferred, particularly if there are worries about the Article 101(3) TFEU decision maker.

KEY DEFINITION Box 2.11

Type 1 and type 2 errors

These terms derive from statistics and are commonly used in the competition law world.

Type 1 error: a false positive, that is, assuming that there is a significant difference in a sample or population when this is not the case. In competition law, it would be finding that an agreement is anti-competitive when it is not.

Type 2 error: a false negative, that is, assuming that there is no significant difference in a sample or population when this is the case. In competition law, it would be finding that an agreement is not anti-competitive when it is.

Questions: What type of error do you think is more damaging for competition law enforcement? Why? What implications does this have for the design of the rules?

Historically, what happened is that the European Commission took a broad view of the notion of restriction of competition, harking back to the Ordo-liberal influences in European Union competition law (discussed in Chapter 1) and a concern with market integration, and started from the assumption that any restriction on the commercial freedom of an undertaking was a restriction on competition. If an agreement was considered to restrict competition this was not the end of the matter, as it would be eligible for an exemption under Article 101(3) TFEU. So one way of viewing the Commission's approach was that it took a wide interpretation of Article 101(1) TFEU, almost as a jurisdictional matter, and considered the substantive question, what is the effect on competition of this agreement, under

Article 101(3) TFEU?[103] In the context of a primary concern with the creation of a common market and the beginnings of a European competition policy, this approach made some sense, because it gave the Commission jurisdiction over a wide range of agreements and, under the original procedural framework, required undertakings to notify agreements to the Commission, so that it could scrutinise them for compatibility with Article 101 TFEU.

Although on a policy basis this approach made some sense, it also created immense practical difficulties because the Commission was unable to process the number of notifications received and take Decisions on them (that is, legally binding Decisions reviewable under Article 263 TFEU [ex Article 230 EC]). In order to try and deal with this problem, as well as trying to dispose of cases informally, general rules were created for categories of agreements, what are known as block exemptions, but these were in turn criticised for being too formalistic and ineffective. In the face of this mounting criticism the Commission has, since the late 1990s, revised its approach to competition policy culminating, in procedural terms, in Regulation 1/2003. The Commission has, however, also altered its approach to the assessment of a restriction of competition, moving away from a jurisdictional approach, to one which examines the agreement in its economic context (Box 2.12):

KEY LEGAL PROVISION   **Box 2.12**

Assessing a restriction on competition

The assessment of whether an agreement is restrictive of competition must be made within the actual context in which competition would occur in the absence of the agreement with its alleged restrictions. In making this assessment it is necessary to take account of the likely impact of the agreement on inter-brand competition (i.e. competition between suppliers of competing brands) and on intra-brand competition (i.e. competition between distributors of the same brand). Article 81(1) [Article 101(1) TFEU] prohibits restrictions of both inter-brand competition and intra-brand competition.

Source: European Commission, *Guidelines on the application of Article 81(3) of the Treaty* [2004] OJ C101/8, para. 17.

Questions: What factors must be considered to evaluate the context? Do you think inter-brand or intra-brand competition is, in general, more important?

It is important to note the first stage of this assessment: the effect of an agreement must be compared to the context within which competition would occur *in the absence* of the agreement (sometimes referred to as the counter-factual). From a student's perspective, a second important point is that Commission decisions prior to around 1999 may be an unreliable guide to how they will approach decisions at the moment. We should also note that the attitude of the European Courts seems to have shifted over time, although it was never entirely clear that they took the same approach to the interpretation of Article 101(1) TFEU as did the Commission; indeed, this was the basis of much of the criticism of Commission practice.

---

[103] D. Goyder, *EC Competition Law* (4th edn, Oxford University Press, 2003) at p. 91 expresses this point clearly.

Having said all this, it is worth considering, what would be the best approach to inter-preting a 'restriction of competition'? There is a tension between the need for legal certainty and the requirements of economic analysis. If one values legal certainty, one wants clear rules, which state whether an agreement is caught by Article 101 TFEU and, if it is, how it will be treated. If concerned with accurate economic analysis, one will want to examine agreements on a case-by-case basis in their economic context and make an assessment that way. Economic analysis also tells us that, in general, horizontal agreements are likely to be more damaging to competition than vertical agreements and therefore the latter should be treated more sympathetically. This is not, however, a distinction which can be found within Article 101(1) TFEU and the suggestion that it should be read in was rejected by the CJEU at an early stage.[104] Nor indeed would a rigid categorisation be helpful as it is possible to accomplish the same commercial ends through a variety of means and the choice adopted by undertakings should not be determined by the legal treatment on the basis of a formal classification. This was one of the criticisms of the block exemption system, which was originally based on setting up exemptions for categories of agreements. What this suggests is that the best approach will be a compromise: there should be clear rules identify-ing agreements that are obviously anti-competitive, some clear rules for excluding agreements that do not raise competition concerns, such as the *de minimis* rules, and then a middle ground, preferably with some sort of filtering system so that not all cases are subjected to an intensive and time-consuming scrutiny. There needs to be flexibility in the system, so that the substance of the rules can be reviewed periodically, in case it is felt that, for example, agreements which were once thought to be obviously anti-competitive might be treated more leniently.[105]

In US antitrust law, historically the solution was to distinguish between agreements which were considered *per se* unlawful, that is, requiring no inquiry into their anti-competitive effects (they were presumed to be harmful), and those which were subject to a rule of reason test, that is, balancing the pro- and anti-competitive effects of the agreement. Over the years, whether a particular type of agreement was *per se* illegal or not has been reviewed in cases and some have been moved from this category to a rule of reason inquiry. At the same time, there have been attempts to develop a structured rule of reason inquiry, that is, to find a somewhat less burdensome form of inquiry for the court to undertake.[106] So US antitrust law has always had a clear category of agreements which are anti-competitive and not much inquiry is needed, a variety of exemptions from the antitrust rules, but a continuing debate over how to deal with agreements which need deeper inquiry because a full rule of reason inquiry is a very unwieldy matter for a court.

Under current EU competition law, a similar structure can be discerned. There is a category of agreements which are held to be in breach of Article 101(1) TFEU without much inquiry being needed: those with the object of restricting competition, which are discussed below. Having said this, recent case law creates some uncertainty and there is no obvious means of reviewing the content of this category. As can be seen from the discussion of appreciability above, there are some reasonably clear exclusions from the ambit of Article 101(1) TFEU and

---

[104] Cases 56 and 58/64 *Consten & Grundig* [1966] ECR 429.

[105] For example, the current US Supreme Court case which changed the rules on resale price maintenance: *Leegin Creative Leather Products, Inc. v PSKS, Inc.* 551 US 877 (2007).

[106] A useful discussion is in H. Hovenkamp, *Federal Antitrust Policy* (11th edn, West Publishing, St Paul, Minnesota, 2011) at Section 5.6.

(as will be seen in Chapter 11) some reasonably clear general exemptions for, in particular, vertical agreements. The greatest controversy arises in the middle ground over those agreements which have the effect of restricting competition, where it is clear that some form of inquiry into the effects of the agreement is needed, but it is not clear just what this entails. In particular, it is not clear to what extent, if at all, the decision maker in an Article 101(1) TFEU case must balance the pro- and anti-competitive effects of an agreement before reaching a decision on whether the agreement restricts competition. An additional problem is that EU competition law has evolved from a model where almost all agreements were seen as, initially, being anti-competitive, there were few clear rules excluding agreements and the filtering and inquiry system did not work in procedural terms. This has left an awkward legacy of cases and decisional practice which are difficult to reconcile with the apparent aims of the system going forward.

Agreements with the object of restricting competition

Article 101 TFEU draws a distinction between agreements with the object of restricting competition and those that have the effect of restricting competition. It is convenient to deal with agreements which have the 'object' of restricting competition first because if an agreement has the object of restricting competition, there is no need to consider whether it has the effect of restricting competition. Whether an agreement has the object of restricting competition is determined not by the intention of the parties, although the intention of the parties may be taken into account, but by examining the aims of the agreement in the light of the economic context of the agreement.[107] The restriction of competition may be direct or indirect. In the *General Motors* case,[108] in order to prevent the export of new cars from the Netherlands, General Motors instituted, among other measures, a bonus system which meant that sales bonuses were not applied to export sales. This was seen as having the object of restricting competition, albeit in an indirect manner because it did not prevent the transaction, simply made it less attractive. If it is found that the object of the agreement is to restrict competition, then there is no need to go further and show that there have been concrete effects in the market; the agreement is taken to be restrictive or distorting of competition by its very nature.[109] Furthermore, the fact that the restriction of competition is not the sole objective is irrelevant; an additional legitimate objective will not save the agreement. As the GC has put it:

> once it has been established that the object of an agreement constitutes, by its very nature, a restriction of competition, such as a sharing of clientele, that agreement cannot, by applying a rule of reason, be exempted from the requirements of Article 81(1) EC [Article 101(1) TFEU] by virtue of the fact that it also pursued other objectives, . . .[110]

The Commission's view of the justification underlying this category is given in Box 2.13.

---

[107] Cases 29 and 30/83 *Compagnie Royale Asturienne des Mines SA v Commission* [1984] ECR 1679 at para. 26.

[108] Case T-368/00 [2003] ECR II-4491 *General Motors Nederland BV v Commission* and Case C-551/03P *General Motors BV v Commission* [2006] ECR I-3173.

[109] A recent example is Case C-209/07 *Competition Authority v Beef Industry Development Society* [2008] ECR I-8637 at para. 16.

[110] Cases T-49–51/02 *Brasserie Nationale v Commission* (judgment of the GC) [2005] ECR II-3033 at para. 85 and Case C-209/07 *Competition Authority v Beef Industry Development Society (BIDS)* [2008] ECR I-8367.

KEY LEGAL PROVISION   Box 2.13

Object of restricting competition

Restrictions of competition by object are those that by their very nature have the potential of restricting competition. These are restrictions which in the light of the objectives pursued by the Community competition rules have such a high potential of negative effects on competition that it is unnecessary for the purpose of applying Article 81(1) [Article 101(1) TFEU] to demonstrate any actual effect on the market. This presumption is based on the serious nature of the restriction and on experience showing that restrictions of competition by object are likely to produce negative effects on the market and to jeopardise the objectives pursued by the Community competition rules.

Source: European Commission, *Guidelines on the application of Article 81(3) of the Treaty* [2004] OJ C101/8, para. 21.

Question: Can you think of examples of restrictions that fit this description?

In order to determine whether an agreement has as its object the restriction of competition the Commission has said that one must consider the agreement's content and its objective aims. In addition, it may be necessary to consider the context in which it is applied and the actual conduct and behaviour of the parties on the market.[111] The Commission goes on to say that non-exhaustive guidance on what constitutes a restriction by object can be found in block exemption regulations, notices and guidelines and that anything identified as a hard-core restriction will generally be found to constitute a restriction by object. This may be true as a matter of fact but in the *Pierre Fabre Dermo-Cosmétique* case, Advocate General Mazák made the point that, conceptually, hard-core restrictions and restrictions of competition by object were different ideas and that it did not necessarily follow that a hard-core restriction would lead to a restriction on competition. This question would require an individual examination of the agreement in question.[112] In terms of horizontal agreements, the Commission states that restrictions by object include price-fixing, output limitation or sharing of markets and customers. As regards vertical agreements, restrictions by object include fixed and minimum resale price maintenance and restrictions providing absolute territorial protection, including restrictions on passive sales.[113] In principle, all such agreements are eligible for an individual exemption under Article 101(3) TFEU but the Commission is very unlikely to give such an exemption.[114]

Case law and Commission guidance on what sort of agreements have the object of restricting competition provides the list in Box 2.14. The list is interesting because it includes what are usually considered the hard-core cartel offences, such as price-fixing, market sharing and output limitations, as well as absolute territorial protection, which can be seen as an issue

---

[111] European Commission, *Guidelines on the application of Article 81(3) of the Treaty* [2004] OJ C101/8 at para. 22.

[112] Case C-439/09 *Pierre Fabre Dermo-Cosmétique SAS* v *Président de l'Autorité de la concurrence and Ministre de l'Économie, de l'Industrie et de l'Emploi* [2011] 5 CMLR 31 (CJEU) at paras 23–30 of the AG's opinion.

[113] Ibid., para. 23.

[114] Case T-17/93 *Matra Hachette* v *Commission* [1994] ECR II-595 at para. 85; Case T-168/01 *GlaxoSmithKline Services* v *Commission* [2006] ECR II-2969 at para. 233; European Commission, *Guidelines on the application of Article 81(3) of the Treaty* (n. 111) at para. 46.

peculiar to European Union competition law. This is not, however, a fixed list as the CJEU has said that the examples in Article 101(3) TFEU do not constitute an exhaustive list.[115] In the *Pierre Fabre Dermo-Cosmétique* case, the CJEU held that a contractual provision in a selective distribution agreement which required sales of cosmetics to be made in a physical space in the presence of a qualified pharmacist (effectively preventing internet selling) constituted a restriction of competition by object.[116]

EXAMPLES   **Box 2.14**

Provisions with the object of restricting competition

Horizontal agreements with the object of restricting competition[117]

- To fix prices [Article 101(1)(a) TFEU]
- To share markets and customers [Article 101(1)(c) TFEU][118]
- To limit output [Article 101(1)(b) TFEU]
- To limit sales
- To exchange price information

Vertical agreements with the object of restricting competition

- To fix minimum resale prices
- To impose export bans/absolute territorial protection

Questions: To what extent do these provisions always have anti-competitive effects? Can you think of any legitimate reasons for engaging in these practices?

Most of these categories are relatively straightforward, although there have been instances where both the Commission and the Courts have been prepared to accept that certain restrictions are not restrictions by 'object'. For example, in the *Visa* case, the European Commission considered that an agreement containing a clause to fix a multilateral interchange fee paid by banks within the Visa system did not have as its object the restriction of competition.[119] By contrast, in its first effort at dealing with the same issue in relation to Mastercard, the OFT took the view that such a multilateral interchange fee could have been characterised as a restriction by object, even though it dealt with it as a restriction by effect, although this decision was subsequently abandoned by the OFT after challenge in the CAT.[120] Equally, in *Erauw-Jacquery*,[121] the plaintiff, an owner of various intellectual property rights relating to

---

[115] Case C-209/07 *Competition Authority v Beef Industry Development Society* [2008] ECR I-8637 at para. 23.

[116] Case C-439/09 *Pierre Fabre Dermo-Cosmétique SAS v Président de l'Autorité de la concurrence and Ministre de l'Économie, de l'Industrie et de l'Emploi* judgment of 13 October 2011 (CJEU) at para. 47.

[117] Adapted from Whish and Bailey (n. 56) at p. 124.

[118] See Case T-360/09 *E.ON Ruhrgas AG v Commission* judgment of 29 June 2012 (GC) for an example of this.

[119] *Visa International Multilateral Exchange Fee* [2002] OJ L318/17, [2003] 4 CMLR 283 at para. 69.

[120] Office of Fair Trading, 'Investigation of the multilateral interchange fees provided for in the UK domestic rules of Mastercard UK Members Forum Limited' (2005) at paras 389–93; *Mastercard UK Members Forum v Office of Fair Trading* [2006] CAT 14.

[121] Case 27/87 *Erauw-Jacquery v La Hesbignonne* [1988] ECR 1919.

certain seeds, authorised the defendant to propagate and sell those seeds in Belgium. In relation to a certain class of seed, the contract provided that the defendant was prohibited from exporting that seed, without the permission of the plaintiff – in other words, something that looks like an export ban. The CJEU, recognising that there may have been considerable financial investment in the development of the seed; that the breeder of the seed should be able to protect themselves against improper handling of the varieties of seed and could therefore place such restrictions in a contract, said that such a clause fell outside of the scope of the prohibition in Article 101(1) TFEU.[122]

More controversial was the approach of the GC in the *GlaxoSmithKline* case.[123] Here GlaxoSmithKline (GSK), a drugs manufacturer, had entered into contracts with its distributors which aimed to prevent parallel trade in its pharmaceutical products, essentially by fixing different prices for the drugs, depending on whether they were going to be used in the Spanish health system or not. In other words, drugs to be used only in the Spanish health system would benefit from a lower price, while those which could be used elsewhere would be charged at a higher price, thus discouraging parallel trading. The Commission took the view in its decision that this was the equivalent of an export ban or a method of impeding parallel trading and was therefore a restriction of competition by object. The GC took the view that, although in principle such agreements had the object of restricting competition, there needed to be more analysis. According to the GC, the purpose of Article 101(1) TFEU was to prevent undertakings from reducing the welfare of the final consumer of the products in question. Although the analysis could be abridged when the clauses of the agreement revealed an alteration of the conditions of competition in themselves, that would need to be supplemented where this was not the case. In particular, the GC interpreted *Consten & Grundig*[124] as a case where the CJEU had carried out an economic analysis of the effects of the agreement, abridged but real, as it put it, during the course of which it became apparent that the purpose of the agreement was to eliminate any possibility of competition at the wholesale level. In the context of GSK's case, the GC came to the conclusion that the prices of drugs depended on the national regulations relating to their prices which were controlled by the public authorities and that it was not obvious that the attempts to restrict parallel trade damaged the final welfare of consumers because the final price was determined by the public authorities, not market forces. The GC went on to consider whether the clauses had the *effect* of restricting competition and held that they did.

The decision by the GC was controversial because it took an approach to agreements that are intended to prevent parallel trade which was very different from that taken in previous court and Commission decisions and the Commission appealed this part of the decision.[125] Although this decision represented a departure from previous interpretations, it could perhaps be reconciled with previous case law as an example of taking seriously the idea of examining the aims of the agreement in the light of its economic context and considering what the state of competition would have been like without the agreement.[126] This does not require a detailed analysis because, even if the agreement does not have the *object* of restricting competition, it may have the *effect* of restricting competition, and this will require a further

---

[122] Ibid., paras 10–11.
[123] Case T-168/01 *GlaxoSmithKline Services v Commission* [2006] ECR II-2969.
[124] Cases 56 and 58/64 *Consten & Grundig* [1966] ECR 429.
[125] Case C-501/06P *GlaxoSmithKline Services v Commission* [2009] ECR I-9291.
[126] Case C-501/06P *GlaxoSmithKline Services v Commission* [2009] ECR I-9291.

detailed analysis, as will be seen below. However, the Advocate General, in her opinion on the appeal, took the view that the GC's approach was legally incorrect, in part because the wording of Article 101(1) TFEU did not mention detriment to the consumer and also because the assessment of consumer benefit was mainly due to be done under Article 101(3) TFEU. The CJEU agreed with the Advocate General, holding that the GC had erred in law and that it was not required to find that there was detriment to consumer welfare before deciding that an agreement had the object of restricting competition. The CJEU emphasised that the purpose of Article 101(1) TFEU was not only to protect the interests of competitors and consumers, but also the structure of the market and that agreements intended to limit parallel trade must in principle be considered to have as their object the restriction of competition.[127]

The GC's judgement in *GlaxoSmithKline* can be seen as an attempt to introduce more economic analysis into the question of whether a restriction was a restriction by object, a development which the CJEU firmly reversed on appeal. In the *BIDS* case,[128] a crisis in the beef processing industry was dealt with by the an industry agreement to reduce capacity through a scheme where those who left the industry were compensated by those who remained in the industry and those who left agreed to, among other things, decommission their plant. The Irish competition authority challenged this agreement, which was disputed in the Irish courts and the case came to the CJEU as a preliminary reference from the Irish Supreme Court. The industry argued that the concept of an agreement having the object of restricting competition should be interpreted narrowly, covering only horizontal price fixing, limitation of output and market sharing. This argument was clearly rejected by the Court, following the Advocate General, which then went on to examine the arrangements before it. Its conclusion was that they patently conflicted with the concept of competition contained in Article 101 TFEU because they substituted practical cooperation for competition and independent decision making by the undertakings concerned. As the Court pointed out, the effect of these arrangements was to protect the profitability of those undertakings who remained in the industry, whereas in a competitive market they would have had to reduce prices and consider the possibility of merging (or simply leaving the market). This case should be linked to the *T-Mobile* case,[129] which involved one meeting between mobile phone providers in the Netherlands, where they discussed the issue of remuneration to their dealers. The Dutch competition authority pursued this case, which came to the CJEU as a preliminary reference from the Dutch courts. The CJEU held that not only was one meeting enough to constitute a concerted practice, but that:

> in order for a concerted practice to be regarded as having an anti-competitive object, it is sufficient that it has the potential to have a negative impact on competition. In other words, the concerted practice must simply be capable in an individual case, having regard to the specific legal and economic context, of resulting in the prevention, restriction or distortion of competition within the Common Market. Whether and to what extent, in fact, such anti-competitive effects result can only be of relevance for determining the amount of any fine and assessing any claim for damages.[130]

Furthermore, it was not necessary for there to be a direct connection between that practice and consumer prices, because the aim of this concept is to protect the structure of the market and competition as such.

---

[127] Ibid., paras 58–64.
[128] Case C-209/07 *Competition Authority* v *Beef Industry Development Society (BIDS)* [2008] ECR I-8367.
[129] Case C-8/08 *T-Mobile Netherlands* v *Raad van Bestur* [2009] ECR I-4529.
[130] Ibid., para. 31.

These developments in the case law have been controversial, because they suggest a wide interpretation of the idea of agreements with the object of restricting competition. Not only is there no exhaustive list of practices but a single event could constitute a concerted practice and it only needs to have the capability of restricting competition to fall foul of Article 101 TFEU.[131] This lack of certainty and potentially wide scope of the concept stand in contrast to the American experience where the category of *per se* restrictions is both well understood and has been shrinking over the years, to be replaced by more rule of reason inquiries.

Agreements which have the effect of restricting competition

For many agreements the critical question will be whether the agreement has the effect of restricting competition. The starting point for any such investigation is to compare the market with the agreement against the market without the agreement (the counter-factual). The issue of effects is not confined to actual effects of the agreement; potential effects of the agreement must also be taken into account. The approach that should be taken was summarised in the *European Night Services* case:

> in assessing an agreement . . . account should be taken of the actual conditions in which it functions, in particular the economic context in which the undertakings operate, the products or services covered by the agreement and the actual structure of the market concerned . . .[132]

What this does not tell us, however, is whether what should be assessed is the net effects of the agreement, that is, the pro-competitive effects netted off against the anti-competitive effects, or whether it is sufficient to find that the agreement has some, or any, anti-competitive effects and then to do any netting off in the context of an inquiry under Article 101(3) TFEU. Very generally, this has been characterised as the question of whether there is a 'rule of reason' in the interpretation of Article 101(1) TFEU and it is possible to point to a number of cases where the European Courts seem to be balancing the pro- and anti-competitive effects of particular agreements.[133]

The effect of adopting such an approach would be to exclude more agreements from the scope of Article 101(1) TFEU because, after analysis, it would be found that their overall effect was pro-competitive and, arguably, to give more power to the Courts to review the Commission's characterisation of the agreement, as they operate some degree of judicial restraint when reviewing decisions under Article 101(3) TFEU. It is not at all clear that the adoption of such an approach would improve the enforcement of EU competition law. American commentators agree that 'it has become something of a commonplace that rule of reason antitrust violations are almost impossible to prove'[134] and that one of the major

---

[131] For discussion see A. Jones, 'Left Behind by Modernisation? Restrictions by Object under Article 101(1)' (2010) 6 *European Competition Journal* 649; S. King, 'The Object Box: Law, Policy or Myth?' (2011) 7 *European Competition Journal* 269; J. Goyder, '*Cet Obscur Objet*: Object Restrictions in Vertical Agreements' (2011) 2 *Journal of European Competition Law and Practice* 327.

[132] Case T-374–375, etc. *European Night Services v Commission* [1998] ECR II-3141 at para. 136.

[133] Arguably, for example, Case T-328/03 *O2 (Germany) v Commission* [2006] ECR II-1231; Case C-250/92 *Gøttrup-Klim Grovvareforening v Dansk Landbrugs Grovvareselskab* [1994] ECR I-564. See R. Nazzini, 'Article 81 EC Between Time Present and Time Past: A normative critique of "restriction of competition" in EU law' (2006) 43 *Common Market Law Review* 497 for further discussion of the case law.

[134] H. Hovenkamp, *The Antitrust Enterprise* (Harvard University Press, Cambridge, Mass., 2005) at p. 8.

difficulties created by this approach is that it mandates a potentially huge, unfocused inquiry which would tend to end with the conclusion that the agreement is legal.[135] Arguably, the deficiencies in the rule of reason approach led to American courts adopting an expanded view of *per se* violations, which, if it happened in the European context, would run against the objectives of rule of reason proponents. Finally, within modern American case law the strict distinction between rule of reason analysis and *per se* violations has been blurred and the American courts appear to be applying more limited and structured approaches rather than the full-blown rule of reason inquiry as described by Whish and Sufrin.[136]

Under the older approach of the Commission and the existing procedural arrangements, the issue of a rule of reason approach generated a large amount of controversy. Much of the heat and interest has been taken out of the debate for three reasons: first, the procedural changes under Regulation 1/2003, which mean notification is not compulsory and the Commission no longer has a monopoly over Article 101(3) TFEU decisions; secondly, the new block exemptions cover a wider range of agreements and, in practice, it is more important to decide if an agreement benefits from an exemption, rather than worry about the Article 101(1) TFEU issue; and, thirdly, the GC has, when asked explicitly about the rule of reason approach, delivered a clear negative answer. This last point can be illustrated by the *Métropole* case.[137] This case involved a joint venture set up by a number of French television companies and companies involved in telecommunications and cable networks with the object of broadcasting programmes by satellite or cable on a pay-per-view basis, primarily in competition with one major undertaking, Canal+. The agreement provided, among other things, that, for a period of *ten* years, the companies involved in the joint venture would not become involved in competing companies (a non-competition clause), that the joint venture would be given first refusal on any special interest programmes that the companies involved in the joint venture had control over (the special interest clause) and that certain general interest channels were to be broadcast exclusively by the joint venture (an exclusivity clause). This agreement was notified to the Commission, which decided that there were no grounds for action in relation to the non-competition clause for *three* years and that the other two clauses would be exempted under Article 101(3) TFEU for a period of *three* years. The parties challenged the decision in relation to the special interest clause and the exclusivity clause on the grounds that the Commission should have applied a rule of reason analysis and, if it had done so, it would have found that the clauses did not restrict competition but actually encouraged it, by allowing a new operator to gain access to a market which, until then, had been dominated by a single operator, Canal+. The GC very clearly rejected this argument (see Box 2.15)[138] and it can be seen that one of the main reasons for rejecting the rule of reason approach is because of the division in Article 101 TFEU between paras (1) and (3) and the GC's view that a comprehensive look at the pro- and anti-competitive effects of the agreement should take place only under Article 101(3) TFEU.

---

[135] E. Gellhorn, W. Kovacic and S. Calkins, *Antitrust Law and Economics* (5th edn, West Publishing, St Paul, Minnesota, 2004) at p. 212.

[136] Ibid. at pp. 222–36 and 259–62. R. Whish and B. Sufrin, 'Art 85 and the Rule of Reason' (1987) *Yearbook of European Law* 1.

[137] Case T-112/99 *Métropole Télévision* v *Commission* [2001] ECR II-2459 and see as well Case T-65/98 *Van den Bergh Foods* v *Commission* [2003] ECR II-4653 at paras 106–7 in similar terms to Box 2.12.

[138] See also Case T-360/09 *E.ON Ruhrgas Ag* v *Commission* judgment of 29 June 2012 at para. 65.

KEY CASE EXTRACT   **Box 2.15**

The GC's approach to a rule of reason

Source: Case T-112/99 *Métropole Télévision* v *Commission* [2001] ECR II-2459, paras 72–6:

> . . . the existence of such a rule has not, as such, been confirmed by the Community courts. Quite to the contrary, in various judgments the Court of Justice and the Court of First Instance have been at pains to indicate that the existence of a rule of reason in Community competition law is doubtful[139] . . . an interpretation of Article 85(1) [Article 101(1) TFEU] in the form suggested by the applicants, is difficult to reconcile with the rules prescribed by that provision . . . Article 85 of the Treaty [Article 101 TFEU] expressly provides, in its third paragraph, for the possibility of exempting agreements that restrict competition where they satisfy a number of conditions, in particular where they are indispensable to the attainment of certain objectives and do not afford undertakings the possibility of eliminating competition in respect of a substantial part of the products in question. It is only in the precise framework of that provision that the pro and anti-competitive aspects of a restriction may be weighed . . . Article 85(3) of the Treaty [Article 101(3) TFEU] would lose much of its effectiveness if such an examination had to be carried out already under Article 85(1) of the Treaty [Article 101(1) TFEU] . . . It is true that in a number of judgments the Court of Justice and the Court of First Instance [General Court] have favoured a more flexible interpretation of the prohibition laid down in Article 85(1) of the Treaty [Article 101(1) TFEU] . . . It must, however, be emphasised that such an approach does not mean that it is necessary to weigh the pro and anti-competitive effects of an agreement when determining whether the prohibition laid down in Article 85(1) of the Treaty [Article 101(1) TFEU] applies.

Questions: Consider whether this interpretation of the case law is accurate. What would be the function of Article 101(3) TFEU if some form of rule of reason was adopted?

How then, should this inquiry be conducted? As noted above, the first stage is the counterfactual: what would the competitive situation be without the agreement in question? As also noted above, the Commission draws a distinction between the effect of the agreement on inter-brand and intra-brand competition. In deciding whether the inter-brand competition is affected, it is necessary to see if the *agreement* would have restricted actual or potential competition that would have existed without it. Thus, the Commission gives the example of where two competing suppliers agree not to sell their products in each other's home state. Here the agreement clearly has the effect of restricting actual or potential competition in the market. As regards intra-brand competition, the question is whether actual or potential competition would have existed in the absence of the restraints contained within the agreement? So, for example, where a supplier restricts its distributors from competing with each other, then this could lead to a restriction of actual or potential competition, for example, through resale price maintenance.[140] However, in regard to intra-brand competition, the Commission points out that certain restraints may in certain cases not be caught by

---

[139] In *van den Bergh* (n. 137) the phrase was 'not accepted'.

[140] For an example, see OFT, 'Price-fixing of replica football shirts' (2003) and 'Hasbro/Argos/Littlewoods' (2003). Upheld ultimately in *Argos and Littlewoods* v *OFT* [2006] EWCA Civ 1318 (CA).

Article 101(1) TFEU when the restraint is objectively necessary for the existence of an agreement of that type or that nature.[141]

How this inquiry is structured was discussed in the *Delimitis* case, which involved beer supply agreements for pubs in Germany and can usefully be contrasted with the views of the European Commission (see Box 2.16) as expressed in its *Guidelines on the application of Article 81(3) of the Treaty*. There is a fair amount of common ground here; indeed, they look to be asking very similar questions, although the Commission makes it clear that what it is really looking for are some signs of market power, albeit less than might be found in an Article 102 TFEU case. As the Commission puts it, '[the agreement] must affect actual or potential competition to such an extent that on the relevant market negative effects on prices, output, innovation or the variety or quality of goods and services can be expected with a reasonable degree of probability'.[142] Furthermore, the Commission states: 'Negative effects on competition within the relevant market are likely to occur when the parties individually or jointly have or obtain some degree of market power and the agreement contributes to the creation, maintenance or strengthening of that market power or allows the parties to exploit such market power.'[143] What is important to remember is that this inquiry is not a case of balancing the anti-competitive effects of an agreement against its pro-competitive effects. All that the competition authorities should be concerned with in this phase of an investigation is whether the agreement may have *negative* effects on competition in the market. If that is found to be the case, then the question of whether there are any positive benefits from the agreement which outweigh the negative effects should be dealt with under Article 101(3) TFEU or via the route of a block exemption.[144] If the agreement does not have any negative effects – in other words, is at least neutral – then it escapes the control of competition law entirely.

KEY CASE EXTRACT Box 2.16

Determining the effect of an agreement: the CJEU and the European Commission

CJEU

Source: Case C-234/89 *Stergio Delimitis v Henniger Brau* [1991] ECR I-935, paras 16–26:

> . . . the relevant market must first be determined:
> What are the possibilities for entry into the market?
> What are the conditions of competition on the market?
> What is the effect of the individual agreement in issue?

---

[141] European Commission, *Guidelines on the application of Article 81(3) of the Treaty* [2004] OJ C101/8 at para. 18(2).

[142] Ibid. at para. 24.

[143] Ibid. at para. 25.

[144] Ibid. at paras 32–3.

European Commission

Source: *Guidelines on the application of Article 81(3) of the Treaty* [2004] OJ C101/8 at para. 27:

Define the market and assess:
    Nature of products
    Market position of parties
    Market position of competitors
    Market position of buyers
    Existence of potential competitors
    Level of entry barriers
    Effect of the agreement in issue.

Questions: What sort of inquiry is needed in this context? How easy is it to conduct this inquiry? Are you inevitably balancing the pro- and anti-competitive effects of an agreement in such an inquiry?

The difficulty with the analysis presented above is that, although arguably logical, it does not seem to be entirely consistent with practice of the European Courts, in particular the CJEU, something which was recognised in passing by the CAT.[145] In a number of cases the Courts have decided that particular agreements, or restrictions within those agreements, do not fall within the prohibition contained in Article 101(1) TFEU and seemingly what has been done is some rough and ready balancing of the pro- and anti-competitive effects of the restriction.

This can be illustrated, first, by a series of cases where the European Courts have been prepared to hold that certain restrictions in an agreement were necessary in order for the undertakings concerned to be willing to enter the market. Or, to put it another way, in the absence of the agreement, there would have been less competition in the market for those particular goods or services. This point is illustrated by the *Nungesser* case,[146] where a French undertaking granted an open exclusive licence to a German undertaking to produce certain new seeds in Germany. The terms of licence included an obligation on the French undertaking and anyone deriving rights from it not to license anyone else in Germany to produce the seeds and not to import seeds it, or anyone else it had licensed, had produced into Germany. In other words, the idea behind these restrictions was to make the German undertaking the sole distributor of these new seeds in Germany. The CJEU concluded that this part of the licence was not in breach of Article 101(1) TFEU:

> . . . in the case of a licence of breeders' rights over hybrid maize seeds newly developed in one member state, an undertaking established in another member state which was not certain that it would not encounter competition from other licensees for the territory granted to it, or from the owner of the right himself, might be deterred from accepting the risk of cultivating and marketing that product; such a result would be damaging to the dissemination of a new technology and would prejudice competition in the Community between the new product and similar existing products.[147]

Perhaps, to put it another way, these restrictions were necessary, otherwise there would have been no new entry into the market or, as was said in an earlier case, 'it may be doubted whether there is an interference with competition if the said agreement seems really necessary for the penetration of a new area by an undertaking'.[148] More recently something like this

---

[145] *Racecourse Association* v *Office of Fair Trading* [2005] CAT 29 at para. 167. See also *Bookmakers Afternoon Greyhound Services et al.* v *Amalgamated Racing Ltd et al.* [2008] EWHC 1978 (Ch), per Mangan J at para. 199.

[146] Case 258/78 *Nungesser* v *Commission* [1982] ECR 2015.

[147] Ibid. at para. 57.

[148] Case 56/65 *Société La Technique Minière* v *Maschinbau Ulm* [1966] ECR 235 at p. 250.

approach seems to have been applied in the *O2* case.[149] Here, in order to provide third generation (3G) mobile phone services, O2 had entered into an agreement with one of its competitors in Germany (T-Mobile) that it could have roaming rights on T-Mobile's network. In other words, it was able to introduce 3G services without having to construct its own network. The Commission examined the agreement and decided that, although Article 101(1) TFEU applied, it would grant an exemption for a limited period of time under Article 101(3) TFEU. O2 challenged this decision, arguing that there was no restriction of competition and that the factual situation had been insufficiently analysed. The GC made it clear that it was not engaged in balancing the pro- and anti-competitive effects of the agreement[150] and that what was required was an examination of the effect of the agreement on existing and potential competition in the absence of the agreement. The GC said that the examination of competition in the absence of an agreement appeared to be particularly necessary as regards markets undergoing liberalisation or emerging markets, as in the case of the 3G mobile communications market, where effective competition may be problematic owing, for example, to the presence of a dominant operator, the concentrated nature of the market structure or the existence of significant barriers to entry.[151] The GC concluded that the Commission had made an insufficient examination of the competitive situation without the agreement and had decided too readily that O2 would be able to enter the 3G market without the roaming agreement and therefore annulled major parts of the decision granting an exemption. The problem with this case, and the others that seem to fall into this category, is that they seem to involve some form of assessing the pro- and anti-competitive effects of an agreement, despite the protestations of the GC. Having said that, it seems that Faull and Nikpay are correct in saying that this balancing approach is only likely to apply in clear-cut cases and also in highlighting that the level of analysis applied in these cases by the European Courts is rather superficial.[152]

Ancillary restraints – the commercial context

The second area where there appears to have been some balancing going on is those cases where there are clauses which are restrictive of competition, but the courts have not been prepared to find a breach of Article 101 TFEU because they are necessary for the implementation of the agreement, often referred to as ancillary restraints. The main agreement must not be restrictive of competition for this approach to apply. The Commission's understanding of the doctrine is set out in Box 2.17.

KEY DEFINITION   **Box 2.17**

Ancillary restraints

In Community competition law the concept of ancillary restraints covers any alleged restriction of competition which is directly related and necessary to the implementation of a main non-restrictive transaction and proportionate to it.

Source: European Commission, *Guidelines on the application of Article 81(3) of the Treaty* [2004] OJ C101/8 at para. 29.

---

[149] Case T-328/03 *O2 (Germany)* v *Commission* [2006] ECR II-1231.
[150] Ibid. at para. 69.
[151] Ibid. at para. 72.
[152] J. Faull and A. Nikpay, *The EC Law of Competition* (2nd edn, Oxford University Press, 2007) at paras 3.222–3.223.

To what extent there is such a doctrine, and how wide it is, is a matter of some controversy amongst the commentators. Whish and Bailey see the cases as falling within a concept of 'commercial ancillarity', which is wider than the ancillary restraints doctrine as defined by the Commission.[153] Bellamy and Child seem, implicitly, to agree with Whish and Bailey, listing a number of cases dealing with restrictions which fall outside Article 101(1) TFEU and having a separate discussion of ancillary restrictions, which they regard as a concept which is 'not always easy to apply'.[154] Faull and Nikpay reckon that the concept 'raises more questions than it answers' and is of limited practical use because of the paucity of case law in this area.[155] It is, nevertheless, worth presenting the cases under this heading in order both to illustrate the narrow version of the doctrine and to see the extent to which the Courts may have gone further.

The basic idea behind the ancillary restraints doctrine can be illustrated by looking at the *Remia* case.[156] Here a subsidiary of a health and baby food manufacturer was sold to an individual and the sales agreements contained clauses which protected the purchaser against competition from the vendor on the same market for ten years after the transfer. There were further promises by the vendor to ensure that the purchasers of another subsidiary would not engage in competition in this market for a period of five years. The agreement was notified to the Commission who took the view that the non-compete obligations were excessive and not eligible for exemption. The applicants appealed to the CJEU arguing, among other things, that Article 101(1) TFEU did not apply to these clauses. The CJEU held that, if the clauses did not exist, then the agreement for the transfer of the undertaking could not be given effect because of the threat of the vendor winning back his former customers. Therefore, such clauses contributed to the promotion of competition by increasing the number of undertakings on the market in question. This comment by the CJEU depends on an assumption that the vendor would have exited the market in the absence of a sale. If an undertaking is sold the number of undertakings on the market does not increase if the vendor exits the market: it remains the same. The number has the potential to increase if, after the end of the non-compete clause, the vendor re-enters the market. The Court went on to say that such clauses must be necessary and strictly limited in their duration and scope and that, in this case, the four-year limitation placed by the Commission on the promises in the clauses was acceptable. In one sense, this is a relatively easy case, because without non-compete provisions the transfer of businesses could not take place and it would seem obvious that such a transfer does not restrict competition on the market, it merely changes the identity of the players.

A more difficult issue was raised in the context of franchising and dealt with in the *Pronuptia* case, which arose out of a contractual dispute between a franchisor and franchisee and resulted in a reference for a preliminary ruling to the CJEU.[157] The contractual provisions in issue did four things, according to the Court: first, they placed restrictions on the franchisee's use of know-how, information and assistance she had obtained from the franchisor; secondly, they also placed certain restrictions on the franchisee relating to the identity and reputation of the network, such as allowing advertising only with the franchisor's consent; thirdly, there were territorial restrictions placed on the franchisee; and, finally, there were provisions relating

---

[153] Whish and Bailey (n. 56) at p. 130, note 444.

[154] P. Roth (ed.), *Bellamy and Child: European Community Law of Competition* (6th edn, Oxford University Press, 2009) at para. 2.113; paras 2.088–2.093 contain the broader list.

[155] Faull and Nikpay (n. 152) at para. 3.213.

[156] Case 42/84 *Remia BV v Commission* [1985] ECR 2545.

[157] Case 161/84 *Pronuptia de Paris GmBH v Pronuptia de Paris Irmgard Schillgallis* [1986] ECR 353.

to price recommendations. The Court took the view that, in general, franchising arrangements did not interfere with competition, although their compatibility with Article 101(1)
TFEU would depend on the provisions within the agreement and the economic context.
Having said that, it decided that provisions which were strictly necessary to ensure that the
franchisor's know-how and assistance did not benefit competitors and were not a restriction
of competition. Nor were provisions which were strictly necessary for maintaining the identity and reputation of the network identified by the common name or symbol. Provisions
which, however, shared markets between the franchisor and franchisees or between franchisees did constitute restrictions on competition. Price recommendations were not a restriction
of competition, so long as there was no concerted practice between the franchisor and the
franchisee or between the franchisees for the actual application of such prices.[158]

One of the more controversial cases in this area is *Gøttrup-Klim*, a case involving a Danish
agricultural purchasing cooperative.[159] This cooperative (DLG) had an objective, among other
things, to provide its members with farm supplies. A number of members were dissatisfied
with the operation of the cooperative, so they set up a rival organisation which began to offer
an alternative for the purchase of certain supplies. As a result DLG changed its membership
rules essentially in order to ensure that its members could not continue to be members of
the competing cooperative and obtain supplies from it in preference to those provided by
DLG. In consequence, a number of members were expelled from DLG and challenged this
expulsion in a Danish court, which referred the question, among others, as to whether these
new rules were compatible with Article 101(1) TFEU to the CJEU. The CJEU took the view
that assessment of the rules could not be conducted in the abstract; it would depend on the
particular clauses and the economic conditions prevailing at the time. It pointed out that, in
a market where prices varied according to the size of order, a purchasing cooperative might
constitute a significant counterweight to the contractual powers of large producers and make
way for more effective competition. Dual membership of competing cooperative associations
could jeopardise the proper functioning of the cooperative and its contractual power in relation to large producers. A rule prohibiting dual membership was therefore not necessarily a
restriction on competition and might even have beneficial effects on competition. Nevertheless,
it was also possible that such a rule could have adverse effects on competition so, in order to
escape the Article 101(1) TFEU prohibition, the rules must be limited to what was necessary
to ensure that the cooperative functions properly and maintains its contractual power in relation to producers. The CJEU went on to assess whether the rules in issue were necessary and
reasonable and therefore not a restriction on competition. This assessment of the rules does
seem to be some form of balancing the anti-competitive effects of the restrictions against pro-
competitive effects (note the reference to beneficial effects on competition) in the context of
the CJEU taking a favourable view of the operation of such cooperatives, by comparison with
collective exclusive dealing. It is also possible to interpret the case as an application of the
ancillary restraints doctrine, although the Court makes no reference to it.[160]

The clearest expression of the ancillary restraints doctrine issue came up in the *Métropole*
case,[161] the facts of which are described above, because the parties argued, in the alternative,
that the exclusivity clauses and the clauses relating to special interest channels were ancillary

---

[158] Ibid., para. 27.
[159] Case C-250/92 *Gøttrup-Klim Grovvareforening v Dansk Landbrugs Grovvareselskab* [1994] ECR I-564.
[160] As Faull and Nikpay (n. 152) suggest at para. 3.258.
[161] Case T-112/99 *Métropole Télévision v Commission* [2001] ECR II-2459.

restrictions. The GC pointed out that for a restriction to be necessary two cumulative conditions had to be met: it had to be objectively necessary for the implementation of the main agreement and proportionate to it. The examination of objective necessity could be done only in a relatively abstract manner. The GC went on to say:

> It is not a question of analysing whether, in the light of the competitive situation on the relevant market, the restriction is indispensable to the commercial success of the main operation but of determining whether, in the specific context of the main operation, the restriction is necessary to implement that operation. If, without the restriction, the main operation is difficult or even impossible to implement, the restriction may be regarded as objectively necessary for its implementation.[162]

This draws a problematic distinction between clauses which are needed for the commercial success of the operation and those which are necessary to implement the operation, particularly as the issues may be interrelated. In *Remia*, the non-compete clause could be seen as going to the commercial success of the sale of the business; if it did not exist, no doubt the purchaser would have negotiated a lower price. A similar argument was made in *Métropole* by the parties who claimed that the exclusivity clause was necessary for the establishment of the joint venture. The GC agreed that the clause was directly related to the joint venture, but held that it was not necessary as a company in the pay TV sector in France could be launched without these rights, as had been the case for the two other operators on the market. Drawing this distinction looks to be difficult in practice. In addition, *Métropole* talks about the main operation being *difficult* to implement,[163] which seems to undermine the notion of objectively necessary because in its usual dictionary meaning 'necessary' means essential in order to achieve something, which is different from the lack of such a clause making it difficult to implement an agreement. In addition, the restrictions must not be disproportionate and in *Métropole* the Court found that the ten-year period of exclusive rights was disproportionate. The answer is perhaps found in an English judgment where it was said:

> In this context, the concept of 'necessity' could be satisfied by something which is not strictly essential. The concept of necessity has some flexibility and in an appropriate case can be satisfied by facts which show that it would be difficult to achieve the commercial objective without the presence of the restriction. The duration and scope of the restriction may be important.[164]

Faull and Nikpay claim that very little is required to take a clause outside the doctrine on this ground.[165]

Ancillary restraints – a wider context

Whatever the interpretation of the ancillary restraints cases, they all take place in a recognisable commercial context and the issue of substance is at least amenable to conventional economic analysis; the problem relates more to whether the analysis should be done under Article 101(1) or (3) TFEU and to what extent the Commission's decision is reviewable. A more difficult problem has arisen in relation to the rules of professional bodies and how they

---

[162] Ibid. at para. 109.
[163] The same point is made in Case T-360/09 *E.ON Ruhrgas AG v Commission* judgment of 29 June 2012 at para. 67.
[164] *Bookmakers Afternoon Greyhound Services et al. v Amalgamated Racing Ltd et al.* [2008] EWHC 1978 (Ch), per Mangan J at para. 452.
[165] Faull and Nikpay (n. 152) at para. 3.211.

relate to the competition law of the EU. In *Wouters*[166] there was a rule of the Dutch bar which prevented members of the bar entering into full partnerships with accountants. The question arose in national proceedings whether this was compatible with the Union rules on competition and this question was referred to the CJEU under Article 267 TFEU. Having decided that the bar was an association of undertakings, the CJEU went on to consider the effect of the rule in issue. It took the view that the rule had an adverse effect on competition.[167] It then went on to say that the rules had to be looked at in their context and that account had to be taken of the objectives of the rules, which were trying to ensure that the ultimate consumers of legal services and the administration of justice were provided with the necessary guarantees in relation to integrity and experience. It then had to be considered whether the consequential effects restrictive of competition were inherent in the pursuit of those objectives. In particular, the Court drew attention to the difference between advocates, who were required to act independently and only in the best interests of their client, and accountants, who were required to carry out certain supervisory activities, such as certifying accounts, and were not bound by strict rules of professional secrecy. The Court concluded that the rule at issue did not infringe Article 101(1) TFEU because the Dutch bar:

> could reasonably have considered that that regulation, despite the effects restrictive of competition that are inherent in it, is necessary for the proper practice of the legal profession, as organized in the Member State concerned.[168]

This is difficult because, as Jones and Sufrin point out, the Court seems to be weighing the anti-competitive effects of the agreement against benefits which were not economic benefits.[169] This raises two, related, conceptual difficulties for the case law. First, it potentially opens up the entire rule of reason or balancing debate again in relation to Article 101(1) TFEU. Secondly, although in principle there are methodologies for balancing the pro- and anti-competitive effects of agreements which can be employed by competition authorities and courts, there is no generally agreed way of balancing the effects of restrictions on competition with non-economic benefits.

The argument has surfaced again in the case of sporting bodies in *Meca-Medina*.[170] Here the appellants had complained to the European Commission that certain rules and practices adopted by the International Olympic Committee and the International Swimming Federation were contrary to Union competition law and the Commission had rejected their complaint. They argued that the anti-doping rules were a restriction of competition, were in no way inherent to the objectives of the rules but were there solely to protect the IOC's economic interests and that the actual limits did not correspond to any scientific evidence and were not necessary. The CJEU took the view that such rules could not be assessed in the abstract, they had to be looked at within their overall context. The Court took the view that the Commission could take the view that the general objective of the rules was to combat doping and to allow competitions to be conducted fairly. In addition, in order to ensure that the rules were effective, the Commission could take the view that penalties were needed. Therefore:

---

[166] Case C-309/99 *Wouters v Algemene Raad van de Nederlandse Orde van Advocaten* [2002] ECR I-1577.
[167] Ibid. para. 86.
[168] Ibid. para. 110.
[169] A. Jones and B. Sufrin, *EU Competition Law* (4th edn, Oxford University Press, 2011) at p. 237.
[170] Case C-519/04P *Meca-Medina v Commission* [2006] ECR I-6991.

even if the anti-doping rules at issue are to be regarded as a decision of an association of under-takings limiting the appellants' freedom of action,[171] they do not, for all that, necessarily con-stitute a restriction of competition incompatible with the common market, within the meaning of Article 81 EC [Article 101 TFEU], since they are justified by a legitimate objective. Such a limitation is inherent in the organisation and proper conduct of competitive sport and its very purpose is to ensure healthy rivalry between athletes.[172]

Nevertheless, the Court went on to examine whether the rules were disproportionate, either in terms of their scope or in terms of the penalties imposed, and decided that they were not disproportionate.

Quite where this case law will go in the future remains a matter of some contention.[173] What it does seem to do is to authorise a more wide-ranging inquiry in cases involving the regulation of activities, so far confined to sport and the professions, as opposed to ordinary commercial activities. Within this area, the case law seems to suggest greater respect for the decisions of national authorities and sporting associations based on balancing the public policy considerations against possible restrictions on competition. However, as has been said, in the context of balancing pro- and anti-competitive effects: 'Meaningful balancing, which involves placing cardinal values on both sides of a scale and determining which is heavier, is virtually never possible.'[174] The problem is even greater when the values on both sides of the scale are not obviously of the same kind.

Summary of Article 101(1) TFEU: restriction of competition

A non-controversial and accurate summary of the case law is difficult. Nevertheless, the posi-tion appears to be:

- If an agreement, or a clause(s) within it, has the object of restricting competition, when looked at properly in its context, then this is a breach of Article 101(1) TFEU, without the need for detailed economic analysis.

- If an agreement, or a clause(s) within it, is alleged to have the effect of restricting competition, then a detailed economic analysis, starting with establishing a counter-factual, must be done to see whether the agreement is likely to have negative effects on competition.[175]

- There are, however, a number of cases where restrictions within agreements have been held to be outside Article 101(1) TFEU on grounds that:
  - they are necessary and proportionate for the penetration of new markets
  - they are necessary and proportionate for the proper functioning of a legitimate com-mercial or regulatory purpose
  - they are mere ancillary restraints.

---

[171] In other words, the Court assumes this without deciding it.

[172] *Meca-Medina* (n. 170) at para. 45.

[173] See E. Szyszczak, 'Competition and Sport' (2007) 32 *European Law Review* 95 and references at 103–5. See also G. Monti, 'Article 81 and Public Policy' (2002) 39 *Common Market Law Review* 1057 at 1086–90.

[174] Hovenkamp (n. 134) at p. 108.

[175] In support of this point see Case T-360/09 *E.ON Ruhrgas AG v Commission* judgment of 29 June 2012 at para. 66.

Individual exemptions

If an agreement is restrictive of competition under Article 101(1) TFEU, the question then arises whether it may benefit from an exemption under Article 101(3) TFEU and, practically, given the uncertainty over the scope of Article 101(1) TFEU this may be the most important question. Under Article 101(3) TFEU there are two different types of exemptions: individual ones and what are called block exemptions. Individual exemptions are typically granted by the Commission, a national competition authority or a national court for a specific agreement, that is, they are individual to that agreement. Block exemptions are a set of general rules, embodied in Union legislation, which apply to categories of agreements. If an agreement meets the criteria embodied in those rules, then it benefits from an exemption, without the need of an explicit decision by a competition authority. Regulation 1/2003 does allow for the possibility of self-assessment of individual exemptions but this is a risky strategy for any undertaking, as will become clear once we discuss the conditions that have to be met for granting an individual exemption.

Under the new arrangements in Regulation 1/2003, the question of whether an agreement benefits from an individual exemption is most likely to arise in two circumstances. First, when the Commission or a national competition authority is taking enforcement proceedings for breach of Article 101(1) TFEU, they will have to consider the question of whether the undertaking is entitled to rely on Article 101(3) TFEU as a defence. Similarly, in private actions against undertakings for breach of Article 101(1) TFEU, the national courts will also have to consider whether Article 101(3) TFEU is available as a defence. It is only on rare occasions outside these contexts that the Commission will pronounce on whether the criteria in Article 101(3) TFEU are satisfied. This contrasts quite strongly with the previous system where agreements were required to be notified to the Commission, which took a broad view of Article 101(1) TFEU, which meant that in principle decisions had to be taken under Article 101(3) TFEU by the Commission. The basic criteria are set out in Box 2.18.

KEY LEGAL PROVISION   Box 2.18

Conditions for an individual exemption

The agreement:

1 must contribute to improving the production or distribution of goods or to promoting technical or economic progress,

2 while allowing consumers a fair share of the resulting benefit, and which does not:

3 impose on the undertakings concerned restrictions which are not indispensable to the attainment of these objectives; and

4 afford such undertakings the possibility of eliminating competition in respect of a substantial part of the products in question.

Source: Article 101(3) TFEU.

Questions: How easy is it to conduct this inquiry? What sort of considerations are relevant?

There are a number of general points to notice about Article 101(3) TFEU. First, the four conditions are cumulative: an agreement has to meet all four of the conditions – if it fails on any one of them, it is not eligible for an exemption.[176] Secondly, the burden of proof as regards meeting the condition is on the undertaking(s) which seeks to rely on them rather than the Commission or the national competition authorities.[177] This is in contrast to Article 101(1) TFEU where the burden of proof is on the European Commission or the national competition authority to show that there has been an infringement. Thirdly, the assessment of agreements is made within the actual context within which they occur and at the time that they are taking place, although there is some element of thinking about or predicting the effect of the agreement in future.[178] Finally, case law makes it clear that, in principle, all types of agreements are eligible to be considered under Article 101(3) TFEU, although it is likely that some forms of agreement, for example, straightforward price fixing or market sharing, will be unlikely to meet the criteria in Article 101(3) TFEU.[179]

The most controversial debate in relation to this Article has been about the breadth of interpretation that should be given to it. On a narrow view, the conditions set out above should be restricted to considering the economic benefits of an agreement against the economic disadvantages, that is, the restriction on competition given by the agreement. The alternative view is that a broader interpretation can be given to the conditions laid down to encompass non-economic matters which are prescribed as aims of the Union in the Treaties.[180] The justification for this is that the European Court of Justice takes a broad, teleological approach to the questions before it. Under the new system of Regulation 1/2003, the broad approach raises potential problems, as it opens the possibility that national courts could apply very wide considerations to criteria for exemption and this could cause some problems in the application of competition law. It is therefore better to take a narrower approach and this is what the European Commission has done in its *Guidelines on the interpretation of Article 81(3)*.[181]

Before discussing the current approach, it is worth looking at past practice because that does seem to show, arguably, a somewhat different approach.[182] The case that is typically cited is the Commission decision in *CECED*.[183] This involved an agreement between washing machine manufacturers not to, among other things, import or produce washing machines

---

[176] See Case C-238/05 *Asnef-Equifax* v *Asociacíon de usuarios de Servicios Bancarios* [2006] ECR I-11125 at para. 65.

[177] Regulation 1/2003, Art. 2.

[178] European Commission, 'Guidelines on the application of Article 81(3) of the Treaty' [2004] OJ C101/8 at para. 44.

[179] Case T-17/93 *Matra Hachette* v *Commission* [1994] ECR II-595 at para. 85; Case T-168/01 *GlaxoSmithKline Services* v *Commission* [2006] ECR II-2969 at para. 233; European Commission, *Guidelines on the application of Article 81(3) of the Treaty* [2004] OJ C101/8 at para. 46.

[180] See G. Monti, 'Article 81 and Public Policy' (2002) 39 *Common Market Law Review* 1057; C. Townley, *Article 81 EC and Public Policy* (2009, Hart Publishing, Oxford); OFT, *Article 101(3) – A Discussion of Narrow versus Broad Definition of Benefits* (2010) and see the OFT roundtable discussion available at: *http://www.oft.gov.uk/ news-and-updates/events/roundtable-article101(3)/* (accessed 18/07/12).

[181] See P. Lugard and L. Hancher, 'Honey I Shrunk the Article . . .' (2004) 25 *European Competition Law Review* 410 for discussion of this point.

[182] Townley (n. 180) estimates non-economic goals were decisive in around one third of Commission decisions between 1993 and 2004 at Annex 1.

[183] Conseil Européen de la Construction d'Appareils Domestiques [2000] OJ L187/47. Faull and Nikpay (n. 152) are of the view that this decision 'does not appear to reflect current Commission thinking as laid down in the Guidelines' (at para. 3.408).

which had low energy efficiency ratings and this part of the agreement was held to have the object of restricting competition because it controlled one important product characteristic on which there was competition in the market.[184] The Commission took the view that washing machines which consumed less energy were objectively more technically efficient and that, although prices might rise, individual consumers would benefit from the savings in electricity and, collectively, there would be a saving from the avoidance of carbon dioxide and sulphur dioxide emission and that these environmental benefits would allow consumers a fair share of the benefits even if no benefits accrued to individual purchasers of machines.[185] It is possible to see this decision as a straightforward application of economic analysis but it is also possible to see it as a case where other Union policies, such as the protection of the environment, were considered relevant and the press release subsequent to the decision encouraged this view by stating, 'This positive contribution to the European Union's environmental objectives is central to the Commission's favourable decision.'[186]

It is not only environmental objectives that have seemed to intrude on particular decisions. There have also been cases where employment issues have been seen to be important, where agreements between competitors to ensure an orderly reduction of capacity were reduced, helping the creation of stronger European firms in the face of competition from the United States and Japan.[187] The Courts' view was expressed in an appeal from a Commission decision in Ford/Volkswagen where the Commission approved the creation of a joint venture in Portugal for the creation of a factory which would produce people carriers (MPVs), in the course of which the Commission took into account the effects on employment, the promotion of the harmonious development of the Union and the reduction of regional disparities.[188] The Commission's decision was challenged by a competitor who claimed, among other things, that the Commission's decision had been based on exceptional circumstances, that is, on the non-competition considerations. The GC rejected this challenge, pointing out that, in its view, the decision to grant an exemption would still have been taken even if the other factors had not been present.[189]

These decisions, and the importance of non-economic considerations, may become more important subsequent to the changes in the Reform Treaty (discussed in Chapter 1), because there may be a greater emphasis, in the Commission as a whole, on a wider range of Union policies in particular cases. At the moment this is only a possibility, so in the following section we examine the current approach of the Commission to individual exemptions, as set out in its *Guidelines*.

Improving efficiency

In order to meet the first condition, any improvements are not looked at simply from the point of view of the parties concerned – they must be capable of benefiting a wider class of people, such as consumers. The Commission's Notice makes it clear that improvements may

---

[184] [2000] OJ L187/47 at para. 33.
[185] Ibid. at para. 56.
[186] European Commission Press Release IP/00/148.
[187] European Commission Decisions Ford/Volkswagen [1993] OJ L20/14, *Synthetic Fibres* [1984] OJ L207/17, *Optical Fibres* [1986] OJ L236/30.
[188] *Ford/Volkswagen* [1993] OJ L20/14 at para. 36.
[189] Case T-17/93 *Matra Hachette* [1994] ECR II-595 at para. 139.

be of broadly two types to qualify under this heading: cost improvements and quality improvements.[190] Cost improvements can arise through new technology or methods, synergies through the integration of existing assets or economies of scale and scope. Improvements to the quality of a product or service are less easy to categorise but may be equally or more important. The Commission takes the view that, in order to substantiate an efficiency claim, the following must be verified:[191]

- the *nature* of the claimed efficiencies,
- the *link* between the agreement and the efficiencies,
- the *likelihood* and *magnitude* of each claimed efficiency, and
- *how* and *when* each claimed efficiency would be achieved.

It is important to stress that there must normally be a direct link between the agreement concerned and the efficiencies claimed. A direct link could be where two undertakings amalgamate their production capacity, thus allowing them to produce the goods for a cheaper cost or where a distribution agreement allows products to be distributed at a lower cost. In addition, the undertakings must also calculate or estimate, that is, quantify, the value of the cost or quality improvements. In the case of new and improved products, the undertakings must describe and explain what the nature of the efficiencies is and how and why they constitute an objective economic benefit.[192]

Indispensability of the restrictions

Although this is the third condition, the European Commission's *Guidelines* treat it as the second one, so we will follow that approach as well. The test applied by the Commission is contained in Box 2.19.

KEY LEGAL PROVISION   Box 2.19

Indispensability of restrictions

First, the restrictive agreement as such must be reasonably necessary in order to achieve the efficiencies. Secondly, the individual restrictions of competition that flow from the agreement must also be reasonably necessary for the attainment of the efficiencies.

Source: European Commission, *Guidelines on the application of Article 81(3) of the Treaty* [2004] OJ C101/8 at para. 73.

Question: Consider the flexibility of the concept of 'reasonable necessity'.

The question to be asked in relation to the first limb is whether the restrictions make it possible to perform the activity in question more efficiently than if they had not been in

---

[190] European Commission, *Guidelines on the Application of Article 81(3) of the Treaty* [2004] OJ C101/08 at para. 59.
[191] Ibid. at para. 51.
[192] Ibid. at para. 57.

place. The European Commission considers it particularly important to consider whether there were less restrictive alternatives that the parties could have chosen or, in other words, that the restrictions are proportional in the context of the agreement. Once the European Commission has decided that the restrictive agreement is necessary in order to produce the efficiencies, it then goes on to assess the indispensability of each of the restrictions imposed in the agreement. 'Indispensability' in Article 101(3) TFEU is turned into 'reasonably necessary' in the *Guidelines*, which means that a restriction is indispensable if 'its absence would eliminate or significantly reduce the efficiencies that follow from the agreement or make it significantly less likely that they will materialise'.[193]

Fair share for consumers

From an economist's point of view, this condition is not actually needed because, if an agreement has both pro- and anti-competitive effects but, on balance, the pro-competitive effects or efficiency gains outweigh the anti-competitive effects, then society as a whole is better off. Who receives the benefits of this improvement is not a matter of concern for economists, as it is a distributional question, which cannot be answered through economic techniques. Here again, EU law differs from economics by imposing a standard which asks the competition authorities to consider the benefits to consumers, defined as all direct or indirect users of the product. In other words, consumer here covers customers who use the good as an input into their own product, wholesalers, retailers and final consumers. In broad terms, the European Commission takes the view that this condition means that the net effect on consumers from the agreement must be neutral. If consumers are worse off following the agreement, then this condition is not fulfilled.[194] What is critical is the overall impact on consumers; they do not have to have a share of every efficiency gain, nor do all individual consumers have to benefit. The European Commission also takes the view that this condition incorporates a sliding scale: the greater the restriction of competition, the greater must be the efficiencies and the pass on to consumers.[195] As regards cost efficiencies, when assessing them the European Commission will look at the characteristics and structure of the market, the nature and magnitude of the efficiency gains, the elasticity of demand and the magnitude of the restriction of competition.[196] The more competitive the market, the more likely cost efficiencies are to be passed on as undertakings try to increase their sales. Economic theory also tells us that consumers are more likely to receive a fair share of cost efficiencies when variable costs are reduced, rather than a reduction in fixed costs. When it comes to qualitative improvements, the European Commission simply says that these must be substantiated.

No elimination of competition

This last condition is a recognition that the process of rivalry and the competitive process should be given priority over potentially pro-competitive efficiency gains which could be

---

[193] Ibid. at para. 79.
[194] Ibid. at para. 85.
[195] Ibid. at para. 90.
[196] Ibid. at para. 96.

potentially reached from agreements. Although this is a concept peculiar to Article 101(3) TFEU, there is a relationship with Article 102 TFEU, on abuse of a dominant position (discussed in Chapters 3 and 4). The position taken by the European Commission in its guidance is that Article 101(3) TFEU must be interpreted in such a way that it cannot apply to restrictive agreements that constitute an abuse of a dominant position. However, in principle, not all agreements concluded by a dominant undertaking will constitute an abuse of a dominant position.[197] Whether competition is being eliminated will depend on the degree of competition that existed prior to the agreement being brought about. This requires a realistic examination of the sources of competition in the market and looking at the actual market conduct of the parties concerned.

Assessment

One of the things that is most evident as regards the European Commission's *Guidelines* is that they are based straightforwardly on an economic approach. The only recognition of other values comes in the statement that: 'Goals pursued by other Treaty provisions can be taken into account to the extent that they can be subsumed under the four conditions of Article 101(3) TFEU.'[198] Whether this represents an accurate picture of previous practice has been discussed above but it certainly lays down a marker for the future. It is worth remembering that Article 101(3) TFEU questions will most likely be raised as a defence to enforcement proceedings or to private actions and are likely to be dealt with by national courts or national competition authorities. Hence the logic is to try and restrict the scope of their inquiry into economic matters. It has, however, been argued that:

> The proposed framework of analysis for Art. 81(3) [Article 101(3) TFEU] goes significantly beyond the requirements the Commission has imposed on itself in the past . . . Therefore, one is left with the impression that the Commission . . . has chosen to issue a gold-plate blueprint of how it considers Art. 81(3) [Article 101(3) TFEU] should ideally be applied by national competition agencies and courts . . . In sum, under the Notice the threshold under Art. 81(3) [Article 101(3) TFEU] is raised significantly, making it questionable whether in practice there is a realistic possibility for firms to establish that the cumulative conditions for exemption under Art. 81(3) [Article 101(3) TFEU] are met.[199]

Even if one's interpretation does not go this far, it should have become clear that there are other avenues for businesses that offer greater degrees of legal certainty in relation to their agreements, notably block exemptions.

Block exemptions

As described above, these are general rules which, if the conditions within them are met, entitle the agreement to an exemption from Article 101(1) TFEU. Currently there are block exemptions in place for vertical agreements, licensing agreements for the transfer of technology,

---

[197] Ibid. at para. 106, citing Joined Cases T-191, 212 and 214/98 *Atlantic Container Line (TACA)* [2003] ECR II-3275 at para. 1456.

[198] [2004] OJ C101/08 at para. 42.

[199] P. Lugard and L. Hancher, 'Honey I Shrunk the Article . . .' (2004) 25 *European Competition Law Review* 410 at 419.

specialisation agreements, and research and development agreements.[200] There are also block exemptions for specific industries or sectors: motor vehicles (a sector dominated by vertical agreements), air and maritime transport. The detail of these block exemptions will be discussed later in the text, whereas here the point is just to make some general observations. The first is that the mere fact that an agreement falls within one of these categories of block exemptions does not imply that it falls within the Article 101(1) TFEU prohibition. It will be caught by the prohibition only if it satisfies the various conditions discussed above.

The previous versions of the block exemptions were heavily criticised for their incomplete coverage of, in particular, vertical agreements, an undue emphasis on meeting formal tests and being too restrictive, as they contained lists of clauses that were forbidden, as well as lists of clauses that were approved. The current sets of block exemptions have been redesigned to meet these problems and they all take, in broad outline, the same approach.

First, all of the exemptions set what is called a 'market share threshold', that is, a percentage share of the market above which the parties to the agreement cannot receive the benefit of the block exemption. So, for example, the exemption for vertical agreements will apply only if neither the supplier nor the buyer has a market share of above 30% (see Box 2.20 for further details). What is being said here is that below certain thresholds there is a presumption that the undertakings do not have market power and therefore may be eligible for an automatic exemption, whereas, above those thresholds, a more detailed inquiry would be necessary, that is, it is a question as to whether an individual exemption could apply.

KEY OFFICIAL GUIDANCE   **Box 2.20**

Market share thresholds

Vertical agreements:	30% (supplier and buyer)
Technology transfer:	20% (where competing undertakings)
	30% (where non-competing undertakings)
Specialisation:	20% (combined market share)
Research and development:	25% (where competing undertakings)

Sources: Commission Regulation (EC) No. 330/2010 of 20 April 2010 on the application of Article 101(3) TFEU to categories of vertical agreements and concerted practices, OJ L102, 23.04.2010, Art. 3; Commission Regulation 1218/2010 on the application of Article 101(3) of the Treaty to categories of specialisation agreements OJ L 335, 18.12.2010, Art. 3; Commission Regulation 1217/2010 on the application of Article 101(3) of the Treaty to categories of research and development agreements OJ L 335, 18.12.2010, Art. 4; Commission Regulation 772/2004 on the application of Article 81(3) of the Treaty to categories of technology transfer agreements, Art. 3.

Question: What do you think the justification for the differing thresholds is or could be?

---

[200] Commission Regulation (EC) No. 330/2010 of 20 April 2010 on the application of Article 101(3) TFEU to categories of vertical agreements and concerted practices, OJ L102, 23.04.2010; Commission Regulation 1218/2010 on the application of Article 101(3) of the Treaty to categories of specialisation agreements OJ L 335, 18.12.2010; Commission Regulation 1217/2010 on the application of Article 101(3) of the Treaty to categories of research and development agreements OJ L 335, 18.12.2010; Commission Regulation 772/2004 on the application of Article 81(3) of the Treaty to categories of technology transfer agreements OJ L 123, 27.04.2004.

Secondly, the Regulations all provide that agreements will not benefit from the exemption if they have as their object certain hard-core restrictions (see Box 2.21). These restrictions are aimed at what are considered to be the most damaging types of restriction under EC competition law, for example, price-fixing, allocation of sales or markets and territorial restrictions on sales. It is important to notice that Box 2.21 does not give a complete list of the hard-core restrictions and that for both allocation of customers and territorial restrictions there are important and detailed exceptions. Arguably some of these restrictions are not as damaging as this classification suggests, but listing them explicitly has the virtue of providing clear rules as to what is forbidden and the lists can be read as general statements about what sort of agreements will have the object of restricting competition. In the case of vertical agreements and technology transfer agreements certain obligations within agreements, such as non-compete obligations in relation to vertical agreements, do not benefit from the exemption but the agreement as a whole can remain in place if the obligations are severable (that is, the agreements can still be operated without them) from the agreement. Finally, the block exemptions make provision for the Commission to withdraw the benefits of the block exemption in relation to particular individual cases or particular markets (in the case of vertical agreements when the agreement, although meeting the terms of the block exemption, still has effects which are incompatible with Article 101(3) TFEU).

KEY CASE EXTRACT   **Box 2.21**

Basic hard-core restrictions

Source: Cases T-374–375 etc. *European Night Services* v *Commission* [1998] ECR II-3141 at para. 136:

- Price-fixing
- Market sharing
- Control of outlets

Questions: What other hard-core restrictions exist? To what extent must the context within which they operate be taken into account?

The block exemptions are very important in terms of the functioning of the system of EU competition law. From the point of view of an undertaking(s), if an agreement is caught by Article 101(1) TFEU, which depends critically on how this is interpreted, the block exemptions offer a predictable safe harbour, if the criteria within them can be met. Given the uncertainties over the scope of Article 101(1) TFEU, the sensible pragmatic choice is to structure agreements in such a way as to meet the block exemption criteria. If this is the case, then it is important that the block exemptions do not artificially force commercial agreements into particular forms. Although it is clear that the new block exemptions are an improvement on the old approach, there are still a number of matters that are inconsistent with modern economic analysis, most notably the treatment of restrictions on selling territories.[201] This is something that we will return to later (Chapter 11).

---

[201] See R. van den Bergh and P. Camesasca, *European Competition Law and Economics* (2nd edn, Sweet & Maxwell, London, 2006) at pp. 235–7.

COMPETITION LAW IN PRACTICE

Cases 56, 58/64 *Etablissements Consten SARL and Grundig* v *Commission* [1966] ECR 299

This case, commonly known as *Consten and Grundig*, has a good claim to being the most important case in the history of EU competition law. It established a number of important principles which moulded the development of EU competition law but, ironically, recent developments have aimed at moving away from the approach in this case.

The facts

In 1957 Grundig, a German undertaking, entered into a contract with Consten, a French undertaking, which appointed Consten the 'sole representative' of Grundig in France for the sale of radios, televisions, tape recorders, dictating machines and their spare parts and their accessories. (This was a vertical agreement, between undertakings operating at different levels of production.) Consten undertook not to sell, either on its own account or on that of another, similar articles liable to compete with the goods which were the subject of the contract and not to make delivery, either direct or indirect, for or to other countries from France. A similar prohibition had already been imposed by Grundig on all its sole concessionaires in other countries, as well as on the German wholesalers. Grundig undertook, for its part, to grant to Consten the retail sale rights and not to deliver, either directly or indirectly, to other persons in the area covered by the contract. For the distribution of the Grundig products, Consten was authorised to use the name and emblem of Grundig, which were registered in Germany and in other Member States. In addition, Consten registered in France, in its own name, the trade mark GINT (Grundig International) which was carried on all appliances manufactured by Grundig, including those sold on the German market.

From early 1961, the company UNEF bought Grundig appliances from German traders who delivered them in spite of the export prohibition imposed by Grundig. UNEF resold these goods to French retailers at more favourable prices than those asked by Consten. Subsequently, Consten brought two actions against UNEF, one for unfair competition and one for infringement of the GINT mark. In the first of these proceedings, Consten won at first instance. However, following an appeal brought by UNEF, the Cour d'Appel de Paris decided to stay proceedings until the decision of the Commission had been given on the claim which UNEF had made to it, on 5 March 1962, for a declaration that the companies Grundig and Consten had infringed the provisions of Article 85 EEC [Article 101 TFEU] through the stipulation in the contract of 1957 and the accessory agreement concerning the registration and use of the GINT mark in France.

In 1963, Grundig notified to the Commission the sole agency contracts concluded with Consten and with its concessionaires in the other Member States. The Commission gave its judgment on the contract concluded between Grundig and Consten. Article 1 of that decision held that the contract in question and the accessory agreement on the registration and use of the GINT mark constituted an infringement of the provisions of Article 85 of the EEC Treaty [Article 101 TFEU]. Article 2 refused to grant the declaration of

➡

inapplicability provided for in Article 85(3) [Article 101(3) TFEU]. Finally, by Article 3, Grundig and Consten were 'required to refrain from any measure tending to obstruct or impede the acquisition by third parties, at their wish, from wholesalers or retailers established in the European Economic Community of the products set out in the contract, with a view to their resale in the contract territory'.

Grundig and Consten brought an action before the CJEU to annul this decision of the European Commission. They argued, among other things, that:

1 Article 85(1) [Article 101(1) TFEU] does not apply to vertical agreements;

2 the restrictions in the contract did not restrict competition;

3 the agreement did not affect inter-state trade.

The CJEU rejected the first argument, holding that there was no such distinction in the wording of Article 85(1) [Article 101(1) TFEU]. In addition, it was possible that such agreements could limit competition between the parties to the agreement and third parties. Finally, on this point, the CJEU said that such agreements between producers and distributors might tend to restore national divisions in trade which was contrary to the basic objects of the EU. As regards the second point, it had been argued that what the Commission needed to do was examine the effect of the agreement on competition between different brands, rather than just its effect on the distribution of Grundig products. The CJEU responded by saying it is superfluous to take account of the concrete effects of an agreement once it appears that it has the object of restricting, preventing or distorting competition. Looking at the agreement in its context, what was intended was the absolute territorial protection for Consten in relation to the Grundig products and this was a restriction of competition contrary to Article 85(1) [Article 101(1) TFEU]. On the third point, the CJEU held that by reserving the market for Grundig products to Consten, the agreement undoubtedly affected trade between Member States, even if it increased the level of trade.

Analysis

The most controversial part of this decision is the approach taken by the CJEU concerning the question of whether the agreement restricted competition. It was argued strongly by the applicants, supported by the German government and accepted by the Advocate General in the case, that what the Commission ought to have done was to have assessed the effects of the agreement on competition on the markets in question. Although there is little hard economic data in the case, the Advocate General points out that Grundig had only a 17% market share in relation to tape recorders, which suggests that they did not have market power. The CJEU rejected this argument, holding that, as the object of the agreement was absolute territorial protection, there was no need to look at its effects. The Court added that the situation results in an insulation of the French market and allows for the products in question the imposition of prices from which is excluded all effective competition.

Questions: How plausible do you think this analysis is? It is worth asking whether Grundig, a German company, could have entered the French market shortly after World War II without this arrangement?

The ruling that Article 85(1) [Article 101(1) TFEU] covered vertical agreements, plus the harsh approach to agreements which looked like they were dividing up the market, were a strong influence on the development of EU competition law up until the late 1990s, when the Commission began to take a different approach to the assessment of vertical agreements, although not to the issue of absolute territorial protection in agreements.

Question: How different would EU competition law have looked if the CJEU had followed the Advocate General's approach?

Summary

➤ In order for an agreement to fall within EU competition law, it must meet a number of criteria:
- there must be an agreement or a decision by an association of undertakings or a concerted practice;
- the agreement, decision or concerted practice must be between *undertakings*;
- the agreement, decision or concerted practice must *affect trade between Member States*;
- the agreement, decision or concerted practice must have as its object or effect the prevention, restriction or distortion of competition, in an appreciable manner, within the common market.

➤ An undertaking is defined as every entity engaged in an economic activity, regardless of the legal status of the entity and the way in which it is financed. Economic activity means any activity which consists in offering goods and services on a given market.

➤ The concept of an agreement centres on the existence of a concurrence of wills between at least two parties, the form in which it is manifested being unimportant so long as it constitutes the faithful expression of the parties' intention.

➤ A concerted practice is a form of coordination between undertakings which, without having reached the stage where an agreement properly so-called has been concluded, knowingly substitutes a practical cooperation between them for the risks of competition.

➤ It is unnecessary to distinguish precisely whether there is an agreement or a concerted practice. What is important is to distinguish collusive from non-collusive behaviour.

➤ To fall within the Article 101(1) TFEU prohibition, an agreement must have an appreciable effect on competition. The Commission's view is that there is no appreciable effect on competition for horizontal agreements if the combined market share of the parties does not exceed 10%. For vertical agreements the combined market share of the parties must not exceed 15%. In addition, the agreements must not contain hard-core restraints.

➤ Agreements which have the object of restricting competition must be distinguished from those with the effect of restricting competition.

117

➤ Restrictions of competition by object are those that by their very nature have the potential of restricting competition and include price-fixing, limitations on output, allocation of customers and restriction of selling territories, although the list is not exhaustive.

➤ If an agreement, or a clause(s) within it, has the object of restricting competition, when looked at properly in its context, then this is a breach of Article 101(1) TFEU, without the need for detailed economic analysis.

➤ If an agreement, or a clause(s) within it, is alleged to have the effect of restricting competition, then a detailed economic analysis, starting with establishing a counter-factual, must be done to see whether the agreement is likely to have negative effects on competition.

➤ There are, however, a number of cases where restrictions within agreements have been held to be outside Article 101(1) TFEU on the grounds that:

● they are necessary and proportionate for the penetration of new markets;
● they are necessary and proportionate for the proper functioning of a legitimate commercial or regulatory purpose;
● they are mere ancillary restraints.

➤ If an agreement falls within the prohibition in Article 101(1) TFEU, it may benefit from the exemption in Article 101(3) TFEU provided four conditions are met. The agreement:

● must contribute to improving the production or distribution of goods or to promoting technical or economic progress,
● while allowing consumers a fair share of the resulting benefit, and which does not,
● impose on the undertakings concerned restrictions which are not indispensable to the attainment of these objectives; and
● afford such undertakings the possibility of eliminating competition in respect of a substantial part of the products in question.

➤ The four conditions are cumulative: an agreement has to meet all four of the conditions – if it fails on any one of them, it is not eligible for an exemption.

➤ In principle, all types of agreements are eligible to be considered under Article 101(3) TFEU, although it is likely that some forms of agreement, for example, straightforward price-fixing or market sharing, will be unlikely to meet the criteria in Article 101(3) TFEU.

➤ A number of block exemptions have been created and, if an agreement meets the criteria in them, it is considered to meet the conditions laid down in Article 101(3) TFEU.

Further reading

Boeger, N., 'Solidarity and EC Competition Law' (2007) 32 *European Law Review* 319. *Puts the case law on solidarity into a wider context which helps explain it.*

Hawk, B., 'System failure: vertical restraints and EC Competition Law' (1995) 32 *Common Market Law Review* 973. *The classic criticism of the old system of enforcement of Article 81.*

Jones, A., 'Analysis of Agreements under US and EC Antitrust Law – Convergence or divergence' (2006) 51 *Antitrust Bulletin* 691. *Long article comparing US and EU practice in a helpful manner.*

Jones, A., 'Left Behind by Modernisation? Restrictions by Object under Article 101(1)' (2010) 6 *European Competition Journal* 649. *Clear discussion of the case law on the restriction of competition by object.*

Lugard, P. and Hancher, L., 'Honey I Shrunk the Article . . .' (2004) 25 *European Competition Law Review* 410. *Detailed critique of Commission Guidelines on Article 81(3).*

Monti, G., 'Article 81 and Public Policy' (2002) 39 *Common Market Law Review* 1057. *Excellent discussion of, in particular, the system of exemptions under Article 81(3).*

Nazzini, R., 'Article 81 EC Between Time Present and Time Past: A normative critique of "restriction of competition" in EU law' (2006) 43 *Common Market Law Review* 497. *Detailed discussion of the case law which argues that there is a balancing test in Article 81(1).*

Odudu, O., *The Boundaries of EC Competition Law: The Scope of Article 81* (Oxford University Press, 2006). *Thought-provoking study on the interpretation of Article 81. Arguments are also elaborated in a number of journal articles.*

Sufrin, B., 'The Evolution of Article 81(3) of the EC Treaty' (2006) 51 *Antitrust Bulletin* 915. *Excellent explanation of the workings of Article 81(3) written for an American audience.*

Townley, C., *Article 81 EC and Public Policy* (Hart Publishing, Oxford, 2009). *Comprehensive examination of the whether non-economic objectives are relevant to Article 101 TFEU and, if so, how they might be incorporated.*

van Gerven, G. and Varona, E., 'The Woodpulp Case and the Future of Concerted Practices' (1994) 31 *Common Market Law Review* 575. *Excellent discussion of law relating to concerted practices.*

Whish, R. and Sufrin, B., 'Art 85 and the Rule of Reason' (1987) *Yearbook of European Law* 1. *Clear introduction to the rule of reason debate in competition law.*

Winterstein, A., 'Nailing the Jellyfish: social security and competition law' (1999) 20 *European Competition Law Review* 324. *European Commission official provides a guide to the case law on the concept of an undertaking in the context of social security. Clear explanation of the cases.*

3 Abuse of a dominant position: introduction and pricing abuses

Chapter outline

This chapter discusses:

➤ Market definition in the context of Article 102 TFEU

➤ The meaning of a dominant position

➤ General considerations regarding the concept of abuse of a dominant position

➤ Objective justification and efficiency

➤ The control of excessive pricing by dominant companies

➤ The law relating to predatory or below cost pricing

➤ The developing doctrine of margin squeeze.

Introduction

In this chapter[1] we will begin to examine the competition rules which attempt to control the behaviour of dominant companies or monopolies; and we will finish this examination in the next chapter. Earlier (Chapter 1) we explained the economic objections to monopoly, namely that the monopolist has an incentive to restrict output and to raise prices, compared to the outcomes that would take place in a competitive market. Having said this, it is unusual for an undertaking to have a complete monopoly of any industry unless that monopoly has been granted to it by the state or it falls within the specialised category of natural monopolies, that is, activities where it is economically efficient to have only one undertaking, such as electricity transmission and distribution. More commonly, we find undertakings with large market shares operating in industries where they have significantly greater market shares than any of the other players, such as Microsoft, which has above 90% of the world market for operating systems for personal computers; or where the industry is divided amongst a number of large operators, such as grocery retailing in the United Kingdom where, although Tesco has around 30% market share, there are three other sizeable competitors (Sainsburys, ASDA and Morrisons) as well as a host of smaller operators. These different types of market structures

[1] Generally see R. O'Donoghue and J. Padilla, *The Law and Economics of Article 82 EC* (Hart Publishing, Oxford, 2006).

raise different policy problems: the former is concerned with the behaviour of individual undertakings, whereas the latter is concerned with the relationships between undertakings and the effect of market structures, which was touched upon earlier (Chapter 2) as the oligopoly problem. With the exception of some discussion of collective dominance below, the discussion of how competition law deals with these market structures will be delayed until later in the text (Chapter 10). The focus of this chapter will be on the controls that competition law places on individual undertakings that are in a dominant position and a definition is provided in Box 3.1. This definition includes undertakings with a monopoly but also extends to those without a monopoly but with significant market power. At what point market power becomes so significant that competition law should intervene is a hotly debated point.

KEY CASE EXTRACT   **Box 3.1**

Definition of dominant position

Source: Case 85/76 *Hoffmann-La Roche* v *Commission* [1979] ECR 461, para. 38:

> . . . a position of economic strength enjoyed by an undertaking which enables it to prevent effective competition being maintained on the relevant market by allowing it the power to behave to an appreciable extent independently of its competitors, its customers and ultimately of the consumers.

Questions: What is meant by economic strength? Is this equivalent to market power? At what level of market power should competition authorities be prepared to intervene?

There are four different ways in which an undertaking can obtain a dominant position, which raise potentially different issues for competition law. First, the undertaking can be a natural monopoly, as mentioned above and discussed in more detail later (Chapter 15). If this is truly the case, then competition law has a limited role to play. Insofar as it is seen as desirable to control the activities of a natural monopoly, this will mean that a regulatory system will have to be created. Secondly, the undertaking might be given a legal monopoly, consistent with the economic market, by the state, which tends to be a deliberate policy decision that competition law should not apply. The third possibility is that in an industry where an undertaking has been given a deliberate monopoly by the state a decision is subsequently taken to liberalise the industry and allow for competition, as happened in the privatisation of telecommunications and electricity in the United Kingdom and is happening in a number of countries throughout the European Union. The previously monopolistic undertaking may, however, retain a dominant market share and this raises a mix of competition law and regulatory issues. These sorts of industries are discussed in detail later in the text (Chapter 15), but specific cases involving them also appear in this chapter. The fourth possibility is that an undertaking may have gained a dominant position through its own conduct, of which a very good example is Microsoft. This conduct might have involved the undertaking being more efficient than its competitors or it may have involved conduct which is regarded as anti-competitive.

It is this fourth category of undertaking which is the main subject matter of this chapter and it raises a difficult policy problem. Insofar as an undertaking has become dominant by being more efficient than its competitors, it would be undesirable to penalise it for its success.

As the American judge, Learned Hand put it, 'the successful competitor, having been urged to compete, must not be turned upon when he wins'.[2] Also in an American context, Hovenkamp has argued that competition law should be less suspicious of unilateral conduct because it is ubiquitous, and therefore monitoring costs are high, and it is very difficult for an undertaking, acting on its own, to create substantial market power.[3] These observations suggest that some caution should be exercised by competition authorities in condemning the unilateral conduct of undertakings because this may end up stifling innovation and normal competitive behaviour; and European Union law has been criticised for going too far in condemning unilateral activities.

The central legal provision which controls this sort of conduct is Article 102 TFEU (ex Article 82 EC), which is replicated at the United Kingdom level by s. 18 of the Competition Act 1998 (see Boxes 3.2 and 3.3). The provision prohibits an abuse of a dominant position and gives some, non-exhaustive, examples of what this might constitute but the text gives no indication, as Monti has noted, of what its purpose is.[4] An important difference with Article 101 TFEU is that there is no equivalent of an exemption as is provided by Article 101(3) TFEU. If we are trying to determine the purpose behind Article 102 TFEU, the text itself can bear multiple meanings and there is substantial controversy over its underlying objectives. Monti, for example, thinks that the abuse doctrine has four possible roles: protecting the market from dominant undertakings when they reduce output or raise prices, protecting the market from dominant undertakings which are harming competitors to obtain the power to reduce output and increase prices, protecting other market participants from the acts of dominant undertakings and protecting the internal market.[5] Nazzini, by contrast, sees the objective as being to maximise long-term social welfare.[6] As regards its enforcement priorities, the European Commission has said that these are to focus on the types of conduct that are most harmful to consumers and safeguarding the competitive process in the internal market.[7] To put it another way, the text is consistent with a number of different interpretations.

KEY LEGAL PROVISION   **Box 3.2**

Article 102 TFEU

Any abuse by one or more undertakings of a dominant position within the internal market or a substantial part of it shall be prohibited as incompatible with the internal market insofar as it may affect trade between Member States. Such abuse may, in particular, consist in:

(a) Directly or indirectly imposing unfair purchase or selling prices or other unfair trading conditions

---

[2] *United States* v *Aluminium Co. of America* 148 F 2d 416 (2nd Cir. 1945) at 430.

[3] H. Hovenkamp, *The Antitrust Enterprise* (Harvard University Press, 2006) at pp. 108–9.

[4] G. Monti, *EC Competition Law* (Cambridge University Press, 2007) at p. 160.

[5] Ibid. at p. 161.

[6] R. Nazzini, *The Foundations of European Union Competition Law* (Oxford University Press, 2011) at Ch. 4. Contrast L.L. Gormsen, *A Principled Approach to Abuse of Dominance in European Competition Law* (Cambridge University Press, 2010).

[7] European Commission, *Guidance on the Commission's enforcement priorities in applying Article 82 of the EC Treaty to abusive exclusionary conduct by dominant undertakings*, COM (2009) 864 final (9 February 2009) at paras 5–6.

(b) Limiting production, markets or technical developments to the prejudice of consumers

(c) Applying dissimilar conditions to equivalent transactions with other trading parties, thereby placing them at a competitive disadvantage

(d) Making the conclusion of contracts subject to the acceptance by the other parties of supplementary obligations which, by their nature or according to commercial usage, have no connection with the subject of such contracts.

KEY LEGAL PROVISION   **Box 3.3**

Competition Act 1998, s. 18

(1) Subject to section 19, any conduct on the part of one or more undertakings which amounts to the abuse of a dominant position in a market is prohibited if it may affect trade within the United Kingdom.

(2) Conduct may, in particular, constitute such an abuse if it consists in –

(a) directly or indirectly imposing unfair purchase or selling prices or other unfair trading conditions;

(b) limiting production, markets or technical development to the prejudice of consumers;

(c) applying dissimilar conditions to equivalent transactions with other trading parties, thereby placing them at a competitive disadvantage;

(d) making the conclusion of contracts subject to acceptance by the other parties of supplementary obligations which, by their nature or according to commercial usage, have no connection with the subject of the contracts.

That a core text of European Union competition law is capable of supporting different objectives is not surprising if we remember that it dates back to 1957 at a time when there was little competition law in Europe and there was ambiguity about the role that competition law should play. Research into the drafting of Article 102 TFEU also indicates that it represented a compromise between different views about the role of competition law.[8] Looking at the history also reminds us that one of the purposes of Article 102 TFEU was to try and ensure that dominant companies could not partition the common market along national lines. Remember as well that German Ordo-liberal conceptions of competition were very important at the time, with their emphasis on economic freedom and protecting the process of competition and this influence can arguably be seen in the list of examples given in Article 102 TFEU, which suggests a concern with the effect of the commercial practices of dominant undertakings on other players in the market. The ambiguity over the purposes of Article 102 TFEU can also be seen in the Commission's rather hesitant steps to enforce it, with its first

---

[8] See H. Schweitzer, 'The History, Interpretation and Underlying Principles of Section 2 Sherman Act and Article 82 EC', in C. Ehlermann and M. Marquis (eds) *European Competition Law Annual 2007* (Hart Publishing, Oxford, 2008); and P. Akman, 'Searching for the Long-lost Soul of Article 82EC' (2009) 29 *Oxford Journal of Legal Studies* 267.

decision not coming until 1971[9] and, up until 1987, the Commission had only taken some 30 decisions on Article 102 TFEU.[10] Although there has been increasing activity throughout the 1990s and the early twenty-first century, the number of cases still remains relatively small, compared to Article 101 TFEU.

Although the number of cases may be small, their importance, and the level of controversy surrounding them, is very high. What we will see in the development of the European Union case law is an initial approach of the European Commission and Courts which has placed less emphasis on the conclusions that might be drawn from economic analysis and more on protecting the commercial interests of competitors to dominant undertakings, as well as a concern with market integration. In recent years the approach of the Commission has apparently changed, following the modernisation of its approach to Article 101 TFEU and merger control and the emphasis on a more economic approach. The Commission initiated a wide-ranging discussion over the modernisation of Article 102 TFEU, which did not lead to any substantive conclusions, but instead to the publication of guidance on its enforcement priorities in relation to exclusionary abuses which signalled an emphasis on protecting consumer welfare and a more economic approach.[11] The guidance paper has had a mixed response.[12] The case law does not unambiguously support the approach of the guidance paper, and in many respects runs counter to it, and, given the limited number of cases and the approach taken by the CJEU, there are significant tensions within the case law and uncertainties over how it should be applied in particular circumstances.

Throughout this chapter, UK law has been treated as identical to EU law, except in those areas where there are specific differences, which are mentioned in the text. For the ease of exposition, this chapter concentrates on general issues in relation to Article 102 TFEU and what I have categorised as 'pricing' abuses. The next chapter looks at 'non-price' abuses, although, as will be seen, the division is somewhat arbitrary.

Article 102 TFEU: market definition and dominance

There are three preliminary points. First, Article 102 TFEU and s. 18 only apply to 'undertakings' and the meaning of this was discussed earlier (Chapter 2), as the same definition applies in Articles 101 and 102 TFEU. Secondly, Article 102 TFEU applies only to conduct which has

---

[9] *GEMA* [1971] OJ L134/71. Case 6/72R *Europemballage Corporation* v *Commission* [1973] ECR 215 (*Continental Can*) was the first case to reach the CJEU.

[10] M. Cini and L. McGowan, *Competition Policy in the European Union* (Macmillan, London, 1998) at p. 94.

[11] European Commission, *DG Competition discussion paper on the application of Article 82 of the Treaty to exclusionary abuses* (Staff discussion paper) (December 2005); European Commission (n. 7).

[12] See D. Ridyard, 'The Commission's Article 102 guidelines: some reflections on the economic issues' (2009) 30 *European Competition Law Review* 230; M. Motta, 'The European Commission's Guidance Communication on Article 102' (2009) 30 *European Competition Law Review* 59; J. Temple Lang, 'Article 102 EC – The Problems and the Solution' (2009) available at: *http://papers.ssrn.com/sol3/papers.cfm?abstract_id=1467747* (accessed 19/07/12); M. Gravengaard and N. Kjaersgaard, 'The EU Commission guidance on the exclusionary abuse of dominance – and its consequences in practice' (2010) 31 *European Competition Law Review* 285; A. Witt, 'The Commission's guidance paper on exclusionary conduct – more radical than it appears?' (2010) 35 *European Law Review* 214; L. Gormsen, 'Why the European Commission's enforcement priorities on Article 82 EC should be withdrawn' (2010) 31 *European Competition Law Review* 45; P. Akman, 'The European Commission's Guidance on Article 102 TFEU: From Inferno to Paradiso?' (2010) 73 *Modern Law Review* 605.

an effect on trade between Member States and what this means was also discussed earlier (Chapter 1). Section 18 is limited to an effect on trade within the United Kingdom. Finally, Article 102 TFEU is limited to conduct within the internal market or a substantial part of it but the notion of 'substantial' has been interpreted broadly to encompass, for example, individual ports.[13] If conduct affects inter-state trade, which has an appreciability test in it, then it should also affect a substantial part of the internal market. Under s. 18, there is no inter-state trade test and this provision has been applied in small local markets: for example, a single crematorium, or an individual bus route.[14]

Since Article 102 TFEU requires the abuse of a dominant position, the first question that has to be asked is: what constitutes a dominant position? This is a question that cannot be answered in the abstract; what is required is a dominant position on a relevant market. Therefore, the first step in an inquiry under Article 102 TFEU is to define the relevant market. Having defined the market, the next step is to consider whether the undertaking concerned has a dominant position and, if so, whether the conduct it has undertaken constitutes an abuse. In practice, the first two steps are almost always hotly contested in cases because conduct that would be an abuse when committed by a dominant undertaking would be lawful, in terms of competition law, if done by a non-dominant undertaking.

Market definition under Article 102 TFEU

The CJEU has made the following comment with regard to market definition (Box 3.4).

KEY CASE EXTRACT   **Box 3.4**

The importance of market definition

Source: Case 6/72R *Europemballage Corporation* v *Commission* [1973] ECR 215 at para. 32:

> the definition of the relevant market is of essential significance, for the possibilities of competition can only be judged in relation to those characteristics of the products in question by virtue of which those products are particularly apt to satisfy an inelastic need and are only to a limited extent interchangeable with other products.

The general approach to market definition which is taken by the competition authorities has been discussed (Chapter 1) and here there are just two additional points. The first is that the European Commission has been criticised for taking too narrow a view of the market in Article 102 TFEU cases with the object of trying to ensure a successful case. Thus it has been criticised for defining a market for bananas, as opposed to fresh fruit, for finding a market for replacement parts for a particular brand of cash register and for limiting geographical markets to the area within which the abuse takes place.[15] Although this seems to be less of an issue in more recent cases,[16] this is an aspect of practice which worries businesses, as it indicates

---

[13] See Case C-179/90 *Merci Convenzionali Porto di Genova SpA* v *Siderurgica Gabriella SpA* [1991] ECR I-5889.
[14] *ME Burgess* v *OFT* [2005] CAT 25; *Arriva Plc and FirstGroup Plc*, OFT Decision of 5 February 2002.
[15] Respectively Case 27/76 *United Brands* v *Commission* [1978] ECR 207; Case 22/78 *Hugin* v *Commission* [1979] ECR 1869; and Case 322/81 *Nederlandsche Banden-Industrie Michelin* v *Commission* [1983] ECR 3461 (*Michelin I*).
[16] Compare the approach to the geographical market in *Michelin I* with Case T-203/01 *Michelin* v *Commission* [2003] ECR II-4071 (*Michelin II*).

potentially a very wide scope for Article 102 TFEU, particularly when combined with a broad definition of dominance, which is discussed below.

The second issue is a more conceptual one, which arises from the use of the hypothetical monopolist, or SSNIP test, as a means of identifying demand substitutability, which is referred to as the 'cellophane fallacy', so-called after a United States case involving this product.[17] The problem is as follows. Typically, the SSNIP test is conducted on the basis of the currently prevailing prices in the economy. As Bishop and Walker point out, the problem is that evidence of substitution at prevailing prices cannot identify whether current competitive constraints are effective in constraining prices to a competitive level rather than simply constraining them from rising any further.[18] They go on to point out that profit-maximising firms will always set prices at a level at which further price increases would be unprofitable. The problem is that if an undertaking already has market power then it will have increased its prices to the point where other products, which would not have constrained its behaviour at lower, competitive price levels now exercise a constraint upon it. We cannot know, therefore, whether prices are at a competitive level. To put the point another way, in the context of an Article 102 TFEU investigation, the hypothetical monopolist test is circular; it assumes that current prices are competitive when this is, among other things, the question that is to be asked.

The issue is recognised in the guidance produced by both the European Commission and the OFT but neither of them give much indication on how they would deal with the problem.[19] Although the problem seems severe theoretically, in practice once it is recognised it is not insurmountable.[20] There are, first, certain inquiries where using the current price is appropriate. As Bishop and Walker point out, if the allegation is that the undertaking is trying to exclude one of its rivals in order to raise prices once they have been excluded, then using current price levels is appropriate.[21] In their view, even if the problem cannot be solved, market definition can still be used in an economically coherent fashion provided that the competition authorities make sure: that their market definitions are consistent with the principles of demand and supply-side substitutability; that the products included in the market definition are at least substitutes at current prices; and that the market definitions are plausible on the basis of an analysis of the characteristics and uses of the products involved.[22] Although, in their view, the result may be that there is more than one market definition, this is better than having one, incorrect, market definition, and a competitive assessment can be carried out of each of the markets.

Establishing dominance

Having established the relevant markets in an Article 102 TFEU inquiry, the next stage is to see if the undertaking concerned is in a dominant position. What this means is set out in Box 3.5.

---

[17] *US v E I du Pont de Nemours* 351 US 377 (1956).

[18] S. Bishop and M. Walker, *The Economics of EC Competition Law* (3rd edn, Sweet & Maxwell, London, 2010) at paras 4.017–4.019.

[19] European Commission, 'Notice on the definition of the relevant market for the purposes of Community competition law', OJ C 372, 09.12.1997, pp. 5–13 (at para. 19); OFT, *Market Definition* (2004), paras 5.4–5.6.

[20] Bishop and Walker (n. 18), paras 4.020–4.022 contain a good discussion of how to deal with the problem, as do O'Donoghue and Padilla (n. 1), pp. 81–4.

[21] Bishop and Walker (n. 18), para. 4.021.

[22] Ibid., para. 4.022.

KEY DEFINITION Box 3.5

Definition of dominance

The dominant position thus referred to [by Article 102 TFEU] relates to a position of economic strength enjoyed by the undertaking which enables it to prevent effective competition being maintained on the relevant market by affording the power to behave to an appreciable extent independently of its competitors, customers and ultimately of its consumers.

Source: Case 27/76 *United Brands* v *Commission* [1978] ECR 207 at para. 65.

Questions: What do you think this means? How would you discover if an undertaking is dominant? How is this different from market power?

This can perhaps best be seen as a statement of the problem, rather than a definition. When economists talk about market power, they mean the ability to raise prices and restrict output, unconstrained by competitive pressures. The problem is that, outside a perfectly competitive market, all undertakings have some market power, indicated formally by their facing a downward sloping demand curve, which means as they raise prices, fewer consumers will purchase their goods and vice versa.[23] So the issue is not whether the undertaking has market power, but at what level of market power the competition authorities should intervene. The formula does not help here, because it contains two elements – the ability to prevent effective competition and the ability to behave independently – but does not explain what these elements mean nor how they relate to each other. Although there is some doubt about whether these are two tests or one test, Jones and Sufrin originally concluded that the better view was that the requirement that the undertaking should be able to exclude competition was descriptive.[24] This places emphasis on the independence aspect of the test, but the qualifying word 'appreciably' does add a large element of uncertainty.

It is important to note that the concept of dominance does not imply that there is no competition in the market. This point is made clear in the *United Brands* case where the CJEU not only makes this point explicitly, but also goes on to mention that, factually, there was a very lively competitive struggle taking place.[25] The point, however, according to the CJEU, is that the dominant position enables the undertaking to at least have an appreciable influence on the conditions under which competition develops and to disregard it so long as it does not operate to its detriment.[26] This, again, does not help in understanding when an undertaking will be considered dominant but it does indicate that the reach of the concept of dominance is rather broad.

Monti has argued that the conception of dominance employed depends on the underlying economic approach which is taken and, in his view, the two main lines in relation to EU law are to see dominance as where the undertaking has greater commercial power than others in the market or when the undertaking is able to devise strategies which can harm rivals and give

---

[23] In a perfectly competitive market, the demand curve of individual undertakings will be horizontal, as if they price their products above the competitive price, they will lose all sales.

[24] A. Jones and B. Sufrin, *EC Competition Law* (2nd edn, Oxford University Press, 2004) at p. 235.

[25] Case 27/76 *United Brands* v *Commission* [1978] ECR 207 at paras 113–18.

[26] Case 85/76 *Hoffmann-La Roche* v *Commission* [1979] ECR 461 at para. 39.

it, in the future, the power to raise prices and restrict output.[27] In his view the commercial power approach has been predominant in the case law of both the European Commission and the European Courts. However, as he points out, the European Commission, in its discussion paper on Article 102 TFEU, seems to be signalling a reassessment of this position and moving towards a more orthodox view of dominance as being equivalent to the power to raise prices and restrict output and this is confirmed by the recent Guidance.[28] Within the UK, the OFT's view is that an undertaking cannot be dominant unless it has 'substantial market power'.[29]

The main approach which has been taken in the European case law has been a structural one, comparing the position in the market of the undertaking under investigation with that of its competitors. This means an assessment of the undertaking's market share. The basic principle is set down in *Hoffmann-La Roche*, where the CJEU said that the view may legitimately be taken that very large market shares are, in themselves, and save in exceptional circumstances, evidence of a dominant position.[30] Later case law has established that if an undertaking has a market share of above 50%, there is a presumption that it is dominant.[31] The case law goes on to suggest that these market shares must be held for some time, that is, they have to be persistent, and that is certainly the way that the Commission and the OFT interpret the cases.[32] An undertaking may also be found to be dominant if its market share is between 40% and 50% of the market depending on the assessment of other factors, which are discussed below.[33] When the market share of an undertaking is below 40%, there are possibly slightly differing views between the European Commission and the OFT. In its recent enforcement guidelines on Article 102 TFEU, the Commission takes the view that dominance is not likely if undertakings have a market share below 40%, although there may be specific cases below that threshold where competitors were not in a position to constrain effectively the activities of a dominant undertaking, and that such cases may deserve the attention of the Commission.[34] By contrast, the OFT's view is that it is unlikely that an individual undertaking will be found to be dominant if its market share is below 40%, although it concedes this may be possible if other relevant factors provide strong evidence of dominance.[35] This difference indicates not only different enforcement priorities between the two agencies, but also shows that there is a significant level of uncertainty with regard to the interpretation of what constitutes dominance. It is worth noting, however, that there has been no decision which has been based on individual dominance where the undertaking has had a market share of below 40%, with the exception of *British Airways* when the market share for one year slipped to 39.7%, having been above 40% for several years before then.[36]

---

[27] G. Monti (n. 4) at pp. 125–6.

[28] European Commission (n. 7) at para. 11.

[29] OFT, *Assessment of Market Power* (2004), para. 2.9.

[30] Case 85/76 *Hoffmann-La Roche v Commission* [1979] ECR 461 at para. 41.

[31] Case C-62/86 *AKZO Chemie BV v Commission* [1991] ECR I-3359.

[32] OFT (n. 29), para. 2.11; European Commission (n. 7) at para. 15.

[33] See Case 27/76 *United Brands v Commission* [1978] ECR 207 (market share between 40% and 45%); Case C-95/04P *British Airways v Commission* [2007] ECR I-2331 (market share between 39.7% and 46.3%); Case 85/76 *Hoffmann-La Roche v Commission* [1979] ECR 461 (dominant position with a market share of 47% for Vitamin A); and Case C-250/92 *Gøttrup-Klim e.a. Grovvareforeninger v Dansk Landbrugs Grovvareselskab AmbA* [1994] ECR I-5641, para. 48 (market shares between 32% and 36% may give rise to a dominant position, depending on strength and number of competitors).

[34] European Commission (n. 7) at para. 14.

[35] OFT (n. 29), para. 2.12.

[36] Case C-95/04P *British Airways v Commission* [2007] ECR I-2331.

In summary, it seems that 40% is a threshold, below which it is very unlikely that an undertaking will be found to have an individual dominant position. Between 40% and 49%, an undertaking may be dominant in the appropriate circumstances, but it will be for the competition authorities or private litigants to prove this. Above 50%, there is a presumption of dominance, and it will be for the undertaking concerned to rebut the presumption. It is worth comparing this approach with that taken in the United States, where it has been said that the courts become much more reluctant to find monopoly power if the market share is below 70%, which supports suggestions that dominance is found too easily in EU competition law.[37] This is important because, as we shall see, there has been much criticism of the abuse doctrine in EU competition law and much of this might be defused if Article 102 TFEU cases were focused more clearly on undertakings with substantial market power, whereas at the moment this is not obviously the case.

It has in addition been suggested that where an undertaking is in a position approaching a monopoly, sometimes referred to as 'super dominance', the obligations on the undertaking not to abuse that position are even more onerous.[38] The CJEU has said that, as a general rule, market strength is significant as regards the effects of the conduct, rather than the question of whether such abuse has occurred. It did, however, say that there may be cases where market strength is relevant to assessing the lawfulness of conduct.[39] A summary of the various thresholds is given in Table 3.1. Calculating a market share is not necessarily an easy or straightforward task and market shares may change over time, sometimes quite dramatically.

Table 3.1 Market share thresholds in Article 102 TFEU

Market share	Possible consequence	Authority
Below 25%	Single firm dominance unlikely	European Commission, *DG Competition discussion paper on the application of Article 82 of the Treaty to exclusionary abuses* (Staff discussion paper) (December 2005), para. 31
25–39%	Single firm dominance possible in specific cases (EU); unlikely unless special circumstances (UK)	European Commission, *Guidance on the Commission's enforcement priorities in applying Article 82 of the EC Treaty to abusive exclusionary conduct by dominant undertakings*, COM (2009) 864 final (9 February 2009), para. 14; OFT, *Assessment of Market Power* (2004), para. 2.12
40–49%	Possibility of dominance, depending on other factors	Case 27/76 *United Brands v Commission* [1978] ECR 207; Case C-95/04P *British Airways v Commission* [2007] ECR I-2331; Case 85/76 *Hoffmann-La Roche v Commission* [1979] ECR 461
50% and above	Presumption of dominance	Case C-62/86 *AKZO Chemie v Commission* [1991] ECR I-3359
90% and above	Possibility of super dominance	Opinion of AG Fennelly in Cases C-395/96P etc. *Compagnie Maritime Belge v Commission* [2000] ECR I-1365

Questions: Are there clear safe areas where an undertaking is not dominant? Is the presumption of dominance set too low?

[37] See H. Hovenkamp, *Federal Antitrust Policy* (4th edn, West Publishing, St Paul, Minnesota, 2011) at s. 6.2a.

[38] See the opinion of AG Fennelly in Cases C-395/96P etc. *Compagnie Maritime Belge v Commission* [2000] ECR I-1365 and, arguably, Case C-333/94P *Tetra Pak II* [1996] ECR I-5951. Note the Court does not use the concept of 'super dominance'.

[39] Case C-52/09 *Konkurrensverket v Telia Sonera Sverige AB* [2011] 4 CMLR 18 at para. 81 citing the cases in note 38 above. In the UK see *Napp Pharmaceuticals v Director General of Fair Trading* [2002] CAT 1 at paras 219 and 337.

Market shares are, in any event, only proxies for market power. It is also necessary to investigate other factors in order to establish dominance.[40] The starting point is to look at the position of the undertaking relative to that of its competitors. This has been particularly important in the EU cases where undertakings have had market shares between 40% and 50% because one of the reasons for finding dominance established has been that these market shares were over twice that of the nearest competitor (*United Brands*) or the share was equal to the aggregate of the next two largest competitors.[41] If this condition is not met, and even if it is, we must go on to consider other factors.

Of these, the most important are barriers to entry into the market. Within the economics literature, the concept is controversial and the debate has polarised around two views. On the one hand, there is the position of Bain, an eminent economist, who defined entry barriers as any market condition that enables an incumbent firm to charge monopoly prices without attracting new entry.[42] On the other hand, there was Stigler's (another eminent economist) definition of entry barriers as 'a cost of producing (at some or every rate of output), which must be borne by firms which seek to enter an industry but is not borne by firms already in the industry.'[43] The latter approach is much narrower than the former and would tend to see entry barriers as restricted to intellectual property rights and government regulation, while the former would include a wider range of factors, such as economies of scale, product differentiation or absolute cost advantages. There is no need to go into this debate in any depth; because competition authorities have taken the view that what matters is not whether something can be defined as an entry barrier but whether, when and to what extent entry into a market is likely to occur, as can be seen in Box 3.6.

KEY OFFICIAL GUIDANCE   Box 3.6

Definitions of entry barriers

Barriers to expansion or entry can take various forms. They may be legal barriers, such as tariffs or quotas, or they may take the form of advantages specifically enjoyed by the dominant undertaking, such as economies of scale and scope, privileged access to essential inputs or natural resources, important technologies or an established distribution and sales network. They may also include costs and other impediments, for instance resulting from network effects, faced by customers in switching to a new supplier. The dominant undertaking's own conduct may also create barriers to entry, for example where it has made significant investments which entrants or competitors would have to match, or where it has concluded long-term contracts with its customers that have appreciable foreclosing effects.

Source: European Commission, *Guidance on the Commission's enforcement priorities in applying Article 82 of the EC Treaty to abusive exclusionary conduct by dominant undertakings*, COM (2009) 864 final (9 February 2009), para. 17.

---

[40] European Commission (n. 7) at para. 10.

[41] Case 85/76 *Hoffmann-La Roche v Commission* [1979] ECR 461 at para. 51. See also Case C-95/04P *British Airways v Commission* [2007] ECR I-2331 and Case T-203/01 *Michelin v Commission* [2003] ECR II-4071.

[42] J.S. Bain, *Barriers to New Competition* (Harvard University Press, 1956) at p. 3.

[43] G. Stigler, *The Organization of Industry* (R.D. Irwin, Homewood, Illinois, 1968) at p. 67.

> Entry barriers arise when an undertaking has an advantage (not solely based on superior efficiency) over potential entrants from having already entered the market and/or from special rights (e.g. to production or distribution) or privileged access to key inputs.
>
> *Source*: OFT, *Assessment of Market Power* (2004), para. 5.5.
>
> Barriers to entry are thus specific features of the market that give incumbent firms advantages over potential competitors.
>
> *Source*: OFT/Competition Commission, *Merger Assessment Guidelines* (2010) at para. 5.8.4.
>
> **Question**: Entry into a market is not a cost-free exercise. At what point does a cost of entry become an entry barrier?

Types of entry barriers

The OFT and the Competition Commission in their joint guidance on mergers list four basic types of barriers to entry: absolute advantages, intrinsic/structural advantages, economies of scale and strategic advantages.[44] This is a useful quick checklist, and many of the ideas within it are incorporated in the discussion below. Strategic advantages deserves some more explanation and the OFT and Competition Commission see this as arising where incumbent firms have advantages over new entrants because of their established position. They go on to say that this can be particularly important in markets which are prone to 'network' effects, which make the market prone to tipping in the direction of an unassailable leader.[45] Although these are the views of the UK authorities, and in the context of merger control, they appear to be consistent with the European Commission's views as expressed in Box 3.6 and are explained in a clear manner.

Legal restrictions

There may be various legal barriers which prevent the entry of competitors into a market. So, for example, entry into a market may require a licence granted by government and the policy may be to license only a limited number of undertakings (as was the case with fixed-line telecommunications in the 1980s in the UK) or, indeed, to have a legal monopoly. Intellectual property rights can also prevent entry into the market if, for example, the incumbent firm has an exclusive patent on a product that is needed to operate in the market.

Sunk costs

There are costs for any undertaking which wishes to enter a market. 'Sunk costs' are defined by the OFT as those costs which must be incurred to compete in a market, but which are not recoverable on exiting the market.[46] The example given is of an entrant to a hypothetical market for long-distance coach services in the North of England which purchases a fleet of vehicles. If it became necessary to exit the market, it is possible that the fleet could be sold to another operator, for example in the South of England, thus recovering some of

---

[44] OFT/Competition Commission, *Merger Assessment Guidelines* (2010) at para. 5.8.5. See also the discussion by the Competition Commission, 'Draft guidelines for market investigations' (2012) at paras 195–210.

[45] Ibid. para. 5.8.6.

[46] OFT (n. 29), para. 5.9.

the costs. Certain other costs, such as painting the coaches in the company colours or advertising, are not recoverable and are referred to as sunk costs. Sunk costs do not necessarily constitute an entry barrier by themselves; the question is whether the scale of sunk costs gives the incumbent an advantage over potential new entrants such that entry becomes unattractive.

Economies of scale

Economies of scale exist where average costs fall as output rises. In an industry where economies of scale are important, for example mass manufacturing, entry may become more difficult and risky. The entrant may have to invest in a large and specialised plant, it will be important to have sufficient contracts and a distribution system that will take advantage of the economies of scale and it may take some time to build up the requisite scale, thus requiring the entrant to operate at a loss for some period of time. These effects may all constitute barriers to entry. Network effects could be considered as a variant of this idea. Network effects exist where the value of the network grows as more people join it. Thus, for example, the value of a phone network, or a social networking site such as Facebook or Twitter, depends on the number of users; the most valuable one being the one which has the greatest number of users. In these circumstances, an incumbent with an established network will have an advantage over an entrant without access to the network that has to establish a new network from scratch.

Absolute cost advantages

According to the European Commission, these may include preferential access to essential facilities, natural resources, innovation and R & D (research and development), intellectual property rights and capital conferring a competitive advantage on the allegedly dominant undertaking, which makes it difficult for other undertakings to compete effectively.[47] This idea is controversial, because it could equally be said that these cost advantages are indicators of an undertaking's efficiency, rather than market power. Nevertheless, this approach has support in the case law of the European Courts: for example, in *Hoffmann-La Roche*, where the CJEU pointed to a technological lead and the existence of a highly developed sales network as being indicators of a dominant position,[48] and in *United Brands*, where the CJEU took into account vertical integration, and research and development, among other factors, as indicators of a dominant position.[49] It is noticeable that absolute advantages are not a factor mentioned by the OFT in its guidance on the assessment of market power, although they are mentioned in the joint OFT/Competition Commission guidance.

Conclusion on entry barriers

This discussion does not purport to be exhaustive but merely to cover some of the more commonly mentioned barriers to entry. It can be seen from the discussion above that the competition authorities have taken a wider view of what constitute entry barriers than some economists.

---

[47] European Commission, op. cit., note 11 at para. 40. European Commission, op. cit., note 7 at para. 17.
[48] Case 85/76 *Hoffmann-La Roche* v *Commission* [1979] ECR 461 at para. 48.
[49] Case 27/76 *United Brands* v *Commission* [1978] ECR 207 at paras 70–85.

Collective dominance[50]

Article 102 TFEU prohibits abuse by one *or more* undertakings of a dominant position. This suggests that the Article can be applied not only to the actions of a single undertaking with a dominant position but also to cases where two or more undertakings together hold a dominant position. Although originally this was interpreted narrowly as it was thought that it was aimed at undertakings and their subsidiaries,[51] the concept has been expanded, both under Article 102 TFEU and the European Merger Regulation, in order to deal with the problem of oligopolistic markets. This has already been discussed briefly (see Chapter 2), and will be discussed in more detail later (Chapter 10), but it is worth remembering what the policy problem is in this context. In brief, there are certain market structures where there is limited competition between the undertakings participating in those markets, but the market could not be described as fully competitive. If there is no contact between the undertakings concerned, it will be very difficult to establish a concerted practice under Article 101 TFEU (as explained in Chapters 2 and 10). At the same time, given the approach to dominance explained above, it is possible that no one undertaking would have a market share above 40% and therefore it would be difficult to find a situation of individual dominance. There is a strong possibility that such a market would fall outside the control of Articles 101 and 102 TFEU and the original version of the Merger Regulation. The European Commission has attempted to develop the notion of collective dominance to catch these sorts of markets under Article 102 TFEU and this development is discussed in more detail later in the text (see Chapters 10 and 13). The first manifestation of this was in *Italian Flat Glass* where the European Commission claimed that three Italian undertakings in the flat glass industry had aggregate market shares of 79% and 95% in the non-automotive and automotive markets respectively and presented themselves on the market as a single entity. Although the GC rejected the factual basis of this contention, and were very critical of the evidential basis of the decision, they went on to say:

> There is nothing, in principle, to prevent two or more independent economic entities from being, on a specific market, united by such economic links that, by virtue of that fact, together they hold a dominant position vis-à-vis the other operators on the same market. This could be the case, for example, where two or more independent undertakings jointly have, through agreements or licences, a technological lead affording them the power to behave to an appreciable extent independently of their competitors, their customers and ultimately of their consumers.[52]

This raised the question of what was meant by 'economic links' and whether this meant some type of formal agreement, in which case it would not have been obvious that this extended the concept beyond Article 101 TFEU. The matter was put beyond doubt in the *CMB* case, which involved a liner conference, that is, an agreement between a number of undertakings. Nevertheless, as regards collective dominance the CJEU said:

---

[50] Generally, see G. Monti, 'The Scope of Collective Dominance under Article 82 EC' (2001) 38 *Common Market Law Review* 131 and R. Whish, 'Collective Dominance', in D. O'Keefe and A. Bavasso (eds) *Judicial Review in European Law* (Kluwer, Deventer, 2000).

[51] Case 85/76 *Hoffmann-La Roche* v *Commission* [1979] ECR 461 at para. 39.

[52] Cases T-68, 77 and 78/89 *Società Italiana Vetro* v *Commission* [1992] ECR II-1403 at para. 358.

it is necessary to consider whether the undertakings concerned together constitute a collective entity vis-à-vis their competitors, their trading partners and consumers on a particular market. It is only where that question is answered in the affirmative that it is appropriate to consider whether that collective entity actually holds a dominant position and whether its conduct constitutes abuse . . . the existence of an agreement or other links in law is not indispensable to a finding of a collective dominant position; such a finding may be based on other connecting factors and would depend on an economic assessment and, in particular, on an assessment of the structure of the market in question.[53]

For present purposes, the important point is to note that undertakings may be caught by Article 102 TFEU even if they do not have a dominant position on their own and without any formal relationship with other undertakings on the market, in circumstances where there are the appropriate market conditions. Again, this indicates the long reach of the idea of dominance and its uncertain scope.

Abuse: introduction

An important introductory point is that possession of a dominant position is not a problem; Article 102 TFEU condemns the abuse of that position.[54] Once an undertaking is found to be in a dominant position, the CJEU has said that it has 'a special responsibility not to allow its conduct to impair undistorted competition on the Common Market'.[55] What this means, in effect, is that there are certain commercial practices which are legitimate if carried out by a non-dominant undertaking but may constitute an abuse if carried out by a dominant undertaking.[56] This is not a matter of the subjective intention of the dominant undertaking because case law establishes that the notion of abuse is an objective one which relates to the behaviour of the undertaking.[57]

Nor does the behaviour have to be successful or have an actual effect on the market. As the GC put it, 'it is not necessary to demonstrate that the abuse in question had a concrete effect on the markets concerned. It is sufficient in that respect to demonstrate that the abusive conduct of the undertaking in a dominant position tends to restrict competition, or, in other words, that the conduct is capable of having, or likely to have, such an effect.'[58] The GC went on to say that the fact that the result hoped for had not been achieved would not prevent a finding of abuse, a point which is supported throughout the case law.[59] Quite what has to be proved here is uncertain, not least because the language used by the European courts varies through the case law.[60] It seems that what is required is both a convincing theory as to why

[53] Case C-395/96 *Compagnie Maritime Belge Transports SA* v *Commission* [2000] ECR I-1365 at paras 39 and 45.
[54] Case C-52/09 *Konkurrensverket* v *TeliaSonera Sverige AB* [2011] 4 CMLR 18 at para. 24.
[55] Case 322/81 *Michelin* v *Commission* [1983] ECR 3461 at para. 10.
[56] See Joined Cases T-191 and 212–214/98 *Atlantic Container Line* v *Commission* [2003] ECR II-3275 at para. 1460.
[57] Case 85/76 *Hoffmann-La Roche* v *Commission* [1979] ECR 461.
[58] Case T-219/99 *British Airways* v *Commission* [2003] ECR II-5917 at para. 293. Upheld on appeal: Case C-95/04P *British Airways* v *Commission* [2007] ECR I-2331. See also Case C-52/09 *Konkurrensverket* v *TeliaSonera Sverige AB* [2011] 4 CMLR 18 at paras 63–4.
[59] Ibid., para. 297. See also Case C-52/09 *Konkurrensverket* v *Telia Sonera Sverige AB* [2011] 4 CMLR 18 at para. 65.
[60] See R. Nazzini (n. 6) at 294–300.

the conduct would cause anti-competitive harm and a convincing explanation of how this might work in the circumstances of the case.[61] The Commission makes a similar point in its guidance, saying that it will intervene in cases where it has cogent and convincing evidence that the alleged conduct is *likely* to lead to anti-competitive foreclosure. Direct evidence of actual foreclosure is considered very helpful, but not necessary.[62] Furthermore, the better view seems to be that there does not have to be a causal link between the dominant position and the abuse committed.[63] In the *Astrazeneca* case, which involved misleading submissions by a dominant undertaking to national patent authorities, the GC said that abuse 'does not necessarily have to consist in the use of the economic power conferred by a dominant position'.[64] This means that the abuse does not have to be committed on the same market as the dominant position. If the effects of the abuse are felt on a separate market, in which the undertaking does not have a dominant position, this may be an abuse, provided that there is a sufficiently close connection between the two markets.[65]

Given the very wide scope of the notion of abuse, it is important to establish what sorts of practices could constitute abuse. Article 102 TFEU gives a list of examples but the CJEU has held that this list is not exhaustive; it needs to be read in the light of Articles 2 and 3 of the EC Treaty [now Article 3 TEU and Articles 3–6 and 8(2) TFEU] requiring harmonious development of economic activities and that competition in the common market is not distorted. Furthermore, Article 102 TFEU, 'is not only aimed at practices which may cause damage to consumers directly, but also at those which are detrimental to them through their impact on an effective competition structure'.[66] It is worth remembering that the *Continental Can* case, from which this quote comes, involved a merger between two undertakings, prior to the merger control Regulation, which the European Commission was trying to control using Article 102 TFEU; in other words, using Article 102 TFEU for a purpose which its drafters certainly had not intended. The CJEU held that, in principle, this could be done, although on the facts the European Commission had not defined the relevant market. The categories of abuse are not, therefore, closed and so, although the following discussion attempts to describe some of the most important types of abuse that have been found in the case law, it is always possible that others will be developed. Quite recently, for example, the Commission has held that an alleged misuse of the patent system could constitute abuse under Article 102 TFEU.[67]

Categorising the types of abuses is quite difficult, but a traditional distinction is between exploitative abuses and exclusionary abuses. Exploitative abuses consist of anti-competitive conduct which exploits consumers directly, such as increasing prices or limiting output.

---

[61] See, for example, the discussion in Case C-52/09 *Konkurrensverket v Telia Sonera Sverige AB* [2011] 4 CMLR 18 at paras 66–7.

[62] European Commission (n. 7) at paras 20–2.

[63] This is controversial: compare R. Whish and D. Bailey, *Competition Law* (7th edn, Oxford University Press, 2012) at 203–4 with R. Nazzini (n. 6) at 176–8 and E. Rousseva, *Rethinking Exclusionary Abuses in EU Competition Law* (Hart Publishing, Oxford, 2010) at 73–4.

[64] Case T-321/05 *AstraZeneca v Commission* [2010] ECR II-2805 at para. 354. On appeal as Case C-457/10P (not yet decided).

[65] Ibid. at para. 127.

[66] Case 6/72R *Europembellage & Continental Can v Commission* [1972] ECR 215 at paras 22–6. See recently Case C-95/04P *British Airways v Commission* [2007] ECR I-2331.

[67] *AstraZeneca*, Commission decision of 15 June 2005, upheld in Case T-321/05 *Astrazeneca v Commission* [2010] ECR II-2805 at para. 354. On appeal as Case C-457/10 P (not yet decided). See also OFT, 'Reckitt Benckiser' (2011).

Exclusionary behaviour is aimed, not directly at consumers, but at excluding competitors from a market, with the intention of obtaining greater market power which can then be used to exploit consumers. Although it might be thought that, if the main objective of competition law is the protection of consumer welfare, the greatest focus would be on exploitative abuses, in fact at European level the vast bulk of case law and decisions is focused on exclusionary abuses. At the UK level, there has been more activity by the OFT and the Competition Commission in relation to exploitative abuses, as we shall see. One explanation for this is that EU competition law has been concerned to protect market access for competitors and to protect them from the abuse of commercial power by dominant companies or, to put it negatively, and controversially, to protect competitors rather than competition, and therefore enforcement effort focused there.[68] The Commission would not accept this argument and has said:

> The aim of the Commission's enforcement activity in relation to exclusionary conduct is to ensure that dominant undertakings do not impair effective competition by foreclosing their competitors in an anticompetitive way, thus having an adverse impact on consumer welfare, whether in the form of higher price levels than would have otherwise prevailed or in some other form such as limiting quality or reducing consumer choice.[69]

In terms of policy areas, the European Commission has also focused on the liberalisation of certain markets, notably in network industries, and seems to have been using Article 102 TFEU as a supplementary enforcement tool and therefore has been largely concerned with foreclosure. Furthermore, as we shall see, proving exploitative abuses may be quite difficult.

Objective justification and efficiency

Before looking at specific abuses, the question of whether there are any general 'defences' should be considered. Article 102 TFEU has no provision which allows for an exemption along the lines of Article 101(3) TFEU. A practical problem arises because Articles 101 and 102 can be applied to the same circumstances, one aimed at the conduct, another at the agreement.[70] This opens up the possibility, in principle, that such conduct could be condemned under Article 102 TFEU but exempted under Article 101(3) TFEU and it is important to avoid inconsistency in the application of the two articles.[71] In addition, it has been argued that, if a more economic approach is taken, this will involve weighing the anti-competitive effects of any conduct against its pro-competitive justifications and that there would be no point in taking action if the latter outweighed the former.[72] So there are strong arguments for recognising some form of defence or justification for conduct under Article 102 TFEU. The Article is not drafted to include such a defence and this creates a conceptual problem. The idea of a defence is that conduct is admitted and excused, because certain conditions have been met. Article 102 TFEU is not drafted in this manner which suggests that any justifications for

---

[68] Schweitzer (n. 8) is dismissive of the negative interpretation.

[69] European Commission (n. 7) at para. 19.

[70] For example, Case 344/98 *Masterfoods Ltd* v *HB Ice Cream Ltd* [2000] ECR I-11639; Cases T-68, 77 and 78/89 *Società Italiana Vetro* v *Commission* [1992] ECR II-1403.

[71] See Case 6/72R *Europemballage & Continental Can* v *Commission* [1972] ECR 215 at para. 25 for this point.

[72] See EAGCP, *An economic approach to Article 82* (2005) available at: *http://ec.europa.eu/competition/antitrust/art82/index.html* (accessed 20/07/12).

the conduct must be incorporated into the concept of abuse.[73] In other words, if conduct has pro and anti-competitive effects, and the former outweigh the latter, then there is no abuse rather than saying that there is an abuse but it meets the condition of an efficiency defence. Recent case law, discussed below, shows the European courts moving towards the acceptance, in principle, of some form of efficiency justification despite the conceptual issues and previous case law.

The starting point is consistent case law which says that if the conduct of which the undertaking is accused is objectively justified, then this does not constitute abuse. It is important to stress that this is not a defence: the claim is that the conduct is not an abuse, because there are objective justifications for it. Although in principle this is a well-accepted point, in practice there does not appear to have been a case where an undertaking has been able to show that its conduct is objectively justified. It has been suggested that there are three broad variants of this defence – legitimate business behaviour, which includes meeting competition, pursuit of a public interest objective, and that the conduct produces efficiency gains – although it is probably helpful to think of this as four categories, splitting legitimate business behaviour into two parts: meeting competition and other justifications.[74]

The first part of legitimate business behaviour would include action that is normal commercial behaviour. Examples of this would include refusing to supply an existing customer because of their poor payment record[75] or because of a lack of capacity. Also included in this category might be pure quantity discounts, that is, discounts granted for large volume orders which are justified by the economic savings made by the undertaking. This type of behaviour is worth distinguishing from the second issue, meeting competition. This has long been accepted by the European Courts as legitimate, at least in principle: 'the fact that an undertaking is in a dominant position cannot deprive it of its entitlement to protect its own commercial interests when they are attacked'.[76] Meeting competition is usually concerned with pricing practices, although this is not always the case. For example, in *United Brands*,[77] the dominant company refused to supply a distributor which had participated in a campaign for a rival undertaking. This was presented as a meeting competition defence, which the CJEU accepted was legitimate, but refused to accept it in this case as the actual purpose was to strengthen the dominant position and, in any event, the response was not proportionate to the threat. More recently, consider *Sot Lelos kai Sia*,[78] which involved the attempts of GlaxoSmithKline

---

[73] P. Akman, *The Concept of Abuse in EU Competition Law* (Hart Publishing, Oxford, 2012) explains this at 115–20. The early case law seems unequivocal on this point: Case 66/86 *Ahmed Saeed v Zentrale zur Bekämpfung unlauteren Wettbewerbs e.V.* [1989] ECR 803 at para. 32 and Case T-51/89 *Tetra Pak Rausing SA v Commission* [1990] ECR II-309 at 25; cases T191/98 and T-212-214/98 *Atlantic Container Line AB and others v Commission* [2003] ECR II-3275 at paras 1109 and 1114.

[74] See Philip Lowe, 'DG Competition's Review of the Policy on Abuse of Dominance', speech at Fordham Corporate Law Institute, 30th Annual Conference on International Antitrust Law and Policy, 23 October 2003, available at: *http://ec.europa.eu/competition/speeches/index_2003.html* (accessed 02/09/12). Although compare: European Commission (n. 11) (objective necessity, meeting competition and efficiency); O'Donoghue and Padilla (n. 1) at pp. 228–9 (objective necessity, reasonable steps to protect commercial interests and efficiency); and G. Monti, *EC Competition Law* (Cambridge University Press, 2007) at pp. 204–10 (economic justification, meeting competition, efficiency and public policy).

[75] As in Cases 29, 30/83 *Compagnie Royale Asturiennes des Mines and Rheinzink v Commission* [1984] ECR 1679, an Article 101 case.

[76] Case T-228/97 *Irish Sugar v Commission* [1999] ECR II-2969 at para. 112.

[77] Case 27/76 *United Brands v Commission* [1978] ECR 207 at para. 189.

[78] Cases C-468/06 to 478/06 *Sot Lelos kai Sia v GlaxoSmithKline AEVE* [2008] ECR I-7139.

to prevent parallel importing by refusing to supply pharmaceuticals to Greek customers who were exporting them to other countries. Although the CJEU held that it was not permissible for such an undertaking in a dominant position to refuse to meet the ordinary orders of existing customers, nevertheless, it was allowed to counter, in a reasonable and proportionate way, threats to its commercial interests by orders which were out of the ordinary course of business and designed essentially for the export market. Whether the conduct was proportional was a matter for the national court. According to the European Commission the constituent elements of proportionality are that the chosen conduct is suitable, indispensable and proportionate.[79]

The issue of meeting competition has been most controversial in relation to pricing practices, that is, what leeway a dominant undertaking has in responding to a competitor undercutting its prices, and relates to the discussion on predatory or below cost-pricing practices which follows below. Although it has often been raised as an issue, there is no example of this argument being successful, which lead Rousseva, a European Commission official, to conclude that this defence is a 'sham'.[80] There are two issues here: how low can price cuts be in response to competition and to what extent do price cuts have to be general, as opposed to targeted at specific customers? In the first place, the European Commission takes the view that if prices are below average avoidable cost (AAC), this indicates that an equally efficient competitor cannot serve the targeted customers without incurring a loss. If prices are above AAC but below long-run average incremental cost (LRAIC) this indicates that an equally efficient competitor could be foreclosed. (The meaning of these concepts is explained below, in the context of predatory pricing.) If either of these situations is the case, then the Commission will integrate this information into a general consideration of anti-competitive foreclosure. If it is clear that an equally efficient competitor can compete, then the Commission will be unlikely to intervene, although it recognises that in certain circumstances less efficient competitors may exercise a constraint.[81] Secondly, the conduct must be a suitable way to achieve this aim, it must be indispensable and it must be proportionate.[82] So it is possible to respond to competition with prices which are above average variable cost (AVC) but below average total cost (ATC), assuming the other conditions for predation are not met. Thirdly, price discrimination does tend to be viewed suspiciously by the European Commission when it comes to meeting competition even though, as O'Donoghue and Padilla suggest, this seems to go too far.[83] In summary, the safest strategy for meeting competition through price cuts would appear to be pricing above AVC, preferably above ATC with those prices being offered to all customers and simply attempting to meet, rather than beat, the competitor's prices. There may be some room for flexibility in light of the CJEU's statement in *Post Danmark*,[84] where it said that a pricing policy cannot be considered to amount to an exclusionary abuse simply because the price charged to a single customer is lower than the average total costs attributed to the activity concerned, but higher than the average incremental costs.

---

[79] European Commission (n. 11) at para. 82.
[80] E. Rousseva, *Rethinking Exclusionary Abuses in EU Competition Law* (Hart Publishing, Oxford, 2010) at 260 and the discussion at 271–81.
[81] European Commission (n. 7) at paras 20–7.
[82] Ibid., para. 82.
[83] O'Donoghue and Padilla (n. 1) at p. 289.
[84] Case C-209/10 *Post Danmark A/S v Konkurrremceådet*, judgment of 27 March 2012 (CJEU) at para. 37.

Pursuit of a public interest objective, for example, would be something related to health or safety or the dangerous nature of the product in question. In the *Hilti* case, the undertaking attempted to justify tying the purchase of Hilti nails to Hilti cartridge strips on the grounds of safety but the CJEU responded by saying that it was not the task of the dominant company to take steps on its own initiative to eliminate products which it regards, rightly or wrongly, as dangerous or inferior to its product.[85] This does seem to suggest that such an argument may be successful only if the dominant undertaking can point to national legislation or regulatory practice which obliges it to behave in a certain way and this is the European Commission's view.[86]

As regards the efficiency defence, the European Commission's guidance claims that there are four conditions (see Box 3.7). As can be seen, these conditions replicate those in Article 101(3) TFEU and the explanation in the guidance suggests that a similar approach would be taken. There are a number of difficulties with such a defence, even if it can be developed on the basis of existing law.[87] Perhaps the most difficult issue is that balancing the pro- and anti-competitive effects of conduct is not a straightforward matter. Hovenkamp, admittedly discussing the American context where it is a question of the competence of the courts, as opposed to an agency like the European Commission, argues that meaningful balancing is virtually never possible because of the difficulties of computing the costs and benefits. He favours an analysis which strips away explanations that are implausible or unproven until a core is reached that characterises the practice as pro- or anti-competitive or, to put it in European terms, whether or not there is an abuse.[88] It is, in any event, unclear how a firm in a dominant position can meet the fourth condition, that competition in a substantial part of the products concerned is not eliminated. By definition, this defence will be invoked in cases where an undertaking has a dominant position and its conduct has been found to have an actual or likely effect of foreclosing competition.[89] The European Commission's discussion paper suggested that this defence will not be available for market shares above 75%[90] but this still looks a difficult hurdle even for market shares below this.

Recent case law of the CJEU confirms the European Commission's view that such an efficiency defence is available. The first clear recognition of this came in the *British Airways* case[91] where, in the context of a rebate system, it said that '[i]t has to be determined whether the exclusionary effect arising from such a system, which is disadvantageous for competition, may be counterbalanced, or outweighed, by advantages in terms of efficiency which also benefit the consumer. If the exclusionary effect of that system bears no relation to advantages for the market and consumers, or if it goes beyond what is necessary in order to attain those advantages, that system must be regarded as an abuse.' This approach has been confirmed in later case law[92] and further developed in the *Post Danmark* case.[93] Here the CJEU said, in terms

---

[85] Case T-30/89 *Hilti* v *Commission* [1991] ECR II-1439 at para. 118; see also Case T-83/91 *Tetra Pak II* [1994] ECR II-755 at paras 83–4 and 138.

[86] European Commission (n. 7) at para. 29.

[87] See O'Donoghue and Padilla (n. 1) at pp. 232–4 for discussion.

[88] H. Hovenkamp, *The Antitrust Enterprise* (Harvard University Press, 2006) at p. 108.

[89] See O'Donoghue and Padilla (n. 1) at pp. 233–4.

[90] Above (n. 11), para. 92.

[91] Case C-95/04P *British Airways* v *Commission* [2007] ECR I-2331 at 86.

[92] Case C-202/07P *France Télécom* v *Commission* [2009] ECR I-2369 para. 111; Case C-52/09 *Konkurrensverket* v *TeliaSonera Sverige AB* [2011] 4 CMLR 18 at para. 76.

[93] Case C-209/10 *Post Danmark A/S* v *Konkurremceådet*, judgment of 27 March 2012 (CJEU) at para. 42.

which were almost identical to the European Commission's guidance set out in Box 3.7 (the numbers in the quote relate to the guidance in Box 3.7):

> ... it is for the dominant undertaking to show that the efficiency gains likely to result from the conduct under consideration counteract any likely negative effects on competition and consumer welfare in the affected markets [3], that these gains have been, or are likely to be, brought about as a result of that conduct [1], that such conduct is necessary for the achievement of those gains in efficiency [2] and that it does not eliminate effective competition, by removing all or most existing sources of actual or potential competition [4].

So it seems as if an efficiency defence has now been established, although it remains unclear whether this is a defence or a justification which means that no abuse has been committed. The problem that a dominant undertaking faces when seeking to rely on this defence is that it has a burden of proof to make out the defence and, in practice, it is likely to be very difficult to convince the European Commission or a national competition agency of this point.[94] Given that there are no examples of an undertaking successfully invoking objective justifications it is critical for dominant undertakings to be clear about the scope of potential abuses, rather than to rely on defences.

KEY OFFICIAL GUIDANCE   Box 3.7

The efficiency defence

1 the efficiencies have been, or are likely to be, realised as a result of the conduct. They may, for example, include technical improvements in the quality of goods, or a reduction in the cost of production or distribution;

2 the conduct is indispensable to the realisation of those efficiencies: there must be no less anti-competitive alternatives to the conduct that are capable of producing the same efficiencies;

3 the likely efficiencies brought about by the conduct outweigh any likely negative effects on competition and consumer welfare in the affected markets;

4 the conduct does not eliminate effective competition, by removing all or most existing sources of actual or potential competition ... In the Commission's view, exclusionary conduct which maintains, creates or strengthens a market position approaching that of a monopoly can normally not be justified on the grounds that it also creates efficiency gains.

Source: European Commission, *Guidance on the Commission's enforcement priorities in applying Article 82 of the EC Treaty to abusive exclusionary conduct by dominant undertakings*, COM (2009) 864 final (9 February 2009), para. 30.

Questions: Can such a defence be established without a court decision? How easy will it be for a dominant undertaking to meet these conditions?

---

[94] See, for example, the discussion in the Commission Decision Comp 37/990 *Intel* 13 May 2009 at s. 4.2.6.3.

Excessive pricing

Excessive pricing can be seen as the classic offence of a monopolist: raising prices by restricting output and thereby harming societal welfare because those consumers who purchase the good or service pay more than they would under competitive conditions and those who would have bought the good or service at a competitive price do not do so. A possible indicator of excessive prices would be high or excessive profitability of the undertaking, although this might simply indicate the undertaking's efficiency or a competitive advantage. The European Commission has, however, shown little appetite for pursuing excessive pricing cases and it has been claimed, with some exaggeration, that it hardly bothers with pursuing excessive pricing cases.[95] In US antitrust law, excessive or monopoly pricing is an issue which is not pursued at all.[96] By contrast, the UK competition authorities have shown much more interest in examining the profitability of undertakings and using this analysis to draw conclusions about the competitiveness of particular markets, an approach which has been heavily criticised as highly misleading and flawed.[97]

There are a number of reasons why it is difficult for a competition authority to pursue excess pricing and profitability cases. First, high profits are not necessarily indicative of a competition problem; they may be a reward for risk taking and innovation or the undertaking may simply be more efficient than its competitors. In both these cases, high profits are not an indication of a problem with the competitive process, but are the rewards of the competitive process for undertakings which are in some sense ahead of the game in their industry (see Box 3.8 for this point from an American context). In the long run, under competitive

---

KEY CASE EXTRACT   **Box 3.8**

The virtues of monopoly prices

Source: Verizon Communications v Trinko 124 S Ct 872 (2004), per Scalia J:

The mere possession of monopoly power, and the concomitant charging of monopoly prices, is not only not unlawful; it is an important element of the free-market system. The opportunity to charge monopoly prices, at least for a short period, is what attracts business acumen in the first place; it induces risk taking that produces innovation and economic growth. To safeguard the incentive to innovate, the possession of monopoly power will not be found unlawful unless it is accompanied by an element of anticompetitive *conduct*.

Questions: How different is this from the attitude of the UK and EU authorities? What sort of conduct would be a competition law problem?

---

[95] Monti (n. 4) at p. 423. A useful discussion is found in B. Lyons, 'The Paradox of the Exclusion of Exploitative Abuse' (2007) available at: *http://papers.ssrn.com/sol3/papers.cfm?abstract_id=1082723* (accessed 23/07/12).

[96] See Hovenkamp (n. 37, 2011) at 292.

[97] See Competition Commission, *Market Investigation References* (2003) at paras 3.81–3.85; D. Morris, 'Dominant Firm Behaviour under UK Competition Law', paper presented to the Fordham Corporate Law Institute, New York, 23–4 October 2003 available at: *http://www.competition-commission.org.uk/our_role/speeches/index.htm* (accessed 20/07/12); and R. Lind and M. Walker, 'The (Mis)use of Profitability Analysis in Competition Law' (2004) 25 *European Competition Law Review* 439 at 445–6.

conditions, these high profits would reduce, as other undertakings learnt the lessons from the innovators and the more efficient (assuming that the innovators and the more efficient remained static). Although a conceptual problem, in practice this is not insurmountable because competition authorities can make judgements about the competitiveness of an industry, the innovativeness of an undertaking and its relative efficiency, although this approach has its own difficulties. The point is that high profits on their own are not a sufficient indication of a competition problem.

There is, however, a second, more difficult problem, namely measuring the profits of an undertaking. In a nutshell, the problem is that undertakings measure accounting profits, whereas competition authorities are interested in economic profits and the two are not the same thing.[98] Accounting measures of profitability are determined by a set of agreed rules and conventions, which both require interpretation and offer some degree of flexibility. So the reported profitability of an undertaking will depend, in part, on the accounting conventions employed and these conventions may vary between undertakings in the same industry for reasons which are not related to the economics of an industry but to other issues, notably the tax treatment of income streams. So, in other words, competition authorities have to translate and interpret the accounts of an undertaking if they are to use it for profitability analysis. Within such a process there is one particularly difficult problem, which is that of cost allocation. To explain, the profitability of an activity will depend on the costs of an activity and almost all undertakings produce more than one product or service. When an undertaking produces more than one product, there will be costs which are peculiar to the production of that product and also costs which are common to the undertaking for the production of its other products. So, for example, banks offer current account services to personal customers and to small businesses.[99] There are a number of costs which are peculiar to each activity, such as the production of statements, printing of cheque books, etc., but there are also costs which are common to these activities, most notably the cost of the bank's branch network. Typically a competition authority will be interested in only one activity, in this case small business banking, and will therefore have to find a way of allocating the common costs between the activity that it is interested in and the one it is not interested in. Although there are a number of ways of allocating common costs, there is no agreed correct way of doing such an allocation and different ways of allocating costs may produce very different results.[100]

Assuming that the competition authority can arrive at a satisfactory number, there is a third obstacle to resolving a case. The competition authority must decide what level of profits is too high and it has been said that this involves 'a high degree of arbitrariness'.[101] Typically, the UK competition authorities would look at the rate of return for the activity against the

---

[98] See F. Fisher and J. McGowan, 'On the Misuse of Accounting Rates of Return to Infer Monopoly Profits' (1983) 73 *American Economic Review* 82 and J. Edwards *et al.*, *The Economic Analysis of Accounting Profitability* (Clarendon Press, Oxford, 1987).

[99] This is a real example: see Competition Commission, 'The supply of banking services by clearing banks to small and medium sized enterprises' (2002). More recently, see Competition Commission, 'Northern Irish Personal Banking' (2007), App. 4.1, paras 16–26: 'There are significant conceptual and practical difficulties in establishing an appropriate basis for allocating the many shared costs that may be attributable to the banks' PCA business in Northern Ireland.'

[100] See Lind and Walker (n. 97) at p. 444 for an example; and OFT, 'Assessing Profitability in Competition Policy Analysis' (2003), ch. 6 for discussion.

[101] M. Motta, *Competition Policy* (Cambridge University Press, 2004) at p. 69.

cost of capital for such an activity, although this has been criticised on the grounds that it is not a like for like comparison; the rate of return is accounting based and the cost of capital is market based, and is therefore flawed, as well as problems with determining the cost of capital.[102] Finally, if the competition authority decides that profitability and hence prices are too high, it will have to decide on a remedy and the obvious remedy is that of price control, which in effect turns the competition authority into a sector regulator, something that the European Commission has been very wary of, saying that it does not normally control or condemn the high level of prices as such.[103] Once a price control is implemented, it has to be monitored and it has to be reviewed to see if it remains appropriate, all activities which take up administrative resources. Having said this, the European Commission has determined prices as part of the remedial process in a number of cases.[104]

This discussion indicates that excessive pricing cases are intrinsically difficult for competition authorities but the UK experience suggests that the problems are not insurmountable. The difference between the UK and the EU approaches may lie more in the administrative capacity of the institutions and the procedures that are followed than in the difficulties of the case. Most excessive pricing cases in the UK have not been dealt with as Article 102 TFEU cases, with one notable exception, but have been market investigations by the Competition Commission (discussed in Chapter 10). The Competition Commission not only has, historically, probably had more economic expertise available to it, but it also has a level of accounting expertise that does not exist in either the European Commission or the OFT and hence has felt more confident in dealing with these issues.[105]

Excessive pricing: the European Union experience[106]

The starting point for looking at the European Union approach to excessive pricing is the *United Brands* case, where United Brands was charging different prices for its bananas in different countries and, in particular, the prices charged for those bananas in certain parts of continental Europe were 100% higher than those sold by United Brands on the Irish market, 20% to 40% higher than the prices of unbranded bananas, with minimal quality differences and 7% higher than other sellers of branded bananas. The European Commission imposed a large fine and suggested a 15% cut in the price of United Brands' bananas. This decision was annulled by the CJEU, primarily on the grounds that the European Commission had provided insufficient proof, as it had not attempted to evaluate the production costs of bananas and the 7% difference could not automatically be regarded as unfair. The CJEU did accept that, in principle, excessive pricing could be an abuse:

---

[102] Bishop and Walker (n. 18) at para. 6.017.

[103] European Commission, *XXIVth Report on Competition Policy* (1994), para. 207.

[104] For example, Commission decision COMP/38.636 *Rambus* 9.12.2009 and the dispute in relation to Microsoft: Commission Press Release IP/07/1567, 22/10/2007.

[105] See Competition Commission, 'Store Card Credit Services' (2006), 'Classified Directory Advertising Services' (2006), 'Home Credit' (2007), 'Northern Irish Personal Banking' (2007), 'Local bus services' (2011), 'Movies on pay-TV' (2012 – revised provisional findings).

[106] Generally, see M. Motta and A. de Streel, 'Excessive Pricing and Price Squeeze under EU Law', in C. Ehlermann and I. Atanasiu (eds) *European Competition Law Annual 2003: What is an Abuse of a Dominant Position?* (Hart Publishing, Oxford, 2006); and P. Oliver, 'The Concept of "Abuse" of a Dominant Position under Article 82 EC: Recent Developments in Relation to Pricing' (2005) 1 *European Competition Journal* 315 at 318–22.

... charging a price which is excessive because it has no reasonable relation to the economic value of the product supplied would be ... an abuse. This excess could, *inter alia*, be determined objectively if it were possible for it to be calculated by making a comparison between the selling price of the product in question and its cost of production, which would disclose the amount of the profit margin ... The questions therefore to be determined are whether the difference between the costs actually incurred and the price actually charged is excessive, and, if the answer to this question is in the affirmative, whether a price has been imposed which is either unfair in itself or when compared to competing products. Other ways may be devised – and economic theorists have not failed to think up several – of selecting the rules for determining whether the price of a product is unfair.[107]

This approach is generally accepted as having created a two-part test:

1 whether the difference between the costs of production and the price charged are excessive and, if so, then,

2 it must be decided if the price is unfair in itself or by comparison to competing products.

It is noticeable that the CJEU gives no guidance as to what is inherently unfair and there are a number of issues in relation to comparisons with competing products. Competing products may offer a different price/quality mixture, which may make such a comparison difficult; or, if we assume an uncompetitive oligopoly, the fact that there is no difference with competing products may conceal a competition problem. In addition, the CJEU suggests that there are other ways for deciding whether a price is unfair without, again, offering any specific guidance.

In subsequent cases the CJEU has been somewhat more helpful, suggesting in *Bodson*,[108] a case involving prices charged for funerals by an undertaking with an exclusive concession in a local area, that the prices charged in that area could be compared with prices charged elsewhere, that is, on a competitive market. In a similar line of thinking, the CJEU has suggested that comparisons could be made between prices charged for a product in one Member State with those charged for a similar product in another Member State but it noted in one of the cases, which involved royalty rates, that the comparison of fee levels had to be on a consistent basis.[109]

Since the *United Brands* case the European Commission has only occasionally brought excessive pricing cases. In the first case, General Motors was charging what the European Commission regarded as excessive prices for vehicle conformity certificates in Belgium, but the CJEU decided that, on the facts, no abuse had been committed, seeing the issue as simply a temporary one while national procedures were changed.[110] In a similar case some years later, British Leyland charged different prices depending on whether the cars were left hand or right hand drive. The European Commission viewed these prices as excessive and discriminatory and the decision was upheld by the CJEU but it is noticeable that there is a distinct element of market partitioning in the case.[111] The other successful case decided by the European Commission was in relation to Deutsche Post, the German post office, which had wrongly classified certain types of mail coming from the UK as having originated in Germany

---

[107] Case 27/76 *United Brands v Commission* [1978] ECR 207 at paras 250–3.
[108] Case 27/86 *Bodson v Pompes Funèbres des Régions Liberées SA* [1988] ECR 2479.
[109] Cases 110, 241 and 242/88 *Lucazeau/Sacem* [1989] ECR 2811.
[110] Case 26/75 *General Motors v Commission* [1975] ECR 1367.
[111] Case 226/84 *British Leyland v Commission* [1986] ECR 3263.

and therefore imposed the full domestic tariff on this mail. In this case, the European Commission could not compare the prices to Deutsche Post's costs as there was no reliable accounting data, nor with its competitors, as it had a statutory monopoly. The European Commission therefore based its judgment on Deutsche Post's own estimate, which was based on international agreements for cross-border mail and indicated an excessive price of some 20%. Given the novelty of the case, a nominal fine was imposed.[112]

The most recent attempt of the European Commission to deal with excessive pricing came in relation to two complaints that a Swedish port had charged excessive prices to ferry operators.[113] Although the European Commission rejected the complaints, the case gives an insight into the methodology that will be employed and into some of the difficulties in trying to prove excessive pricing. Most importantly, in this case the European Commission employed the two-stage test mentioned above. The European Commission had great difficulty in determining costs, partly because most of them were indirect, and therefore it was a question of cost allocation, and also because the largest proportion of the costs were fixed, while the variable costs were relatively small. Secondly, the European Commission was not able to find a sufficient benchmark for what constituted an excessive price. It was unable to make a comparison with other ports, nor was it able to decide what a 'reasonable' profit margin for such a port would be.

The European Commission's decision in relation to the German system for the recycling of packaging for consumer products also raised the issue of excessive pricing and was appealed to the GC and the CJEU. Under the relevant German law, manufacturers or distributors of such packaging could either provide their own means of recycling the packaging or could join in a scheme which ensured the recycling of their packaging, as well as combining the two solutions. One nationwide scheme for recycling packaging was created by Duales Systemes Deutschland (DSD), whereby all packaging which was eligible for this system bore a green dot as a label (Der Grüne Punkt). Manufacturers and distributors were charged a fee for the use of this symbol based on the amount of packaging that they put into circulation in Germany, regardless of the amount that was actually recycled by DSD, and the core of the abuse was that the fee was not linked to the use of the system, as well as it actually making it more difficult for competitors to enter the market. The GC upheld the decision on this point, although without needing to comment in any detail on the issue of excessive pricing, beyond simply saying that it was an abuse to charge fees for services which were disproportionate to the economic value of the service provided.[114]

This survey supports Motta and De Streel's conclusion that the European Commission has used its power sparingly and originally focused on cases where there was a legal monopoly and barriers to the creation of an internal market (e.g. *British Leyland*), while more recently it has been active on markets opened to competition (such as telecommunications) as part of its programme of liberalisation.[115] Both the Swedish Port case and the DSD case can be seen as part of this second group of cases, with the former case indicating how difficult it is for the

---

[112] *Deutsche Post* [2002] OJ L331/40.

[113] *Scandlines and Sundbussern* v *Helsingborg*, 23 July 2004; see also M. Lamalle *et al.*, 'Two important rejection decisions on excessive pricing in the port sector' (2004) *Competition Policy Newsletter*, No. 3, p. 40.

[114] Case T-151/01 *Duales System Deutschland* v *Commission* [2007] ECR II-1607 at para. 121. Upheld on this point in Case C-385/07P *Der Grüne Punkt – Duales System Deutschland* v *Commission* [2009] ECR I-6155 at paras 141–7.

[115] Motta and de Streel (n. 106) at p. 107.

European Commission to establish a case of excessive pricing where there is no clear comparison or benchmark.

Excessive pricing: the UK experience under s. 18[116]

Within the United Kingdom, the first major decision under s. 18 was in the *Napp* case.[117] Napp produced sustained release morphine tablets, used for treating moderate and severe pain. There were two relevant markets for this drug – the community market for patients under the care of their GPs and the hospital market – and Napp had a market share of over 90% in both markets. In relation to the community market, the Director General of Fair Trading (DGFT) had decided that Napp had abused its dominant position by charging excessive prices. The DGFT took the view that a price would be excessive if it was above that which would be found in a competitive market and that there was no effective competitive pressure which would bring the prices down to competitive levels, nor was there likely to be any. The CAT accepted that this was a sound basis on which to proceed in the present case.[118] In one sense, this was a relatively easy case as the DGFT was able to compare the prices of the same product produced by the same undertaking in two different markets, one being more competitive than the other, where, among other factors, the list prices on some of the items sold on the less competitive market were more than 1,400% higher than on the other market.

The difficulty in bringing excessive pricing cases under s. 18 can be illustrated by two more recent cases: *Attheraces* and *Albion Water*.[119] *Attheraces* involved a dispute between the British Horse Racing Board (BRB) which organises horse racing in the UK and Attheraces (ATR), which was essentially a company broadcasting horse races to overseas bookmakers, over the provision of pre-race data (number and names of horses running, etc.) from BRB to ATR. ATR claimed, among other things, that the price charged for this data was excessive and a breach of s. 18 of the Competition Act 1998, and this claim succeeded at first instance when the judge held that the competitive price was the cost of producing the data plus a reasonable return on that cost. The Court of Appeal overturned the first instance decision on this point, holding that this approach was too narrow and that it did not take into account the economic value of the data to the purchaser and that economic value would depend on market conditions. Although the Court of Appeal did not adopt any one methodology, it emphasised that there was no evidence that ATR's competitiveness was being damaged, which was important, since the object of Article 102 TFEU was not to regulate prices, but to protect and promote competition, specifically the interests of consumers.

By contrast, the claimant was successful in *Albion Water*, albeit after protracted litigation which took around four years. In this case, Albion wished to supply water to a paper mill, using Welsh Water's (Dŵr Cymru) transportation system and it complained, among other

---

[116] Generally, see N. Green, 'Problems in the Identification of Excessive Prices: The United Kingdom Experience in the Light of *Napp*' in C. Ehlermann and I. Atanasiu (eds) *European Competition Law Annual 2003: What is an Abuse of a Dominant Position?* (Hart Publishing, Oxford, 2006); and S. Kon and S. Turnbull, 'Pricing and the Dominant Firm: Implications of the Competition Commission Appeal Tribunal's Judgment in the *Napp Case*' (2003) 24 *European Competition Law Review* 70.

[117] *Napp Pharmaceuticals* v *Director General of Fair Trading* [2002] CAT 1.

[118] Ibid. at para. 391.

[119] *Attheraces Ltd* v *British Horse Racing Board* [2007] EWCA Civ 38; *Albion Water* v *Water Services Regulation Authority* [2008] CAT 31.

things, that the price it was being charged for the use of this system was excessive and an abuse of dominance. The complaint was first made to the regulator, who has concurrent competition powers with the OFT, and then, after the regulator rejected the complaint, Albion Water appealed to the CAT, which found in its favour. This case was factually very complex and the CAT was assisted by having a detailed report on the costs of the service provided from the regulator. The CAT held that the price charged was excessive in relation to costs and that, in the particular circumstances of the water industry where Welsh Water had a monopoly on these services, the economic value of these services was to be judged in relation to the cost of the services. In other words, this was a very different market to *Attheraces* and there was no competitive constraint on Welsh Water. Most usefully, the CAT summarised (Box 3.9) the legal test adopted by the European Commission, the OFT and the UK judicial authorities.

KEY CASE EXTRACT **Box 3.9**

The test for excessive pricing

Source: *Albion Water* v *Water Services Regulation Authority* [2008] CAT 31, para. 20:

  (a) an analysis of the costs incurred in producing the product or service;

  (b) a comparison of those costs with the price charged and an assessment of whether the resulting difference, i.e. the profit, is such that the price charged is excessive; and if so

  (c) an assessment of whether the excessive price bears no reasonable relation to the economic value of the product or service supplied and is an abuse of a dominant position, with the consequence that it is either:

    (i) unfair in itself; or

    (ii) unfair when compared with competing products.

Questions: How easy is it to work out the cost of producing a product or service? What constitutes excessive profit? How do you work out the economic value of the product? If an abuse is found, what is the appropriate remedy?

Low or predatory pricing

We now come to the first of the exclusionary abuses, that of low or predatory pricing.[120] The idea behind this category is that it can be a competition problem if an undertaking prices so low that it is able to drive its competitors out of the market, thus leaving it with market power, which it can then exploit by raising prices to a monopoly level. This is a counter-intuitive idea, as low prices would normally be taken to be a sign of a competitive market, since the standard criticism of monopolies is that they restrict output and raise prices. Indeed, price competition is normal competitive behaviour. This has led economists to argue, at one extreme, that predatory pricing either does not exist or, if it does, it is extremely difficult to distinguish it from competitive price behaviour.[121]

---

[120] 'Predatory pricing' has been the standard term used. We will see, however, that it is possible that prices may be too low, and thus constitute an abuse of dominant position, yet not be predatory.

[121] R. Bork, *The Antitrust Paradox* (2nd edn, Free Press, New York, 1993) at p. 154.

The argument that predatory pricing is not a rational or sensible strategy to engage in runs like this: first, predatory pricing involves the undertaking concerned in making losses on its sales, because it will price below cost. These losses may be substantial if the undertaking has a large market share, cannot engage in price discrimination and the strategy takes some time to have an effect. This can be a sensible strategy only if, after its competitor leaves the market, it prices above cost and thereby recoups its losses. However, by raising prices, it indicates that there is a profitable opportunity in this market, thereby encouraging other undertakings to enter, which will force it to lower prices. Thus, the undertaking engaged in predatory conduct can never recover its losses. This argument depends on a number of assumptions: first, it uses a very restrictive notion of entry barriers and assumes that entry into a market is easy; secondly, it assumes perfect information on the part of both undertakings and other market participants; and, thirdly, it is premised on operations within one market.

In particular, once the assumption of perfect information is relaxed, a number of economic theories have developed to explain why predatory pricing may be a perfectly rational strategy for an undertaking. They are normally classified into three types: reputational, signalling and deep pockets.[122] The reputational theory is relatively simple to explain. If an undertaking has a reputation as a predator, or an aggressive competitor, this may deter other undertakings from entering that market because they will look at entry in the light of all their investment opportunities and conclude that there are other markets where the possibility of profitable entry is greater. If we also consider that undertakings may operate in a number of different markets, such as local bus services in the UK, it becomes even clearer that it may be sensible for the dominant undertaking to establish a reputation as an aggressive or predatory competitor in order to defend all the markets. To put it another way, it may be worth the dominant undertaking making losses in one or two markets if, by establishing a reputation as a predatory incumbent, it deters entry into the other markets. Note that it is assumed in this model that the entrant does not know what the incumbent's costs are and therefore will find it difficult to judge whether the incumbent can maintain the low prices.

The table below[123] helps to illustrate this argument. The numbers in the table indicate the profit that, respectively, the incumbent and the new entrant will obtain depending on whether the incumbent fights or accommodates the entrant. As can be seen in this example, if it is a case of one-off entry, it makes sense for the incumbent to accommodate entry, as the incumbent continues to make profits, unlike the situation where the incumbent fights entry, where losses are made. If, however, to take Bishop and Walker's example,[124] the incumbent has a dominant position in ten separate geographical markets, such as might be the case in relation to local bus services, then it might make sense to fight in some of the markets if this deters entry into others. So, in the example below, accommodating entry into ten markets leads to a profit of 10 but predating (fighting) in three and remaining dominant in seven (no entry) leads to a profit of 11.

---

[122] For discussion, see Motta (n. 101) at pp. 412–43; Bishop and Walker (n. 18) at paras 6.088–6.095 and R. Van den Bergh and P. Camesasca, *European Competition Law and Economics* (2nd edn, Sweet & Maxwell, London, 2006) at pp. 280–99. Competition Commission, 'Local bus services' (2011) at para. 9.38 discusses this.

[123] Adapted from Bishop and Walker (n. 18), para. 6.093.

[124] Bishop and Walker (n. 18) at para. 6.094.

Possible incumbent responses to entry

		Fights	Accommodates
No entry	2, 0	N/A	N/A
Entry		−1, −1	1, 1

Source: Adapted from Bishop, S. and Walker, M. *The Economics of EC Competition Law* (3rd edn, Sweet & Maxwell, London, 2010) at 98.

Signalling models[125] develop the notion of imperfect information to explain why predatory pricing might be a rational strategy. The basic idea behind them is that the potential entrant does not know whether the incumbent has high or low costs and may be uncertain itself about what costs it will have when it enters the industry. In these circumstances, instances can be imagined where it makes sense not only for a low cost incumbent to set low prices to deter entry, but also for a high cost incumbent to mimic the behaviour of a low cost incumbent. In all these cases, the intended effect is to deter new entry into the market by making it seem as if the opportunity is not profitable.

Finally, there is the so-called 'deep pockets' theory of predatory pricing. This begins with the idea that the dominant firm has access to greater financial resources than the entrant, either through the capital markets or because it operates in more than one market and can use the profits in one market to subsidise artificially low prices in another. The objection to this argument has typically been that, if capital markets are efficient, there is no reason why the new entrant should not have access to sufficient resources, to keep it in the market until the predatory pricing ceases. The problem is that the institutions who lend the money have imperfect information and cannot know for certain whether the losses incurred by the entrant are due to the predatory pricing or other reasons (e.g. managerial inefficiency). In addition, it seems to be the case that predatory pricing can raise the cost of capital for new entrants and thus deter entry into markets.

This discussion leads to the conclusion that predatory pricing may be a sensible strategy in certain circumstances. An OFT research paper gave some indication of what those circumstances might be:[126]

- Is competition localised through a narrow geographic or product market definition, such that the alleged predator can target its prey?
- Is the alleged predator capable of forcing the prey into loss?
- Does the alleged predator have a deep pocket or the ability to cross-subsidise necessary to force out the competition?
- What is the relevant market share of the alleged predator and of its competitors in the relevant market?
- Are there sufficient barriers to entry, including those created by reputation effects, that are likely to provide the alleged predator with market power to allow losses to be recouped?
- Does the alleged predator operate in a number of different markets that might benefit from any reputation effect created in the market under consideration?

[125] Discussed in Motta (n. 101) at pp. 418–20.
[126] OFT, 'Predatory Behaviour in UK Competition Policy' (1994) Research Paper 5 at pp. 25–6.

In the UK, many allegations of predatory pricing, and other anti-competitive behaviour, have arisen in relation to the market for local bus services after privatisation in 1985. At the time of privatisation the market was quite fragmented but, in a relatively short time afterwards, the industry nationwide was dominated by four groups: Stagecoach, First, Arriva and National Express (in the form of Travel West Midlands). There was substantial controversy over the tactics used by these undertakings to increase their market share, in particular those of Stagecoach and there were numerous allegations of predatory pricing. Most of this market consolidation happened prior to the implementation of the Competition Act 1998 and it became evident that the pre-1998 Act procedures were not effective in dealing with allegations of predatory pricing, even though there were a number of formal inquiries.[127] The point is that the market for local bus services is a good example of a market where predation would be a feasible and rational strategy. It is a narrow market, there are large national undertakings, with access to large financial resources, competing in numerous local markets against locally based undertakings with less access to capital. Indeed, recently it was claimed unsuccessfully, in a private action, that Arriva was engaged in predatory behaviour seeking to drive a local bus company out of business, and the OFT has taken action against Cardiff Buses for predatory behaviour.[128] The OFT referred the local bus market, outside London, to the Competition Commission for a market investigation (discussed in Chapter 10), partly on the basis of its experience with bus cases and allegations of predatory behaviour.[129] The Competition Commission found that there were certain features of the market that restricted competition and led to an adverse effect on competition.[130] Although the report does not identify specific issues of predatory pricing, the discussion implies that this is a sensible strategy for incumbent operators who wish to deter new entry.

As we have seen from our discussion, the issue of predation arises when an undertaking charges prices that are below cost. This raises the question, what costs do the prices need to be below? As can be seen from Box 3.10, there are a number of alternatives. The standard test derives from an academic article by Areeda and Turner,[131] where they proposed that prices were predatory if they were below the short-run marginal cost of providing the product or service. Since it is very difficult to measure short-run marginal costs, they proposed using average variable costs as a proxy. Their basic view was that prices below average variable cost should be considered predatory and prices above average variable cost should not be considered predatory. This approach has been very influential in the US, and, as we shall see, forms the basis of the test applied by the courts and the competition authorities in the UK and European Union. Despite its influence, the test remains controversial and there are a number of difficulties with it.[132] Three important criticisms are that, first, it is difficult to draw a clear distinction between fixed and variable costs because this depends on the industry in question and the time period that is being considered. On a long enough time period, it is a truism

---

[127] Generally, see T. Prosser, *Law and the Regulators* (Clarendon Press, Oxford, 1997) at pp. 200–12.

[128] *Chester City Council* v *Arriva* [2007] EWHC 1373 (Ch); OFT, 'Cardiff Bus' (2008). In the follow-on action, the plaintiff was awarded exemplary damages against Cardiff Bus: *2 Travel Group plc* v *Cardiff City Transport* [2012] CAT 19.

[129] OFT, 'Local bus services' (2009).

[130] Competition Commission 'Local bus services' (2011).

[131] P. Areeda and D. Turner, 'Predatory Pricing and Related Practices under Section 2 of the Sherman Act' (1975) 88 *Harvard Law Review* 697.

[132] See J. Brodley and D. Hay, 'Predatory Pricing: Competing Economic Theories and the Evolution of Legal Standards' (1981) 66 *Cornell Law Review* 738 for discussion.

that all costs are variable. Secondly, there are a number of reasons why prices might be below average variable costs, such as promotional pricing, end of line clearances, using spare capacity in an economic downturn, etc. Thirdly, in certain markets where AVC may be minimal, but fixed costs are high, notably new economy and network markets, the test does not work well. For example, the fixed costs of a telecommunications network are very high but the variable costs of a phone call are very low and therefore do not accurately reflect the costs that a provider incurs in providing telecommunications services. It is for this reason that the Commission suggested a better test in the context of telecommunications would be the use of long-run average incremental costs.[133]

KEY DEFINITION   Box 3.10

Different definitions of cost

Total cost: The total costs of production.

Average total cost (ATC): The total costs involved in the production of one unit of output, i.e. total cost divided by the number of units produced.

Fixed costs: Those which do not change with output over a given time period.

Variable costs: Those which do change with output.

Average variable cost (AVC): The variable costs involved in the production of one unit, i.e. variable costs added up and divided by the number of units produced.

Marginal cost: The increase in total costs of a firm caused by increasing its output by one extra unit.

Short-run marginal cost (SRMC): The marginal cost based on a firm's existing plant and output, not on that which would be the most efficient.

Avoidable costs: The costs that will not be incurred if an undertaking ceases a particular operation.

Long-run incremental cost (LRIC): The total long-run costs of supplying a specified additional unit of output, taking into account both capital and operating costs.

Long-run average incremental cost (LRAIC): The average of all the (variable and fixed) costs that an undertaking incurs to produce a particular product.

Stand-alone costs: The costs which are involved in producing a product without taking into account that some of these costs are shared with the production of other products.

Source: A. Jones and B. Sufrin, *EU Competition Law* (4th edn, Oxford University Press, 2011) at pp. 389–90. By permission of Oxford University Press.

Questions: Which approach produces the highest cost? Which one produces the lowest cost?

---

[133] European Commission, 'Notice on the application of the competition rules to access agreements in the telecommunications sector' OJ C265, 22.08.1998, pp. 2–28 (at paras 110–16).

EU case law on predatory pricing

The starting point for discussion is the *AKZO* case.[134] AKZO was a multinational chemicals company which produced benzoyl peroxide, which was used as a catalyst in plastics production and as a bleaching agent in flour. ECS was a small UK undertaking that produced benzoyl peroxide and conducted most of its business in the flour sector. ECS then decided to expand into the plastics sector and AKZO retaliated by threatening to attack ECS's business in the flour sector by offering low prices, in particular to ECS's best customers. After litigation in the UK, ECS complained to the European Commission, which ultimately held that AKZO had abused its dominant position, imposing a fine of ECU 10 million and ordering it to cease the infringement, which meant to refrain from offering or applying prices which would result in customers in respect of whose business it was competing with ECS paying dissimilar prices to those paid to comparable customers. The European Commission did not base its decision on any view as regards AKZO's prices in relation to costs, but focused on what it saw as the intent behind AKZO's actions. On appeal to the CJEU, the court found that AKZO was guilty of predatory pricing but set out a different test to that adopted by the European Commission (see Box 3.11).

KEY CASE EXTRACT   Box 3.11

Test for predatory pricing

Source: Case C-62/86 *AKZO Chemie v Commission* [1991] ECR I-3359 at paras 71–2:

Prices below average variable costs (that is to say, those which vary depending on the quantities produced) by means of which a dominant undertaking seeks to eliminate a competitor must be regarded as abusive. A dominant undertaking has no interest in applying such prices except that of eliminating competitors so as to enable it subsequently to raise its prices by taking advantage of its monopolistic position, since each sale generates a loss, namely the total amount of fixed costs (that is to say, those that remain constant regardless of the quantities produced) and, at least, part of the variable costs relating to the unit produced. Moreover, prices below average total cost, that is to say, fixed costs plus variable costs, but above average variable costs, must be regarded as abusive if they are determined as part of a plan for eliminating a competitor. Such prices can drive from the market undertakings which are perhaps as efficient as the dominant undertaking but which, because of their smaller financial resources, are incapable of withstanding the competition waged against them.

Questions: Are there any circumstances in which a business would think it was a good idea to price below average variable cost? How do you prove that someone has a plan for eliminating competition? How is this different from normal market behaviour?

This seems to set down a test which says that prices below AVC *are* predatory ('must be regarded as abusive') but that prices above AVC but below ATC are predatory only if they are part of a plan to eliminate a competitor. A number of comments can be made about this test.

[134] Case C-62/86 *AKZO Chemie v Commission* [1991] ECR I-3359.

First, the language of the CJEU is seemingly absolute as regards prices below AVC[135] but all the commentators on the case find this uncomfortable and extreme and translate this into a rule that prices below AVC are *presumed* to be predatory, albeit taking the view that this is a very strong presumption, something which, as we shall see, has also been picked up by the GC and European Commission.[136] Secondly, when prices are between AVC and ATC what becomes crucial is the intent of the undertaking in the particular circumstances and this opens up a very difficult area because the intent of all profit-seeking undertakings is to beat, or outperform, their competitors. It may in practice prove very difficult to distinguish between the ordinary intentions of competition and those which are judged to be predatory, in particular as business people can engage in colourful phraseology. In one US case, the Chief Executive of a company accused of predatory pricing advised that, 'when you see the competition drowning . . . stick a water hose down their throats'. The Court responded that, 'The antitrust statutes do not condemn, without more, such colorful, vigorous hyperbole; there is nothing to gain by using the law to mandate "commercially correct" speech within corporate memoranda and business plans.'[137] In the EU context, what is important is the intention of the undertaking, not the effects of the behaviour; the fact that the hoped for result is not achieved is not relevant.[138] Thirdly, as we have seen above, for predatory pricing to be a rational strategy it must be possible for the undertaking engaging in it to recoup its losses – the *AKZO* case says nothing about the possibility of this. Finally, the case itself illustrates the difficulty of apportioning costs because the Commission and AKZO submitted very different cost estimates, with AKZO arguing that its labour costs were fixed, rather than variable, a point with which the CJEU agreed.

Nor is it obvious that the best explanation for this case was predatory pricing; it seems equally possible that the intervention of the European Commission simply brought to an end a competitive price war in a bilateral oligopoly.[139] ECS and AKZO had had previous commercial links before ECS entered into manufacturing, there are some doubts that AKZO could have maintained its pricing strategy given the market share of ECS, it is not clear that entry barriers into the market were high and there were a number of large buyers in the market which could have, if genuinely faced with a monopoly, kept ECS in business if they had felt threatened. The important point about this interpretation is that it shows that the main thrust of the case is in protecting smaller competitors against commercial harm visited on them by a larger undertaking. It certainly makes it very difficult for a dominant undertaking to decide how to respond to its competitors.

The next major case in front of the CJEU was *Tetra Pak*, where an undertaking had a dominant position in the aseptic carton market, with a market share of over 90%, but was fined for predatory pricing in a different market, for non-aseptic cartons, on which it was not

---

[135] And even stronger subsequently in Case C-333/94P *Tetra Pak International* v *Commission* [1996] ECR I-5951 at para. 41: 'prices below average variable costs must always be considered abusive'.

[136] For example, A. Jones and B. Sufrin, *EU Competition Law* (4th edn, Oxford University Press, 2011) at p. 396; Case T-340/03 *France Télécom SA* v *Commission* [2007] ECR II-107 at para. 227; Case C-202/07P *France Télécom SA* v *Commission* [2009] ECR I-2369 at para. 109 ('prima facie abusive'); European Commission (n. 7) at para. 64. In the UK, see *Aberdeen Journals* v *Director General of Fair Trading* [2003] CAT 11 at para. 357.

[137] *Advo, Inc.* v *Philadelphia Newspapers, Inc.* 854 F Supp 367 (3rd Cir. 1995).

[138] Case T-340/03 *France Télécom SA* v *Commission* [2007] ECR II-107 at para. 196. European Commission (n. 7) at para. 69.

[139] Van den Bergh and Camesasca (n. 122) at pp. 296–8.

dominant. One of the issues argued in the case was that, since the European Commission had not shown that Tetra Pak could recoup its losses, it was not guilty of predation. The CJEU firmly rejected this argument:

> . . . it would not be appropriate, in the circumstances of the present case, to require in addition proof that Tetra Pak had a realistic chance of recouping its losses. It must be possible to penalize predatory pricing whenever there is a risk that competitors will be eliminated.[140]

This marks a significant difference between the EU approach to predatory pricing and that within the US, making it in principle easier to prove such a case in the EU. This has led to some debate within the academic literature, which has spilled over into the work of the CJEU. Broadly, there are two positions: there are those who feel that recoupment should be part of the test for predatory pricing under EU law because it is the essence of the practice;[141] and there are those who argue that, as the undertaking must be in a dominant position in order to bring the case, this means that the possibility of recoupment can be presumed.[142] The most authoritative supporter of the former position was Advocate General Fennelly, who thought that it was implicit in the *AKZO* test.[143] The problem with the latter position is that, although it may well be true in the cases with very high market shares, say over 75%, undertakings have been found to have a dominant position with market shares in the range of 40%–49% and the European Commission continues to argue that dominance is possible below the 40% mark. In addition, given that predatory pricing can be committed on a market where the undertaking is not dominant, as in *Tetra Pak*, the dominance found in one market does not imply recoupment on the other.

The recoupment issue was discussed in the co-called 'Wanadoo' case, where[144] Wanadoo, a subsidiary of France Télécom, was accused of predatory pricing by the European Commission in relation to the prices it charged for ADSL (i.e. broadband) internet for a period of around 18 months. For part of the period prices were below AVC; for the remaining part of the period they were below the full costs (ATC) of the service. The European Commission claimed that this was a deliberate policy, which was part of a company plan to pre-empt the market for high speed internet access. As a result of its policy, the undertaking's market share rose from 46% to 72% in the context of a rapidly growing market. By contrast, at the end of the period of the abuse no competitor had more than a 10% share of the market and one had gone out of business. A fine of €10.35 million was imposed. Wanadoo appealed to the GC on a number of grounds including that the European Commission had to provide evidence of recoupment of losses. The GC took the view that it was not necessary for proof of recoupment of losses to be found before taking a decision of predatory pricing.[145] This should perhaps be seen in the context of the GC's comment that case law established that if a dominant undertaking implemented a practice which intended to eliminate competitors, the fact that they were unsuccessful is irrelevant.[146] This was affirmed as the correct position

---

[140] Case C-333/94P *Tetra Pak International v Commission* [1996] ECR I-5951 at para. 44.

[141] See Bishop and Walker (n. 18) at para. 6.102; Van den Bergh and Camesasca (n. 122) at 294; L. Bravo and P. Siciliani, 'Exclusionary Pricing and Consumers Harm: The European Commission's Practice in the DSL Market' (2007) 3 *Journal of Competition Law and Economics* 243 at 254–5.

[142] See European Commission (n. 11) at para. 122.

[143] See Cases C-395 and 396/96 *Compagnie Maritime Belge v Commission* [2000] ECR I-1365 at para. 136 of the AG's opinion.

[144] Case T-340/03 *France Télécom SA v Commission* [2007] ECR II-107.

[145] Ibid., para. 228.

[146] Ibid., para. 196.

by the CJEU on appeal in this case, contrary to the views expressed by Advocate General Mazák.[147]

To end this section it should be noted that the European Commission has experimented with different cost standards in its decisional practice and in guidance that it has issued in telecommunications and, most recently, in its guidance on exclusionary abuses. In its 'Notice on the application of competition rules to access agreements in the telecommunications sector', the European Commission suggested that it would be appropriate to apply a cost standard of long-run average incremental costs in telecommunications because in network industries there are much larger common and joint costs.[148] In a decision relating to Deutsche Post, it found predatory pricing on the grounds that the prices charged were below the long-run average incremental costs, that is the costs incurred in providing a specific service.[149] In its guidance on Article 102 TFEU, the Commission says that the appropriate cost benchmark is average avoidable costs, which means that the price it is charging for part of its output is not covering the costs that could have been avoided by not producing that output. This may be a stricter test because, in certain circumstances, such as where capacity is expanded in order to predate, the average avoidable costs will include this element of investment, which would not be included under the AVC test.[150]

UK case law on predatory pricing

Although accusations of predatory pricing are not uncommon in a UK context, there are only three examples of cases where a breach of the s. 18 prohibition has been found: *Napp Pharmaceuticals, Aberdeen Newspapers* and *English, Welsh and Scottish Railway (EWS)*.[151]

Napp was the first case before the CAT and involved a pharmaceutical firm which produced sustained release morphine tablets, which it sold into the community and hospital markets and had a market share, across the two markets, of around 95%. The hospital market was critical for Napp because, if a patient was prescribed its drug in hospital, the patient would continue to be prescribed the drug once he or she returned to the community. Although Napp accepted that it was pricing below cost in the hospital sector, it argued that the *AKZO* approach was inappropriate here because, although sales in the hospital segment were unprofitable, when these sales were combined with sales in the community segment, the business as a whole was profitable. For example, a patient in a hospital would be prescribed Napp's drug and then, on leaving hospital, would continue taking it. The combined revenue of sales to this patient in the hospital and community would be profitable. The CAT rejected this defence largely because Napp produced no evidence that this reasoning was part of its rationale at the time of sale (it was produced for the purposes of the tribunal hearing), although there were also some important conceptual weaknesses in the defence.[152] It confirmed the DGFT's finding of an abuse of a dominant position on the basis of predatory pricing.

[147] Case C-202/07P *France Télécom SA* v *Commission* [2009] ECR I-2369.

[148] [1998] OJ C265/2 at paras 113–14.

[149] Case COMP/35.141 *Deutsche Post*, OJ L125/27, 5.5.2001.

[150] European Commission (n. 7) at para. 64.

[151] *Aberdeen Journals* v *Director General of Fair Trading* [2003] CAT 11; *Napp Pharmaceuticals* v *Director General of Fair Trading* [2002] CAT 1; *English, Welsh and Scottish Railways Ltd* decision of the Office of Rail Regulation available at: *http://www.oft.gov.uk/OFTwork/competition-act-and-cartels/ca98/decisions/ews-rail* (accessed 02/09/12).

[152] *Napp* (n. 117) at paras 251 and 258–66.

Aberdeen Journals was a case which involved the owner of three papers in the Aberdeen area, two of which customers paid for, one of which was free, incurring losses on the free paper in relation to its prices for advertising in order to expel a new entrant on the market for free newspapers. Here, ultimately, after substantial argument,[153] the case came down to pricing below AVC for one month in 2000 (just after the Competition Act 1998 came into force) and the CAT upheld the DGFT's decision.

EWS was a decision of the Office of Rail Regulation (ORR) which found that EWS, which provided rail freight transport, had abused its dominant position by engaging in exclusive contracts, discriminatory behaviour and predatory pricing in order to protect its competitive position. A penalty of £4.1 million was imposed. Interestingly, the predatory pricing here was found to be between AVC and ATC, although closer to the former than the latter, and that, combined with the evidence of appropriate intention, convinced the ORR that predation had occurred.[154]

US case law on predatory pricing

Having looked at the EU and UK case law, it is worth briefly discussing the American experience because this offers an important contrast to the European approach as it is much more difficult to prove a case of predatory pricing under American law.[155] As a preliminary point, the Supreme Court has expressed some scepticism about the prevalence of predatory pricing: 'predatory pricing schemes are rarely tried, and even more rarely successful' and they are concerned that the costs of an erroneous finding of liability are high.[156] *Brooke Group* sets out two prerequisites for proving predatory pricing: first, the prices complained of must be below an appropriate measure of its rivals costs and, secondly, a demonstration that a competitor had a dangerous probability of recouping its investment in below-cost prices. The general consensus is that the combination of these two tests has made it very difficult or almost impossible for plaintiffs to prove predatory pricing cases.[157] The first hurdle will be proving that prices are below an appropriate measure of costs. Although the American federal courts do not appear to have adopted a common test, the Areeda–Turner test has been very influential and they began, it has been said, by embracing it.[158] One of the consequences of this was said to be that at high output levels the test was a paradise for defendants and virtually none lost a case.[159] In applying this test, the courts have faced a number of difficulties in applying the test but this has still provided the basic framework for their inquiry. The second hurdle,

---

[153] *Aberdeen Journals v Director General of Fair Trading* [2002] CAT 4; *Aberdeen Journals v Office of Fair Trading* [2003] CAT 11.

[154] *English, Welsh and Scottish Railways Ltd* decision of the Office of Rail Regulation available at: *http://www.oft. gov.uk/OFTwork/competition-act-and-cartels/ca98/decisions/ews-rail* (accessed 02/09/12) at 144 (all cost and price numbers are redacted).

[155] The focus is on the Sherman Act, not the Robinson-Patman Act, which has somewhat different conditions for liability.

[156] *Brooke Group Ltd v Brown & Williamson* 509 US 209 (1993) citing *Matsushita Electrical Industries Co Ltd v Zenith Radio Corp*, 475 US 574 at 589 (1986). Although compare *United States v AMR Corp*, 335 F 3rd 1109 (2003): 'Although this court approaches the matter with caution, we do not do so with the incredulity that once prevailed.' At para. 16.

[157] Although see D. Crane, 'The Paradox of Predatory Pricing' [2005] 91 *Cornell Law Review* 1 at 4–5, who suggests a more nuanced picture.

[158] See H. Hovenkamp (n. 37).

[159] Ibid., p. 388.

proving recoupment, has proved difficult for plaintiffs because they have to be able to show that the market structure makes recoupment feasible. In addition, as Hovenkamp points out, the length of the claimed period of predation is relevant because, the longer the alleged period of predation, the longer a period of recoupment is needed. Given that predation is a costly strategy, allegations of long periods of predation seem implausible.[160] It is worth pointing out that this approach makes evidence of the defendant's intent much less relevant to any case, unlike EU law, where it becomes critical when prices are between AVC and ATC. In addition, this approach precludes any inquiry into above-cost predatory pricing, again unlike the position in EU law, which is discussed above.

What should be evident from this discussion is that the legal principles behind predatory pricing in the EU, as expressed in Box 3.11, are reasonably clear. They are, however, not aligned with the insights of economic analysis. Economists often insist on a requirement of recoupment and proof that the conduct has had actual effects on competition. The law does not require proof of recoupment and simply a demonstration that the conduct was likely to have had an effect on competition. In addition, as recent cases illustrate, applying these principles is fraught with practical difficulties. Although the problems with this test are exacerbated by the cases on selective low pricing, discussed below, it is worth noting that the competition authorities have brought relatively few such cases. It is a very popular allegation, but the private litigation reported so far has not yielded any notable successes, with perhaps the exception of the follow-on action in the Cardiff Bus case.[161]

Selective low pricing

Although predatory pricing is controversial, even more difficult is the idea that it may be an abuse for a dominant undertaking to price *above* average total cost when this is part of a plan to eliminate competition. This issue arose in the case of *Compagnie Maritime Belge*,[162] which involved a liner conference (that is, a group of shipping companies which had agreed to pool services on a particular route) operating on routes between Europe and Zaire with a market share of 90% that responded to the presence of its sole competitor by engaging in a practice known as 'fighting ships'. This involved the conference scheduling its sailings at or around the same time as its competitor and offering favourable rates for shipping. Any losses on the voyages of the fighting ships were apportioned between the members of the liner conference, although the European Commission did not do an analysis of the costs. Although the arrangement looks like an anti-competitive agreement, it was allowed under a block exemption for maritime transport. The European Commission condemned this as an abuse of a collective dominant position and the conference appealed, arguing that its prices were not predatory under the test in *AKZO*. When this case reached the CJEU, the Court pointed out that the list of practices mentioned in Article 102 TFEU was not exhaustive and that the scope of the special responsibility imposed on dominant undertakings had to be considered in the light of the special circumstances of each case. Here the Court emphasised the special circumstances of the case and specifically said that it was not making a general ruling. Instead, the

---

[160] Ibid. at 394.
[161] *Chester City Council v Arriva* [2007] EWHC 1373; *Arkin v Borchard* [2003] EWHC 687 (Comm); 2 *Travel Group plc v Cardiff City Transport* [2012] CAT 19.
[162] Cases C-395 and 396/96 *Compagnie Maritime Belge v Commission* [2000] ECR I-1365.

Court pointed out that the conference had over 90% of the market, only one competitor and the purpose of the conduct was to eliminate the competitor and that this constituted an abuse of a dominant position.[163]

This approach can also be seen in the *Irish Sugar* case,[164] where Irish Sugar, the sole producer of sugar beet in Ireland and Northern Ireland, reacted to import competition by, among other things, dropping its prices to consumers seen as most vulnerable to imports, although again the prices do not appear to have been below total costs. The European Commission condemned the practice as an abuse of a dominant position because of the intent to exclude competition and its decision was upheld by the GC, which said that it was necessary to consider all the circumstances and whether the practice took place in the context of a plan aimed at eliminating competition.[165]

It is perhaps best to view these cases as involving exceptional circumstances, as the European Commission put it in its discussion paper on exclusionary abuses,[166] or, alternatively, that they all involved cases where the undertakings concerned had very high market shares, above 90%, or that the undertakings were involved in a range of exclusionary practices and that therefore there was a cumulative effect from a number of abuses.[167]

Margin squeeze

This is an abuse which has come into greater prominence recently, largely because of claims that it has been occurring in regulated industries, notably telecommunications. As O'Donoghue and Padilla explain,[168] this abuse may occur when there are two markets, an upstream and a downstream one, and the upstream product is a necessary component in the good or service provided on the downstream market. If there is a vertically integrated undertaking which has a dominant position in an upstream market, there may be allegations that either (1) it is charging too high a price for the upstream input which it is selling to its downstream competitors, or (2) it is charging too low a price for its downstream products. The result of such practices will be that the downstream rivals are driven out of the market or become marginal competitors. Figure 3.1 illustrates the factual situation that this entails.

A simple example from one of the earliest cases will illustrate this, so far abstract, discussion. In the *Industrie des Poudres Sphériques (IPS)* case,[169] IPS marketed broken calcium metal (the downstream product), which was a derivative of primary calcium metal (the upstream product). Within the EU primary calcium metal was produced only by Péchiney Électrométallurgie (PEM), which also marketed broken calcium metal – in other words, it was vertically integrated. IPS complained to the Commission that, among other things, the price at which PEM offered to sell the primary calcium metal to it was too high. The

---

[163] Ibid. at paras 112–20.

[164] Case T-228/97 *Irish Sugar* v *Commission* [1999] ECR II-2969.

[165] Ibid. at para. 114. As the CAT put it in *Aberdeen Journals* v *Office of Fair Trading* [2003] CAT 11 (at para. 358): 'An objective justification will normally be particularly difficult to establish if there is evidence of selective price cutting by a dominant undertaking that is targeted specifically towards the customers or potential customers of a competitor.'

[166] European Commission (n. 11) at para. 127.

[167] See O'Donoghue and Padilla (n. 1), pp. 281–3.

[168] Ibid. at p. 304.

[169] Case T-5/97 *Industrie des Poudres Sphériques* v *Commission* [2000] ECR II-3755.

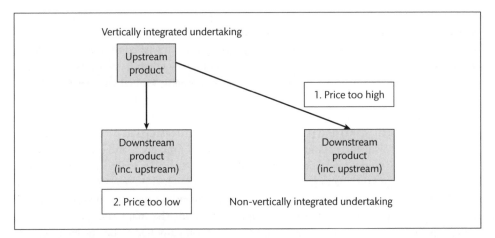

Figure 3.1 The margin squeeze problem

Commission rejected the complaint, and this rejection was upheld by the GC on a number of grounds, of which two are particularly relevant: first, that there were alternative sources of primary calcium metal available from suppliers outside the EU; and, secondly, that the price charged was not too high, especially because certain adaptations had to be made to the manufacturing process to meet IPS's needs.

It will be apparent that a number of conditions have to be met before a margin squeeze becomes, even theoretically, a plausible strategy for an undertaking. First, the undertaking must have significant upstream market power through the provision of some input for the downstream product that is essential for its production. This can be a raw material, as above, or access to a network in order to provide telecommunications services or to transport gas or electricity. Secondly, the undertaking will need to have the ability in the downstream market to profit from the raising of rivals' costs. A clear example would be if the firm was dominant in the downstream market as well, but this does not appear, as we shall see, to be a requirement of the law. Thirdly, there need to be barriers to entry at both the upstream and the downstream levels either to prevent upstream competition for the essential product or to prevent entry downstream or, indeed, re-entry if competitors are driven off the downstream market.

As is evident from this description, a margin squeeze incorporates elements of other offences. In its second version, too low a price for downstream products, this looks similar to predatory pricing, while in its first version it resembles a form of constructive refusal to supply.[170] It is also possible for there to be elements of price discrimination or excessive pricing, as the vertically integrated undertaking may charge different prices for the upstream input to its own downstream division or subsidiary than it charges to its downstream competitors. Nevertheless, case law has confirmed the guidance from both the OFT and the European Commission which treat this as a separate form of abuse, with its own conditions.[171]

---

[170] European Commission (n. 7) at para. 80.

[171] OFT, 'Assessment of Conduct: Draft competition law guideline for consultation' (London, 2004), pp. 24–6; European Commission, 'Notice on the application of the competition rules to access agreements in the telecommunications sector', OJ C265, 22.08.1998, pp. 2–26 (at paras 117–18). Case C-52/09 *Konkurrensverket* v *Telia Sonera Sverige AB* [2011] 4 CMLR 18. Although compare European Commission (n. 7) at para. 79.

These conditions can be illustrated by the most important UK case, that of *Albion Water*.[172] Here there was a paper mill, Shotton Paper, which was one of the largest industrial customers of water from its local company Welsh Water (Dŵr Cymru). It wished to move from having water supplied by Welsh Water to using the services of a new entrant, Albion Water. Albion proposed to purchase this water from another water company, United Utilities (which had provided this water to Welsh Water), and transport it to Shotton Paper using the existing pipes of Welsh Water. Welsh Water offered to provide transportation services (the upstream product for these purposes) at a price which Albion Water regarded as excessive and also as producing a margin squeeze, because the combined price of the water and the transportation services meant that it could not operate profitably. Albion Water originally made these claims of abuse to the regulator, the Office of Water Services, but, when these claims were rejected, appealed to the CAT, which ruled in its favour,[173] but this ruling was in turn appealed to the Court of Appeal, primarily on the margin squeeze ground. The main argument for Welsh Water was that, for there to be a margin squeeze, the company had to be engaged in some form of 'transformative' activity in relation to the downstream product or service, whereas here all that Albion Water was doing was supplying the same water and services as Welsh Water had done in the past. The Court of Appeal did not accept that this was part of the test, instead holding that its main elements were as follows:[174]

- the existence of two markets (an upstream market and a downstream market);
- a vertically integrated undertaking which is dominant on the upstream market and active (whether also dominant or not) on the downstream market;
- the need for access to an input from the upstream market in order to operate in the downstream market; and
- the setting of upstream and downstream prices by the dominant undertaking that leave an insufficient margin for an efficient competitor to operate profitably in the downstream market.

As regards the question of what is meant by an efficient competitor, the Court of Appeal followed the decision of the GC[175] and held that the test was that of an equally efficient competitor; in other words, the question was whether the downstream operations of the vertically integrated undertaking could make a profit if they were charged the same input prices as the competitor. The benefit of this approach is that it allows the vertically integrated undertaking to take a view based on its own prices, rather than having to calculate whether a notional or real competitor could operate profitably.

There have been a number of cases, largely in the regulated sectors in the UK, where allegations of a margin squeeze have been made, usually unsuccessfully. Rather than going into them here, this discussion will be postponed until later (Chapter 15), when it will be dealt with in the context of telecommunications, which will also deal with the main EU case law. We should note at this point, however, that the Supreme Court in the US has rejected a margin squeeze claim in terms that make it very difficult, if not impossible, to bring such a case under US law.[176]

---

[172] *Dŵr Cymru v Albion Water* [2008] EWCA Civ 536.
[173] *Albion Water v Water Services Regulation Authority* [2006] CAT 23 and 36.
[174] *Dŵr Cymru v Albion Water*, paras 88–9.
[175] Case T-271/03 *Deutsche Telekom v Commission* [2008] ECR II-477.
[176] *Pacific Bell Telephone Co v linkLine Communications*, 129 S. Ct. 1109 (2009).

COMPETITION LAW IN PRACTICE

Bananas versus other fruit[177]

United Brands (UB) was a major US fruit company (its successor is Chiquita Brands) and one of its important activities was the export of bananas from Central America to Europe. In 1975 the European Commission decided that United Brands had abused its dominant position in four ways:

1 by preventing its distributors and ripeners from reselling its bananas while still green;

2 by charging, in respect of Chiquita bananas, trading partners other than one group dissimilar prices for equivalent transactions;

3 by imposing unfair (excessive) prices for the sale of Chiquita bananas; and

4 refusing to supply bananas to a particular distributor.

The Commission imposed a fine of around 3 million Dutch guilders and ordered UB to reduce its prices by around 15%. United Brands challenged this decision before the CJEU, arguing, among other things, that it was not in a dominant position and that the practices identified did not constitute abuses.

Market definition and dominance

The first issue was whether UB was in a dominant position and, in order to determine this, a relevant market had to be defined. UB argued that bananas competed with other types of fresh fruit, while the European Commission argued that bananas were in a market of their own. The CJEU said that there was a limited degree of substitutability for bananas because of their specific characteristics (appearance, taste, softness, seedlessness) which satisfied the needs of an important section of the population, namely the very young, the old and the sick. UB also disputed that it was dominant, even if the market was defined as bananas. On this market, UB had a market share of between 40% and 45%, which was a share several times greater than that of its closest competitor. The CJEU also pointed to a number of factors in relation to the way UB was organised which supported the finding of dominance. It was vertically integrated: it grew the bananas, packaged them, transported them and sold them. It was the only undertaking that had its own large fleet of ships (the so-called Great White Fleet) which could carry up to two-thirds of its exports. It was technologically advanced, in various ways, and had a strong brand position (Chiquita). As was said, 'It has thus attained a privileged position by making Chiquita the premier banana brand name . . .'[178] The CJEU concluded that, even though there was evidence of lively competition on the market, the cumulative effect of all the advantages was that UB had a dominant position.

The prohibition on selling green bananas

The CJEU held that this was a restriction of competition because it cut down on the ability of the ripeners to compete with UB and because it limited markets to the prejudice of

➡

---

[177] Case 27/76 *United Brands* v *Commission* [1978] ECR 207.
[178] Ibid. at para. 93.

consumers, in particular by partitioning markets. The point here is that UB exported to several markets: Belgium/Luxembourg, Denmark, Germany, Ireland and the Netherlands, and charged different prices in each market. By prohibiting their ripeners from selling the green bananas, this prevented the ripeners from taking advantage of the different prices so that a ripener in a cheap UB country could have sold to an expensive UB country (a process known as arbitrage).

Unfair prices

The Commission examined the price differentials between the various markets and decided that the highest prices were excessive as compared to the lowest ones, which yielded a profit. The CJEU said that the appropriate approach was to ask, first, whether the difference between the costs of producing the product and the price actually charged is excessive and, if so, secondly, whether a price has been imposed which is unfair in itself or when compared to competing products. The Commission did not have any evidence in relation to UB's costs and, therefore, this part of the decision could not stand.

The discriminatory prices

There were quite significant price differences between the various national markets. At the extreme end, customers in Belgium were asked to pay prices on average 80% higher than those in Ireland. UB argued that the prices that they charged simply reflected the prices that they anticipated in the ripe, or yellow, banana market in the various national markets. The difference in prices reflected the different circumstances of the national markets. The CJEU did not accept this argument, saying that the interplay of supply and demand should only be applied to each stage where it is really manifest, in other words, at the retail level, not at the wholesale level. The discriminatory prices were just obstacles to the free movement of goods and their effect was intensified by the clause forbidding the resale of bananas while still green.

The refusal to supply a distributor

UB had done this because the distributor had taken part in a promotional campaign for a rival brand of bananas. The CJEU said, as a general principle, that an undertaking in a dominant position cannot stop supplying a customer who abides by regular commercial practice, if the orders placed by that customer are in no way out of the ordinary. Although the CJEU accepted that an undertaking could protect its own commercial position, it said that such actions must be proportionate to the threat and that this behaviour was in excess of what might reasonably be contemplated. It was a serious interference with the independence of small- and medium-sized firms in their commercial relations with the undertaking in a dominant position.[179]

Summary

The CJEU upheld the European Commission's decision on all the points bar excessive pricing.

---

[179] Ibid. at para. 193.

Analysis

This is one of the most famous and controversial cases in relation to Article 102 TFEU. As background, it is worth pointing out that UB was a very controversial company,[180] particularly in relation to its practices within Central America. It was also a company that had had run-ins in the United States as regards antitrust law. So it was a company that did not have a wholly favourable reputation.

Having said this, the judgment of the CJEU has been subjected to robust criticism on almost all of the points.[181] On the definition of the relevant market, referring to the needs of the very young, the old and the sick is not an appropriate way to define a market, because there are always some consumers who cannot or will not switch products. The question is whether there are sufficient other consumers who would make a price rise unprofitable by switching to alternative products. On the issue of dominance, even with the narrow market definition, UB was said to have only between 40% and 45% market share and there was admittedly lively competition. Furthermore, some of the other factors the CJEU relies on to establish dominance, such as technological advantage, seem to indicate that UB was simply more efficient than its competitors.

It is also evident, from the terms of the judgment, that one of the issues that the CJEU is really concerned about is market partitioning, as opposed to the economic effects of the practices which are condemned. It is noticeable that there is little analysis of the actual effects of the conduct which had been condemned by the Commission. The comments by the CJEU on refusal to supply are very broad, while the comments on discriminatory pricing are, in economic terms, very odd. As we have seen earlier in this chapter, the approach to excessive pricing raises more questions than it answers; something, to be fair, the CJEU seemed aware of in this judgment.

Summary

➤ Case law under Article 102 TFEU has focused primarily on exclusionary, rather than exploitative practices, and there has been a primary concern with protecting the competitive structure of markets through protecting the rights of access to the markets of competitors of dominant undertakings and protecting them against what are seen as anti-competitive practices. This case law has been criticised on the grounds of ignoring the insights of modern economic analysis and the European Commission has proposed an approach to Article 102 TFEU in its discussion paper and guidance which adopts a more economic approach.

[180] See P. Chapman, *Jungle Capitalists* (Canongate, London, 2007).
[181] See V. Korah, 'Concept of a dominant position within the meaning of Art 86' (1980) 17 *Common Market Law Review* 395; C. Baden Fuller, 'Article 86 EEC: Economic analysis of the existence of a dominant position' (1979) 4 *European Law Review* 423; W. Bishop, 'Price Discrimination under Article 86' (1981) 41 *Modern Law Review* 282.

➤ Dominance was defined as: a position of economic strength enjoyed by the undertaking which enables it to prevent effective competition being maintained on the relevant market by affording the power to behave to an appreciable extent independently of its competitors, customers and ultimately of its consumers.

➤ The case law takes a structural approach, focusing first on absolute and then on relative market shares as a filter. There is a presumption that market shares above 50% indicate dominance. For cases where undertakings have market shares between 40% and 49% other factors have to be analysed, of which the most important is entry barriers. Although there is some uncertainty in principle, there is no case where an undertaking with a market share of below 40% on its own has been held to be dominant.

➤ Dominant undertakings have a special responsibility not to abuse this position, which means that there are certain commercial practices which they cannot carry out that would be legal for a non-dominant undertaking. The test for abuse is objective and what matters is whether the conduct would be likely to have an anti-competitive effect – its actual effect is not relevant, even if unsuccessful.

➤ The European Commission has proposed an efficiency defence, which seems to have been approved in recent case law, modelled on Article 101(3) TFEU, which would have four conditions:

1. that efficiencies are realised or likely to be realised as a result of the conduct concerned;
2. that the conduct concerned is indispensable to realise these efficiencies;
3. that the efficiencies benefit consumers; and
4. that competition in respect of a substantial part of the products concerned is not eliminated.

➤ The test for excessive pricing is as follows:

(a) an analysis of the costs incurred in producing the product or service;
(b) a comparison of those costs with the price charged and an assessment of whether the resulting difference, i.e. the profit, is such that the price charged is excessive; and if so
(c) an assessment of whether the excessive price bears no reasonable relation to the economic value of the product or service supplied and is an abuse of a dominant position, with the consequence that it is either:
  (i) unfair in itself; or
  (ii) unfair when compared with competing products.

➤ There is a strong presumption that prices below average variable cost are predatory. Prices between AVC and average total cost are considered predatory if they are part of a plan for eliminating a competitor. There is no requirement that the dominant company has to be able to recoup any losses it makes. The Commission's guidance suggests using average avoidable costs.

➤ Selective low pricing, even though not below cost, may also be considered an abuse of a dominant position. The cases where this has been found seem to be exceptional, involving undertakings with very high market shares which are engaged in a number of abuses and a clear plan to exclude competitors from the market.

➤ The test for a margin squeeze is as follows:

- the existence of two markets (an upstream market and a downstream market);
- a vertically integrated undertaking which is dominant on the upstream market and active (whether also dominant or not) on the downstream market;

- the need for access to an input from the upstream market in order to operate in the downstream market; and
- the setting of upstream and downstream prices by the dominant undertaking that leave an insufficient margin for an efficient competitor to operate profitably in the downstream market.

Further reading

General

Nazzini, R., *The Foundations of European Union Competition Law: The Objectives and Principles of Article 102* (OUP, 2011). *Scholarly and sophisticated attempt to provide a coherent reworking of Article 102 TFEU. A complex argument which is not always obviously consistent with the case law.*

O'Donoghue, R. and Padilla, J., *The Law and Economics of Article 82 EC* (Hart Publishing, Oxford, 2006). *Comprehensive but advanced work. Views may be controversial.*

Market definition

Baker, J., 'Market Definition: An Analytical Overview' (2007) 74 *Antitrust Law Journal* 129. *Very clear explanation of the mechanics of market definition from an American perspective. Views on supply-side substitutability are very controversial and do not represent European practice.*

Bishop, S. and Walker, M., *The Economics of EC Competition Law* (3rd edn, Sweet & Maxwell, London, 2010), ch. 4. *Clear explanation of issue by two leading economic consultants.*

European Commission, 'Notice on the definition of the relevant market for the purposes of Community competition law', OJ C372, 09.12.1997, pp. 5–13. *The Commission's approach to this issue.*

Office of Fair Trading, *Market Definition* (2004). *A clear explanation of the OFT's approach to the issue.*

Dominance

Monti, G., 'The Concept of Dominance in Article 82' [2006] 2 *European Competition Journal* 31. *Analyses different concepts of dominance.*

Collective dominance

Monti, G., 'The scope of collective dominance under Article 82 EC' (2001) 38 *Common Market Law Review* 131. *Good discussion of case law and underlying issues.*

Whish, R., 'Collective Dominance' in D. O'Keeffe and M. Andenas (eds) *Liber Amicorum for Lord Slynn* (Kluwer, Amsterdam, 2000). *Clear discussion of issues by one of the leading UK commentators in the area.*

Abuse: general

Akman, P., *The Concept of Abuse in EU Competition Law* (Hart Publishing, Oxford, 2012). *Offers a new approach to the concept of abuse.*

Eilmansberger, T., 'How to Distinguish Good from Bad Competition Under Article 82 EC' (2005) 42 *Common Market Law Review* 129. *Advanced discussion, which takes a somewhat different approach to economic analysis than others. Important example of way of thinking about abuse not often seen in English language literature.*

European Commission, *Guidance on the Commission's enforcement priorities in applying Article 82 of the EC Treaty to abusive exclusionary conduct by dominant undertakings,* COM (2009) 864 final (9 February 2009). *The Commission's official position.*

Gormsen, L.L., *A Principled Approach to Abuse of Dominance in European Competition Law* (Cambridge University Press, 2010) *An interesting attempt to argue that there are wider objectives than just consumer welfare for Article 102 TFEU.*

Oliver, P., 'The Concept of "Abuse" of a Dominant Position under Article 82 EC: Recent Developments in Relation to Pricing' [2005] 1 *European Competition Journal* 315. *Good survey of case law by a European Commission official.*

Rousseva, E., *Rethinking Exclusionary Abuses in EU Competition Law* (Hart Publishing, Oxford, 2010). *Offers a new approach to exclusionary abuses through a systematic examination of the case law. Clear on where the division is between her views and the case law.*

Vickers, J., 'Abuse of Market Power' (2005) 115 *Economic Journal* F244–F261. *Past Chairman of OFT's views on what should be the principles underlying abuse of dominance. Clear and non-technical.*

Excessive pricing

Furse, M., 'Excessive Prices, Unfair Prices and Economic Value: The Law of Excessive Pricing Under Article 82 EC and the Chapter II Prohibition' (2008) 4 *European Competition Journal* 59. *Clear overview of the case law arguing for greater enforcement.*

Kon, S. and Turnbull, S., 'Pricing and the Dominant Firm: Implications of the Competition Commission Appeal Tribunal's Judgment in the *Napp* Case' (2003) 24 *European Competition Law Review* 70. *Good survey of UK law put into context of EC law.*

Lind, R. and Walker, M., 'The (Mis)use of Profitability Analysis in Competition Law' (2004) 25 *European Competition Law Review* 439. *Discussion of problems of profitability analysis.*

Morris, D., 'Dominant Firm Behaviour under UK Competition Law', paper presented to the Fordham Corporate Law Institute, New York, 23–4 October 2003 available at: *http://www.competition-commission.org.uk/our_role/speeches/index.htm* (accessed 02/09/12). *Clear explanation from ex-Chairman of Competition Commission as to why, among other things, analysis of excess profitability is possible and useful.*

Motta, M. and de Streel, A., 'Excessive Pricing and Price Squeeze under EU Law' in C. Ehlermann and I. Atanasiu (eds) *European Competition Law Annual 2003: What is an Abuse of a Dominant Position?* (Hart Publishing, Oxford, 2006) at pp. 91–113. *Excellent survey of EU case law up until 2002.*

Predatory pricing

Areeda, P. and Turner, D., 'Predatory Pricing and Related Practices under Section 2 of the Sherman Act' (1975) 88 *Harvard Law Review* 697. *Classic article which sets out framework adopted in law today.*

Brodley, J. and Hay, D., 'Predatory Pricing: Competing Economic Theories and the Evolution of Legal Standards' (1981) 66 *Cornell Law Review* 738. *Comprehensive discussion of problems with the Areeda/Turner test.*

Ritter, C., 'Does the Law of Predatory Pricing and Cross-Subsidisation Need a Radical Rethink?' (2004) 27 *World Competition* 613. *Advanced critique of law on predatory pricing.*

Margin squeeze

Auf'mkolk, H., 'The "Feedback Effect" of Applying EU Competition Law to Regulated Industries: Doctrinal Contamination in the Case of Margin Squeeze' (2012) 3 *Journal of European Competition Law & Practice* 149. *Interesting argument contrasting 'regulatory' and 'competition law' approaches to margin squeeze.*

Dunne, N., 'Margin Squeeze: theory, practice, policy' (2012) 33 *European Competition Law Review* 29 and 61. *Good discussion of EU and US case law, contrasting different approaches.*

Faella, G. and Pardolesi, R., 'Squeezing Price under EC Antitrust law' (2010) 6 *European Competition Journal* 255. *Balanced discussion of the economic issues surrounding margin squeeze cases and early case law.*

4

Abuse of a dominant position: exclusive dealing and non-pricing abuses

Chapter outline

This chapter discusses:

➤ Exclusive dealing, price discrimination, discounts and rebates

➤ The approach to tying and bundling

➤ The controversial case law on refusals to supply and essential facilities.

Introduction

In the previous chapter we discussed pricing practices which could constitute an abuse of a dominant position. In this chapter we move on to discuss practices which can be seen as non-price based. The division adopted between the two chapters is somewhat arbitrary and has been done for presentational purposes. In particular, the first section on exclusive dealing covers matters which are clearly price based, such as price discrimination.

Exclusive dealing, price discrimination, discounts and rebates

In this section the text will examine certain practices that tend to be treated separately by economists but which the case law of the European Courts tends to see as related: namely exclusive dealing, price discrimination and discounts and rebates, which are an element of price discrimination. Exclusive dealing has been discussed earlier (Chapter 2), in the context of Article 101 TFEU, but it has also been treated as an Article 102 TFEU issue, as a practice by which a dominant firm may seek to exclude its rival from a market. From a commercial point of view, there are a number of reasons why an undertaking might wish to enter into an exclusive supply arrangement with its customers. Such an arrangement helps to provide a guaranteed level of sales, important for recovering fixed costs, it may incentivise the customer to promote sales of the product and exclusive sales for a period of time may be necessary to ensure that the arrangement is profitable for the seller if an initial investment is needed.

Looking at how commonplace such arrangements are has in part influenced analysis by Chicago School economists who have argued that exclusive dealing does not raise competition problems. Their argument is that, first, a buyer would only enter into an exclusive arrangement if they felt that it was of some advantage to them or they could obtain what they regarded as a favourable price. If you imagine a situation with an existing monopoly seller, a buyer and a potential entrant who was more efficient than the existing monopoly seller, the buyer would only enter into an exclusive arrangement with the existing monopoly seller if the buyer was guaranteed a better price than could be obtained from the potential entrant. This is not possible because, under monopoly, the seller obtains a surplus *and* there is a deadweight loss to society. The monopoly seller will only be able to compensate the buyer to the extent of its surplus, whereas the new entrant can offer a price which allows the buyer to gain from *both* the monopoly surplus and the deadweight loss. Hence exclusive dealing cannot exclude more efficient entrants from the market and is not something that the competition authorities should be worried about.[1]

Inevitably, further economic analysis suggests that the issue is not so clear-cut. First, if the monopoly supplier is active on two markets and able to increase profit on both by excluding the new entrant on one market, it might be possible for the offer to be high enough to the buyer to exclude the new entrant. Secondly, if there is more than one buyer (and there is no coordination between them), and there is a minimum viable scale of entry, then the current monopoly supplier can deter entry by offering to compensate just enough buyers to make it unprofitable for the new entrant. If, at the extreme, all the buyers assume that all the other buyers are going to enter the exclusive contract, it may be that the existing monopoly supplier will not have to compensate any of them.[2] Now, although these arguments suggest that there are circumstances where exclusive dealing is a competition problem, it requires the competition authorities to establish that the conditions for this strategy exist, for example, that a sufficient amount of the market is foreclosed, and why the affected parties could not enter into non-exclusive contracts.[3] As we shall see, EU law on this issue has taken a much stronger line than the economics suggests.

We now turn to the issue of price discrimination which is an area where EU competition law diverges both from the recommended approach of economists and from US antitrust law, and is therefore highly controversial. There have been few cases in UK law dealing with this issue, which is presumably in part a reflection of the enforcement priorities of the OFT.[4]

Price discrimination is usually defined as where different customers are offered different prices for the goods or services that they buy, unrelated to the costs of production.[5] So, for example, one buyer might be offered a cheaper price than another because they had signed an exclusive contract. This is a practice which happens quite regularly in the economy. So, for example, rail tickets are cheaper for off-peak trains than for peak trains and students with a

---

[1] See M. Motta, *Competition Policy* (Cambridge University Press, 2004) at pp. 363–4 for this argument and R. O'Donoghue and J. Padilla, *The Law and Economics of Article 82 EC* (Hart Publishing, Oxford, 2006) at p. 355.

[2] See Motta (n. 1) at pp. 365–6 and O'Donoghue and Padilla (n. 1) at pp. 355–6 for this argument. Also European Commission Economic Advisory Group on Competition Policy (EAGCP), 'An economic approach to Article 82' (2005) at pp. 47–9. Available at: *http://ec.europa.eu/competition/antitrust/art82/index.html* (accessed 22/07/12).

[3] See O'Donoghue and Padilla (n. 1) at p. 357; EAGCP (n. 2) at pp. 49–50.

[4] Although see *Attheraces Ltd v British Horse Racing Board* [2007] EWCA Civ 38.

[5] Price discrimination would also occur if different customers were offered the same price for goods or services which had different costs of production for each customer.

railcard get a further discount. The price of an airline ticket on a budget airline varies dramatically depending on when you book your flight, so passengers sitting on the same flight may have paid dramatically different prices. Off-peak telephone calls cost more than peak time telephone calls. Buy one, get one free offers are another example of price discrimination, as the price paid for each of the two units is different, lower, than the price paid if just one unit is purchased. Discounts and rebates of this sort are in general forms of price discrimination – those who purchase more tending to get higher discounts.

Economists typically divide price discrimination into three categories (see below), but competition law is really only interested in second and third degree price discrimination, because first degree price discrimination is impossible in the real world. It is accepted that price discrimination can occur in a competitive market[6] but it is critical for its success that customers are unable to arbitrage between themselves. In other words, those customers who pay the lower price must not be able to sell the product to those who would be prepared to pay the higher price. Note as well that price discrimination is not necessarily something imposed by the seller. Large supermarkets will typically ask for a discounted price from their suppliers because of the volumes that they order.

Types of price discrimination

- *First degree price discrimination*: this occurs when an undertaking can discriminate perfectly between its consumers and charge each one of them the price they are willing to pay.

- *Second degree price discrimination*: this occurs when each customer is offered the same price schedule but the customers can decide how much they pay. So, for example, most electricity is offered on the basis of a two-part tariff: a (fixed) standing charge and a price per unit consumed. All consumers pay the standing charge, but the overall price paid depends on consumption.

- *Third degree price discrimination*: this occurs when different prices are offered to consumers, depending on the characteristics of the consumers: for example, discounts for children or the elderly.

Why would an undertaking engage in price discrimination? The issue relates mainly to the recovery of fixed costs, where an undertaking has large fixed costs but small or low variable costs: for example, a phone network.[7] If it costs an undertaking £1 to produce its good, which it sells for £2 in general, it would also be commercially sensible to discount that offer down to £1.01 in order to generate additional sales, as each additional sale will help to cover the fixed costs. So if the undertaking's total costs were £1 million, but it could sell only 450,000 units at £2, it would recover only £900,000. If it could sell 200,000 additional units at £1.50, that would enable it to cover its costs. An alternative strategy would be to keep a uniform higher price, such as £2.25, but this would work only if the undertaking was able to sell at least 445,000 units, as, on any quantity below this, it cannot cover its costs. This example would be seen by economists as a pro-competitive outcome, because output has increased because of the discriminatory pricing, and it is taken to be the general test for whether price

---

[6] See S. Bishop and M. Walker, *The Economics of EC Competition Law* (3rd edn, Sweet & Maxwell, London, 2010) at para. 6.029.

[7] Explained very well in D. Ridyard, 'Exclusionary Pricing and Price Discrimination Abuses under Article 82 – An Economic Analysis' (2002) 23 *European Competition Law Review* 286.

discrimination is harmful.[8] This does not, however, mean that price discrimination is always welfare enhancing because the circumstances may be such that output is not greater. Therefore, economists would argue that competition authorities should look at the economic effects of price discrimination practices, rather than concentrating on the form that the practice takes.[9]

The commercial connection between price discrimination and exclusive dealing is worth noting. Exclusive dealing has certain benefits for the supplier but, in addition to those benefits, it will be in their interest to come to an arrangement with the buyer which provides an incentive for the buyer to improve their performance. An easy example would be if some rebate or discount is granted for meeting a particular sales target. Indeed, the contract could be structured in such a way, through the use of discounts and rebates, that, although it is not expressed as an exclusive deal, it only makes commercial sense for the buyer if they buy all or almost all of their requirements from the seller.

The legal position in the EU

The text of Article 102 TFEU states that abuse may consist in: (a) directly or indirectly imposing unfair purchase or selling prices or other unfair trading conditions; and (b) applying dissimilar conditions to equivalent transactions with other trading parties, thereby putting them at a competitive disadvantage. This can be seen as a distinction between primary line injury, that is, something which prejudices the supplier's competitors in (a), and secondary line injury, that is, something which prejudices the supplier's customers when they are competing against each other. Although there has been a number of cases where action has been taken against secondary line injury,[10] the main concern of the European authorities has been with primary line injury.

The starting point is the CJEU's decision in *Hoffmann-La Roche*, where it stated as follows (in Box 4.1):

KEY CASE EXTRACT   Box 4.1

Fidelity arrangements

Source: Case 85/76 *Hoffmann-La Roche* v *Commission* [1979] ECR 461 at paras 89–90:

> An undertaking which is in a dominant position on the market and ties purchasers – even if it does so at their request – by an obligation or promise on their part to obtain all or most of their requirements exclusively from the said undertaking abuses its dominant position . . . whether the obligation in question is stipulated without further qualification or whether it is undertaken in consideration of the grant of a rebate . . . Obligations of this kind to obtain supplies exclusively from a particular undertaking . . . are incompatible with the objective of undistorted competition within the Common Market, because . . . they are not based on an economic transaction which justifies this burden of benefit but are designed to deprive the purchaser of or restrict his possible choice of sources of supply and to deny

---

[8] See Bishop and Walker (n. 6), para. 6.036; Motta (n. 1), pp. 493–7; R. Van den Bergh and P. Camesasca, *European Competition Law and Economics* (2nd edn, Sweet & Maxwell, London, 2006) at pp. 256–7; EAGCP (n. 2) at p. 31.

[9] EAGCP (n. 2) at p. 34; Bishop and Walker (n. 6), para. 6.036; Ridyard (n. 7) at p. 301.

[10] This is discussed in O'Donoghue and Padilla (n. 1) at pp. 573–91.

other producers access to the market. The fidelity rebate, unlike quantity rebates exclusively linked with the volume of purchases from the producer concerned, is designed through the grant of a financial advantage to prevent customers from obtaining their supplies from competing producers. Furthermore, the effect of fidelity rebates is to apply dissimilar conditions to equivalent transactions with other trading parties in that two purchasers pay a different price for the same quantity of the same product depending on whether they obtain their supplies exclusively from the undertaking in a dominant position or have several sources of supply. Finally, these practices by an undertaking in a dominant position and especially on an expanding market tend to consolidate this position by means of a form of competition which is not based on the transactions effected and is therefore distorted.

Questions: To what extent is it necessary to show that fidelity rebates actually restrict competitors entering the market? What is the difference between a quantity and a fidelity rebate?

It is worth quoting this extract at length because it has been highly influential, if not decisive, in subsequent case law and because it provides a good contrast with the economic approach to matters of price discrimination. The major concern of the CJEU is in a dominant company foreclosing the market to new entrants, or to existing entrants expanding their business by contractual arrangements which encourage customers to purchase all or most of their requirements from the dominant undertaking; either explicitly through an exclusive supply arrangement or implicitly through fidelity rebates which encourage customers to purchase all their requirements from the dominant undertaking. Note that this is a tough rule, which does not require proof of anti-competitive effects or, seemingly, any real analysis of market conditions beyond the establishment of dominance. In so doing, the CJEU draws a distinction between quantity rebates (linked to volumes of purchases) and fidelity rebates, which are not so linked. The former would be lawful, because the rebate is linked to the economic efficiencies that the supplier gains from volume, while the latter would not.

Hoffmann-La Roche was followed by the first *Michelin* case (*Michelin I*),[11] which involved the sale of new replacement truck tyres in the Netherlands. Michelin offered dealers a discount linked to an annual sales target which was personal to each dealer. Part of this was paid in advance, but the dealer got the full sum only if the annual target was met. Neither the discount system as a whole, nor the annual targets were published by Michelin. The individual sales targets were confirmed only orally by Michelin's representatives. So, in summary, this was a set of individualised discounts for the buyers, applying to all their purchases, set on a non-transparent basis, covering a whole year's purchases, with certain amounts paid in advance. Given that the discount applied to all purchases from Michelin, one of the effects of this system would be to put pressure on the buyers at the end of the year to obtain their full discount by making sure that they ordered enough tyres to meet the sales target. The CJEU pointed out that this effect was accentuated by Michelin's high market share, which meant that a competitor to Michelin would have to offer a discount which compensated the buyer for losing their full Michelin discount and do this in the context of a non-transparent system, that is, it would be very difficult to calculate an appropriate price.[12] The Court took the view that such a system was designed to prevent the dealers from selecting the most

[11] Case 322/81 *Nederlandsche Banden-Industrie Michelin v Commission* [1983] ECR 3461.
[12] Ibid. paras 82–3.

economically favourable offers and by a wish to sell more or to spread production more evenly, i.e. there was no economic justification for the practice.

In the next important case, the European Commission took action against British Plasterboard (BPB), which had reacted to increasing competition from imports by introducing a range of promotional and discount practices. BPB's competitors complained to the European Commission. One of the practices operated by BPB was a discount available only in Hampshire and Dorset for builders merchants that bought in large loads. Part of this discount was justified by cost savings and part, described by the European Commission as 'a small price reduction', was not. These arrangements were held not to be an abuse of a dominant position.[13] However, BPB's other practice, which was to make payments of promotional and advertising expenses to merchants that purchased exclusively from it, was held to be an abuse of a dominant position and this was supported by the GC. Although the Court accepted that such discounts were part of normal commercial practice, it said that, when an undertaking has a 'strong' position (in this case over 95% market share), the conclusion of exclusive supply contracts in respect of a substantial proportion of purchases constitutes an unacceptable obstacle to entry to the market. Even if this were a response to requests from the buyers, it did not justify an exclusivity clause. In addition, the GC condemned the withdrawal of discounts from merchants in Northern Ireland[14] who intended to import plasterboard and its replacement with a higher discount for those who remained loyal to BPB. Again, it can be seen that the Court's approach is to see the issue as being primarily about an undertaking with a very large market share trying to prevent entry by tying its customers to it by exclusivity arrangements. There is no attempt by the Court to look at the economic effects of the practices; once they are classified as loyalty inducing, that is enough.

The controversy over the treatment of this issue has been reignited by two recent cases: *Michelin II* and *British Airways*.[15] In *Michelin II* the European Commission took a decision that Michelin was in breach of Article 102 TFEU in respect of its pricing schemes for replacement tyres for heavy vehicles in France – in other words, a very similar issue to the case that had previously arisen in the Netherlands. The details of the schemes are complex but they involved four basic schemes: a quantity rebate, a progress bonus, a service bonus, and an arrangement known as the 'Michelin Friends Club'. The quantity rebates were based on a scale, whereby the rebate increased with the volume purchased by the dealer during the past year and the rebate applied to all purchases made in that year. There were a large number of thresholds within the conditions, between 47 and 54 within the general conditions, and the rebates were larger at the lower end of the scale and decreased as purchases increased. The service bonus depended on the dealer reaching a minimum annual turnover and entering into a number of commitments to Michelin and the extent to which those commitments were fulfilled; in other words, an assessment of the dealer's performance. The commitments included matters such as promoting Michelin's products, providing market information and providing tyres for retreading. The progress bonus was an individually negotiated target with a dealer to exceed a minimum purchase level, based on past performance and future prospect.[16] In the

[13] *BPB Industries* [1989] OJ L10/50 at para. 134.

[14] Case T-65/89 *BPB Industries v Commission* [1993] ECR II-389.

[15] Case T-203/01 *Manufacture Française Des Pneumatiques Michelin v Commission* [2003] ECR II-4701; Case T-219/99 *British Airways v Commission* [2003] ECR II-5917 (GC), on appeal Case C-95/04P *British Airways v Commission* [2007] ECR I-2331.

[16] The European Commission decision on this was not appealed to the GC.

Michelin Friends Club, Michelin made a financial contribution to the dealers in return for certain obligations, revolving partly around providing Michelin with information about their business and also in promoting Michelin products. It can be seen from this description that three of these arrangements look close to the individualised loyalty-inducing schemes that were condemned in previous case law, while the quantity rebates look to be the sort of arrangements which were, in principle, acceptable.

The GC held that the service bonus was an abuse of a dominant position because it depended on the subjective assessment of Michelin in regard to the dealer's performance, and that it was aimed at inducing loyalty in the dealers and tying them to Michelin.[17] Similarly, it held that the Michelin Friends Club was, in the circumstances, an attempt to protect Michelin's position on the market and to exclude other manufacturers from access to dealers who were members of the club.[18] Given the way that the GC characterised the facts in relation to these issues, the result is in line with previous case law.

More surprising was the issue regarding the quantity rebates that Michelin claimed were just ordinary quantity rebates, which it was entitled to grant to its customers. The European Commission claimed that the system was loyalty inducing because it was based on a dealer's entire turnover with Michelin and the reference period was a year, which it considered an excessive length of time. The GC, after examining the working of the system, took the view that a quantity rebate system in which there is a significant variation in the discount rates between the lower and higher steps, which has a reference period of one year and in which the discount is fixed on the basis of total turnover achieved during the reference period, has the characteristics of a loyalty-inducing discount system.[19] The key point here is that if the rebate applies to all the purchases from Michelin over a year, this will be a large number of purchases and this will place a substantial incentive on the dealer to reach a higher threshold. A competitor to Michelin who wishes to enter the market, will thus have to compensate the dealer not simply for the loss of discount on the tyres that they order from the competitor rather than Michelin, but for the loss of a discount, or part of it, on all the dealer's purchases of Michelin tyres. Given that Michelin had a market share of somewhere over 50%, five to six times greater than its closest competitor, this potentially makes it very costly for a competitor to supply a Michelin dealer.[20] According to the GC, such rebates could be acceptable only if they were economically justified, but Michelin had provided insufficient evidence to make this out. Finally, the Court reiterated that it is not necessary for the European Commission to show actual effects of the conduct complained about; it was enough that the conduct was capable of having that effect.[21]

The *British Airways* case arose through a complaint from Virgin Airlines about the commission scheme which BA offered to travel agents for selling BA tickets. The scheme offered extra payments in return for the agents' meeting or exceeding their previous year's sale of tickets. The increase in commission applied to all the BA tickets sold by the agent, not just those above the target level. So, although the target level was transparent, this system provides a strong incentive for travel agents to meet their targets and it is correspondingly

[17] Case T-203/01 *Manufacture Française Des Pneumatiques Michelin* v *Commission* [2003] ECR II-4701 at paras 136–67.

[18] Ibid., paras 168–226.

[19] Ibid., para. 95.

[20] See Commission Decision [2002] OJ L143/1 at paras 174–80. No publicly available information was given as to Michelin's market share – this was presumably available to the GC.

[21] Case T-203/01 *Manufacture Française Des Pneumatiques Michelin* v *Commission* [2003] ECR II-4701 at para. 239.

more difficult for competitors to take away this business. Unlike Michelin, BA had a market share over the five years covered by the European Commission of 46% at the maximum, which had declined to just under 40% by the time of the decision condemning these practices. Both the GC and the CJEU took the view that this form of discount scheme was an abuse of a dominant position because it exerted a particularly strong pressure on the travel agents, particularly when it came to the purchase of tickets which would make a difference to the attainment of the targets, because the commission then applied to all tickets, not just those purchased after the attainment of the target. This is further strengthened by the fact that BA held a much larger position on the market than its competitors, which meant that they could not establish a reward scheme which was equivalent to BA's. In addition, the GC repeated the point that the question was whether the conduct was capable of having an effect on the market, not whether it did, and that the fact that BA's market share had fallen during the period under issue was not relevant as it could be inferred that, if it were not for these practices, the market shares of its competitors would have grown even further.[22]

The approach taken in these cases has continued in the *Tomra* case.[23] Tomra was the manufacturer of what are called 'reverse vending machines', that is, in countries where the price of drinks in containers contains a deposit element, the container can be returned to a reverse vending machine which identifies the container and returns the appropriate deposit. The case involved the operations of Tomra in Germany, the Netherlands, Austria, Sweden and Norway between 1998 and 2002 and, during that period, the Commission estimated that Tomra had a market share exceeding 95%. Tomra was fined €24 million for operating an exclusionary strategy which involved exclusivity agreements, individualised quantity commitments and individualised retroactive rebate schemes. Tomra challenged this decision on a number of grounds, two of which are particularly interesting in this context. First, they argued that the Commission had not conducted a sufficient examination of the market context in which the agreements operated, a point dismissed by the General Court, which pointed out that there was significant examination of context in the decision, as well as a discussion of the actual effects of Tomra's practices.[24] Secondly, they argued that the agreements in question had not foreclosed a sufficient amount of the market to prevent competitors entering it. The GC commented that Tomra has foreclosed about 40% of total demand in that period, which it said was far from small. In addition, it made the point that:

> . . . customers on the foreclosed part of the market should have the opportunity to benefit from whatever degree of competition is possible on the market and competitors should be able to compete on the merits for the entire market and not just for a part of it. Second, it is not the role of the dominant undertaking to dictate how many viable competitors will be allowed to compete for the remaining contestable portion of demand.[25]

Before the CJEU, Tomra produced an additional argument, that the retroactive rebates had not led to prices which were below costs. The CJEU responded by saying that a finding of prices below costs was not a prerequisite to a finding that the retroactive rebates were an abuse of a dominant position. The Court added, following the GC, that the exclusionary

---

[22] See Case T-219/99 *British Airways v Commission* [2003] ECR II-5917 at paras 293–8. Upheld on appeal in Case C-95/04P *British Airways v Commission* [2007] ECR I-2331.

[23] Case T-155/06 *Tomra Systems ASA v Commission* [2010] ECR II-4361(GC), confirmed on appeal Case 549/10P judgment of 19 April 2012 (CJEU).

[24] Ibid. paras 217–219.

[25] Ibid. para. 241. This was approved by the CJEU.

effect of the rebates did not require a sacrifice of profits and it was possible that they might lead to a high average profit for the supplier. The Commission was entitled to point to various other considerations to establish the exclusionary effect of the rebates, such as the strong incentive provided by retroactive rebates, their individualised nature, the application of the rebates to the largest customers and the failure to show any objective justifications.[26]

The case law in this area does take a very strict and formalistic view of these practices, contrary to the approach which is favoured by many economists.[27] In part, this reflects the origins of Article 102 TFEU and a concern to protect the competitive structure of a market and a wariness of practices that are not seen as normal competition. The European Commission in its enforcement guidelines has tried to take these points on board, while remaining true to the case law. The Commission says that it will focus its enforcement efforts on those cases where the loyalty obligations will prevent the entry or expansion of competing undertakings which would have represented an important competitive constraint. When investigating this, particularly in relation to rebates, the Commission will look to see whether equally efficient competitors to the dominant undertaking could enter the market, given the effect of these rebates. In a new departure, the Commission will examine the effective price of the product (that is, taking into account the rebate) and, if the effective price is below average avoidable cost, as a general rule that will be exclusionary, whereas if it is above long-run average incremental cost, this will normally not be exclusionary. Prices between these two points will require looking at other factors.[28] The problem for an undertaking accused of these practices is that the Commission's standards are higher than those required by the case law.

The issue of the proper approach to discounts and rebates is likely to remain highly controversial after the Commission fined the computer chip maker Intel €1.06 billion for abusing its dominant position. The Commission found that Intel engaged in two specific forms of illegal practice. First, Intel gave wholly or partially hidden rebates to computer manufacturers on condition that they bought all, or almost all, their x86 CPUs (a common computer chip) from Intel. Intel also made direct payments to a major retailer on condition that it stock only computers with Intel x86 CPUs. Secondly, Intel made direct payments to computer manufacturers to halt or delay the launch of specific products containing competitors' x86 CPUs and to limit the sales channels available to these products.[29] In the context of a market for computer chips where Intel has a market share of around 80% and its main competitor, AMD, has a share of around 20%, the Commission found that such practices would have made it impossible for competitors to compete for customers' orders. The Commission found that, in order to be able to compete with the Intel rebates, for the part of the computer manufacturers' supplies that was 'up for grabs', a competitor that was just as efficient as Intel would have had to offer a price for its CPUs lower than its costs of producing those CPUs, even if the average price of its CPUs was lower than that of Intel. For example, according to the Commission, rival chip manufacturer AMD offered one million free CPUs to one particular computer manufacturer. If the computer manufacturer had accepted all of these, it would have lost Intel's rebate on its many millions of remaining CPU purchases, and would

---

[26] Ibid. paras 73–81 (CJEU).

[27] See, for example, EAGCP (n. 2) at pp. 37–8.

[28] European Commission, *Guidance on the Commission's enforcement priorities in applying Article 82 of the EC Treaty to abusive exclusionary conduct by dominant undertakings*, COM (2009) 864 final (9 February 2009) at paras 32–46.

[29] See Commission Press Release IP/09/745, 13 May 2009.

have been worse off overall simply for having accepted this highly competitive offer. In the end, the computer manufacturer took only 160,000 CPUs for free. Intel has denied that its practices harmed consumers and has appealed the Commission's decision.[30]

US law on exclusive dealing and discounts

In US antitrust law, exclusive dealing can be dealt with under ss. 1 and 2 Sherman Act, s. 3 Clayton Act and s. 5 Federal Trade Commission Act, all of which have somewhat different wording and standards to apply. The focus here is on the case law under s. 1 Sherman Act and s. 3 Clayton Act. The starting point for discussion is the *Standard Oil* case[31] in which Standard Oil's practice of requiring independent petrol stations in the Western United States to take all their requirement from Standard Oil was challenged under the Clayton and Sherman Acts. To give this some context, Standard Oil also operated its own petrol stations as well and its competitors also operated a system composed of their own petrol stations and independents. Standard sold just under 7% of petrol in the geographic area covered. The Supreme Court dealt with the question under s. 3 Clayton Act which says:

> It shall be unlawful for any person engaged in commerce, in the course of such commerce, to lease or make a sale or contract for sale of goods, wares, merchandise, machinery, supplies, or other commodities, whether patented or unpatented, for use, consumption, or resale within the United States . . . on the condition, agreement, or understanding that the lessee or purchaser thereof shall not use or deal in the goods . . . of a competitor or competitors of the . . . seller, where the effect of such lease, sale, or contract for sale or such condition, agreement, or understanding may be to substantially lessen competition or tend to create a monopoly in any line of commerce.

The majority of the court saw the question as being whether this statutory provision could be met simply by proving that a substantial proportion of commerce was affected or whether it had to be shown that actual competitive activity had diminished. Despite recognising the pro-competitive justifications for exclusivity contracts, the Court held that, for the purposes of the Clayton Act, competition had been foreclosed in a substantial share of commerce. If the US courts had continued with this approach it would have created a rule arguably stricter than that developed by the European courts. The Supreme Court did seem to retreat somewhat in the later case of *Tampa Electric*, which involved a twenty-year exclusive supply contract for coal to an electricity generating station.[32] The case was actually resolved by a process of market definition that reduced the area of the market below 1%, hence it failed on the substantial proportion of commerce. But the Court also added that:

> To determine substantiality in a given case, it is necessary to weigh the probable effect of the contract on the relevant area of effective competition, taking into account the relative strength of the parties, the proportionate volume of commerce involved in relation to the total volume of commerce in the relevant market area, and the probable immediate and future effects which preemption of that share of the market might have on effective competition therein.[33]

---

[30] Case T-286/09 *Intel v Commission* (not yet decided).
[31] *Standard Oil Co. v United States*, 337 US 293 (1949).
[32] *Tampa Electric Co. v Nashville Coal Co.* 365 US 320 (1961).
[33] Ibid. at 329.

This seems to have created a two-part test. First, there must be foreclosure of a sufficient part of the market which, according to Hovenkamp's summary of the case law, would seem to be around 40%.[34] If that level of foreclosure is found, then the other factors mentioned in *Tampa* have to be examined to discover whether there is a substantial lessening of competition including looking, for example, at the duration of the contracts and the pro- and anti-competitive effects. It can be seen that this is a very different approach from that taken by the European courts and, in particular, the European courts do not undertake any examination of the extent to which the market has been foreclosed, although in *Tomra* they accepted the estimation that about 40% of the market had been foreclosed without going into any of the other factors that would be relevant in US law.

Discounting practices by dominant companies are treated in the US as a price practice and are therefore not considered a problem unless the resultant price is below some measure of cost. Although this seems to be the case in relation to simple discount and rebate cases, bundled ones have caused more difficulty, as illustrated by *LePages Inc* v *3M*.[35] 3M manufactured Scotch tape for home office use in the US and had, at the time of the case, a market share of around 90%. It also manufactured other office supplies and equipment. LePages had decided to enter the tape market in relation to office supplies through making an unbranded private label tape which would compete with that offered by 3M. 3M responded to this by offering its customers a set of bundled rebates which gave them significant discounts if they bought a variety of office products from them, including but not limited to tape. The problem for LePages was that they did not offer the range of products that 3M did and so they could not offer an alternative bundle. LePages brought action under s. 2 Sherman Act which was successful in front of the jury.[36] 3M appealed the jury verdict, arguing that there was no anti-trust violation because it had never sold its tape below cost. The US Court of Appeals in the Third Circuit did not accept 3M's argument, holding that its conduct, when looked at as a whole, was sufficient for the jury to find that there had been exclusionary anti-competitive practices. This case has been controversial and heavily criticised on the grounds that the court did not assess whether 3M's bundled rebates constituted competition on the merits, focusing instead on the harm that the practice had caused to LePages.[37] Interestingly, the CJEU reached a similar conclusion in relation to the rebate systems used by Hoffmann-La Roche in relation to the purchase of vitamins.[38]

Tying and bundling[39]

In this section we examine a commercial practice which is commonplace, namely, selling different products or services together. Classic examples are shoes and shoelaces, automobiles (with tyres, radios, different options, accessories, etc.) and season tickets for football matches.

---

[34] H. Hovenkamp, *Federal Antitrust Policy* (4th edn, West Publishing, St Paul, Minnesota, 2011) at s. 10.9e.

[35] *LePages Inc* v *3m*, 324 F 3rd 141 (2003).

[36] The s. 1 Sherman Act and s. 3 Clayton Act claims were not successful.

[37] See Antitrust Modernisation Commission (2007) *Final Report* at 94–99 available at: *http://govinfo.library.unt.edu/ amc/report_recommendation/toc.htm* (accessed 22/07/12).

[38] Case 85/76 *Hoffmann-La Roche* v *Commission* [1979] ECR 461 at paras 110–111.

[39] Generally, see B. Nalebuff, *Bundling, Tying and Portfolio Effects* (2003) DTI Economics Paper No. 1 available at: *http://www.bis.gov.uk/files/file14774.pdf* (accessed 22/07/12).

Table 4.1 Options available to buyers under tying and bundling

	Options available to buyers
Tying	X + Y
	Y
Bundling	X + Y
Mixed bundling	X + Y
	X
	Y

Source: Bishop and Walker (n. 6) at p. 209.

Three types of bundling and tying can be distinguished: pure bundling, when none of the components of a package are offered separately; mixed bundling, where both elements of the package are offered separately but the consumer receives an advantageous price by buying the package; and tying, where one of the elements is available separately (the tying product), but another is available only in combination with the first element (the tied product). The options for buyers are illustrated in Table 4.1. Tying and bundling can be accomplished either through the terms of the contract ('if you buy our photocopier, you must buy our paper as well') or it may be technological (for example, if you buy one games console, then you can buy only games which are designed to work on that console).

There are a number of reasons why it makes sense for undertakings to engage in these practices. First, it may give rise to both economies of scale and scope in production and distribution if, for example, the same machines are used to make the goods or putting them together reduces marketing and distribution costs. Secondly, this may also be used as a means of protecting the undertaking's reputation and brand, through ensuring that products of the appropriate quality are used together. An example would be branded printer cartridges. Thirdly, tying may also be used as a way of establishing how often one of the products is used. If you buy a printer and have to buy all your paper from the manufacturer, it is easy for the manufacturer to monitor your usage. Fourthly, bundling may also allow the producers to sell more of their product through price discrimination. Imagine[40] that a manufacturer sells two products, A and B, which are sold separately at £10 but in a bundle at £15. Consumers who value A and B at more than £10 but the bundle at less than £15, will buy the good separately. Those who value A and B at less than £10, but the bundle at more than £15, will buy the bundle. In the absence of bundling, these consumers would not purchase the good at all and overall societal welfare is increased because output is raised. It is not, however, necessarily the case that price discrimination will increase consumer welfare, as we have seen earlier.

Looking at the prevalence of the practice, and the fact that there may be good commercial reasons for this activity, it has been argued by the Chicago School of economists that tying is not anti-competitive because it is possible to charge only one monopoly price; this cannot be extended to the tied good.[41] Without going into detail, this argument rests on the assumptions that the tied good market is competitive and that the two products are used in fixed proportions. Once these assumptions are relaxed, it becomes evident that bundling and tying can be used in an anti-competitive manner either to exclude or deter rivals from entering a

---

[40] The example is in Bishop and Walker (n. 6) at 6.067.
[41] Van den Bergh and Camesasca (n. 8) discuss these points at section 7.3.

market or to soften price competition. If an undertaking produces two products in two different markets and engages in mixed bundling, this may make it more difficult for someone who wants to enter just one of the markets, as those consumers who want both products will buy the bundle, leaving only those who do not value one of the products very highly available for the new entrant. Alternatively, if an undertaking has a monopoly in product A, but is subject to competition in relation to product B and bundles the two together, it has an incentive to price very aggressively because every lost sale now means loss of the profit on B and loss of the monopoly profit on A. The result might be to drive competitors from the market or to deter entry – in other words, it looks similar to predation. Price competition can be softened because tying can allow product differentiation, which can soften the competition between two products and allow the prices of both to rise.

Putting all these points together, there seems to be a consensus amongst the economists that tying and bundling may give rise to efficiencies.[42] However, there are circumstances where such practices may lead to anti-competitive effects. It is important therefore that each case should be considered on its merits, even though balancing efficiency gains against possible anti-competitive effects is complex. By contrast, competition authorities have traditionally been very suspicious of tying arrangements. In the United States, tying arrangements were, from the later 1940s, subject to a *per se* prohibition which was quite strict until the mid 1980s, when the Supreme Court appeared to move towards a rule of reason test, although currently the test is still characterised as a *per se* one.[43] In Europe, the European Commission has traditionally been hostile to tying practices engaged in by a dominant undertaking, largely because of worries that the undertaking would be able to leverage its position of dominance from one market into another, and has taken the view that the market has been foreclosed once bundling has been proved, without the need for more analysis.[44] There are relatively few decided cases in European Union law and none in the UK under the competition Act 1998. There have been a number of settlements between the European Commission and undertakings, which give an indication of its approach.[45]

The starting point is the *Hilti*[46] case, where a manufacturer supplied nail guns to the construction industry and it attempted to tie the purchase of its nails and cartridges to the guns through a variety of practices, including making the sale of cartridges conditional upon taking a supply of nails. Independent manufacturers complained about these practices and the European Commission decided that Hilti had abused its dominant position. The European Commission took the view that there were separate markets for Hilti compatible nails and cartridges, as well as nail guns more generally, and that Hilti was, not surprisingly, dominant on this market with a market share of around 70–80%. Although Hilti appealed to the GC, it based its case primarily on arguments relating to market definition and objective justifications for the practices it engaged in, whilst conceding that such behaviour could constitute an abuse of a dominant position. There was, therefore, no discussion by the GC of the approach that should be taken.

---

[42] See EAGCP (n. 2) at pp. 38–42; O'Donoghue and Padilla (n. 1) at p. 491; Bishop and Walker (n. 6) at para. 6.065–6.068; Van den Bergh and Camesasca (n. 8) at pp. 275–6; Motta (n. 1) at pp. 467–8.

[43] See E. Gellhorn, W. Kovacic and S. Calkins, *Antitrust Law and Economics* (5th edn, West Publishing, St Paul, Minnesota, 2004) at pp. 378–94.

[44] Case Comp/C-3/37 *Microsoft*, Commission Decision of 24 March 2004 at para. 841.

[45] See O'Donoghue and Padilla (n. 1) pp. 491–6 for examples.

[46] Case T-30/89 *Hilti* v *Commission* [1991] ECR II-1439.

The second major case was *Tetra Pak*,[47] where the undertaking supplied carton packaging machines and the cartons for the packaging of liquid and semi-liquid food. This market is divided into aseptic and non-aseptic processes, so there were four relevant markets: aseptic packaging machines; non-aseptic packaging machines; aseptic cartons; and non-aseptic cartons. At the time of the case, the undertaking had a market share of above 90% in aseptic packaging and 45–50% in non-aseptic packaging. We have dealt with the predatory pricing aspects of this case in the section above; here we concentrate on the issue of tying because, in a standard clause in its contract, Tetra Pak insisted that purchasers and lessees of its machines should use only Tetra Pak cartons in them. The GC took the view that the contractual clauses had to be looked at in combination and as part of an overall strategy to make customers totally dependent on Tetra Pak for the life of the machine, while the clauses in relation to the cartons were intended to make the carton market wholly dependent on the machine market.[48] On the GC's view, this was a practice that attempted to deprive customers of choice and prevent other suppliers entering the market and it was neither normal commercial practice nor objectively justified.[49] The CJEU upheld the GC's judgment, commenting that 'even where tied sales of two products are in accordance with commercial usage or there is a natural link between the two products in question, such sales may still constitute abuse within the meaning of Article 86 [Article 102 TFEU] unless they are objectively justified'.[50]

The final, and perhaps most controversial case, is Microsoft and fuller details of the context of the case are given below. Here the European Commission decided that the practice of bundling Microsoft Media Player with Microsoft Windows, which had over 90% of the market for operating systems, was an abuse of a dominant position because it protected Microsoft's position in the media player market, protecting it from potentially more efficient competitors, deterred innovation and allowed it to expand its position in adjacent, related markets.[51] In order to establish this, four criteria had to be met (Box 4.2).

KEY CASE EXTRACT   Box 4.2

Criteria for unlawful tying

Source: Case T-201/04 *Microsoft* v *Commission* [2007] ECR II-3601 at para. 862:

1 the tying and tied products are two separate products;

2 the undertaking concerned is dominant in the market for the tying product;

3 the undertaking concerned does not give customers a choice to obtain the tying product without the tied product; and

4 the practice in question forecloses competition.

Questions: How easy is it to show that there are two separate products? What has to be proven to show a foreclosure of competition?

---

[47] Case T-83/91 *Tetra Pak* v *Commission* [1994] ECR II-755 (GC); Case 333/94P *Tetra Pak* v *Commission* [1996] ECR I-5951 (CJEU).

[48] Ibid. (GC) at para. 135.

[49] Ibid. at para. 137.

[50] Ibid. (CJEU) at para. 37.

[51] Case Comp/C-3/37 *Microsoft*, Commission Decision of 24 March 2004 at paras 978–84.

The decision was appealed to the GC, which upheld the European Commission's findings in relation to tying. The GC agreed that Windows Media Player and Windows Operating System were two separate products and that Microsoft held a dominant position in the market for operating systems. The bundling did, in the GC's view, entail coercion, primarily of the original equipment manufacturers who, if they wished to install the Windows Operating System, had to install Windows Media Player and this coercion thereby found its way to the end consumers.[52] Interestingly, the GC took the view that the bundling of Windows Media Player with the Windows Operating System, without being able to remove the Media Player, allowed Media Player to benefit from the ubiquity of the operating system, which could not be counterbalanced by other methods of distributing media players and was enough on its own to demonstrate foreclosure.[53] Although the European Commission went on to examine whether the bundling was capable of having an effect on content providers and software designers and the actual effect of the bundling on the market, both of which the GC upheld, this was not strictly necessary.

The Commission's approach in its guidance on enforcement priorities is presented in a different manner from *Microsoft*, although it refers to that case as authority for its approach. The Commission says that it will normally take action where an undertaking is dominant in the tying market and the tying and tied products are distinct products and the tying practice is likely to lead to anti-competitive foreclosure.[54] The Commission takes the view that there are certain factors which help to identify possible anti-competitive foreclosure.[55] First, the risk is greater where the tying or bundling strategy is a lasting one, for example through technical tying, as in Microsoft. Secondly, in relation to bundling, if the undertaking has a dominant position for more than one product in the bundle, the greater the number of such products, the stronger the likely anti-competitive foreclosure. Thirdly, if the tying leads to fewer customers interested in buying the tied product alone to sustain competitors of the dominant undertaking in the tied market. Fourthly, if the tying and tied product can be used in variable proportions as inputs to a production process, tying can prevent customers substituting the tied product for the tying product. Fifthly, if prices on the tying market are regulated, tying may allow the dominant firm to raise prices on the tied market. Finally, if the tying product is an important complementary product for customers of the tying product, reducing alternative suppliers of the tied product can make entry to the tying market alone more difficult. As regards multi-product rebates,[56] if competitors cannot sell competing bundles, the Commission will look at the incremental price that customers pay for each of the products in the bundle. If the incremental price for each of the products in the bundle is above long-run average incremental cost (LRAIC) the Commission will not normally intervene since an equally efficient competitor, producing only one product, should be able to compete. If the incremental price is below LRAIC, enforcement action may be warranted. If competitors are selling identical bundles, the question becomes whether the price of the bundle as a whole is predatory. This is a different approach from that taken by the CJEU in *Hoffmann-La Roche*, as discussed above.[57]

---

[52] Ibid. at para. 962.
[53] Ibid. at paras 1036 and 1048.
[54] European Commission (n. 28) at para. 50.
[55] Ibid. at paras 52–8.
[56] Ibid. paras 59–61.
[57] Op. cit., note 38.

US law on tying

There is a long history of challenging tying arrangements under a variety of provisions of US antitrust law. The prevailing approach, which is a *per se* test, is summarised by Hovenkamp:[58]

1 There must be separate tying and tied products

2 There must be 'evidence of actual coercion by the seller that in fact forced the buyer to accept the tied product'

3 The seller must possess 'sufficient economic power in the tying product market to coerce purchaser acceptance of the tied product'

4 There must be 'anticompetitive effects in the tied market', and

5 There must be 'involvement of a "not insubstantial" amount of interstate commerce in the tied product market'.

Leaving aside the fifth condition, which is peculiar to the requirements of a federal system,[59] the four conditions put forward by the US courts look quite similar to the GC's conditions in *Microsoft*, which are set out below. One of the things that is interesting about this approach is that, although it is described as a *per se* test, it does require a determination of market power as is made clear in the Supreme Court decision of *Jefferson Parish Hospital District*[60] where the hospital had tied the use of operating rooms to a particular firm of anesthesiologists. Here the Court made it clear that some form of market power was needed and, in the case in hand, found that a 30% market share was insufficient. The court did say that tying arrangements should be condemned when the seller has sufficient 'market power to force a purchaser to do something that he would not do in a competitive market'.[61]

COMPETITION LAW IN PRACTICE

Microsoft

Microsoft is an American software company whose products are ubiquitous – it has been estimated that it has a 90% market share in relation to operating systems for home PCs and has had such a share for some time. In 2007 it had global revenues of over US$50 billion (in 2012 it was over US$70 billion). It has also been the subject of two major competition law cases in the United States and Europe, as well as one in Korea,[62] which raise interesting issues about the application of competition law in high-technology industries, the approach of US and European competition law and about the development of certain competition law doctrines.

In the United States there was a series of cases and investigations into Microsoft during the early 1990s. The most celebrated case was that started by the Justice Department

---

[58] Hovenkamp (n. 34) at s. 10.1.

[59] The equivalent provision for Article 102 TFEU is the requirement for an effect on inter-state trade and an effect on a substantial part of the internal market.

[60] *Jefferson Parish Hospital District* v *Hyde*, 466 US 2 (1984).

[61] Ibid. at 14.

[62] See *International Herald Tribune*, 17 October 2007.

and 20 states based on, among other things, illegal tying of Windows and Internet Explorer and attempted monopolisation of the browser market. After a lengthy trial and an attempt at settlement, the trial judge accepted the government's request to divide Microsoft into an operating systems business and an applications business. This decision was appealed to the Court of Appeals for the District of Columbia which confirmed that Microsoft had violated the Sherman Act, upholding the finding of monopolisation, but rejected the remedy of divestiture.[63] The result was a complicated settlement, embodied in a Final Judgment that was reviewed and approved by the district court. A related Court of Appeals decision in 2004 confirmed the relief. The Final Judgment protects consumers by protecting competition in middleware: for example, it prohibits Microsoft from using exclusive contracts that inhibit competition, and it requires Microsoft to provide information to allow interoperability of competitors' software. The US government continues to enforce the Final Judgment, which it claims has resulted in substantial changes to Microsoft's business practices, benefiting United States consumers.

Following the American case, it has been claimed that those complainants who were unhappy with the outcome of that case encouraged the European Commission to take action, although the first complaints were made in 1998. Eventually, the European Commission brought a case against Microsoft in 2000, alleging that it had abused its dominant position by refusing to provide information which would allow interoperability between Microsoft servers and others and by bundling Windows Media Player with the Microsoft operating system so that anyone who bought a computer with Microsoft Windows installed would also receive Media Player. These two abuses were categorised as a refusal to supply and unlawful tying, contrary to Article 82(b) [Article 102(b) TFEU] and Microsoft was fined €497 million in 2004, at the time, the largest fine ever levied on a single undertaking and the largest fine in the history of EU competition law.[64] Microsoft was also ordered by the European Commission to disclose the necessary information to its competitors and to begin providing a version of Windows without the Media Player, which became known as Windows XP N and has sold very few copies.

The issue of disclosing information necessary for interoperability has been a very difficult one. The European Commission took action against Microsoft for failing to comply with the 2004 decision on interoperability, citing the view of the Monitoring Trustee, appointed to advise the European Commission, that the documentation was 'fundamentally flawed', and ultimately imposed a penalty of €280.5 million in July 2006. It was not until October 2007 that the Commission announced that it was satisfied that Microsoft had complied with the 2004 decision. Then in February 2008 it imposed a further penalty of €899 million on Microsoft for non-compliance with the 2004 decision. Microsoft appealed this decision to the GC, but only succeeded in reducing the fine to €860 million.[65] It is worth noting that one of the issues in the case was the reasonableness, or otherwise, of the prices that Microsoft was charging for access to the information.

---

[63] *Microsoft Corporation* v *United States* 253 F 3rd 34 (DC Cir. 2001).
[64] Case Comp/C-3/37 *Microsoft*, Commission Decision of 24 March 2004.
[65] See European Commission Press Release IP/08/318, 27 February 2008 and Case T-167/08 *Microsoft* v *Commission*, judgment of 27 June 2012.

Microsoft appealed against the 2004 decision and, in September 2007, the GC upheld the European Commission's decision in substance, although it overturned part of the remedy.[66] Discussion of the legal issues is contained in the sections of tying and bundling and refusal to supply.

The GC's decision has been highly controversial and has again raised the issue of different standards being used in Europe and the United States. The American Assistant Attorney General for antitrust, Tom Barnett, said that he was 'concerned that the standard applied to unilateral conduct by the CFI [GC], rather than helping consumers, may have the unfortunate consequence of harming consumers by chilling innovation and discouraging competition'.[67] The Competition Commissioner, Neelie Kroes, responded by saying, 'It is totally unacceptable that a representative of the U.S. administration criticized an independent court of law outside its jurisdiction . . . The European Commission does not pass judgment on rulings by U.S. courts, and we expect the same degree of respect.'[68] It is not, however, clear that Barnett's view is shared by the entire American antitrust community, as the American Antitrust Institute made clear:

> The oddity of Barnett's statement is that both Europe and the US found that Microsoft was a monopolist which had acted to harm competition, and both insisted on interoperability in framing a remedy. Both jurisdictions concluded that Microsoft exercised market power in personal computer operating systems, though the specifics of its anticompetitive conduct differed (in one case, protecting its monopoly position by preventing Internet browsers from replacing the operating system as a way for applications programs to run; in the other, leveraging the operating system monopoly into the media player market). And in fashioning a remedy, both required interoperability to assure that independent suppliers of application software can work with the monopoly. The real difference is over the appropriate remedy. Frankly, neither the US remedy nor the European remedy has proven to be very effective. It may be necessary at some point for the Europeans to impose even stronger remedies against Microsoft, such as the break-up originally contemplated by our government. As the inconsistency from one US Administration to the next might suggest, Barnett is far from speaking for a unified US antitrust community.[69]

At the beginning of 2008, the Commission opened another investigation against Microsoft in relation to complaints about interoperability and tying.[70] One complaint about tying related to the tying of Internet Explorer to Windows. This case was settled when Microsoft gave commitments to the Commission to provide a choice screen to users of Windows which would allow them to choose their browser.[71] The Commission has, however, opened further proceedings against Microsoft to check whether it has complied with the commitments decision.[72] Another complaint about tying and the interoperability complaint are still continuing.

---

[66] Case T-201/04 *Microsoft v Commission* [2007] ECR II-3601.

[67] Available at: *http://www.usdoj.gov/atr/public/press_releases/2007/226070.htm* (accessed 22/07/12).

[68] Available at: *http://www.iht.com/articles/2007/09/19/business/msft.php* (accessed 22/07/12).

[69] Available at: *http://www.antitrustinstitute.org/~antitrust/node/10879* (accessed 22/07/12).

[70] See European Commission Press Release MEMO/08/19, 14 January 2008 and see Press Release IP/09/1941 16 December 2009.

[71] Case COMP/C-3/39.530 *Microsoft (tying)* European Commission Decision of 16 December 2009.

[72] European Commission Press Release IP/12/800, 17 July 2012.

Questions: Microsoft obtained its market position through its own efforts. To what extent are these cases simply penalising a company for being successful? Is this a case about competition in the market or competition for a market? Is it possible that Microsoft could see its market position eroded very quickly, in a similar manner to what happened to IBM? How effective do you think the remedies have been?

Refusals to supply and essential facilities

This section brings us to another controversial area, namely the requirement of a dominant company to supply its customers. There is a strong intuitive feeling that commercial relations are founded on the basis of freedom of contract, which means that consumers have the freedom to choose with whom they wish to contract and whom they wish to reject. When an undertaking becomes dominant, this freedom is in some sense curtailed by competition law and this is perhaps one of the clearest examples of where the special responsibility placed on a dominant undertaking is most clearly felt.

The concern in this area is with the behaviour of undertakings that are vertically integrated and operate in two markets, commonly referred to as an upstream and a downstream market. The problem typically arises when a competitor of the vertically integrated undertaking needs access to some product, service or facility in order to reach customers on the downstream market. Consider, for example, a vertically integrated electricity company which generates electricity and then supplies it to customers through its distribution and supply network. A competitor, which only generates electricity, would be able to reach customers only through having access to the distribution and supply network. The relationship is set out schematically in Figure 4.1.

Why should this be a problem for competition law? As the example of electricity suggests, there may be circumstances where a vertically integrated undertaking controls some asset, without which it is impossible for a competitor to enter the downstream market, and it is not possible for the competitor to duplicate that asset. In the case of electricity it is because the distribution and supply system, i.e. the wires, is a natural monopoly; in other cases it might be because the asset is protected by intellectual property rights. If competitors cannot get access to these assets then, in these circumstances, the downstream market would remain uncompetitive because it would be, on this simplified example, a monopoly.

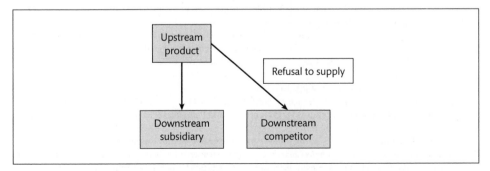

Figure 4.1 Standard essential facilities case

The analysis so far suggests that the appropriate policy would be to allow access for competitors in these situations as a general rule, despite concerns over freedom of contract. Economists would, however, suggest that a different approach should be taken, primarily because of the negative effects that such a general rule would have on innovation.[73] When the vertically integrated undertaking creates a downstream asset, it does this through investment of its own resources, on which it expects to earn a return, which will be calculated, in part, on the basis of the amount of competition it faces in the downstream market. If competitors are allowed access to those assets, this would reduce the return and the incentive on the vertically integrated undertaking to create those assets. The vertically integrated undertaking could charge a price for access to its assets, which would allow it to earn what it regards as an acceptable return, but, in the first instance, this should be a matter for the undertaking to decide, rather than the competition authorities. This argument has been taken to suggest that where the undertaking has obtained the asset not through its own efforts but through, for example, inheritance when it was a previously state-owned enterprise, or when the property right in the asset is weak in some sense, then a different approach should be taken and access granted more freely.[74] This is controversial and, although it might provide an explanation for some of the cases discussed below, it has been argued that this does not provide a useful legal test for deciding when access should be granted.[75]

Before looking at the case law, there are some preliminary distinctions that are worth making. First, a distinction has been drawn between assets protected by intellectual property (IP) rights and assets which are not so protected. The relationship between IP rights and competition law is discussed in more detail later in the text (see Chapter 12), so here it is simply worth pointing out that IP rights are typically granted by legislation as a reward for the innovation by the holder. One of the fundamental characteristics of an IP right is the ability to control the use of the property and to exclude others from it. In the context of refusal to supply, this has been taken to mean that competition law should be more cautious in cases of IP rights, than in non-IP cases. The rationale for such a distinction is debatable, but it is well entrenched in the case law.[76] Secondly, there may be a distinction between cases where an existing arrangement is terminated and those where a new relationship is sought to be created. This is again controversial,[77] but since the European Commission takes the view that the termination of an existing supply relationship is more likely to be abusive, than the refusal to create a new one, it is worth bearing in mind.[78] By contrast, in the context of a margin squeeze case, the CJEU has said that whether the operators affected by the margin squeeze are existing or potential customers was of no relevance in assessing the abuse.[79]

---

[73] See O'Donoghue and Padilla (n. 1) at pp. 411–14 for a list of objections, and AG Jacobs in Case C-7/97 *Oscar Bronner* v *Mediaprint* [1998] ECR I-7791.

[74] See Motta (n. 1) at p. 68. European Commission, *Guidance on the Commission's enforcement priorities in applying Article 82 of the EC Treaty to abusive exclusionary conduct by dominant undertakings* COM (2009) 864 final (9 February 2009) at para. 82. See also Case C-209/10 *Post Danmark A/S* v *Konkurrencadet* judgment of 27 March 2012 (CJEU) at para. 23.

[75] See O'Donoghue and Padilla (n. 1) at pp. 462–3.

[76] See Case C-7/97 *Oscar Bronner* v *Mediaprint* [1998] ECR I-7791 at para. 41; Case T-201/04 *Microsoft* v *Commission* [2007] ECR II-3601 at para. 334. O'Donoghue and Padilla (n. 1) at pp. 421–3 give the alternative argument.

[77] See O'Donoghue and Padilla (n. 1) at pp. 458–61 for an overview of the competing views.

[78] European Commission, *Guidance on the Commission's enforcement priorities in applying Article 82 of the EC Treaty to abusive exclusionary conduct by dominant undertakings* COM (2009) 864 final (9 February 2009) at para. 84.

[79] Case C-52/09 *Konkurrensverket* v *Telia Sonera Sverige AB* [2011] 4 CMLR 18 at paras 90–5.

The starting point for all the case law is the *Commercial Solvents* case.[80] Here CSC supplied aminobutanol, a raw material from which a derivative, ethambutol, could be produced. CSC's Italian subsidiary sold the raw material to an Italian company, Zoja, which used it to make ethambutol. Zoja cancelled its order when independent distributors offered it a better deal. This did not work out and Zoja sought further supplies from CSC. In the meantime, CSC had decided to stop supplying the raw material in the European Union, and that its Italian subsidiary would make the derivative. It therefore refused to supply Zoja, which complained to the European Commission, which found that there had been an abuse of a dominant position. The CJEU upheld the decision, making the statement set out in Box 4.3. This approach was followed by the CJEU in a later case, where a television station had refused to allow telemarketers to advertise unless they used the station's subsidiary, where the first statement in Box 4.3 was put in general terms, also quoted in Box 4.3. Both of these cases are examples of vertically integrated undertakings which have cut off supply to existing customers,[81] and they suggest the conditions for abuse are the existence of two markets and the possibility of eliminating all competition on the downstream market.

KEY CASE EXTRACTS   Box 4.3

Refusal to supply

Source: Cases 6 and 7/73 *Istituto Chemioterapico and Commercial Solvents* v *Commission* [1974] ECR 223 at para. 25:

> . . . an undertaking which has a dominant position in the market in raw materials and which, with the object of reserving such raw materials for manufacturing its own derivatives, refuses to supply a customer, which is itself a manufacturer of these derivatives, and therefore risks eliminating all competition on the part of this customer, is abusing its dominant position . . .

Source: Case 311/84 *Centre Belge d'Etudes du Marché-Télémarketing* v *CLT* [1985] ECR 3261 at para. 27:

> . . . an abuse within the meaning of Article 102 [Article 82 TFEU] is committed where, without any objective necessity, an undertaking holding a dominant position on a particular market reserves to itself or to an undertaking belonging to the same group an ancillary activity which might be carried out by another undertaking as part of its activities on a neighboring but separate market, with the possibility of eliminating all competition from such undertaking.

Questions: Compare with Box 4.4. Which test is easier to meet? Would the result be different if new customers were involved?

These cases were followed by two preliminary references relating to spare parts for cars, that is, items that were protected by IP rights.[82] The question was whether it would be an abuse of a dominant position for a car manufacturer to refuse to license the design rights on its spare parts to third parties wishing to manufacture and sell such parts. The CJEU held that

---

[80] Cases 6 and 7/73 *Istituto Chemioterapico and Commercial Solvents* v *Commission* [1974] ECR 223.

[81] This appears to be how the Court in *Commercial Solvents* treated Zoja.

[82] Case 238/87 *AB Volvo* v *Erik Veng* [1988] ECR 6211; Case 53/87 *CICCRA and Maxicar* v *Renault* [1988] ECR 6039.

such a refusal would be an abuse only if it involved conduct such as the arbitrary refusal to supply spare parts to independent repairers, fixing of prices at an unfair level or ceasing to manufacture certain spare parts, even though the model was still in circulation.[83] One of the striking elements of this decision, aside from the difficulties caused by the examples given, is that there is no consideration about the possibility of eliminating competition in the downstream market.

The Commission and essential facilities[84]

Outside the European Courts, the European Commission began to develop a doctrine called essential facilities, which was based on the refusal to supply case law. Although there are a number of Commission decisions which are regarded, by the Commission, as examples of the essential facilities doctrine, even though it is not explicitly mentioned, the doctrine was first developed explicitly in a series of cases involving access to port facilities, starting with *B&I Holyhead/Sealink*.[85] Here Sealink owned and operated the port of Holyhead as well as running ferries on what the Commission called the 'central corridor' route between Wales and Ireland (i.e. Holyhead to Dublin and Dun Laoghaire) and it was held to be in a dominant position. B&I also ran ferries from Holyhead, using a particular berth where its operations had to cease every time a Sealink ferry went past because of the physical characteristics of the harbour. B&I complained that Sealink intended to introduce a new timetable which would cause greater disruption to its activities. The Commission adopted a decision providing for interim measures ordering Sealink to return to its previous timetable and laid down the matter of principle as set out in Box 4.4.

KEY OFFICIAL GUIDANCE   **Box 4.4**

Commission definition of essential facilities

A dominant undertaking which both owns or controls and itself uses an essential facility, i.e., a facility or infrastructure without access to which competitors cannot provide services to their customers, and which refuses competitors access to that facility or grants access to competitors only on terms less favourable than those which it gives its own services, thereby placing the competitors at a competitive disadvantage, infringes Article 86 [Article 102 TFEU], if the other conditions of that Article are met . . . A company in a dominant position may not discriminate in favour of its own activities in a related market.

Source: Commission Decision of 11 June 1992, *B&I Holyhead/Sealink* [1992] 5 CMLR 255 at para. 41.

Question: Compare with Box 4.3. What are the differences between the two tests?

This case involved an existing relationship between B&I and Sealink but in two later cases, one involving a new competitor who wanted access to Holyhead, the Commission made it

---

[83] *Volvo* v *Veng* at para. 9.

[84] Generally, see A. Jones and B. Sufrin, *EU Competition Law* (4thd edn, Oxford University Press, 2011) at pp. 487–89; P. Larouche, *Competition Law and Regulation in European Telecommunications* (Hart Publishing, Oxford, 2000) at pp. 179–88.

[85] Decision of 11 June 1992 [1992] 5 CMLR 255.

clear that the principle applied to new as well as existing customers.[86] If this is compared with the statement in *Commercial Solvents*, it can be seen that the European Commission's view was much broader than that of the Courts as the issue was framed as one of discrimination, without any reference to the possibility of competition being eliminated and it seems aimed at allowing new entry.

The essential facilities doctrine has been invoked by the European Commission in a series of cases related to railways[87] but most important were a number of cases in the telecommunications sector which the Commission views as having discussed regulatory principles and served as the basis for the 1998 Guidelines on access agreements in the telecommunications sector.[88] The Commission set out the basic principles as follows:

> (a) access to the facility in question is generally essential in order for companies to compete on that related market . . . The key issue here is therefore what is essential. It will not be sufficient that the position of the company requesting access would be more advantageous if access were granted – but refusal of access must lead to the proposed activities being made either impossible or seriously and unavoidably uneconomic . . . (b) there is sufficient capacity available to provide access; (c) the facility owner fails to satisfy demand on an existing service or product market, blocks the emergence of a potential new service or product, or impedes competition on an existing or potential service or product market; (d) the company seeking access is prepared to pay the reasonable and non-discriminatory price and will otherwise in all respects accept non-discriminatory access terms and conditions; (e) there is no objective justification for refusing to provide access.[89]

It can be seen that the Commission is attempting to develop a general principle of competition law which will be useful, in particular, in relation to the liberalisation of certain industries, such as energy and telecommunications (discussed in more detail in Chapter 15). As will be seen in the discussion of the Courts' case law below, this approach has not been taken up wholeheartedly by them although the existing case law on refusal to supply has been expanded.

The case law of the European Courts

After the IP cases, the next major case in front of the CJEU was *Magill*,[90] again an intellectual property case. At the time of the case, television guides in Ireland and Northern Ireland were published by the broadcasters and limited to giving the schedules for the programmes that they broadcast. This information was covered by copyright. Magill wanted to publish a television guide which gave a comprehensive listing of all the television programmes, on all the channels, that would be shown in the coming week. In order to do this, it had to be given

---

[86] *Sea Containers Ltd/Stena Sealink* [1994] OJ L15/8, [1995] 4 CMLR 84; *Port of Rødby* [1994] OJ L55/52, [1994] 5 CMLR 457.

[87] *HOV SVZ/MCN*, Decision 94/210 of 29 March 1994, [1994] OJ L104/34; *ACI*, Decision 94/594 of 27 July 1994, [1994] OJ L224/28; and *Night Services*, Decision 94/663 of 21 September 1994, [1994] OJ L259/20. See also: *Eurotunnel*, Decision 94/894 of 13 December 1994, [1994] OJ L354/66; *GVG/FS*, Decision of 27 August 2003, COMP37/685.

[88] The cases are: *Eirpage* [1991] OJ L306/22; *Atlas and Phoenix/GlobalOne* [1996] OJ L239/23 and 57; and *Unisource* [1997] OJ L318/1.

[89] European Commission, 'Notice on the application of the competition rules to access agreements in the telecommunications sector', OJ C265, 22.08.1998, pp. 2–28 (at para. 91).

[90] Cases C-241–242/91 *RTE & ITP v Commission* [1995] ECR I-743.

the information by the broadcasters, who refused to provide it and took out an injunction against Magill, preventing it from publishing. Magill complained to the European Commission, which decided that there had been an abuse of a dominant position and that the broadcasters should provide Magill with the information it sought about their television programmes. The broadcasters appealed against this decision to the GC and, ultimately, to the CJEU. The CJEU held that, in exceptional circumstances, the exercise of exclusive rights by an IP right holder could constitute an abuse. In this case, the exceptional circumstances were that the broadcasters were the only source of the indispensable raw material, that their refusal prevented the emergence of a new product, which they did not offer and for which there was potential consumer demand, that there was no objective justification for such a refusal, and, finally, that the broadcasters had reserved for themselves a secondary market by excluding all competition on the market.[91]

This decision encouraged the European Commission in its attempt to create an essential facilities doctrine, but the next time the issue came before the CJEU, a more restrictive approach was taken in the *Oscar Bronner* case.[92] This case involved an Austrian daily newspaper, published by Mediaprint, which was the largest selling daily newspaper in Austria. It delivered its papers through a home delivery service. Oscar Bronner published a competing newspaper, with a much smaller circulation and sought access to Mediaprint's home delivery service, using a court action in Austria, arguing that there was no alternative means of delivery and that it would be unprofitable for it to create its own home delivery system given its small size. The Austrian court asked for a preliminary ruling on the question of whether this behaviour constituted an abuse. The CJEU firmly answered this question negatively. After referring to *Magill*, the Court said that in order to rely on that case, assuming an IP case was relevant here, three conditions had to be met:

1 that the refusal of service must be likely to eliminate all competition in the daily newspaper market;

2 that the refusal could not be objectively justified; and

3 that the service was indispensable, as there was no actual or potential substitute for the home delivery scheme.[93]

This was not the case here, as there were other methods of distributing newspapers and it had to be shown that it was impossible or unreasonably difficult to create an alternative system, which meant, not that it was impossible for a newspaper with a small circulation but that it would not be economically viable to create a second home delivery system for a newspaper with an equivalent circulation.

The next major case was *IMS Health*,[94] where the European Commission intervened to try and ensure access to information or a way of structuring information for new entrants in the market. Here, data on the purchasing habits of German pharmacies was collected in a particular format, called the 1860 brick format, which had been developed by the incumbent in collaboration with the industry and was subject to protection under IP law, and was then sold to the pharmaceutical industry. A competitor of IMS Health, having failed to create an

---

[91] Ibid., paras 50–6.
[92] Case C 7/97 *Oscar Bronner* v *Mediaprint* [1998] ECR I-7791.
[93] Ibid., para. 41.
[94] Case C-418/01 *IMS Health* v *NDC Health* [2004] ECR I-5039.

alternative structure, sought access to this format, which was refused by the incumbent. The competitor then took action in the German courts and complained to the European Commission. The Commission took a decision which required access, but was unsuccessful in adopting interim measures to enforce this decision, which the incumbent had appealed. In the meantime, the issue arrived at the CJEU, via a preliminary reference. The Court took the view that in order for the refusal by an undertaking which owns a copyright to give access to a product or service to be treated as abusive there were four conditions that had to be met:

1 the product or service had to be indispensable for carrying on a particular business;
2 the refusal prevents the emergence of a new product for which there is potential consumer demand;
3 there is no objective justification for the refusal; and
4 the refusal excludes any competition on a secondary market.[95]

There is a significant lack of clarity about the scope of the principles. First, in *IMS*, there is the requirement of the emergence of a new product, which is not referred to in *Bronner*. This seems to be because *IMS* involved intellectual property, unlike *Bronner*, although it is possible that a different newspaper was assumed to be a new product.[96] In any event, what constitutes a new product? These appear to be services of a 'different nature'[97] but that in itself begs a question. Is a simpler, cheaper version of the copyrighted product something of a different nature? Alternatively, is a more expensive, more complicated version something of a different nature?

A second difficult issue is that relating to the secondary market. First, there is the question of what exactly is a secondary market. The Court talks about two different stages of production that are interconnected at para. 45 of its judgment, which seems to mean that the upstream goods are used for the production or supply of the downstream goods or services as suggested in para. 42. This seems consistent with the Advocate General's opinion at para. 55. This suggests that we have to be careful to distinguish cases involving complementary markets and after-markets from these situations and thus exclude cases like *Hugin*[98] (spare parts for cash registers) from consideration under this doctrine. Secondly, as the Court points out in para. 44, it appears to be sufficient to identify a potential or indeed even a hypothetical market. It does not matter whether the product is marketed independently, and this was confirmed in the *Microsoft* case.[99] As Jones and Sufrin put it, the market so identified in *IMS* 'was a very artificial one'.[100]

Even if these issues were resolved, there is still the key problem of what should be considered as 'indispensable'. It seems that the idea is wider than that of a natural monopoly.[101] According to the Court in *Oscar Bronner*, indispensable means that there must be no actual or potential substitute for the product or service in question. In particular, it must not be possible for an undertaking, in a similar economic position to the undertaking controlling

---

[95] Ibid. at para. 38.
[96] See the opinion of Advocate General Tizzano at para. 61.
[97] See the opinion of Advocate General Tizzano at para. 62.
[98] Case 22/78 *Hugin Kassaregister v Commission* [1979] ECR 1869.
[99] Case T-201/04 *Microsoft v Commission* [2007] ECR II-3601 at para. 335.
[100] Jones and Sufrin (n. 84) at p. 508.
[101] See J. Temple Lang, 'Defining Legitimate Competition: Companies' Duties to Supply Competitors and Access to Essential Facilities' (1994) 18 *Fordham International Law Journal* 437 at 490.

the facility, to be able to replicate it. It is not a good argument for a small competitor to say that it, because of its size, is unable to create the alleged essential facility.

The *Microsoft* decision[102] is also careful not to use the concept of essential facilities explicitly and may perhaps be considered to fall into a special case of refusing to supply information needed for interoperability, as seems to be suggested in the Commission's discussion paper on Article 102 TFEU.[103] Here the issue was Microsoft's refusal to supply information about interoperability in the work group server operating systems (in essence, a network of computers) that it had developed to its competitors so that they could develop competing products. The information was protected by IP rights, so the fundamental question was whether a refusal to license intellectual property rights to competitors would constitute an abuse of a dominant position. Although the European Commission contended in this case that the tests set down in *IMS Health* needed to be broadened,[104] the GC disposed of the case by applying the four tests mentioned above. The Court found that the information was indispensable for competitors to operate on the market, that the refusal to supply it prevented the emergence of new products[105] and that there was no objective justification for the refusal.[106] As regards the elimination of competition, the GC took the view that:

> . . . [it was not] necessary to demonstrate that all competition on the market would be eliminated. What matters, for the purpose of establishing an infringement of Article 82 EC [Article 102 TFEU], is that the refusal at issue is liable to, or is likely to, eliminate all effective competition on the market. It must be made clear that the fact that the competitors of the dominant undertaking retain a marginal presence in certain niches on the market cannot suffice to substantiate the existence of such competition.[107]

From the GC's point of view, action could be taken before competition was eliminated on the market, as long as the conduct made it likely that effective competition would be eliminated. The formulation of this test is slightly different from that in *IMS Health* (see below) but the consensus of opinion is that the legal test is the same in the two cases; but it has been suggested that the GC too easily accepted the factual points underpinning the Commission's case.[108] It is important to add, as a final point, that a delay in granting access or supply can also constitute an abuse.[109] A good example of this is the decision of the European Commission in the Telekomunikacja Polska case where it found an abuse of dominant position because the undertaking had proposed unreasonable access conditions, delayed the negotiation process, limited access to its network and subscriber lines and refused to provide important information.[110]

---

[102] COMP/C-3/37.792, *Microsoft*, Commission Decision of 24 March 2004.

[103] European Commission, *DG Competition discussion paper on the application of Article 82 of the Treaty to exclusionary abuses* (Staff discussion paper) (December 2005) at para. 241.

[104] Case T-201/04 *Microsoft* v *Commission* [2007] ECR II-3601 at para. 316.

[105] Ibid., paras 621–65.

[106] Ibid., paras 666–712.

[107] Ibid., para. 563.

[108] P. Larouche, 'The European Microsoft Case at the Crossroads of Competition Policy and Innovation' (May 2008) TILEC Discussion Paper No. 2008-021, available at SSRN: *http://ssrn.com/abstract=1140165* (accessed 02/09/12); J. Vickers, 'A Tale of Two Cases: IBM and Microsoft' (2008) 4 *Competition Policy International* 3; C. Ahlborn and D. Evans, 'The Microsoft Judgment and its Implications for Competition Policy Towards Dominant Firms in Europe' (2009) 75 *Antitrust Law Journal* 1.

[109] See Case T-301/04 *Clearstream Banking* v *Commission* (GC) [2009] 5 CMLR 24 at para. 151.

[110] COMP/39.525, *Telekomunikacja Polska*, Commission Decision of 22 June 2011.

KEY CASE EXTRACT   Box 4.5

Refusal to supply test

Source: Case T-201/04 *Microsoft* v *Commission* [2007] ECR II-3601 at paras 332–3:

1 the refusal relates to a product or service indispensable to the exercise of a particular activity on a neighbouring market;

2 the refusal is of such a kind as to exclude any effective competition on that neighbouring market;

3 the refusal prevents the appearance of a new product for which there is potential consumer demand; and

4 the refusal is not objectively justified.

Questions: What counts as a separate market? What counts as a new product? What is meant by 'effective' competition?

In its guidance on enforcement priorities, the Commission focuses, in the section refusal to supply, on cases where the dominant undertaking competes on the downstream market with other undertakings. The Commission's approach in these cases is that it will consider them an enforcement priority if three conditions are met:[111]

1 the refusal relates to a product or service that is objectively necessary to be able to compete effectively on a downstream market,

2 the refusal is likely to lead to the elimination of effective competition on the downstream market, and

3 the refusal is likely to lead to consumer harm.

The Commission goes on to to say that these criteria apply to bother termination of an existing arrangement as well as refusal to provide new supplies, although the former is more likely to be found abusive. Objective necessity arises when there is no actual or potential substitute for the input. If the conditions for criteria (1) above are met, the Commission's view is that, in general, this means that there will be an elimination of effective competition.[112] Consumer harm may arise, in particular, when competitors are prevented from bringing new or innovative goods or services to the market, so a relevant inquiry is just how different will be the products or services provided by competitors.[113] Although the structure of this test is clearly based on the case law of the Courts, the inclusion of the consumer harm criteria is an amendment of the Courts' approach, albeit a sensible position for an enforcement agency to take. It will be interesting to see whether the enthusiastic approach taken by the Commission in the past to refusals to supply will continue into the future. The guidance does suggest a more circumspect position.

---

[111] European Commission (n. 28) at para. 81.
[112] Ibid. para. 85.
[113] Ibid. para. 87.

UK cases on refusal to supply

There is very limited case law on refusal to supply in the UK and no such cases appear to have been brought by the OFT.[114] The main case is *Burgess*,[115] which is a case involving access to a crematorium in Stevenage. The plaintiffs, funeral directors in Hertfordshire, complained to the OFT that Austins, also funeral directors in Hertfordshire, which owned the crematorium in Stevenage, had refused to allow them access to it and this was an abuse under s. 18 Competition Act 1998. When the OFT decided that no abuse had been committed, this decision was appealed to the CAT. The CAT took a different position from the OFT, basing itself on these principles (references omitted):[116]

1 An abuse of a dominant position may occur if a dominant undertaking, without objective justification, refuses supplies to an established existing customer who abides by regular commercial practice, at least where the refusal of supply is disproportionate and operates to the detriment of consumers.

2 Such an abuse may occur, in particular, if the potential result of the refusal to supply is to eliminate a competitor of the dominant undertaking in a neighbouring (e.g. downstream) market where the dominant undertaking is itself in competition with the undertaking potentially eliminated, at least if the goods or services in question are indispensable for the activities of the latter undertaking, and there is a potential adverse effect on consumers.

3 It is not an abuse to refuse access to facilities that have been developed for the exclusive use of the undertaking that has developed them, at least in the absence of strong evidence that the facilities are indispensable to the service provided, and there is no realistic possibility of creating a potential alternative.

The CAT added that these principles were not exhaustive and that there might be abuse if a competitor were substantially weakened, but not eliminated. In the circumstances of the case, the CAT found that there had been abuse because there were barriers to entry into the market, the refusal eliminated one of only two competitors in the downstream market (funeral directing), there was no evidence that the refusal to supply was part of normal business practice, the refusal potentially strengthened a dominant position and there was significant consumer detriment.[117] The issue was also raised in *Purple Parking* where there was a dispute over access to forecourts at Heathrow for meet and greet services for passengers arriving there.[118] The case was decided in favour of the plaintiffs on the basis of unlawful discrimination in favour of their own services by Heathrow but it does contain an interesting discussion of the case law and, in particular, the judge's refusal to accept that the plaintiffs are required to show elimination of competition, as opposed to distortion.

---

[114] For more cases see R. Whish and D. Bailey, *Competition Law* (7th edn, Oxford University Press, 2011) at 710.

[115] *M E Burgess and others* v *OFT* [2005] CAT 25.

[116] Ibid. at para. 311.

[117] Ibid. para. 330.

[118] *Purple Parking Ltd* v *Heathrow Airports* [2011] EWHC 911.

US law on refusal to supply and essential facilities

US antitrust law starts from the presumption that everyone is free to choose their own business dealings. This point was made clearly in an old case:[119]

> In the absence of any purpose to create or maintain a monopoly, the [Sherman] Act does not restrict the long recognized right of trader or manufacturer engaged in an entirely private business freely to exercise his own independent discretion as to parties with whom he will deal, and, of course, he may announce in advance the circumstances under which he will refuse to sell.

This is qualified by the phrase, 'in the absence of any purpose to create or maintain a monopoly' and the US courts have recognised a number of exceptions to this general principle. The cases which recognise exceptions are sporadic and some of the earlier ones are not good examples of a refusal to deal by a single, dominant undertaking.[120] Nevertheless, more recent cases seemed to suggest a wider doctrine of refusal to deal, which was labelled 'essential facilities'.

The starting point was a case called *Aspen Skiing*.[121] This case involved two companies, Aspen and Highlands, who controlled downhill skiing in Aspen, Colorado, a very famous high-quality ski resort. Aspen controlled three of the mountains in the area, while Highlands controlled only one. They agreed between themselves to produce 'All Aspen' tickets which allowed skiers to use all four mountains, usage was monitored and revenues were split in proportion to usage. The arrangement broke down because Aspen wanted a greater share of the revenue and, when Highlands refused to do this, Aspen then exited the sharing arrangement and produced its own deal for its three mountains. It also refused to cooperate with Highlands in any arrangements to allow Highlands customers access to Aspen's mountains. Highlands brought an action against Aspen for breach of s. 2 Sherman Act and was successful at trial. The decision was eventually heard by the Supreme Court which decided the case in favour of Highlands. Although the Supreme Court accepted that Aspen had a right to choose its business partners, that right was not unqualified. Here Aspen had made an important change in a pattern of distribution that had originated in a competitive market[122] and had persisted for several years. The question the Supreme Court asked was whether the record supported the jury's implied conclusion that there were no good business justifications for the refusal. The Supreme Court found that this was the case, founding itself on the superiority of the All Aspen ticket, the effect of the refusal to cooperate on Highlands and the lack of business justification for the behaviour. It concluded: 'the evidence supports an inference that [Aspen] was not motivated by efficiency concerns and that it was willing to sacrifice short-run benefits and consumer goodwill in exchange for a perceived long-run impact on its smaller rival.'[123] There was no recourse to the essential facilities doctrine in this case.

---

[119] *United States* v *Colgate & Co.*, 250 US 300 (1919) at 307. See also Antitrust Modernisation Commission op. cit., note 37 at 101.

[120] For example, *United States* v *Terminal Railroad Association*, 224 US 383 (1912); *Associated Press* v *United States*, 326 US 1 (1945).

[121] *Aspen Skiing Co* v *Aspen Highlands Skiing Corp*, 472 US 585 (1985). See also *Otter Tail Power* v *United States*, 410 US 366 (1973).

[122] Originally each mountain had been owned by a separate company.

[123] Ibid. at 610–611.

The *Aspen* case has been heavily criticised and the Supreme Court in *Trinko* described it as being at the limit of antitrust liability under s. 2 Sherman Act.[124] In terms of its own facts, it seems defensible as involving the termination of an existing relationship, without any business justification that clearly harmed consumers.[125] The approach taken in *Aspen* found its way into cases which argued for an essential facilities doctrine of which perhaps the most influential was the *MCI* case, a decision of the Seventh circuit.[126] This was described as an 'extraordinary' antitrust case brought by a new entrant in the telecommunications industry, MCI, against the incumbent monopoly, AT & T, alleging, among other things, that AT & T had not allowed it to interconnect with the appropriate networks. The court said that there were four requirements for the doctrine:[127]

1   control of the essential facility by a monopolist;
2   a competitor's inability practically or reasonably to duplicate the essential facility;
3   the denial of the use of the facility to a competitor; and
4   the feasibility of providing the facility.

It took the view that the network that MCI wanted to connect to was a natural monopoly and that it would not be economically feasible to duplicate it and nor would regulatory permission have been given.

A very different attitude was seen in the Supreme Court case of *Verizon v Trinko*.[128] Here the Telecommunications Act 1996 had imposed a duty on incumbent local telephone exchange carriers to provide access to, among other things, unbundled network elements, including access to operating support systems. An interconnection agreement was approved by Federal and State regulators and, when competitors complained that Verizon had failed to meet its obligations, the regulators investigated, found a breach, and imposed penalties and remedial measures. The plaintiffs sued on the basis that Verizon had responded to competitors' orders in a discriminatory manner as part of an anti-competitive scheme to prevent customers moving and that this was a violation of s. 2 of the Sherman Act. Justice Scalia, writing the opinion of the court, distinguished these facts from previous case law because the services allegedly withheld were not otherwise marketed or available to the public absent the scheme under the Telecommunications Act. The Act created a brand new obligation to share something which existed 'only deep within the bowels of Verizon'. One of the Supreme Court's points is that there is a difference between a company producing a product or service for consumption by consumers, to which it refuses a competitor access, and where what is being asked for is access to something new. Although the Court did not comment on the essential facilities doctrine, its holding places strong limits on any further development.

It is often said that US antitrust law takes a very different attitude to refusal to supply cases then EU law and certainly, if *Trinko* is focused on, this appears to be the case. The US case law is more nuanced than this and cases can certainly be found which go as far as some of the European court decisions.[129] One of the important differences seems to have been the enthusiasm of the European Commission to push for a broad approach to this doctrine, which is

---

[124] *Verizon Communications v Trinko*, 124 S Ct 872 (2004).
[125] See Hovenkamp (n. 34) at s. 7.5.
[126] *MCI Communications Corp v AT & T* 707, F 2d 1081 (1983).
[127] Ibid. at 1132–3.
[128] *Verizon Communications v Trinko*, 124 S Ct 872 (2004).
[129] For example, *Hecht v Pro-Football*, 570 F 2d 982 (1977) – access to the Washington Redskins football stadium.

related to pushing for the liberalisation of certain sectors in advance of specific legislation and the lack of a careful inquiry into factual circumstances by the GC in the *Microsoft* case. There are a number of good and compelling reasons why an expansive interpretation of the refusal to supply case law would be a negative development for competition law. Saying that, however, is not the same thing as saying that it should be interpreted out of existence.

Conclusions

Article 102 TFEU is a provision which is drafted in quite broad terms. Although there was initially uncertainty about its scope, the history of its enforcement by the European Commission and the Courts shows a primary concern with exclusionary behaviour which damages the competitive structure of markets and involves the unfair use of commercial power. In the earlier cases this seemed to involve a lack of economic analysis, focusing on the particular circumstances of the case and a more general approach where certain forms of conduct were viewed with suspicion. The difficulties with this approach have been exacerbated by a broad and uncertain concept of dominance which has arguably captured too many undertakings. Recently there has been a move towards greater economic analysis and a greater emphasis on consumer welfare, best exemplified by the European Commission's discussion paper and subsequent guidance on exclusionary abuses, which in many ways take a very different approach to Article 102 TFEU and one that is in line with other steps towards the modernisation of EU competition law, notably in relation to Article 101 TFEU and vertical agreements, as well as merger control. This new approach is controversial and, unlike Article 101 TFEU, changing the interpretation of Article 102 TFEU is more of a task for the Courts rather than the European Commission. What this means is that we are at a very interesting point in the evolution of Article 102 TFEU, which could go in different directions, an issue which may also be influenced by the changes in the objectives of the European Union contained in the reform treaty.

Summary

➤ Exclusive dealing, price discrimination and discounts and rebates tend to be treated as similar phenomena by the case law. The economic evidence suggests that such practices may be both pro- and anti-competitive and a careful case-by-case analysis is needed. The law on the subject takes a different approach and both the European Commission and the Courts have been very suspicious of such practices. It is an abuse of a dominant position if undertakings promise to obtain all or most of their requirements exclusively from a dominant undertaking whether the obligation in question is stipulated without further qualification or whether it is undertaken in consideration of the grant of a rebate. Fidelity rebates are to be distinguished from quantity rebates, exclusively linked with the volume of purchases from the producer concerned, which are generally considered not to have this effect, although *Michelin II* suggests that the issue is not entirely straightforward.

➤ Tying and bundling can be seen to be common commercial practices which may give rise to efficiencies. There are, however, circumstances in which these practices can be anti-competitive. For tying and bundling to be an abuse of dominant position, four criteria have to be met:

1   the tying and tied products are two separate products;
2   the undertaking concerned is dominant in the market for the tying product;
3   the undertaking concerned does not give customers a choice to obtain the tying product without the tied product; and
4   the practice in question forecloses competition.

➤ Competition law doctrines relating to refusal to supply and essential facilities are in tension with general views about freedom to choose contracting partners and intellectual property rights. Nevertheless, case law has developed specifying that, in certain circumstances, dominant undertakings must not refuse supply or must allow access by new customers. The case law suggests that four conditions must be met:

1   the refusal relates to a product or service indispensable to the exercise of a particular activity on a neighbouring market;
2   the refusal is of such a kind as to exclude any effective competition on that neighbouring market;
3   the refusal prevents the appearance of a new product for which there is potential consumer demand (this appears only in the IP cases); and
4   the refusal is not objectively justified.

Further reading

Price discrimination, loyalty, discounts and rebates

Ridyard, D., 'Exclusionary Pricing and Price Discrimination Abuses under Article 82 – An Economic Analysis' (2002) 23 *European Competition Law Review* 286. *Excellent explanation of relevant economic issues in the context of EU law.*

Tying and bundling

Langer, J., *Tying and Bundling as a Leveraging Concern under EC Competition Law* (Kluwer, Deventer, 2007). *Comprehensive monograph.*

Nalebuff, B., *Bundling, Tying and Portfolio Effects* (2003) DTI Economics Paper No. 1, available at: *http://www.bis.gov.uk/files/file14774.pdf* (accessed 22/07/09). *Difficult to find but an excellent introduction to the economic issues.*

Refusals to supply and essential facilities

Areeda, P., 'Essential Facilities: An Epithet in Need of Limiting Principles' (1990) 58 *Antitrust Law Journal* 841. *Classic article on problems with the doctrine.*

Geradin, D., 'Limiting the Scope of Article 82EC: What can the EU learn from the US Supreme Court's judgment in Trinko in the wake of Microsoft, IMS and Deutsche Telekom?' (2004) 41 *Common Market Law Review* 1519.

Ridyard, D., 'Essential Facilities and the Obligation to Supply Competitors' (1996) 8 *European Competition Law Review* 438. *Clear explanation of the economic issues in the context of the case law.*

Temple Lang, J., 'Defining Legitimate Competition: Companies' Duties to Supply Competitors and Access to Essential Facilities' (1994) 18 *Fordham International Law Journal* 437. *Influential article by senior European Commission official.*

Objective justification

Albors-Llorens, A., 'The role of objective justification and efficiencies in the application of Article 82 EC' (2007) 44 *Common Market Law Review* 1727. *Overview of the case law.*

Loewenthal, P.-J., 'The defence of "objective justification" in the application of Article 82 EC' (2005) 28 *World Competition* 455. *Overview article.*

Reform

Akman, P., 'The European Commission's Guidance on Article 102 TFEU: From Inferno to Paradiso?' (2010) 73 *Modern Law Review* 605.

Bishop, S. and Marsden, P., 'The Article 82 Discussion Paper: A Missed Opportunity' (2006) 2 *European Competition Journal* 1–7. *Criticises Discussion Paper for not placing more emphasis on harm to competition as opposed to competitors.*

EAGCP, *An Economic Approach to Article 82 EC* (2005). *Report by panel of economists to DG Comp on their preferred approach to Article 82.*

European Commission, *Discussion paper on the application of Article 82 of the Treaty to exclusionary abuses* (2005). *The Commission's discussion of how Article 82 might be reformed.*

European Commission, *Guidance on the commission's enforcement priorities in applying Article 82 of the EC Treaty to abusive exclusionary conduct by dominant undertakings* (2008). *The Commission's statement of its approach to Article 82 and its enforcement priorities in the light of discussion about the reform of Article 82.*

European Commission, Public Hearing on Article 82, available at: *http://ec.europa.eu/competition/antitrust/art82/hearing.html. Web broadcast of public discussion of Article 82 and proposals in Discussion Paper. Need to understand basic issues before listening to this.*

Gormsen, L., 'Why the European Commission's enforcement priorities on Article 82 EC should be withdrawn' (2010) *European Competition Law Review* 45.

Gravengaard, M. and Kjaersgaard, N., 'The EU Commission guidance on the exclusionary abuse of dominance – and its consequences in practice' (2010) *European Competition Law Review* 285.

Motta, M., 'The European Commission's Guidance Communication on Article 102' (2009) 30 *European Competition Law Review* 59.

Ridyard, D., 'The Commission's Article 102 guidelines: Some reflections on the economic issues' (2009) 30 *European Competition Law Review* 230.

Sher, B., 'The Last of the Steam-Powered Trains: Modernising Article 82' (2004) 25 *European Competition Law Review* 243–6. *Short piece setting down principles for modernising Article 82.*

Temple Lang, J., 'Article 102 EC – The Problems and the Solution' (2009) available at: *http://papers.ssrn.com/sol3/papers.cfm?abstract_id=1467747* (accessed 19/07/12).

Witt, A., 'The Commission's guidance paper on exclusionary conduct – more radical than it appears?' (2010) 35 *European Law Review* 214.

5

Public enforcement of competition law

Chapter outline

This chapter discusses:

➤ The aims of enforcement
➤ The rules and practice of the European Commission
➤ Judicial review of Commission decisions by the Union Courts
➤ The allocation of cases between the Commission and national competition authorities
➤ The enforcement of competition law in the UK by the OFT
➤ Judicial review of OFT decisions by the CAT.

Introduction

The aims of enforcement

It does not matter how well designed the substantive rules of competition law are, if there are no mechanisms for their effective enforcement. The rules governing the procedures for the enforcement of EU and UK competition law are complex and the aim of this chapter is to provide an overview of the major provisions and the underlying policy issues surrounding them, rather than a comprehensive exposition.[1] We can start by asking, what are the aims of an effective system of competition law enforcement? In general terms, these can be said to be as follows:

1 to deter undertakings from committing breaches of competition law;

2 to compensate undertakings and individuals who are damaged by breaches of competition law; and

3 to work in an efficient and procedurally fair manner.

---

[1] See L. Ortiz Blanco, *EC Competition Procedure* (2nd edn, Oxford University Press, 2006) and M. Brealey, N. Green and K. George, *Competition Litigation: UK Practice and Procedure* (Oxford University Press, 2010).

In order to accomplish these aims, enforcement can be undertaken by the public authorities, such as the European Commission and the Office of Fair Trading (OFT), or by those individuals or undertakings who are damaged by anti-competitive actions, which is referred to as private enforcement. Historically, enforcement activity in the EU and UK has been undertaken almost entirely by public agencies, rather than through private enforcement. This contrasts very strongly with the US, where it has been estimated that 95% of antitrust cases are brought by private actions and the system as a whole has been described as relatively decentralised, with enforcement split between two government agencies – the Department of Justice and the Federal Trade Commission – the attorney generals of the respective states and private plaintiffs.[2] In addition, the sanctions for breach of antitrust law in the US are very tough: breach of the rules may be a criminal offence which, as well as leading to fines, may also result in the imprisonment of individuals. As regards civil cases, plaintiffs may claim treble damages for breach of antitrust law. Add this incentive to a contingency fee system for lawyers, as well as the possibility of class actions, and it can be seen that there are large incentives for people to bring private actions. However, recently there has been a concerted effort at both EU and UK level to encourage greater use of private actions to enforce competition law and move to something which is closer in appearance to the American system, although probably still with a greater emphasis on public enforcement. Private enforcement is discussed subsequently (see Chapter 6) but one of the underlying aims of this and the following section is to get the reader thinking about what should be the relationship between public and private enforcement.[3]

The structure of this chapter is that a brief introductory discussion of the aims of enforcement is followed by a detailed explanation of the law and practice of the European Commission relating to enforcement. The next section of the chapter discusses enforcement in the UK by the OFT.

Enforcement aims: general reflections

From the point of view of economists, the main damage done by anti-competitive practices is a societal one – the deadweight loss to consumer welfare that occurs under monopoly – rather than a concern with damage to individual consumers or competitors. Therefore the primary issue is how to deter this sort of conduct, rather than provide compensation for damage. In terms of deterrence, the law and economics literature starts from the assumption that businesses aim to maximise their profit and take decisions in accordance with this view.[4] If that is the case, then they will engage in anti-competitive activity if it is profitable to them. They will be deterred from acting anti-competitively if they think that the likelihood of detection and punishment will impose greater costs on them than the profitability of the activity. This can be expressed as a formula (see Box 5.1).

---

[2] See H. Hovenkamp, *The Antitrust Enterprise* (Harvard University Press, 2005) at p. 58; C. Jones, *Private Enforcement of Antitrust Law in the EU, UK and USA* (Oxford University Press, 1999), ch. 2.

[3] For a stimulating overview, see C. Hodges, 'European Competition Enforcement Policy: Integrating Restitution and Behavioural Control' (2011) 34 *World Competition* 383.

[4] The classic statement is G. Becker, 'Crime and Punishment: An Economic Approach' (1968) 76 *Journal of Political Economy* 169. See also OFT, *OFT's Guidance as to the appropriate amount of a penalty: A consultation on OFT guidance* (2011) at para. 3.9.

EXAMPLE   **Box 5.1**

Rational deterrence formula[5]

If A stands for gains of anti-competitive activity, B stands for the monetary sanction (fine) and C for the probability of detection then if $B \times C > A$, the business will not engage in the activity. If $B \times C < A$, then it is profitable to engage in the activity.

Questions: How easy is it to make this calculation? Is the only loss for a business the monetary sanction? What about business reputation?

This is a commonsense intuition but it has dramatic repercussions in terms of fixing the levels of fines because it suggests that the appropriate way to set the fine is to multiply the expected gain in inverse proportion to the probability of detection, thus ensuring that the fine exceeds the gains for the business. The point is made neatly by Veljanovski, a well-known senior economics consultant and expert witness:

> . . . if the fine is €100 million but only one in three cartels are successfully prosecuted, then the *expected* fine is 33 percent of the €100 million, or only €33 million. The corollary is that in order to deter price-fixers, the fine must be grossed-up (multiplied) so that the *expected* fine equals the aggregate consumers' loss. Taking the same figures and assuming that the €100 million measures consumers' loss, the optimal fine with a conviction rate of 33 percent is three times loss i.e. €300 million.[6]

More recently, the same point was put in an *Economist* blog:[7]

> One rule of thumb antitrust economists use is that cartels can achieve overcharges of 20–30%. But the agencies that police cartels use fines of between 10–40% (Britain's watchdog is at the weak end of the scale, America's is more beefy). Mr Becker's crime calculus shows the problem with this: with a 50% detection rate, and fines ranging between 10–40%, the expected cost of cartel crime is in the 5–20% range. Use a 10% detection rate, and expected punishment costs fall to 1–4%. So the expected benefits outweigh the costs. At the moment, it seems, some corporate crimes pay handsomely.

This idea is familiar from the United States, where treble damages are available for breaches of antitrust law in civil proceedings and, in criminal proceedings, fines of twice the gross gain to the offender or twice the gross loss to the victims can be imposed. As we shall see later, policy in the EU has never been as clear-cut as this, and there is a cap on fines, which are not allowed to exceed 10% of the worldwide turnover of an undertaking. A crucial variable in this equation is the detection rate of cartels and there is, unsurprisingly, no robust data on this. Veljanovski refers to some estimates of cartel detection, from the US, which suggest that

---

[5] Compare with *Fight Club*: 'A new car built by my company leaves somewhere traveling at 60 mph. The rear differential locks up. The car crashes and burns with everyone trapped inside. Now, should we initiate a recall? Take the number of vehicles in the field, A, multiply by the probable rate of failure, B, multiply by the average out-of-court settlement, C. A times B times C equals X. If X is less than the cost of a recall, we don't do one.'

[6] C. Veljanovski, 'Cartel Fines in Europe' (2007) 30 *World Competition* 65 at 80–1. Emphasis in original.

[7] http://www.economist.com/blogs/freeexchange/2012/07/economics-crime?fsrc=scn/tw/te/bl/iscrimerational (accessed 26/07/12).

between one in seven or one in ten cartels were detected, and a French paper estimates a detection rate of around 13% in Europe based on a sample between 1969 and 2007.[8] If these figures are applied to the example above, the fine rises to over €600 million or €1,000 million, which might raise questions about the continuing viability of an undertaking subjected to such a fine.

A second aim of competition law enforcement would seem to be ensuring that those who are damaged by anti-competitive action receive sufficient compensation. This implies the need for effective private actions, as the fines imposed by public agencies are paid into the public purse, rather than as compensation to those who have been injured by the behaviour. Here the calculation of the appropriate amount will be done on a different basis from that of the public agency because the primary aim is not deterrence, although the provision for treble damages in American law combines both deterrence and compensation. Compensating all the victims of anti-competitive activity can lead to difficult calculations. Imagine a price-fixing cartel, where the victims are the direct purchasers of the good, who will have paid a higher price, those people who purchased the good from the direct purchasers and those people who would have bought the good if the price had been at a competitive level. Those direct purchasers who resell the good may also claim damage due to loss of profits because of lower profits either through selling less at higher prices or because they absorbed the higher, non-competitive price. Calculating damages in these contexts is a very complex exercise and (as we shall see in Chapter 6) not one that either European or British law has yet got to grips with. American law, by contrast, operates a number of pragmatic rules which deny recovery to certain classes and thus make the calculation easier.

The third aim for enforcement is procedural fairness. The problem here comes about because in EU and UK law the European Commission and the OFT combine a number of enforcement functions. They investigate potential breaches of competition law, decide whether a breach has occurred and impose a penalty if one has occurred. They are effectively police, prosecutor and judge in one institution, subject to control only by appeal to the European Courts and the Competition Appeal Tribunal (CAT). There have consistently been complaints over the years that this institutional arrangement, at European level, is in breach of the guarantees in the European Convention on Human Rights, in particular Article 6. Such generalised complaints have not been successful in front of the European Courts, but the European Commission has modified its procedure over the years in order, partly, to meet some of these objections. In addition, there are more specific complaints that existing procedures breach specific human rights protections, notably the right to privacy and the right against self-incrimination. This has been much less of an issue at the UK level, where the system has been designed quite carefully to be compatible with the European Convention on Human Rights because it is clear that, under the Human Rights Act 1998, the OFT, as a public body, is required to comply with these rights. At the EU level, the European Convention is not yet part of European Union law, although it is recognised that the rights it protects form part of Union law. The interpretation of these rights has, however, at times seemed to be at odds with that of the European Court of Human Rights.

---

[8] Ibid. at 81. E. Combe, C. Monnier and R. Legal, 'Cartels: The probability of getting caught in the European Union', available at *http://papers.ssrn.com/sol3/papers.cfm?abstract_id=1015061*. See also P. Ormosi, 'How Big is a Tip of the Iceberg? A Parsimonious Way to Estimate Cartel Detection Rate' (between 10 and 20%) available at: *http://papers.ssrn.com/sol3/papers.cfm?abstract_id=1851309* (both accessed 27/07/12).

European Commission procedures[9]

Starting the process

Figure 5.1 gives an overview of the process.

An investigation into whether there has been a breach of Articles 101 and 102 TFEU can be started by the European Commission either on its own initiative or in response to a complaint. In practice, this division is not clear-cut, as the European Commission claims that it encourages the submission of information about anti-competitive practices which falls short of a complaint.[10] Although there is not much public information about how the European Commission decides on its enforcement priorities, it does seem that complaints from consumers and customers are an important factor as well as, more recently, the conclusions of sectoral inquiries under Article 17 of Regulation 1/2003. An example of the latter is where, in July 2007, proceedings were initiated against E.ON and Gaz de France for a market-sharing agreement in relation to the French and German gas markets, partly because of information that came about from the sectoral inquiry into the energy industry in Europe. The two companies were ultimately fined a total of €553 million for breaching Article 101 TFEU.[11]

As regards complaints, these can be initiated by any natural or legal person who can show a legitimate interest and by Member States, using the form prescribed by the European Commission.[12] According to the European Commission, undertakings are entitled to claim a legitimate interest if they are operating on the same market and the conduct complained of directly and adversely affects their interests. This can include parties to an agreement, competitors affected by the conduct complained about or undertakings excluded from a distribution system.[13] Consumer associations can also claim a legitimate interest, as can consumers, insofar as they are the buyers of goods or services that are affected by the claimed infringement.[14] If a person does not meet these criteria, the information provided can still be considered by the European Commission, although they will not have further procedural rights.[15]

When the European Commission receives a complaint, it has been established in the case law that the Commission has discretion to decide what to do about the complaint.[16] According to its guidelines, the European Commission must carefully examine the factual

---

[9] Generally see European Commission, 'Notice on best practices for the conduct of proceedings concerning Articles 101 and 102 TFEU', OJ 2011 C 308/06 20.10.2011.

[10] See European Commission, 'Notice on the handling of complaints by the Commission under Articles 81 and 82 of the EC Treaty', OJ C101, 27.04.2004, paras 3–4.

[11] European Commission Case Comp/39.401, *E.ON/GDF collusion*, 8 July 2009 (the full decision is only available in German and French) and Case T-360/09 *E.ON Ruhrgas AG v Commission*, judgment of 29 June 2012 (GC). See also the sending of a statement of objections to Lundbeck and others for preventing market entry of generic anti-depression medicine following the pharmaceutical sector enquiry: Commission Press Release IP/12/834 25 July 2012.

[12] Council Regulation (EC) No. 1/2003 of 16 December 2002 on the implementation of the rules on com-petition laid down in Articles 81 and 82 of the Treaty OJ L1, 04.01.2003, pp. 1–25 at Art. 7(2) (hereafter 'Regulation 1/2003'); European Commission, 'Notice on the handling of complaints by the Commission under Articles 81 and 82 of the EC Treaty' (n. 10), para. 26.

[13] European Commission, 'Notice on the handling of complaints by the Commission under Articles 81 and 82 of the EC Treaty' (n. 10) para. 36.

[14] Ibid., para. 37.

[15] European Commission (n. 9) at note 18.

[16] Case T-24/90 *Automec Srl v Commission* [1992] ECR II-2223.

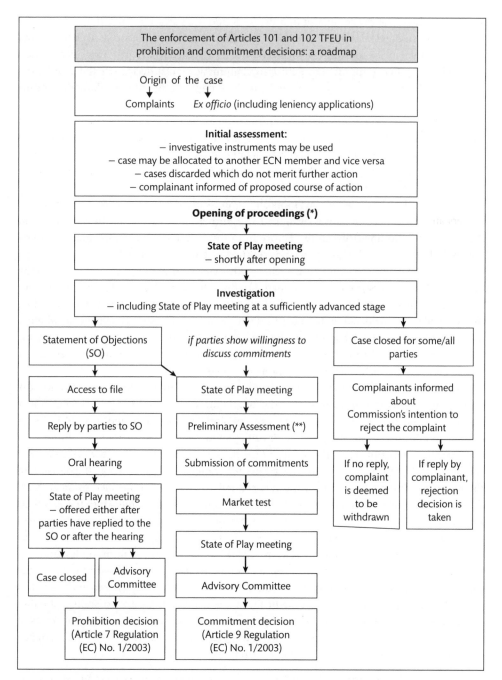

Figure 5.1 European Commission procedures in Articles 101 and 102 TFEU cases

Notes: (*) With the exception of cartel proceedings, where the opening of proceedings normally takes place simultaneously with the adoption of the Statement of Objections.

(**) If an SO has already been issued, a Preliminary Assessment is not required.

Source: European Commission, 'Notice on best practice for the conduct of proceedings concerning Articles 101 and 102 TFEU', OJ C308/06 20.10.2011.

and legal elements of the complaint in order to decide what action to take. It is not required to undertake further investigation, nor is it required to make a decision as to whether the conduct complained of constitutes a breach of Articles 101 and 102 TFEU.[17] Considering itself as an administrative authority, the European Commission must decide whether it is in the interests of the European Union to investigate the complaint. Broadly speaking this means that the Commission must take into account the duration and extent of the infringements alleged, their effect on the internal market, the probability of establishing the infringement and the difficulty of conducting such an investigation. Complaints are usually rejected if the European Commission feels that the complainant could bring an action to assert their rights before a national court, if the conduct complained of has ceased or if a national competition authority is dealing with the case.[18]

When a complaint is received the European Commission operates a three-stage procedure.[19] In the first stage, the complaint is examined and further information may be collected, and there may be a meeting between the European Commission and the complainant at which the preliminary view of the Commission is communicated. In the second stage, the European Commission may investigate the case further, with a view to initiating proceedings, or it may decide no further investigation is warranted. If it does the latter, then it will inform the complainant and give them a chance to make further observations. If no reply is received, then the complaint is considered withdrawn. In the third stage, a decision is taken as to whether to proceed further with the complaint. The importance of the decision at this stage is that this is an act of the European Commission which may be the subject of a judicial review under Article 263 TFEU, which is discussed in more detail later.

This process can be summarised by saying that complainants have no right for the European Commission to investigate their complaint, let alone initiate proceedings under Articles 101 and 102 TFEU. The European Commission has a broad discretion to decide what cases it should investigate and what its priorities should be. What it is required to do is to consider the complaints properly and give reasons, via a judicially reviewable act, as to why it has decided to reject a complaint. This allows the complainant to challenge the decision in the European Union Courts. Under the very centralised system that operated prior to 2004, the rights of complainants was a very controversial topic as many undertakings felt that their only chance of challenging anti-competitive practices was through getting the European Commission to investigate them. The European Commission was reluctant to take up these cases in a number of areas, notably selective distribution systems for automobiles, and was ultimately supported in this by the European Courts, whilst being criticised in terms of the procedures it operated for dealing with complaints.[20] Since 2004, this has become much less of a live issue, partly because it is evident that there is a much greater possibility of either private actions or getting national competition authorities to investigate alleged breaches of competition law and partly because the case law makes it clear that, ultimately, the European Commission may make its own decision on what cases to pursue.

---

[17] European Commission, 'Notice on the handling of complaints by the Commission under Articles 81 and 82 of the EC Treaty' (n. 10), paras 41–42.

[18] Ibid., para. 44; Regulation 1/2003, Art. 13. Generally, see European Commission, *Annual Report on Competition Policy* (2005), ch. 3.2, point 26.

[19] 'Notice on the handling of complaints by the Commission under Articles 81 and 82 of the EC Treaty' (n. 10), paras 55–7.

[20] C.S. Kerse, 'The complainant in competition cases: a progress report' (1997) 34 *Common Market Law Review* 213 discusses the development of the case law.

Investigation and fact-finding by the European Commission

Once the European Commission has decided to investigate an agreement or conduct, the first stage is to obtain information. Like all regulatory authorities, the European Commission suffers from what is called 'information asymmetry', that is, the best information about the allegedly anti-competitive practices is in the hands of the undertakings being investigated, rather than the authority. It is critical, therefore, that the European Commission has sufficient information-gathering powers, particularly as undertakings which are engaging in anti-competitive practices may go to some lengths to hide the evidence of their misbehaviour. For example, in the elevators and escalators cartel, the participants took a number of steps to avoid being detected such as meeting outside their own country, using private and pre-paid mobiles, not keeping written notes of meetings, submitting false expenses claims and pretending to meet as a trade association.[21]

The starting point of the powers is Article 18 of Regulation 1/2003 which allows the European Commission, by simple request or by decision to require undertakings and associations of undertakings to provide all necessary information. Such a request or decision must state the legal basis and purpose of the request, specify the information which is required and the time limit within which it is to be provided. Regardless of whether it is a request or a decision, Article 17(4) states that the recipients of the request *shall supply* the information requested and the case law makes it clear that undertakings are under an obligation to cooperate actively with the investigation.[22] There are penalties for supplying incorrect or misleading information, and, as regards decisions to require information, there is scope for periodic penalty payments to be fixed. Decisions to require information must make it clear that the decision can be reviewed by the Court of Justice. In addition, Article 19 provides that there is a power to interview persons, if they consent, for the purpose of collecting information for an investigation.

Such powers would not be enough on their own, as undertakings will have a strong incentive to conceal information from the European Commission when it is investigating. Therefore, under Article 20 of Regulation 1/2003, the European Commission has the power to conduct necessary inspections of undertakings and associations of undertakings without giving advance notice of the inspection and Article 20(4) specifies that undertakings are required to submit to these inspections. These are popularly referred to as 'dawn raids', although they do not necessarily take place at dawn, more likely at the beginning of business hours.[23] The officials conducting the investigation must produce a written authorisation specifying the subject matter and purpose of the investigation and outlining the possible penalties. Article 20(2) empowers an official to:

- enter any premises, land and means of transport of undertakings;
- examine the books and other records related to the business;
- take or obtain in any form copies or extracts from the books or records;
- seal business premises and books or records (to prevent tampering); and
- ask any representative or member of staff of the undertaking for explanations on facts or documents relating to the inspection.

---

[21] European Commission Case COMP/E-I/38.823 *Elevators and Escalators*, 21 February 2007, paras 153, 219–21, 304–7 and 583.

[22] Case 374/87 *Orkem* v *Commission* [1989] ECR I-3283 at para. 27.

[23] The Dutch Competition Authority has produced a video which illustrates the process from the Dutch perspective: *http://www.youtube.com/watch?v=5diFAaJdweI* (accessed 05/09/12).

The power to enter premises has been extended by Article 21 of Regulation 1/2003 to any other premises, land and means of transport, including the homes of directors, managers and other members of staff of undertakings and associations of undertakings if reasonable suspicion exists that books or other records relating to the business, which may be relevant to prove a serious violation of Articles 101 and 102 TFEU, are being kept there.

These are extensive powers to gather information and they are exercised on a regular basis by the European Commission. For example, in July 2012 the European Commission announced that it had carried out unannounced inspections on the premises of undertakings involved in plastic pipes and plastic pipe fittings in the sewerage sector.[24] Not surprisingly, the exercise of these powers has been challenged by undertakings on a regular basis, primarily on human rights grounds, especially regarding breach of privacy, breach of the right against self-incrimination and a lack of judicial supervision.

Enforcement and human rights

Before discussing this case law in more detail, the relationship between the European Convention on Human Rights (ECHR) and European Union law needs to be explained. The European Convention is an international treaty which is binding on its signatories, which include the Member States of the European Union[25] but not the European Union itself as an international organisation. Indeed, the case law of the CJEU held that the EU was not entitled to become a signatory of the ECHR.[26] Article 6 of the *old* Treaty on European Union did say, however, that the Union shall respect fundamental rights, as guaranteed by the ECHR and as they result from the constitutional traditions common to the Member States, as general principles of Community [Union] law. The European Union Courts have also consistently held that, as part of the general principles of Community law, there is respect for fundamental human rights within the Union legal order.[27] So what this means is that, in principle, challenges on human rights grounds are legitimate but that the interpretation of human rights obligations will not necessarily be the same in EU law as under the ECHR, as decisions of the European Court of Human Rights are not binding on the CJEU and GC. This position is set to change after the European Reform Treaty, as the new Article 6 of the Treaty on European Union recognises the rights and principles set out in the EU's Charter of Fundamental Rights and gives them the same legal value as the Treaties. The Charter itself says that, insofar as such rights correspond to those in the European Convention, they shall have the same meaning and scope. In addition, Article 6(2) says that the EU 'shall' accede to the European Convention. There are, however, various issues which will need to be resolved before the EU can accede to the Convention.[28] The process of accession has proved to be a protracted one and the details still remain to be resolved.[29] So, although in principle the legal position has not changed, it is reasonable to

---

[24] See European Commission Press Notices MEMO/12/549 11 July 2012.

[25] As well as a number of states that are not members of the EU, such as Turkey and Russia.

[26] Opinion C-2/94 *Accession of the Community to the ECHR* [1996] ECR I-1759.

[27] See Case 4/73 *Nold* v *Commission* [1974] ECR 491.

[28] See R. White, 'The Strasbourg Perspective and its Effect on the Court of Justice: Is Mutual Respect Enough?' in A. Arnull, P. Eeckhout and T. Tridimas (eds) *Continuity and Change in EU Law. Essays in Honour of Sir Francis Jacobs* (Oxford University Press, 2008).

[29] A good description of the process is at: *http://blogg.uio.no/jus/smr/multirights/content/the-eus-accession-to-the-echr-negotiations-to-resume-after-7-month-hiatus* (accessed 26/07/12).

think that the EU courts will be more careful to ensure that their judgments are consistent with the case law of the European Court of Human Rights. To make matters more difficult, the ECHR was signed in 1950, before any modern competition law regimes were created and its provisions, which were aimed at defending citizens against totalitarian regimes, do not mesh that easily with modern regulatory agencies, as we shall see. There has been a substantial debate over whether EU decision making procedures are compatible with the obligations contained in the ECHR, but this is dealt with below, after discussion of the working of the decision making process.

Privacy

As regards investigations under Article 20, a good starting point is the issue of privacy. Article 8 of the ECHR provides for a right of respect for private life and a set of conditions under which a public authority may interfere with the exercise of this right, and is outlined in Box 5.2.

KEY LEGAL PROVISION   **Box 5.2**

European Convention on Human Rights and Fundamental Freedoms, Article 8

1 Everyone has the right to respect for his private and family life, his home and his correspondence.

2 There shall be no interference by a public authority with the exercise of this right except such as is in accordance with the law and is necessary in a democratic society in the interests of national security, public safety or the economic well-being of the country, for the prevention of disorder or crime, for the protection of health or morals, or for the protection of the rights and freedoms of others.

Question: What does the word 'necessary' mean?

Whether the provisions of what is now Article 20 constituted a breach of Article 8 was considered in some depth in *Hoechst*.[30] This was a case involving an investigation into a suspected cartel in the material PVC which involved price-fixing and market sharing. When the European Commission's inspectors arrived at the offices of Hoechst, they were refused entry, on the grounds that this was an unlawful search. After a couple more fruitless attempts, the European Commission adopted a decision imposing periodic penalty payments on Hoechst and Hoechst challenged the decisions imposing the penalty, as well as the original decision to order an investigation. The CJEU held that Article 8 did not apply to business premises and that the European Commission was entitled to call for the assistance of the national authorities, which means that it was required to respect the relevant procedural guarantees laid down by national law. This meant that, ultimately, the decision whether to allow the inspection would be up to the national body that could authorise such an action. However, the CJEU pointed out that the national body could not substitute its own assessment of the need for the investigation for that of the European Commission, although it could decide whether the investigation was arbitrary or excessive.

---

[30] Cases 46/87 and 227/88 *Hoechst AG v Commission* [1989] ECR 2859.

The case law of both the CJEU and the European Court of Human Rights has developed on this issue, with it becoming clear from decisions under the ECHR that Article 8 does apply to business premises.[31] As regards the role played by national bodies in authorising inspections, this was discussed again in *Roquette Frères*,[32] a case where the European Commission had asked the French authorities for assistance in an inspection and the French authorities had applied to the relevant French court for permission, which was granted. The undertaking challenged the authorisation, on the ground that it should not have been granted, given the limited information provided to the court. The issue was referred to the CJEU by means of a preliminary reference from the French Cour de Cassation, roughly the equivalent of the Court of Appeal. The CJEU accepted that case law subsequent to *Hoechst* had established that, in certain circumstances, Article 8 protection could extend to business premises, but it also pointed out that the right of interference established in Article 8(2) could be more extensive in these circumstances.[33] In deciding this issue, the CJEU reiterated that it was the job of the national court to ensure that there was nothing arbitrary about the coercive measures that the European Commission intended to employ. In order to ensure that was the case, the European Commission was required to provide explanations showing that they were in possession of evidence and had reasonable grounds for suspecting an infringement of the competition rules. What the European Commission did not have to do was to provide the actual evidence and information that it had in its possession.[34] In addition, the CJEU also recognised that the national court could examine the proportionality of the inspection request, taking into account the seriousness of the suspected infringement, the involvement of the undertaking concerned and the importance of the evidence sought and, in principle, a request for an authorisation could be refused on these grounds.[35] These rules are now effectively summarised in Article 20(8) of Regulation 1/2003 (see Box 5.3).

KEY LEGAL PROVISION   Box 5.3

Regulation 1/2003, Article 20(8)

Where [an] authorisation . . . is applied for, the national judicial authority shall control that the Commission decision is authentic and that the coercive measures envisaged are neither arbitrary nor excessive having regard to the subject matter of the inspection. In its control of the proportionality of the coercive measures, the national judicial authority may ask the Commission, directly or through the Member State competition authority, for detailed explanations in particular on the grounds the Commission has for suspecting infringement of Articles 81 and 82 of the Treaty [101 and 102 TFEU], as well as on the seriousness of the suspected infringement and on the nature of the involvement of the undertaking concerned. However, the national judicial authority may not call into question the necessity for the inspection nor demand that it be provided with the information in the Commission's file. The lawfulness of the Commission decision shall be subject to review only by the Court of Justice.

Question: How effective is this provision in protecting undertakings from unjustified investigations?

---

[31] *Nimitz* v *Germany* [1992] ECHR 80.
[32] Case C-94/00 *Roquette Frères* v *Directeur Général de la Concurrence* [2002] ECR I-9011.
[33] Ibid., para. 29.
[34] Ibid., paras 60–70.
[35] Ibid., paras 79–86. See also Case T-339/04 *France Telecom* v *Commission* [2007] ECR II-521.

Self-incrimination

Given the amount and type of questions that the European Commission may ask of under-takings, the next question relates to the privilege against self-incrimination. Article 6 of the ECHR guarantees the right to a fair trial, but does not say anything explicitly about self-incrimination. However, the European Court of Human Rights has held that anyone charged with a criminal offence within the meaning of Article 6 had the right to remain silent and not contribute to incriminating themselves and that included the right not to produce incriminat-ing documents.[36] In a subsequent case, the Court of Human Rights also ruled that the use of incriminating statements in a criminal trial obtained by Department of Trade and Industry inspectors through the use of their compulsory powers of investigation under the Companies Act was oppressive and undermined the defendant's right to remain silent.[37] This right only applies to respecting the will of the accused and his or her decision to remain silent; it does not apply to material which might be obtained through compulsory powers but has an independent existence, such as, among other things, documents acquired pursuant to a warrant.[38]

The Courts of the European Union have addressed this issue on a number of occasions. Before looking at this case law, a preliminary issue must be dealt with because the protection of Article 6 against self-incrimination applies only in relation to criminal charges, a concept which has its own meaning under the law of the European Convention. According to Article 23(5) of Regulation 1/2003, penalties imposed under this article are not of a criminal law nature and the CJEU has also said that competition law is distinct from criminal law.[39] On the other hand, fines for substantive breaches of the competition rules can be substantial, running into millions of euros and do have the purpose, as expressed by the European Commission, of deterring undertakings from committing further breaches of the rules. These certainly look like the characteristics of criminal penalties. Furthermore, in *Société Stenuit* v *France*,[40] the European Commission *of Human Rights* (as distinct from the Commission of the European Union) held that a fine imposed on undertakings by the French competition authorities was criminal in nature; and when the issue has been raised in front of the CAT in the UK it has been assumed by all concerned that the proceedings are criminal in nature.[41] The weight of opinion does seem to be against the view of the European Union Courts, which suggests that the principle against self-incrimination should apply in these cases.

The issue was dealt with first in the *Orkem* case,[42] which involved the European Com-mission's investigation into a suspected PVC cartel, and was decided before the relevant decisions of the European Court of Human Rights. The Commission sent a number of questions to Orkem, the company, asking for:

- factual information about a meeting;

- clarification on every step or concerted measure which may have been envisaged or adopted;

[36] *Funke* v *France* (1993) 16 EHRR 297.
[37] *Saunders* v *United Kingdom* (1997) 23 EHRR 313.
[38] Ibid., para. 69.
[39] Case 374/87 *Orkem* v *Commission* [1989] ECR 3283 at para. 31. But compare with the opinion of AG Sharpston in Case C-272/09P *KME Germany and others* v *Commission* [2012] 4 CMLR 10.
[40] (1992) 14 EHRR 509.
[41] *Napp* v *Director General of Fair Trading* [2002] CAT 1 at para. 98. See also the discussion in *Safeway* v *Twigger* [2010] EWHC 11 Comm.
[42] Case 374/87 *Orkem* v *Commission* [1989] ECR 3283.

- details of any system or method which made it possible to attribute sales or targets or quotas to the participants; and

- details of any methods facilitating annual monitoring of compliance with any system of targets in terms of volumes or quotas.

The decision to ask these questions was challenged on the basis that it breached a general principle against self-incrimination. The CJEU held that the principle against self-incrimination was only relevant in criminal law, not competition law and that, although undertakings could rely on Article 6 ECHR in competition proceedings, neither the wording of the Article nor decisions of the European Court of Human Rights indicated that the principle against self-incrimination was included within it. Nevertheless, the CJEU held that the rights of an undertaking to defend itself must not be irremediably impaired during the investigative procedure. Therefore, although the undertaking could be compelled to provide documents to the European Commission, it could not be compelled to provide answers to questions which might involve an admission on its part of the existence of an infringement. On this basis, the CJEU annulled all but the first of the questions listed above.

The reasoning of the CJEU in this case, insofar as it was based on its views about the place of self-incrimination in Article 6, was obviously not accurate, so the question was raised again in *Mannesmannröhren-Werke v Commission*.[43] Here the European Commission was conducting an investigation into an alleged cartel in the seamless tube industry and asked a number of questions relating to meetings. They asked for dates, places, names of participants, copies of agendas, minutes, and records relating to them and, 'in the case of meetings for which you are unable to find the relevant documents, please describe the purpose of the meeting, the decisions adopted and the type of documents received before and after the meeting'. The undertaking refused to answer these questions and the European Commission adopted a decision requiring answers and imposing periodic penalty payments for the period the questions remained unanswered. This decision was appealed to the GC, which applied the test in *Orkem* and held that the question asking about the purpose of the meetings and the decisions adopted went beyond mere factual information as they might compel the undertaking to admit to participation in an unlawful agreement and were thus annulled.

Subsequent case law has not deviated from this position, even though the CJEU has recognised that the case law of the European Court of Human Rights has developed, the principle established in *Orkem* did not require modification and the European Commission's powers as regards the production of documents had not been limited.[44] The CJEU held that, if the European Commission requests the documents, they must be provided by the undertaking, even if they could be used to establish the existence of an infringement. The CJEU pointed out that the undertaking is still able to argue, in proceedings before the European Commission or the Courts, that the documents do not have the meaning that the European Commission ascribes to them.[45]

The position of the Courts is understandable, as the European Commission's position would be made impossible if undertakings could refuse to provide documents on the grounds of self-incrimination. Although it has been claimed that this position is incompatible

---

[43] Case T-112/98 *Mannesmannröhren-Werke v Commission* [2001] ECR II-729.
[44] Case C-301/04P *Commission v SGL Carbon* [2006] ECR I-5915 at para. 43.
[45] Ibid., paras 44 and 49.

with the case law of the European Court of Human Rights,[46] there are some grounds for thinking that the conflict is not that severe. First, the ECHR case law, albeit with some inconsistency, seems to suggest that there is a legitimate distinction between documents (which have an independent existence) and testimony (which depends on the person's willingness to consent). Secondly, the ECHR cases have all involved individuals, as opposed to companies, and it is at least arguable that a less strict standard should apply in the context of competition law, where there is no threat of imprisonment. However, the European Court of Human Rights dismissed this type of argument in the *Saunders* case, where the defendant was convicted of criminal offences in relation to, among other things, share dealing, on the basis of evidence he had been compelled to provide in a previous investigation.

Legal privilege[47]

One further point to be noted is that it has been recognised that, in European Union competition law, there is legal privilege between lawyers and their clients.[48] In other words, communications between an undertaking and their lawyers are confidential and do not have to be disclosed to the European Commission. However, unlike the principle within English law which applies to communications with all lawyers, the EU rule only applies to communications between undertakings and their *external* lawyers;[49] communications with in-house lawyers are not protected by legal privilege. This ruling has, not surprisingly, generated a substantial amount of controversy and is regularly opposed by lawyers' associations. It still remains the rule and this was confirmed in *Akzo Nobel*,[50] where the dispute was over the treatment of an internal memorandum which the undertaking claimed had been created in order to seek legal advice and copies of emails to an in-house lawyer. The GC held that documents prepared exclusively for the purpose of seeking legal advice from a lawyer for exercising an undertaking's rights of defence could be covered by privilege, but that this exception to the European Commission's power to obtain documents should be interpreted restrictively.[51] As regards communications with in-house lawyers, the GC reiterated the rule in *AM&S v Commission*, finding that there were no reasons to change it and that changes in EU competition law, notably the ending of the notifications systems and the need for undertakings to self-assess agreements and conduct, did not require an extension of privilege to in-house lawyers.[52] This position was affirmed by the CJEU.

The decision making process

Once the European Commission has obtained the information, analysed it and decided that the undertaking(s) have a case to answer, then the second stage of proceedings begins. Article 27 of Regulation 1/2003 states that before taking decisions which have a negative

---

[46] A. Riley, 'Saunders and the Power to Obtain Information in Community and United Kingdom Competition Law' (2000) 25 *European Law Review* 264.

[47] European Commission (n. 9) at paras 51–8 explains the Commission's practice.

[48] Case 155/79 *AM&S v Commission* [1982] ECR 1575.

[49] Reports and summaries of external legal advice are covered by privilege: Case T-30/89 *Hilti v Commission* [1990] ECR II-163.

[50] Case T-125/03 *Akzo Nobel v Commission* [2007] ECR II-3523, [2008] 4 CMLR 3. On appeal, Case C-550/07P *Akzo Nobel v Commission* [2010] ECR I-8301.

[51] Ibid., paras 123–4.

[52] Ibid., paras 169–77.

impact on an undertaking, the European Commission shall give them an opportunity to be heard on the matters it objects to and that its decisions shall be based only on objections to which the parties concerned have been able to comment. Article 27(2) says that the rights of defence of the parties shall be fully respected and they shall be entitled to access to the European Commission's file, subject to the legitimate interests of undertakings in the protection of their business secrets. The right of access to the file does not extend to confidential information and internal documents of the European Commission and the national competition authorities. These rules are underpinned by general principles of European Union law that parties who are affected by decisions of the Union authorities must be able to make their views known and, in order to do so, must know the case against them.[53]

It is easy to state these general principles, but implementing them in practice has proved to be highly controversial. First, the combination of functions within the European Commission means that often the same officials who do the investigations and decide that there is a potential competition law problem are the ones who assess the response of the undertakings to their concerns. As Wils, a senior European Commission official, has pointed out, this leads to a suspicion that there is a confirmation bias, in other words that the officials only look for evidence that supports their initial hypotheses.[54] Secondly, there are a number of tensions surrounding the right of access to the file. The European Commission may have based its case in part on information received from other undertakings, notably competitors and customers, who would be unhappy, to put it mildly, if their input became known to the subjects of competition investigations. In addition, there is also the issue as to what extent the European Commission must give details of its thinking and analysis to the parties, in order to allow them to defend themselves effectively. Finally, there has been the suggestion that there is a significant amount of lobbying in important competition cases and that this is not properly regulated in the decision making process.[55]

The starting point for this part of the procedure is the issue by the European Commission of a Statement of Objections (SO), which is given to the parties and notified to the Member States. This is a critical document because it sets out the case against the parties, both factually and legally, and any decision must be based on material in the SO. The parties are given a time limit to reply and may request an oral hearing, which must be granted if requested.[56] As well as setting out the case against the parties, the SO also includes a list of the documents that the European Commission is relying on in its proposed decision.

The basic principle regarding access to the file is that this must be available to the parties who are subject to the procedure, but not the complainants.[57] The file consists of all the documents which have been obtained, produced or assembled by the European Commission during their investigation[58] and access must be given to documents regardless of whether, in the opinion of the European Commission, those documents represent evidence against the

---

[53] Case 17/74 *Transocean Marine Paint Association* v *Commission* [1974] ECR 1063.

[54] W. Wils, *Principles of European Antitrust Enforcement* (Hart Publishing, Oxford, 2005), ch. 6 at pp. 164–5.

[55] See J Temple Lang, 'Three Possibilities for Reform of the Procedure of the European Commission in Competition Cases under Regulation 1/2003' (Centre for European Policy Studies, 2011).

[56] Commission Regulation (EC) No. 773/2004 relating to the conduct of proceedings by the Commission pursuant to Articles 81 and 82 of the EC Treaty, OJ L123, 27.04.2004, pp. 18–24, Art. 12 (hereafter Regulation 773/2004).

[57] Regulation 1/2003, Art. 27(2); Regulation 773/2004, Art. 15.

[58] Commission, 'Notice on the rules for access to the Commission file in cases pursuant to Articles 81 and 82 of the EC Treaty and Council Regulation (EC) No. 139/2004', OJ C325, 22.12.2005, p. 7 (at para. 8).

parties or evidence which would go in their favour.[59] Article 15 of Regulation 773/2004 makes clear the limits on access to the file (see Box 5.4).

KEY LEGAL PROVISION   **Box 5.4**

Access to the file

The right of access to the file shall not extend to business secrets, other confidential information and internal documents of the Commission or of the competition authorities of the Member States. The right of access to the file shall also not extend to correspondence between the Commission and the competition authorities of the Member States or between the latter where such correspondence is contained in the file of the Commission.

Source: Regulation 773/2004, Article 15.

A failure to communicate a document constitutes a breach of the rights of the defence, and so allows the decision to be annulled, only if the European Commission relies on that document to support its case concerning the existence of an infringement and if the objection could only be proved by reference to that document.[60] The case law also draws a distinction between incriminating and exculpatory (i.e. something which shows innocence) documents. In the former case, if there is other evidence, the undertaking has to show that the decision would have been different. In the latter case, the undertaking simply has to show that it would have been able to use the exculpatory material in its defence and it would have had some influence on the European Commission's assessment.[61]

As will be evident from the discussion so far, the bulk of the procedures are conducted in written form, although there is a provision for an oral hearing. Oral hearings are conducted under the auspices of the Hearing Officer, a post created in 1982 with the aim of providing further procedural guarantees for the parties being accused of breaches of competition law. The Hearing Officer, while a member of staff of the European Commission, is independent of the case team in a particular investigation. The Hearing Officer is responsible for organising the oral hearing, deciding which parties may appear, dealing with disputes over access to the file and writing a report, which is meant to cover both the procedural aspects of the hearing, as well as the objectivity of the inquiry as regards any commitments proposed in relation to the proceeding.[62] The Hearing Officer also deals with disputes over claims to legal professional privilege, disputes over access to the file and disclosure of business secrets and confidential information, requests for extensions of time and requests by third parties to participate in the process.

Decisions by the European Commission

Having started the process, for the European Commission there are a number of possible outcomes:

---

[59] Cases C-204–5, 211, 213, 217 and 219/00P *Aalborg Portland A/s v Commission* [2004] ECR I-123 at para. 68.
[60] Ibid., para. 71.
[61] Ibid., paras 72–7.
[62] Decision of the President of the European Commission 13 October 2011 on the function and terms of reference of the hearing officer in certain competition proceedings [2011] OJ L275/29.

- it may reach a settlement with the parties (only in relation to cartels);
- the parties may agree to enter into legally binding commitments to resolve the identified problem.

If the European Commission decides that there has been an infringement of Articles 101 and 102 TFEU:

- it may order the undertakings to cease their behaviour;
- it may impose fines for the breach of competition law; or
- it may impose behavioural or structural remedies.[63]

Before discussing these matters, we need to examine two other issues: the power of the European Commission to order interim measures and the possibility of the undertakings entering into commitments rather than seeing the adoption of a formal decision.

Interim measures

Article 8 of Regulation 1/2003 provides that in cases of urgency due to the risk of serious and irreparable damage to competition, the European Commission may, on the basis of a *prima facie* finding of infringement, order interim measures. The basic idea here is that, because competition proceedings may be protracted and take several years, it must be possible to prevent further harm to competition taking place during the course of the proceedings. Although this power was not recognised explicitly in the old procedural Regulation (17/62), case law of the European Courts had established that the European Commission could take action on an interim basis.[64] Typically this happened at the request of a competitor and this was reflected in the test applied by the Courts, which stated that there must be a situation of proven urgency where there would otherwise be serious and irreparable damage to the party seeking the measure or damage which would be intolerable to the public interest.[65] Under the new provision, where the European Commission can take action under its own initiative, this has been interpreted by the European Commission as meaning that complainants cannot apply for interim measures but should look to their national courts for help in such circumstances.[66] We should note as well that the power in Article 8 is confined to cases where the problem is damage to *competition*, which is not necessarily the same as damage to a competitor, although there may be some overlap. The European Commission did not take any interim measures decisions between 2004 and 2009 and does not appear to have taken any since 2009.[67]

Commitments by undertakings to solve the problem

Article 9 of Regulation 1/2003 is a new provision, which states as follows (in Box 5.5).

---

[63] Regulation 1/2003, Art. 7.
[64] Case 792/79R *Camera Care* v *Commission* [1980] ECR 119.
[65] Case T-44/90 *La Cinq SA* v *Commission* [1992] ECR II-1.
[66] Commission, 'Notice on the handling of complaints' (n. 10), para. 80.
[67] See European Commission, 'Staff working paper accompanying the Communication from the Commission to the European Parliament and Council report on the functioning of Regulation 1/2003' COM (2009) 206 final, para. 111.

KEY LEGAL PROVISION   **Box 5.5**

Power to accept undertakings

Where the Commission intends to adopt a decision requiring that an infringement be brought to an end and the undertakings concerned offer commitments to meet the concerns expressed to them by the Commission in its preliminary assessment, the Commission may by decision make those commitments binding on the undertakings.

Source: Regulation 1/2003, Article 9.

Questions: What does a preliminary assessment mean? What sort of commitments might be acceptable?

The idea behind this provision is that infringements, where a fine is not appropriate,[68] can be brought to an end without the European Commission having to prove its case and go through the time and expense of a formal decision. Since it obtained this power, the European Commission has used it regularly to resolve cases under both Articles 101 and 102 TFEU. In the UK, the most high-profile case was the one affecting the FA's Premier League and the collective selling of media rights to broadcast football matches: that is, the Premier League sells the rights to broadcast the matches as a package, rather than the clubs selling their matches on an individual basis. The European Commission was concerned that this collective selling, which at the time was done exclusively to one broadcaster, Sky, led to foreclosure of the downstream media markets, that is, television broadcasting. The FA therefore offered a deal whereby, from 2007, competing packages of live matches would be offered, so that there would be at least two broadcasters of live matches, which were initially Sky and Setanta.[69]

This procedure has also been used in a number of cases such as Coca-Cola's policy in relation to the distribution of its products in the EU and the liberalisation of the gas market in Belgium.[70] Their use in the energy sector is discussed in more detail later (see Chapter 15). There are, however, a number of uncertainties about how this procedure should work. An important one is what is meant by the term 'preliminary assessment' in Article 9. It has been suggested that this does not have to be a Statement of Objections, as this involves a great deal of work by the European Commission, which may not be necessary in order to let the undertaking know its concerns.[71] This does not, however, seem to be correct in the light of the *Alrosa* case.[72] This case involved agreements for the sale of rough diamonds between De Beers,

---

[68] Regulation 1/2003, Recital 13.

[69] European Commission, 'Notice published pursuant to Article 19(3) of Council Regulation No. 17 concerning case COMP/C.2/38.173 and 38.453 – joint selling of the media rights of the FA Premier League on an exclusive basis' [2004] OJ C115/02. A similar decision was reached in relation to the German Bundesliga in the first ever decision using Article 9: see Press Release IP/05/62 of 19 January 2005, which contains a link to the detailed commitment, summarised in OJ L134/46. Setanta's rights in the UK have been taken over by ESPN.

[70] European Commission, 'Decision relating to a proceeding pursuant to Article 82 of the EC Treaty Case COMP/A.39.116/B2 Coca-Cola, 22 June 2005, COMP/37.966 Distrigaz, 11 October 2007'. See R. Whish and D. Bailey, *Competition Law* (7th edn, Oxford University Press, 2012) at pp. 259–60 for a list of cases up until 2010.

[71] L. Ortiz Blanco (n. 1) at para. 13.10.

[72] Case T-170/06 *Alrosa v Commission* [2007] ECR II-2601; on appeal, Case C-441/07P *Commission v Alrosa* [2010] ECR I-5949. And see the Advocate General's Opinion of 17 September 2009.

a South African undertaking which is the world's largest diamond producer, and Alrosa, a Russian company which is the other main producer of diamonds in the world. The two undertakings agreed that Alrosa would supply to De Beers effectively all of the production that it would make available outside Russia, thus enabling De Beers to maintain control of the rough diamond market. Alrosa and De Beers initially offered joint commitments, which would lead to a progressive reduction in De Beers' purchases of rough diamonds from Alrosa, but the European Commission preferred a later commitment, made by De Beers alone, which ultimately led to De Beers agreeing not to purchase any diamonds from Alrosa. This was challenged in the General Court (GC) by Alrosa on the grounds that it was, among other things, disproportionate. The GC said that the European Commission must:

> establish the reality of the competition concerns which justified its envisaging the adoption of a decision under Articles 81 EC and 82 EC [101 and 102 TFEU] and which allow it to require the undertaking concerned to comply with certain commitments. This presupposes an analysis of the market and an identification of the infringement envisaged which are less definitive than those which are required for the application of Article 7(1) of Regulation No. 1/2003, although they should be sufficient to allow a review of the appropriateness of the commitment.[73]

This seems to suggest that what is required is a Statement of Objections and that anything less formal will be insufficient. The GC went on to annul the decision for breach of the principle of proportionality because other, less onerous solutions to the problem of exclusive purchasing could have been adopted, rather than prohibiting transactions between De Beers and Alrosa.[74] The case was appealed to the CJEU, which reversed the decision, taking a different view on proportionality.[75] The CJEU said that remedies under Article 7 have to be proportionate to the infringement that has been established while remedies under Article 9 aim to address the Commission's concerns following its preliminary assessment. As the Court put it:

> Undertakings which offer commitments on the basis of Article 9 of Regulation No. 1/2003 consciously accept that the concessions they make may go beyond what the Commission could itself impose on them in a decision adopted under Article 7 of the regulation after a thorough examination. On the other hand, the closure of the infringement proceedings brought against those undertakings allows them to avoid a finding of an infringement of competition law and a possible fine.[76]

In particular, the Commission is not required to seek out less onerous commitments than the parties have offered to it; the only question is whether the commitments offered meet its concerns.[77]

The second issue is that Regulation 1/2003 makes it clear, in Recitals 13 and 22, that decisions about commitments are reached without the European Commission concluding that there is an infringement of either Article 101 or 102 TFEU. Therefore, those decisions are without prejudice to the powers of national competition authorities and national courts to make a finding and decide upon the case. Although clear, this is surprising because it opens up the possibility that, in private litigation, a national court might come to the conclusion that the commitments do not meet the competition issues and that an infringement continues

---

[73] Ibid., para. 100.
[74] Ibid., para. 126.
[75] Case C-441/07P *Commission v Alrosa* [2010] ECR I-5949.
[76] Ibid., para. 48.
[77] Ibid., para. 61.

to exist.[78] This in turn leads to the possibility of divergent interpretations of EU competition law, depending on which forum the dispute is decided in and, as we will see later when discussing the *Crehan* case (Chapter 6), it is not a fanciful speculation.

Fines

The European Commission's power to impose fines for a substantive breach of competition law is probably the most high-profile of its enforcement powers. The starting point is Article 23(2) of Regulation 1/2003, which provides that the Commission *may* impose fines where undertakings either intentionally or negligently infringe Article 101 or 102 TFEU, contravene a decision imposing interim measures or fail to comply with a binding commitment under Article 9. In fixing the amount of the fine, the European Commission must have regard to the gravity and the duration of the infringement. There is an upper limit of 10% of the total turnover in the preceding business year of each undertaking taking part in the infringement. These provisions, which are similar to the older arrangements under Regulation 17/62, give the Commission a substantial amount of discretion in determining the level of the fine that it will impose for an infringement and its policy has developed over the years, beginning with a low level of fines originally and gradually becoming tougher to the point where, in absolute terms, the fines look to be very high, as is illustrated by Tables 5.1 and 5.2.

The European Commission has been criticised for a lack of transparency in its fining practice and it first responded to this with a set of Guidelines in 1998, which have been replaced by a new set in 2006, which have been presented as representing a tougher approach to fining policy. A preliminary point is that the Commission has always wanted to retain some level of discretion in its fining practice, so that it would not be possible for undertakings to do a precise calculation of the cost of their infringement and set that against the potential profits. The guidelines have always, therefore, contained a number of elements which are open to interpretation.

Table 5.1 Ten largest fines by company

Case	Fine (€ millions)	Date	Case	Fine (€ millions)	Date
Intel	1,006	2009	Microsoft	497	2004
Microsoft	899	2008	Thyssenkrupp I	480	2007
St Gobain	896	2008	Hoffmann-La Roche	462	2001
E.On	553	2009	Siemens AG 1	397	2007
GDF Suez	553	2009	Pilkington	370	2008

Table 5.2 Ten largest fines by sector

Case	Fine (€ millions)	Date	Case	Fine (€ millions)	Date
Car glass	1,383	2008	Paraffin waxes	676	2008
Gas	1,106	2009	Butadiene rubber	519	2006
Elevators and escalators	992	2007	Flat glass	487	2007
Vitamins 2	790	2001	Plasterboard	458	2002
Gas insulated switchgear	750	2007	Hydrogen peroxide	388	2006

Source: http://ec.europa.eu/competition/cartels/overview/faqs_en.html (accessed 26/07/12) with Intel and Microsoft cases added. These figures are before court judgments, which have tended to reduce them.

[78] Generally, see Ortiz Blanco (n. 1) at paras 13.21–13.26. In theory, this might be open to a national competition authority as well, but this is unlikely in practice.

The new Guidelines are deceptively simple in their principles.[79] The European Commission determines a basic amount and then it adjusts that amount up or down to take into account aggravating or mitigating circumstances. The first step in determining the basic amount is to take the value of the sales to which the infringement directly or indirectly relates with the relevant geographic area. Once this is established, a proportion of the value will be taken, depending on the gravity of the infringement, up to a maximum of 30%, which will be multiplied by the duration of the infringement. In addition, the European Commission will also include an additional sum, what has been called the 'entry fee', of between 15 and 25% of the value of sales to deter undertakings from entering into horizontal price-fixing, market sharing and output limitation agreements, although the entry fee is not limited to horizontal agreements and could apply to, for example, a vertical agreement with absolute territorial restrictions.

Having determined the basic amount, this is then adjusted in the light of aggravating or mitigating circumstances. Aggravating circumstances includes repeat offences, which can result in the basic amount being increased by up to 100%, refusal to cooperate with the Commission or obstructing its investigations, being the leader or instigator of the infringement or taking action to penalise other members of the cartel. In addition, there may be a specific increase to ensure that the fines have sufficient deterrent effect or to ensure that the fine exceeds the amount of gains made. Mitigating circumstances, which are separate from the leniency programme discussed below, include where the undertaking provides evidence that it terminated the infringement as soon as the Commission intervened, where it has committed the infringement negligently, where its involvement was substantially limited, where it has cooperated outside the leniency Notice and beyond its legal obligations, and where the conduct has been authorised or encouraged by the public authorities. In exceptional circumstances the Commission may take into account the undertaking's ability to pay the fine.

From this brief description it can be seen that important elements in the calculation of a fine will depend on the judgment of the Commission, for example on the gravity of the infringement, whether an entry fee should be applied and whether an undertaking is a leader in the cartel. There are a number of ambiguities in the Guidelines and certain factors seem to be taken into account in more than one place: for example, the deterrent effect of a fine. It is also not clear that they will be able to reflect either the loss to consumers from the practices or the gains of the undertakings, particularly if we bear in mind that there is a 10% cap on fines, based on an undertaking's turnover. For an overall assessment of fining policy, it is important to consider the leniency programme and its effects as well.

The leniency programme

The leniency programme addresses a problem faced by all competition authorities, which is that they have very limited information about what is happening in industry and that it can be very difficult for them to detect the existence of cartels, particularly if those cartels are trying to avoid detection. The basic idea behind the policy of leniency is that, if an undertaking notifies the competition authorities of an infringement of competition law, that undertaking should receive a lesser penalty, or no penalty at all, because without its cooperation the infringement would not have been detected. Economic theory suggests that cartels are unstable and a leniency programme provides an incentive on participants to break the cartel

---

[79] European Commission, *Guidelines on the method of setting fines imposed pursuant to Article 23(2)(a) of Regulation No. 1/2003*, OJ C210, 01.09.2006.

arrangements. Because of its importance in relation to cartel enforcement, this programme is discussed later in the text (see Chapter 8).

Settlement procedures

The European Commission has recently introduced procedures for settlement in cartel cases which is in addition to the leniency programme.[80] The idea behind this is that, in cartel cases, there is not much dispute about the substance of the case once the European Commission has gathered the appropriate evidence but undertakings are concerned about the level of the fine and, procedurally, the case can be complex because of concerns about confidentiality and requests for the use of multiple different languages.[81] The details of this are discussed later (see Chapter 8).

Judicial review of European Commission decisions

Decisions by the European Commission are subject to challenge in front of the GC under the grounds set out in Article 263 TFEU (see Box 5.6).

KEY LEGAL PROVISION   **Box 5.6**

Article 263 TFEU (ex Article 230 EC)

The Court of Justice shall review the legality of acts adopted . . . by the . . . Commission . . . , other than recommendations and opinions, . . .

It shall for this purpose have jurisdiction in actions brought by a Member State, the European Parliament, the Council or the Commission on grounds of lack of competence, infringement of an essential procedural requirement, infringement of the Treaties or of any rule of law relating to their application, or misuse of powers.

. . . Any natural or legal person may, under the same conditions, institute proceedings against a decision addressed to that person or against a decision which, although in the form of a regulation or a decision addressed to another person, is of direct and individual concern to the former.

The proceedings provided for in this article shall be instituted within two months of the publication of the measure, or of its notification to the plaintiff, or, in the absence thereof, of the day on which it came to the knowledge of the latter, as the case may be.

Questions: What is the difference between review of legality and an appeal on the merits? What might direct and individual concern mean?

---

[80] European Commission, 'Notice on the conduct of settlement procedures in view of the adoption of Decisions pursuant to Article 7 and Article 23 of Council Regulation (EC) No. 1/2003 in cartel cases', OJ C167, 02.07.2008, pp. 1–6; 'Commission Regulation (EC) No. 622/2008 of 30 June 2008 amending Regulation (EC) No. 773/2004, as regards the conduct of settlement procedures in cartel cases', OJ L171, 01.07.2008, pp. 3–5. For discussion, see A. Stephan, 'The Direct Settlement of EC Cartel Cases' (2009) 58 *International and Comparative Law Quarterly* 627.

[81] See N. Kroes, 'Assessment of and perspectives for competition policy in Europe', speech given on 19 November 2007, Barcelona. Available at *http://ec.europa.eu/competition/speeches/index_2007.html* (accessed 05/09/12).

There is provision as well to challenge the Commission's failure to act under Article 265 TFEU (ex 232 EC) on the basis that the rules of the EU Treaties have been infringed. In relation to decisions by the Commission to impose a fine, the European Courts are stated to have 'unlimited jurisdiction' to review these decisions and may cancel, reduce or increase them.[82]

A number of points are worth bearing in mind. First, note that Member States and EU institutions are always allowed to challenge decisions[83] of the Commission, as well as natural or legal persons who are the subject of decisions. So, undertakings which are the subject of a Commission decision stating that they have infringed either Article 101 or 102 TFEU may challenge such decisions in front of the GC, as well as decisions in relation to a merger. Undertakings that are not the subject of a Commission decision may challenge a decision if they have 'direct and individual concern'. In the context of competition cases, this has been interpreted to cover undertakings that had complained to the Commission, those that had taken part in the proceedings and those that could have taken part in the Commission's proceedings.[84] Simply being a competitor that might be indirectly affected by a decision is not, however, sufficient.[85] Secondly, the initial challenge is made to the GC, from which there is an appeal on a point of law to the CJEU. Factual matters are, therefore, dealt with by the GC, rather than the CJEU, which has been keen to maintain this division of labour.[86] Cases before the GC can take some time (between 2007 and 2011 completed competition cases averaged 45 months)[87] but the CJEU has held that cases must be decided within a reasonable time, which will depend on the circumstances of the case. However, this will only lead to setting aside of the GC's judgment if the length of time had an effect on the outcome of the dispute.[88]

The key question is the standard of review applied by the European courts and the approach is set out in Box 5.7. It is worth reiterating that, although the Courts have consistently stated that the Commission has a margin of appreciation when making complex technical and economic assessments, they have also been prepared to look closely at the factual basis of the decision, as well as the reasoning behind the decision.[89] A more detailed discussion, in the context of mergers is found later in the text (see Chapter 13).

KEY CASE EXTRACT   Box 5.7

Standard of review

Source: Case C-12/03P *Commission* v *Tetra Laval* [2005] ECR I-987 at paras 38–9:

[T]he basic provisions of the Regulation, in particular Article 2, confer on the Commission a certain discretion, especially with respect to assessments of an economic nature, and that,

---

[82] Regulation 1/2003, Art. 31.

[83] 'Decision' covers any measure which produces binding legal effects: Joined Cases T-125/97 and T-127/97 *Coca-Cola* v *Commission* [2000] ECR II-1733.

[84] Case 26/76 *Metro* v *Commission (No. 1)* [1977] ECR 1875; Case 75/84 *Metro* v *Commission (No. 2)* [1986] ECR 3021; Cases T-528/93 etc. *Métropole* v *Commission* [1996] ECR II-649.

[85] Case C-70/97P *Kruidvat* v *Commission* [1998] ECR I-7183.

[86] See Cases 204/00P etc. *Aalborg Portland* v *Commission* [2004] ECR I-123.

[87] CJEU *Annual Report 2011* at 201.

[88] See Case C-185/95P *Baustahlgewebe* v *Commission* [1998] ECR I-8417; Case C-385/07P *Der Grüne Punkt – Duales System Deutschland* v *Commission* [2009] 5 CMLR 19 (five years and ten months was a procedural irregularity but did not lead to overturning the decision).

[89] Generally, see Case C-12/03P *Commission* v *Tetra Laval* [2005] ECR I-987.

consequently, review by the Community [Union] Courts of the exercise of that discretion, which is essential for defining the rules on concentrations, must take account of the margin of discretion implicit in the provisions of an economic nature which form part of the rules on concentrations. Whilst the Court recognises that the Commission has a margin of discretion with regard to economic matters, that does not mean that the Community [Union] Courts must refrain from reviewing the Commission's interpretation of information of an economic nature. Not only must the Community [Union] Courts, inter alia, establish whether the evidence relied on is factually accurate, reliable and consistent but also whether that evidence contains all the information which must be taken into account in order to assess a complex situation and whether it is capable of substantiating the conclusions drawn from it.

Question: How much discretion is left to the Commission under this test?

Human rights and EU enforcement procedures

We have seen that the European Commission has the power to impose substantial fines on undertakings, as well causing them to make important changes in their business practices. The European Commission has also become more active on its own initiative since 2004 and the Modernisation Regulation. The process by which its decision making operates has, however, been subject to substantial criticism because it combines the functions of investigator, prosecutor and decider in one body. The combination of more activism and concerns over process has led to a substantial body of criticism of the European Commission's decision making procedures.[90] One of the Commission's responses to this criticism was to give more responsibilities to the Hearing Officer. One of the key questions has been whether the process, as a whole, is compatible with Article 6 of the ECHR (see Box 5.8).

KEY LEGAL PROVISION   **Box 5.8**

European Convention on Human Rights and Fundamental Freedoms, Article 6(1)

In the determination of his civil rights and obligations or of any criminal charge against him, everyone is entitled to a fair and public hearing within a reasonable time by an independent and impartial tribunal established by law. [words omitted]

There are a number of issues that need to be unpicked here. First, can the European Commission be regarded as an independent and impartial tribunal? Secondly, in competition cases, when a sanction is imposed, is this a criminal or a civil matter? Finally, is the

---

[90] I. Forrester, 'Due Process in EC Competition Cases: A distinguished institution with flawed procedures' (2009) 34 *European Law Review* 817; W. Möschel, 'Fines in European Competition Law' (2011) 32 *European Competition Law Review* 369; Editorial, 'Towards a more judicial approach? EU antitrust fines under the scrutiny of fundamental rights' (2011) 48 *Common Market Law Review* 1405.

decision making process as a whole, including any appeal rights before the European Courts, compatible with Article 6 ECHR?

The first question seems relatively easy to answer. Given that the European Commission chooses the cases to investigate, investigates them and decides on the outcome, it is difficult to see it as impartial. The rather hazy role of the Commissioners, as whole, in the decision making process also raises questions as regards its independence. Furthermore, there is no clear internal separation between the investigation/prosecution function and that of making decisions on the evidence before them. The entire process is handled, largely, by the same case team.

If the European Commission cannot be viewed, for the purposes of Article 6(1) ECHR, as independent and impartial, the next question becomes whether the imposition of sanctions is a civil or criminal matter, because greater protections attach to criminal matters. As discussed above, the consensus of opinion is that the imposition of sanctions under Articles 101 and 102 TFEU is a criminal matter.[91] This is not, however, the end of the debate, because the case law of the European Court of Human Rights distinguishes between criminal matters which are part of the 'hard core' of criminal law as opposed to those matters which are not part of the hard core.[92] Again, the difference is that less procedural protections apply to those criminal matters outside the hard core. This becomes particularly important in relation to the third question, which is whether any issues with the decision making process can be cured by a subsequent appeal?

This issue was addressed in *Menarini Diagnostics SRL v Italy*.[93] In this case the plaintiff, a company engaged in marketing diagnostic tests for diabetes, was fined €6 million by the Italian competition authority for engaging in price-fixing practices contrary to the relevant Italian legislation. The plaintiff unsuccessfully appealed this decision to the relevant administrative tribunal and then to the Italian Conseil D'Etat and, finally, to the Court of Cassation. Under Italian law, the administrative tribunal only had power to review the legality of the decision made by the Italian competition authority, not the merits of the decision. The plaintiff brought the case to the European Court of Human Rights, arguing that the sanction imposed was of a criminal nature, which engaged the protection of Article 6 and that Italy was in breach of Article 6 because of the limited jurisdiction of the reviewing tribunal. The Court held that the sanction imposed on the plaintiff was of a penal nature, although not characterised in that manner under Italian domestic law. The Court then held, by six votes to one, that there was not a breach of Article 6(1). There was no difficulty in finding that the administrative tribunal and the Conseil d'Etat were independent judicial bodies; the key question was whether they had sufficient scope to review the decisions of the Italian competition authority. The Court noted that administrative procedures could be different from criminal law in the strict sense and that, although that did not excuse a breach of the protection guaranteed by Article 6, these protections could be provided in different ways. The Court noted that the reviewing powers of the administrative tribunal and the Conseil D'Etat were not limited to a simple control of legality. They could assess whether the Italian competition authority had exercised its powers in an appropriate manner, the grounds of the complaint, the proportionality of the sanction and even the technical [economic] evaluation.

---

[91] The prohibition of a merger would seem to be a civil matter.
[92] *Jussila* v *Finland* (ECHR) at para. 43.
[93] Judgment of 27 September 2011.

There was, therefore, no breach of Article 6(1) ECHR. The importance of this case is that, first, it confirms the view that competition law sanctions are to be considered as criminal sanctions for the purposes of the European Convention on Human Rights and, secondly, that institutional arrangements which combine an administrative body imposing the sanction followed by something short of a full merits appeal to a court are not a breach of Article 6(1).

A similar point arose in the *KME Germany* case,[94] which was an appeal against a decision of the European Commission imposing fines of around €65 million on the group for participating in a cartel in relation to copper plumbing tubes. Among other points, the applicants argued before the CJEU that the GC had not applied the appropriate standard of review to the European Commission's decision and that the GC had been too deferential. The CJEU rejected this argument, pointing out that the review of legality is done on the basis of evidence adduced by the applicant and that the courts could not use the Commission's margin of discretion as a basis for dispensing with the conduct of an in-depth review of the law and of the facts. The review of legality was supplemented by the unlimited jurisdiction provided in Article 17 of Regulation 1/2003 but that this could, in general, only be done on the basis of the points raised by the applicant. The CJEU concluded that the review of legality provided for under Article 263 TFEU, supplemented by the unlimited jurisdiction in respect of the amount of the fine, provided for under Article 31 of Regulation 1/2003, is not therefore contrary to the requirements of the principle of effective judicial protection in Article 47 of the Charter of Fundamental Rights (the equivalent of Article 6(1) ECHR).[95]

Allocation of cases between the European Commission and national competition authorities[96]

Regulation 1/2003 allows national competition authorities (NCAs) and national courts to apply Articles 101 and 102 TFEU, in addition to the European Commission, and therefore one of the issues that arises is that of case allocation, that is, which authority should decide a case? An anti-competitive agreement may cover the territory of one or more Member States. As there has been no harmonisation of procedures, remedies or sanctions, it is important in practical terms to know which competition authority will have the responsibility for investigation of an agreement or conduct.[97] Regulation 1/2003 makes certain provision for the allocation of cases, which has been expanded upon by the creation of the European Competition Network (ECN) and the Commission's 'Notice on cooperation within the Network of Competition Authorities'.[98]

---

[94] Case C-272/09P *KME Germany AG and others* v *Commission* [2012] 4 CMLR 10.

[95] Ibid. para. 133.

[96] Generally, see See European Commission, 'Staff working paper accompanying the Communication from the Commission to the European Parliament and Council report on the functioning of regulation 1/2003' (COM (2009) 206 final), section 5.

[97] European Commission, 'Results of the questionnaire on the reform of Member States (MS) national competition laws after EC Regulation No. 1/2003' (2007) illustrates some of the differences. Available at *http://ec.europa.eu/competition/ecn/index_en.html* (accessed 05/09/12).

[98] European Commission, 'Notice on cooperation within the Network of Competition Authorities', OJ C101, 27.04.2004, pp. 43–53.

The powers within Regulation 1/2003 are available to NCAs, which are designated by the Member States under Article 35. Article 35 simply requires that designation is done to ensure that the provisions of the Regulation are effectively complied with and makes it clear that courts may be designated as well as NCAs. In the UK, the OFT has been designated under Regulation 1/2003, but *not* the Competition Commission, so only the former has powers to apply Articles 101 and 102 TFEU. All the designated competition authorities are members of the ECN, which is a forum for discussion and cooperation in the application and enforcement of EU competition policy. It also provides a framework for the cooperation of European competition authorities in cases where Articles 101 and 102 TFEU are applied.

Although it is expected that, in general, the competition authority that receives the complaint or starts an investigation will be best placed to complete the process, provision is made for the reallocation of cases, preferably at the outset of the procedure. The idea is that a case should be dealt with by the authority best placed to deal with it and there are three cumulative criteria that need to be met by an NCA (Box 5.9).

KEY LEGAL CONCEPT   Box 5.9

Criteria for allocation of cases

- the agreement or practice has substantial direct actual or foreseeable effects on competition within its territory, is implemented within or originates from its territory;

- the authority is able to effectively bring to an end the entire infringement, i.e. it can adopt a cease-and-desist order the effect of which will be sufficient to bring an end to the infringement and it can, where appropriate, sanction the infringement adequately;

- it can gather, possibly with the assistance of other authorities, the evidence required to prove the infringement.

Source: European Commission, 'Notice on cooperation within the Network of Competition Authorities', para. 8.

Questions: How easy do you think these criteria are to operate in practice? To what extent do NCAs have an incentive to claim cases?[99]

Parallel action is also envisaged, for example where there is an agreement between two undertakings in two different Member States, dividing the national markets between themselves. The Commission is said to be well placed if one or several agreement(s) or practice(s), including networks of similar agreements or practices, have effects on competition in more than three Member States (cross-border markets covering more than three Member States or several national markets).[100] To ensure that the Commission knows what NCAs are doing, Regulation 1/2003 provides, under Article 11, that before commencing formal investigative procedures, NCAs must inform the Commission and they must also give it advance notice

---

[99] See European Commission, 'Commission Staff Working Paper accompanying the Report on the functioning of Regulation 1/2003' (SEC 2009) 574 final at Section 5.2.2.

[100] Ibid., para. 14.

before they make a decision. Article 11(6) provides that the initiation of proceedings by the Commission relieves the NCAs of their competence to act on a case under Articles 101 and 102 TFEU, although if the NCA has already started a case, the Commission will only do this after consulting with it. Similarly, Article 13 provides that where an NCA is acting under Articles 101 or 102 TFEU this is sufficient for either another NCA or the Commission to reject the complaint. If the matter has already been dealt with by another NCA, the Commission or an NCA may reject it.

Provision is also made for the sharing of information between NCAs and between NCAs and the European Commission, subject to certain safeguards.[101] Surprisingly, given the emphasis on the importance of leniency programmes, there has been no attempt to harmonise leniency programmes or provide a one-stop shop for leniency applications. There is, however, a model leniency programme which has been launched by the ECN.[102] The Commission Notice makes it clear that an application for leniency to a given NCA is not to be considered as an application to another NCA. It is therefore in the interests of undertakings to apply for leniency to all the relevant competition authorities and, given the importance of timing, probably to do this simultaneously.[103]

Conclusions on enforcement by the European Commission

The reforms instituted by Regulation 1/2003, in particular the end of the notification system, have had, in the Commission's view, a significant and positive effect on its enforcement practice. The Commission's view is that not only has it been able to issue more decisions, particularly in relation to cartels, but also it has been able to take a more proactive stance and to investigate areas which it regards as important to the European economy.[104] In addition, the new procedure for commitment decisions has helped to increase the output of the Commission. Although the absolute number of decisions taken by the Commission is relatively small – for example, the Commission adopted 33 decisions on cartels between 2004 and 2009, and 15 from 2010 to the middle of 2012 – this is buttressed by the work of the national competition authorities, which concluded 50 such cases in the period.[105] This level of enforcement does, however, suggest that there is a valuable supplemental role that could be played by private enforcement (discussed in Chapter 6).

Nevertheless, questions still remain about the enforcement process. There are still questions about whether the level of fines is a sufficient deterrent and whether fines should be reinforced by some form of individual criminal sanction, as is the case in the UK and a couple of other European countries. The enforcement process as a whole, taking into account the time in front of the Commission and the European Courts, is often very lengthy and this raises questions about its effectiveness, particularly in industries which are undergoing rapid change. Finally, there has been a continuing debate over the fairness of the procedures used by the European Commission and it is unlikely that this will disappear.

---

[101] Regulation 1/2003, Art. 12; European Commission, 'Notice on cooperation within the Network of Competition Authorities', paras 26–8.

[102] Available at *http://ec.europa.eu/competition/ecn/documents.html* (accessed 05/09/12).

[103] European Commission, 'Notice on cooperation within the Network of Competition Authorities', para. 38.

[104] See European Commission, 'Staff working paper accompanying the Communication from the Commission to the European Parliament and Council report on the functioning of regulation 1/2003' (COM (2009) 206 final).

[105] Ibid., para. 188.

Enforcement in the United Kingdom by the OFT[106]

Within the UK, the OFT is responsible for the enforcement of the Chapters I and II prohibitions of the Competition Act 1998 as well as enforcement of Articles 101 and 102 TFEU. In a very general sense, the OFT's powers of enforcement and procedures are similar to those of the European Commission but there are also important differences, which stem from it being a domestic authority and decisions made about enforcement in the UK.[107] An outline of the process is contained in Figure 5.2. The OFT is due to be replaced by the Competition and Markets Authority (CMA) in 2014, formed by merging the OFT and the Competition Commission, which will probably lead to some changes in procedures. One of the major reasons behind this change was dissatisfaction with the OFT's enforcement record, both in terms of the number of cases and the amount of time that the process took and this must be borne in mind when reading the subsequent material.[108]

Unlike the European Commission, the OFT has been more explicit in explaining the thinking behind its decisions on which cases it will pursue, spurred on by criticism from the House of Commons Public Accounts Committee, which said that it had been too reliant on complaints and did not start enough investigations on its own initiative.[109] The OFT responded by publishing a competition prioritisation framework in 2006,[110] which has subsequently been updated.[111] The new guidance goes wider than just competition law powers and asks the following questions:

1 What would be the likely direct effect on consumer welfare of an intervention?

2 What would be the likely indirect effect on consumer welfare of an intervention?

3 What would be the additional economic impact on efficiency and/or productivity?

4 Does the work fit in with the OFT's strategy?

5 Is the OFT best placed to act?

6 What would be the impact of the new work on the OFT's current portfolio of work?

7 What is the likelihood of a successful outcome?

8 What are the resource implications of doing the work?

As the guidance makes clear, this is just a framework for thinking about the issues, which requires judgement, rather than a hard and fast set of rules. Consumer welfare here means the benefit to consumers including changes in price, quality and terms of service. The indirect impact of the OFT's work is meant to cover, among other things, the deterrent effect of the work. Like the European Commission, the OFT can act on its own initiative or in response to complaints.

---

[106] Generally, see OFT, *A guide to the OFT's investigation procedures in competition cases* (2011).

[107] A number of regulatory bodies also have concurrent jurisdiction in competition matters with the OFT. For convenience, only the OFT is referred to throughout.

[108] Enterprise and Regulatory Reform Bill, BIS *A Competition Regime for Growth: A consultation on options for reform* (2011).

[109] Public Accounts Committee, *Enforcing competition in markets* (2006, HC 841).

[110] OFT, *Competition prioritisation framework* (2006).

[111] OFT, *Prioritisation Principles* (2008).

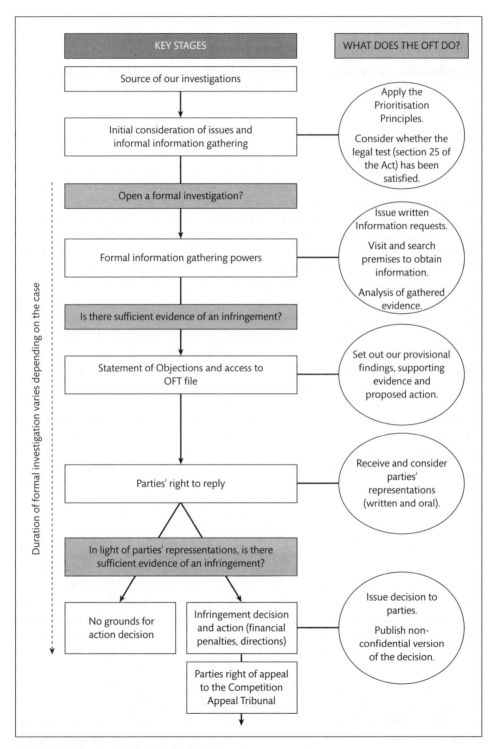

Figure 5.2 Key stages in an investigation

Source: A guide to the OFT's investigation procedures in competition cases (2011)

Complaints to the OFT

There are two categories of complaints to the OFT:

1 individual complaints by consumers or businesses that there has been a breach of competition law; and

2 'super-complaints' by consumer organisations, which have their own statutory regime and are discussed later.

As regards individual complaints, the OFT seems to receive about 1,000 each year but an internal report found that the quality of the complaints was low, that is, they did not provide any sufficient information and only 2% of complaints from consumers and small businesses warranted setting up an investigation as opposed to 10% from large enterprises.[112] There is no guidance in either the legislation or the OFT's Rules on how complaints should be dealt with and the rights of complainants. This topic was addressed in the CAT decision in *Pernod Ricard*,[113] a case where there had been complaints about the commercial practices of Bacardi. Here Pernod, a competitor, had been closely involved in the case as a complainant, giving evidence and making its views known to the OFT. The OFT decided, after around three years of investigation, to accept assurances from Bacardi that it would cease certain activities and closed the file. It did not, however, give Pernod a copy of the statement of objections nor did it consult Pernod about this decision to close the file. Pernod asked the OFT to change its decision, but it refused to do so, so Pernod challenged both the decision to close the file and the refusal to vary the decision. The CAT took the view that, in the absence of any legislative guidance specifically on complaints, and the presence of s. 60 of the Competition Act 1998 which provided for consistency with EU competition law, complainants under the domestic system should have equivalent procedural rights to those which existed under Union law. They therefore took the view that the OFT had been wrong not to allow Pernod to see a non-confidential version of the statement of objections and Pernod should have been asked for their views before a decision on whether to accept the assurances and close the file was taken. The CAT commented that, having regard to the general system of the Competition Act, it was desirable that complainants be given a structured right to be heard before the OFT, rather than having to raise their points at the Tribunal stage.[114]

Perhaps partially as a result of this case,[115] the OFT has revised its guidance for complainants indicating the sort of information that it will require in order for complainants to be given the status of *formal complainants*, which will allow them to comment on certain parts of the OFT procedure, as well as information that the OFT will find useful.[116] In order to become a formal complainant, it is necessary to request this status, to submit a formal written complaint containing information specified in general terms by the OFT and to be a party whose interests are materially affected by the agreement or conduct complained of. Examples of parties who are materially affected would include:

---

[112] National Audit Office, *Enforcing Competition in Markets* (2005, HC 593) at Fig. 13.

[113] *Pernod Ricard* v *Office of Fair Trading* [2004] CAT 10.

[114] Ibid., para. 241.

[115] The OFT's view appears to be that the points of principle in the case were wrongly decided: see Press Release, 1 July 2004, available at *http://www.oft.gov.uk/news/press/2004/bacardi-martini* (accessed 05/09/12).

[116] OFT, *Involving Third Parties in Competition Act Investigations* (2006), Annexes A–C.

- actual or potential competitors denied access to a market,
- a competitor affected by predatory behaviour,
- a customer denied a choice of supplier, and
- a consumers' association whose members are materially affected by the behaviour of which they complain.

Conferral of this status means that complainants will be consulted before a decision to close the file is taken, via a provisional closure letter, and will receive a copy of the final decision to close the file. They will also be sent a copy of any statement of objections issued by the OFT and given a chance to submit their own comments. These rights may be limited in relation to certain cartel cases where the OFT considers that this may give rise to a risk of prejudice to criminal investigations. The OFT may also, at this stage, invite comments from other parties that are materially affected by the behaviour at issue, even if they have not complained. As can be seen, the result is a procedural system which is similar to that operated by the European Commission although, under domestic administrative law, it is clear that a decision on whether to open an investigation is a matter for the discretion of the OFT and that a complainant has no right to have an investigation begun, let alone receive a decision that there has been a breach of competition law.

Super-complaints

The second type of complaint is a super-complaint, a specific statutory procedure set up by s. 11 of the Enterprise Act 2002 which allows selected consumer bodies to submit a complaint to the OFT that any feature, or combination of features, of a market in the UK for goods or services is or appears to be significantly harming the interests of consumers.[117] The Secretary of State selects appropriate bodies and these include Consumer Focus, the Consumers' Association, Citizens' Advice and the Campaign for Real Ale (CAMRA).[118] Super-complaints get a fast track response, as the OFT must respond to them within 90 days. If there is felt to be merit in the complaint, then a variety of outcomes are possible, not all of which will result in action that falls within competition law. Of the fourteen super-complaints that have been received by the OFT,[119] only three have resulted in competition law action in the form of references to the Competition Commission requiring it to undertake a market investigation.[120] Some, such as doorstep selling and private dentistry have resulted in the OFT launching consumer information campaigns (involving the production of OFT leaflets), while the complaint about the methods used to calculate interest on credit cards resulted in a programme of work between the OFT, the industry and consumer bodies to make the calculations easier to understand. This led to recommendations for an independent price comparison website,

---

[117] Generally, see OFT, *Super-complaints – guidance for designated consumer bodies* (2003) and *http://www.oft.gov.uk/advice_and_resources/resource_base/super-complaints/* (accessed 27/07/12).

[118] See *http://www.bis.gov.uk/policies/consumer-issues/enforcement-of-consumer-law/super-complaints* for the current list (accessed 27/07/12). What Car? applied for designation but this was refused.

[119] As of 27/07/12.

[120] Home collected credit, Northern Ireland banking, and payment protection insurance. This procedure is discussed later (see Chapter 10). For the outcomes, see Competition Commission, 'Home Credit' (2007), 'Northern Irish Personal Banking' (2008) and 'Payment Protection Insurance' (2009). In all the cases the CC found that there were competition problems.

standardised terminology and better summary boxes. What this statutory provision has done is to allow consumer bodies a route through which to raise what they regard as important issues and to get a timely response from the relevant authorities. What this has not done is provide a new means of bringing complaints about restrictive agreements and abuse of dominant position to the notice of the OFT, as none of the super-complaints have resulted in such an investigation, although arguably this was not the point of the new procedure.[121]

Obtaining information

In the same way as the European Commission, the OFT suffers from the problem of information asymmetry, that is, undertakings have much more information about their activities than the competition authority. So, although the OFT may make informal requests for information, the legislation provides it with a wide range of powers to obtain information, going, in fact, further than the European Commission's powers.[122] The trigger point for the exercise of the statutory powers is when the OFT decides to launch an investigation under s. 25 of the Competition Act 1998 on the grounds that it has reasonable grounds for suspecting that an agreement falls within the prohibition in Chapter I or Article 101(1) TFEU or that there is conduct which is a breach of Chapter II or Article 102 TFEU. The starting point is s. 26, which enables the OFT to require that any person produces documents or information that it requests, upon receipt of a written notice. Document is defined widely, as information recorded in any form[123] and the OFT may also ask people to explain documents in their possession or to indicate where they think that the documents are. Failure to respond to these requests or wilful obstruction opens the undertaking to the possibility of criminal penalties, although the OFT has not used these provisions because it is worried about the proportionality of imposing such a penalty and the difficulty of proving such a case in the criminal courts.[124]

In addition to the powers to obtain information, the OFT also has powers to enter business premises, both with and without a warrant. When it enters business premises without a warrant, it must give two days' notice to the occupant, who need not be the person suspected of the infringement, but could be a supplier or a customer. On entering the premises, the officer can require the production of documents or information, an explanation of them, ask for answers as to where certain documents are kept, and may take copies, or extracts from the documents, and steps to preserve or prevent interference with them. The OFT's guidelines allow the undertakings concerned to contact their legal advisers and set out procedures to maintain the status quo while waiting, a reasonable time, for the advisers to arrive.

This procedure is limited to business premises and requires, in general, that the OFT announces its inspection in advance. Like the European Commission, the OFT also has the power to enter premises unannounced, once it has obtained a warrant from a High Court judge,[125] and this power extends explicitly to domestic premises as well. Such inspections are only possible under three conditions:

---

[121] Although the super-complaint by CAMRA invited the investigation of agreements between pubs and their landlords.

[122] Generally, see OFT, *Powers of investigation* (2004).

[123] Competition Act 1998, s. 59.

[124] See Public Accounts Committee (n. 109), para. 18.

[125] Court of Session in Scotland.

1 if the OFT has requested information under ss. 26 or 27 and it has not been provided;

2 if the OFT thinks that if it used its powers under ss. 26 and 27 the information would be concealed, altered or destroyed; or

3 where the information is such that it could have been produced under s. 27 but the officer has been unable to enter the premises.

On entering the premises, in addition to the powers under s. 27, officers of the OFT may enter the premises by force and may take possession of the documents and remove them, as well as taking any necessary steps to preserve them or prevent them being tampered with, such as putting a seal on them.[126]

The exercise of these powers raises human rights issues, in the same way as they do for the European Commission. An important difference is that, under the Human Rights Act 1998, s. 6, public bodies are required to have regard to the human rights obligations implemented under that Act. There is thus no question that both the legislation and the OFT's exercise of its powers under that legislation must be consistent with the case law under the European Convention on Human Rights. In general terms, this issue was addressed in *Office of Fair Trading v X*,[127] where Morison J addressed the issue of whether the powers of investigation contained in the Competition Act 1998 were compatible with Articles 6 and 8 of the European Convention and, in particular, whether any rules against self-incrimination were breached. His view was that they were not breached as the legislative rights were conferred in pursuit of a legitimate aim and were proportionate to that aim. In addition, the framework of procedural protection surrounding these provisions meant that there was no breach of the defendants' rights. It is worth pointing out that this is a judgment made in very general terms, on the basis of an OFT application for a warrant, as opposed to a defendant claiming a specific breach of their human rights.

The United Kingdom has also made certain types of anti-competitive activity a criminal offence (the cartel offence – discussed in Chapter 8), so this has led to an extension of the OFT's investigatory powers in relation to the cartel offence. Broadly speaking, in addition to having powers very similar to those mentioned above,[128] the OFT now has power to carry out a variety of means of covert surveillance when investigating the cartel offence.[129] This can include what is called 'directed intelligence', that is surveillance which is covert but not intrusive, such as taking pictures from a concealed location. The powers do go further to cover intrusive surveillance, which includes entry in a covert manner on to property and placing devices, such as telephone tapping, or the use of directional microphones from outside, and the use of covert human intelligence sources, such as informers. Authorisation for the use of these powers is a matter for the OFT itself, either the Director of Cartel Investigations or, in the case of intrusive surveillance, the Chairman of the OFT. Failure to comply with the provisions of the legislation will put the OFT at risk of having the information declared to be inadmissible in any subsequent criminal prosecution, although this is not an automatic outcome. It should also be noted that there is specific protection in this context for statements

---

[126] The European Commission imposed a fine of €38 million on E.ON for tampering with the seal during an investigation: see Commission Press Release IP/08/108, 30 January 2008.

[127] [2003] EWHC 1042.

[128] Enterprise Act 2002, ss. 193–194.

[129] Generally, see OFT, *Powers for investigating criminal cartels* (2003), *Covert surveillance in cartel investigations* (2004) and *Covert human intelligence sources in cartel investigations* (2004).

which people make in response to the exercise of compulsory powers by the OFT not to be used in court against them, except when it is a case of prosecuting them for making a false statement.[130] In other words, there is specific statutory protection for the right against self-incrimination.

Decision making procedures

The OFT's decision making process has been criticised for lacking transparency, confirmation bias and for a lack of speed. The OFT published a guide to its processes, as well as instituting a trial of a Procedural Adjudicator, as a response to the criticisms about transparency.[131] Investigations can be very lengthy and the OFT has been criticised by the Public Accounts Committee for the length of its investigations, which seem to last between one and five years, depending on the case, and the OFT has promised to work more quickly and this seems to have been an important reason for the replacement of the OFT with the new Competition and Markets Authority from 2014.[132] Having received a complaint which may meet the OFT's prioritisation principles (or suggestions for an own-initiative investigation), OFT officials will then consider whether the OFT should open an investigation. Documentation prepared for these purposes will include an analysis of whether there are reasonable grounds for suspecting that an infringement has occurred or is occurring. If, on investigation, the case still is seen to have merit and to be consistent with the prioritisation principles and the legal test,[133] a formal investigation will be opened, which allows the OFT to use its formal information-gathering powers. Just before that point, the case will be allocated to a Team Leader (responsible for the day-to-day running of the case), a Project Director (who directs the case) and a Senior Responsible Officer (SRO) with the SRO deciding if there are sufficient grounds to open a formal investigation and whether the evidential requirements of an infringement are met.[134] At this point, the businesses under investigation will be sent a case initiation letter setting out details of the conduct being examined, an indicative timescale and who the decision maker is. Typically the decision maker is the SRO, although this need not be the case. As the investigation proceeds, the SRO seeks internal advice, in particular from the specialist lawyers and economists employed by the OFT. Before issuing a statement of objections or a final decision, the decision maker will consult with a steering committee which is made up a range of senior OFT officials and other relevant staff who provide strategic advice and guidance.[135] If the OFT thinks, provisionally, that the conduct under investigation amounts to an infringement, a statement of objections will be sent to the parties which will state the facts and evidence on which the OFT relies, its objections, the action it proposes to take and the reasons for the action. At this point, the OFT may invite the recipients of a statement of objections to discuss an early resolution of the case, although the OFT would prefer to have these discussions at

---

[130] Enterprise Act 2002, s. 197.
[131] OFT, *A guide to the OFT's investigation procedures in competition cases* (2011).
[132] Public Accounts Committee (n. 109), para. 15; and see National Audit Office (n. 112), Section 3 for a more general discussion. National Audit Office, *Progress Report on Maintaining Competition in Markets* (2009, HC 127) at 3.7. Enterprise and Regulatory Reform Bill, BIS *A Competition Regime for Growth: A consultation on options for reform* (2011).
[133] Competition Act 1998, s. 25.
[134] OFT, *A guide to the OFT's investigation procedures in competition cases* (2011) at para. 5.1
[135] Ibid. at paras 9.7–9.10.

an earlier stage.[136] The OFT has no statutory time limit within which it has to issue a statement of objections. The parties will have a right of access to the OFT's file and a time limit to respond. If they so request, the parties are entitled to an oral hearing. After that a final decision is made and, again, there is no statutory time limit within which the OFT has to make this final decision.

Although the time limits are a matter of concern for businesses and their advisers, as well as the OFT,[137] there has been much less argument over the rights of the parties within these procedures, in particular as regards access to the information that the OFT holds. The explanation for this seems to be partly because the OFT has built on well-understood procedures operated by the European Commission and partly because it is easier to challenge the decision on substantive grounds before the CAT.

The OFT issued a consultation paper on changes to its procedures as response to a number of criticisms.[138] The major change is described as a move towards collective judgment and the separation of investigation and decision making in antitrust cases. The way that this will work is that the OFT will establish a committee, the Decision Making Committee, composed of the Chief Executive, Chief Economist, General Counsel, the head of policy and other executive members of the OFT Board. In cases where a statement of objections has been issued, or where a decision is required in relation to commitments or an early resolution prior to the issue of a statement of objections, the Committee would appoint a three-member group, called the Case Decision Group.[139] The Case Decision Group would include at least one member of the Decision Making Committee and at least one member would be legally qualified.[140] The Case Decision Group would review the statement of objections, the parties' written representations and the key underlying evidence. It would also attend the, enhanced, oral hearing, actively engaging with the parties through asking questions. In addition, the Chief Economist and General Counsel would attend the oral hearing and would be able to ask questions of the parties.[141] Before taking a decision, the Case Decision Group would consult the Decisions Committee before taking what is called a Collective Decision, which is designed to provide an opportunity for the General Counsel, Chief Economist, head of policy and other senior officials to provide their views.[142] These proposals have already been criticised on the grounds that the Case Decision Group will not be sufficiently independent.[143] The argument is that the third member of the Case Decision Group would be an OFT member of staff, in addition to the lawyer and the member of the Decisions Committee, and that consultation with the Decisions Committee would bring back in people that were involved earlier in the case and that members of the Decision Group may have involvement with other people involved in the decision process, for example, the staff members of the Decision Group will depend on decisions by people in the Decisions Committee for the progression of their careers.

---

[136] Ibid. at para. 11.2. See OFT, 'Loan products to professional service firms' (2011) for a good example of an early resolution – RBS agreeing to pay a penalty of £28.5 million.

[137] The Enterprise and Regulatory Reform Bill gives the Secretary of State a power to set statutory time limits for OFT and, later, CMA investigations.

[138] OFT, *Review of the OFT's investigation procedure in competition cases* (2012).

[139] Ibid. para. 3.2.

[140] Ibid. para. 3.6.

[141] Ibid. para. 3.8.

[142] Ibid. para. 3.10.

[143] See *http://competitionpolicy.wordpress.com/2012/06/08/ofts-proposed-reforms-fall-short-of-ensuring-independence-in-antitrust-decision-making/* (accessed 16/06/12).

Decisions by the OFT

The OFT has a similar range of powers to the European Commission: it may accept binding commitments from the parties, order the infringement to cease and impose fines. It also has the power to order interim measures.

The OFT may also resolve or dispose of a case where, as a result of the investigation, the undertaking concerned has changed its behaviour. It has done this in a number of cases.[144] One was where there was a concern over the contracts for street furniture (roadside advertising) between the two major companies involved and individual local authorities. The OFT was concerned that the terms of the contracts would make it more difficult for rival providers to enter the market. The two companies concerned agreed to give the OFT voluntary assurances about their future conduct and interpretation of the terms of existing contracts and, therefore, the OFT closed the investigation.

Commitments

The power to accept commitments is modelled on the similar power given to the European Commission in Regulation 1/2003 and is contained in ss. 31A–31E of the Competition Act 1998. Commitments may be accepted from any person that the OFT considers appropriate at any time between the beginning of an investigation and the decision that there has been an infringement of the competition rules. The OFT's guidance states that it will only accept commitments where:

- the competition concerns are readily identifiable;
- the competition concerns are fully addressed by the commitments offered; and
- the proposed commitments are capable of being implemented effectively and, if necessary, within a short period of time.[145]

The OFT goes on to state that it will not accept commitments, except in very exceptional cases, where there are secret cartels engaged in price-fixing, bid-rigging, restrictions on production or output, sharing or dividing markets or serious abuses of a dominant position.[146] Commitments will not be accepted where it would be difficult to monitor their effectiveness or if the OFT considers that not to complete its investigation and make a decision would be to undermine deterrence. Commitments can be structural, such as divesting a particular factory or operation, or behavioural, that is, promising to behave in a particular way, in nature and will usually be given for a specific period of time. Once binding commitments have been accepted, the OFT will cease its investigation and can only make a decision on this issue if there has been a material change of circumstances, there are reasonable grounds for suspecting that the person has not adhered to the commitments or the information on which the commitments are based is incomplete or false in a material particular. Acceptance of binding commitments simply meets the OFT's competition concerns; it is not a statement about whether there has been an infringement and therefore, as in relation to the European Commission's practice on commitments, the issue as to whether there is

---

[144] See OFT, *Case Closure Summaries*, available at: *http://www.oft.gov.uk/OFTwork/competition-act-and-cartels/ca98/closure/* (accessed 27/07/12).

[145] OFT, *Enforcement* (2004) at para. 4.3.

[146] Ibid., para. 4.4.

a breach of competition law could rise in a private action. There are provisions in the legislation for public consultation.[147]

A good example of the commitments was the Associated Newspapers (AN) case,[148] which arose from a complaint from a competitor that the exclusive contracts AN had reached with Network Rail, London Underground and some train operating companies for space to sell the Metro newspaper had prevented them from establishing competing free newspapers and that this had foreclosed the market and constituted an abuse of dominant position under the Chapter II prohibition. After the OFT had opened a formal investigation, AN offered commitments to meet the competition concerns which, in essence, involved waiving its exclusive rights and offering its competitors appropriate access to its distribution racks. The OFT took the view that these agreements were likely to affect inter-state trade, as they covered all of London, which was a substantial part of the EU, and therefore accepted these commitments as dealing with the Article 101 and 102 TFEU issues which may have arisen as well.

Directions

When the OFT finds that there has been an infringement of the competition rules, it may give directions to such persons as it considers appropriate.[149] The OFT takes the view that directions may require the agreement or conduct to be terminated, that they may require positive action by the person concerned and the directions may also require structural alterations to a business.[150] Directions requiring structural alterations to a business have never been given and under Article 7 of Regulation 1/2003, the European Commission is restricted in its use of structural remedies to where there is either no equally effective behavioural remedy or any effective behavioural remedy would be more burdensome than the structural one. These restrictions are likely to apply to the OFT's use of its power as well.

Interim measures

The OFT also has power to give interim measures directions before it reaches a final decision.[151] Interim measures directions will be given where the OFT considers that it is necessary to act urgently either to prevent serious, irreparable damage to a particular person or category of persons, or to protect the public interest.[152] What constitutes serious damage is a question of fact, but it means something like serious competitive disadvantage and a serious financial loss, and the damage must irreparable.[153] The direction may require termination or modification of the agreement or conduct and before it is issued the person affected must be given an opportunity to comment upon it.

The first, and so far only, case where the OFT has issued interim directions concerned the London Metal Exchange (LME).[154] Here, acting on complaints from a competitor of LME about its allegedly predatory and discriminatory pricing, the OFT issued an interim measures

---

[147] Competition Act 1998, Sch. 6A.
[148] See 'Associated Newspapers Limited', 1 March 2006. Two other cases are: 'TV Eye', 24 May 2005 (offer of terms and conditions by broadcasters to media agencies) and 'British Horseracing Board and Jockey Club' (2004) (governance of racing and competition between racetracks).
[149] Competition Act 1998, ss. 32 and 33.
[150] OFT, *Enforcement* (n. 145), para. 2.3.
[151] Competition Act 1998, s. 35.
[152] OFT, *Enforcement* (n. 145), para. 3.3.
[153] Ibid., paras 3.5 and 3.6.
[154] *London Metal Exchange* v *Office of Fair Trading* [2006] CAT 19.

direction ordering LME not to increase its trading hours beyond those it had already established, in other words, preventing it from trading during Asian opening hours and thus, allegedly, taking business away from its competitor, the complainant. The basis of this decision was both the potential damage to the competitor and to the public interest, in threatening the existence of a competitor to the LME. This decision was appealed to the CAT and the OFT withdrew the direction, without reaching any conclusion in respect of LME's conduct. The LME applied for its costs and one of the questions in the costs application was whether the OFT had acted properly in imposing the direction. The CAT was very critical of the process that the OFT had followed and the quality of the evidence that it had relied on before issuing the interim direction. All of the evidence had come from LME's competitor, on an informal basis and not in response to a s. 26 request for information, and no evidence from customers had been sought. The CAT was particularly concerned that the OFT had only a limited understanding of the competitor's business and, by extension, the market, yet had nevertheless gone ahead and issued an interim measures direction and, overall, that its investigative process was superficial and flawed.[155] In terms of action for the future, the CAT's judgment indicates that the OFT will need to rely on better evidence, ideally gathered in response to s. 26 requests, and to ensure that it does not rely on the views of simply one party.

Fines

Like the European Commission, the OFT also has a power to impose financial penalties and this is the sanction most frequently used. There is also a leniency programme, which is discussed later. According to the OFT, the objective behind its policy is:

- to impose penalties on those undertakings that breach competition law which reflect the seriousness of the infringement; and

- to ensure that the threat of penalties will deter undertakings from engaging in anti-competitive practices.[156]

The OFT intends, where appropriate, to impose severe penalties, particularly as regards secret cartels and price-fixing and serious abuses of dominant position. The Guidelines date from 2004 and were drafted to be consistent with the European Commission's 1998 Penalty Guidelines because they are intended to apply to both breaches of domestic and EU competition law. The European Commission issued new guidelines in 2006, which take a different approach than the OFT's 2004 Guidelines. It is not obvious which method of calculation will be used if an undertaking is penalised by the OFT for a breach of the domestic prohibitions and Articles 101 and 102 TFEU, or for simply a breach of Articles 101 and 102 TFEU, except that the undertaking cannot be penalised twice for the same conduct. Examples of some of the fines levied in the UK are set out in Table 5.3. The OFT consulted on a revision to the guidelines from October 2011 to mid 2012 and it is expected that there will be certain changes of detail in their application.[157]

---

[155] Ibid., paras 144 and 170.
[156] OFT, *OFT's Guidance as to the appropriate amount of a penalty* (2004) at para. 1.4.
[157] OFT, *OFT's Guidance as to the appropriate amount of a penalty: A consultation on OFT guidance* (2011).

Table 5.3 Examples of fines levied in the UK[158]

OFT Case	Fine (£ million)	Offence	Year
Retail pricing of tobacco	225	Price-fixing of tobacco products	2011
Construction Industry	129.2	Bid rigging	2009
British Airways	58.5	Fixing long-haul passenger fuel surcharges	2012
Construction Industry Recruitment forum	39.3	Price fixing and collective boycott	2011
Agreements between Hasbro, Argos and Littlewoods	22.65	Price-fixing of Hasbro toys and games	2003
Replica football kit	18.587	Price-fixing	2003
Genzyme	6.8	Bundling and margin squeeze	2003
Napp Pharmaceuticals	3.2	Predatory and excessive pricing	2001
UOP Ltd *et al.*	1.707	Price-fixing	2004
Aberdeen Journals	1.328	Predatory pricing	2001

The OFT sets out a five-step approach to calculating the penalty:

- calculation of the starting point, having regard to the seriousness of the infringement and the relevant turnover of the undertaking;

- adjustment for duration;

- adjustment for other factors;[159]

- adjustment for further aggravating or mitigating factors; and

- adjustment if the maximum penalty of 10% of the worldwide turnover of the undertaking is exceeded and to avoid double jeopardy, that is, the undertaking being penalised twice for the same offence.[160]

The seriousness of the offence will be determined on a case-by-case basis but the most serious infringements are considered to be cartels engaging in price-fixing and particularly serious abuses of a dominant position which will damage competition. When making its assessment of the starting point, the OFT says that it will consider a number of factors including the nature of the product, the structure of the market, the market share(s) of the undertaking(s) involved in the infringement, entry conditions, and the effect on competitors and third parties, as well as the damage caused to consumers whether directly or indirectly.[161] Although in the past it has used a maximum starting point of 10% of relevant turnover, it is proposing to increase this to 30%, which will bring it more in line with other competition authorities.[162] Once the basic amount is determined, it is then adjusted for the duration of the offence, and may be multiplied by the number of years the activity has carried on; and is then further adjusted to take into account other factors. These include the OFT's objective estimate of any economic or financial benefit made or likely to be made by the infringing undertaking

---

[158] Fines are given as in the original OFT decision. A number of these have been reduced on appeal to the CAT.

[159] The intention is to reverse the order of steps 3 and 4 so that adjustments for specific deterrence and proportionality are carried out after considering aggravating and mitigating factors: ibid. paras 5.27–5.28.

[160] OFT, *OFT's Guidance as to the appropriate amount of a penalty* (2004), para. 2.1.

[161] OFT, *OFT's Guidance as to the appropriate amount of a penalty* (2004), para. 2.5.

[162] OFT, *OFT's Guidance as to the appropriate amount of a penalty: A consultation on OFT guidance* (2011), paras 3.15–3.22 and 5.19–5.14.

from the infringement, as well as the special characteristics, including the size and financial position of the undertaking in question. Where relevant, the OFT's estimate would account for any gains which might accrue to the undertaking in other product or geographic markets as well as the 'relevant' market under consideration.[163] There will then be an adjustment for aggravating and mitigating factors, such as being the leader of a cartel, or being under pressure to enter the cartel.[164] Finally, there is an adjustment to prevent the maximum fine of 10% of turnover being exceeded and to prevent the undertaking being penalised twice.

There is a limited immunity from penalties for small agreements and conduct which is of minor significance, which means agreements where the combined turnover does not exceed £20 million a year and for conduct where the turnover of the undertaking concerned does not exceed £50 million.[165] There have been some exceptional cases where no penalty was imposed. An interesting example is the Northern Ireland Livestock Association where the Association recommended the introduction of a standard commission for buyers from its members, that is, price-fixing. Although the Director General of Fair Trading took the view that this was an example of a serious infringement, because it was not covert and because of the exceptional circumstances due to the effects of BSE and foot and mouth disease, no penalty was imposed in these circumstances.[166] Also interesting is the *Cardiff Bus* case where the OFT did not impose a penalty but, in the subsequent private action, the CAT awarded exemplary damages.[167]

One of the most interesting cases in relation to the OFT's policy on sanctions arose in relation to the exchange of information between independent schools on fee levels.[168] Here some 50 schools circulated information on their current and prospective fee levels, which the OFT saw as a serious infringement of the Chapter I prohibition, being a practice which had as its object the restriction of competition. It only imposed a fine of £10,000 on each of the schools, taking into account their cooperation with the investigation, the fact that they were non-profit-making and their agreement to make an ex gratia payment of £3 million to a trust fund for the benefit of the pupils who attended the schools during the years the arrangement operated, which the OFT saw as indirectly benefiting those whom the legislation was designed to protect.

The leniency programme

The OFT also has a leniency programme, similar to that of the European Commission, and details are discussed later in the text (see Chapter 8).

Individual sanctions

The UK system of public enforcement for competition law is different from the EU system because there is the possibility of sanctions for individuals who have been responsible for

---

[163] OFT, *OFT's Guidance as to the appropriate amount of a penalty* (2004), para. 2.10.

[164] Persistent delay will be added as an aggravating factor: OFT, *OFT's Guidance as to the appropriate amount of a penalty: A consultation on OFT guidance* (2011), para. 1.16.

[165] Competition Act 1998, ss. 39–40 and the Competition Act 1998 (Small Agreements and Conduct of Minor Significance) Regulations 2000, SI 2000/262.

[166] 'Northern Ireland Livestock and Auctioneers Association' (2003).

[167] OFT, 'Cardiff Bus' (2008); *2 Travel Group plc v Cardiff Transport* [2012] CAT 19.

[168] 'Schools: exchange of information on future fees' (2006).

breaches of competition law. This brings the UK system closer to the American one and, arguably, adds another level to deterrence. There are two main provisions, which are discussed in detail later (see Chapter 8):

1 disqualification orders for directors;[169]
2 the criminalisation of cartel behaviour.[170]

Judicial review of OFT decisions by the Competition Appeal Tribunal

Challenges to decisions that the prohibitions under Articles 101 and 102 TFEU or that Chapters I and II of the Competition Act have been breached, the imposition of penalties and cancelling block or parallel exemptions, as well as withdrawing the benefit of a Commission Regulation taken by the OFT,[171] may be subject to an appeal to the Competition Appeal Tribunal (CAT).[172] The CAT is directed to determine such an appeal on the merits, by reference to the grounds of appeal.[173] The CAT is allowed to confirm or set aside the decision which is the subject of the appeal, or any part of it, and may remit the matter to the OFT, impose or revoke, or vary the amount of, a penalty, give such directions, or take such other steps, as the OFT could itself have given or taken, or make any other decision which the OFT could itself have made. Even if it confirms the decision, it may still set aside a finding of fact made by the OFT, for example, that a firm is in a dominant position.[174]

The CAT has made it clear that, when the appeal is on the merits, the CAT's function is not limited to applying the principles of judicial review nor to the heads of review contained in Article 263 TFEU.[175] Regardless of whether there is a decision of an infringement, or non-infringement, hearing an appeal on the merits means that the CAT may decide whether the OFT or an economic regulator has made an error of fact or law, or an error of appraisal or of procedure, or whether the matter has been sufficiently investigated.[176] The CAT has said that a convenient check list of points for an appellant was: that the decision is incorrect or, at the least, insufficient, from the point of view of (i) the reasons given; (ii) the facts and analysis relied on; (iii) the law applied; (iv) the investigation undertaken; or (v) the procedure followed.[177]

The CAT went on to emphasise in the same case that it was an appellate tribunal and that if it felt the OFT was incorrectly informed, it should in general remit the matter to the OFT to decide again, rather than make its own decision. Although, in the *Burgess* case, the CAT set aside the OFT's decision that there had been no abuse of a dominant position and decided

---

[169] Company Directors Disqualification Act 1986, s. 5A.
[170] Enterprise Act 2002, s. 188.
[171] As well as those regulators that have competition law powers.
[172] Competition Act 1998, s. 46.
[173] This is different from the provisions concerning decisions relating to merger control and market references, where the CAT applies judicial review principles: Enterprise Act 2002, s. 120.
[174] Competition Act 1998, Sch. 8, para. 3.
[175] *Freeserve.com* v *Director General of Communications* [2003] CAT 5 at para. 106.
[176] Ibid., para. 110.
[177] Ibid., para. 114.

that there had been such an abuse, refusal to supply, without remitting the matter back to the OFT.[178] The CAT took the view that it should, if necessary, take its own decision rather than remit if (i) it has or can obtain all the necessary material, (ii) the requirements of procedural fairness are respected and (iii) the course the Tribunal proposes to take is desirable from the point of view of the need for expedition and saving costs.[179]

Undertakings which are subject to the relevant decisions may appeal to the CAT as well as third parties, provided that the CAT feels they have sufficient interest in the matter.[180] Decisions of the CAT may be appealed, on a point of law, to the Court of Appeal.[181]

Conclusions on public enforcement in the UK

The record of the OFT in enforcing competition law since the Competition Act 1998 came into force in 2000 does seem to be mixed. It has had success in a number of high-profile cases, both initially and more recently, but the absolute number of infringement decisions is quite low. For example, between 2008 and 2012, the OFT only took seven formal decisions and three early resolution decisions.[182] Although it is important not to place too much emphasis on the number of decisions, for example, the construction industry decision involved over one hundred firms but counts as only one decision, this does seem to be a low level of activity. The OFT's recent activity appears to be concentrated almost exclusively on Chapter I and Article 101 TFEU cases and a perception has grown up that the OFT is not interested in small markets.[183] It has only used the criminal cartel offence successfully once (see Chapter 8 for a discussion). There are still concerns over the amount of time it takes in dealing with cases. Its record in front of the CAT has also been mixed. Although it has very rarely been reversed as regards liability, there have been some high profile failures as well as the CAT having some issues with the OFT's approach to certain matters.[184]

Overall, this mixed record of performance seems to be one of the reasons that the Government has decided to undertake a major reform of competition policy by merging the OFT with the Competition Commission to create a Competition and Markets Authority (CMA).[185] It must be remembered that enforcing competition law is a challenging task and that the OFT has been exercising some powers which are very new in a European context, such as the powers in relation to criminal law. The key question is whether the OFT and then the new CMA will be seen to have become more effective in the near future.

---

[178] *ME Burgess* v *Office of Fair Trading* [2005] CAT 25. See also *Floe Telecom* v *Ofcom* [2005] CAT 14.

[179] Ibid., para. 132.

[180] Competition Act 1998, s. 47.

[181] Competition Act 1998, s. 49.

[182] OFT *Annual Report 2011–12*, Annex C.

[183] Although OFT, 'Cardiff Bus' (2008) involves the Chapter II prohibition and a local market. See National Audit Office, *Progress Report on Maintaining Competition in Markets* (2009, HC 127) at para. 5 for the perception on local markets. Also OFT, 'Reckitt Benkiser' (2012) involves the Chapter II prohibition.

[184] Perhaps the two most important were: *Imperial Tobacco and others* v *Office of Fair Trading* [2011] CAT 41 and *Mastercard UK Members Forum* v *OFT* [2006] CAT 14. In the construction industry case, fines totalling £63.5 million were appealed and these were reduced to around £9.8 m, which included a few findings of infringement which were set aside. The most important example is *Kier Group and others* v *Office of Fair Trading* [2011] CAT 3.

[185] Enterprise and Regulatory Reform Bill and BIS, *A Competition Regime for Growth: A consultation on options for reform* (2011). See also Secretary of State for Innovation, Business and Skills, HC Debs 11 June 2012 col 73.

Summary

➤ Historically, in the EU and UK the enforcement of competition law has been the responsibility of the public authorities. There is now a policy to encourage the development of private litigation.

➤ There are three main aims for enforcement: deterrence, compensation and procedural fairness. These have to be balanced against one another.

➤ European Commission investigations can be started either on the initiative of the Commission or in response to a complaint. There is no right to have a complaint investigated.

➤ The European Commission has wide powers to obtain information, including the power to enter premises, take copies of documents and ask questions of individuals.

➤ There is no privilege against self-incrimination under EU competition law, but the rights of an undertaking to defend itself cannot be irremediably impaired during an investigation. This places some limits on the questions that the Commission may ask.

➤ The decision procedure starts with the issue of a Statement of Objections (SO) and is primarily written. Subject to some limitations, parties have a right of access to the Commission's file. They also have a right to oral hearings, which are conducted by the Hearings Officer.

➤ Rather than issue a formal decision, the Commission may accept commitments from undertakings to bring an infringement to an end. This decision is not binding on national courts in private litigation.

➤ The Commission has power to impose fines for breach of Articles 101 and 102 TFEU, up to a limit of 10% of the total turnover in the preceding business year of each undertaking taking part in the infringement.

➤ The Commission calculates fines by deciding on a basic amount and then adjusting that amount to take into account aggravating or mitigating circumstances.

➤ The Commission also operates a leniency programme, which allows undertakings to benefit from full or partial immunity from a fine, depending on whether they meet the appropriate conditions.

➤ Enforcement of the Chapters I and II prohibitions and Articles 101 and 102 TFEU within the UK is the responsibility of the OFT.

➤ Complaints may be individual, or there is a special process for 'super-complaints' from designated consumer bodies. Super-complaints do not have to lead to action under competition law.

➤ The OFT has wide powers to obtain information, including the right to enter premises and question individuals. When it comes to the cartel offence, the OFT also has powers to carry out covert surveillance.

➤ If the OFT carries out a formal investigation and decides to proceed with the case, it will issue a statement of objections. Parties have a right of access to the file and an oral hearing.

➤ The OFT may resolve cases informally and may also accept commitments. These are not binding in private actions.

➤ The OFT has power to impose fines and has a five-step approach: calculation of the starting point, having regard to the seriousness of the infringement and the relevant turnover of the undertaking; adjustment for duration; adjustment for other factors; adjustment for further aggravating or mitigating factors; and adjustment if the maximum penalty of 10% of the worldwide turnover of the undertaking is exceeded and to avoid double jeopardy.

➤ The OFT operates a leniency programme which offers total immunity and relief from fines of up to 100% provided the appropriate conditions are met. The OFT also operates Amnesty Plus.

➤ Unlike the system in the EU, individuals in the UK can be subject to sanctions for breach of competition law. In the appropriate circumstances, they can be disqualified from being directors. Certain breaches of competition law have now become a criminal offence.

Further reading

Reference works

Brealey, M., Green, N., and George, K., *Competition Litigation: UK Practice and Procedure* (Oxford University Press, 2010). *Comprehensive discussion of UK procedures.*

Ortiz Blanco, L., *EC Competition Procedure* (2nd edn, Oxford University Press, 2006). *Comprehensive coverage by a team of, primarily, Commission officials.*

Other reading

Andreangeli, A., *EU Competition Enforcement and Human Rights* (Edward Elgar, Cheltenham, 2008). *Monograph looking in detail at human rights issues and competition law enforcement.*

Jones, C., 'Private Antitrust Enforcement in Europe' (2004) 27 *World Competition* 13. *A reply to Wils (2003), arguing the contrary.*

Kerse, C.S., 'The complainant in competition cases: a progress report' (1997) 34 *Common Market Law Review* 213. *Clear overview of the cases.*

National Audit Office, *Enforcing Competition in Markets* (2005, HC 593). *Critical examination of the OFT's enforcement record.*

National Audit Office, *Progress report on maintaining competition in markets* (2009, HC 127). *An update of previous report, noting substantial positive progress.*

Public Accounts Committee, *Enforcing competition in markets* (2006, HC 841). *Very critical report on the OFT's enforcement record.*

Riley, A., 'Saunders and the Power to Obtain Information in Community and United Kingdom Competition Law' (2000) 25 *European Law Review* 264. *Controversial argument about the effect of European Court of Human Rights decisions on EC competition law.*

Segal, I. and Whinston, M., 'Public vs Private Enforcement of Antitrust Law: A Survey' (2007) 28 *European Competition Law Review* 306. *Survey of economic issues relating to public and private enforcement.*

Veljanovski, C., 'Cartel Fines in Europe' (2007) 30 *World Competition* 65. *Careful and clear empirical examination of Commission's fining practice.*

Vesterdorp, B., 'Complaints concerning infringements of competition law within the context of EC law' (1994) 31 *Common Market Law Review* 77. *Overview by President of the GC.*

Wils, W., 'Should Private Anti-trust Enforcement be Encouraged in Europe?' (2003) 26 *World Competition* 1. *Strong argument by Commission official that the answer is 'No'.*

Wils, W., *Principles of European Antitrust Enforcement* (Hart Publishing, Oxford, 2005). *Collection of essays on a variety of relevant issues.*

Yeung, K., 'Privatizing Competition Regulation' (1998) 18 *Oxford Journal of Legal Studies* 581. *Dated, but still a balanced discussion of the pros and cons of private enforcement.*

6

Private enforcement of competition law

Chapter outline

This chapter discusses:

➤ Using competition law as a defence

➤ Bringing an action for breach of competition law

➤ The conditions that need to be established for a successful action

➤ Actions following decisions of the competition authorities or courts.

Introduction

Increasing private enforcement of competition law has been a policy goal of the European Commission and the OFT for some time, as can be seen by the number of papers and investigations into the topic that they have published.[1] It is evident that there is much less use of private litigation in the UK and Europe than in the United States. Table 6.1 below gives data

Table 6.1 US Federal antitrust cases

	Antitrust cases	Private	US	% private
2011	475	452	23	95
2010	544	523	21	96
2009	812	792	20	98
2008	1,318	1,287	31	98
2007	1,038	1,018	20	98

Source: Judicial Business of the US Courts: *http://www.uscourts.gov/Statistics/JudicialBusiness.aspx*, Tables C2 and C2A (accessed 20/04/12).

---

[1] Most recently, see European Commission, Green Paper on *Damages actions for breach of EC antitrust rules*, COM (2005) 672; OFT, *Private actions in competition law: effective redress for consumers and business* (2007); European Commission, White Paper on *Damages actions for breach of the EC antitrust rules*, COM (2008) 165. European Commission, *Towards a Coherent European Approach to Collective Redress: Next Steps* (2010) available at: *http://ec.europa.eu/competition/antitrust/actionsdamages/index.html* (accessed 20/04/12); BIS, 'Private actions in competition law – a consultation on options for reform' (2012).

for federal antitrust actions over the last five years. This shows that, on average, there are around eight hundred private actions per year, although the last two years show a significant decline, and that private actions make up over 95% of the federal courts' work. There are, however, no equivalent databases for the UK courts (and the CAT) nor for antitrust enforcement in the EU as a whole. The impression is that activity in the UK is very limited, perhaps between ten and twenty cases a year,[2] but that this may not be representative of the situation in the rest of Europe as Peyer has found significant activity in Germany.[3] If it is true that there is less activity in the EU then some of this is no doubt a historical legacy of having centrally enforced systems, and some is no doubt due to litigation being more commonplace in the United States than in Europe, but there are also a number of difficulties in the existing law which make it difficult to bring private actions. Bringing such cases is costly, there are problems about obtaining the necessary information, proving a case may be difficult and, as will be seen, there are a number of uncertainties in relation to the law. A key question for this chapter is, to what extent are these just the inevitable problems of litigation and to what extent are they peculiar to competition law?

The rationale behind the policy of trying to encourage private actions is broadly twofold. First, the public authorities – the OFT and the European Commission – inevitably have limited resources and limited information. Their enforcement efforts will have to focus on a limited number of cases. Actions by private parties can be a valuable supplement to this enforcement activity, which will raise the chances of detection of anti-competitive activity. Private parties will, however, have their own motivation, which is not necessarily aligned with the public interest; a point well recognised in the United States. Secondly, although anti-competitive action damages people, public enforcement does not provide compensation for that damage. So, for example, the first high-profile case under UK law involved the price-fixing of replica football shirts. The OFT imposed a penalty on the undertakings concerned but there were numerous individuals who had paid more than the market price for their shirts.[4] Without some form of private action, they would not obtain compensation (what actually happened is discussed later in this chapter). So this justification is essentially a rights based one.

Before discussing the law relating to private actions, a number of introductory points should help to clarify the discussion. First, three types of litigants can be distinguished: competitors, customers and consumers. The incentive on competitors to take action against anti-competitive behaviour is obvious; they are being damaged by the conduct or the agreement and want it to stop. It may, however, be in the interests of a competitor to use competition law to try and disrupt the business strategies of a rival, regardless of their effects on competition. For example, responding to low pricing by claiming that it is predatory is a common

---

[2] There were eleven competition cases in the Chancery Division of the High Court in 2010 and seven follow-on actions in the CAT over a similar period. See *http://www.justice.gov.uk/statistics/courts-and-sentencing/judicial-annual* (accessed 20/04/12) for the High Court and CAT *Annual Review 2010–11* at p. 43. There were four competition cases in the High Court in 2011.

[3] S. Peyer, 'Myths and Untold Stories – Private Antitrust Enforcement in Germany' (2010) University of East Anglia CCP Working Paper 10–12 available at: *https://ueaeprints.uea.ac.uk/29237/1/Peyer_-_Myths_and_Untold_Stories-Private_Antitrust_Enforcement_in_Germany.pdf* (accessed 20/04/12).

[4] See OFT Press Release, 1 August 2003, available at *http://www.oft.gov.uk/news/press/2003/pn_107-03* and OFT, 'Football kit price fixing' (2003), available at *http://www.oft.gov.uk/OFTwork/competition-act-and-cartels/ca98/decisions/football-kit* (both accessed 20/04/12).

issue, as illustrated in the bus industry cases discussed earlier (see Chapter 3).[5] For the purposes of this chapter it is worth distinguishing customers from consumers, even though all consumers are also customers of some undertaking. Customers, for our purposes, are those undertakings that buy inputs from other undertakings, that is, they are in a vertical relationship with those other undertakings that are involved in the anti-competitive behaviour.[6] They will have less incentive to take action than competitors, because of the problem of disrupting existing relationships, but will be in a better position to understand the market than consumers. Consumers are in much the weakest position of these three parties. The damage to an individual consumer from anti-competitive action is small,[7] there are problems in coordinating a collective response and consumers have very little information readily available about how an industry or an undertaking operates. As we shall see, there have been a number of efforts to try to strengthen the consumers' position in private litigation in the UK, and some evidence that this has begun to have an effect. The overall conclusion, though, is that those who are most harmed by anti-competitive actions, the consumers, are in the weakest position to bring enforcement actions, while those whose motivations can be mixed, competitors, will be in the best position. Does this mean, therefore, that encouraging more private actions may have mixed results?

Secondly, we can also distinguish two different ways in which private parties may use competition law in disputes between them. The first is to use competition law as a defence against a claim. For example, if a claim is brought under a contract for monies owed, you might defend this action by claiming that the contract is in breach of competition law, therefore void, and so it cannot be enforced in court. Historically, in the UK most private litigation on competition law has involved it being used as a defence.[8] The second way of using competition law is as a basis for your action. So, if you feel that you are being or have been damaged by anti-competitive action, you might bring a case against the alleged perpetrators seeking to stop the practice and/or trying to obtain compensation for the damage done to you. Although we will discuss competition law as a defence, recent policy discussion has focused much more on using competition law as the basis for an action, that is, on the ability of plaintiffs to claim that they have been damaged by anti-competitive activity which must cease and they must be given compensation for the damage. As we shall see, this raises a number of difficult questions.

Thirdly, a distinction has grown up between 'stand-alone' actions and 'follow-on' actions (see Box 6.1). A stand-alone action is where a plaintiff alleges that there has been anti-competitive behaviour and has to prove that this has occurred before obtaining a remedy. A follow-on action occurs where a competition authority, or a court, has decided that some behaviour is anti-competitive and the plaintiff claims that they have been damaged by this behaviour. In these situations UK law makes provision for the decisions of the competition authority or court to be binding in subsequent proceedings, and provides a special procedure for these sorts of claims, so that it is much easier for a plaintiff to be successful.[9]

---

[5] See *Chester City Council* v *Arriva* [2007] EWHC 1371 (Ch).

[6] Customers who buy from undertakings not involved in the anti-competitive behaviour may still suffer damage and this issue is discussed in more detail below.

[7] Those who would have purchased, but for a monopoly price, can also be considered to have been damaged.

[8] See B. Rodger, 'Competition law litigation in the UK courts: a study of all cases to 2004, Part 2' (2006) 27 *European Competition Law Review* 279.

[9] Competition Act 1998, ss. 47A, 47B, 58 and 58A.

> **KEY DEFINITIONS**   Box 6.1
>
> ### Stand-alone and follow-on actions
>
> **Stand-alone action**: this is an action brought by a private party against an undertaking which claims that the undertaking has breached competition law and that this breach has caused some damage to the party. Such actions may only be brought in the High Court.[10]
>
> **Follow-on action**: this is an action by a private party against an undertaking which is based on ('follows on from') a decision that there has been an infringement of competition law by the OFT, the European Commission or a UK court. Such an action may be brought in the High Court or the Competition Appeal Tribunal.
>
> **Questions**: Why would you prefer to use one procedure rather than the other? What might be the pros and cons of arguing your case in the High Court as opposed to the Competition Appeal Tribunal?

The final point to tackle is the relationship between UK and EU law in this area. It is obvious that, in principle, a private right of action for breach of competition law could be created under UK legislation although, as we shall see, the legislation says nothing explicit about this. The position under EU law is more complicated. The basis of EU law is a set of treaties agreed between the Member States, which are binding upon the Member States. EU law has developed to say that, regardless of the domestic law of Member States, certain obligations contained in EU law have direct effect, that is, they can be enforced by individuals within their national courts, although this developed in the context of enforcing individual rights derived from EU law against Member States, what has been known as vertical direct effect.[11] It has, however, become clear that rights derived from Treaty articles, such as Articles 101 and 102 TFEU, are enforceable by individuals against individuals but this is done through the national court system, using national procedures and remedies.[12] The European Courts have made it clear that national procedures for the enforcement of EU rights must be equivalent to procedures for the enforcement of national rights and must also be effective, which means that there must be real protection of Union rights.[13] The question of whether this meant that there should be a right for damages actions under Union law has only been decided recently, as we shall see. Given these principles, and s. 60 of the Competition Act 1998, the expectation must be that the grounds for private actions, and procedures, under Articles 101 and 102 TFEU and the Chapters I and II prohibitions should be identical.

Therefore, unlike some of the previous chapters, there is not a hard and fast distinction between domestic and Union law. Accordingly, the plan is as follows in this chapter. First,

---

[10] In general, this will be either the Chancery Division or the Commercial Court: see Civil Procedure Rules, r. 30.8 and CPR Practice Direction – Competition Law – claims relating to the application of Articles 81 and 82 of the EC Treaty and Chapters I and II of Part I of the Competition Act 1998. Section 16 of the Enterprise Act 2002 allows the Lord Chancellor to make regulations for the transfer of stand-alone cases to the CAT, but this has not been done. The BIS consultation paper (n. 1) suggests that this should be done at para. 4.17 and that stand-alone actions should be allowed in the CAT at para. 4.19.

[11] Case 26/62 *Van Gend en Loos* [1963] ECR 1.

[12] Case 127/73 *BRT v Commission* [1974] ECR 51, paras and 16. National courts are given the power to apply Article 101(3) TFEU under Regulation 1/2003, Art. 6, although this is controversial.

[13] Case /83 *Van Colsen v Land Nord-rhein-Westfalen* [1984] ECR 1891.

we deal with the issue of competition law as a defence, which primarily relates to anti-competitive agreements. Secondly, we discuss the basis of original or stand-alone actions in domestic and then Union law. Thirdly, having established the cause of action, we examine the conditions which have to be met for a successful claim. Finally, the law and practice relating to follow-on actions is discussed.

Using competition law as a defence

Article 101(2) TFEU states that agreements or decisions prohibited under Article 101(1) TFEU are automatically void, as long as they do not meet the conditions in Article 101(3) TFEU. Despite the wording, the CJEU has ruled that this only applies to individual clauses in the agreement, therefore if those clauses are removed ('severable' being the technical term) from the agreement, the agreement can still stand.[14] Where the clauses or the agreement are held to be void, they can have no effect between contracting parties and cannot be invoked against third parties. It has been quite common for parties to agreements to claim that the agreement is in breach of Article 101 TFEU and is therefore unenforceable against them. The UK courts have generally been very unsympathetic to such claims, tending to see them as attempts by parties to evade bargains that they have freely entered into, when they did not turn out to their advantage.[15] In principle, if the court finds a breach of Article 101(1) TFEU, the sanction of nullity must be applied: this means that the contract is not enforceable in the courts, which will not recognise it as having any legal effects.

Counter-intuitively, it seems that nullity is not a once and for all decision. It will be remembered that, for an agreement to fall foul of Article 101(1) TFEU, a number of conditions must be met (as discussed in Chapter 2). As circumstances in a market change, it may be possible for an agreement which was not in breach of Article 101(1) TFEU to become in breach and for one that did breach Article 101(1) TFEU to fall out of it. For example, an agreement could be made by a small undertaking which did not have an appreciable effect on trade and therefore was not in breach of Article 101(1) TFEU. That undertaking could grow, or be taken over, to the point where it did have an appreciable effect on competition and therefore the agreement, or the relevant clauses within it, would be void. Given the policy objectives underlying Article 101 TFEU, this is sensible as originally the agreement had no appreciable effect on competition and later it did have such an effect. The logic also works the other way – if an agreement is made which does have an appreciable effect on competition and is therefore in breach of Article 101(1) TFEU, if the undertaking shrinks in size, the agreement may no longer have an appreciable effect on competition and therefore will not be void.[16] This would again seem a sensible outcome given the policy objectives – there is no point in being concerned with an agreement which does not have an appreciable effect on competition.[17]

---

[14] Case 56/65 *Société La Technique Minière* v *Maschinbau Ulm* [1966] ECR 234 at 250.

[15] See, e.g., *Gibbs Mew* v *Gemmell* [1999] 1 EGLR 43.

[16] See *Passmore* v *Morland* [1999] 3 All ER 1005.

[17] Although in Case C-295/04 *Manfredi* [2006] ECR I-6619 at para. 57 the CJEU refers to the invalidity as being 'absolute' and 'capable of having a bearing on all the effects, past or future of the agreement'. This suggests a different conclusion but was not said in response to the type of examples given in the text. The analysis in the text would seem to fit the policy objectives of Article 101 TFEU better.

Although Article 102 TFEU does not provide explicitly for a sanction of nullity, it has been held that if a contract is, or terms of a contract are, in breach of the prohibition in Article 102 TFEU, they are illegal and void.[18]

As regards severance, this is again a matter for the domestic rules. The English rules on this are that the courts will sever parts of a contract where sufficient consideration remains and they can simply delete the offending clauses, and the contract, as broadly envisaged by the parties, will remain in place.[19] The UK courts are, however, very reluctant to engage in this process if they think that the effect will be to rewrite the contract and alter the bargain between the parties.

Competition law as the basis for an action

The position in the UK

The Competition Act 1998 makes no explicit provision for private actions to enforce the Chapters I and II prohibitions. During the passage of the Act, the government rejected an amendment which would have made it clear that private actions were available.[20] It is, nevertheless, clear that the intention behind the Act was that private actions would be available, as was stated at various points in the passage of the Act. In addition, particular provisions of the Act indicate that private actions were envisaged. For example, s. 47A, which deals with follow-on actions, is stated as applying to any claim for damages which a person who has suffered loss or damage due to an infringement of the relevant prohibitions may make in civil proceedings: that is, it assumes that such claims are possible. It would, in any event, be odd if it were possible to claim damages under EU law but not under domestic law and probably contrary to s. 60 of the Competition Act 1998.

The position in EU law

Although the issue in relation to the availability of damages for breach of the Competition Act 1998 was slightly problematic, the issue in relation to damages for breach of Union law was, initially, even more difficult. The European Union Treaties only provide, explicitly, a right to damages in relation to unlawful acts of the European Commission; they make no reference to unlawful acts of Member States or individuals in breach of Union law.[21] However, in a series of cases, starting with *Francovich*,[22] the European Courts held that, where there was a breach of European law by a Member State, compensation had to be available. There were three conditions which had to be met:

1 the Member State had to have infringed a rule of Union law which was intended to confer rights on the applicant;

2 the infringement had to be sufficiently serious; and

---

[18] *English, Welsh & Scottish Railways v E.ON UK* [2007] EWHC 599.
[19] The rules are complex: see *Chitty on Contracts* (31st edn, Sweet & Maxwell, London, 2012), ch. 16.
[20] See Lord Simon, HL Debs, Vol. 586, cols 1325–6, 5 March 1998.
[21] Article 340 TFEU.
[22] Cases C-6/90 *Francovich v Italy* [1991] ECR I-5357.

3 in circumstances in which there was a direct causal link between the breach of Union law and the applicant's loss.[23]

Once this principle had been established, it was a small step to argue that, as a natural extension, such liability ought to be imposed on private individuals who had acted in breach of Union law or, to put it in a more limited way, actions for damages for breach of Union competition law ought to be available.[24]

The issue was finally addressed in the case of *Courage* v *Crehan* (the whole story being told in the 'Competition law in practice' feature at the end of the chapter).[25] In this case the defendant, Crehan, had leased a pub from a pub company, Inntrepreneur, and had committed himself to buying only Courage beer. The pub was not a success and went out of business. Courage sued for the recovery of money which it claimed that Crehan had not paid it for the beer and Crehan defended himself by claiming that the beer tie was in breach of Article 101 TFEU and counter-claimed for damages, arguing that the failure of the business had been caused by the anti-competitive clause. It is worth noting that this was a test case, which started in 1993, because the exclusive supply arrangements contained in the Inntrepreneur lease were common throughout the industry at the time. When the case came to the English courts, the claim for damages was dismissed, at first instance, primarily on the ground that it was based on an illegal act, breach of Article 101 TFEU, and that reliance on an illegal act could not ground a claim for damages, basing the decision on a general principle of policy found in the case law. The Court of Appeal did, however, recognise that the policy arguments might be different in the area of competition law and within EU law and so referred a series of questions to the CJEU under Article 267 TFEU (ex Article 234 EC).[26]

The CJEU decided that there was a Union right to damages in these sorts of cases. Box 6.2 provides an extract of the salient points.

KEY CASE EXTRACT   **Box 6.2**

Source: Case C-453/99 *Courage* v *Crehan* [2001] ECR I-6297:

26 The full effectiveness of Article 85 [Article 101 TFEU] of the Treaty and, in particular, the practical effect of the prohibition laid down in Article 85(1) [Article 101(1) TFEU] would be put at risk if it were not open to any individual to claim damages for loss caused to him by a contract or by conduct liable to restrict or distort competition.

27 Indeed, the existence of such a right strengthens the working of the Community [Union] competition rules and discourages agreements or practices, which are frequently covert, which are liable to restrict or distort competition. From that point of view, actions for damages before the national courts can make a significant contribution to the maintenance of effective competition in the Community [Union] . . .

29 However, in the absence of Community [Union] rules governing the matter, it is for the domestic legal system of each Member State to designate the courts and tribunals

---

[23] Cases C-46 and 48/93 *Brasserie du Pêcheur* v *Germany* [1996] ECR I-1029.
[24] See the Advocate General's opinion in Case C-128/92 *Banks* v *British Coal* [1994] ECR I-1209.
[25] Case C-453/99 [2001] ECR I-6297.
[26] *Courage* v *Crehan (No. 1)* [1999] ECC 455.

having jurisdiction and to lay down the detailed procedural rules governing actions for safeguarding rights which individuals derive directly from Community [Union] law, provided that such rules are not less favourable than those governing similar domestic actions (principle of equivalence) and that they do not render practically impossible or excessively difficult the exercise of rights conferred by Community [Union] law (principle of effectiveness) . . .

31 Similarly, provided that the principles of equivalence and effectiveness are respected . . . Community [Union] law does not preclude national law from denying a party who is found to bear significant responsibility for the distortion of competition the right to obtain damages from the other contracting party. Under a principle which is recognised in most of the legal systems of the Member States and which the Court has applied in the past . . . a litigant should not profit from his own unlawful conduct, where this is proven.

32 In that regard, the matters to be taken into account by the competent national court include the economic and legal context in which the parties find themselves and, as the United Kingdom Government rightly points out, the respective bargaining power and conduct of the two parties to the contract.

33 In particular, it is for the national court to ascertain whether the party who claims to have suffered loss through concluding a contract that is liable to restrict or distort competition found himself in a markedly weaker position than the other party, such as seriously to compromise or even eliminate his freedom to negotiate the terms of the contract and his capacity to avoid the loss or reduce its extent, in particular by availing himself in good time of all the legal remedies available to him.

Questions: Would the effectiveness of Article 101 TFEU really be hurt if people who were party to anti-competitive contracts could not challenge them? What does significant responsibility for a distortion of competition mean?

The basic principle laid down by the CJEU was that an individual should be able to claim damages for loss caused to him or her by an agreement or conduct liable to restrict competition. In the case where parties to contracts made a claim on the basis of the anti-competitive nature of the contract that they had entered into, the CJEU said that relief could be denied if the party bore significant responsibility for the breach of competition law. To determine this, it would be justified for the national court to look at the relevant bargaining power of the parties to the contract and determine whether the claimant was in a significantly weaker position which would compromise or eliminate their freedom to determine the terms of the contract or to mitigate any potential losses.

This position was confirmed in the *Manfredi* case.[27] Here the Italian competition authority had ruled that an information exchange between insurance companies in relation to the terms of motor insurance was unlawful under Italian law and had had the effect of raising premiums in the sector. Manfredi and others had sued in the Italian courts for return of the overcharge and the Italian court took the view that there was a breach of Article 101(1) TFEU as well and referred a number of questions under Article 267 TFEU to the CJEU. Here the

---

[27] Case C-295/04 *Manfredi v Lloyd Adriatico Assicurazioni SpA* [2006] ECR I-6619.

CJEU stated plainly that 'any individual can claim compensation for the harm suffered where there is a causal relationship between that harm and an agreement or practice prohibited under Article 81 [Article 101 TFEU] EC [EU]'.[28] This, however, must be done using national rules on procedure and jurisdiction. These national rules for actions under Article 101 TFEU must not be less favourable than for equivalent domestic actions (principle of equivalence), and they must not make it practically impossible or excessively difficult for the plaintiff to exercise those rights (principle of effectiveness).[29]

Conditions for liability

These cases establish the general principle that there is a private right of action for damages for breach of Article 101 TFEU and, it is assumed, Article 102 TFEU. This is, however, only the start of the story because, having established the principle, we need to look at the detailed conditions that have to be met before liability can be successfully established. In the UK context, the basis for the action is breach of statutory duty, an action in tort, which has four conditions:

1 the damage suffered falls within the scope of the statute;

2 the statutory duty was breached;

3 the breach caused the loss; and

4 there are no applicable defences.

The discussion above indicates that damage caused by anti-competitive action does fall within the terms of Articles 101 and 102 TFEU, although it is worth noting that there can be some argument about this. When the *Crehan* case returned to the Court of Appeal after the CJEU reference,[30] it was argued that if there had been a breach of Article 101 TFEU, this had taken place at the distribution level of trade, not the retail level at which Crehan operated and sustained his losses; therefore, he was not protected against such loss by Article 101 TFEU. The Court of Appeal rejected this suggestion because, although it was right as a matter of English law, it would have rendered the practical application of Article 101 TFEU ineffective and prevented Crehan from protecting his rights.

To prove that the statutory duty has been breached, the plaintiff will have to show an infringement of Articles 101 and 102 TFEU or their domestic equivalents and the law relating to this is discussed above (see Chapters 2 to 4). Where the plaintiff has contracted with the defendant, allegedly in breach of competition law, then, as seen above, the CJEU has said that relief can be denied to a party with significant responsibility for the distortion of competition. What this will mean in practice will need some working out. If we think of the facts of *Courage* v *Crehan*, someone leasing a couple of pubs will clearly be in a weaker position, but what about an undertaking that leases 100 pubs from a brewery? At what point between one and 100 pubs would we draw the line?

---

[28] Ibid., para. 61.

[29] Ibid., para. 62. For what happened after the case, see P. Nebbia, '. . . so what happened to Mr Manfredi? The Italian decision following the ruling of the European Court of Justice' (2007) 28 *European Competition Law Review* 591.

[30] As *Crehan* v *Inntrepreneur* [2004] EWCA 637.

How, then, does a claimant go about proving the infringement? The easiest way is if either the OFT or the European Commission has made a decision in the case that the conduct or agreement complained of is an infringement of competition law because s. 58A of the Competition Act 1998 makes OFT or CAT decisions binding in subsequent actions for damages. As regards Union law, Article 16(1) of Regulation 1/2003 states that, when taking decisions under Articles 101 and 102 TFEU national courts cannot take decisions running counter to a decision adopted by the Commission.[31] These are clear examples of follow-on claims and the procedure which needs to be followed is discussed later.

When it comes to proceedings before a national court that take place at the same time as proceedings before the European Commission, but before the Commission has decided the case, Article 16 of Regulation 1/2003 says that national courts must avoid giving decisions that would conflict with a decision contemplated by the Commission. The national court is entitled to ask the Commission about whether it has initiated proceedings and the timetable for a decision in the case. When such a request is made, the proceedings in the case will be adjourned or stayed. The Commission has stated that it will endeavour to give priority to cases for which it has decided to initiate proceedings and that are the subject of national proceedings stayed in this way, in particular when the outcome of a civil dispute depends on them.[32] The same Notice suggests that if the national court is confident about the decision the Commission is going to take, it can decide the case without waiting for the final decision, although in practice a court would probably be reluctant to take this course. Despite this, the sensible course in this situation is for the national court to stay the proceedings to await the outcome of the Commission's decision. The same outcome could be expected in domestic proceedings, if a case was before the court and the OFT at the same time.

A real problem has arisen in the case of consecutive proceedings between different parties, as illustrated in the *Crehan* case on its return from the CJEU (discussed in full at the end of the chapter).[33] It will be recalled that the basis of Crehan's claim was that the beer tie was contrary to Article 101(1) TFEU. In a number of cases involving other brewers in the UK, the Commission had decided that similar agreements were in breach of Article 101(1) TFEU, although it had never reached a decision on the Inntrepreneur agreement.[34] When the case returned from the CJEU to the first instance judge, Park J, he held that the UK market for the distribution of beer to licensed premises was not foreclosed to new entrants and that therefore there was no breach of Article 101(1) TFEU. This was a surprising decision, seeming to run contrary to Commission decisions, as well as the views of the UK authorities and the other UK courts. It was reversed by the Court of Appeal, which held that Park J ought to have given more deference to the decisions of the European Commission, but this decision was reversed in its turn by the Supreme Court (at the time the House of Lords).[35] The Supreme Court took the view that this was not a case where there was a conflict of views between the Commission and the national court, in which case the national court would be obliged to follow the Commission. Instead, this was a case which had been left, by the Commission, for

[31] See also on this, Case 344/98 *Masterfoods* [2000] ECR I-11369.

[32] European Commission, 'Notice on the co-operation between the Commission and the courts of the EU Member States in the application of Articles 81 and 82 EC', OJ C101, 27.04.2004, para. 12.

[33] *Crehan v Inntrepreneur* [2006] UKHL 38.

[34] 'Whitbread' [1999] OJ L88/26; 'Bass' [1999] OJ L186/1; and 'Scottish and Newcastle' [1999] OJ L186/28.

[35] Respectively: *Crehan v Inntrepreneur* [2003] EWHC 1510 (Ch); *Crehan v Inntrepreneur* [2004] EWCA Civ 637 (CA); *Crehan v Inntrepreneur* [2006] UKHL 38.

the national court to decide and the Commission's view on the legality of the agreement was simply evidence before the English judge, on the basis of which, in part, he would have to make up his mind. If the decision went the other way, holding that the judge was bound by the Commission's view, this would mean that Inntrepreneur would be unable to defend itself, because the basis of its argument had always been that the agreement was lawful.[36]

So, in private actions involving agreements or conduct which have not been the subject of a decision by the competition authorities, it will be up to the party alleging the infringement to prove the basis of their claim, both factually and legally. The major problem for private litigants is that of information asymmetry: in other words, that the undertaking that is alleged to have committed the breach will have much more information about its activities than the person bringing the action. The OFT's view is that English law has wide disclosure provisions, which means that this is less of a problem than in other jurisdictions. In particular, the OFT highlights provision for pre-disclosure orders, that when litigation commences parties not only have to disclose documents on which they wish to rely but also documents which adversely affect their own case and that there is provision for obtaining information from people who are not parties to the case.[37] Although this is true, it will still require a major commitment of resources by a litigant to establish their case.

An illustration can be given in the case of *Chester City Council* v *Arriva*.[38] Here the City Council owned a bus company, which claimed that it had been subject to predatory pricing by Arriva, a fairly common accusation in this industry; and, as an industry, bus services have been subject to numerous competition investigations, so neither the legal grounds, nor the industry presented any novel problems. As a preliminary step in this claim, it was necessary for the plaintiffs to define the market, both product and geographical, so that they could show that Arriva was dominant and had, by its behaviour, abused its dominance. The plaintiffs failed to show that the product market was limited to local bus services, that is, did not include cars and rail transport, and the judge did not accept their views on the geographic market, preferring the defendants' view which gave Arriva a market share of around 30%, which did not constitute dominance. As a result, the plaintiffs lost the case. What this illustrates is that each stage of a private action will be hard-fought and even a relatively well-resourced litigant may find it difficult to establish the basis for a claim. The judge also commented that, 'This case showed the inadequacy of the adversarial system of litigation for an inquiry into markets and market shares.'[39] This is hardly an encouraging comment for would-be private litigants.

Even if the infringement can be established, it will also have to be proved that it is the breach of competition law that has caused the loss to the claimant, not some other intervening factors. The problem was raised directly in *Arkin* v *Borchard Lines (No. 4)*,[40] which was a case where the allegation was that the operation of a liner conference had caused the collapse of a shipping group by acting in breach of Article 102 TFEU. Here the judge held, not only that there was no breach of Article 102 TFEU but also, if there had been, that the plaintiff's loss had been caused by its own actions, essentially running a pricing policy that was bound to lead to losses. The judge made it clear that the onus of proof was on the claimant to show

---

[36] See, especially, Lord Hoffmann at paras 67–70.
[37] OFT, *Private actions in competition law: effective redress for consumers and business* (2007) at para. 6.5.
[38] [2007] EWHC 1373 (Ch).
[39] Ibid. at para. 182.
[40] [2003] EWHC 687.

that the conduct had caused the claimed loss. The judge thought that in these sorts of cases the most helpful approach was simply asking whether the breach of duty was the predominant cause of the loss.[41] Here the plaintiff's actions had been so unreasonable that he had broken the chain of causation between the alleged breaches and the damage caused because no sensible operator would have continued operating given the level of losses that were being incurred.

Who can claim?

Even if the case can be proved, and causation can be shown, there are also currently unresolved issues over who can claim and how damages may be quantified. The former issue has been seen as the more pressing problem, although the two are interrelated, and can be explained through an example. Assume that there is a cartel of food producers, who charge monopoly prices to their customers, the supermarkets. The supermarkets may respond to this pricing policy in a number of ways: they could simply 'pass-on' the extra cost to consumers; they could maintain prices and take reduced profits; or they could stock less of the particular item while raising its price, on the assumption that they would sell more of something else. Consumers who purchase the item on the first and third assumptions are damaged because they pay more than they would have in a competitive market. There will also be some consumers who will not purchase the item because the price is now too high, which means that the supermarkets will have lost sales. If we assume that the supermarkets bring an action against their suppliers, one defence of the suppliers will be that the supermarkets have reduced their damage by passing on the increased costs to consumers and, at its most extreme, they have suffered no damage because they have passed on the entire overcharge. Supermarkets would legitimately respond by arguing that they had lost sales because of the overcharge and the proper measure of damages should be the profits that they would have obtained if the goods had been sold at competitive prices. This line of argument invites the court to enter into a complex discussion which involves determining what a competitive price would have been (remember competition authorities are reluctant to pursue cases on excessive prices) and what would have happened on the market had a competitive price been charged, and then comparing that with what did happen. Further complications are raised if consumers who have not purchased directly from the suppliers (indirect purchasers), then bring actions for damages. In particular, it looks as if the suppliers will end up paying twice for their offences – one set of compensation to the supermarkets and one set of compensation to the consumers – unless the court can find a way of apportioning the damages. This also does not take into account those consumers who would have purchased the good at a competitive price.

In order to avoid these complexities, the US federal courts have developed two basic rules: the passing-on defence is not allowed[42] and indirect purchasers are not allowed to sue for damages.[43] The policy reasons behind this approach are that, in essence, it restricts the inquiry that the court has to make to a manageable one, even if it deprives indirect purchasers, typically consumers, of a right to compensation. The question of what approach to take has not been litigated under competition law in either the UK or the EU courts but there are

---

[41] Ibid. at para. 537.
[42] *Hanover Shoe Inc.* v *United Shore Machinery Corp*, 392 US 481 (1968).
[43] *Illinois Brick Co.* v *Illinois*, 431 US 720 (1977).

indications that the UK courts are reluctant to enter into complex assessments of damages and that there are policy arguments for adopting the US approach.[44] On the other hand, US opinion has moved against the approach suggested above. A substantial number of states have enacted legislation allowing indirect purchasers to sue and the Antitrust Modernisation Commission has recommended that Congress overrule the Supreme Court's decisions to the extent necessary to allow both direct and indirect purchasers to recover.[45] EU law outside the competition area does not provide a clear answer either.[46]

The European Commission and the OFT have taken a different approach from the current US law. Although one reading of the staff paper accompanying the Green Paper from the European Commission was that the preferred option was to follow the US model, on the grounds that this would lead to more effective enforcement of Union law,[47] the White Paper takes a different view. The White Paper's opinion is that, as the case law says that any individual can claim damages for loss caused to them, this covers indirect purchasers.[48] Defendants in antitrust cases should be able to rely on the passing on defence against a claim for overcharging brought by a plaintiff who is not a final consumer but the burden of proving the passing on will lie on the defendant.[49] Indirect purchasers should be able to rely on a rebuttable presumption that the overcharge was passed on in its entirety.[50] Similarly, the OFT took the view that:

> There is increasing consensus that the focus of competition law should be on protecting consumer welfare. In the light of this, it is likely to be inappropriate in policy terms to deny consumers and other end-users the right to sue for damages arising from breach of the competition rules.[51]

As regards passing on, the OFT takes the view that the defendant should only be liable for the loss that he or she has caused to a person and therefore should be allowed to rely on the passing on defence, but that the burden of proof on making this defence will be on the defendant, with the implication being that this will be a difficult burden to overcome.[52] To explain this in the context of the supermarket example above, what this means is that the food producers cartel would have to prove that the supermarkets had passed on the extra costs to consumers, which would require knowledge, among other things, of the supermarkets' costs. Whatever option is chosen, the possibility of legislative action is some years away and the issue of how the courts will respond remains open. Such a significant uncertainty will act as a deterrent for those who are thinking of bringing private actions, whether they be direct or indirect purchasers.

---

[44] See *Re Televising Premier League Football Matches* [2000] EMLR 78; *Crehan v Inntrepreneur* [2004] EWCA Civ 637 at paras 179–80; M. Brealey, 'Adopt Permalife but follow Hanover Shoe to Illinois?' (2002) 1 *Competition Law Journal* 127.

[45] See *http://govinfo.library.unt.edu/amc/report_recommendation/toc.htm* (accessed 20/04/12), Recommendation 47; and H. Hovenkamp, *The Antitrust Enterprise* (Harvard University Press, 2005) at pp. 306–7.

[46] See European Commission, 'Damages actions for the breach of EC antitrust rules' (2005) Commission Staff Working Paper, paras 164–75.

[47] Ibid. at para. 180. The Green Paper is neutral between the various options.

[48] European Commission, 'Staff Working Paper accompanying the White Paper on damages actions for breach of the EC antitrust rules', SEC (2008) 404 at paras 33–7.

[49] Ibid., paras 208–14.

[50] Ibid., paras 215–20.

[51] OFT, *Private actions in competition law: effective redress for consumers and business* (2007) at para. 6.

[52] Ibid. at para. 6.

Assessing damages

The basic principle in terms of assessing damages is that they should be compensatory, that is, they should put the defendant in the position that he or she would have been in had it not been for the unlawful action. Although it is easy to state the principle, it has been said by the European Commission that:

> Quantification of damages in competition litigation can be particularly complex given the economic nature of the illegality and the difficulty of reconstructing what the situation of the claimant would have been absent the infringement . . .[53]

There is a variety of methods of calculating damages, ranging from the simple to the very complex.[54] The 'before and after' approach and the yardstick method are two of the most common and relatively simple. The former compares the prices during the infringement with the situation before and after the infringement to provide a reasonable assumption of the real price levels in the absence of an infringement. Although this is relatively simple, Hovenkamp points out that it usually requires the use of a multiple regression analysis,[55] which considers other factors that might explain differences in the period.[56] This requires the input of economics experts and may be very controversial because the data will almost certainly be imperfect and various assumptions will have to be made to compensate for this. The latter compares the distorted market with similar markets which are not affected by the infringement. The problem here will be finding similar markets and a multiple regression analysis may also be required to control for differences between the markets. So, even after a breach has been established, it will not necessarily be easy to quantify the damages. The Commission's White Paper acknowledges the problem and promises non-binding guidance for quantifying damages in antitrust cases.[57] The BIS consultation document suggests introducing a rebuttal presumption of loss in cartel cases. This is likely to be a presumption that a cartel had affected prices by 20%.[58]

A controversial question in this area has been whether exemplary or punitive damages are available for private actions. In the United States, private plaintiffs may claim treble damages in their suits and this has been seen as a large encouragement to plaintiffs in that jurisdiction. Within the UK, the closest that we would get to that would be an award of exemplary damages and the courts have been generally reluctant to develop this head of damages. Nevertheless, it is clear that exemplary damages may be available where damage has been caused by an action calculated to make a profit and that the categories of cases where

---

[53] European Commission, 'Damages actions for breach of EC antitrust rules' (2005) Staff Working Paper at para. 125.

[54] European Commission, 'Damages actions for breach of EC antitrust rules' (2005) Staff Working Paper at paras 130–144 has some discussion. A more detailed discussion can be found in Ashurst, 'Analysis of economic models for the calculation of damages' (2005), available at *http://ec.europa.eu/comm/competition/antitrust/actionsdamages/study.html* (accessed 20/04/12).

[55] This is a statistical technique used for modelling and analysing several variables, when the focus is on the relationship between a dependent and an independent variable(s). In the example above, the prices are the dependent variables and the independent variable is the infringement but there will be other independent variables, such as labour or raw material costs and the problem will be isolating their effects.

[56] Hovenkamp (n. 45) at p. 86.

[57] European Commission, 'Staff Working Paper accompanying the White Paper on damages actions for breach of the EC antitrust rules', SEC (2008) 404 at paras 198–200.

[58] BIS (n. 1) at para. 4.40.

exemplary damages may be awarded are not closed.[59] European Union law leaves the issue of exemplary damages to the question of national rules, although the UK is one of the few European jurisdictions which leaves open this possibility. The matter was discussed in *Devenish Nutrition*,[60] a case which arose out of the vitamins cartel, where the European Commission had fined a number of undertakings substantial amounts for engaging in activity in breach of Article 101 TFEU. Devenish was one of a number of users who claimed that they had been damaged by this activity, that is, they had paid higher prices for the vitamins that they used in their activities. This case was focused on whether exemplary damages could be claimed in this situation. The judge, Lewison, J, decided that such damages were not available for two reasons. The first was a principle of Union law known as *non bis in idem*, or, to put it another way, the rule against double jeopardy. The rule here was that a person should not be sanctioned more than once for the same unlawful conduct and since the purpose of exemplary damages was to punish and deter, and this was the same aim as fining the offenders, the principle would be infringed if exemplary damages were awarded in addition to a fine imposed by the European Commission, even if the defendant benefited from the leniency policy. The second reason was that, if a national court were to award exemplary damages, this could only be because it thought that the fines were insufficient to punish and deter and the national court would not be in a position to reach this conclusion as it would be running counter to the Commission's decision.

A contrasting outcome occurred in the *Cardiff Bus* case.[61] Here the defendant had been found guilty by the OFT of engaging in predatory pricing, but the OFT had not imposed a penalty because it had decided that the defendant benefited from an exemption within the Competition Act 1998[62] for conduct of minor significance and decided not to withdraw the benefit of the exemption. The plaintiff brought a follow-on action, based on the OFT decision claiming damages and, in particular, exemplary damages. After reviewing the case law, the CAT considered that what was required was a conscious disregard of an unacceptable risk and that, in terms of the Chapter II prohibition, this would only apply in circumstances where the proposed conduct was probably or clearly unlawful.[63] After reviewing the evidence, the CAT concluded that the defendant's conduct was only consistent with that of an organisation that had deliberately decided to disregard the law, and that this conduct was done in cynical disregard of the plaintiff Travel's rights.[64] There were no pro-competitive effects to the conduct and this was not a case involving leniency, as was *Devenish*. The CAT went on to to award exemplary damages of £60,000.

Follow-on actions

Under Union law, if an infringement decision has been taken by the European Commission, then domestic courts are bound to follow that decision and such a claim can be brought in

---

[59] See *Rookes* v *Barnard* [1964] AC 1129; *Kuddus* v *Chief Constable of Leicestershire* [2002] 1 AC 122.
[60] *Devenish Nutrition and others* v *Sanofi Aventis and others* [2007] EWHC 2394 (Ch).
[61] *2 Travel Group PLC* v *Cardiff City Transport* [2012] CAT 19.
[62] Competition Act 1998, s. 40.
[63] Ibid. paras 486–490.
[64] Ibid. para. 593.

the High Court.[65] Section 58 of the Competition Act 1998 provides that findings of fact by the OFT in proceedings based on UK or EU competition law are binding in other court proceedings. Section 58A of the Competition Act 1998 provides that findings of an infringement by either the OFT or the CAT of UK or EU competition law are binding in courts in which damages or other sums of money are claimed. In other words, it is possible to bring a follow-on action in the High Court, relying on the findings made by the competition authorities.

In addition to these provisions, s. 47A of the Competition Act 1998 provides that a person who has suffered loss or damage as a result of the infringement of the provisions of UK or EU competition law may bring an action in front of the CAT provided that a decision has been made that an infringement has been committed by the OFT, the CAT or the European Commission. Section 47B of the Competition Act 1998 extends this provision to what it calls 'consumer claims', which allows specified bodies to bring, or continue, damages actions on behalf of individual consumers. Damages awarded are paid to the individual, rather than the body which may receive its costs. At the moment, only the Consumers Association has applied for and been granted this status.[66] It is worth noting here that it is difficult under English law to combine a number of individual claims into one action in the context of competition law, unlike the US where class actions are more common.[67]

Before discussing the use of this provision in practice, it is important to notice that the follow-on action is allowed only when one of the competition authorities has made a decision that the competition rules have been infringed. This is neatly illustrated by the *Enron* case.[68] Here the Office of Rail Regulation (ORR) had decided that English, Welsh and Scottish Railways (EWS) had abused its dominant position by discriminatory behaviour on the part of EWS in relation to prices offered to Enron. On the basis of this ruling, Enron brought an action against EWS claiming, among other things, damages for being overcharged for coal haulage by EWS. EWS defended itself on this point by arguing that there had been no finding that the prices charged were excessive and the Court of Appeal agreed. Patten LJ made the point that:[69]

> No right of action exists unless the regulator has actually decided that such conduct constitutes an infringement of the relevant prohibition as defined. The corollary to this is that the [CAT] (whose jurisdiction depends upon the existence of such a decision) must satisfy itself that the regulator has made a relevant and definitive finding of infringement.

This provision has been used with some success in front of the CAT.[70] The most high-profile example came in the aftermath of the OFT's decision that certain undertakings had engaged in the price-fixing of replica football shirts between 2000 and 2001. The OFT's decision was appealed to the CAT and from there to the Court of Appeal, and was upheld by the latter in 2006. Subsequent to this decision, in early 2007, the Consumer's Association brought an

---

[65] Regulation 1/2003, Art. 16(1); and see *Devenish Nutrition and others* v *Sanofi Aventis and others* [2007] EWHC 2394 (Ch) as an example of such a claim.

[66] Specified Body (Consumer Claims) Order 2005, SI 2005/2365. Compare with the number of bodies that can make super-complaints.

[67] See *Emerald Supplies* v *British Airways* [2011] Ch 345. R. Mulheron, *The Class Action in Common Law Legal Systems* (Hart Publishing, Oxford, 2004) and R. Mulheron, *Reform of Collective Redress in England and Wales* (Civil Justice Council, London, 2008) give a wider context.

[68] *Enron Coal Services* v *English, Welsh and Scottish Railways* [2009] EWCA Civ 647.

[69] Ibid. at para. 31.

[70] There have been twelve cases since 2008: CAT *Annual Review 2010–11* at p. 43.

action against JJB Sports on behalf of some 130 individual consumers who had purchased individual replica shirts, seeking both compensatory and exemplary or restitutionary damages from JJB. The case was settled in January 2008 and JJB agreed to pay £20 to those who had joined the action initially and £10 to those who did not join the action but still had proof of purchase (rather unlikely some six or seven years later). Press reports suggested that there were 600 consumers who had joined the action and that the total cost to JJB would be in the region of £20,000, as opposed to the original fine of £6.7 million.[71] This is noteworthy as the first such case, but the sums involved for individual consumers are quite small, as is the total bill.

By contrast, also in January 2008, it was announced that BA and Virgin Airways had settled a class action suit in the United States brought in the wake of fines of approximately £270 million levied by the US authorities in relation to a cartel over fuel surcharges between 2004 and 2006. In relation to flights from the UK, the companies set aside a fund of more than £73.5 million to compensate passengers for the overcharging (there is a separate fund for flights originating from the United States).[72] Although the individual sums per consumer will be quite small, the overall figure does seem to be significant, particularly when combined with the fines that have been levied by the Department of Justice, and one press report estimated that the case had cost BA around £338 million.[73]

This provision has also been used by competitors who have been damaged by anti-competitive activities. Following on from the OFT's decision in the *Genzyme* case, which related to the pricing of certain drugs supplied to both the NHS and the home health care market, an action under s. 47A was brought by Healthcare at Home against Genzyme for damages for, among other things, loss of margin on their sales in April 2006. The case was settled, on confidential terms, at the beginning of 2007. Similarly, following on from the decision in the *Burgess* case,[74] which involved a finding by the CAT that a crematorium had abused its dominant position by refusing access to its facilities, an action was brought some two years later by the party who was claiming to be damaged.[75] This case was settled in early 2008.

Both of these cases have been relatively straightforward in terms of the affected parties being able to gain some redress. This need not always be the case, as can be illustrated by *Emerson Electric* v *Morgan Crucible*, a case which arose following the decision of the European Commission (in December 2003) in the electrical and carbon graphites case that there had been a cartel amongst a number of English, French and German undertakings in relation to these products in breach of Article 101 TFEU.[76] All the participants in the cartel had been subject to fines, with the exception of Morgan Crucible, which had benefited from the leniency policy and had had its fine reduced to zero. Emerson Electric, and some other companies, brought an action against Morgan Crucible under s. 47A, alleging that they had been damaged by the actions of the participants in the cartel. However, since some of the participants in the cartel, not including Morgan Crucible, had appealed the European Commission's decision to the GC, the question arose as to whether the plaintiffs

---

[71] See *The Financial Times*, 10 January 2008.

[72] See *https://www.airpassengerrefund.co.uk/* (accessed 20/04/12).

[73] *Daily Telegraph*, 17 February 2008.

[74] *M E Burgess* v *OFT* [2005] CAT 25.

[75] Case No. 1088/5/7/07 *M E Burgess et al.* v *W Austin*.

[76] Commission Decision, Case C.38.359, *Electrical and mechanical carbon and graphite products* (3 December 2003). Proceedings were also taken against this cartel in the United States, both by the Department of Justice and private litigation.

needed the permission of the CAT to bring the action, as s. 47A provides that such permission is needed in circumstances where an appeal has been lodged, but not determined. The CAT decided that, on a plain reading of s. 47A, it covered this situation and that permission needed to be sought to bring the action.[77] The CAT did, however, in a later judgment grant permission for this action to be brought.[78] The appeals by the other parties to the cartel were unsuccessful before the GC and the CJEU.[79] The plaintiffs then sought and were granted the CAT's permission to join as additional defendants Schunk, SGL, Carbone Lorraine and Le Carbone (Great Britain) Ltd. Le Carbone (Great Britain), which had become Mersen UK Portslade, then applied to have the claim against it struck out, on the ground that it was not named within the Commission decision, although it had been part of the Carbon Lorraine group at the time of the European Commission's decision. The CAT accepted this argument and struck out the claim against Mersen UK Portslade and the plaintiffs appealed this decision to the Court of Appeal.[80] It is worth noting that this claim is founded on a decision in 2003 (in relation to a cartel running from 1988 to 1999), the claim was made in 2007 and that, at best, the CAT might make a decision towards the end of 2012.

Conclusions on private enforcement

While it is true that, in principle, actions for damages for breach of competition law can now be brought by private plaintiffs, what the discussion above indicates is that, outside the sphere of follow-on actions, there are a number of difficulties which make private actions unattractive. It is only worth bringing an action, in economic terms, if the benefits will outweigh the costs and potential benefits will be discounted by the chance of success. Competition law cases are very costly: they are often factually complex, expert evidence is usually required and they tend to be lengthy. In addition, if the plaintiff fails, they are likely to have to pay the other side's costs. These problems are even more daunting for consumers and small businesses, particularly in the absence of class actions which are common in the United States. Even if some of these problems were to be rectified,[81] there will still be problems of proof, causation, quantum of damages and the availability or not of a passing-on defence, to mention some examples. Although these obstacles suggest that stand-alone private actions are difficult and that we might expect the main burden of enforcement to fall on the public authorities, there is evidence that this may be too pessimistic a view.[82]

In order to reform the UK law relating to private actions, BIS has suggested that the law should be changed to allow stand–alone actions in the CAT, provide a fast-track procedure

---

[77] [2007] CAT 28, paras 62–73.

[78] [2007] CAT 30.

[79] Case T-68/04 *SGL Carbon v Commission* [2008] ECR II-2511, Case T-69/04 *Schunk GmbH v Commission* [2008] ECR II-2567, Case T-73/04 *Le Carbone-Lorraine v Commission* [2008] ECR II-2661 (all GC), Case C-554/08P *Le Carbone-Lorraine SA v Commission* [2009] ECR I-189 and Case C-564/08P *SGL Carbon AG v Commission* [2009] ECR I-191 (both CJEU).

[80] *Emerson Electric Co v Morgan Crucible* [2011] CAT 4.

[81] See OFT, *Private actions in competition law: effective redress for consumers and business* (2007) for proposals for a representative action and for some changes to the costs rules.

[82] B. Rodger, 'Private enforcement of competition law, the hidden story: competition litigation in the United Kingdom, 2000–2005' (2008) 29 *European Competition Law Review* 96 provides information on 43 settlements during that period.

for small business competition cases, introduce a rebuttable presumption of a 20% loss for cartel cases, encourage the use of alternative dispute resolution and introduce an opt-out collective action which will be available for consumer and business claims.[83] Although there are a number of sensible suggestions in this consultation paper, the important question is whether these reforms will change the incentives sufficiently for potential plaintiffs to encourage more private litigation.

COMPETITION LAW IN PRACTICE

Courage v Crehan[84]

We have discussed the *Crehan* case at a number of different places in this chapter. It is, however, worth putting the entire sequence of events together because it illustrates how private enforcement has developed and also the various obstacles to even a determined litigant.

Facts

In 1991 Mr Crehan entered into leases for two pubs in West London with a pub leasing company, Inntrepreneur. These leases contained a provision which was standard in such leases between breweries and their tenants, known as a 'beer tie'. Essentially this provision provided that the lessee, Crehan, would purchase all the beers needed for the pub from a brewer nominated by Inntrepreneur, who nominated Courage. In other words, it was an exclusive supply arrangement. Crehan ran the pubs and made large losses until, in 1993, he surrendered the leases. Courage brought an action against him for an unpaid debt for beer and other supplies. He then counter-claimed against Courage, alleging that because he had to purchase all his beers from Courage at list prices he was unable to compete against other pubs in the area. The beer tie had made his pub fail and it was in breach of Article 101 TFEU.

This relatively simple set of facts has led to a significant change in the law relating to private enforcement, as well as being an indication of the major changes which the UK brewing industry has undergone since the early 1990s, largely in response to changes brought about by competition law. Crehan, although an individual litigant, also represented a number of tenants of Inntrepreneur who found themselves in a similar position and thus this was a test case for a substantial group.

Context

The context of this case was the rapid changes in the brewing industry in the early 1990s.[85] At the end of the 1980s, the brewing industry in the UK was vertically integrated and dominated by six national brewers, which accounted for 75% of beer production, owned over 50% of the pubs and had substantial interests in wholesaling of beer. The industry was investigated by the then Monopolies and Mergers Commission (MMC), the forerunner of the Competition Commission, which concluded that a complex monopoly

➡

---

[83] See: BIS (n. 1).

[84] Much of the factual background is drawn from *Crehan v Inntrepreneur* [2003] EWHC 1510 (Ch).

[85] See Trade and Industry Select Committee, *Pub Companies* (2004), paras 7–25 for a description of developments.

existed in favour of brewers that owned tied houses or that had tying agreements with free houses in return for loans (brewer loans) at favourable interest rates.[86] The main recommendation of the MMC was that a ceiling be introduced restricting any one brewing company, or group, from owning more than 2,000 on-licensed outlets (the majority of which were public houses), thereby increasing competition in brewing, wholesaling and retailing. These recommendations were not fully implemented, but, through a set of statutory instruments known as the Beer Orders, the government in essence said that brewers could not own more than 2,000 pubs each.[87]

In response, the major brewers largely divested their pubs and a new entity sprung up, the so-called Pubcos, which were the companies that owned the pubs, but did not brew beer. Inntrepreneur was one such company which, having been created through a deal between Courage and Grand Metropolitan, took over the management of the pubs. Courage took over the brewing of beer and Grand Metropolitan withdrew from brewing. Inntrepreneur had its own form of lease for its tenants, which was different from other industry leases, being for a longer term, for a higher rent and obliging its tenants to buy their beer from Courage at list prices, that is, the tenants were not able to obtain any discounts, unlike some of their competitors which were not subject to such ties. Although there was a high demand for this type of lease initially, relations between the tenants and Inntrepreneur seemed to have gone very badly wrong in the early 1990s leading to a substantial amount of litigation between Inntrepreneur and its tenants, usually over unpaid debts to Courage or regarding the forfeiture of leases. One of the standard defences raised was that the beer tie obligations were contrary to Article 101 TFEU and this therefore made the contract unenforceable.

Although Inntrepreneur was winning these cases, it decided to go to the European Commission, notifying their agreement in 1992, and seek either a decision that its leases were not in breach of Article 101 TFEU, or that they fell within the Block Exemption for beer supply, or that they could be granted an individual exemption. (All of this was conducted under the old procedures contained in Regulation 17/62.) The issue of the compatibility of beer supply agreements with competition law had been a major issue for the European Commission for some time. The *Delimitis*[88] case in the CJEU had provided a twofold test for the compatibility of such agreements with Article 101 TFEU:

1 Having regard to the economic and legal context of the agreement at issue, is it difficult for competitors that could enter the market or increase their market share to gain access to the national market for the distribution of beer in premises for the sale and consumption of drinks? This is usually called market foreclosure.

2 Did the agreement in question make a significant contribution to the sealing off effect brought about by the totality of those agreements in their economic and legal context?

Ultimately, the Commission never made a decision on this notification but it did grant an individual exemption to a modified version of the standard tenancy agreements in

---

[86] Monopolies and Mergers Commission, 'The Supply of Beer: A report on the supply of beer for retail sale in the United Kingdom' (1989).

[87] These have since been revoked.

[88] Case C-234/89 *Stergios Delimitis* v *Henniger Brau* [1991] ECR I-935.

1997, but this only applied prospectively, so did not answer the question of whether the original agreement was in breach of Article 101 TFEU. In a letter to Inntrepreneur, the Commission said that no Union interest would be served by making a decision and that the question of whether Article 101(1) TFEU applied to the old lease was a matter a national court could decide. In 1999, the Commission came to a decision on three other brewers' leases that, although they fell foul of Article 101(1) TFEU and did not meet the terms of the block exemption, they were entitled to an individual exemption.[89]

The case

The case began as a claim by Courage in 1993 against Crehan for an unpaid debt for beer and other goods. Crehan counter-claimed that the beer tie was a breach of Article 101 TFEU and that he was entitled to damages. Proceedings in the case were informally suspended between the parties while the Commission was considering the issue but the case was revived in 1997. The case came before Carnwath J in November 1998: see *Courage Ltd v Crehan*.[90] He held, following obiter dicta of the Court of Appeal in *Gibbs Mew v Gemmell*:[91] (1) that Article 101 TFEU was designed, not to protect the parties to an unlawful agreement themselves (i.e. in the present context not to protect tied tenants), but rather to protect the competitors of parties to an unlawful agreement (i.e. to protect other brewers who wished to enter the market or to expand their market shares); and (2) that in any case a party to an unlawful agreement could not claim damages from the other party for loss caused to himself by being a party to it. Crehan then appealed to the Court of Appeal, which, among other things, decided to refer certain questions in the case to the CJEU in May 1999.[92] The CJEU came to a decision in February 2001, saying that a party to a contract in breach of Article 101 TFEU could rely on that breach to obtain relief from the other contracting party.

The case then came back to the English courts and was heard in the High Court before Park J, who decided the case in March 2003.[93] Crehan claimed that both the *Delimitis* conditions were met which was, in essence, proved by the Commission decisions in 1999 and that the judge should accept the Commission's view. The judge disagreed, holding that he was entitled to address the issue of market foreclosure, and came to the conclusion that Crehan had not established that the first *Delimitis* condition had been met in relation to the UK beer market between 1991 and 1993; and therefore the claim failed.

There was then an appeal by Crehan to the Court of Appeal, which reversed the first instance judgment in 2004.[94] It ruled that the first instance judge was obliged to follow the view of the Commission expressed in the other brewers' cases and that he had not shown sufficient deference to the Commission's views. Crehan was awarded damages in the sum of £131,336. This was then followed by a further appeal to the House of Lords,[95]

---

[89] *Whitbread* [1999] OJ L88/26; *Bass* [1999] OJ L186/1; and *Scottish and Newcastle* [1999] OJ L186/28.
[90] [1999] EuLR 409.
[91] [1998] EuLR 588.
[92] *Crehan v Courage* [1999] EWCA Civ 1501.
[93] *Crehan v Inntrepreneur* [2003] EWHC 1510 (Ch).
[94] *Crehan v Inntrepreneur* [2004] EWHC Civ 637.
[95] *Inntrepreneur v Crehan* [2006] UKHL 38.

which was decided in 2006 and reversed the decision of the Court of Appeal, restoring the first instance decision. The House of Lords held that the duty of national courts not to make decisions which contradicted decisions of Union institutions on the same subject matter between the same parties did not extend to requiring national courts to accept the factual basis of a decision reached by a Union institution when considering an issue arising between different parties in respect of a different subject matter. One of the reasons behind this was that it meant that, in the circumstances, to decide otherwise would have meant that Inntrepreneur would have had no venue in which to raise its main defence.

Analysis

The first point to notice is that this case took thirteen years to reach a final, unsuccessful, conclusion for the applicant. Is this a good advertisement for private enforcement? Would subsequent cases take that amount of time given the new system of enforcement in Regulation 1/2003 and the decision of principle by the CJEU in this case? Such cases are, however, expensive: for the final hearings in the Court of Appeal and the House of Lords, Inntrepreneur claimed costs of just over £2 million.[96] Secondly, the case shows the limits to the UK courts' duty to follow decisions of the CJEU and, more importantly, the European Commission. Do you prefer the House of Lords or the Court of Appeal on this point? Private litigants will not be able to rely on a decision in a factually similar case with different parties but must rely on decisions in their case, in other words, follow-on actions. Finally, there is an argument that the CJEU decision in *Courage* v *Crehan* was not desirable from the point of view of competition law as Crehan essentially was seeking to escape a bad bargain.[97] In terms of private enforcement, should we really be interested in encouraging those who are damaged by anti-competitive behaviour to take action, as opposed by those who entered into anti-competitive agreements and then found that they did not work out as expected?

Summary

➤ Individuals may either use competition law as a defence in actions brought against them or may bring an action to obtain damages for breach of competition law.

➤ Actions to obtain damages can either follow the decision of a competition authority or court (follow-on actions) or be an original claim.

➤ It has been established that individuals may bring original actions in national courts for breach of EU competition law and UK competition law and obtain damages to compensate them for their losses.

[96] See *Crehan* v *Inntrepreneur* [2007] EWHC 90081 (Costs) at para. 8.
[97] See G. Monti, 'Anti-Competitive Agreements: The Innocent Party's Right to Damages' (2002) 27 *European Law Review* 282.

➤ In order to establish a successful claim for damages, individuals will have to prove that an anti-competitive agreement or conduct has taken place and that it has caused the loss. Both of these may be difficult to accomplish.

➤ It has not yet been decided whether it is a defence to a private action that the plaintiff has passed on the losses to people who have purchased from it. It is also not clear whether indirect purchasers will be allowed to bring claims.

➤ Assessment of damages is a complex procedure. Two common methods are the before and after approach and the yardstick approach. Both will require expert economic evidence.

➤ It is unlikely that the UK courts will be sympathetic to claims for exemplary damages.

➤ Follow-on actions have begun to be used regularly in the UK and claimants have had some success with them.

➤ Given all the obstacles to successful private actions, the Commission, BIS and the OFT have proposed certain reforms.

Further reading

Komninos, A., 'New Prospects for Private Enforcement of EC Competition Law' (2002) 39 *Common Market Law Review* 447. *Positive discussion of* Courage v Crehan.

Monti, G., 'Anti-Competitive Agreements: The Innocent Party's Right to Damages' (2002) 27 *European Law Review* 282. *Critical examination of* Courage v Crehan, *arguing that the decision was undesirable.*

Rodger, B., 'Competition law litigation in the UK courts: a study of all cases to 2004' (Parts I–III) (2006) 27 *European Competition Law Review* 241, 279 and 341. *Discusses litigation trends from the 1970s until 2004.*

Rodger, B., 'Private enforcement of competition law, the hidden story: competition litigation settlements in the United Kingdom, 2000–2005' (2008) 29 *European Competition Law Review* 96. *Useful discussion of competition cases that were brought but never reached trial and so were not reported.*

Rodger, B., 'Competition law litigation in the UK courts: a study of all cases 2005–2008: Part 1' (2009) 2 *Global Competition Litigation Review* 93. *Updates previous work.*

Official publications

BIS, 'Private actions in competition law – a consultation on options for reform' (2012).

European Commission, Green Paper on *Damages actions for breach of EC antitrust rules*, COM (2005) 672. *The European Commission's first thoughts on how to encourage damages actions.*

European Commission, White Paper on *Damages actions for breach of the EC antitrust rules*, COM (2008) 165. *The European Commission's developed proposals for improving private enforcement.*

European Commission, *Towards a Coherent European Approach to Collective Redress: Next Steps* (2010) available at: *http://ec.europa.eu/competition/antitrust/actionsdamages/index.html* (accessed 20/04/12).

OFT, *Private actions in competition law: effective redress for consumers and business* (2007). *The OFT's view on how to encourage private actions.*

BIS, 'Private actions in competition law – a consultation on options for reform' (2012).

7 Competition law and the state

Chapter outline

This chapter discusses:

➤ The problems of controlling state action

➤ When is action by a state contrary to competition law? – the state action doctrine

➤ Article 106(1) TFEU – when does the creation of a monopoly by the state contravene competition law?

➤ Article 106(2) TFEU – when is there an exception to the application of competition law?

➤ The control of state aids:

  ● What is a state aid?
  ● What types of aid are exceptions and exemptions to the control regime?
  ● Where are services of general economic interest treated?
  ● The enforcement of the rules by the European Commission.

Introduction

One of the peculiarities of EU competition law, when compared with American law and UK law prior to 1998, is that it is concerned to ensure that the activities of the state are compatible with the rules of competition law. This is unusual because, historically, in most states there has been an assumption that once the state intervenes, for example to create a publicly owned monopoly, then there is no room for competition law. This was the case in the past with nationalised industries in the United Kingdom which had monopoly status, such as British Gas, and US law assumes that certain activities can be removed from the scope of antitrust law if the federal and state authorities think this is appropriate and, in the case of state authorities, the appropriate conditions are met.[1] As regards the European Union, however, where one of the main objectives has been to create a common or internal market, it has always been recognised that actions by Member States could form an obstacle to the creation of an internal market. The EU Treaties therefore place limitations on state action which will impede the creation of an internal market, but more often this is done through provisions

---

[1] See H. Hovenkamp, *Federal Antitrust Policy* (4th edn, West Publishing, St Paul, Minnesota, 2011) at chs. 19–20.

relating to free movement, rather than competition. Nevertheless, state intervention can be damaging to the competitive process through, for example, limiting entry to a market or placing restrictions on competition within it, as well as to the creation of an internal market, and so it is not surprising that the EU Treaties seek to place some limits on this intervention.

This does, however, raise a difficult problem as to what should be the appropriate limits on intervention? The Member States of the EU have different traditions in relation to state intervention. The United Kingdom and the Scandinavian countries are characterised as on the free market end of the spectrum, with France, Belgium and Greece at the more interventionist end, but this is very simplistic and also ignores the experiences of the newer members, such as Poland, Hungary and the Czech Republic, which only entered into a free market system after 1998. The point is that there is not, and has never been, a consensus amongst the Member States about the appropriate place for state intervention in the economy. This disagreement was reflected in debates over the European Reform Treaty where the French President Nicholas Sarkozy apparently engineered the removal of the part of Article 3 EC speaking of a commitment to 'undistorted competition', saying that 'Competition as an ideology, as a dogma, what has it done for Europe?'[2] although the outcome is more nuanced than this public statement suggests (as was discussed in Chapter 1). At the EU level the issue becomes more complicated because it is inevitably intertwined with the issue of national versus EU powers. Member States intervene in economic matters for a variety of reasons but one overarching explanation is that they are unhappy with the workings of the existing market and seek to alter its outcomes, typically for social reasons. To what extent is it legitimate for Union law to say that a Member State cannot undertake this intervention or place limits upon it?

The problem is made yet more complex by the myriad means of intervention in the economy that are open to the state and, in particular, a growing trend towards privatisation and liberalisation of state enterprises. What has been happening in Europe, at different speeds, has been the movement of public bodies into the private sector, notably in the UK between 1984 and 1992, and a consequent liberalisation of these markets: for example, the opening up of the postal services market. In addition, private sector ideas are sometimes introduced into the public sector, such as the introduction of market-like mechanisms within the NHS. For our purposes, what this means is that there is no longer a clear divide between sectors which are non-market based and those which are market based. States are trying in certain areas to combine the benefits of market disciplines while at the same time maintaining non-market goals or policies. Producing such a balance is inherently difficult and we will see that EU law has struggled with this question when it has been raised. It has equally struggled with the question of whether competition law is appropriate at all, as can be seen by the earlier discussion of the concept of an 'undertaking' (see Chapter 2).

There are three areas to discuss here. There is, first, the question of whether state measures which allow or encourage anti-competitive behaviour contrary to Articles 101 and 102 TFEU can be held to be unlawful under Union law, given that Articles 101 and 102 TFEU only apply to undertakings. Secondly, there is the question as to what extent certain types of undertakings, which are entrusted by the state with certain activities, may avoid the application of the competition rules. This is the area of law covered by Article 106 TFEU (ex Art. 86 EC). Thirdly, there is the question as to what extent the state may provide aids to industry. This area is covered by Articles 107–109 TFEU (ex Articles 87–89 EC).

---

[2] *The Financial Times*, 22 June 2007.

State actions contrary to Articles 101 and 102 TFEU

It will be recalled that Articles 101 and 102 TFEU only apply to agreements or conduct by *undertakings*, not to action by a state. Having said this, Article 4 para. 3 TEU provides that Member States shall abstain from measures which could jeopardise the attainment of the objectives of the Treaty and one of those objectives has been the creation of a system of undistorted competition (Box 7.1).

KEY LEGAL PROVISION   **Box 7.1**

Article 4 para. 3 TEU (ex Article 10 EC)

The Member States shall take any appropriate measure, general or particular, to ensure fulfilment of the obligations arising out of the Treaties or resulting from the acts of the institutions of the Union. The Member States shall facilitate the achievement of the Union's tasks and refrain from any measure which could jeopardise the attainment of the Union's objectives.

Question: How much weight, in practice, will a Member State give to this obligation?

On the basis of these provisions, the CJEU developed a concept of 'effet utile', initially stating it in very wide terms, in *GB-Inno*, a case which involved a legislative scheme fixing prices for tobacco products (minimum and maximum retail price maintenance):

> While it is true that Article 86 [102 TFEU] is directed at undertakings, nonetheless it is also true that the Treaty imposes a duty on member states not to adopt or maintain in force any measure which could deprive that provision of its effectiveness . . . Likewise, Member States may not enact measures enabling private undertakings to escape from the constraints imposed by Articles 85 to 94 [101–109 TFEU] of the Treaty.[3]

The CJEU came to this conclusion by reading Articles 101 and 102 TFEU in conjunction with what is now Article 4 para. 3 TEU and Protocol 27 (ex Article 3(f) EC), which states that one of the objectives of the European Union is a system of undistorted competition. This wide approach to the issue was slightly narrowed in the *Asjes* case,[4] which involved the fixing of prices for air transport. Here the CJEU said that the effectiveness of the competition provisions would be undermined, in particular, if a Member State were to require or favour the adoption of agreements, decisions or concerted practices contrary to Article 101 TFEU or to reinforce their effects.[5]

This approach opened up the possibility of challenging a wide variety of state measures and can be illustrated by *Vlaamse Reisbureaus*,[6] a case where a Belgian law prevented travel

---

[3] Case 13/77 *GB-Inno* [1977] ECR 2115 at paras 31 and 33.

[4] Cases 209–213/84 *Asjes* [1986] ECR 1425.

[5] Ibid. at para. 72. The formulation was originally that of the Commission in Case 229/83 *LeClerc v Au blé vert* [1985] ECR 1 at para. 12 where it was envisaged as happening only in exceptional circumstances.

[6] Case 311/85 *Vlaamse Reisbureaus v Sociale Dienst* [1987] ECR 3801.

agents from sharing their commission with consumers, as an inducement to use their services. The Association of Flemish Travel Agencies brought an action against a social services office, which arranged travel and offered rebates to its clients. The Belgian court referred the issue of whether this was a breach of Union competition rules to the CJEU under Article 267 TFEU. The CJEU held that there was a system of anti-competitive agreements in place between travel agents and that the legislation had reinforced the effect of the agreement because it converted the contractual provisions into a legislative provision with a permanent character. It allowed those travel agents who were party to the agreement to bring actions against those who did not abide by it and provided an effective sanction against those who did not adhere to the agreement, by making this a ground for removing their licence as a travel agent.[7] Such legislative provisions were therefore incompatible with the Union rules on competition. A similar result was reached in *BNIC* v *Aubert*[8] which concerned the French rules on production quotas for cognac.

The test to be applied was narrowed in *Van Eyck*.[9] In this case the plaintiff wanted to open a savings account at a Belgian bank but found that they would not be paid the advertised rate of interest but only a lower rate, because the Belgian bank was prevented from offering a higher rate of interest by Belgian legislation. The legislation was put in place because a previous self-regulatory regime amongst financial institutions had not been adhered to by all the participants. The plaintiff brought an action in the national courts seeking a declaration that Belgian law was contrary to Union competition law and the issue reached the CJEU by way of a preliminary reference. After reciting the formula mentioned above from *GB-Inno*, the CJEU said that legislation could deprive the competition provisions of their effectiveness 'if a Member State were to require or favour the adoption of agreements, decisions or concerted practices contrary to Article 85 [Article 101 TFEU] or to reinforce their effects, or to deprive its own legislation of its official character by delegating to private traders responsibility for taking decisions affecting the economic sphere'.[10] The CJEU said that legislation may be regarded as intended to reinforce the effects of pre-existing agreements, *only* if it incorporates either wholly or in part the terms of agreements concluded between undertakings and requires or encourages compliance on the part of those undertakings and neither had been shown to be the case here.[11]

The effect of this approach was to encourage a number of private litigants to challenge state regulation of commercial matters, combining this with use of the freedom of movement provisions (the European Commission has never taken action on these grounds). Ironically, given the current policy to encourage private litigation, such litigants have been looked on with disapproval in the academic literature, being described as 'opportunistic' or offending the principle of democratic federalism and representative democracy.[12] The upshot of this was a set of decisions in 1993[13] which confirmed the *Van Eycke* formula, and this is set out in Box 7.2.

---

[7] Ibid. at para. 23.

[8] Case 136/86 *BNIC* v *Aubert* [1987] ECR 4789.

[9] Case 267/86 *Van Eycke* v *ASPA* [1988] ECR 4769.

[10] Ibid. at para. 16.

[11] Ibid. at para. 18.

[12] See E. Szyszczak, *The Regulation of the State in Competitive markets in the EU* (Hart Publishing, Oxford, 2007) at p. 50 for references.

[13] Case C-2/91 *Meng* [1993] ECR I-5797; Case C-185/91 *Reiff* [1993] ECR I-5847; Case C-245/91 *Ohra* [1993] ECR I-5878; J.L. Buendia Sierra, *Exclusive Rights and State Monopolies under EC Law* (Oxford University Press, 1999) at p. 26.

KEY CASE EXTRACT   Box 7.2

When does state action breach Article 101 TFEU combined with Article 4 para. 3 TEU?

Source: Case 267/86 *Van Eycke* v *ASPA* [1988] ECR 4769 at para. 16:

- it imposes on undertakings the entering into of agreements contrary to Article 101 TFEU; or
- it favours the entering into of such agreements; or
- it reinforces the effects of such agreements; or
- it delegates to private operators the responsibility for adopting decisions concerning economic intervention.

Questions: How easy is it to put these guidelines into practice? Can you think of examples that might be relevant? Consider the regulation of the legal profession.

What is noticeable about the case law is that, since 1993, there has been no decision of the CJEU that national regulations are contrary to Article 101 TFEU, when read in conjunction with Article 4 para. 3 TEU and Protocol 27 (ex Article 3(f) EC). The CJEU has been very reluctant either to expand these categories or to look very closely at the factual situation in the cases before it, although, since almost all these cases have been brought under Article 267 TFEU, it is somewhat limited in reviewing the facts. This approach has been severely criticised by Buendia Sierra, a leading commentator, as being very formalistic ('infantile') and having no regard to economic reality, for example through excluding the possibility of delegation of public powers to private operators because the representatives of the sector in a tariff-fixing commission are formally independent of the undertakings which propose them and the decision can be theoretically changed by a minister.[14]

The most interesting recent case was the *CIF* case, which involved the Italian competition authority and the Italian match monopoly.[15] The basic idea behind the legislation, which initially came into force in 1923, was that all match manufacturers were required to be members of a consortium which, among other things, set production and monitored quotas. Prices for the sale of matches were set by the Italian government. The arrangements governing this consortium were liberalised in the 1980s and 1990s, allowing new companies to become members and, ultimately, abolishing the monopoly. A German match company complained to the Italian competition authority about certain practices which it alleged had made it difficult for it to distribute its matches. The Italian competition authority investigated and decided that the relevant legislation was contrary to Article 101 TFEU when read in conjunction with Article 4 para. 3 TEU because it required anti-competitive conduct and, after the reforms, facilitated it. In addition, independently of the legislation, the consortium had made certain anti-competitive decisions relating to the production of matches. The consortium

---

[14] Buendia Sierra (n. 13) at p. 265. For a more recent example, see Case C-94 and 202/04 *Cipolla* [2006] ECR I-11421 [2007] 4 CMLR 8.

[15] Case C-198/01 *Consorzio Industrie Fiammiferi* v *Autorità Garante della Concorrenza e del Mercato* [2003] ECR I-8055.

challenged the decision in the Italian administrative tribunal, arguing that the competition authority had no power to disapply the Italian legislation. Two questions were referred to the CJEU: first, could the competition authority disapply the Italian legislation and, if so, what penalties could be imposed? Secondly, would it be possible to regard national legislation under which competence to fix the retail prices of a product is delegated to a ministry and power to allocate production between undertakings is entrusted to a consortium to which the relevant producers are obliged to belong, as precluding undertakings from engaging in autonomous conduct which restricts competition?

The CJEU responded to the first question by saying that the rules would be less effective if a national competition authority could not declare that national legislation was contrary to the EU rules on competition. As regards the penalties, the CJEU drew a distinction between conduct before and after the competition authority decided that the national law was in breach of EU law. For conduct prior to the decision, undertakings would not be regarded as acting autonomously and thus had a defence against a charge of breach of Article 101 TFEU where that conduct was required by the national legislation. Once the decision is made to disapply the national law, undertakings can no longer claim that they are required to follow it, so consequently can be penalised. Where past conduct was merely facilitated or encouraged by the national legislation, then penalties could be imposed, although the context of the national legislation should be taken into account as a mitigating factor. As regards the second question, although this was ultimately up to the national court to decide, there are indications in the CJEU's discussion that it thought there was room for independent conduct by the undertakings concerned, as the Italian government only controlled price and this was just one aspect of the competition process.

What seems to have happened in this area is that the CJEU has pulled back from following the logic of its initial case law. Explanations for this development have been varied,[16] ranging from the technical, such as the inability to use the Article 101(3) TFEU exemption procedure in this context, to the more political. This latter is the explanation favoured by Ehle,[17] a German lawyer, who says that the doctrine is not really about competition but about the distribution of political power, or, in other words, to what extent Member States may engage in the regulation of economic affairs without falling foul of EU competition law. He concludes that as long as the state retains effective control over the regulation of its economy, the CJEU will honour the decision to restrain market forces.[18] Regardless of the explanation, the focus of interest has shifted to the rules in Article 106 TFEU and this is the next topic.

Article 106 TFEU

Article 106 TFEU is a strange and unclear provision which was originally twinned with what is now Article 37 TFEU (ex Article 31 EC) (adjustment of state monopolies of a commercial character) and the text is given in Box 7.3.[19]

[16] See Szyszczak (n. 12) at pp. 74–5 for some of the explanations.
[17] D. Ehle, 'State Regulation under the US Antitrust State Action Doctrine and under EC Competition Law: A Conceptual Analysis' (1998) 19 *European Competition Law Review* 380.
[18] Ibid. at 396.
[19] See the opinion of AG Tesauro in Case C-202/88 *France v Commission* [1991] ECR I-1223 at para. 11: 'clear obscurity'.

KEY LEGAL PROVISION   Box 7.3

Article 106 TFEU

1   In the case of public undertakings and undertakings to which Member States grant spe-
    cial or exclusive rights, Member States shall neither enact nor maintain in force any
    measure contrary to the rules contained in this Treaty, in particular to those rules
    provided for in Article 18 and Articles 101 to 109.

2   Undertakings entrusted with the operation of services of general economic interest
    or having the character of a revenue-producing monopoly shall be subject to the rules
    contained in the Treaties, in particular to the rules on competition, in so far as
    the application of such rules does not obstruct the performance, in law or in fact, of the
    particular tasks assigned to them. The development of trade must not be affected to such
    an extent as would be contrary to the interests of the Union.

3   The Commission shall ensure the application of the provisions of this Article and shall,
    where necessary, address appropriate directives or decisions to Member States.

Questions: Who are these provisions aimed at? Who can rely on them?

Buendia Sierra, a European Commission official and leading academic commentator, takes
the view that the ambiguity was deliberate, as it represented a compromise between the
founding states over different views on the limits of national economic policy in a common
market.[20] It is found in a section of the Treaty addressed to undertakings, but Article 106(1)
TFEU is addressed to *states* and prohibits them, in relation to certain types of undertakings,
from enacting measures contrary to the Treaties. So it contains a prohibition, but the content
of the prohibition depends on the interpretation of other articles which need not be provisions on competition law but could include, for example, the free movement of goods.
Secondly, Article 106(2) TFEU allows for a derogation[21] from the rules of the Treaties for
certain types of undertakings when the application of the rules obstructs their performance
in some manner. This is a derogation that can be relied on by both states and undertakings.
Finally, Article 106(3) TFEU allows the Commission to take decisions or issue Directives in
order to ensure the application of this Article. Having given this very basic outline of the
Article, it is now necessary to explore it in more depth.

Article 106(1) TFEU

Application of Article 106(1) TFEU

This part of the Article applies to public undertakings and undertakings which are granted
special and exclusive rights. The question of whether an entity is an undertaking is something

---

[20] Buendia Sierra (n. 13).

[21] Although there is some controversy over how to categorise Article 106(2) TFEU, the case law and the bulk of
academic opinion sees it as a derogation: see Buendia Sierra (n. 13), ch. 8; AG Jacobs in Case C-67/96 *Albany
International* v *Stichting Bedrijfspensioenfonds* [1999] ECR I-5751; Case 127/73 *BRT* v *SABAM* [1974] ECR 313
at para. 19. J. Baquero Cruz rather mysteriously refers to it as a binary or switch rule in 'Beyond Competition:
Services of General Interest in European Community Law' in G. de Búrca (ed.) *EU Law and the Welfare State*
(Oxford University Press, 2005).

that we have discussed previously (see Chapter 2) and it is worth referring back to that. The basic rule is that an undertaking is every entity engaged in an economic activity, regardless of the legal status of the entity and the way that it is financed.[22] This question has been particularly important in this area as controversial cases have arisen in relation to bodies which have some of the characteristics of a private sector commercial organisation and some of the characteristics of a public sector, non-commercial operation. If such a body is not characterised as an undertaking, then competition law does not apply to it, and the Member State can implement whatever social policy it likes, whereas if it is characterised as an undertaking, then its activities can be scrutinised for compatibility with the EU competition rules, with the ultimate say vesting in the European Courts. Certainly, some commentators think that there are a number of cases where the European Courts have deliberately limited the scope of competition law by saying that particular entities do not constitute undertakings, notably in the area of health services.[23]

Article 106(1) TFEU only applies to public undertakings and undertakings granted special and exclusive rights. In *Commission* v *France* it was made clear that 'public undertaking' is a concept of Union law which should be given a uniform interpretation for all member states;[24] and the CJEU approved the Commission's view that a public undertaking is 'any undertaking over which the public authorities may exercise, directly or indirectly, a dominant influence by virtue of their ownership of it, the financial participation therein, or the rules which govern it'.[25] The important point to note about this definition is that it does not turn on the legal form of the undertaking but on the ability of the state to control its activities.

If an undertaking is not a public one, it may still fall within Article 106(1) if it has been granted special or exclusive rights. In *France* v *Commission*, where the issue was squarely raised, the CJEU made it clear that special and exclusive rights were two different concepts, although in subsequent cases the Court appears not to have used this distinction quite so carefully.[26] The notion of exclusive rights is relatively easy to grasp: they are those rights where the state has granted a monopoly to the undertaking in question. The notion of special rights is more difficult but seems to cover the situation where the state has given to a limited number of undertakings concerned legal or regulatory advantages which substantially affect the ability of other undertakings to provide the same service and have done this on criteria which are not objective, proportional or non-discriminatory.[27] The idea here is that the state has selected an undertaking and given it an advantage over its competitors but the selection has been done on the basis of some non-objective policy reason.

However, most recently the CJEU seems to have changed its mind and come to the conclusion that special and exclusive rights constitute one concept. In *Ambulanz Glöckner*,[28] one of the questions was whether a provision of German legislation which said that only medical

---

[22] Case C-41/90 *Höfner and Elser* v *Macroton* [1991] ECR I-1979.

[23] See Szyszczak (n. 12) at p. 116; A. Winterstein, 'Nailing the Jellyfish: Social Security and Competition Law' (1999) 20 *European Competition Law Review* 324 at 327; V. Hatzopoulos, 'Health Law and Policy: The Impact of the EU' in G. de Búrca (ed.) *EU Law and the Welfare State* (Oxford University Press, 2005) at p. 157.

[24] Reischl AG in Case 188/80 *Commission* v *France* [1982] ECR 2545.

[25] Commission Directive 80/723 on the transparency of financial relations between Member States and public undertakings [1980] OJ L195/35, amended by Commission Directive 85/413 [1985] OJ L229/20.

[26] Case C-202/88 *France* v *Commission* [1991] ECR I-1223.

[27] This is based on Commission Directive 94/46 amending Commission Directives 88/301 and 90/388 in particular with regard to satellite communications [1994] OJ L268/15.

[28] C-475/99 *Ambulanz Glöckner* [2001] ECR I-8089.

aid organisations, such as the German Red Cross, could provide ambulance services and that, therefore, independent operators were excluded, granted special or exclusive rights to the medical aid organisations. In his discussion of the criteria, AG Jacobs took the view that the idea of granting rights on the basis of criteria which are not objective, proportional or non-discriminatory was only relevant in the context of the liberalisation of telecommunications services[29] because they were aimed at distinguishing legitimate from illegitimate special rights, whereas here it was just a matter of determining the scope of Article 106(1) TFEU. Therefore special *and* exclusive rights were rights granted by the authorities of a Member State to one undertaking or to a limited number of undertakings which substantially affect the ability of other undertakings to exercise the economic activity in question in the same geographical area under substantially equivalent conditions.[30] This formulation was endorsed by the CJEU (see Box 7.4).[31]

KEY CASE EXTRACT | **Box 7.4**

Definition of special or exclusive rights

Source: C-475/99 *Ambulanz Glöckner* [2001] ECR I-8089 at para. 24:

> [P]rotection . . . conferred by a legislative measure on a limited number of undertakings which may substantially affect the ability of other undertakings to exercise the economic activity in question in the same geographical area under substantially equivalent conditions.

Questions: Is a legislative measure always necessary? Consider the BBC's Royal Charter. What sort of rights might such a provision entail?

This seems incorrect because implicit in the notion of 'special' rights is some sense that they are not granted on objective criteria; if they were granted on objective criteria, then how could they be special? In any event, in this case, what was being contested was the exclusivity of the rights being granted to the medical aid organisations in relation to the ability to tender for ambulance services. It is, however, not obvious that this has made a difference in practice, as there has been no case law which has turned on the definition of special rights.

Infringement of Article 106(1) TFEU

Much more difficult than this is the question of whether Article 106(1) TFEU has been infringed when its prohibition is combined with the prohibition in Article 102 TFEU. Article 106(1) TFEU may also be invoked in relation to other articles of the Treaties, notably the free movement of goods and services, but this is outside the scope of this book.[32] The question in this context is whether a Member State, which grants exclusive rights to an undertaking, public or private, has breached these provisions. The answers that have been given to this question by the courts have varied and the reasons for particular decisions are not explained

---

[29] Contrast A. Jones and B. Sufrin, *EU Competition Law* (4th edn, Oxford University Press, 2011) at p. 576.
[30] Advocate General Jacobs: Opinion (n. 28), paras 88–9.
[31] C-475/99 *Ambulanz Glöckner* [2001] ECR I-8089 at para. 24.
[32] For discussion, see Buendia Sierra (n. 13), ch. 6.

in much depth, causing one commentator to regard the case law as 'opaque, if not erratic'.[33] The problem was summarised by AG Jacobs as a dilemma:

> On the one hand, the grant of exclusive rights, or in other words the creation of a statutory monopoly, is a structural State measure which typically facilitates anticompetitive behaviour. On the other hand, the wording of Article 90 EEC [Article 106 TFEU] seems to imply that the grant of exclusive rights *as such* can in principle not have been the kind of measures which the authors of the Treaty intended Article 90(1) [Article 106(1) TFEU] to prohibit.[34]

In the initial phase of thinking about Article 106(1) TFEU, both academic commentary and the case law seemed to take the view that the grant of exclusive rights could not, on its own, be a measure infringing the Treaties.[35] As the CJEU put it, 'the fact that an undertaking to which a member state grants exclusive rights has a monopoly is not as such incompatible with Article 86 [Article 106 TFEU]. It is therefore the same as regards an extension of exclusive rights following a new intervention by the state.'[36] This approach was rejected in *France* v *Commission* where France challenged the competence of the Commission to adopt the tele-communications terminal Directive which, among other things, imposed an obligation on Member States to abolish national monopolies in relation to telecommunications terminals. The French government argued that Article 106(1) TFEU presupposed the existence of such exclusive rights and therefore the grant of such rights could not be subject to Union control. The CJEU rejected this, holding that, 'even though that article presupposes the existence of undertakings which have special and exclusive rights, it does not necessarily follow that all the special or exclusive rights are necessarily compatible with the Treaty.'[37]

This case was then followed by a series of decisions in the early 1990s, which found that the grant of exclusive rights constituted a breach of Article 106(1) TFEU. One of the most well known is *Höfner*,[38] which was a case where a German law had established that an executive job seekers agency had a monopoly in filling such positions in Germany. Despite the law, a number of private agencies were running in competition with the statutory agency and Höfner had found a candidate for a post at Macrotron, which did not appoint the candidate and then refused to pay the agreed fees. When this was challenged in the German courts, the question was raised whether these arrangements were contrary to Article 106(1) TFEU. The CJEU held that there was a breach only if:

> the undertaking in question, merely by exercising the exclusive right granted to it, cannot avoid abusing its dominant position. Pursuant to Article 82(b) [Article 102(b) TFEU], such an abuse may in particular consist in limiting the provision of a service, to the prejudice of those seeking to avail themselves of it. A Member State creates a situation in which the provision of a service is limited when the undertaking to which it grants an exclusive right extending to executive recruitment activities is manifestly not in a position to satisfy the demand prevailing on the market for activities of that kind and when the effective pursuit of such activities by private companies is rendered impossible by the maintenance in force of a statutory provision under

---

[33] L. Hancher, 'Community, State and Market' in P. Craig and G. de Búrca (eds) *The Evolution of EU Law* (Oxford University Press, 1999); Buendia Sierra (n. 13) at p. 187: 'far from satisfactory'.

[34] Case C-67/96 *Albany International* v *Stichting Bedrijfspensioenfonds* [1999] ECR I-5751 at para. 389.

[35] See Buendia Sierra (n. 13) at paras 4.15 and 4.16.

[36] Case 155/73 *Sacchi* [1974] ECR 430 at para. 14.

[37] Case C-202/88 *France* v *Commission* [1991] ECR I-1223 at para. 22.

[38] Case C-41/90 *Höfner and Elser* v *Macroton* [1991] ECR I-1979.

which such activities are prohibited and non-observance of that prohibition renders the contracts concerned void.[39]

Shortly after this case, the CJEU decided the *ERT* case.[40] Here ERT had been given a statutory monopoly in the broadcasting and transmission of television programmes, both its own and others, in Greece. It brought proceedings in a national court to prevent a municipality from also broadcasting television programmes. One of the questions was whether this was a breach of Article 106(1) TFEU and the CJEU held that it was, where those rights (to broadcast) are liable to create a situation in which that undertaking is led to infringe Article 106 TFEU by virtue of a discriminatory broadcasting policy which favours its own programmes.[41]

The next case was the *Port of Genoa* case,[42] where an Italian law had stipulated that all unloading of ships had to be done by particular dock work companies, which were allowed to employ only Italian nationals. In the course of a dispute between the dockworkers company and a shipping company, the question was raised whether these arrangements were contrary to Article 106(1) TFEU. The CJEU held that these arrangements were such a breach. They took the view that there was such a breach:

- if simply by exercising those rights undertakings would be led to a breach (*Höfner*), or
- if the arrangements were such as to be liable to create a situation in which the undertaking would be induced to commit an abuse.

In the circumstances, this seems to have fallen within the second category as the CJEU said that the undertakings were induced either to demand payment for services which have not been requested, to charge disproportionate prices, to refuse to have recourse to modern technology, which involved an increase in the cost of the operations and a prolongation of the time required for their performance, or to grant price reductions to certain consumers and at the same time to offset such reductions by an increase in the charges to other consumers.[43]

The final case to examine here is the *RTT* case,[44] which was where RTT, the Belgian telecommunications monopoly, which also had a monopoly over the approval of telephones for their connection to the network, brought an action to try to prevent a supermarket chain from selling unapproved telephones. The CJEU saw this as equivalent to those situations where an undertaking with a monopoly in one market, reserves for itself a neighbouring market and eliminates all competition on that neighbouring market. RTT argued that this provision could be applied only if RTT had acted in an abusive manner and it denied that it had done so. The CJEU firmly rejected this argument, pointing out that it was the extension of the monopoly that was the problem. In order to create a system of undistorted competition there needed to be equality between operators on the market and a system which allowed one of the producers of telecommunications equipment to certify the products of other producers gave that undertaking an obvious advantage over its competitors and should be replaced by a system of independent approvals.[45]

---

[39] Ibid. at paras 29–31.
[40] Case C-260/89 *Elliniki Radiophonia Tileorassi (ERT) v Dimotiki Etairia Pliroforissis* [1991] ECR I-2925.
[41] Ibid. at para. 37.
[42] Case C-179/90 *Merci Convenzionali Porto di Genova v Siderurgica Gabrielli* [1991] ECR I-5889.
[43] Ibid. at para. 19.
[44] Case C-18/88 *RTT v GB-Inno-BM SA* [1991] ECR I-5973.
[45] Ibid. at paras 23–6.

In all these cases the CJEU is trying to find a link between the grant of exclusive rights and a situation where there was an abuse under Article 102 TFEU, either because the grant of rights made that abuse inevitable or because it made the undertaking liable to commit an abuse. Although the application of this approach to the facts of each case may be difficult, there is an attempt to draw a connection. In the *Corbeau* case, this attempt to draw a connection disappeared.[46] Here Corbeau provided postal services in Liege, Belgium, contrary to a Belgian law which gave the Belgian postal services an exclusive right to deliver mail. Corbeau was prosecuted for breach of the exclusive rights and one of the questions was whether these arrangements were compatible with Article 106(1) TFEU. The CJEU answered this by saying that Article 106(1) TFEU had to be read in conjunction with the derogation in Article 106(2) TFEU. Without reaching a conclusion about the Article 106(1) TFEU point, the Court went on to see if the conditions for the application of Article 106(2) TFEU were made out, but left this as a matter for the national court, which ultimately decided that they were not. As Buendia Sierra interprets this approach, it means that in principle all grants of exclusive rights are contrary to Article 106(1) TFEU, unless they can be justified under the exception in Article 106(2) TFEU.[47] The problem with the judgment in this case is that, aside from the grant of the exclusive rights, there is no indication of what the possible problem might be. There is no suggestion that there is a conflict of interest, that the prices charged by the Belgian postal service were excessive or that a monopoly was being extended from one market to another. Those who have attempted to organise the case law have struggled to find a place for *Corbeau*[48] and, as we shall see, although it has never been overruled, the European Courts have not applied this approach in subsequent cases.

A different approach was evident in *La Crespelle*.[49] Here French law had created a network of centres which provided artificial insemination services to farmers and each centre had a regional monopoly. Farmers could, however, ask for artificial insemination to be provided from cattle outside the region, which was charged at a higher rate than artificial insemination from within the region. The CJEU analysed the position by saying that these regional exclusive rights had created a dominant position but that the mere creation of such a dominant position was not incompatible with Article 102 TFEU. The question was if, in merely exercising the exclusive right, the undertaking could not avoid abusing its dominant position. In this case the national law allowed the centres to charge for the additional costs entailed by the choice of cattle from outside the region. Although the centres could calculate the costs, the law did not lead them to charge disproportionate costs and thereby abuse their dominant position.[50] Unlike *Corbeau*, the analysis explicitly recognises that there has to be some linkage, at least at a theoretical level, between the grant of a dominant position and something which would constitute an abuse.

This now seems to be the position taken by the European Courts. We can contrast the decision in *Deutsche Post*[51] with that in *Corbeau*. In this case, credit card companies electronically

---

[46] Case C-320/91 *Corbeau* [1993] ECR I-2533.

[47] Buendia Sierra (n. 13) at para. 5.103.

[48] See AG Jacobs' opinion in Case C67/96 *Albany International v Stichting Bedrijfspensioenfonds* [1999] ECR I-5751; and D. Edward and M. Hoskins, 'Article 90: Deregulation and EC Law' (1995) 32 *Common Market Law Review* 157–86.

[49] Case C-323–93 *Société Civile Agricole du Centre d'Insémination de la Crespelle v Coopérative d'Elevage et d'Insémination Artificielle du Département de la Mayenne* [1994] ECR I-5077.

[50] Ibid., paras 18–22.

[51] Cases C-147–148/97 *Deutsche Post v GZS and Citicorp* [2000] ECR I-825, [2000] 4 CMLR 838.

transmitted their data from Germany to Denmark, where the bills were prepared and posted back to Germany, because it was cheaper to use international mail than pay the German rates. The relationship between national postal services is governed by the Universal Postal Convention, which provides that national postal services are required to deliver mail from other countries addressed to their residents. In the case of mail originating in the domestic country, but which is posted in bulk outside that country, the domestic carrier is entitled to charge its full internal rate or to return the items to the sending country. In this case Deutsche Post demanded the full internal rate from the credit card companies, which refused to pay. The question was whether it was contrary to Articles 106 and 102 TFEU for Deutsche Post to exercise its rights under the Universal Postal Convention. The CJEU started by reciting the *Corbeau* formula that Article 106(1) TFEU had to be read in conjunction with Article 106(2) TFEU but, unlike in that case, it went on to analyse whether there was a potential abuse. It said that the grant of the right to treat international items of mail as internal post creates a situation where Deutsche Post may be led to abuse its dominant position, resulting from the exclusive rights granted to it. Therefore, the next question was whether the exercise of that right was necessary for the body to carry out its task of general interest and operate under economically acceptable conditions: that is, could it rely on the exception in Article 106(2) TFEU?[52]

The approach in principle is summarised in Box 7.5.

KEY CASE EXTRACT   **Box 7.5**

Infringement of Article 106(1) TFEU combined with Article 102 TFEU

Source: Case C-475/99 *Ambulanz Glöckner* [2001] ECR I-8089 at para. 39:

> . . . the mere creation of a dominant position through the grant of special or exclusive rights within the meaning of Article 90(1) of the Treaty [Article 106(1) TFEU] is not in itself incompatible with Article 86 of the Treaty [Article 82 TFEU]. A Member State will be in breach of the prohibitions laid down by those two provisions only if the undertaking in question,
>
> – merely by exercising the special or exclusive rights conferred upon it, is led to abuse its dominant position, or
> – where such rights are liable to create a situation in which that undertaking is led to commit such abuses

Questions: How easy is it to apply this test to prospective cases? Do not all monopolies provide an incentive to commit an abuse?

Although the principle may be relatively clear, another problem with the case law is that its application in practice may be difficult. Compare, for example, *La Crespelle* with the *Port of Genoa* case, as in both cases there were allegations that the grant of exclusive rights had led to excessive pricing. In the *Genoa* case, the CJEU sees this as a consequence of the national law, while in *La Crespelle* this is not a consequence of the national law, yet in both cases the

---

[52] Ibid., paras 47–9.

incentives from the national law seem to be similar. Leaving aside such factual issues, which might be said to be an inherent problem, Jones and Sufrin have neatly categorised the types of measures whose results would infringe Article 106(1) TFEU, although they caution that the categories are not closed, and there are some cases where the nature of the abusive conduct is not clear, notably *Corbeau*.[53] They distinguish six cases:

- inability to meet demand,[54]
- conflict of interest cases,[55]
- inequality of opportunity,[56]
- extension of monopoly into a neighbouring market,[57]
- pricing abuses, in particular price discrimination,[58]
- refusal to supply.[59]

Article 106(2) TFEU: the exception

Once a breach of the prohibition in Article 106(1) TFEU is established, the next question is whether the exception in Article 106(2) TFEU can be invoked (see Box 7.6).

KEY LEGAL PROVISION   Box 7.6

Article 106(2) TFEU

Undertakings entrusted with the operation of services of general economic interest or having the character of a revenue-producing monopoly shall be subject to the rules contained in the Treaties, in particular to the rules on competition, in so far as the application of such rules does not obstruct the performance, in law or in fact, of the particular tasks assigned to them. The development of trade must not be affected to such an extent as would be contrary to the interests of the Union.

Questions: What does a service of general economic interest mean? To what extent does its performance have to be obstructed?

This exception may be invoked either by undertakings or by Member States, even though the provision simply talks about undertakings. It applies, however, only to undertakings entrusted with the operation of a service of general economic interest or to undertakings with the character of a revenue-producing monopoly. Undertakings with the character of a

---

[53] Jones and Sufrin (n. 29) at pp. 596–98.
[54] Case C-41/90 *Höfner* v *Macrotron* [1991] ECR I-1979, [1993] 4 CMLR 306. This was also an issue in Case C-475/99 *Ambulanz Glöckner* [2001] ECR I-8089.
[55] Case C-260/89 *ERT* v *DEP* [1991] ECR I-2925, [1994] 4 CMLR 540; Case C-163/96 *Silvano Raso* [1998] ECR I-533.
[56] Case C-49/07 *MOTOE* v *Ellinikia Dimitri* [2008] ECR I-4863.
[57] Case C-18/88 *RTT* v *GB-Inno-BM SA* [1991] ECR I-5973.
[58] Case C-266/96 *Corsica Ferries* [1998] ECR I-3949, [1998] 5 CMLR 402.
[59] Cases C-147–148/97 *Deutsche Post* v *GZS and Citicorp* [2000] ECR I-825, [2000] 4 CMLR 838 (although this could equally be considered a case of pricing abuses).

revenue-producing monopoly may also constitute commercial monopolies and will be subject to Article 37 TFEU. Buendia Sierra gives as an example of the latter, the French and Italian match monopolies.[60] There has been little academic discussion or case law on these sorts of undertakings and most interest has focused on undertakings entrusted with services of general economic interest.

Services of general economic interest

The notion of an undertaking is the same as has been discussed previously (see Chapter 2). Here, however, certain functions have to be entrusted to it; there has to be a positive action by the state imposing certain obligations on the undertaking in the general economic interest.[61] It is not enough simply to approve or endorse the activities of the undertaking; there has to be some delegation of a task to them.[62] What is meant by the term 'service of general economic interest'? According to the European Commission, 'the term refers to services of an economic nature which the Member States or the Community [Union] subject to specific public service obligations by virtue of a general interest criterion'.[63] Public service obligations refer to requirements that are imposed by public authorities on the provider of the service in order to ensure that certain public interest objectives are met. An example of this, from the same paper, would be the idea of universal service, that is, that certain services are made available at a specified quality to all consumers and users throughout the territory of a Member State, regardless of geographical location, and at an affordable price.[64] Examples of this would be the requirements placed on gas, electricity and water companies to provide a connection to their networks to all consumers who are within a reasonable distance of the networks and require access. The postal service supplied in the United Kingdom for letters can also be seen as an example of a universal service, which is available to all at the same price, regardless of geographical location and offering the same quality of service. Case law has expanded this definition and the Courts have accepted numerous activities as constituting services of general economic interest, including waste processing, mooring services in ports and the provision of emergency ambulance services, to give some examples.[65]

These are, however, only examples of what might be services of general economic interest. The GC has stated in *British United Provident Association (BUPA)* that there is no clear and precise definition of this concept in EC law and that therefore Member States have a wide discretion to define what they regard as services of general economic interest.[66] The control that EU institutions could exercise was limited to that of manifest error. There was, nevertheless, some minimum content to the notion and the GC found this in the idea that there had to be universal service for there to be a service of general economic interest. This did not mean that a service had to be offered to an entire population or territory, nor did it mean that any particular content to the service had to be prescribed by the state. The key point was that the service was compulsory,

---

[60] Buendia Sierra (n. 13) at p. 287.

[61] See AG Jacobs at para. 103 in Case C-203/96 *Chemische Afvalstoffen Dusseldorp v Minister van Vlokhuisvesting* [1998] ECR I-4075.

[62] See Case 127/73 *BRT v SABAM* [1974] ECR 313; Case 7/82 *Gesellschaft zur Verwertung Von Leistungsschutzrechten mbH (GVL) v Commission* [1983] ECR 483.

[63] European Commission, *Green Paper on Services of General Interest*, COM (2003) 270 final at para. 17.

[64] Ibid. at para. 50.

[65] Case C-203/96 *Chemische Afvalstoffen Dusseldorp v Minister van Vlokhuisvesting* [1998] ECR I-4075; Case C-266/96 *Corsica Ferries* [1998] ECR I-3949; Case C-475/99 *Ambulanz Glöckner* [2001] ECR I-8089.

[66] Case T-289/03 *British United Provident Association (BUPA) v Commission* [2008] ECR II-81.

that is, the undertaking offering it was under an obligation to provide the service to any user requesting it.[67] In the *BUPA* case, it was offering private medical insurance.

Article 14 TFEU

Before discussing the case law, Article 14 TFEU needs a mention.

KEY LEGAL PROVISION **Box 7.7**

Article 14 TFEU (ex Article 16 EC)

Without prejudice to Article 4 of the Treaty on European Union or to Articles 93, 106 and 107 of this Treaty, and given the place occupied by services of general economic interest in the shared values of the Union as well as their role in promoting social and territorial cohesion, the Union and the Member States, each within their respective powers and within the scope of application of the Treaties, shall take care that such services operate on the basis of principles and conditions, particularly economic and social conditions, which enable them to fulfil their missions. The European Parliament and the Council, acting by means of regulations in accordance with the ordinary legislative procedure, shall establish these principles and set these conditions without prejudice to the competence of Member States, in compliance with the Treaties, to provide, to commission and to fund such services.

Questions: Does Article 14 say anything that can be converted into a legal principle? Why do you think it was inserted into the Treaty?

This is a gnomic provision which was inserted by the Treaty of Amsterdam and came into force in 1999. It has been much discussed by academics,[68] although it has not appeared in the case law of the European Courts; and has also been the site of much political debate over the text. The Reform Treaty amended Article 16 EC [Article 14 TFEU] by inserting the words, 'particularly economic and financial conditions' after 'conditions' and added a new sentence allowing the Council and European Parliament to pass legislation which will establish the principles and set the conditions to provide, commission and fund such services. This is expressed as being without prejudice to the competence of the Member States.[69] What is at stake here is the question of the extent of competition law and the ability of Member States to organise various matters on their own territory. The argument is that in order to carry out certain activities in the public interest, those undertakings which have that responsibility cannot do so if they are subjected to the full rigours of a competitive market. Although Article 106(2) TFEU offers a derogation, this is neither a positive recognition of the place of services of general economic interest, nor, arguably, does it go far enough in exempting them. Although it is easy to state this criticism in broad terms, coming up with a positive solution has proved much more difficult.

---

[67] Ibid., paras 186–90.

[68] See M. Ross, 'Article 16 and Services of General Interest: From Derogation to Obligation?' (2000) 25 *European Law Review* 22; W. Sauter, 'Services of general economic interest and universal service in EU Law' (2008) 33 *European Law Review* 167; M. Krajewski, 'Providing legal clarity and securing policy space for public services through a legal framework for services of general economic interest: squaring the circle?' (2008) 14 *European Public Law* 377; N. Boeger, 'Solidarity and EC competition law' (2007) 32 *European Law Review* 319.

[69] See also the Protocol (No. 26) on Services of General Interest.

The case law on Article 106(2) TFEU

As Article 106(2) TFEU is a derogation or exception from the usual Treaty rules, the Court has ruled that it should be construed narrowly,[70] a line which has been followed by both the Commission and the Union Courts. In addition to providing a defence against an allegation of breach of the rules on competition, it may also provide a defence to both the state and the undertaking against allegations of a breach of other provisions of the Treaties.[71] Early attempts to rely on the exception tended to be unsuccessful. For example, in *Air Inter*[72] the French Airline TAT claimed that it needed its exclusive rights on certain French air routes in order to subsidise flights on other, less profitable ones. The General Court responded that, on a strict interpretation, it was not sufficient for such performance simply to be hindered or made more difficult. Furthermore, it was for the applicant to establish obstruction of its task.[73] In this respect, the company had merely asserted its case; it had not put a figure on the scale of losses nor had it shown that the losses were so great it would have to abandon certain routes. In addition, it had not argued that there was no appropriate alternative system which would ensure regional development and that the routes continued to operate.

An alternative approach sometimes taken by the Court has been to send the substantive issue of whether the derogation has been made out to the national court. This was the case in *Corbeau*, where the Court accepted in principle that there might need to be protection for the Belgian Post Office against 'cream-skimming'. It has, however, been argued by Whish and Bailey[74] that the Court gave a strong indication that it should not be possible to maintain a monopoly over express courier services in order to sustain the basic service of the daily delivery of letters. The passage he refers to is worth citing:

> the exclusion of competition is not justified as regards specific services dissociable from the service of general economic interest which meet special needs of economic operators and which call for certain additional services not offered by the traditional postal service, such as collection from the senders' address, greater speed or reliability of distribution or the possibility of changing the destination in the course of transit, in so far as such services, by their nature and the conditions in which they are offered, such as the geographical area in which they are provided, do not compromise the economic equilibrium of the service of general economic interest performed by the holder of the exclusive right.[75]

This is certainly a powerful statement and we should note that, in the *Almelo* case,[76] although the issue was returned to the national court, that court ruled that the exception had not been made out.

There is, however, a series of cases where the exception has been made out. The first case was *Corsica Ferries*.[77] Here the Italian government had given an undertaking the exclusive rights to provide mooring services for ships over a certain weight. The applicants complained that this was an abuse of a dominant position because it prevented them from using their own staff, that the price of the service was excessive and that the tariffs charged varied from

---

[70] Case 127/73 *BRT v SABAM* [1974] ECR 313, [1974] 2 CMLR 238.
[71] See Case C-157/94 *Commission v Netherlands* [1997] ECR I-5699, [1998] 2 CMLR 373 (Article 37).
[72] Case T-260/94 *Air Inter v Commission* [1997] ECR II-997, [1997] 5 CMLR 851.
[73] Ibid., para. 138.
[74] R. Whish and D. Bailey, *Competition Law* (7th edn, Oxford University Press, 2012) at p. 240.
[75] *Corbeau* (n. 46), para. 19.
[76] Case C-393/92 *Almelo* [1994] ECR I-1477; and see L. Hancher (1997) 34 *Common Market Law Review* 1509.
[77] Case C-266/96 *Corsica Ferries France v Gruppo Antichi Ormeggiatori del Porto di Genova* [1998] ECR I-3949.

port to port. In response, the mooring undertaking argued that the tariffs were indispensable if a universal mooring service was to be maintained. Included in the tariff was a component that corresponded to the additional cost of providing a universal service. The variation of the tariffs was to take into account the differing circumstances of each individual port. The Court pointed out that mooring groups were obliged to provide at any time and to any user a universal mooring service, *for reasons of safety*, in port waters.[78] In any event, the Court thought that the Italian government was justified, on grounds of public security, to grant the exclusive right. In those circumstances it was not incompatible:

> . . . to include in the price of the service a component designed to cover the cost of maintaining the universal mooring service, inasmuch as it corresponds to the supplementary cost occasioned by the special characteristics of that service, and to lay down for that service different tariffs on the basis of the particular characteristics of each port.[79]

Note that this is expressed narrowly. The universal service component must correspond to the special characteristics of the service and the differing tariffs must take into account the different characteristics of the ports in question. In other words, the tariffs must be cost based and the Court is not intervening with the discretion given to Italy on grounds of public security.

In the *Albany* case[80] the Court was faced with the question of whether a Dutch rule relating to compulsory membership of a supplementary pension fund scheme could fall within the exception. In dealing with this, the Court stressed that the derogation sought to reconcile the States' interest in using certain undertakings as instruments of economic or fiscal policy with the Union's interest in ensuring compliance with the competition rules. The Court pointed out that the supplementary pension scheme fulfilled an essential social function by reason of the limitations on the amount of the statutory pension. As regards the exception, in order for its conditions to be fulfilled, it was not necessary:

> that the financial balance or economic viability of the undertaking entrusted with the operation of a service of general economic interest should be threatened. It is sufficient that, in the absence of the rights at issue, it would not be possible for the undertaking to perform the particular tasks entrusted to it . . . or that maintenance of those rights is necessary to enable the holder of them to perform tasks of general economic interest which have been assigned to it under economically acceptable conditions.[81]

In the circumstances, the removal of the exclusive right would mean that undertakings with young employees engaged in non-dangerous occupations would seek more advantageous insurance from the private sector. So the departure of 'good' risks would leave the sectoral pension funds with an increasing proportion of 'bad' risks, thereby increasing the cost of pensions. This was particularly a problem in relation to a case where the fund displayed a high degree of solidarity and where contributions did not reflect the risk, there was an obligation to accept all workers without a prior medical examination, pension rights were accrued even where employees did not contribute due to incapacity, pensions were indexed and the fund made up the arrears of employers that had gone insolvent. Those constraints were said to make the fund less competitive than a private insurance company

---

[78] Ibid. at para. 45 (emphasis added).
[79] Ibid. at para. 46.
[80] Case C-67/96 *Albany International v Stichting Bedrijfspensioenfonds* [1999] ECR I-5751.
[81] Ibid. at para. 107.

and, therefore, the removal of the exclusive right *might* make it impossible for the fund to perform its tasks.[82]

The third case is the *Deutsche Post* case, which involved international re-mail. The court here took the view that if Deutsche Post were obliged to forward and deliver mail to German residents posted outside Germany, without any provision allowing for financial compensation for all the costs occasioned by the obligation, the performance, *in economically balanced conditions*, of that task would be jeopardised.[83] Postal services of Member States could not, in the Court's view, simultaneously bear the costs while at the same time losing the income, so they were entitled to charge internal postage. However, insofar as part of the costs were offset by the terminal dues, it was not necessary to charge the *full* internal postage for such items. So, Deutsche Post was only allowed to charge a proportion of the costs.

Finally, it is worth comparing two cases in the area of waste management. The first was *Dusseldorp*.[84] Here the Dutch government had organised a long-term waste disposal plan, one of the elements of which, prohibited the export of oil filters for reprocessing outside the Netherlands and gave an exclusive right to reprocess such filters to a Dutch undertaking. This was challenged by an undertaking which wanted to export its oil filters to Germany for processing. Leaving aside the major issue of the export ban, on this particular point the Court held that there was a breach of Article 106(1) TFEU because the ban resulted in the restriction of outlets. Could the derogation apply? The Dutch government submitted that the rules in question were meant to reduce the costs of the undertaking and make it economically viable. However, the Court pointed out that it was up to the Dutch government to show to the satisfaction of the national court that the objective could not be achieved equally well by other means. The exception could apply only if it were shown that, without the contested measure, the undertaking would be unable to carry out the task assigned to it.[85]

Entreprenorforeningens Affalds[86] involved the arrangements for the recycling of building waste in Copenhagen. Here the Copenhagen municipality had authorised three undertakings to receive building waste from within Copenhagen, thus preventing any other undertaking in Denmark from receiving that waste. The benefit of the exclusive right was to be reviewed at the end of the normal writing-off period for the plant of the undertaking, which benefited from the restriction; in other words, the restriction was limited in time. The applicant undertaking was a competing waste-recycling undertaking that claimed breach of Articles 102 and 106 TFEU. The Court began this section of the judgment by pointing out that, in order to establish breach of Article 102 TFEU, it was for the national court to define the relevant market in order to see whether there is a dominant position. Once that has been defined, only then can the question of whether there is an abuse be raised. The Court, again, avoided the issue of whether there was an abuse of dominant position[87] and went on to consider whether the exception had been made out. The Court pointed out that the Municipality was faced with a serious environmental problem and considered that, in order to deal with the problem, a high-capacity centre would need to be

---

[82] Ibid. at para. 111 (emphasis added). See now, to similar effect, Case C-437/09 *AG2R Prévoyance v Beaudout Père et Fils Sarl* [2011] 4 CMLR 19.

[83] *Deutsche Post* (n. 50) at para. 50 (emphasis added).

[84] Case C-203/96 *Chemische Afvalstoffen Dusseldorp v Minister van Vlokhuisvesting* [1998] ECR I-4075.

[85] Ibid., para. 67.

[86] Case C-209/98 *Entreprenorforeningens Affalds* [2000] ECR I-3743.

[87] Although it did say, 'Nor is there anything in the documents . . . to suggest that the exclusive right granted in the present case is such that it will necessarily lead the undertakings in question to abuse their dominant position' (para. 82), which suggests it did not think there was an abuse.

set up and that, in order to ensure the centre was profitable, this meant granting it an exclusive right, which was limited in time to the period over which the investments could be written off and in space to the boundaries of the Municipality. A measure that would have had a less restrictive effect on competition would not necessarily ensure that most of the waste produced in the Municipality would have been recycled, due to lack of capacity. Therefore, even if the grant of an exclusive right infringed the competition rules it would have benefited from the exception.

The important point in these cases relates to the burden of proof. The burden is initially on the undertaking or state that wishes to rely on this provision to make out a case. It is not enough simply to assert that this is the case. It is, however, not necessary to show that the undertaking's survival would be threatened if it were subjected to the competition rules, nor is it necessary to prove that there is no other conceivable measure which could ensure that the task in question is carried out.[88] Having said this, it seems as if the Court will not undertake a searching review of the reasoning behind the state's action, as is evidenced by the *Corsica Ferries* and the *Deutsche Post* cases, where the Court accepted reasoning which was plausible but did not go behind it. Box 7.8 summarises the approach.

KEY CASE EXTRACT   Box 7.8

Conditions for meeting Article 106(2) TFEU derogation

- The entity concerned must be an undertaking.
- There must be a service of general economic interest (SGEI).
- The SGEI must be explicitly entrusted to the undertaking (e.g. through legislation).
- Any derogation from the rules on competition must be necessary and proportionate.
- The development of trade must not be affected contrary to the interests of the EU.

Questions: How easy is it to prove these points? Have the Courts become more liberal in allowing undertakings to rely on this derogation?

Article 106(3) TFEU

Article 106(3) TFEU provides the Commission with the means to ensure that the obligations in Article 106(1) and (2) TFEU are followed by taking decisions or, indeed, creating Directives (see Box 7.9).

KEY LEGAL PROVISION   Box 7.9

Article 106(3) TFEU

The Commission shall ensure the application of the provisions of this Article and shall, where necessary, address appropriate directives or decisions to Member States.

Question: Why might the Commission be reluctant to use the power to issue Directives under this provision?

---

[88] See Case C-157/94 *Commission v Netherlands* [1997] ECR I-5699, [1998] 2 CMLR 373.

The power of the Commission to take decisions on individual cases is not controversial in itself and the Commission has taken a number of decisions under this power.[89] An example concerned a French law which allowed three banks in France, and only those three banks, to offer specific types of tax-free savings accounts.[90] France argued, in part, that these arrangements met the criteria for the Article 106(2) TFEU derogation as the banks which offered these accounts were undertaking a service of general economic interest of financing social housing and providing access to banking services. The Commission rejected these arguments on the grounds, among others, that such arrangements were not necessary to finance social housing and the general economic interest of providing access to bank accounts was stated too vaguely.

The power to issue Directives under Article 106(3) TFEU

Much more controversial has been the power of the Commission to issue Directives under Article 106(3) because this is the only provision of the Treaties which gives the Commission power to pass legislation on its own initiative. Normally the Commission must make proposals for Directives to the Council, which will then decide, in cooperation with the Parliament, whether to accept the proposal; and the Council may make amendments to a Commission draft Directive. In other words, the usual procedure allows the Member States to have significant input into the content of the final measure, whereas Article 106(3) TFEU does not allow such input. This power became particularly controversial when the Commission used it to issue two Directives which were aimed at liberalising the telecommunications terminals market (that is, telephones) and liberalising telecommunications services themselves. The exercise of this power was challenged by a number of Member States in *France v Commission* and *Spain v Commission*.[91] The CJEU upheld the Commission's power to act in both cases, although it annulled certain articles of the telecommunications terminals Directive on the ground that the Commission had not sufficiently established whether the rights concerned were special or exclusive. The longer term importance of these cases is that, by establishing its right to act unilaterally, the Commission found that the Member States were more amenable to discussions on the liberalisation of telecommunications, and ultimately energy, which paved the way for a series of Directives liberalising these industries and the current position is discussed later in the text (see Chapter 12).

State aids

The law relating to the control of state aids is peculiar to European Union competition law as opposed to UK domestic law or, indeed, American antitrust law. UK readers may not appreciate it at first glance, but the control of state aids is a major area of activity for the European Commission, comprising about a quarter of its staff in 2006, and the European Courts, comprising the third largest category of cases for the GC, after competition and intellectual property. It would, however, be a mistake to regard this as an area of no concern

---

[89] See *http://ec.europa.eu/competition/liberalisation/cases.html* (accessed 05/09/12) for a list.

[90] European Commission, 'Decision of 10 May 2007, on the special rights granted to La Banque Postale, Caisses d'Epargne and Crédit Mutuel for the distribution of the *livret A* and *livret bleu*', COM (2007) 2110 final.

[91] Case C-202/88 *France v Commission* [1991] ECR I-1223 (terminal equipment) and Cases C-271/90 etc. *Spain, Belgium, Italy v Commission* [1992] ECR I-5833 (telecommunications).

to the UK. First, although the UK has provided a relatively smaller proportion of its GDP as state aid than a number of other Member States, it still provided some €4.9 billion in non-financial crisis state aid in 2010, excluding railways. Secondly, in response to the financial crisis, the UK government set up guarantee and recapitalisation schemes worth just under €360 billion, which in percentage terms was just under 20% of GDP, to provide support for bank borrowing and inject new capital into banks.[92] Thirdly, state aid given by other countries to their own undertakings may have a detrimental effect on UK companies which are trying to compete abroad and put them at a competitive disadvantage. This, then, is an important and, as we shall see, complex area of the law. In the space available within this chapter, all that can be done is to give an outline of the substantive law and procedures and highlight major issues. For fuller detail, the reader will need to refer to practitioner works, which cover the area more fully.[93]

Reasons for state aid

The issues and the context of state aid law are slightly different from other parts of competition law. There are many reasons why states might provide economic aid to undertakings, but two broad categories can be identified: market failure and social policy or equity.[94] The sort of market failures which might necessitate state intervention could include the problem of externalities, for example, where the market does not ensure that polluters pay the cost for their activities, or public goods, where it is difficult or impossible to prevent anyone from using the goods, and hence paying for them, of which free to air broadcasting would be an example. On the other hand, states might want to provide economic advantages for reasons of equity, for example, to encourage economic development in a poor region or to deal with the problems occurring in a particular sector of the economy. Although market failure rationales for intervention can be analysed on an economic basis, this is more difficult in relation to the social or equity based intervention because it is ultimately based on a judgment about what should be the appropriate distribution of economic goods, something which economic analysis is silent about. Decisions about state aid therefore have a political dimension; they are often deliberate decisions made for particular policy reasons, and weighing up the pros and cons of such a decision is not necessarily susceptible to an objective economic analysis, although this is not to say that such analysis is irrelevant. As one of the leading practitioner books put it, 'State aid control remains beset by political and social considerations'.[95]

The regulation of state aid

From the point of view of the EU, the problem with such interventions by Member States is that they may create an obstacle to the creation of an internal market, particularly if they

---

[92] European Commission, 'State aid scoreboard – Spring 2009 update – Special edition on state aid interventions in the current financial and economic crisis', COM (2009) 164, Tables 2 and 3.

[93] See C. Quigley, *European State Aid Law and Policy* (2nd edn, Hart Publishing, Oxford, 2009); L. Hancher, P. Jan Slot and T.R. Ottervanger, *European State Aids* (4th edn, Sweet & Maxwell, London, 2012); M. Heidenhain, *European State Aid Law* (Hart Publishing, Oxford, 2010).

[94] See H. Friederiszick and Lars-Hendrik Röller, 'European State Aid Control: an economic framework', in P. Buccirossi (ed.) *Handbook of Antitrust Economics* (MIT Press, Harvard, Mass, 2006). An earlier version is available at: *http://ec.europa.eu/dgs/competition/economist/publications.html* (accessed 06/08/09).

[95] Hancher, Jan Slot and Ottervanger (n. 93) at para. 1-008.

favour national undertakings, rather than being applied more generally. From its inception, the EU has always had rules relating to state aids, the main provisions of which are now contained in Articles 107–109 TFEU and the key prohibition is set out in Box 7.10.

KEY LEGAL PROVISION   Box 7.10

Article 107(1) TFEU

Save as otherwise provided in the Treaties, any aid granted by a Member State or through State resources in any form whatsoever which distorts or threatens to distort competition by favouring certain undertakings or the production of certain goods shall, insofar as it affects trade between Member States, be incompatible with the internal market.

Questions: What do you think constitutes aid? Why would a Member State give aid to an undertaking? Can you think of recent examples? Why have this prohibition in the EU Treaties?

The basic rule is that state aid, which distorts competition by favouring certain undertakings and affects trade between Member States, is prohibited unless it falls within certain approved categories. Procedurally, Member States are required to notify the European Commission of new state aid and the Commission must decide whether that aid is compatible with the internal market. A limited set of categories are stated to be compatible with the internal market, while the Commission has discretion to decide whether a wider group of types of state aid is compatible with the internal market. On the basis of this discretion, a complicated set of rules and guidelines has been issued, which give guidance as to how the Commission will approach the issue, although they have recently been simplified through a general block exemption.[96] If the Commission decides that state aid has been unlawfully paid to an undertaking, it *may* require its repayment. Commission decisions are reviewable by the European Courts, which have exercised a close scrutiny of the decisions and certain issues are enforceable by the national courts.

The State Aid Action Plan

How these provisions have been implemented has, not surprisingly, changed substantially over the years. A major change came about after the accession in 2004 of the central and eastern European states with the adoption of the State Aid Action Plan.[97] The broad aims of this strategy were as follows:

1 less and better targeted state aid;

2 a refined economic approach;

3 more effective procedures, better enforcement, higher predictability and enhanced transparency;

4 a shared responsibility between the Commission and Member States.

---

[96] European Commission Regulation (EC) No. 800/2008 of 6 August 2008 declaring certain categories of aid compatible with the common market in application of Articles 87 and 88 of the Treaty (General block exemption Regulation), OJ L214, 09.08.2008, pp. 3–47.

[97] European Commission, 'State Aid Action Plan: Less and better targeted state aid: a roadmap for state aid reform 2005–2009' (Consultation document (2005) COM 107).

One of the aims in particular of this approach has been to try to adopt a more economic, and hopefully more objective, approach to questions of assessing the effect of state aids, something which is in line with general developments in competition policy. The Commission has described this as asking the following questions:[98]

1 Is the aid measure aimed at a well-defined objective of common interest?

2 Is the aid well designed to deliver the objective of common interest, i.e. does the proposed aid address the market failure or other objectives?

   (a) Is the aid an appropriate policy instrument to address the policy objective concerned?

   (b) Is there an incentive effect, i.e. does the aid change the behaviour of the aid recipient?

   (c) Is the aid measure proportionate to the problem tackled, i.e. could the same change in behaviour not be obtained with less aid?

3 Are the distortions of competition and effect on trade limited, so that the overall balance is positive?

Progress towards achieving these aims has been mixed and overtaken by the economic and financial crisis which started in 2007–08 in the financial and banking sector. This produced a major challenge for the Commission because of the scale of the problems and the need for rapid decision making and it is discussed in more detail below. In part because of this experience, and also because of continuing economic problems in the EU, the Commission has launched a major initiative to modernise state aid control.[99] The objectives of the reform are (i) to foster sustainable, smart and inclusive growth in a competitive internal market; (ii) to focus Commission *ex ante* scrutiny on cases with the biggest impact on internal market whilst strengthening the Member States' cooperation in state aid enforcement; (iii) to streamline the rules and provide for faster decisions.[100] In order to accomplish these objectives, the Commission wants to develop common principles for the assessment of aid, revise and simplify the rules that it operates and improve the decision making process. Proposals for reform are mentioned at relevant points later in this chapter but we now turn to the first issue, determining whether something constitutes state aid.

The concept of aid

This is a key concept because, if a measure is not state aid, it does not fall to be controlled by the Commission. The Treaty does not give a definition of state aid and interpreting the concept is by no means straightforward. As part of its drive to modernisation, the Commission would like to provide better clarification of the concept. Stemming from the wording of Article 107(1) TFEU, there are usually said to be four elements although, as Richard Plender QC has commented, the elements are interrelated.[101] The elements are as follows:

---

[98] European Commission, 'Common principles for an economic assessment of the compatibility of state aid under Article 87.3' (Non-Paper) (2009) at para. 9. Available at *http://ec.europa.eu/competition/state_aid/reform/economic_assessment_en.pdf* (accessed 31/07/12).

[99] Generally see *http://ec.europa.eu/competition/state_aid/modernisation/index_en.html* (accessed 31/07/12).

[100] European Commission 'Communication from the Commission on EU State Aid Modernisation (SAM)' COM(2012) 209 final 08.05.2012 at para. 8.

[101] R. Plender, 'Definition of Aid' in A. Biondi, P. Eeckhout and J. Flynn (eds) *The Law of State Aid in the European Union* (Oxford University Press, 2005).

- there must be aid, that is, there must be a benefit or an advantage;
- it must be granted by a Member State or through state resources in any form whatsoever;
- it must distort or threaten to distort competition by favouring certain undertakings or the production of certain goods; and
- it must affect trade between Member States.

When we think of state aid, we typically think of the grant of money from the state to an undertaking. The notion is, however, wider than this and can cover such things as exemptions from tax and social security rules, equity investments, guarantees by the state, or selling goods or services to the undertaking for less than the market value. In short, anything which can give an undertaking a financial advantage in the marketplace may count as a state aid, as the CJEU has said:

> The concept of aid . . . embraces not only positive benefits, such as subsidies themselves, but also interventions which, in various forms, mitigate the charges which are normally included in the budget of an undertaking and which, without, therefore, being subsidies in the strict meaning of the word, are similar in character and have the same effect.[102]

In addition, the CJEU has made it clear that it is the effect of the measure granted, not the purpose for which it is granted, that will determine whether it is to be categorised as aid. By effect, what is meant is whether the action gives an advantage to the undertaking(s) that receive it. Having said this, there are a number of cases where the Courts have taken into account the nature of the scheme and decided that it did not constitute aid. For example, in *Sloman Neptun*,[103] German employment and social security legislation was not entirely applicable to the foreign crews of vessels flying the German flag. The effect of this was that the owners of seafaring vessels which employed non-German nationals had to pay reduced social security contributions and it was argued that, therefore, this constituted state aid. The CJEU took the view that this was not state aid:

> The system at issue does not seek, through its object and general structure, to create an advantage which would constitute an additional burden for the State or the abovementioned bodies, but only to alter in favour of shipping undertakings the framework within which contractual relations are formed between those undertakings and their employees. The consequences arising from this, in so far as they relate to the difference in the basis for the calculation of social security contributions, mentioned by the national court, and to the potential loss of tax revenue because of the low rates of pay, referred to by the Commission, are inherent in the system and are not a means of granting a particular advantage to the undertakings concerned.[104]

There have been a number of cases where this idea of the object and general structure of the system has been used to carve out an exemption to the idea of state aid.

State investments

Another area which has been controversial as regards the definition of aid revolves around those cases where the state has invested in an enterprise, for example, through taking a shareholding. This can be seen as a subset of a more general problem, which is where the state has

---

[102] Case 30/59 *De Gezamenlijke Steenkolenmijnen in Limburg v High Authority* [1961] ECR 1, a case under the European Coal and Steel Treaty but applied to aids under the EU Treaties.

[103] Cases C-72–73/91 *Sloman Neptun Shiffarhts AG v Seebetireibsrat Bodo Ziesemer der Sloman Neptun Schiffahrts AG* [1993] ECR I-887.

[104] Ibid. at para. 21.

granted a benefit to the undertaking but has received something in return for it. Typically, when we think of aid, we think of something being granted for nothing, but in these cases the state has received something. Does the transaction count as aid, given that the state has received some value? In order to deal with this problem, the Courts have developed what has been called the private market investor principle, which also has counterparts in the private purchaser, vendor or creditor tests. The idea here is that if the state makes an investment, or a financial decision, which would have been made by a private investor, then what has happened is not state aid, but simply a normal commercial decision. Originally this seems to have developed in the context of restructuring plans for unprofitable undertakings, where the state invested in them, but it has been extended to profitable ones as well.

This point can be illustrated by a case from Germany involving the banking sector, referred to as *WestLB*.[105] This case involved the financial restructuring of a German bank, wholly owned by the public sector, through the incorporation into it of a body, also owned by the state, which offered loans for housing at low interest rates. The assets transferred were ring-fenced within the bank to continue the provision of housing loans but also served as an injection of equity capital for the bank which served, in part, as a further guarantee of the commercial operations of the bank. The reason for this capital restructuring was the requirements of certain EU Directives relating to the solvency ratios of banks. This process of restructuring was undertaken for seven public banks in Germany and *WestLB* was a test case. In this case, it was agreed that, if there was a profit, the bank would provide a return of 0.6% on those assets to the public authorities. The private banks in Germany complained that the public banks had received an unfair advantage through this injection of capital, as they had to raise their capital through commercial means. The Commission took the view that the capital injection constituted state aid and decided that the appropriate rate of return would have been in the region of 9%, obviously higher than what had been agreed.[106] This decision was challenged by the German authorities on the grounds, among others, that the state aid rules could not be applied to profitable undertakings and that the average rate of return used by the Commission was not appropriate in the case. The GC took the view that the profitability of an undertaking was not decisive for establishing whether the undertaking had obtained an advantage. It did, however, have to be taken into account in order to determine whether the public authorities had behaved like an investor in a market economy.[107] As regards the application of an average return, the GC said that this was an appropriate analytical tool but it did not absolve the Commission from looking in depth at the circumstances of the case. Ultimately, the GC annulled the decision on the grounds that the Commission had not explained the reasoning behind the adoption of the rates of return properly, in breach of Article 296 TFEU (ex Article 253 EC). After the case, the Commission revised its estimate of state aids downwards and required repayment of the state aids from the German authorities, after a process of negotiation.

One of the difficulties with this approach is that it may have to be applied in the context of cases where there is no private sector equivalent. A good example of this is the dispute that arose between the French post office and its competitors over the assistance offered by the

---

[105] Cases T-228 and 233/99 *WestLB and Land Nordrhein-Westfalen v Commission* [2003] ECR II-435. See European Commission, Press Notice IP/04/1261, 20 October 2004 for the background.

[106] The Commission decision gives precise figures for return.

[107] [2003] ECR II-435 at para. 208.

French post office to its express courier service.[108] The complaint, in essence, was that the express courier service paid less for the services it received, which included access to the infrastructure of the post office, than would be charged in a commercial setting and that this constituted unfair state aid. The Commission decided that there was no state aid in this case because the assistance had been provided to the express courier service under normal business conditions. This decision was challenged before the GC, which annulled the Commission's decision on the grounds that the analysis undertaken did not consider whether the terms of the transaction were comparable to those between undertakings operating in normal market conditions, specifically the situation where there was a holding company with a monopoly and a subsidiary operating in a competitive market. This decision was appealed to the CJEU, which overturned the GC's decision because La Poste's situation was very different from that of a private undertaking operating under normal market conditions. Given that La Poste had an obligation to collect, carry and deliver mail for all users in France at uniform tariffs and with similar quality requirements, the creation and maintenance of the postal network could not be assessed purely in line with a commercial approach. Instead, the assessment must be based on the objective and verifiable elements that were available. In this case, that meant the costs incurred by La Poste in providing assistance to its subsidiary and whether these covered variable costs, an appropriate element for fixed costs, an adequate return on capital investment, and that the calculation of these costs was not too low or arbitrary.[109]

The point of this decision would seem to be that the Commission does not have to compare the workings of what might be called a public service enterprise with a comparable private sector operation but should instead make an objective assessment of whether the costs of support are covered. The difficulty with this approach, leaving aside the difficulty of calculating costs, is the suggestion that there must be an adequate return on investment. Calculating this will depend, presumably, on making a reference to rates of return on comparable projects in the private sector although, if they do not have the same public service obligations, this implies that a lower rate of return will be acceptable. Certainly what the case does imply is that the Commission's assessment is more important than any private sector comparisons.

Aid from a Member State or through state resources

There are two preliminary points here which should be noted. First, aid counts as coming from a Member State if it comes direct from the state (for example, through a government department) or if it comes through an agency over which the state has a measure of control. Secondly, the transfer of resources may be either through a positive action, such as granting or loaning of money, or through the state receiving less money than it would otherwise do so in the absence of the aid, through, for example, exempting an undertaking from paying certain taxes or charges. There have been two areas of particular controversy.

One issue concerns charges that are levied by bodies on undertakings, which can be illustrated by looking at two cases. In *Steinike*,[110] the plaintiff, who imported fruit from Italy, was required to pay a levy which went into a fund for the promotion of the German food and agricultural industries and the plaintiff challenged this levy before a national court on the

---

[108] Case C-83/01P *Chronopost SA, La Poste and French Republic v Commission* [2003] ECR I-6993.
[109] Ibid. at paras 38–41.
[110] Case 78/76 *Steinike and Willig* [1977] ECR 595.

grounds that it was unlawful state aid. Here the CJEU said that if the financing was wholly or partially by means of contributions imposed by a public authority and levied on the under-takings concerned it could still constitute aid.[111] This should be contrasted with the more recent case of *Pearle*,[112] which involved a situation in the Netherlands where the trade association for opticians, established under Dutch legislation, levied a charge on opticians which it used to fund a collective advertising campaign. Here the CJEU held that this did not constitute state aid; as the costs of the advertising campaign were fully covered by the levies, there was no advantage gained or additional burden put on the state. Furthermore, the campaign had been under-taken at the request of an association of private undertakings and the board acted for a purely commercial purpose which had nothing to do with a policy determined by the Dutch authorities. By contrast, in *Steinike*, the CJEU said that the fund had been financed by state subsidies and contributions and it was a means for implementing a policy determined by the state.

More controversially, there has been an argument that no transfer of resources from the state is required for there to be state aid and that a broad interpretation of the concept is needed.[113] This issue seems to have been resolved in the *Preussen Elektra* case.[114] In this case electricity supply companies in Germany were required, by legislation, to purchase certain amounts of renewable energy and a minimum fixed price was set by the legislation based on the general prices charged, the effect of which was that producers of renewable energy were able to charge higher prices. It was strongly argued by the Commission and other interveners that this arrangement constituted state aid, even though the money did not come from state resources, and that the Court should take a broad view of the concept and depart from previous case law.[115] The CJEU rejected this argument, holding that only advantages granted directly or indirectly through state resources would fall within the concept of state aid. Here there was no direct or indirect transfer of state resources because the money was paid by private under-takings; therefore, even though the scheme gave an advantage to the producers of renewable electricity, it could not be classified as state aid.

Just how difficult the distinction can be to operate can be seen in *Netherlands v Commission*, often referred to as the 'Dutch Nox' case.[116] Here the Dutch authorities had established an emissions trading system for nitrogen oxide for plants producing above a certain capacity of emissions. Plants which produced below a certain level of emissions would obtain certificates, which could be sold to plants that were above their target. Failure to comply with the emission standards could lead to the imposition of a fine. One of the arguments in the case was whether the creation of these tradable certificates was a state aid matter. The Netherlands argued that it was not, because there was no transfer of state resources. Ultimately, the CJEU disagreed with this, saying that in creating such certificates the state had forgone the right to auction or sell them and that this loss of revenue was not inherent in the design of the system. Although in *Preussen Elektra* the scheme led to a loss of tax revenue, because it reduced the profits of those undertakings paying the higher price, that was inherent in the design of the scheme.

---

[111] Ibid. at para. 22.

[112] Case C-345/02 *Pearle BV v Hoofdbedrijfschap Ambachten* [2004] ECR I-7139.

[113] See, for example, P. Slotboom, 'State Aid in the Community: A broad or narrow definition' (1995) 20 *European Law Review* 289.

[114] Case C-379/98 *Preussen Elektra* [2001] ECR I-2099.

[115] See the opinion of AG Jacobs, ibid., at paras 134–59.

[116] Case C-279/08P *Netherlands v Commission* judgment of 8 September 2011 (CJEU).

Distortion of competition

The key issue under this heading is whether the aid has been selective, that is, has it benefited an undertaking, or class of undertakings, in some way that has not been available to other undertakings? If selectivity is shown, it is relatively easy to show that there is a distortion of competition according to the case law. The case law makes the point that there is no obligation to show an actual distortion of competition, simply that it must 'threaten' to distort competition.[117] One of the reasons given for this is a procedural one: if the Commission had to show a real effect on competition, this would favour those states that pay the aid without notifying the Commission, because in essence it would put the burden of proof on the Commission.[118] So the important question is whether the aid is selective.

Where aid is granted to a specific undertaking or to a class of undertakings the issue of selectivity is reasonably straightforward. More difficult is the case where a discretionary power to grant aid is given but this can be exercised in favour of specific undertakings. It has become clear that the exercise of that power may constitute state aid. In the *Ecotrade* case,[119] Italian law created a special insolvency procedure for large industrial companies, which, among other things, allowed them to carry on trading. In order to benefit from this procedure, a number of conditions needed to be satisfied, including a decision by the relevant Ministers. The CJEU took the view that, in these circumstances, having regard to the class of undertakings covered by the legislation and the scope of the discretion enjoyed by the Minister when authorising an insolvent undertaking to continue trading, the legislation met the condition that it should relate to a specific undertaking.[120]

Trade between Member States

Although the wording of the test is slightly different in Article 107 TFEU from Article 101 TFEU, the CJEU has read this test expansively. It is not necessary to demonstrate any actual effect on trade within the Union but simply that there is a reasonable prospect. The expansive interpretation can be seen in the *Altmark* case,[121] where the CJEU was asked by a national court whether subsidies for local public transport services would affect trade between Member States. The CJEU pointed out that the fact that a transport undertaking only operates in one Member State does not make it impossible for a subsidy system to have an effect on trade between Member States because the subsidy to a local operator may make it more difficult for an undertaking from outside that Member State to bid to run those operations. In addition, the CJEU said that according to the Court's case law there is no threshold or percentage below which it may be considered that trade between Member States is not affected. The relatively small amount of aid or the relatively small size of the undertaking which receives it does not as such exclude the possibility that trade between Member States might be affected.[122]

---

[117] Case T-298/97 *Alzetta* [2000] ECR II-2319 at paras 78–80.
[118] Case T-214/95 *Vlammse Gewest v Commission* [1998] ECR II-717 at para. 67.
[119] Case C-200/97 *Ecotrade v Altiforni e Ferriere di Servola* [1998] ECR I-7907.
[120] Ibid., para. 40.
[121] Case C-280/00 *Altmark TransGmbH* [2003] ECR I-7747.
[122] Ibid., para. 81, citing Case C-142/87 *Belgium v Commission (Tubemeuse)* [1990] ECR I-959; Joined Cases C-278–280/92 *Spain v Commission* [1994] ECR I-4103.

This approach by the CJEU creates a practical problem for the Commission and Member States because state aid must be notified to the Commission and the Commission must decide whether notified aid meets the criteria in Article 107 TFEU. The problem with not having a *de minimis* rule is that the Member States will spend time and resources on notifying small grants of aid, while the Commission also expends time and resources on checking them. In practice, the Commission has adopted a policy for some time that small grants of aid are not considered by it as falling within the terms of Article 107 TFEU. The rules are now set out in a 2006 Commission Regulation on *de minimis* aid,[123] which in broad terms sets a ceiling of €200,000 over any period of three fiscal years although there are a number of exceptions to this provision as well as certain monitoring requirements laid on the Member States. It is possible that this Regulation will be reviewed under the modernisation process. It has also made a number of decisions concluding that certain activities were purely local and did not have an affect on trade, for example local swimming pools.[124]

Exceptions and exemptions

Not all state aid is incompatible with the EU Treaties because Article 107 TFEU makes provision for aid which *shall* be compatible with the common market and aid which *may be considered* to be compatible with the common market (see Box 7.11 for text).

Decisions on both categories of aid are made by the Commission but the difference is that in the former instance there is no discretion for the Commission to approve the aid if it falls within that category while in the latter case there is, and a complicated set of rules has arisen in these areas. In addition, it is also clear now that the derogation in Article 106(2) TFEU may be used in the context of the financing of services of general economic interest.

KEY LEGAL PROVISION   **Box 7.11**

Article 107(2) and (3) TFEU

2 The following shall be compatible with the internal market:

(a) aid having a social character, granted to individual consumers, provided that such aid is granted without discrimination related to the origin of the products concerned;

(b) aid to make good the damage caused by natural disasters or exceptional occurrences;

(c) aid granted to the economy of certain areas of the Federal Republic of Germany affected by the division of Germany, insofar as such aid is required in order to compensate for the economic disadvantages caused by that division. Five years after the entry into force of the Treaty of Lisbon, the Council, acting on a proposal from the Commission, may adopt a decision repealing this point.

➡

---

[123] Commission Regulation (EC) No. 1998/2006 of 15 December 2006 on the application of Articles 87 and 88 of the Treaty to de minimis aid. See M. Berghofer, 'The New De Minimis Regulation: Enlarging the Sword of Damocles?' [2007] 1 *European State Aid Law Quarterly* 11.

[124] Commission Communication on the application of the European Union State aid rules to compensation granted for the provision of services of general economic interest, OH C 8/4, 11.01.2012, at para. 40.

3 The following may be considered to be compatible with the interal market:

(a) aid to promote the economic development of areas where the standard of living is abnormally low or where there is serious underemployment and of the regions referred to in Article 349, in view of their structural, economic and social situation;

(b) aid to promote the execution of an important project of common European interest or to remedy a serious disturbance in the economy of a Member State;

(c) aid to facilitate the development of certain economic activities or of certain economic areas, where such aid does not adversely affect trading conditions to an extent contrary to the common interest;

(d) aid to promote culture and heritage conservation where such aid does not affect trading conditions and competition in the Union to an extent that is contrary to the common interest;

Question: How much room for interpretation is there in these various criteria?

Article 107(2) TFEU

Article 107(2) TFEU provides for three compulsory exceptions, which can be dealt with quickly.[125] Aid to make good damage caused by natural disasters or exceptional circumstances is self-explanatory. By its nature, this is a relatively small category and there have been about thirty decisions between 2007 and mid 2012 approving aid of this nature and covering such events as earthquake, flood and fire disasters. Aid granted to certain areas of the Federal Republic of Germany is a category which was intended to deal with areas of the former West Germany which bordered on the former East Germany and West Berlin. After German reunification, the Commission has tried to deal with state aid through the normal processes of control and this category is now only of historical interest. The final category, aid having a social character granted to individual consumers, covers such schemes as the home owners mortgage support scheme in the UK. This is again a relatively small category of aid, judging by the number of cases on the Commission's website, around twenty-eight between 2007 and mid 2012, covering a variety of measures.

Article 107(3) TFEU

Much more important are the discretionary exemptions in Article 107(3) TFEU. Not only has the Commission taken numerous individual decisions on these exemptions but it has been empowered by the Council to implement regulations which provide for block exemptions for certain categories of aid and this now takes the form of one general block exemption Regulation.[126] It has also published guidelines on how it will apply its discretion in certain categories of cases. The result is a very complex series of rules and the aim of this section is

---

[125] For more detail, see Hancher, Jan Slot and Ottervanger (n. 93) at paras 4-003 to 4-010.

[126] European Commission Regulation (EC) No. 800/2008 of 6 August 2008 declaring certain categories of aid compatible with the common market in application of Articles 87 and 88 of the Treaty (General block exemption Regulation), OJ L214, 09.08.2008, pp. 3–47.

to try and give a general overview of the approach taken by the Commission, rather than a detailed discussion in relation to each area.

Regional aid[127]

One of the most important areas of activity of the Commission is in relation to regional aid. This is based on Article 107(3)(a) and (c) TFEU and the distinction between the two parts of the Article is that Article 107(3)(a) TFEU is aimed at areas where the standard of living is abnormally low and this must be judged in relation to the European Union as a whole, whereas Article 107(3)(c) TFEU is wider, relating to certain economic activities or economic areas, so long as the aid does not adversely affect trading conditions contrary to the common interest, and therefore allows the authorisation of aid to an area which is disadvantaged in relation to the rest of that Member State.[128] So, Article 107(3)(a) TFEU covers the poorest areas in the Union and allows aid to them, while Article 107(3)(c) TFEU covers the poorest areas in a particular country and allows aid to them. This basic distinction has been further developed by the Commission through its guidance on regional aid schemes. In general, this aims to approve aid for investment by an undertaking that is part of a multi-sectoral aid scheme as part of a coherent strategy for regional development.[129] Regions will fall within the Article 107(3)(a) TFEU criteria if they have a per capita gross domestic product of less than 75% of the Union average. As regards the Article 107(3)(c) TFEU criteria, the Commission determines, first, the eligible amount of population that can be covered and the Commission approves proposals made by Member States. Broadly speaking, these can be economic development regions or regions which have a low population, relatively low GDP, relatively high unemployment or are geographically isolated.[130] In relation to the UK, only two areas have been approved under Article 107(3)(a) TFEU: Cornwall and the Isles of Scilly, and West Wales and the Valleys, with a total population of just under 2.4 million. Under Article 107(3)(c) TFEU areas covering around 7 million people were proposed, including parts of South Yorkshire, North Nottinghamshire, East Derbyshire, Merseyside, parts of Scotland, Cumbria and Tyneside.[131]

The category into which a region falls is important because it affects the amount of aid which can be granted, primarily for investment projects. The amount of aid is calculated in relation to the costs of the investment and the recipient of the aid must put in a contribution of at least 25% of the eligible costs and undertake to maintain that investment for at least five years. The maximum amount of aid that can be given is defined as a percentage of the relevant costs and is referred to as the 'intensity' of aid. For Article 107(3)(a) TFEU regions, the intensity of aid can vary from 30% to 50% of the eligible costs, depending on the relative level of GDP in the region. For Article 107(3)(c) TFEU regions, the percentages vary from 10% to 20%, so roughly half that of the poorest regions.[132] It should be noted that operating aid, aid aimed at reducing a firm's current expenses, is usually prohibited. Exceptionally,

---

[127] Hancher, Jan Slot and Ottervanger (n. 93), ch. 21.
[128] Case 248/84 *Germany* v *Commission* [1987] ECR 4013 at para. 19.
[129] European Commission, *Guidelines on national regional aid 2007–2013*, OJ C54/13, 04.03.2006, pp. 13–45 (at para. 10). The guidelines do not apply to fisheries, coal, agriculture and steel.
[130] Ibid., paras 24–32.
[131] European Commission, *UK Regional Aid Map 2007–2013*, N673/2006.
[132] *Guidelines* (n. 129), paras 42–9.

however, such aid may be granted in regions eligible under the derogation in Article 107(3)(a) TFEU provided that (i) it is justified in terms of its contribution to regional development and its nature, and (ii) its level is proportional to the handicaps it seeks to alleviate.[133]

The general block exemption Regulation[134]

One of the longer term issues for the Commission has been to try find a way of administering the state aid regime efficiently. One way of dealing with the number of notifications was to create a series of block exemptions, under authority granted by the Council, so that aid schemes which met these criteria did not have to be notified to the Commission before implementation. A number of Regulations have now been consolidated into one general block exemption Regulation which covers aid to regions, small and medium-sized enterprises, female entrepreneurs and environmental protection, among other categories.[135] The Regulation covers aid schemes, aid awarded on the basis of a scheme ('individual aid') and aid awarded outside a scheme ('ad hoc aid'). The general rules for qualification are that the aid must be transparent (and the types of aid that meet this criteria are listed in Article 5) and must fall below particular thresholds, normally ranging from €2 million to €10 million.[136] The aid must also have an incentive effect which, in terms of SMEs simply means that they must submit an application, while for large enterprises it must be shown that the aid will lead to an increase in activity.[137] In addition to these general requirements, there is a set of detailed specific requirements that have to be met for each category of aid, which are beyond the scope of this book. There is likely to be some change to this Regulation under the modernisation proposals.

Commission guidelines

As well as guidelines on regional aid, the Commission has also issued guidelines on aid for research and development and innovation, environmental protection, rescue of enterprises and risk capital. The guidelines on research and development are interesting because they provide two routes by which such aid can be approved.[138] First, it may be approved under Article 107(3)(b) TFEU if it is an important project of European interest. For this to be the case it must be clearly defined, with an advantage for the Union as a whole, represent a substantive leap forward for Union objectives, the project must involve a high level of risk, the aid must be necessary as an incentive and overall the project must be meaningful and of great importance. According to Hancher *et al.*, a group of eminent practitioners and academics, no Member State has tried to make use of these provisions.[139]

In order to qualify under Article 107(3)(c) TFEU, aid must lead to increased research and development and innovation without adversely affecting trading conditions, contrary to the

---

[133] Ibid., para. 76.

[134] European Commission Regulation (EC) No. 800/2008 of 6 August 2008 declaring certain categories of aid compatible with the common market in application of Articles 87 and 88 of the Treaty [107 and 108 TFEU] (hereafter GBER), OJ L214, 09.08.2008, pp. 3–47.

[135] It does not apply to agriculture, coal, steel and shipbuilding, among others.

[136] Although aid for research projects has higher thresholds, especially under the Eureka scheme.

[137] GBER (n. 134), Art. 8.

[138] European Commission, *Community framework for State aid for research and development and innovation* [2006] OJ C323/01. Generally, see Hancher, Jan Slot and Ottervanger (n. 93), ch. 23.

[139] Ibid. at para. 23-006.

common interest. This is decided on the basis of what the Commission calls a 'balancing test', which has three parts:

(1) Is the aid measure aimed at a well-defined objective of common interest (e.g. growth, employment, cohesion, environment)?

(2) Is the aid well designed to deliver the objective of common interest, i.e. does the proposed aid address the market failure or other objective?

   (i)   Is state aid an appropriate policy instrument?

   (ii) Is there an incentive effect, i.e. does the aid change the behaviour of firms?

   (iii) Is the aid measure proportional, i.e. could the same change in behaviour be obtained with less aid?

(3) Are the distortions of competition and effect on trade limited, so that the overall balance is positive?[140]

The amount of aid intensity allowed varies, from 65% to 100%, depending on the type of research (fundamental, industrial or experimental) and the size of the enterprise carrying it out. Aid may also be given for a variety of other research and development activities: for example, innovation clusters, technical feasibility studies, industrial property right costs for SMEs and the loan of highly qualified personnel. For larger projects, the Commission may undertake a more detailed assessment and it gives detailed guidance on the methodology that it will follow in these circumstances. The Commission is has undertaken a review of the operation of these guidelines and they are likely to be amended in the near future.[141]

There is also a set of guidelines on aid for environmental purposes, which has the overall aim of integrating environmental protection into competition policy, in particular to promote sustainable development.[142] The Commission says that the primary objective of state aid control in the field of environmental protection is to ensure that state aid measures will result in a higher level of environmental protection than would occur without the aid and to ensure that the positive effects of the aid outweigh its negative effects in terms of distortions of competition, taking account of the polluter pays principle.[143] The approach outlined in these guidelines is a balancing test, based on the State Aid Action Plan, but adapted for environmental protection. Broadly speaking, the questions to be asked are: is the aid measure aimed at a well-defined area of common interest? Is the aid well designed to deliver this objective, that is, is it an appropriate instrument, will it change the behaviour of the undertakings concerned and is it proportional? Finally, are the distortions on competition and trade limited, so that the overall balance is still positive? The guidelines also identify a series of measures which may, under specific conditions, be compatible with Article 107(3)(c). These include aid for firms that aim to go further than existing EU standards, early adaptation to Union standards, environmental studies, energy saving and renewable energy sources.[144]

---

[140] European Commission, *Community framework for state aid for research and development and innovation* [2006] OJ C323/01 at para. 1.3.1.

[141] See *http://ec.europa.eu/competition/consultations/2012_stateaid_rdi/index_en.html* (accessed 31/07/12).

[142] European Commission, *Community guidelines on State aid for environmental protection*, OJ C 82/1 01.04.2008. Generally, see Hancher, Jan Slot and Ottervanger (n. 93), ch. 20.

[143] European Commission, *Community guidelines on State aid for environmental protection*, OJ C 82/1 01.04.2008 (at para. 6).

[144] Ibid. paras 42–57.

Rescuing and restructuring aid

Guidelines have also been adopted for dealing with state aid to rescue and restructure firms which are in difficulty.[145] This is a highly controversial area, as there is a history of state owned or controlled undertakings getting into financial difficulties and being bailed out by governments, often more than once. An example of this would be the saga of the French computer group, Bull, which had received aid in 1993 and 1994, which the Commission decided was compatible with the internal market, so long as the restructuring plan, among other requirements, was carried out. In 2001, France paid a further cash advance to Bull of €450 million, again as part of a restructuring operation which the Commission ruled as compatible with the internal market, so long as the advance was repaid within about a year, although this was not done and the Commission brought an action against France. Subsequently, the Commission took a fresh decision in this case, approving an aid of €517 million subject to the implementation of a restructuring plan.[146] Restructuring can also be undertaken on a large scale, as in the mid-1990s when there was a large-scale restructuring of almost the entire chemical industry in former East Germany.[147] As these two examples indicate, the issue of state support for particular companies or sectors of industry can be politically very important. At the same time, as the Commission points out in the guidelines, the exit of inefficient firms from the market is a critical part of the normal operation of a competitive market. It regards this sort of state aid as being potentially one of the types which can have the severest effects on competition. Nevertheless, the Commission accepts that rescue aid can be legitimate, if it meets certain conditions, of which there are five (see Box 7.12). To summarise them:

- the firm in question must be in difficulty;[148]
- the support must be in the form of loans or loan guarantees at a commercial rate;
- the aid must be needed to avert serious social difficulties;
- a restructuring plan must be put in place;
- the aid must be proportionate to the problem and the aid should only be granted once.

A similar approach is taken to restructuring aid,[149] where the basic idea is that any distortions of competition are offset by the benefits flowing from the firm's survival, although this is a controversial idea in itself. In order to avoid undue distortion of competition, the restructuring plan must include compensatory measures, such as the divestment of assets, reductions in capacity or market presence and reductions in barriers to entry. The aid must be limited to what is necessary and the beneficiaries are expected to make a significant contribution

---

[145] European Commission, *Community guidelines on State aid for rescuing and restructuring firms in difficulty*, OJ C244, 01.10.2004, pp. 2–17. They have been extended until at least October 2012 because of the current economic crisis.

[146] See Decision 2003/599 (EC) *Bull* [2003] OJ L209/1 and Decision 2005/94 (EC) *Bull* [2005] OJ L342/81.

[147] Hancher, Jan Slot and Ottervanger (n. 93) at para. 24–005; and Decision 96/545 (EC) *Leuna-Werke* [1996] OJ L239/1.

[148] There is no Union definition of a firm in difficulty. The Commission regards a firm as in difficulty if it is unable to stem losses which, without outside intervention by the public authorities, will almost certainly condemn it to going out of business in the short or medium term.

[149] European Commission, *Community guidelines on State aid for rescuing and restructuring firms in difficulty*, OJ C244, 01.10.2004, pp. 2–17 (at paras 33–54).

to the restructuring plan from their own resources. The Commission may also impose additional conditions on the grant of restructuring aid. The plan must be implemented and its progress will be monitored by the Commission through regular reports presented by the Member State.

KEY OFFICIAL GUIDANCE   Box 7.12

Conditions for the grant of rescue aid

It must:

(a) consist of liquidity support in the form of loan guarantees or loans; in both cases, the loan must be granted at an interest rate at least comparable to those observed for loans to healthy firms, and in particular the reference rates adopted by the Commission; any loan must be reimbursed and any guarantee must come to an end within a period of not more than six months after the disbursement of the first instalment to the firm;

(b) be warranted on the grounds of serious social difficulties and have no unduly adverse spillover effects on other Member States;

(c) be accompanied, on notification, by an undertaking given by the Member State concerned to communicate to the Commission, not later than six months after the rescue aid measure has been authorised, a restructuring plan or a liquidation plan or proof that the loan has been reimbursed in full and/or that the guarantee has been terminated; in the case of non-notified aid the Member State must communicate, no later than six months after the first implementation of a rescue aid measure, a restructuring plan or a liquidation plan or proof that the loan has been reimbursed in full and/or that the guarantee has been terminated;

(d) be restricted to the amount needed to keep the firm in business for the period during which the aid is authorised; such an amount may include aid for urgent structural measures; the amount necessary should be based on the liquidity needs of the company stemming from losses; in determining that amount regard will be had to the outcome of the application of the Commission's formula; any rescue aid exceeding the result of that calculation will need to be duly explained;

(e) respect the one time, last time condition.

Source: European Commission, *Community guidelines on State aid for rescuing and restructuring firms in difficulty*, OJ C244, 01.10.2004, pp. 2–17 (at para. 25).

Questions: How objective do you think these conditions are? How quickly, and under what political pressure, do governments have to take these decisions?

Responding to the financial crisis[150]

The financial crisis of 2007–08 started by affecting a number of individual financial institutions and the Commission dealt with these cases under Article 107(3)(c) TFEU. The first example of this in the UK was the rescue of Northern Rock in late 2007. Northern Rock got into trouble because it had financed its mortgage lending by securitising its assets[151] and, when there was a worldwide credit squeeze, it was unable to continue to raise the money to support its activities. The Bank of England stepped in with an emergency liquidity facility, followed by state guarantees for the existing accounts at Northern Rock, an additional injection of money and a guarantee for new accounts. All these measures were duly notified to the Commission, which took the view that the initial emergency liquidity facility was not state aid because it was secured by high quality collateral and against a very high interest rate. The other measures did, however, constitute state aid but, as they met the conditions for rescue aid, were considered compatible with the internal market under Article 107(3)(c) TFEU.[152] The UK was required to present a plan for restructuring Northern Rock to the Commission which was altered in the light of deteriorating financial conditions and investigated by the Commission. The restructuring plan, among other things, split Northern Rock into two operations, one of which was potentially commercially viable ('a good bank') and the other part of which was not ('a bad bank'). After some discussion, the Commission approved this plan, now under Article 107(3)(b), and Northern Rock's good assets were sold to Virgin Money.[153]

By the autumn of 2008, it became apparent that an individualised response was no longer adequate, so the Commission switched the legal basis of its intervention to Article 107(3)(b) TFEU, which refers to remedying serious disturbances in the economy of a Member State. On the back of this, the Commission produced four communications for financial institutions dealing with their rescue, recapitalisation and the treatment of impaired assets.[154] A fifth

---

[150] Hancher, Jan Slot and Ottervanger (n. 93) at ch. 19; C. Ahlborn and D. Piccinin, 'The application of the principles of restructuring aid to banks during the financial crisis' [2010] *European State Aid Law Quarterly* 47; P. Werner and M. Maier, 'Procedure in Crisis? Overview and assessment of the Commission's state aid procedure during the current crisis' [2009] *European State Aid Law Quarterly* 177; U. Soltész and C. Von Köckritz, 'From State Aid Control to the Regulation of the European Banking System – DG Comp and the Restructuring of Banks' (2010) 6 *European Competition Journal* 285. For discussions about why the financial crisis happened see: Bank of England, *Financial Stability Report*, October 2008, available at: *http://www.bankofengland.co.uk/ publications/fsr/2008/fsr24.htm*, which gives a detailed, official and authoritative version while M. Lewis, *The Big Short* (2011, Penguin) is a non-technical explanation. B. Lyons, 'Competition Policy, Bailouts and the Economic Crisism,' March 2009, available at: *http://competitionpolicy.ac.uk/publications/working-papers-2009* (accessed 31/07/12) is a good explanation of the underlying issues.

[151] It pooled its mortgages and used the pool to raise money.

[152] European Commission State aid NN 70/2007 (ex CP 269/07) – United Kingdom Rescue aid to Northern Rock.

[153] European Commission State Aid Case C14/2008 Restructuring aid to Northern Rock, UK Financial Investments, Press Release 17 November 2011 available at: *http://www.ukfi.co.uk/index.php?URL_link= press-releases&Year=2011* (accessed 31/07/12).

[154] European Commission, 'Communication – The application of State aid rules to measures taken in relation to financial institutions in the context of the current global financial crisis', OJ C270, 25.10.2008, pp. 8–14; 'Communication – Recapitalisation of financial institutions in the current financial crisis: limitation of the aid to the minimum necessary and safeguards against undue distortions of competition' OJ C10, 15.01.2009, pp. 2–10; 'Communication from the Commission on the Treatment of Impaired Assets in the Community Banking sector' OJ C72, 26.03.2009, pp. 1–22; 'Communication on the return to viability and the assessment of restructuring measures in the financial sector in the current crisis under the State aid rules' OJ C 195/9 19.08.2009.

communication explains the approach going forward.[155] Outside the financial sector, the Commission has adopted a temporary framework for access to finance to help provide finance to companies because of the problems of obtaining bank finance due to the economic crisis which expired at the end of 2011. This framework has been regularly amended in the course of its existence.[156] The scale of the interventions has been remarkable. In spring 2009 the Commission estimated that it has approved aid of around €3,000 billion, corresponding to around a quarter of EU GDP.[157] In addition, decision making in this area has been significantly speeded up, as compared with the normal processes which are discussed below.[158] It is too early to assess the repercussions that this might have for state aid procedure in general but it is a significant achievement for the Commission to have been able to respond to the financial crisis in a timely manner and thus maintain the structure of state aid control.

Although the details of the approach taken by the Commission are too complicated to go into here,[159] a number of comments are worth making. First, the Commission approved almost all of the measures that Member States proposed to support their banks and financial institutions.[160] Secondly, although it approved the state aid, the Commission did try to do this on the basis of some principles so that competition was not distorted. In legal terms the Commission either imposed conditions or obtained the Member States' commitments on certain matters. For example, in relation to the recapitalisation of RBS and Lloyds TSB,[161] the Commission insisted on the government obtaining a proper return for its investment and that there was a charge for participating in the asset protection scheme. Thirdly, as part of the price for state aid, the Commission has often insisted on the restructuring of banks and the disposal of assets. Again, to take RBS and Lloyds as examples, RBS has sold off its insurance businesses (Direct Line and Churchill) as well as selling some bank branches to Santander. Lloyds has been required to divest itself of a number of retail branches which will most likely go to the Co-operative Group. It looks as if these measures, when combined with the Northern Rock sell-off, may ensure a higher level of competition in retail banking in the UK.

Perhaps unsurprisingly, Commission decisions have not often been challenged in the European courts. In *Netherlands and ING Groep v Commission*,[162] the General Court gave its first decision on measures taken as a result of the financial crisis. This case involved state aid given by the Netherlands to ING during the financial crisis. The Netherlands supported ING through a capital injection, an impaired assets merger and certain guarantees, all of which were approved by the Commission, subject to certain conditions, notably a restructuring plan and certain behavioural conditions. The key point of contention involved the capital injection which had initially been given in November 2008, subject to certain repayment

---

[155] European Commission, 'Communication on the application, from 1 January 2012, of State aid rules to support measures in favour of banks in the context of the financial crisis' OJ C 356/7, 06.12.2011.

[156] For the current framework and the amendments, see *http://ec.europa.eu/competition/state_aid/legislation/temporary. html* (accessed 01/08/12).

[157] European Commission, 'State aid scoreboard – Spring 2009 update – special edition on state aid interventions in the current financial and economic crisis' COM (2009) 164.

[158] See P. Werner and M. Maier, 'Procedure in Crisis? Overview and assessment of the Commission's state aid procedure during the current crisis' [2009] 2 *European State Aid Law Quarterly* 177.

[159] Hancher, Jan Slot and Ottervanger (n. 93) at ch. 19 give details.

[160] The one exception was a Portuguese bank: SA 28787 'Restructuring of BPP' 20.07.2010.

[161] Case N428/2009 *Restructuring of Lloyds Banking Group* 18.11.2009, N422/2009; *RBS Restructuring Plan* 22.04.2010.

[162] Cases T-29 and 33/10, judgment of 2 March 2012 (GC).

terms. The initial terms were that the securities could either be repurchased at €15 (a 50% redemption premium) or, after three years, converted into ordinary shares. If this latter option were chosen, the Dutch authorities would have the choice of opting for the alternative redemption of the securities at a price of €10 plus interest. A coupon would be paid to the Netherlands only if a dividend was paid by ING on ordinary shares. The repayment terms were then amended, providing that ING could repurchase up to 50% of the securities at issue price plus accrued interest in relation to the annual coupon of 8.5% and an early redemption premium, which would vary between €340 million and a maximum of €705 million, ensuring a minimum internal rate of return of 15%. This option was then exercised towards the end of 2009. The plaintiffs challenged the Commission decision on the ground that the amendment to the repayment terms did not constitute state aid. The argument was, in essence, that the amendment met the private market investor test and therefore this was not state aid. The GC upheld this argument, essentially on the grounds that the Commission had not considered properly whether the amendment to the capital injection would have passed the test and annulled the decision and, probably most importantly, the commitments that went with it. The case also contains an interesting description of the procedure followed in approving these measures, which indicates the time pressure that the authorities were under and culminated in an email sent by the Commission to the Netherlands at 4.12 am, asking them to check the draft of the final decision which was to be issued later that day!

Services of general economic interest

The issue of state aids and services of general economic interest has been particularly controversial within the European Union. The typical problem arises when the state provides a subsidy to a private undertaking in return for that undertaking carrying out an activity that it would be unlikely to do otherwise. A simple example is the subsidy provided by local authorities for uneconomic bus routes; without the subsidy, the bus company would not operate the route. At first sight, this situation looks like a clear case where state aid has been given to one undertaking, which gains an advantage over others and so competition is distorted.[163] There might be questions about the effect on inter-state trade, given the bus example, and the size of the aid, but in principle it should be notified to the Commission, which will need to take a decision on its compatibility with the common market. If, however, such subsidy cannot fit within the exemptions within Article 107 TFEU, it could be saved by the derogation in Article 106(2) TFEU but this would, again, be a decision for the Commission to make. Alternatively, it might be argued that these payments are not aid at all but they are compensation for the bus company taking on these uneconomic routes. If this was the case then the payments would escape from control of the Commission under the state aids regime.

The former approach was taken in the *FFSA*[164] case decided by the GC, where tax concessions granted to the French post office were challenged by its competitors on the grounds that they were unlawful state aid. The Commission, in its decision, took the view that the concessions were not state aid because they were justified under the derogation in Article 106(2)

---

[163] The Commission also seemed to take this view: see 'Communication from the Commission on the application of State aid rules to public service broadcasting' [2001] OJ C320/04 at para. 19: 'any transfer of State resources to a certain undertaking – also when covering net costs of public service obligations – has to be regarded as State aid'.

[164] Case T-106/95 *Fédération Française des Sociétés d'Assurances (FFSA)* v *Commission* [1997] ECR II-229.

TFEU as not being greater than the amount needed to carry out the public service tasks. These tasks included having a network of post offices, stretching into rural areas, some of which would be loss making. The GC took a different approach, seeing the tax concession as a state aid and then discussing whether the derogation in Article 106(2) TFEU could apply and deciding that it could not overturn the Commission's analysis (this is referred to in the literature as the 'state aid' approach). Subsequently, the CJEU took a different approach to the question in the *Ferring* case.[165] Here wholesale distributors of medicines were exempted from a tax imposed on pharmaceutical laboratories when they made direct sales to pharmacies. The wholesale distributors were required under French law to have adequate stocks of medicines for specific geographical areas and to deliver those stocks at short notice. In principle, these facts look similar to the *FFSA* case, and the CJEU pointed out that, leaving aside the public service obligations, the tax exemption did meet the state aid criteria. Nevertheless, the CJEU decided that, provided the tax corresponded to the additional costs actually incurred by the wholesalers in discharging their public service obligations, not assessing them for the tax could be regarded as compensation for the services provided (this is referred to in the literature as the 'compensation approach'). They thus did not enjoy any advantage, the state had in effect purchased a service and this was, therefore, not state aid. Insofar as the subsidy exceeded the additional costs, it could not benefit from the derogation in Article 106(2) TFEU.

This decision was highly controversial and was criticised in both academic literature and by Advocate Generals in subsequent cases because it confused looking at the aims of a measure with its effects, it deprived Article 106(2) TFEU of any useful function and undermined the Commission's supervisory powers, because if something is not state aid, it does not need to be notified.[166] The issue came up again in the *Altmark* case, which involved the question of subsidies to local bus operators and whether this constituted state aid.[167] The CJEU took the view here that compensation for public service activities did not constitute state aid, provided that four conditions were met (see Box 7.13).

KEY CASE EXTRACT   **Box 7.13**

The *Altmark* criteria

Source: Case C-280/00 *Altmark TransGmbH* [2003] ECR I-7747:

First, the recipient undertaking must actually have public service obligations to discharge, and the obligations must be clearly defined . . .

Second, the parameters on the basis of which the compensation is calculated must be established in advance in an objective and transparent manner, to avoid it conferring

➡

---

[165] Case C-53/00 *Ferring* [2001] ECR I-9067.

[166] Generally, see C. Rizza, 'The Financial Assistance Granted by Member States to Undertakings entrusted with the Operation of a Service of General Economic Interest', in A. Biondi, P. Eeckhout and J. Flynn (eds) *The Law of State Aid in the European Union* (Oxford University Press, 2005); P. Nicolaides, 'Distortive Effects of Compensatory Aid Measures: A Note on the Economics of the Ferring Judgment' (2002) 23 *European Competition Law Review* 313; Szyszczak (n. 12) at pp. 222–36; AG Jacobs in Case C-126/01 *GEMO* [2003] ECR I-13769; AG Stix-Hackl in Case C-34/01 *Enirisorse* [2003] ECR I-14243.

[167] Case C-280/00 *Altmark TransGmbH* [2003] ECR I-7747.

an economic advantage which may favour the recipient undertaking over competing undertakings . . .

Third, the compensation cannot exceed what is necessary to cover all or part of the costs incurred in the discharge of public service obligations, taking into account the relevant receipts and a reasonable profit . . .

Fourth, where the undertaking which is to discharge public service obligations, in a specific case, is not chosen pursuant to a public procurement procedure which would allow for the selection of the tenderer capable of providing those services at the least cost to the community, the level of compensation needed must be determined on the basis of an analysis of the costs which a typical undertaking, well run and adequately provided with means . . . so as to be able to meet the necessary public service requirements, would have incurred in discharging these obligations, taking into account the relevant receipts and a reasonable profit for discharging the obligation.

Questions: What is the relationship of these criteria to Article 106(2) TFEU? How do you determine the costs of discharging public service obligations? What constitutes a typical well-run (efficient) undertaking for the purposes of comparison? What if there is no equivalent?

A very detailed discussion and application of the *Altmark* criteria can be seen in the *BUPA* case.[168] This case came from Ireland where, on top of the national health scheme, there were two systems of private medical insurance (PMI): one run by the Voluntary Health Insurance Board (VHI) covering about 85% of the relevant population; and one run by BUPA covering about 15% of the relevant population.[169] The Irish government decided to introduce a risk equalisation scheme (RES) between PMI providers. The basic idea of this was that those PMI providers that had a better risk profile than the market average would make payments to those that had a lower profile than the market average. In practice, this meant that BUPA would be making payments to VHI. The scheme was notified by the Irish government to the Commission, which concluded that this was not state aid and that, even if it was, it met the conditions in Article 106(2) TFEU – and it was this decision that BUPA challenged in the GC. BUPA argued that the PMI schemes were not services of general economic interest but this was rejected by the GC because the PMI providers had to offer cover to anyone who applied, for their lifetime, with the provision of specified minimum benefits and at a uniform rate regardless of the personal circumstances of the applicant. As regards the four *Altmark* conditions, the GC found that the legislation had clearly entrusted such a mission to the PMI providers, that there were objective and transparent criteria for the calculation of compensation under the RES and that the system put in place was necessary and proportionate. As regards the fourth *Altmark* criterion, in this particular case there was no need to draw a comparison between the efficiency of the recipient of the RES payments and an efficient operator. This was due to the neutrality of the particular RES scheme, which focused on the risk profile of the provider, rather than the actual costs incurred.[170] Having done this analysis, the GC then went on to consider whether the derogation in Article 106(2) TFEU applied and held that it might meet these criteria as well.[171]

[168] Case T-289/03 *British United Provident Association (BUPA) v Commission* [2008] ECR II-81.
[169] These PMI schemes only covered about half of the Irish population.
[170] Paras 246–9.
[171] Ibid., paras 259–310.

The Commission built upon *Altmark* by producing a framework for state aid in the form of public service compensation and a decision on the application of Article 106(2) TFEU to such cases.[172] This package of measure has subsequently been revised.[173] The arrangements work in this manner. Where the *Altmark* criteria are met, then there is no state aid and nothing has to be notified. If the *Altmark* conditions are not met, there is state aid, but it will be considered compatible with the internal market and exempt from notification if the criteria in the Decision and the *de minimis* Regulation are met. If the measure falls outside the *Altmark* criteria, the Decision, and the *de minimis* Regulation, then it may be considered compatible with the internal market if it meets the criteria set out in the Framework. The measure will still, however, have to be notified.

The Decision applies to public service compensation granted in relatively small amounts, for hospitals, social needs, such as childcare and social housing, air or maritime links to islands with relatively low usage and relatively low used ports and airports. The criteria in the Decision are as follows:

- There is a genuine service of general economic interest.
- There needs to be an instrument specifying the public service obligations and the methods for calculating compensation.
- The amount of compensation must not exceed what is necessary to cover the costs incurred in discharging the obligations.
- Member States must monitor the arrangements to ensure that there is no over-compensation.

Aid which falls outside the Decision does have to be notified to the Commission, which will then check whether it meets the criteria. As can be seen, these criteria look very similar to the *Altmark* criteria, the main difference being that the financing under the Decision's criteria does not have to be arranged by a public procurement exercise or by comparison with the costs of a well-run undertaking so long as the compensation corresponds to the net costs estimated by the instrument. In addition, there is now a *de minimis* Commission Regulation which says that aid to services of general economic interest which is under €500,000 over a three-year period is deemed not to meet all the criteria for state aid and thus is also exempt from notification.[174] There are a number of exceptions to this rule, for example fishery and agriculture, and the Member States must monitor and record the provision of this aid.

---

[172] European Commission, *Community framework for State aid in the form of public service compensation* [2005] OJ C29, 29.11.2005; 'Decision on the application of Article 86(2) of the EC Treaty to State aid in the form of public service compensation granted to certain undertakings entrusted with the operation of services of general economic interest' OJ L312, 29.11.2005.

[173] Commission Communication, European Union framework for State aid in the form of public service compensation, OJ C 8/15 11.01.2012; Commission Communication on the application of the European Union State aid rules to compensation granted for the provision of services of general economic interest OJ C 8/4, 11/01.2012; Commission Decision on the application of Article 106(2) TFEU to State aid in the form of public service compensation granted to certain undertakings entrusted with the operation of services of general economic interest OJ L7/3, 11.01.2012; Commission Regulation No. 360/2012 on the application of Articles 107 and 108 TFEU to de minimis aid granted to undertakings providing services of general economic interest, OJ L 114/8 26.04.2012 at Art 2. All available at: *http://ec.europa.eu/competition/state_aid/legislation/sgei.html* (accessed 01/08/2012).

[174] Commission Regulation No. 360/2012 on the application of Articles 107 and 108 TFEU to de minimis aid granted to undertakings providing services of general economic interest, OJ L 114/8 26.04.2012 at Art 2.

If a measure does not qualify under any of the criteria just discussed, then it must be notified to the Commission, which will assess it under the criteria contained in the Framework. The Commission views this as explaining how it interprets the derogation contained in Article 106(2) TFEU.[175] In order to qualify, there must be a genuine service of general economic interest, a proper act of entrustment, the duration of entrustment should not exceed the period required for the depreciation of the most significant assets required to provide the SGEI, the rules on transparency of financial relations with Member States and public procurement should be complied with and there should be no discrimination.[176] The Framework is, however, most concerned with ensuring that the amount of compensation provided does not exceed what is necessary to cover the net cost of discharging the public service obligations, including a reasonable profit. The Commission's preferred methodology is what it calls 'net avoided cost' which, put simply, is the difference between operating with and without the public service obligations.[177] Other cost allocation methods are acceptable, and the Commission also gives details of how it would expect a reasonable profit to be calculated and emphasises that Member States should introduce efficiency incentives.[178] Finally, the Commission adds that there may be exceptional cases where, even though all the normal criteria are met, there is still a risk of serious competition distortions, which may require a more detailed assessment which will need to be remedied by conditions imposed on or commitments accepted by the Member States.[179]

Although the case law and the rules published by the Commission seem difficult and technical, there are important issues of principle underlying this area, with which the EU has struggled to deal. At the heart of this is the question of to what extent Member States may subsidise the provision of public services, or services of general economic interest, in order to make up for market imperfections or more general reasons of social policy. The European Commission is concerned to ensure that such subsidies do not distort competition, while at the same time respecting Member States' social policy choices. It may be that as public expenditure becomes squeezed across many European states in the future that this becomes less of a lively issue.

Council decisions in exceptional cases

Article 108(2) TFEU (ex Article 88(2) EC) provides that the Council may, in exceptional circumstances, decide that aid is compatible with the internal market, outside the general rules, and that, if the Commission has started proceedings, those proceedings will be suspended while the Council is deciding the matter.

---

[175] Commission Communication, European Union framework for State aid in the form of public service compensation, OJ C 8/15 11.01.2012 at para. 7.

[176] Ibid. paras 12–20.

[177] Ibid. para. 25.

[178] Ibid. paras 28–43.

[179] Ibid. paras 51–59.

Council powers in exceptional circumstances

On application by a Member State, the Council may, acting unanimously, decide that aid which that State is granting or intends to grant shall be considered to be compatible with the internal market, in derogation from the provisions of Article 107 or from the regulations provided for in Article 109, if such a decision is justified by exceptional circumstances. If, as regards the aid in question, the Commission has already initiated the procedure provided for in the first subparagraph of this paragraph, the fact that the State concerned has made its application to the Council shall have the effect of suspending that procedure until the Council has made its attitude known.

Source: Article 108(2) TFEU (part).

Question: What might constitute exceptional circumstances?

This provision has caused some controversy as there have been occasions when Member States have used it in an attempt to avoid the application of the state aid rules. The most high-profile example is the so-called Portuguese Pigs case. Here Portugal had granted aid to its pig farmers in 1994 and 1999. In 2000 and 2001, the Commission declared most of the aid to be illegal and ordered it to be repaid to the Portuguese government. In 2002, Portugal asked the Council to adopt a decision, allowing them to grant aid to pig farmers equivalent to the amount of aid which was required to be repaid, on the grounds that the repayment of aid would threaten the viability of a significant number of pig farmers. The Council agreed and adopted a decision allowing this, which was challenged by the Commission in the CJEU. The CJEU agreed with the Commission and held that the Council could not validly declare compatible with the internal market an aid which allocates to the beneficiaries of an unlawful aid, which a Commission decision has previously declared incompatible with the internal market, an amount designed to compensate for the repayments which they are required to make pursuant to that decision.[180]

Enforcement procedures for state aid

Enforcement of the rules on state aid is centralised and the responsibility of the Commission, which is required not only to examine new aids but also to keep under review existing state aids (see Box 7.15 for the key provisions).[181]

When granting new aids, regardless of whether they are individual aids or more general aid schemes,[182] Member States are required to notify the Commission of their intention to grant aid and may not implement the aid before the Commission has made a decision. On

[180] Case C-110/02 *Commission v Council* [2004] ECR I-6333 at para. 47.
[181] Council Regulation No. 659/1999 laying down detailed rules for the application of Article 93 of the EC Treaty, OJ L83/1, 22.03.1999; Article 1(b) defines existing aid.
[182] On the distinction between new aid, existing aid and existing aid *schemes*, see: Hancher, Jan Slot and Ottervanger (n. 93) at 25-014–25-019.

receipt of notification, the Commission conducts a preliminary investigation, which must be completed within two months,[183] otherwise the aid is deemed to be approved (see Figure 7.1 for an overview of the procedure). The two-month period only starts running from when the Commission has received a complete notification and this is defined as being when the Commission does not ask for further information.[184] It has been said that in practice this preliminary stage is significantly longer than two months (although this comment was presumably made in relation to aid granted outside the financial crisis).[185]

KEY LEGAL PROVISION   **Box 7.15**

Procedure for control of aid

1   The Commission shall, in cooperation with Member States, keep under constant review all systems of aid existing in those States. It shall propose to the latter any appropriate measures required by the progressive development or by the functioning of the internal market.

2   If, after giving notice to the parties concerned to submit their comments, the Commission finds that aid granted by a State or through State resources is not compatible with the internal market having regard to Article 107, or that such aid is being misused, it shall decide that the State concerned shall abolish or alter such aid within a period of time to be determined by the Commission.

> If the State concerned does not comply with this decision within the prescribed time, the Commission or any other interested State may, in derogation from the provisions of Articles 258 and 259, refer the matter to the Court of Justice direct.

> [. . . (see Box 7.14)]

3   The Commission shall be informed, in sufficient time to enable it to submit its comments, of any plans to grant or alter aid. If it considers that any such plan is not compatible with the internal market having regard to Article 107, it shall without delay initiate the procedure provided for in paragraph 2. The Member State concerned shall not put its proposed measures into effect until this procedure has resulted in a final decision.

4   The Commission may adopt regulations relating to the categories of state aid that the Council has, pursuant to Article 109, determined may be exempted from the procedure provided for by paragraph 3 of this Article.

Source: Article 108 TFEU.

Questions: How does the Commission find out about state aid? What sanctions does the Commission have if Member States do not obey the rules?

---

[183] Case 120/73 *Lorenz v Germany* [1973] ECR 1471.

[184] Council Regulation No. 659/1999, op. cit., note 181, Article 4(5). The Commission and the Member State may also agree an extension of the time limit.

[185] M. Schütter, 'Procedural Aspects of EU State Aid law and practice', in E. Szyszczak, *Research Handbook on European State Aid Law* (Edward Elgar, Cheltenham, 2011) at 340.

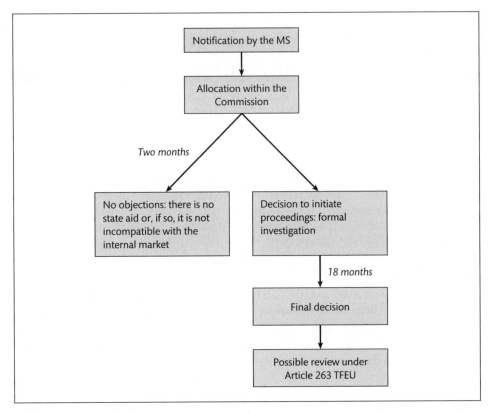

Figure 7.1 The notification/investigation procedure

At the end of the preliminary investigation, the Commission may decide either that the measure is not aid, that it is aid but there are no doubts as to its compatibility with the internal market, or that there are doubts as to its compatibility with the internal market. If there are doubts, then the Commission will open a formal investigation.

The decision to open a formal investigation is published and asks for comments from the Member State and all other interested parties, such as competitors. Interested parties only have the right to be involved in the administrative procedure to the extent appropriate in the light of the circumstances of the case.[186] The Commission will endeavour to make a decision within 18 months of the opening of the procedure, although the time limit may be extended with the agreement of the Member State concerned. At the end of the procedure the Commission may decide:

- the measure does not constitute aid;
- after modification by the Member State, doubts as to its compatibility have been removed;

---

[186] Cases T-371 and 394/94 *British Airways v Commission* [1998] ECR II-2405.

- the aid is compatible with the internal market (positive decision), although conditions may be attached to this decision;
- the aid is not compatible with the internal market.[187]

If aid is not notified to the Commission, the CJEU has held that the Commission is obliged to proceed to examine the compatibility of the aid with the internal market via the procedure discussed above, i.e. a preliminary investigation followed by, if necessary, a formal investigation. If it is clear that the aid has been granted or altered without notification or misused, the Commission may issue an injunction requiring the Member State to suspend the unlawful or misused aid until the Commission has taken a decision on its compatibility with the internal market.[188] If a negative decision is made then the Commission is required to decide that the Member State concerned shall take all necessary measures to recover the aid from the beneficiary, including interest fixed at an appropriate rate. Recovery of aid is not required if this would be contrary to a general principle of Union law.[189] There is a limitation period of ten years on recovery decisions.[190]

Recovery of unlawful state aid

The general principle is that where the Commission has decided that state aid is unlawful, it is required to decide that the Member State shall take all the necessary measures to recover the aid, which will include interest at an appropriate rate.[191] There is a limitation period of ten years and the Commission shall not order recovery if it is contrary to a general principle of EU law. Typically the general principle invoked is that of legitimate expectations or of legal certainty. These generally involve cases where the undertaking argues that it had an expectation that the aid had been lawfully granted (for example, on the basis of a statement by the Commission), or where there has been undue delay by the Commission in taking a decision. The case law has, however, been very generous to the Commission on this latter point.[192] The other exception is if it would be 'absolutely impossible' for the Member State to recover the aid and, according to the Commission, this has been interpreted in a very restrictive manner by the Courts; there do not appear to be any examples of when this has been accepted.[193]

Recovery is undertaken by the Member States, using national procedures, and they have a duty to do this without delay and an obligation to cooperate under Article 4 para. 3 TEU.[194] In general, the Commission takes the view that recovery should take place within four

---

[187] Council Regulation No. 659/1999 laying down detailed rules for the application of Article 93 of the EC Treaty, OJ L83/1, 22.03.1999, Art. 7.

[188] Ibid., Art. 11(1).

[189] Ibid., Art. 14.

[190] Ibid., Art. 15.

[191] Ibid., Arts 14 and 15. See also European Commission, 'Notice – Towards an effective implementation of Commission decisions ordering Member States to recover unlawful and incompatible State aid', OJ C272, 15.11.2007, pp. 4–17.

[192] See Case T-126/96 *Breda Fucine* v *Commission* [1998] ECR II-3427; Case C-408/04P *Commission* v *Slazgitter* [2008] ECR I-2767.

[193] European Commission, 'Notice – Towards an effective implementation of Commission decisions ordering Member States to recover unlawful and incompatible State aid', OJ C272, 15.11.2007, pp. 4–17 at para. 20. See also J. Faull and A. Nikpay, *The EC Law of Competition* (2nd edn, Oxford University Press, 2007) at para. 16.345.

[194] See European Commission, 'Notice – Towards an effective implementation of Commission decisions ordering Member States to recover unlawful and incompatible State aid', OJ C272, 15.11.2007, pp. 4–17.

months of a decision that the aid is unlawful. Failure to take action may lead to the Commission launching infringement proceedings against the Member State and also, if the unlawful aid has not been recovered, the Commission may not allow new, lawful, aid to be given to an undertaking until this has been done.[195]

Role of national courts[196]

The role of the national courts in this area is more limited than in other areas of EU competition law. Essentially, the national courts are limited to three roles: deciding whether there is aid; ordering recovery of illegal aid; and, in exceptional cases, dealing with claims for damages by third parties against the state for payment of unlawful aid. We deal with these three issues in turn.

The starting point is Article 108(3) TFEU, which provides that aid shall not be put into effect by a Member State until the Commission has made a decision. This provision has been held to have direct effect[197] and, as a consequence, national courts are required to order recovery of the aid, and possibly interim measures, even if the Commission is still considering the issue. It follows from this that the national court may also have to decide whether the measure concerned constitutes aid because if the measure is not aid, there is no breach of the prohibition.[198]

As regards damages to competitors, it has been held that competitors can claim damages from the state, but only if they meet the restrictive criteria laid down in *Francovich* that the rule of law infringed was intended to confer rights on individuals, that the breach is sufficiently serious and that there is a direct causal link between the breach and the damage caused.[199] Proving the causal link may be difficult and the Commission makes the following points:[200]

- damage can be loss of an asset or preventing the claimant from improving their position;
- lost profit is easiest to calculate where the claimant has lost a contract or an opportunity;
- it is more difficult to quantify the claim from loss of market share; and
- damage suffered may exceed the lost profit, for example if it leads to insolvency.

Damages cannot be claimed from the recipient of the aid on the basis of Union law alone; this can only be done when the liability would have arisen in national law.[201] In the UK context, this was confirmed in the *Betws Anthracite* case, where a Welsh coal producer claimed that a German coal producer, which imported its coal into the UK, had misused state aid, allowing it to sell its coal at cheaper prices in the UK.[202] The Commission had decided that Germany had breached the state aid rules in this case. The English court ruled that there was no action in English or Union law available against the German producer; at best there might be an action against the German state.[203]

---

[195] Ibid., paras 72–78.
[196] See European Commission, 'Notice on the enforcement of State aid law by national courts', OJ C85, 09.04.2009, pp. 1–22.
[197] Case 120/73 *Lorenz v Germany* [1973] ECR 1471.
[198] Case C-39/94 *SFEI v La Poste* [1996] ECR I-3547.
[199] Cases C-6 and 9/90 *Francovich v Italy* [1991] ECR I-5357.
[200] See European Commission, 'Notice on the enforcement of State aid law by national courts', OJ C85, 09.04.2009, pp. 1–22 (at para. 49).
[201] Case C-39/94 *SFEI v La Poste* [1996] ECR I-3547 at para. 75.
[202] *Betws Anthracite v DSK Anthrazit Ibbenburen* [2004] 1 All ER 1237.
[203] Ibid. at para. 37.

COMPETITION LAW IN PRACTICE

State aid and Ryanair

Ryanair is a well-known low-cost airline in Europe. In 2000 it began negotiations to establish a base on the continent at Charleroi in Belgium (just outside Brussels). It entered into negotiations with the Walloon Region, a public body which owned Charleroi Airport and Brussels South Charleroi Airport (BSCA), a public sector company controlled by the Walloon Region which operated the airport. The Walloon Region agreed to change the airport opening hours and to grant Ryanair a 50% reduction on the normal landing fees. BSCA agreed to contribute slightly over €1 million to the costs of establishing the base, as well as providing some benefits in kind, such as the provision of office space, and to provide a 90% discount on ground handling services. Ryanair agreed to base between two and four aircraft at Charleroi and operate at least three rotations a day out of the airport. BSCA and Ryanair also formed a joint company to promote the use of the airport.

The European Commission investigation

After press reports about this and having received complaints, the European Commission decided in 2002 to investigate the arrangements and made a decision in 2004 that these constituted illegal state aid and should be recovered.[204] In evaluating these arrangements, the Commission distinguished between the position of the Walloon Region and the BSCA. It treated the Walloon Region's actions as actions of a public authority, which were not subject to the private investor in a market economy test. In other words, the Walloon Region was not carrying out an economic activity but exercising its public authority. On this approach the arrangements were clearly state aid because the resources came from a state authority, they affected inter-state trade, Ryanair had gained an advantage over its competitors and these arrangements threatened to distort competition. In relation to the actions by BSCA, the Commission assessed these separately on the basis of the private investor in a market economy principle and found that this had been breached because BSCA took risks that no private sector investor would have taken.

The GC Decision

This decision was challenged by Ryanair in front of the GC, arguing that the Walloon Region and BSCA should be treated as one entity and that, if this was done, the Commission should have employed the private investor in a market economy principle to the transaction as a whole.[205] As it had not done so, the decision was unlawful and should be annulled. The GC pointed out that around 96% of BSCA's share capital was owned by the Walloon Region and that the Commission had concluded that the two

---

[204] European Commission, 'Decision 2004/393 concerning advantages granted by the Walloon Region and Brussels South Charleroi Airport to the airline Ryanair in connection with its establishment at Charleroi' [2004] OJ L137/1.

[205] Case T-196/04 *Ryanair* v *Commission* [2008] ECR II-3643.

entities were very closely linked. The GC made the point that it was necessary, when applying the private investor test, to envisage the commercial transaction as a whole in order to determine whether the public entity and the entity which is controlled by it, taken together, have acted as rational operators in a market economy.[206] The two entities therefore should have been considered as one for the purposes of applying this test. The GC then went on to consider whether the Commission had been correct in refusing to apply the test to the activities of the Walloon Region. The GC held that the activities of the Walloon Region were economic activities, that is, offering goods and services on a given market. The reason for this was that the airport charges fixed by the Walloon Region had to be regarded as remuneration for the provision of services within Charleroi airport, notwithstanding the fact that a clear and direct link between the level of charges and the service rendered to users is weak. Just because the Walloon Region was a public authority did not mean that it could not carry out economic activity. As a result, therefore, the GC annulled the Commission's decision.

Developments after the case

Subsequent to this case, the Commission has investigated the arrangements that Ryanair has with airports in Finland, France, Germany, Italy and Slovakia,[207] although at the time of writing the Commission has only reached a decision not to raise objections to the arrangements for Toulon. Ryanair, for its part, has launched a series of complaints to the European Commission about illegal state aid given to other airlines, as well as challenging various decisions that the Commission has made, most notably its approval of the rescue of Alitalia by the Italian government.[208]

Questions: Are there economically rational reasons for airports offering Ryanair incentives to use them as a destination? Are there wider public interest reasons? Do you think that Ryanair has a litigation strategy? If so, what is it?

---

[206] Ibid., para. 59.

[207] Cases C25/2007, *Alleged state aids involving Ryanair at Tampere-Pirkkala Airport* – met private investor test; N563/2005, *Aid to Ryanair* (Toulon–London) – no objections; C53/2007, *Airport Marketing Services* (France–Pau); C29/2008, *Frankfurt-Hahn, Alleged State aid to the airport and the agreement with Ryanair* (Germany); C37/2007, *Air One/Ryanair – Aéroport d'Alghero* (Italy); C12/2008, *Possible state aid involving Bratislava Airport and Ryanair* (Slovakia) – decided no state aid; Case C24/2007, *Lübeck–Blankensee*; Case SA 18857, *Västerås*; Case SA 24221, *Klagenfurt*; Case SA 26494, *Charente-Maritime*; Case SA 26500, *Aéroport á Alkenburg Nobitz*.

[208] Case T-423/07 *Ryanair v Commission*, unsuccessful, judgment of 19 May 2011; Case T-442/07 *Ryyanair v Commission*, successful, judgment of 29 September 2011 (GC) on appeal Case C-615/11P (not yet decided); Case T-123/09 *Ryanair v Commission*, case rejected, judgment of 28 March 2012 (GC), on appeal Case C-287/12 (not yet decided).

Summary

➤ EU competition law is concerned to control state intervention in the market. This requires answers to three difficult questions:

- What is the scope of competition law?
- How do you balance non-economic policy objectives against possible anti-competitive effects?
- To what extent is this a decision for Member States as opposed to the EU and its institutions?

➤ A state measure will only breach Article 101 TFEU in conjunction with Article 4 para. 3 TEU if:

- it imposes on undertakings the entering into of agreements contrary to Article 101 TFEU;
- it favours the entering into of such agreements;
- it reinforces the effects of such agreements;
- it delegates to private operators the responsibility for adopting decisions concerning economic intervention.

These criteria are interpreted restrictively.

➤ Under Article 106(1) TFEU the mere creation of a dominant position through the grant of special or exclusive rights is not in itself incompatible with Article 102 TFEU. A Member State will be in breach of the prohibitions laid down by those two provisions only if the undertaking in question:

- merely by exercising the special or exclusive rights conferred upon it, is led to abuse its dominant position, or
- where such rights are liable to create a situation in which that undertaking is led to commit such abuses.

➤ There are five areas where these criteria are likely to be met:

- inability to meet demand;
- conflict of interest cases;
- extension of monopoly into a neighbouring market;
- pricing abuses, in particular price discrimination;
- refusal to supply.

➤ The derogation in Article 106(2) TFEU is interpreted strictly. The burden of proof is initially on the undertaking or state that wishes to rely on this provision. It is, however, not necessary to show that the undertaking's survival would be threatened if it were subjected to the competition rules, nor is it necessary to prove that there is no other conceivable measure which could ensure that the task in question is carried out. The Court will not undertake a searching review of the reasoning behind the state's action, but the case law is very unpredictable.

➤ State aid, which distorts competition by favouring certain undertakings and affects trade between Member States, is prohibited unless it falls within certain approved categories.

➤ Member States are required to notify the European Commission of new state aid and the Commission must decide whether that aid is compatible with the internal market.

➤ A limited set of categories are stated to be compatible with the internal market, while the Commission has discretion to decide whether a wider group of types of state aid is compatible with the internal market. On the basis of this discretion, a complicated set of rules and guidelines has been issued, giving guidance as to how the Commission will approach the issue, although it has recently been simplified through a general block exemption.

➤ If the Commission decides that state aid has been unlawfully paid to an undertaking, it *may* require its repayment. Commission decisions are reviewable by the European Courts, which have exercised close scrutiny of the decisions; and certain issues are enforceable by the national courts.

Further reading

Reference works

Buendia Sierra, J.L., *Exclusive Rights and State Monopolies under EC Law* (Oxford University Press, 1999). *Although somewhat dated now, still the most comprehensive discussion of the topic.*

Hancher, L., Jan Slot, P. and Ottervanger, T.R., *EC State Aids* (4th edn, Sweet & Maxwell, London, 2012). *Comprehensive discussion of all issues of state aids. Pre-dates the 2008 Block Exemption Regulation.*

Quigley, C., *European State Aid Law and Policy* (2nd edn, Hart Publishing, Oxford, 2009). *Up-to-date discussion of the area by an eminent practitioner.*

Articles

Bacon, K., 'State Regulation of the Market and EC Competition Rules: Article 85 and 86 Compared' (1997) 18 *European Competition Law Review* 283. *Good, albeit dated, overview of the area.*

Baquero Cruz, J., 'Beyond Competition: Services of General Interest in European Community Law', in G. de Búrca (ed.) *EU Law and the Welfare State* (Oxford University Press, 2005). *Good, although slightly controversial, overview of the area.*

Edward, D. and Hoskins, M., 'Article 90: Deregulation and EC Law' (1995) 32 *Common Market Law Review* 157. *Comprehensive review of the case law, and a suggested categorisation by a judge and legal secretary of the GC.*

Hancher, L., 'Case note on *Corbeau*' (1994) 31 *Common Market Law Review* 105. *Excellent discussion of a problematic case.*

Hancher, L., 'Community, State and Market', in P. Craig and G. da Burca (eds) *The Evolution of EU Law* (Oxford University Press, 1999). *Excellent introduction to the general issues in this area. Not up to date on the case law, but sets out the issues well.*

Hancher, L., 'Towards a New Definition of a State Aid under European Law: Is there a New Concept of State Aid Emerging?' (2003) *European State Aid Law Quarterly* 365. *Good discussion of the vexed issue of definition.*

Hoffmann, A., 'Anti-competitive State Legislation Condemned under Articles 5, 85 and 86 of the EEC Treaty: How far should the Court go after Van Eycke?' (1990) 11 *European Competition Law Review* 11. *Thorough discussion of the Article 101 TFEU cases with brief comparison with US doctrine.*

Lynskey, O., 'The application of Article 86(2) to measures which do not fulfil the Altmark criteria' (2007) 30 *World Competition* 153. *Excellent and clearly written article explaining the issues and background.*

Ross, M., 'Article 16 and Services of General Interest: From Derogation to Obligation?' (2000) 25 *European Law Review* 22. *Comprehensive overview of the legal issues surrounding Article 14 TFEU.*

Winter, G., 'Re(de)fining the notion of State aid in Article 87(1) of the EC Treaty' (2004) 41 *Common Market Law Review* 407. *Critical review of the most recent case law.*

8　The control of cartels

Chapter outline

This chapter discusses:

➤ Economic issues surrounding cartels

➤ Legal issues in cartel enforcement

➤ Different types of cartel

➤ The enforcement record in the EU and UK

➤ The leniency programmes

➤ The EU's settlement procedure

➤ The criminal cartel offence in the UK

➤ Directors' disqualification.

Introduction

This chapter examines a topic which has always been a central concern of competition policy, that is, the prohibition on cartels. A cartel has been defined as 'an agreement among otherwise competing firms to reduce their output to agreed upon levels or sell at an agreed upon price'[1] by a leading American academic, whereas the European Commission has put the idea slightly differently, 'A cartel is a group of similar, independent companies which join together to fix prices, to limit production or to share markets or customers between them'[2] and it is worth contrasting these definitions with the one given by the OECD in Box 8.1 below. Interestingly, the notion of a cartel does not appear explicitly in Article 101 TFEU and nor does it appear in the US Sherman Act. In UK law, s. 188 Enterprise Act 2002 provides a definition of the cartel offence, breach of which is a crime, but, as we shall see below, this is a narrower definition than these alternatives given here. Despite some uncertainty over definitions, cartels are widely recognised as being damaging to competition and the fight against them is today seen as a major priority for competition authorities.

In order to discuss this issue, this chapter starts by looking at why and when firms enter into cartels, the problems created by cartels and how cartels are organised. This is followed

---

[1] H. Hovenkamp, *Federal Antitrust Policy* (4th edn, West Publishing, St Paul, Minnesota, 2011) at 158.

[2] *http://ec.europa.eu/competition/cartels/overview/index_en.html* (accessed 02/05/12).

by a relatively short section discussing the general legal approaches in the EU and UK and then an examination of specific types of cartel behavior. Having done this, the chapter then looks at the enforcement record, leniency, the use of settlements and, in the UK, the criminal cartel offence and disqualification of directors.

KEY DEFINITIONS Box 8.1

Cartel and oligopoly

Cartel: A cartel is a formal agreement among firms in an oligopolistic industry. Cartel members may agree on such matters as prices, total industry output, market shares, allocation of customers, allocation of territories, bid-rigging, establishment of common sales agencies, and the division of profits or combination of these.

Oligopoly: An oligopoly is a market characterized by a small number of firms who realize they are interdependent in their pricing and output policies. The number of firms is small enough to give each firm some market power.

Source: OECD at *http://stats.oecd.org/glossary/index.htm* (accessed 14/08/09).

Questions: In order to make a cartel effective, which elements listed above do you have to agree upon? What is a small number of firms in this context? Examples of markets which *might* fit this description would be: retail banking, electricity supply and supermarkets.

Economic issues surrounding cartels

As we have seen, under monopoly as opposed to perfect competition, prices are higher, output is lower and there is a dead-weight loss to society (see Chapter 1). It is possible, through agreement between undertakings, to produce effects which are similar to a monopoly. The reason why undertakings have an incentive to enter into cartels can be illustrated by the following example. Imagine an industry with two firms, which produce the same product, with the same costs of production, and between them can meet all consumer demand but consumers can switch, without cost, between the two firms. Assume that there are only two price points for the product, £5 and £10, which produces a profit of £4 or £9 per sale. Assume as well that this is a single game: the firms may only make the choice once; there is no possibility of recovering from a pricing error. There is a market demand of 100. The total profit that is yielded by adopting either pricing point depends on what price the other firm adopts. If the low price is adopted and the other firm adopts a high price, the firm with the lower price will capture all the market and vice versa. If they adopt the same prices, then the market will be split between them. This gives the following property space:

	Firm A – low price	*Firm A – high price*
Firm A	£5, £10	£10, £5
Profit	£400, £0	£0, £400
Firm B	£5, £5	£10, £10
Profit	£200, £200	£450, £450

From the point of view of the firms jointly, the ideal outcome will be if they both charge the higher price, then they will make the maximum profit (£450). The danger for each firm individually is, if they charge the higher price, then their competitor will charge the lower price and obtain all the market and drive them out of this business. In these circumstances the rational decision, if you cannot communicate with your competitor, is to price low, because this produces the best outcome no matter what the competitor does (if the competitor prices high, you obtain all the market; if they price low, you remain in the market). If the firms were able to communicate with each other, it would be in their interests to reach an agreement to charge the higher price: in other words, to establish a cartel. If we relax the assumption about this being a once-and-for-all game and assume that the property space above represents one time period, then it is also in the firms' interests to agree to charge the higher prices.

Strategically, firms could reach the same position either through a merger or through one of the two firms being more successful in the long run and obtaining a monopoly. A merger is, however, a public process and, these days, almost all countries have systems of merger control which are meant to prevent these sort of outcomes. Outcompeting your rivals is a possible strategy but it will take some time and the outcomes are uncertain, as your rivals are trying to outcompete you. The attraction of a cartel is that it can be set up relatively quickly, and in secret, so that the participating firms can receive the benefits of the agreement. The example given above is very simplified and, to understand how cartels work, a number of the assumptions have to be relaxed. Typically cartels involve more than one firm and the firms will have different costs of production. This means that any agreement on prices will be a compromise amongst the firms, although it will still be above the competitive price. This leads to two problems, which are similar to that caused by a monopoly. Output is restricted, which means that some consumers pay higher prices than they would in a competitive market and some cannot purchase the good or service at all because of the higher price and, secondly, to the extent the cartel succeeds, this diminishes any incentive on high cost firms to improve their efficiency. In addition, it may be that the products in the industry are not homogeneous. This may create some difficulties for coordinating prices, although not necessarily insurmountable, but it leads to another disadvantage which is that in the absence of price competition resources will be diverted, wastefully, into non-price competition.[3]

As a result of these effects, competition law in all countries prohibits competitors from communicating with each other and making such agreements. By doing this, the idea is that a position is created where the two companies have to decide independently what price to charge, without being able to agree. In these circumstances, as the example above suggests, the outcome will be that both firms will choose the lower price point, because no matter what the other firm does, this will provide the best outcome.

Although it can be seen that, in general, there are incentives for firms to enter into cartels, there are also a number of problems with organising and maintaining them. The first problem is what Hovenkamp has called the virtual universality of cartel cheating.[4] The reason for this is that, if the cartel price is a compromise, there is likely to be one or more member firms who may make profitable sales, even supra-competitive profits, while charging below the cartel price. In order to do this without risking retaliation from other cartel members, this will have to be done secretly. There are many ways of disguising price reductions but just look at

---

[3] See M. Utton, *Cartels and Economic Collusion* (Edward Elgar, Cheltenham, 2011) at 2–3.
[4] Hovenkamp (n. 1) at 161.

a simple example. Often, especially with intermediate products, that is, products used in making the final good, the published price list is just a starting point for negotiations between the buyer and the seller and the final price is confidential to the two parties. In these circumstances, monitoring the price actually paid becomes very difficult. Although this suggests that there is an element of instability in all cartels, the members of a cartel are equally aware of this problem and will try to deal with it through the organisation of the cartel. Organising a successful cartel is a complex matter. Although cartels are often thought of as simply agreements to fix prices, in order to do this successfully a number of issues have to be addressed. First, fixing prices is not necessarily straightforward when products are not homogeneous and the firms may operate in different currencies. Secondly, fixing prices is not enough in itself; the output of the participants has to be controlled and this can be done through a variety of measures. There can simply be limitations on output and/or particular territories or customers may be allocated to members of the cartel. Thirdly, once these rules are agreed upon, there has to be some means of ensuring that everyone is abiding by the rules, so there has to be some form of communication and monitoring of the activities of the cartel. The members of a cartel can do this by meeting on a regular basis or by delegating these tasks to a third party, often in the past a trade association. In the marine hoses case, one of the defendants was employed full-time to organise the cartel. The judge's sentencing remarks illustrate the organisational issues:[5]

> The cartel was run as it had to be with meticulous attention to detail. Code names were used, clandestine meetings were organised and held, agreements were reached, both in relation to the market share and for the bogus contract bids. All of this was illustrated and monitored by monthly reports. There was a formally agreed decision-making process by which the successful company would be nominated as the champion for that contract. There were rules for compliance. The parties communicated through the use of code names when they or their companies became more concerned about compliance; and they disguised their contact with one another and with you [the defendant] through the use of email accounts that, of course, had no connection with the companies they represented. Then, all of the bid documentation had to be prepared.[6] I have seen an illustration of this and can well believe that this was indeed a labour intensive exercise, time consuming and highly sophisticated.

Finally, there has to be some means of disciplining errant cartel members or ensuring that they compensate other members. Disciplining errant members would typically take the form of price competition, which assumes some spare capacity is available. Compensation can mean simply the payment of money from one cartel member to another.

Organising a cartel is not a straightforward matter and there are a number of factors which would seem necessary to make cartel formation successful. It is also worth noting that research suggests that one of the drivers for forming cartels is when conditions are more competitive, that is, a decline in prices, possibly linked to a decline in demand. Harrington says that 'there is no case in which it was documented that a cartel formed amidst rising profit'.[7] This is particularly relevant in the midst of difficult economic circumstances in Europe. The sort of factors which make cartel formation easier can be summarised as:

---

[5] See: *http://www.oft.gov.uk/shared_oft/prosecutions/remarks.pdf* (accessed 05/09/12).
[6] This was in essence a bid-rigging cartel.
[7] J. Harrington, 'How do Cartels operate?' *Foundations and Trends in Microeconomics*, Vol. 2, No. 1 (2006) 1 at 56.

- market concentration – relatively few undertakings active in the market (which means that agreement is only needed amongst a few firms to control a market);

- symmetry between market participants (this makes agreement easier – it may be impossible if there is one significant firm with a very different business model);

- barriers to entry (so that new entrants cannot come in and undercut the cartel price);

- price and market transparency (makes it more difficult to cheat);

- lack of buyer power;

- stable pattern of demand;

- product homogeneity (this makes it easier to coordinate prices).

Can you think of industries which have these characteristics? Cement is often used as an example.

Legal issues in the control of cartels

Article 101 TFEU lists three examples of cartel behaviour which it prohibits: directly or indirectly fixing purchase or selling prices; limiting or controlling production, markets, technical development or investment; and sharing markets or sources of supply.[8] The issue in relation to all of these breaches of Article 101 TFEU is not whether they will have an effect on competition, because they are considered as agreements which have the object of restricting competition,[9] but whether it is possible for the Commission to prove that such an agreement has been reached. The onus of proof, under Regulation 1/2003, is on the party alleging breach of the provision. The standard of proof is not specified in Regulation 1/2003 but the European Courts have consistently held that the Commission must produce 'precise and consistent evidence' in order to prove the allegations.[10] What this does not mean is that every item of evidence produced by the Commission has to meet that standard. The European Courts have recognised that cartels are complex arrangements, which the participating undertakings will have gone to some lengths to conceal. Therefore, they give some leeway to the Commission, requiring simply that the body of evidence, as a whole, meets this requirement. As it was put, 'in most cases, the existence of an anti-competitive practice or agreement must be inferred from a number of coincidences and indicia which, taken together, may, in the absence of another plausible explanation, constitute evidence of an infringement of the competition rules'.[11] So, for example, minutes of meetings may be fragmentary or incomplete; there might not be a complete record of contacts between the undertakings. In addition, it is clear that participants in a cartel cannot plead that they merely attended meetings, without participating in the events afterwards. In order for this plea to be accepted, they must publicly distance themselves from the activities of the cartel.[12]

---

[8] For present purposes, UK law will be assumed to be the same as EU law.

[9] As the Commission puts it, they are 'by their very nature, among the most harmful restrictions of competition': European Commission, *Guidelines on the method of setting fines imposed pursuant to Article 23(2)(a) of Regulation No 1/2003*, OJ C210, 01.09.2006 (at para. 23).

[10] Joined Cases T-44, 54, 56, 60 *Dresdner Bank v Commission* [2006] ECR II-at para. 62.

[11] Case T-53/03 *BPB v Commission* [2008] ECR II-1333 at para. 63.

[12] Case C-49/92P *Commission v Anic* [1999] ECR I-4125 at para. 96; Cases C-204P etc. *Aalborg Protland v Commission* [2004] ECR I-123 at paras 81–6.

Given that cartel activities are clearly unlawful, the participants tend to take care to try to avoid detection through, for example, meeting discreetly, referring to the meetings through code names, not keeping notes of meetings, not using their work telephones, etc. The problems created are the justification for the wide investigatory powers of the European Commission and the OFT (discussed in Chapter 5). In addition, as has been discussed above, cartels are not necessarily stable as the participants may be inclined or have the incentive to cheat on the arrangements. To encourage this propensity, competition authorities have adopted leniency programmes which allow those undertakings providing information about a cartel to escape a penalty or obtain a reduction in the penalty, and these are discussed below. Indeed, the OFT has gone further and is prepared to offer a financial reward of up to £100,000 for information about cartels.[13] It is, however, worth looking in a bit more depth at examples of the various types of cartel that can exist, using the above categories from Article 101 TFEU and adding two more: collusive tendering or bid-rigging[14] and hub and spoke cartels. Leaving aside collusive tendering, which can be treated as a category on its own, it is important to remember that complex cartels will have to engage in price-fixing, restrictions on output and market sharing at the same time; they will not engage in just one of these activities. The reason is quite simple: all these activities are needed to make the cartel work effectively. In the copper tubes cartel, the participants fixed prices by agreeing on price lists, price line increases and the discount scheme. In addition, each producer was allocated a share of national demand and customers were also allocated to the producers. There were also arrangements for monitoring the workings of the cartel.[15]

Price-fixing

According to Article 101 TFEU, price-fixing can be direct or indirect. In other words, there can be an agreement over which prices to charge, which would be direct price-fixing. Alternatively, there might be an exchange of information with the expectation that this will influence pricing policies so that there is no significant difference between the undertakings. This would be indirect price-fixing. There are many examples of price-fixing between competitors in the case law of the European Commission, although typically price-fixing is also combined with other restrictions on competition, such as sharing markets and limits on output. Price-fixing cartels between competitors have been uncovered on a regular basis in both the European Union and the UK. So, for example, the European Commission fined four Dutch brewers over €250 million for a cartel which coordinated prices and price increases on the Dutch beer market and this is discussed in more detail in 'Competition law in practice' at the end of this chapter.[16] More recently, the Commission fined nine producers of window mountings €86 million for fixing prices for the buyers of windows across the EU, in an arrangement that had lasted from 1999 to 2007.[17]

---

[13] See *http://www.oft.gov.uk/OFTwork/competition-act-and-cartels/cartels/rewards* for information about this policy (accessed 03/05/12).

[14] That is, the practice among companies making tenders for a job of sharing inside information between themselves, with the objective of fixing the end result.

[15] European Commission, Case COMP/E–1/38.069, *Copper Plumbing Tubes*, 3 September 2004, at section 6.4.1.1 to 6.4.1.3.

[16] Press Notice IP/07/509, 18 April 2007.

[17] Press Notice IP/12/313, 28 March 2012.

The paraffin waxes case is a good example of the workings of a cartel. The product is used for a variety of purposes: mainly making candles, but also in chemicals, tyres and automotive products. According to the Commission this was a cartel between ten groups of companies which lasted from 1992 to 2005. There were two to six meetings a year at hotels around Europe, referred to as 'Technical Meetings'.[18] At these meetings they would discuss such matters as price-fixing, market and customer allocations, and exchange and disclosure of commercially sensitive information including present and future pricing policies, customers, production capacities and sales volumes. The meetings would agree not only on price increases, in this case in absolute rather than percentage terms, but also minimum prices if this was necessary, for example, when demand was falling. Occasional cases of cheating or non-implementation would be discussed at these meetings. The pricing would be implemented through announcements to customers and the participants in the cartel would be informed of these announcements, usually orally. There was also an agreement that the companies represented should not benefit from an increase in price to increase their market share. The Commission fined the participants €676 million, although the decision has been appealed to the GC.[19] As well as noting that price-fixing here goes along with market and customer allocation, it is interesting that this is, allegedly, a cartel with a significant number of participants (ten), which brings with it coordination problems in principle – yet it lasted for over ten years, which is a long period.

In the UK, the first high-profile price-fixing case did not involve a horizontal arrangement but occurred in the context of vertical arrangements, that is, resale price maintenance in relation to replica football shirts.[20] Resale price maintenance occurs where the manufacturer and the distributor or retailer agree to sell the product at a particular price. Here the agreement was not to sell replica football kits below certain prices. The economic issues in relation to resale price maintenance and vertical arrangements are different from those in cartels because there is not the same level of agreement that this practice is damaging to the competitive process. Indeed, the US Supreme Court recently changed the US rules on resale price maintenance, which has sparked a large debate on this issue, illustrating the difference with horizontal cartels.[21] The second big price-fixing case in the UK involved Argos and Littlewoods and Hasbro toys and games.[22] This was interesting because Hasbro, the manufacturer, entered into separate price-fixing arrangements with Argos and Littlewoods, the retailers. The aim of these arrangements was not, however, simply resale price maintenance, but to prevent price competition taking place at the retail level and is discussed below. So, instead of Littlewoods and Argos agreeing directly to fix prices, this was done through the separate agreements with Hasbro. The OFT has fined BA £121.5 million (later reduced to £58.5 million) for colluding over long-haul passenger surcharges with Virgin Atlantic (which benefited from the leniency programme) and pursued a criminal case (unsuccessful) against those BA executives that it alleges were involved in the practices.[23]

---

[18] European Commission, Case COMP/39181, *Candle Waxes*, 1 October 2008 at paras 98–116.

[19] See Cases T-540/08 *Esso*; T-543/08 *RWE*; T-548/08 *Total*; T-550/08 *Tudapetrol*; T-544/08 *Hansen*; T-558/08 *ENI*; T-562/08 *Repsol* – all brought against the Commission and not yet decided.

[20] OFT, 'Football kit price-fixing' (2003).

[21] *Leegin Creative Leather Products, Inc.* v *Psks, Inc.* 127 S Ct 2705 (2007).

[22] OFT, 'Hasbro/Argos/Littlewoods' (2003).

[23] OFT Press Notice 113/07, 1 August 2007; and see *http://www.oft.gov.uk/OFTwork/competition-act-and-cartels/civil-cartels-complete/fuel-surcharges/* (accessed 05/09/12).

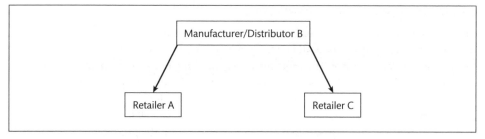

Figure 8.1 Illustrative hub and spoke cartel

Hub and spoke cartels[24]

A particular issue which has come up in UK competition law are the so-called hub and spoke cartels. These have occurred in situations where A communicates information to B, who then communicates it to C and vice versa. Typically, the relationship in this situation between A and B and B and C is a vertical one, for example B is a manufacturer and A and C are retailers. Figure 8.1 illustrates the relationship.

The clearest example of this type of cartel arose in the Hasbro/Argos/Littlewoods case. Hasbro is the manufacturer of a number of toys and games including, ironically, Monopoly. Argos and Littlewoods were well known 'catalogue' retailers at the time that saw themselves as in competition with each other, whilst Hasbro was keen generally to maintain the prices of its products. Although there was no evidence of direct contact between Argos and Littlewoods, there was evidence that Hasbro facilitated the flow of information in order to ensure that the pricing policies of the retailers on Hasbro products were coordinated. The OFT concluded that the agreements between Hasbro and Argos and Hasbro and Littlewoods were interlinked and each retailer maintained the agreement on the basis that the other would as well.[25] Argos and Littlewoods were fined around £17 million and £5 million respectively, while Hasbro's penalty was reduced to nil because it had given information about the cartel and cooperated with the investigation. Argos and Littlewoods appealed to the Competition Appeal Tribunal which ultimately upheld the decision on liability.[26] There was a further, unsuccessful appeal to the Court of Appeal.[27] The case was controversial because suppliers and retailers do have conversations about a number of issues, including price, and the possibility that this could lead to liability, even though no contact with competitors had been made, was worrying. The Court of Appeal put the proposition thus:

> . . . if (i) retailer A discloses to supplier B its future pricing intentions in circumstances where A may be taken to intend that B will make use of that information to influence market conditions by passing that information to other retailers (of whom C is or may be one), (ii) B does, in fact, pass that information to C in circumstances where C may be taken to know the circumstances in which the information was disclosed by A to B and (iii) C does, in fact, use the information in determining its own future pricing intentions, then A, B and C are all to be regarded as parties to a concerted practice having as its object the restriction or distortion of competition.[28]

---

[24] For Discussion see O. Odudu, 'Indirect Information Exchange: The Constitutent Elements of Hub and Spoke Collusion' (2011) 7 *European Competition Journal* 205.

[25] OFT, 'Hasbro/Argos/Littlewoods' decision of 2 December 2003 at para. 96.

[26] *Argos Ltd* v *Office of Fair Trading* [2004] CAT 24.

[27] *Argos Ltd and JJB Sports* v *Office of Fair Trading* [2006] EWCA Civ 1318.

[28] Ibid. para. 141.

Restrictions on output and related matters

In order to maintain prices, it is important for the participants in a cartel to limit production because, once a firm has produced certain goods, there is an incentive to sell them, even if this is below an agreed price. The most direct way of doing this is to set production or sales quotas which are typically based on the market shares of the participating undertakings. A nice example of this comes from the *Cartonboard* case, which involved a large cartel, around a dozen producers of cartonboard in Western Europe in the late 1980s and early 1990s. One of the features of this industry was that it was more efficient for the producers to operate their plant at near to full capacity which meant that, in order to control prices, it was also necessary to control output. This involved freezing the market share levels of the producers at their existing levels and a complicated system for reporting on production levels and monitoring the implementation of this agreement.[29]

Sharing of markets

In order for a cartel to work properly, the markets also have to be shared out, which can be done on a customer or a geographic basis. A good example of this came in one of the first Competition Act investigations and relates to market sharing between bus companies in Leeds.[30] Here, Arriva had one service from Leeds to Holt Park in competition with FirstGroup which was unprofitable. It decided to withdraw from that service and use the buses on a service from Leeds to Halifax, also in competition with FirstGroup. Before so doing, managers from the companies had discussions about this and the process by which it would take place, at which FirstGroup indicated that it would withdraw from the Leeds to Halifax service. The result was that on two services, where the companies had previously been competitors, they were competitors no longer; and the OFT held that the aim of the agreement was market sharing and, effectively, a hard-core cartel. Ultimately, Arriva was fined around £300,000 and FirstGroup around £500,000 but these penalties were reduced because the companies had cooperated with the investigation. Since FirstGroup was the first company to provide information about the cartel, its fine was reduced 100% to nil, while Arriva received a 36% reduction to around £200,000. This is a very small example but it is a clear illustration of geographic market sharing in a local market.

At a European level, one of the most well-known examples was the agreement between two producers of soda ash, which is used in glass manufacture. ICI of the UK and Solvay of Belgium agreed to divide the European market into two: ICI would supply the UK and Solvay would supply the rest of Europe. This agreement seems to have started before World War II and was restarted shortly after the war. When the UK entered the European Union in 1972, the agreement was formally terminated, as it would obviously be in breach of EU competition rules. When the Commission investigated, however, it found that even though the agreement had been terminated, this had not led to any change in commercial behaviour by the companies concerned. The Commission took the view that there was complete cooperation between the two parties and that there were continuing contacts between them where they discussed commercial policy and, in these circumstances, there was at least a concerted

---

[29] European Commission, IV/C/33.833, *Cartonboard*, 13 July 1994 at paras 51–71. A similar idea was behind the arrangements in Case C-209/07 *Competition Authority v Beef Industry Development Society* [2008] ECR I-8637.

[30] OFT, 'Market sharing by Arriva plc and FirstGroup plc' (2002).

practice, working on the basis that the pre-WWII policies would continue.[31] This decision was overturned on procedural grounds by the GC but it serves as a good example of geographical market division which is contrary to the competition rules and, indeed, to the basic principle of market integration which lies behind the European Union. The case was more complicated as the Commission brought Article 102 TFEU actions against ICI and Solvay, as well as an additional Article 101 TFEU action against Solvay in relation to an agreement with a German company relating to a minimum volume of sales. These were also annulled by the GC on, different, procedural grounds and unsuccessfully appealed by the Commission to the CJEU.[32] Here, however, the Commission re-adopted the decisions after the CJEU had made its ruling, because the procedural breaches were technical.[33]

A recent example of market allocation comes in the E.ON/GDF case where the European Commission fined E.ON and GDF Suez €553 million each for sharing the German and French gas markets. The two companies had agreed to build a pipeline from Russia to France, going through Germany, in order to import Russian gas. As part of this arrangement, they agreed not to sell gas transported over this pipeline into each other's home markets.[34] This arrangement meant that they were able to maintain monopolies in their respective areas and they kept these arrangements in place even after the markets were liberalised (see Chapter 15 for details). What is interesting about this case, and indeed the soda ash case, is that the aim of the geographic market sharing was to prevent the development of competitive pressures and give the undertakings concerned freedom to price without having to worry about the activities of a competitor.

A good example of customer allocation comes from the cartel on industrial thread, covering the UK and the Nordic and Benelux countries. Industrial thread is used in a variety of industries, such as leather goods, automotive products or mattresses; and this cartel had 13 participants. The arrangements as regards prices were organised through a series of meetings, as well as bilateral contacts between the undertakings involved. Here there was a basic understanding not to undercut the incumbent supplier's prices to customers and participants in the cartel would contact each other to exchange information about prices to customers and to complain if they felt that this was taking place.[35] The producers were fined a total of around €43 million.

Collusive tendering or bid-rigging

This occurs when companies agree together to try to fix the outcome of a tendering process, which is equivalent to price-fixing or market allocation. There are a number of ways in which this can be done, as the OFT has explained in its decision on collusive tendering in relation to flat roof contracts in the West Midlands. First, there may be the practice of cover bids or cover pricing. This is where a tenderer submits a bid which is not intended to win the contract but is decided upon with another contractor, that does wish to win the contract. In other words, it is a token bid, at too high a price. Secondly, there is bid suppression when the suppliers agree among themselves either not to bid or to withdraw bids. Thirdly, there is bid

[31] Commission Decision of 19 December 1990 (IV/33.133-A: *Soda-ash – Solvay, ICI*) [1991] OJ L152/1.

[32] Case T-30/91 *Solvay v Commission* [1995] ECR II-1775; Cases C-287–288/95P *Commission v Solvay* [2000] ECR I-2391.

[33] Commission Press Release IP/00/1449, 13 December 2000; and see OJ L10/1, 15.12.2003 for the decisions.

[34] See European Commission Press Release IP/09/1099, 8 July 2009; Case No. COMP/39.401. The decision on liability was upheld by the GC: Case T-360/09 *E.ON Ruhrgas AG v Commission* judgment of 29 June 2012 (GC).

[35] European Commission, COMP/38.337, *Thread*, 14.09.2005 at paras 124–7, 173–4, 179, 198–202 and 215.

rotation, which happens when the suppliers decide that the lowest bid will be made on a systematic or rotational basis.[36] Finally, there can also be market division, for example when certain companies agree not to bid in certain geographical areas.[37]

Within the UK there have been a number of cases of collusive tendering, mainly between 2004 and 2006, involving the construction industry and bidding for contracts for flat roofs and car park surfacing contracts. Following on from this work, the OFT has fined 103 firms in the construction industry in England a total of £129.5 million, for engaging in bid-rigging activities when making tenders for, among other projects, the construction of schools, hospital and university buildings.[38] Twenty-five of the firms appealed this decision on a penalty to the CAT, with six of them also challenging their liability. The CAT upheld the decisions on liability but reduced the fines of a number of the undertakings.

The major EU case on collusive tendering was the pre-insulated pipes cartel case,[39] which involved the manufacturers of pipes that were used for district heating schemes, primarily in public housing projects. Typically contracts were awarded by competitive tender and the aim of the cartel, which started in Denmark and then became EU-wide, was to stabilise existing market shares and maintain prices. National quotas were fixed by the chairmen or managing directors of the producers and were implemented in Member States by the local sales managers. The general idea was that the traditional supplier of a customer was the favourite on a project and other producers should either decline to bid or provide a cover bid. For major projects, the work would be shared out between the normal suppliers. New projects would be allocated to the producers in line with the remainder of their agreed annual quota.[40] This cartel is also interesting because it had sophisticated arrangements for monitoring compliance with the obligations, which involved auditing of the information by a firm of Swiss accountants, as well as provisions for payment of compensation by more successful to the less successful members.

Information sharing

For cartels to work properly, there needs to be sharing of information between their members, so that they can be confident that everyone is sticking to the agreed deal. On the other hand, one of the assumptions underlying perfect markets is that there is perfect information for both consumers and producers, which allows them to make the optimal choices. It is also important to distinguish between markets where transparency of information is a normal part of business (for example, in the sale of groceries to individual consumers)[41] and those where it is not (for example, in the sale of items to grocery retailers by the suppliers) (see, in Box 8.2, the discussion of category management). A good example from the UK of this sort of practice involved the selling of loans to professional service firms (for example, lawyers and accountants) by RBS and Barclays in 2007–08. In this case there were a number of contacts, for example at social events, between the relevant employees of the banks where pricing matters, both general and specific, were discussed between them. The OFT decided that this

---

[36] OFT, 'Flat roofing contracts in the West Midlands' (2004) at para. 18.

[37] OFT, 'Flat roof and car park servicing contracts in England and Scotland' (2006) at para. 68.

[38] See http://www.oft.gov.uk/OFTwork/competition-act-and-cartels/ca98/closure/construction/ (accessed 05/09/12).

[39] [1999] OJ L24/1. Another example is Commission Decision Case COMP/E-1/38.823, *Elevators and Escalators* 21.02.2007, imposing an aggregate fine of over €990 million. Largely upheld on appeal in Case T-138/07 et al *Schindler v Commission* judgment of 13 July 2011 (GC), on appeal Case C-501/11P.

[40] Ibid., para. 68.

[41] See Competition Commission, 'Groceries' (2008) at para. 8.25.

was a breach of both the Competition Act and Article 101(1) TFEU and reached an early resolution agreement, fining RBS some £28 million, while Barclays benefited from leniency, having brought the issue to the OFT's attention.[42] Whether the transparency is a normal part of business is not always easy to determine: in the *Wood Pulp* case,[43] the European Commission thought that the price transparency was indicative of a concerted practice within an oligopolistic market, whereas the CJEU, relying on its economic experts, thought that this was just a natural outcome of the market.

KEY DEFINITION   **Box 8.2**

Category management

Category management is a relatively common practice within grocery retailing that aims to improve a grocery retailer's sales or performance in a particular product category through collaboration between that grocery retailer and its suppliers. To this end, a grocery retailer may exchange information with its suppliers on sales volumes and trends, consumer demographics, profiles and preferences, and a retailer may take advice from suppliers on the range of products displayed, placement and size of the product displays, pricing, promotion, supply chain improvements and stock management.

Category management can introduce efficiencies as a result of suppliers' better knowledge of consumer demand. For example, a supplier is likely to be better positioned from its consumer research to provide advice on the products in a category most likely to appeal to different types of consumers, and can lead to better market information or trading advantages being available to a particular supplier . . . This may directly benefit consumers and result in increased total sales in the category. However, extensive use of category management might also bring about an environment which could facilitate collusion between retailers, between suppliers, and collusion involving both retailers and suppliers.

For example, a supplier providing the same category management advice to a number of retailers may dampen competition between those retailers. Alternatively, category management could give rise to collusion by facilitating an indirect exchange of information between competing retailers through suppliers. Similarly, category management may provide increased opportunities to exchange information between suppliers, whether directly or indirectly via retailers.

Analysis

The Competition Commission looked at category management in fresh fruit and yogurt and came to the conclusion that the degree of interaction between suppliers because of category management was a cause for concern. They thought that given the level of interaction among suppliers, and the large amount of information that is passed between retailers and suppliers, there was an opportunity for competitive harm.

Source: Competition Commission, 'The supply of groceries in the UK market investigation' (2008), paras 8.13–8.15.

Questions: Are there examples of practices with the same effect in other industries? What sorts of roles might trade associations play?

---

[42] OFT, 'Loan products to professional services firms' (2011) available at: *http://www.oft.gov.uk/OFTwork/ competition-act-and-cartels/ca98/decisions/loan-services* (accessed 05/09/12).

[43] Cases C-89/85 etc. *Ahlström Oy* v *Commission (Wood Pulp II)* [1993] ECR I-1307.

So, when assessing information sharing arrangements, it is necessary to look carefully at the context within which they take place. The discussion here overlaps with the discussion of information exchanges later in the text (see Chapter 9), to which reference should be made. There is clearly a breach of the competition law rules when they are tied into price-fixing, output limitation or market sharing but more difficult is a situation where there is information sharing without any such explicit agreement. When looking at the context of an information sharing agreement, there are three important factors: the structure and characteristics of the market; the type of information; and the way that it is exchanged.[44] As the CJEU put it:

> the compatibility of an information exchange system . . . with the Community [Union] competition rules cannot be assessed in the abstract. It depends on the economic conditions on the relevant markets and on the specific characteristics of the system concerned, such as, in particular, its purpose and the conditions of access to it and participation in it, as well as the type of information exchanged – be that, for example, public or confidential, aggregated or detailed, historical or current – the periodicity of such information and its importance for the fixing of prices, volumes or conditions of service.[45]

As the OFT in its guidelines makes clear, information which is aggregated is unlikely to be in breach of Article 101(1) TFEU while, if it is disaggregated, it might be saved if it is sufficiently historical.[46]

Two cases can be used to illustrate these points. In the UK Agricultural Tractors Registration Exchange, the Commission condemned an information agreement between eight UK manufacturers and importers as a breach of Article 101(1) TFEU.[47] Relevant factors were that the market was highly concentrated (covering 87–88% of the relevant market), there were high barriers to entry, there were insignificant intra-Union imports, the information exchanged was detailed and identified the exact retail sales and shares of the firms, and the members met regularly. This analysis was accepted by the GC, when the Commission decision was challenged.[48] By contrast, in the *Asnef-Equifax* case, the exchange of information between financial institutions of information on the credit records of customers was challenged in front of a Spanish court, which referred the issue under Article 267 TFEU to the CJEU. Here the CJEU took the view that, provided the markets were not highly concentrated, the system did not permit lenders to be identified and the conditions of access and use by financial institutions were not discriminatory, then such information exchange systems did not, in principle, have the effect of restricting competition.[49] Of course the difference here is between a credit register, which gives information about potential customers, but does not tell the financial institution anything about decisions taken by competitors, nor decisions likely to be taken by competitors, as this will depend on their individual policies, and, in contrast, the tractor exchange scheme, which clearly allowed competitors to monitor each other's sales and prices.

---

[44] OFT, *Agreements and Concerted Practices* (2004) at para. 3.19.

[45] Case C-238/05 *Asnef-Equifax v Asociación de Usuarios de Servicios Bancarios (Ausbanc)* [2006] ECR I-11125 at para. 54.

[46] OFT, 'Agreements and Concerted Practices' (2004) at paras 3.21–3.23.

[47] [1977] OJ L242/10.

[48] Case T-35/92 *John Deere v Commission* [1994] ECR II-957.

[49] Ibid. at para. 61.

Exemptions under Article 101(3) TFEU

In theory it is possible for all agreements to benefit from the exemption under Article 101(3) TFEU[50] but that requires meeting the four conditions, namely: improvement of production, distribution or technology; while allowing consumers a fair share of the resulting benefit; not imposing restrictions which are not indispensable for the agreement; and not affording the possibility of eliminating all competition. To put this another way, the agreement has to offer some efficiency benefits to compensate for its anti-competitive effects. When put this way, it seems very implausible that either collusive tendering or market-sharing agreements could be justified as bringing any benefits to consumers. However, price-fixing agreements and output restrictions raise more difficult issues because it is possible to combine these facets with arguments about efficiency. In the context of discussing whether the Multilateral Interchange Fee (MIF) for the Visa system could benefit from an exemption under Article 101(3) TFEU, the Commission made the point that an agreement concerning prices is not always to be classified as a cartel and inherently non-exemptible.[51] The Commission does say, however, that severe restrictions of competition are unlikely to meet the conditions in Article 101(3) TFEU.[52] Such restrictions are referred to by the Commission as 'hard-core' restrictions and are identified in block exemption regulation and Commission guidance and notices. Typically, these would include clauses in agreements which fix prices, limit output or sales and allocate markets or customers.

Enforcement in the EU and UK

History[53]

Although the modern understanding of cartels is that they are clearly detrimental to society, this is a relatively recent development. Certainly within twentieth-century Europe, there has been a history of seeing cartels as being, in certain circumstances, a positive thing, as they allowed a more rational response, arguably, to conditions of economic slowdown than the unfettered play of competitive forces. It is worth remembering that the UK legislation against cartels only makes an appearance after World War II, the German legislation against restraints on competition dates from 1958 and the Treaty of Rome from 1957. In other words, it is only since the 1950s that European countries have adopted an explicit competition policy.

Enforcement activity in the EU

Enforcement action by the European Commission against cartels started slowly and it has been claimed that the initial period, in the early to mid 1960s, was an era of low-profile

---

[50] Case T-17/93 *Matra Hachette* v *Commission* [1994] ECR II-995.

[51] *Visa International Multilateral Interchange Fee* [2002] OJ L318/17 at para. 79. The Commission has, however, opened proceedings against Visa in relation to the multilateral interchange fee, among other issues: see Press Release MEMO/08/170, 26 March 2008. Visa agreed to cut its interchange fees and this commitment was accepted, but the Commission has also sent a supplementary statement of objections to Visa: Commission Decision COMP/39/398 *Visa – MIF* 08.12.2010 and Press Release IP/12/871 31.07.2012.

[52] European Commission, *Guidelines on the application of Article 81(3) of the Treaty*, OJ C101, 27.04.2004, pp. 97–118 (at para. 46).

[53] See M. Utton (n. 3), ch. 3, and L. McGowan, *The Antitrust Revolution in Europe* (Edward Elgar, Cheltenham, 2010), chs 3–4.

negotiation, leading to agreed terminations or modifications of agreements with minimal publicity.[54] The first decision imposing a fine on a cartel, on the basis of an own-initiative investigation by the Commission, was not until 1969, in the case of the Quinine cartel, where the value of the fines was approximately 500,000 European units of account (one of the forerunners of the euro), which has been described as 'quite substantial' for the time.[55] Activity for the next 30 years can best be described as sporadic. As the Commission itself has said, in the 30 years prior to 2001 it averaged around 1.5 decisions in cartel cases per year.[56]

There are a number of possible explanations for this lack of activity but the most plausible seems to be that the notification system set up under Regulation 17/62 did divert much of the Commission's resources into the examination of notifications, rather than uncovering cartels. The so-called modernisation of competition law started with the block exemption for vertical agreements in 1999, which removed a substantial administrative burden from the Commission, and was followed by the adoption of Regulation 1/2003, which came into force in 2004, and abolished the notification system. Internally, the Commission created a task force dedicated to cartel enforcement in 2005. The change in the level of enforcement decisions can be seen in Table 8.1 below, which shows that, since 2002, the Commission has taken just over six cartel decisions a year, although each decision involves a number of undertakings. This certainly represents a major change in enforcement practice[57] but does still seem a low level of activity, particularly if compared to the annual number of criminal cases filed under the Sherman Act, s. 1 by the Antitrust Division of the US Department of Justice, also shown in Table 8.1.[58] These statistics are quite crude and do not take into account informal settlements, Commission's activity under Article 102 TFEU and, importantly, decisions taken by national competition authorities under Article 101 TFEU, which would have no analogue in the US system. In the period 2004–08, the Commission reports that national competition authorities have taken more than 50 decisions on cartels, which would need to be added to the Commission's 33.[59] Although these figures represent the lower end of any assessment of enforcement activity, there would seem to be scope for more enforcement of European Union competition law against cartels.

Enforcement in the UK

It is very difficult to provide an accurate description of the OFT's enforcement record in relation to cartels. OFT annual reports only give numbers specifically for cartel cases up until the reporting year 2007–08. After that, the statistics put together all investigations and formal decisions, in other words, cartel investigations are combined with abuse of dominance cases. It is also important to understand that, because investigations take some time, the OFT's workload is comprised of new investigations and those which have been opened in previous years. In the last three years, there have been between 10 and 12 such continuing investigations

---

[54] C. Harding and J. Joshua, *Regulating Cartels in Europe* (Oxford University Press, 2003) at pp. 112–13.

[55] Ibid. at p. 121. [1969] OJ L192/5, 16.07.1969.

[56] European Commission, *Annual Report on Competition Policy* (2003) at para. 26.

[57] See also E. Gippini-Fournier, 'The Modernisation of European Competition Law: First Experiences with Regulation 1/2003', available at SSRN: *http://ssrn.com/abstract=1139776* (accessed 05/09/12), a Commission official who tells a similar story.

[58] Section 1 of the Sherman Act deals with anti-competitive agreements, i.e. cartels.

[59] European Commission, 'Commission Staff working paper accompanying the Communication from the Commission to the European Parliament and Council Report on the functioning of Regulation 1/2003', COM (2009) 206 final (at para. 188).

Table 8.1 Cartel enforcement by the European Commission and the US Department of Justice

Year	Number of decisions	US DoJ, s. 1 Sherman Act cases filed (Criminal)
2011	4	63
2010	7	41
2009	6	37
2008	7	26
2007	8	25
2006	7	21
2005	5	23
2004	6	28
2003	5	23
2002	9	23
2001	10	37
2000	2	52
1999	2	53

Source: European Commission, *Annual Reports on Competition Policy, 2007* (author's own calculation from Commission website) and Department of Justice, 'Ten Year Workload Statistics Report', available at *http://www.justice.gov/atr/public/workload-statistics.html* (accessed 05/09/12).

each year. If this is combined with the figures in Table 8.2, this suggests that the OFT has about twenty formal investigations being carried out currently. As regards the OFT, since about 2004, it seems to have made on average two or three decisions on cartel cases per annum, although some of these have been the result of fairly lengthy inquiries: for example, aluminium spacer bars (used to separate the panes of glass in double glazing) was an investigation that took four years.[60] Having said that, there seems to have been an upsurge in activity since 2007, with cases being taken against British Airways for fuel surcharges, various supermarkets and milk producers in relation to milk pricing, a very large case in relation to bid-rigging in the construction industry (although this dates back to 2004), a large fine being imposed on firms involved in recruitment in the construction industry and one relating to the prices of tobacco products in various supermarkets and retail chains.[61] So it may be that we have seen a change in enforcement practice from the OFT, although the tobacco and dairy products cases are not classic cartel cases but involve vertical relationships and there have been a number of difficulties in bringing these cases to a successful conclusion. For example, the OFT's decision in the tobacco case was quashed by the CAT and Tesco has appealed aspects of the dairy case.[62] The OFT has not, however, had any real success in using the criminal offence which was created in the Enterprise Act 2002 (this is discussed below).

The OFT's record in terms of cartel enforcement is mixed and this seems to have been one of the concerns behind the government's review of competition policy in 2011–2012. In terms of antitrust cases in general, the government was concerned that the OFT brought fewer antitrust cases than other European countries and took longer to complete.[63] On the latter

[60] OFT, 'Aluminium double glazed spacer bars' (2006).

[61] See OFT, 'Construction recruitment forum' (2009), 'Bid-rigging in the construction industry in England' (2009), 'Tobacco' (2010), 'Dairy products' (2011); see *http://www.oft.gov.uk/OFTwork/competition-act-and-cartels/ca98-current/dairy-products/* (accessed 06/09/12).

[62] *Imperial Tobacco* v OFT [2011] CAT 41; Case 1188/1/1/11 *Tesco* v OFT (not yet decided).

[63] BIS, 'A Competition Regime for Growth: A consultation on options for reform' (2011).

Table 8.2 Cartel Enforcement in the UK by the OFT

Year	Cartel case opened	Formal investigation opened	Formal decision
	NA	10	1
2009–10	NA	5	2
2008–09	NA	3	1
2007–08	12	2	0
2006–07	20	6	2
2005–06	23	7	6
2004–05	27	13	4

Source: OFT, Annual Reports.[64]

point, the government calculated that infringement decisions took on average 38 months, including the appeal stage.[65] The main changes proposed in the Enterprise and Regulatory Reform Bill are to merge the OFT and the Competition Commission to form a new CMA, to speed up the decision making process and reform the criminal cartel offence (this last point is discussed below). Enforcement of the law will remain challenging, not least because of the information problems suffered by the OFT (and all enforcement agencies), which leads to a discussion of the leniency programmes.

Leniency programmes

The basic idea behind the policy of leniency is that, if an undertaking notifies the competition authorities of an infringement of competition law, that undertaking should receive a lesser penalty, or no penalty at all, because without its cooperation the infringement would not have been detected. This approach was originally pioneered in the United States by the Antitrust Division of the Department of Justice and it has claimed that its leniency programme has significantly enhanced its enforcement of competition law. The European Commission first adopted such a programme in 1996 and has since revised its approach in 2002 and, most recently, in 2006. Both the 1996 and the 2002 Notices were seen by the Commission and commentators as having been highly successful in raising the number of cartel cases and allowing the Commission to take action against them. A number of issues relating to the design of the 2002 Notice have been addressed in the latest version.

The European Union

Under the current policy, undertakings can benefit from either full immunity from a fine or a reduction of the fine imposed. In order to qualify for full immunity, the undertaking must be the first to submit evidence to the Commission which will allow the Commission either to carry out a 'targeted inspection'[66] in connection with the alleged cartel or to find an infringement of Article 101 TFEU. The undertaking must provide a detailed description of the cartel, the corporate members of the cartel, the individuals who were involved in the

[64] OFT reporting prior to 2004 does not clearly separate out cartel from non-cartel activity.

[65] Ibid. Appendix 1.

[66] It is not clear what this means. The Commission says that the undertaking 'should therefore be in a position to provide to the Commission such "insider" information on the cartel that would allow the Commission to better target its inspection with more precise information as to, for instance, what to look for and where in terms of evidence.' Memo 06/469, 07.12.06.

operation of the cartel, information on which other competition authorities are going to be approached for leniency and any other information. In addition, the undertaking must fully cooperate with the European Commission throughout the investigation, which includes making employees and directors available for interview, end its participation in the cartel and not destroy incriminating evidence. An undertaking that took steps to coerce other undertakings to participate in the cartel or to remain in it is not eligible for immunity, although it may be eligible for a reduction in its fine. An undertaking making such an application may be granted a 'marker', preserving its place in the queue and allowing it to obtain further information or it may present a hypothetical case to the Commission.

If an undertaking is not eligible for immunity, it may gain a reduction in the fine if it provides evidence of the alleged infringement which adds 'significant added value' to the evidence already in the Commission's possession; in other words, it must strengthen the Commission's ability to prove its case. The first undertaking to provide such evidence can obtain a reduction of 30–50%, the second one a reduction of 20–30% and subsequent undertakings can obtain reductions of up to 20%, providing that they qualify.

The leniency programme is used quite regularly. An example is where Sony, Fuji and Maxell were fined, respectively, €36.3 million, €22 million and €18 million for fixing prices for professional customers of videotape in Europe. Fuji received a reduction of 40% and Maxell a reduction of 20% for cooperating with the Commission, while Sony's fine was increased by 30% for obstructing the Commission's investigation. The ultimate result was that their fines were, respectively, €47.19 million, €13.2 million and €14.4 million (see Table 8.3), which indicates that there are substantial benefits to undertakings in cooperating with the Commission or exposing cartels.[67]

An important issue for the leniency programme is its relationship with private enforcement. An applicant for leniency only obtains a benefit in relation to any sanctions which the European Commission might impose; it does not gain any immunity from private enforcement actions. A particular issue is to what extent a plaintiff in private action is able to obtain the documents that an undertaking submitted in its leniency application to the European Commission, or indeed any national competition authority. This came up in the *Pfleiderer* case[68] where Pfleiderer was bringing a damages action against certain undertakings that had been found to be operating a cartel in Germany. As part of this action, it requested access to the leniency applications and documents submitted in support of those applications which had been submitted to the German competition authority. The CJEU took the view that Regulation 1/2003 did not preclude such an application, but that it was for the courts of the Member States, on the basis of their national law, to determine the conditions under which such access must be permitted or refused by weighing the interests protected by EU law. What

Table 8.3 An example of the effects of leniency

	Original fine (€ millions)	Increase or reduction	Final fine (€ millions)
Sony	36	+30%	47
Fuji	22	–40%	13
Maxell	18	–20%	14

[67] Commission Press Release IP 07/1725, 20 November 2007. The calculations were done under the 2002 guidelines.

[68] Case C-360/09 *Pfleiderer AG v Bundeskartellamt* [2011] 5 CMLR 7.

is being weighed here is the interests in an effective leniency programme, against the rights of those that have suffered damage from anti-competitive activity.

The United Kingdom[69]

The OFT's leniency programme offers three levels of incentive: total immunity to an undertaking that comes forward with evidence of cartel activity before the OFT has started an investigation, relief of up to 100% of financial penalties to the first undertaking to come forward after an investigation has begun, and relief of up to 50% for undertakings that come forward before a statement of objections is issued but do not qualify under the other two headings. There are four general conditions which have to be met to qualify for this relief. Undertakings must:

1 provide the OFT with all the information, documents and evidence available to them regarding the cartel activity;

2 maintain continuous and complete cooperation throughout the investigation and until the conclusion of any action by the OFT arising as a result of the investigation;

3 refrain from further participation in the cartel activity from the time of disclosure of the cartel activity to the OFT (except as may be directed by the OFT); and

4 not have taken steps to coerce another undertaking to take part in the cartel activity.[70]

The last condition does not apply to undertakings seeking up to a 50% reduction. Unlike the European Commission, the OFT also operates what is referred to as an 'Amnesty Plus' system. Under this policy, if an undertaking is being investigated for cartel activities in market A, and is cooperating with that investigation, and tells the OFT about cartel activities in market B, of which the OFT had no knowledge, then, in addition to getting total immunity for its activities in market B, the undertaking will also receive a discount for its activities in market A. To try and encourage individuals to give information to the OFT, it now offers a reward of up to £100,000 (in exceptional circumstances) for information about cartel activity.[71]

A good example of the use of leniency in practice occurred in September 2007. The OFT issued a statement of objections which provisionally found that certain large supermarkets (Asda, Morrisons, Safeways, Sainsburys and Tesco) and dairy processors had colluded to fix the retail prices of milk, value butter and UK cheese. The OFT reached early resolution agreements with some, but not all, of the parties, which admitted liability and agreed to pay penalties of over £116 million.[72] They will receive significant reductions in their penalties due to their cooperation with the investigation. One party will receive complete immunity because it had previously applied for leniency. Rather embarrassingly for the OFT, Morrisons sued for libel because of the original press release, which suggested that Morrisons was involved in the cartel.[73] The OFT settled the case with an apology and a payment of £100,000 but not until after a High Court judge had accused it of trying to attract 'sensationalist publicity'.[74]

---

[69] Generally see OFT, 'Leniency and no action' (2008) and 'Applications for leniency and no action in cartel cases: A consultation on OFT guidance' (2011).

[70] OFT, *Guidance as to the appropriate amount of a penalty* (2004), para. 3.9.

[71] See *http://www.oft.gov.uk/OFTwork/competition-act-and-cartels/cartels/rewards* (accessed 07/09/12).

[72] OFT Press Release, 7 December 2007.

[73] See *The Financial Times*, 10 February 2008.

[74] *The Daily Telegraph*, 24 April 2008; and see *http://www.oft.gov.uk/news/press/2008/54-08* (accessed 07/09/12).

Settlement procedures

The European Commission has recently introduced procedures for settlement in cartel cases which is in addition to the leniency programme.[75] The idea behind this is that, in cartel cases, there is not much dispute about the substance of the case once the European Commission has gathered the appropriate evidence but undertakings are concerned about the level of the fine and, procedurally, the case can be complex because of concerns about confidentiality and requests for the use of multiple different languages.[76] So, after the investigation but before issuing a statement of objections, there will be discussions between the parties and the Commission where the parties will hear about the case against them and the level of sanctions that are envisaged. When progress has been made to the point of a common understanding of the case, the parties may produce a written settlement submission which acknowledges liability, indicates a maximum amount of fine that the parties would accept, confirms that they have had a sufficient right to be heard, do not require further access to the file and will accept an SO and decision in a single Union language.[77] The Commission does not have to accept the settlement proposal but, where it does not, the procedure reverts to the normal one, but the settlement proposals cannot be used against the parties. Where it does accept the proposal, it moves straight to a decision, without an oral hearing. The reward for the parties is a 10% reduction to the fine, which may be in addition to any reductions granted under the leniency programme. The benefits of this procedure to the European Commission seem obvious through faster settlement of cases and a freeing up of resources.[78] The benefits to the parties involved are less clear and depend on the percentage reward for a reduction that is available. It is not necessarily in the interests of parties to an anti-competitive practice for there to be a speedy decision on their activities. It may be in their interests to delay, by legitimate means, decisions of competition authorities as this allows them to continue to reap the profits of unlawful action, which might be more attractive in the context of a fining system that does not fully take into account their level of benefit.

A further potential problem arises if this proposal is looked at in the context of fining policy overall. Veljanovski has argued that the leniency programme is over-generous, that the fines imposed do not reflect the harm imposed by cartels and they are not likely to deter price-fixing.[79] Although his research was based on cases under the pre-2006 system, he takes the view that this conclusion is not likely to change under the new system. The proposals for settlements would further exacerbate the issue.

---

[75] European Commission, 'Notice on the conduct of settlement procedures in view of the adoption of Decisions pursuant to Article 7 and Article 23 of Council Regulation (EC) No. 1/2003 in cartel cases', OJ C167, 02.07.2008, pp. 1–6; Commission Regulation (EC) No. 622/2008 of 30 June 2008 amending Regulation (EC) No. 773/2004, as regards the conduct of settlement procedures in cartel cases, OJ L171, 01.07.2008, pp. 3–5. For discussion, see A. Stephan, 'The Direct Settlement of EC Cartel Cases' (2009) 58 *International and Comparative Law Quarterly* 627.

[76] See N. Kroes, 'Assessment of and perspectives for competition policy in Europe', speech given on 19 November 2007, Barcelona. Available at *http://ec.europa.eu/competition/speeches/index_2007.html* (accessed 05/09/12).

[77] European Commission, 'Notice on the conduct of settlement procedures . . .' (n. 74), para. 20.

[78] Since it was introduced in 2008, the Commission has used this in five cases up until the end of 2011, see: *http://ec.europa.eu/competition/cartels/legislation/cartels_settlements/settlements_en.html* (accessed 05/09/12).

[79] C. Veljanovski, 'Cartel Fines in Europe' (2007) 30 *World Competition* 65 at 85. R. Van den Bergh and P. Camesasca, *European Competition Law and Economics* (2nd edn, Sweet & Maxwell, London, 2006) have a similar critique in ch. 8.

Criminal sanctions

In a European context, the United Kingdom is unusual because it has introduced criminal sanctions for certain breaches of competition law. Although this has always been a central part of the US system for the enforcement of antitrust law, there is no such jurisdiction in EU competition law. Some Member States of the EU have criminalised breaches of competition law, notably France and Ireland, and this has also been introduced in some other countries, such as Australia and Canada. The introduction of criminal sanctions for the breach of competition law was one of the most controversial parts of the Enterprise Act 2002. The main provisions of s. 188 are set out in Box 8.3.[80]

KEY LEGAL PROVISION   **Box 8.3**

The cartel offence[81]

(1) An individual is guilty of an offence if he dishonestly agrees with one or more other persons to make or implement, or to cause to be made or implemented, arrangements of the following kind relating to at least two undertakings (A and B).

(2) The arrangements must be ones which, if operating as the parties to the agreement intend, would –

  (a) directly or indirectly fix a price for the supply by A in the United Kingdom (otherwise than to B) of a product or service,

  (b) limit or prevent supply by A in the United Kingdom of a product or service,

  (c) limit or prevent production by A in the United Kingdom of a product,

  (d) divide between A and B the supply in the United Kingdom of a product or service to a customer or customers,

  (e) divide between A and B customers for the supply in the United Kingdom of a product or service, or

  (f) be bid-rigging arrangements.[82]

(3) Unless subsection (2)(d), (e) or (f) applies, the arrangements must also be ones which, if operating as the parties to the agreement intend, would –

  (a) directly or indirectly fix a price for the supply by B in the United Kingdom (otherwise than to A) of a product or service,

  (b) limit or prevent supply by B in the United Kingdom of a product or service, or

  (c) limit or prevent production by B in the United Kingdom of a product.

Source: Enterprise Act 2002, s. 188.

---

[80] R. Williams, 'Cartels in the Criminal Law Landscape', in C. Beaton-Wells and A. Ezrachi (eds) *Criminalising Cartels* (Hart Publishing, Oxford, 2011) is a good discussion of the cartel offence in the wider criminal law context.

[81] See OFT, *Proposed criminalisation of cartels in the UK* (2001); C. Harding and J. Joshua, 'Breaking up the Hard Core: The Prospects for the Proposed Cartel Offence' [2002] *Criminal Law Review* 933.

[82] Defined as arrangements where, in response to tenders, only one of either A and B can make a bid or, if they can both bid, this is only done in accordance with their arrangement (for example, one is the specified low bidder): Enterprise Act 2002, s. 188(5).

Breach of these provisions can lead to liability to imprisonment for up to five years or a fine or both. Prosecutions can be brought only by the OFT or the Serious Fraud Office.

A number of things need to be noticed about these provisions. First, the sanctions only apply to individuals, not undertakings. Secondly, it is only a criminal offence to dishonestly agree to the arrangements spelled out under s. 188, which is a more limited set of breaches of competition law than is encompassed by, for example, the Chapter I prohibition. The offence does not apply to vertical agreements, that is, agreements between undertakings at different levels in the supply chain.[83] In a broad sense, this provision is aimed at what are regarded as the most damaging types of behaviour, namely price-fixing, the limitation of supply or production of products or services, the division of markets in terms of products, service or customers, and bid-rigging. Thirdly, the offence is only committed if the person has acted 'dishonestly', which has a well-known meaning within criminal law. The test today is set out in *R* v *Ghosh*[84] and is a two-part one. First, what must be considered is whether, by the ordinary standards of reasonable people, what was being done was dishonest (an objective test). If that can be established, the next question is whether the defendant must have realised that what he or she was doing was dishonest (a subjective test).

In a similar vein to the leniency programme, the OFT also wants to encourage individuals to come forward with evidence of cartel activity, so it has published guidelines as to when individuals may gain immunity from prosecution.[85] In order to obtain a no-action letter, which will effectively grant immunity from prosecution, the individual must be at risk of prosecution for the criminal offence and the OFT must not have, or be in the course of gathering, sufficient information to prosecute an individual. In order to obtain a letter, the individual must:

- admit participation in the criminal offence;
- provide the OFT with all information available to them regarding the existence and activities of the cartel;
- maintain continuous and complete cooperation throughout the investigation and until the conclusion of any criminal proceedings arising as a result of the investigation;
- not have taken steps to coerce another undertaking to take part in the cartel; and
- refrain from further participation in the cartel from the time of its disclosure to the OFT (except as may be directed by the investigating authority).[86]

The OFT will also not seek a disqualification order against anyone who benefits from a no-action letter. It does not appear that these provisions have been used yet in practice.

The cartel offence is generally considered to have been ineffective.[87] The first, and so far only successful, charges under these provisions were brought in December 2007 against three businessmen accused of dishonestly participating in a cartel to allocate markets and customers, restrict supplies, fix prices and rig bids for the supply of marine hose and ancillary equipment in the UK. This investigation was carried out in cooperation with the US authorities and

---

[83] Enterprise Act 2002, s. 189.

[84] [1982] QB 1053.

[85] OFT, *The Cartel Offence: Guidance on the issue of no action letters* (2003) and OFT, *Leniency and no action* (2008).

[86] Ibid., para. 3.3.

[87] M. Furse, 'The cartel offence – "great for a headline but not much else"?' (2011) 32 *European Competition Law Review* 223 gives an excellent overview of the experience of enforcing the cartel offence.

the European Commission. Under UK law they were convicted and sentenced to terms of imprisonment between two and a half and three years, reduced by around six months on appeal, as well as being disqualified from being directors for between five and seven years.[88] The OFT suffered a major embarrassment when its attempt to prosecute some British Airways executives collapsed in the Crown Court due to problems over the availability of evidence to the defence. Equally problematic has been the fact that the marine hoses and British Airways cases were the only criminal prosecutions that the OFT has brought since the provisions came into force in 2003.

Because of the failure to enforce these provisions, the government's recent consultation on the reform of competition policy devoted a significant amount of discussion to reform of the criminal cartel offence.[89] The government accepted the argument that the problem with the offence was the requirement of dishonesty[90] and it has decided to remove the dishonesty element of the offence and provide that it does not include cartel agreements where the parties have published details of those arrangements before they are implemented.[91] Clause 40 of the Enterprise and Regulatory Reform Bill accomplishes this by simply deleting the word 'dishonesty' from s. 188 and then inserting a new s. 188A. This provides that an individual does not commit an offence if customers are given relevant information about the arrangements before they enter into agreements for the supply of the product or service concerned; for bid-rigging arrangements the person requesting the bids must be given relevant information at or before the time when a bid is made or relevant information is publicised before the arrangements are made in a manner specified by the Secretary of State. What counts as 'relevant information' will be defined in secondary legislation, although this will include the names of the participating undertakings, a description of the arrangements which is sufficient to show why they are or might be arrangements to which s. 188 applies and the products or services covered by the arrangements. The rationale for undertakings to be obliged to publish details of commercial arrangements in order to avoid a criminal prosecution is questionable. It also looks as if the published details will have to be periodically updated, for example, if the membership of the arrangements changes. Broadening the offence in this manner is likely to be unpopular with the business community and may well cause some practical difficulties when it comes to putting the legislation through Parliament. The new provisions are unlikely to have come into force before some time in 2014.

Disqualification of directors

A person may be disqualified from acting as a director by a court after an application from relevant bodies, typically the Insolvency Service but in this context the OFT. Under the Company Directors Disqualification Act 1986, the court must make a disqualification order against a person if an undertaking of which that person was a director commits a breach of competition law[92] and the court considers that that person's conduct makes them unfit to be a director of a company.[93] This sanction only applies to directors of companies, but this

---

[88] See OFT Press Release, 11 June 2008; *The Times*, 14 November 2008; *http://www.oft.gov.uk/about-the-oft/legal-powers/enforcement_regulation/prosecutions/marine-hose* (accessed 18/04/12).

[89] Department of Business, Industry and Skills (BIS), *A Competition Regime for Growth* (2011); BIS, *Growth, Competition and the Competition Regime: Government Response to Consultation* (2012).

[90] A. Stephan, 'How Dishonesty Killed the Cartel Offence' [2011] *Criminal Law Review* 446.

[91] BIS, *Growth, Competition and the Competition Regime: Government Response to Consultation* (2012), para. 7.26.

[92] Breach of the Chapters I and II prohibitions and Articles 101 and 102 TFEU.

[93] Company Directors Disqualification Act 1986, s. 5A.

concept could stretch to include people who act as directors of companies, even though they are not formally appointed as such. In deciding whether a person's conduct makes them unfit to be a director the court must take into account whether their conduct contributed to the breach or, if it did not, whether they had reasonable grounds to suspect that the conduct constituted a breach and did nothing about it, or whether they did not know but ought to have known that the conduct constituted a breach of competition law. Disqualification can be for a maximum period of 15 years and makes it a criminal offence for, among other things, a disqualified person to be a director of a company during that period or to be involved in the management of a company.

This is potentially a very serious sanction and the OFT has given guidance as to when it will seek a disqualification order.[94] There must, first, be a breach of competition law. Typically, this will be through a decision of the OFT, the European Commission or the Courts, although the OFT does not rule out taking action in exceptional cases outside these circumstances. Secondly, the OFT will consider the seriousness of the breach. Typically that will be where a financial penalty has been or would have been imposed. Thirdly, no order will be sought if the undertaking has benefited from the application of the leniency policy. Fourthly, the extent of the director's involvement in the breach must be taken into account, with the OFT saying that it is 'likely' to apply for a disqualification order against a director who was directly involved in the breach or when it considers that the director had reasonable grounds to know about the breach but failed to take corrective action or where the director ought to have known that there was a breach. Finally, the OFT will consider any aggravating or mitigating factors. In lieu of applying for an order, the OFT may accept an undertaking from a director not to act as director of a company.[95] The first use of this power came in relation to the marine hose cartel, discussed above.

COMPETITION LAW IN PRACTICE

Beer and cartels

Background
Luxembourg is one of the smallest countries in the EU but its inhabitants are the second largest consumers of alcohol in the world, per head, according to the World Health Organization.[96] So the price of alcohol is of great public interest. This case concerned an agreement between the five main brewers in Luxembourg with a view to ensuring the mutual observance and protection of beer ties which they imposed on drinks outlets.[97] A beer tie is an exclusive dealing clause by which the owner of the outlet agrees to sell only that brewery's products in return for certain financial advantages.

Commission investigation
The agreement was concluded in 1985 and sent to the European Commission in 2000 by the Belgian parent company, which had recently acquired two of the Luxembourg

➡

---

[94] OFT, *Director Disqualification Order in Competition Cases* (2010), Chapter 4.
[95] Ibid., paras 3.1–3.5.
[96] WHO, *Global Status report on alcohol* (2004).
[97] 'Outlets' was widely defined, including boarding houses, campsites and wholesalers.

companies (remember, at this point the notification system was still in place). The main aim of the agreement was to prevent each of the signatories from poaching one of the other's outlets. In addition, the agreement provided for penalties for its breach, as well as a system of settling disputes. The agreement was terminable with a brewery if it became foreign owned and there were provisions which aimed at protecting the market against incursion by foreign brewers. The European Commission had no difficulty in finding that this agreement had the object of restricting competition between the breweries and making it more difficult for foreign brewers to enter this market. Three of the brewers were fined in total around €450,000 at the end of 2001, while the main two, which were owned by the Belgian company, escaped a fine of €2.5 million because of their cooperation.

Appeal to the GC

The fines were appealed to the GC, the appellants arguing that the agreement had not been examined in its proper context and did not have the object of restricting competition. They argued, among other things, that the purpose of the agreement was to ensure that contracts were adhered to and to deal with the implications of certain decisions by the Luxembourg courts, which had set aside such agreements (not on competition grounds) and created legal problems in this sector. The GC rejected this argument, saying that, 'it is unacceptable for undertakings to attempt to mitigate the effects of legal rules which they consider excessively unfavourable by entering into restrictive arrangements intended to offset those disadvantages on the pretext that they have created an imbalance detrimental to them' and that, 'the conclusion that the Agreement had the object of restricting competition within the common market cannot be invalidated by the supposed fact that it also pursued a legitimate object'.[98]

Other continental European cases

Similar problems in relation to cartels have arisen in other European beer markets. In 2001 the Commission fined four brewers over €91 million for organising cartels on the Belgian beer market.[99] The cartel was involved in price-fixing, market allocation (referred to as respect for each other's market position) and the exchange of information about sales volumes. Unusually, the Chief Executive Officers and other top management of the companies were involved in these practices. One of the companies concerned appealed to the GC, which found that the Commission had not applied its fining guidelines properly and reduced the fine from €44 million to €42.4 million.[100] The company then appealed to the CJEU, which dismissed the appeal.[101]

In 2004, the European Commission found that Heineken and Kronenbourg, at the time the two main French brewers, with around 70% of the market, had breached competition law.[102] Here the two brewers had entered into a so-called 'armistice agreement'

---

[98] Case T-49/02 *Brasserie National* v *Commission* [2005] ECR II-3033 at paras 81 and 85.
[99] See European Commission, Press Release IP/01/1739, 5 December 2001. Belgium is 22nd on the WHO list.
[100] Case T-38/02 *Groupe Danone* v *Commission* [2005] ECR II-4407.
[101] Case C-3/06 *Groupe Danone* v *Commission* [2007] ECR I-1331.
[102] European Commission, Case COMP/C.37.750/B2 *Brasseries Kronenbourg, Brasseries Heineken*, 29 September 2004. France is 7th on the WHO list.

in relation to the acquisition of wholesalers, which was aimed at preventing too much competition over the acquisition of wholesalers and ensuring equal shares in the distribution of their respective beers. The Commission found no evidence that the agreement had been implemented, although there was evidence of contact between the parties and the agreement. The Commission found that this was an agreement having the object of restricting competition and fined the two brewers €2.5 million.

In 2007, the European Commission fined Heineken, Grolsch and Bavaria a total of over €273 million for a cartel on the Dutch beer market.[103] At meetings called 'agenda meeting', 'Catherijne meeting' or 'sliding scale meeting', the brewers coordinated prices, and price increases of beer in the Netherlands, both in the on-trade segment of the market – where consumption is on the premises – and the off-trade market segment – consumption off the premises (mainly sold through supermarkets), including private label beer. Private label beer is either sold under a supermarket chain's own brand, or under a brand name unsupported by advertising.

In the on-trade market segment the brewers coordinated the rebates granted to pubs and bars, which are the main element of pricing, using the 'sliding scale'. Moreover, there was proof that they occasionally coordinated other commercial conditions offered to individual customers in the on-trade segment in the Netherlands, and engaged in customer allocation, both in the on-trade and the off-trade segment.

The Commission had evidence that in all three brewery groups, high-ranking management (such as board members, the managing director and national sales managers) participated in the cartel meetings and discussions. There was also evidence that the companies were aware that their behaviour was illegal and took measures to avoid detection, such as using a panoply of code names and abbreviations to refer to their unofficial meetings and holding these meetings in hotels and restaurants. The companies concerned appealed the decision to the GC. In the *Grolsch* case[104] the GC found that the Commission had not proved the participation of Grolsch in the infringement and annulled the decision as concerned them. In the *Bavaria and Heineken* cases,[105] the GC decided that the length of time taken by the European Commission was excessive, 65 months between the opening of the investigation and the issuing of a statement of objections and 20 months from the statement of objections to the decision. It also decided that it had not been established that Bavaria and Heineken had engaged in occasional coordination to individual customers in the on-trade segment. The fines levied on the undertakings were reduced. Both cases have been appealed.[106]

Analysis

A number of interesting points arise in these cases. The cartel arrangements vary between those which were very explicit, and indeed were embodied in a written agreement, in Luxembourg, to those which were known to be illegal and efforts were made to conceal their existence, in the Netherlands. The Luxembourg cartel is perhaps quite unusual in

---

[103] The Netherlands are 29th on the same list relating to alcohol consumption. See European Commission, Press Release IP/07/509, 18 April 2007. The text of the decision is in Dutch.

[104] Case T-234/07 *Grolsch v Commission*, judgment of 16 September 2011 (GC).

[105] Cases T-235 and 240/07 *Bavaria and Heineken v Commission*, judgments of 16 June 2011.

[106] Cases C-445 and 452/11 P (not yet decided).

its implementation and suggests that, when entered into, the participants did not properly understand the reach of EU competition law. All of these are cartels with the object of restricting competition, which constitutes a breach of Article 101(1) TFEU, even if it pursues another legitimate object (Luxembourg) and even if it is not implemented (France). It is worth noting that in most of these cases the companies concerned have appealed to the European Courts, if only to challenge the level of fines imposed, thus adding more time before the case is ultimately concluded. Finally, it is worth noting that it was some of the cartel participants themselves who drew the attention of the practices to the Commission. Thus, in the Luxembourg case the agreement was notified to the Commission after a change in control of one of the companies and the French case came about because one of the Belgian brewers pointed out that they had modelled their practices on the French market.

The structure of the beer industry in the UK is different from that in continental Europe, in part because of the operation of competition law which placed a limit on the number of pubs that brewers could own. This has led to the rise of the pub company or 'pubco' which controls a number of pubs, either by management or leasing and often involving the obligation to buy particular products. These arrangements and their effects are controversial and, arguably, raise competition issues but not cartel problems.[107] However, one common response to the problem of alcohol-related crime is to call for a minimum price and to ban loss-leading promotions, and this has been adopted as a policy in Scotland.[108] Such a policy could not be implemented by agreement between the companies concerned, as this would be a breach of competition law, but would require government action of some sort. The Scottish Whisky Association has apparently complained to the European Commission about the policy.[109]

Summary

➤ A cartel is a formal agreement among firms in an oligopolistic industry. Cartel members may agree on such matters as prices, total industry output, market shares, allocation of customers, allocation of territories, bid-rigging, establishment of common sales agencies, and the division of profits or a combination of these.

➤ Cartels are unlawful under both EU and UK competition law.

[107] See Business and Enterprise Committee, 'Pub Companies' (2007–08) HC 26; Business, Innovation and Skills Committee, 'Pub Companies' (2010–12) HC 1369; generally see CAMRA at: *http://www.camra.org.uk/beertie* (accessed 05/09/12). The UK is 18th on the WHO list.

[108] See, for example, Home Affairs Select Committee, 'Policing in the 21st Century' (2007–08) HC 364 at para. 124; Scottish Government, 'Changing Scotland's Relationship with Alcohol: A Framework for Action'. Although see *http://news.scotsman.com/alcoholandbingedrinking/Happy-hours-stretch-to-.5620582.jp* for efforts at avoidance (accessed 05/09/12). See now: Alcohol (Minimum Pricing) (Scotland) Act 2012.

[109] See: *http://www.bbc.co.uk/news/uk-scotland-scotland-politics-18898024* (accessed 05/09/12).

➤ Typical types of cartel activity involve:

- price-fixing;
- restrictions on output;
- market sharing;
- collusive tendering or bid-rigging;
- information sharing.

➤ 'Hub and spoke' cartels have been a feature of enforcement activity in the UK.

➤ Participants in cartel activity typically try and conceal their actions.

➤ The European Commission and the OFT operate leniency programmes under which undertakings may obtain complete immunity from fines or a reduction in the penalty if they meet the appropriate conditions.

➤ The European Commission has introduced a settlement procedure for cartel cases. The OFT also operates a similar process, sometimes called 'early resolution'.

➤ It is a criminal offence under UK law for an individual to dishonestly make or agree to make certain arrangements between two undertakings such as price-fixing, market sharing and bid-rigging.

➤ The government plans to remove the dishonesty requirement from the cartel offence.

Further reading

Connor, J., 'Cartels and Antitrust Portrayed', available at *http://www.slideshare.net/jmconnor/cartels-portrayed-1609-presentation?type=presentation* (accessed 17/08/09). *Presents very comprehensive data on cartel enforcement worldwide.*

Department of Justice, 'Lysine cartel', actual footage and recordings of cartel participants in meetings used by the US Department of Justice in a prosecution. Obtained via hidden cameras and recording devices. Available at *http://www.bepress.com/jioe/vol1/iss1/6/* (accessed 18/08/09).

Furse, M., 'The cartel offence – "great for a headline but not much else"?' (2011) 32 *European Competition Law Review* 223. *An excellent overview of the experience of enforcing the cartel offence.*

Harrington, J., 'How do Cartels operate?' *Foundations and Trends in Microeconomics* Vol. 2, No. 1 (2006) 1–105. *Lengthy paper based on Commission cartel cases between 2000 and 2004. Very clear discussion of operational issues.*

Levenstein, M. and Suslow, V., 'What determines cartel success?' available at *http://papers.ssrn.com/sol3/papers.cfm?abstract_id=299415* (accessed 17/08/09). *Paper written in 2002 which surveys the literature on cartels up to that point. Non-technical and very accessible.*

Utton, M., *Cartels and Economic Collusion* (Edward Elgar, Cheltenham, 2011). *Excellent non-technical overview of the issues surrounding cartels by an economist. Limited legal analysis, although includes sections on fining policy and leniency.*

9 Horizontal cooperation arrangements

Chapter outline

This chapter discusses:

➤ Horizontal agreements which may be pro-competitive or neutral and their treatment under Article 101 TFEU

➤ The general approach taken by the European Commission to such agreements

➤ The treatment of:

- information exchanges
- research and development agreements
- Production agreements
- purchasing agreements
- commercialisation agreements, and
- standardisation agreements.

Introduction

In the previous chapter agreements between competitors which were clearly damaging to the competitive process, cartels, were examined. However, not all agreements between competitors ('horizontal agreements') are necessarily so damaging. One reason for entering such an agreement might be to improve efficiency. So, for example, two undertakings may produce the same product in two different factories, both operating at 50% capacity. If they were to combine their operations, and only use one factory, then their production costs would be lower, and they might also engage in joint distribution to further lower their costs. If the market for the product remained competitive, and they had spare capacity in the one remaining factory, they would have an incentive to lower prices to consumers in order to gain more market share and greater profits. The difficulty lies in distinguishing a situation where the efficiencies outweigh the damage to competition. Consider the above example, but where the two undertakings had 40% market shares each. What would be their incentive to lower prices if they combined their operations? Would the combination of operations make it more difficult for new entrants on to the market? The other difficulty is in finding a set of rules and procedures which will identify agreements which are beneficial, without being too costly to administer by either the European Commission or the undertakings concerned. On this point, cooperation between undertakings may take a variety of forms. One particular type, referred to as a full function joint venture, falls to be examined under the European Merger Control Regulation (discussed in Chapter 13). Broadly speaking, this is where what is proposed has the characteristics of a merger of operations between undertakings, rather than an agreement between them. Such an operation will have to be notified to the European Commission which will be obliged to make a decision on it within a relatively brief timescale. Where cooperation between undertakings does not fall within the Merger Regulation, Regulation 1/2003 has removed the notification procedure which means that undertakings must initially make their own assessment of agreements which they have entered into or wish to enter into.

European Commission Guidelines on horizontal cooperation agreements

For the purposes of this chapter, the treatment of horizontal agreements under Article 101 TFEU will be examined and the material discussed earlier (see Chapter 2) should be recalled. The European Commission[1] has produced rules on horizontal agreements which are found in a general set of Guidelines (hereafter 'Guidelines on Horizontal Agreements') and two block exemptions for agreements on specialisation and research and development.[2] Three questions need to be asked about these rules. First, are they sufficiently clear for undertakings to know whether their agreements fall inside or outside them? Secondly, do the rules, in substance, deter undertakings from entering into pro-competitive or neutral agreements? Thirdly, and alternatively, are they likely to allow undertakings to enter into agreements which are anti-competitive? The Guidelines are focused on the most common types of horizontal agreements:

- Information exchanges,
- research and development (R&D),
- production,
- purchasing,
- commercialisation, and
- standardisation agreements.[3]

For Article 101 TFEU to apply to agreements, they must affect trade between Member States and must have an appreciable effect on competition, which, in terms of horizontal agreements,

---

[1] Agreements that benefit from the block exemptions, or would do if they affected inter-state trade, would have a parallel exemption under UK law. There have been few decisions on horizontal agreements under the Competition Act 1998 and those have involved very specific arrangements: e.g. OFT, 'Memorandum of Understanding on the Supply of Oil Fuels in an Emergency' (2001).

[2] European Commission, *Guidelines on the applicability of Article 101 TFEU to horizontal co-operation agreements*, OJ C11, 14.01.2011, p. 1; European Commission Regulation (EC) No. 1218/2010 on the application of Article 101(3) TFEU to categories of specialisation agreements, OJ L335, 18.12.2010, p. 43; European Commission Regulation (EC) No. 1217/2010 on the application of Article 101(3) TFEU to categories of research and development agreements, OJ L335, 18.12.2010, p. 36.

[3] Guidelines on Horizontal Agreements (n. 2), para. 5.

means that if they are below a threshold of a 10% market share and do not contain restrictions relating to price-fixing, limitation of outputs or sales or the allocation of markets or customers within the agreement, then they escape the prohibition in Article 101(1) TFEU and there is no need to consider the Guidelines on Horizontal Agreements or the specific block exemption Regulations.[4]

When analysing horizontal agreements, assuming that they have an appreciable effect on competition, the following questions need to be asked:

1 Does the agreement fall within Article 101(1) TFEU? If yes, then

2 Are the block exemption criteria met? (R&D and specialisation agreements only.) If no, then,

3 Does the agreement meet the criteria in Article 101(3) TFEU for an exemption? (See Box 9.1 for the criteria.)

KEY LEGAL PROVISION   Box 9.1

Article 101(3) TFEU criteria for an individual exemption[5]

The agreement must:

Contribute to improving the production or distribution of goods or to promoting technical or economic progress (economic benefits);

While allowing consumers a fair share of the resulting benefit, and it must not (fair share for consumers);

Impose on the undertakings concerned restrictions which are not indispensable to the attainment of these objectives (indispensability);

Afford such undertakings the possibility of eliminating competition in respect of a substantial part of the products in question (no elimination of competition).

Question: Remember that these conditions are cumulative and exhaustive. What sort of evidence would be needed to make a case?

The Guidelines offer some basic principles for analysis, followed by a description of how they should be applied to specific types of agreements. As regards the first question, the Guidelines take a standard approach, distinguishing between agreements with the object of restricting competition and those that have the effect of restricting competition. The former are those which by their very nature have the potential to restrict competition. As regards the latter, it must have an appreciable adverse impact on one of the parameters of competition, such as price, quality or output. Whether the agreement will have a restrictive effect must be judged against the economic or legal context that would have existed in the absence of the agreement.

---

[4] European Commission 'Notice on agreements of minor importance which do not appreciably restrict competition under Article 81(1)' OJ C368, 22.12.2001, p. 13.
[5] The text of Article 101(3) TFEU has been edited for the purposes of this box. Words in brackets are common shorthand used by the Commission for each of the conditions.

This means that horizontal cooperation agreements between competitors that, on the basis of objective factors, would not be able to independently carry out the project or activity covered by the cooperation, for instance due to the limited technical capabilities of the parties, will normally not give rise to restrictive effects on competition within the meaning of Article 101(1) unless the parties could have carried out the project with less stringent restrictions.[6]

The Guidelines go on to try to explain in what circumstances an agreement may have the effect of restricting competition. This requires looking at the nature and content of the agreement, as well as the market power of the parties and the characteristics of the market. In terms of horizontal agreements, these may have the effect of restricting competition through limiting the competition between parties or through reducing independent decision making either through requiring a sharing of assets or financial interests.[7] In addition, such an agreement may lead to a sharing of strategic information either between the parties or wider or ensure that they achieve commonality of costs.[8] Whether the parties have market power is a matter that needs assessment. The Guidelines contain some 'safe harbours' as regards market shares, discussed below, as does the *de minimis* guidance.[9] The Commission does, however, say that the threshold for a finding of market power in an Article 101 TFEU case is less than that required in an Article 102 TFEU case or, to put it another way, undertakings with market shares between 10 and 39% of a market must consider themselves at risk of being found to have suitable levels of market power.[10]

If an agreement falls within Article 101(1) TFEU, it may qualify for an exemption if it meets the Article 101(3) TFEU criteria (as discussed in Chapter 2). In this context, the Commission makes the point that the block exemption Regulations on specialisation and R&D are premised on the idea that the combination of complementary skills can be the source of efficiencies; therefore, horizontal cooperation agreements which do not involve complementary skills or assets are less likely to lead to efficiencies.[11]

Although the Guidelines categorise horizontal agreements, they also recognise that, in practice, commercial arrangements do not necessarily fall into such clear categorisation. For example, a research and development agreement may also include provisions relating to the production of products developed through the research and development side of the agreement. In these circumstances, the Guidelines say that when particular parts of them contain 'graduated messages', such as a safe harbour or an assessment of whether something has the object or effect of restricting competition, then what is set out in that section of the guidelines applying to that part of the operation which can be considered its 'centre of gravity' applies to the whole operation.[12] Two factors are relevant for determining the centre of gravity: the starting point of the cooperation and the degree of integration of the different functions.[13] To take the example of a research and development venture combined with subsequent production, if production can only take place if the research and development is successful, then this places the centre of gravity as research and development, whereas if the production

---

[6] Guidelines on Horizontal Agreements (n. 2) at para. 30.
[7] Ibid., para. 33.
[8] Ibid., para. 35.
[9] European Commission 'Notice on agreements of minor importance which do not appreciably restrict competition under Article 81(1)' OJ C368, 22.12.2001, p. 13.
[10] Guidelines on Horizontal Agreements (n. 2) at para. 42.
[11] Ibid. paras 50–53.
[12] Ibid. para. 13.
[13] Ibid. para. 14.

is going to take place in any event, then this places its centre of gravity as a production agreement.

In discussing horizontal agreements, this chapter follows the structure set out in the Guidelines and discusses the block exemption Regulations within the appropriate categories set out in the Guidelines.

Information exchanges

The first part of the Guidelines discusses information exchanges, which have already been touched on (see Chapter 8), in the context of cartels. The Commission sees three common means of sharing information: between the parties, through a common agency, such as a trade association, or through a third party, for example a marketing agency.[14] An information exchange can only be caught under Article 101 TFEU if it constitutes an agreement, decision or a concerted practice. A concerted practice may arise where only one undertaking discloses information, as this may reduce strategic uncertainty and increase risks of collusion.[15] One instance may constitute a concerted practice.[16] Genuinely public announcements will not constitute concerted practices.

As regards the restriction of competition by object, the Commission takes the view that information exchanges of individualised data between competitors on intended future prices and quantities should be treated as restrictions of competition by object and will in fact be treated as cartels.[17] As regards information exchanges having the effect of restricting competition, this will depend in part on the characteristics of the market, although the information exchange may change these characteristics. According to the Commission, 'Companies are more likely to achieve a collusive outcome in markets which are sufficiently transparent, concentrated, non-complex, stable and symmetric.'[18] The Commission goes on to make the point that collusion is more likely among companies that recognise that they will continue to operate on the market together for a long time. In addition, there needs to be a credible threat of retaliation if collusion is to be maintained.[19]

The Guidelines also contain discussion of the type of information that will be more or less problematic. At the top of the list is strategic data, for example pricing data, customer lists, production costs, quantities, turnover, sales and capacity, among other things.[20] Genuinely aggregated data is less likely to lead to restrictive effects than individualised company data. Generally, swapping aggregated data, unless it occurs in a tight oligopoly, is not likely, according to the Commission, to lead to a restriction on competition.[21] Historical data is likely to be less of a problem than contemporary data, as is the exchange of genuinely public information.[22]

The information exchange is more likely to be problematic if the companies exchanging information cover a sufficiently large part of the market. What this means depends on the

[14] Ibid. para. 55.
[15] Ibid. para. 62.
[16] As in Case C-8/08 *T-Mobile Netherlands* [2009] ECR I-4529 where there was one meeting.
[17] Guidelines on Horizontal Agreements (n. 2) at para. 74.
[18] Ibid. para. 77.
[19] Ibid. paras 84 and 85.
[20] Ibid. para. 86.
[21] Ibid. para. 89.
[22] Ibid. paras 90, 92 and 93.

context, but the Commission's view is that where an information exchange takes place in the context of another type of horizontal cooperation agreement and does not go beyond what is necessary for its implementation, market coverage below the market share thresholds set out in the relevant part of the Guidelines, the relevant block exemption regulation or the *de minimis* Notice pertaining to the type of agreement in question will usually not be large enough for the information exchange to give rise to restrictive effects on competition.[23] Frequent exchanges of information are considered to increase the risks of collusion.[24] Information exchange which takes place publicly, that is, so all competitors and customers also have access to it, will reduce the risks of collusion, although the Commission warns that even genuinely public exchanges of information may lead to collusive outcomes.[25]

Even if the information exchange is restrictive of competition it may still qualify for an exemption under Article 101(3) TFEU if it meets the criteria and the Commission devotes some space in the Guidelines to discussing this issue. Information exchange can lead to efficiency gains through benchmarking, allowing companies to direct production to high demand areas, provide customers with incentives to change behaviour (for example, through the exchange of credit data) and genuinely public information can help consumers make a more informed choice.[26] The restrictions must be necessary to achieve the efficiency gains, the benefits must be passed on to consumers and there must be no elimination of competition.[27]

What is evident from this discussion is that information exchange can cover a wide range of practices, from those which constitute a cartel to others which are much more benign, indeed, pro-competitive. Perhaps because of the wide range of practices caught under this heading, the Guidelines do not provide clear safe harbours or market share thresholds. They do provide some general guidance but the clear message is that all such information exchanges have to be assessed in their context.

Research and development (R&D) agreements

For the purposes of the block exemption, R&D agreements are divided into two types, with two stages: joint R&D or paid-for R&D (that is, where the R&D is contracted out) and the two stages are the actual research and development and the exploitation of the resulting products.[28] The Commission's Guidelines make the point that R&D agreements can affect competition in three ways; through affecting competition on existing product markets, on existing technology markets and also in relation to the market for innovation. As regards the last point, the example is given of the pharmaceutical industry, where it is said that the process of innovation is structured in such a way that it is possible to identify so-called 'R&D poles', that is, efforts directed towards a new product or technology and the substitutes for that R&D. So the question here would be whether, after an agreement, there were sufficient numbers of R&D poles left.[29] Where there is not such a clear structure, the Commission says that it will limit its investigation to the existing product and/or technology markets.[30]

[23] Ibid. para. 88.
[24] Ibid. para. 91.
[25] Ibid. para. 94.
[26] Ibid. paras 95–100.
[27] Ibid. paras 101–104.
[28] Block Exemption on R&D Agreements (n. 2), Article 1(a).
[29] Guidelines on Horizontal Agreements (n. 2) at para. 120.
[30] Ibid. para. 122.

How the market should be defined in relation to R&D and new technology markets has been a matter of some controversy,[31] but the Guidelines stick to a conventional approach, although recognising that there is a distinction between existing markets and competition for innovation. If the agreement aims at improving or replacing existing products, then the starting point for analysis is the sales of existing products. If, however, the agreement is about creating a completely new product, then the analysis will be based on the effects on competition in innovation.[32] Where agreements fall between these two extremes, then the analysis will have to cover both aspects.[33]

What sort of R&D agreements might fall within Article 101(1) TFEU? Agreements between competing undertakings are eligible for the benefit of the block exemption, provided that their combined market share does not exceed 25%. This does not, however, mean that an agreement between competitors, where the combined market share is above 25%, automatically falls within Article 101(1). The Commission's view is that there is no absolute threshold above which an R&D agreement creates market power and therefore can be presumed to have restrictive effects on competition, although the stronger the position of the parties on the markets, the more likely this is.[34] The Commission's view is that most R&D agreements do not fall within Article 101(1), especially where the agreement is in relation to 'pure' R&D without covering the exploitation of the results. The Commission makes a distinction in general terms between 'pure' R&D agreements and those where there is joint production, marketing or licensing of the improved products where there must be a closer scrutiny of the effects on competition. If the R&D agreement is concentrated on producing an entirely new product, then the analysis shifts on to whether or not there is an effect on markets for innovation. The view is taken that this is unlikely to lead to a restriction on competition unless only a limited number of credible R&D poles exist.[35] Insofar as agreements combine elements of improving existing products and creating new ones, both aspects must be investigated. Even if the agreement has a negative effect on competition, it will still be possible to gain an exemption if either the conditions under the block exemption or under Article 101(3) TFEU are met.

For agreements where the parties are competitors, and their combined market share is below 25%, the block exemption for R&D agreements may be available.[36] It applies to agreements which relate to the conditions under which those undertakings entering into the agreements pursue:

1 joint research and development of contract products or contract technologies and joint exploitation of the results of that research and development;

2 joint exploitation of the results of research and development of contract products or contract technologies jointly carried out pursuant to a prior agreement between the same parties;

---

[31] See, for example, D. Teece and M. Coleman, 'The meaning of monopoly: Antitrust analysis in high-technology industries' (1998) *The Antitrust Bulletin* 801; C. Ahlborn, D. Evans and A. Padilla, 'Competition Policy in the New Economy: Is European Competition Law up to the Challenge?' (2001) 22 *European Competition Law Review* 156; C. Veljanovski, 'EC Antitrust in the New Economy: Is the European Commission's View of the Network Economy Right?' (2001) 22 *European Competition Law Review* 115.

[32] Guidelines on Horizontal Agreements (n. 2) at paras 123–6.

[33] Ibid. para. 112.

[34] Ibid. paras 134–5.

[35] Ibid. para. 138.

[36] Where the parties are not competitors, the exemption applies for the duration of the R&D.

3 joint research and development of contract products or contract technologies excluding joint exploitation of the results;

4 paid-for research and development of contract products or contract technologies and joint exploitation of the results of that research and development;

5 joint exploitation of the results of paid-for research and development of contract products or contract technologies pursuant to a prior agreement between the same parties; or

6 paid-for research and development of contract products or contract technologies excluding joint exploitation of the results.[37]

In addition to the market share thresholds, the Regulation also sets out certain other criteria that have to be met for the agreement to benefit from the block exemption. First, the agreement must stipulate that the parties to it have full access to the final results for the purpose of further R&D or exploitation. However, parties which specialise in either exploitation or research may limit their access to the results for these purposes. There may be provisions in the agreement providing that the parties have to pay for access to the results, but such payments must not be so high as to effectively impede access. Secondly, where the agreement relates to joint R&D or contract R&D access must be granted to the pre-existing know-how of the other party, if that is indispensable to the exploitation of the results. Again, this may have to be paid for, so long as the payments are not such as to effectively impede access. Thirdly, any joint exploitation may only pertain to results which are protected by intellectual property rights or constitute know-how and which are indispensable for the manufacture of the contract products or the application of the contract technologies. Finally, parties that manufacture the products by way of specialisation must be required to fulfil orders from those products from other parties, unless there is joint distribution or the parties have agreed that only the party manufacturing the products may distribute them.[38] In addition, the exemption does not apply to agreements which have as their object a number of things, referred to as 'hard-core restrictions'. There are seven:[39]

- the restriction of the freedom of the parties to carry out research and development independently or in cooperation with third parties in a field unconnected with that to which the research and development agreement relates or, after its completion, in the field to which it relates or in a connected field;
- limitation of output or sales except for:
  - the setting of production and sales targets,
  - practices constituting specialisation, and
  - restricting the freedom of the parties to manufacture, sell, assign or license products, technologies or processes which compete with the contract products or technologies during the period the parties have agreed to jointly exploit the results;
- price-fixing for selling or licensing (excepting certain joint arrangements);
- restriction of passive sales by customer or territory with the exception of the requirement to exclusively license results to another party;

[37] European Commission Regulation (EC) No. 1217/2010 on the application of Article 101(3) TFEU to categories of research and development agreements, OJ L335, 18.12.2010, p. 36, Art. 1.
[38] Ibid. Art. 3.
[39] Ibid. Art. 5.

- restriction of active sales to customers or territories not exclusively allocated to the parties;

- a requirement to refuse to meet demand from customers in the parties' respective territories or form customers otherwise allocated to the parties;

- a requirement to make it difficult for customers to meet their demands from other resellers.

In addition, Article 6 says that the benefit of the block exemption will not extend to certain obligations placed in agreements, referred to as excluded restrictions. These are prohibitions on challenging the validity of the intellectual property rights and the requirement not to grant licences to third parties to manufacture the contract products or to apply the contract processes unless the exploitation by at least one of the parties of the results of the joint research and development is provided for and takes place in the internal market. Outside the block exemption, an individual exemption is possible if the criteria of Article 101(3) TFEU are met but the Commission suggests that any agreement containing the individual clauses listed in Article 5 of the block exemption Regulation will make an individual exemption less likely and it will generally be necessary for the parties to the agreement to show that such restrictions are indispensable to the cooperation.[40]

Production agreements

Production agreements are the next major category, and three main types can be distinguished:

1 joint production agreements, whereby the parties agree to produce certain products jointly, possibly through a joint venture;

2 specialisation agreements (unilateral or reciprocal), whereby the parties agree unilaterally or reciprocally to cease production of a product and to purchase it from the other party; and

3 subcontracting agreements whereby one party (the 'contractor') entrusts to another party (the 'subcontractor') the production of a product.[41]

The Commission makes the point that, in general, agreements which involve price-fixing, limiting output or sharing markets or customers have the object of restricting competition. In relation to production agreements, it feels that there are two exceptions to this: first, where the parties agree on the output directly concerned by the production agreement, provided that the other parameters of competition are not eliminated and, secondly, a production agreement that also provides for the joint distribution of the jointly manufactured products envisages the joint setting of the sales prices for those products, and only those products, provided that that restriction is necessary for producing jointly, meaning that the parties would not otherwise have an incentive to enter into the production agreement in the first place.[42] In these circumstances, the question is whether such agreements have the *effect* of restricting competition.

Deciding whether a production agreement has the effect of restricting competition depends on the characteristics of the market and what would have happened if the agreement had not been entered into (the so-called counter-factual). In particular, if the agreement gives

---

[40] Guidelines on Horizontal Agreements (n. 2) at para. 142.
[41] Ibid. at paras 150–54.
[42] Ibid. at para. 160.

rise to a new market or product that the parties were unable to do without the cooperation, such an agreement will not be restrictive of competition.[43] The Commission also makes the point that production agreements, which also involve commercialisation functions, such as joint distribution and marketing, carry a higher risk of restricting competition because this usually involves the joint setting of prices, which carries the highest risk for competition.[44] A key question for considering restrictive effects is whether the parties have market power. If they do not have market power, then restrictive effects are unlikely. The starting point for this analysis is the market share of the parties and the Commission's view is based on the specialisation Regulation, which states that certain agreements can have the benefit of the block exemption if the combined market share of the parties is below 20%. The Commission takes the view that the same approach can be taken to horizontal subcontracting agreements with the aim of increasing production: if the market share of the parties does not exceed 20%, it is unlikely market power exists.[45] The Commission suggests that market shares which are slightly above 20% may not be a concern if the market is not highly concentrated.[46] The question that the Commission addresses is whether the market is highly concentrated and how dynamic it is, that is, how frequently is there entry and how often do market positions change?

The Commission is particularly concerned with agreements that directly limit competition between parties and those that might lead to collusive outcomes. In relation to the former, it gives as an example, that the parties to a production joint venture could, for instance, limit the output of the joint venture compared to what the parties would have brought to the market if each of them had decided their output on their own.[47] As regards the latter, it is particularly concerned with agreements that increase the commonality of the costs of the parties participating in them. The problem is greatest for the Commission where production costs constitute a large proportion of the variable costs of the product or where there is joint production of an intermediate product, or a horizontal subcontracting relationship that accounts for a large proportion of the variable costs of the final product with respect to which the parties compete downstream.[48] The Commission also recognises that information exchanges between competitors may give rise to collusive outcomes.[49]

Agreements below the market share threshold will benefit from the block exemption regulation provided that they do not include clauses which fix prices, limit output or sales and allocate markets or customers.[50] Agreements above the threshold may, in principle, be exempted under Article 101(3) TFEU, provided that they meet the conditions for exemption.[51]

Joint purchasing agreements

The next category of agreements dealt with by the Guidelines is joint purchasing agreements. This type of agreement arises where two or more parties find it useful to combine their buying

---

[43] Ibid. para. 163.
[44] Ibid. para. 167.
[45] Ibid. para. 169.
[46] Ibid. para. 170.
[47] Ibid. para. 174.
[48] Ibid. paras 178–80.
[49] Ibid. paras 181–82.
[50] European Commission Regulation (EC) No. 1218/2010 on the application of Article 101(3) TFEU to categories of specialisation agreements, OJ L335, 18.12.2010, p. 43, Art. 5.
[51] Guidelines on Horizontal Agreements (n. 2) paras 183–86.

power: for example, if they buy a greater quantity together, they can get a better price. An example would be a group of farmers banding together to buy fertiliser and seeds. It is clear that, in general, joint purchasing agreements will fall under Article 101(1) TFEU because they will have an effect on competition. Whether that effect is negative will depend on the context of the agreement. In terms of these agreements, the Commission points out that there are two markets which have to be considered: first, the relevant purchasing market; and, secondly, the downstream market where the relevant purchasers are active as sellers.[52] The combination of the purchasers may create competition problems where the purchasers have market power on the selling markets or where they are able to use their buying power to foreclose competitors' access to efficient suppliers.[53] The problem for the Commission for these arrangements is if they facilitate collusion between the parties on the selling market, either because of common costs or exchanging commercially sensitive information.[54] The Commission takes the view that market power is unlikely to exist if the parties to the agreement have a combined market share of below 15% on the purchasing market(s) as well as a combined market share of below 15% on the selling market(s).[55] Below these thresholds the conditions of Article 101(3) TFEU are likely to apply and, again, in principle above these thresholds an exemption is available.

Commercialisation agreements

Commercialisation agreements have been more controversial. These are agreements which involve cooperation between competitors in the selling, distribution or promotion of their products, of which perhaps the best-known example is the joint selling of broadcasting packages by various football leagues in Europe. As the Commission points out, agreements limited to joint selling have, as the rule, the object and effect of coordinating the pricing policy of competing manufacturers as well as controlling the output of the participants.[56] They therefore fall under Article 101(1) TFEU. If they fall short of joint selling, then the Commission has two major potential concerns. The first is the opportunity provided for the exchange of sensitive commercial information; and the second is, depending on the cost structure of the commercialisation, a significant input to the parties' final cost may be common.[57] Where, however, the parties have a combined market share of below 15%, then those agreements which do not involve price-fixing will not be considered by the Commission to fall within Article 101(1) TFEU. Again, in principle, commercialisation agreements may be exempt under Article 101(3) TFEU, although the Commission makes it clear that in general price-fixing cannot be justified. Claimed efficiencies must be demonstrated and must result from the integration of economic activities, rather than from the elimination of costs which are inherently part of competition. The example given by the Commission is that of reducing transport costs by customer allocation, rather than integration of logistical systems.

---

[52] Ibid. para. 197.
[53] Ibid. at paras 200–204.
[54] Ibid. paras 213–216.
[55] Ibid. at para. 208.
[56] Ibid. at para. 143.
[57] Ibid. at para. 146.

Agreements on standards[58]

Agreements on standards are a particularly important part of a modern economy, which may relate to a number of different issues. These agreements deal with the technical or quality requirements of products and are particularly important where products have to be compatible or interoperability is required. For example, the same SIM card can be used in a number of different mobile phones. Although the Commission is generally positive about the effects of standard setting agreements, it also identifies a number of potential problems.

The Commission's Guidelines make the point that standard setting agreements can have effects on four possible markets:[59]

1 The product or service market to which the standard relates.

2 Where standard setting involves the selection of technology and the marketing of IP rights, the technology market may be affected.

3 The market for standard setting may be affected if there are different standard setting bodies.

4 A market for testing and certification may be affected.

The Commission identifies three main potential risks to competition through standard setting: a reduction in price competition, foreclosure of innovative technologies and the exclusion of or discrimination against certain companies through refusing to allow them access to the standard.[60] Agreements which are either part of a wider arrangement to exclude competitors or a disguised means of price-fixing will constitute, in the Commission's opinion, agreements with the object of restricting competition and will thus be in breach of Article 101(1).[61] For other types of agreements, the question will be whether they have the effect of restricting competition. If the agreement does not create market power, then it is not capable of producing restrictive effects on competition. In the context of standardisation agreements, the Commission does not give any precise guidance as to what constitutes market power. Broadly speaking, market power in the context of an Article 101(1) agreement may occur when the parties' combined market share is less than a dominant position, but more than the thresholds in the *de minimis* Notice, that is, between 10% and 40%. For agreements within and above this range, if they meet certain conditions, they will normally be considered to fall outside Article 101(1). The conditions are that:

> . . . participation in standard-setting is **unrestricted** and the procedure for adopting the standard in question is **transparent**, standardisation agreements which contain **no obligation to comply** with the standard and provide **access to the standard on fair, reasonable and non-discriminatory terms** will normally not restrict competition within the meaning of Article 101(1).[62]

A key part of these requirements is that that there is access to the standard and any relevant IP rights on fair, reasonable and non-discriminatory (FRAND) terms, although this will require some provision amongst the participants for ensuring that the prices charged are reasonable.

---

[58] Generally, see D. Geradin and M. Rato, 'Can standard-setting lead to exploitative abuse? A dissonant view on patent hold-up, royalty stacking and the meaning of FRAND' (2007) 3 *European Competition Journal* 101.

[59] Guidelines on Horizontal Agreements (n. 2) at para. 261.

[60] Ibid. para. 264.

[61] Ibid. paras 273–4.

[62] Ibid. para. 280 (emphasis in original).

The Commission also accepts that there may be standardisation agreements which do not meet this model but nevertheless do not have a restrictive effect on competition. There are a number of factors here that the Commission says it would consider, such as the market share of the goods or services affected by the standardisation agreement, access to the standard, openness of the standard setting process and whether or not participants are free to develop alternative standards or products.[63] A final point is that standard setting agreements providing for *ex ante* disclosures of most restrictive licensing terms, will not, in principle, restrict competition within the meaning of Article 101(1).[64]

This normally applies to standards applied by recognised standards bodies, such as the British Standards Institute. Agreements on standards are clearly a problem where they are part of a broader restrictive agreement which is aimed at excluding actual or potential competitors. Outside these situations, they may create problems depending on the extent to which parties are free to develop alternative products or standards that do not comply with the agreed standard. Unlike other horizontal agreements, high market shares are not necessarily a concern because for standard setting to be effective good coverage of the industry is needed. They will be a concern where the standards discriminate against third parties, or prevent their access to the market, or segment markets on a geographical basis.[65] Again, such standards may benefit from an exemption under Article 101(3) TFEU.

This section of the Guidelines also sets out the concerns that the Commission may have with standard terms. They may, in the appropriate circumstances, limit product choice and innovation, restrict price competition or restrict access to an industry if they become standard practice.[66] Determining whether they are restrictive of competition requires assessing them in the light of the appropriate economic context and the market conditions. The Commission's view is that as long as participation in the actual establishment of standard terms is unrestricted for the competitors in the relevant market (either by participation in the trade association or directly), and the established standard terms are non-binding and effectively accessible for anyone, such agreements are not likely to give rise to restrictive effects on competition.[67] The Commission does, however, suggest that it will look more closely at standard terms which limit product choice or are an important part of the transaction for the consumer and, if the terms are binding, their effect on product quality, choice and innovation.[68]

Conclusions on horizontal arrangements

As can be seen from the discussion above, there is a wide variety of horizontal agreements which are seen as pro-competitive or, at worst, as neutral and therefore should not be caught by competition law. The Commission's Guidelines recognise that the assessment of such agreements can only sensibly take place by examining their economic context but, at the same time, they attempt to define an area where an in-depth assessment is not needed using market shares as a proxy for market power. We should note, however, that the inclusion of

---

[63] Ibid. paras 292–99.
[64] Ibid. para. 299.
[65] Ibid. at para. 168.
[66] Ibid. paras 270–72.
[67] Ibid. para. 301.
[68] Ibid. paras 302–307.

certain clauses in an agreement, such as price-fixing, output limitation or market or customer allocation, will mean that the Commission will consider the agreement in breach of competition law, almost regardless of market power. It is interesting, however, to compare the differences in market thresholds for different types of agreement, set out below in Box 9.2, while bearing in mind that for vertical agreements (discussed in Chapter 11) the threshold is 30% and so is more generous.

KEY LEGAL PROVISION   Box 9.2

Market share thresholds for horizontal cooperation agreements

R&D agreements:	25%
Production agreements:	20%
Purchasing agreements:	15% on purchasing and selling markets
Commercialisation agreements:	15%
Standardisation agreements:	'high market shares . . . will not necessarily lead to the conclusion that the standard is likely to give rise to restrictive effects on competition'

Source: European Commission Regulation (EC) No. 1218/2010 on the application of Article 101(3) TFEU to categories of specialisation agreements, OJ L335, 18.12.2010, p. 43, Art. 3; European Commission Regulation (EC) No. 1217/2010 on the application of Article 101(3) TFEU to categories of research and development agreements, OJ L335, 18.12.2010, p. 36, Art. 4; Guidelines on Horizontal Agreements (n. 2) at paras 169, 208, 240, 296.

Questions: Why are the market share thresholds lower for horizontal than vertical agreements? Why are there different thresholds for different types of agreements?

Summary

➤ Horizontal agreements are regulated under Article 101(1) TFEU. The Commission has issued Guidelines on their treatment as well as block exemptions for research and development agreements and specialisation agreements.

➤ Information exchanges need to be assessed in their context considering the market position of the parties and the type of information being exchanged.

➤ The Commission's view is that most research and development agreements do not fall within Article 101(1).

➤ Research and development agreements between competitors may benefit from a block exemption provided that their combined market share is below 25% and the agreement does not contain any hard-core restrictions.

➤ Specialisation agreements may benefit from a block exemption provided that the combined market share of the parties is not above 20% and the agreement does not contain any hard-core restrictions.

➤ Horizontal subcontracting agreements with the aim of increasing production are not seen to be restrictive of competition by the Commission if the parties combined market share is below 20%.

➤ The Commission takes the view that market power is unlikely to exist in purchasing agreements where the market share of the parties is below 15% on the purchasing and selling markets.

➤ Commercialisation agreements where the parties have a combined market share of below 15% will not be considered by the Commission to fall within Article 101(1) TFEU.

➤ Standard setting agreements will normally be considered to fall outside Article 101(1) if participation in standard setting is unrestricted and the procedure for adopting the standard in question is transparent, there is no obligation to comply with the standard and the agreement provides access to the standard on fair, reasonable and non-discriminatory terms.

Further reading

Official literature

European Commission, *Guidelines on the applicability of Article 101 TFEU to horizontal co-operation agreements*, OJ C11, 14.01.2011, p. 1.

European Commission Regulation (EC) No. 1218/2010 on the application of Article 101(3) TFEU to categories of specialisation agreements, OJ L335, 18.12.2010, p. 43.

European Commission Regulation (EC) No. 1217/2010 on the application of Article 101(3) TFEU to categories of research and development agreements, OJ L335, 18.12.2010, p. 36.

Journal articles

Bennett, M. and Collins, P., 'The Law and Economics of Information Sharing: The good, the bad and the ugly' (2010) 6 *European Competition Journal* 311. *Excellent discussion by two OFT officials of the issues around information exchanges.*

Seitz, C., 'One Step in the Right Direction – The New Horizontal Guidelines and the Restated Block Exemption Regulations' (2011) 2 *European Journal of Competition Law & Practice* 452. *Clear explanation and discussion of the Guidelines and the block exemptions.*

10 The control of oligopolies

The economic problem: the prisoner's dilemma

Cartels are in a sense the 'easy' part of enforcing competition law because it is clear that they are harmful and that they are prohibited. The difficult part is discovering their existence and proving that they have been in operation and then dealing with the appeals against penalties. There is, however, an issue that is more difficult, which arises from oligopolistic market structures.

In a market where there are few firms (which is referred to as an oligopoly), for example between four and ten, these firms will be aware of each other and also that the decisions they each make on price, quantity and quality will affect their performance. In other words, they all have some level of market power and, for example, if one firm lowers its prices it will take market share from the other firms. Equally, if only one firm raises its prices, it will lose market share to the others, all things remaining equal. At the extremes, such industries can be either highly competitive or have outcomes very similar to a cartel.

A way of understanding the outcomes is to think of the firms as being subject to the prisoner's dilemma. In its simplified version, this is where there are two prisoners, held separately, who cannot communicate with each other, who are each charged with a crime and they may either confess or remain silent. If one confesses and the other does not, then the one who confesses is freed and the other is sent to jail for ten years. If they both confess, they each get five-year prison terms. If neither confess, they cannot be found guilty. The situation is illustrated in Table 10.1.

The outcome for each prisoner thus depends on what the other one does; and game theory,[1] a branch of mathematics often used in economics, tells us that, in these circumstances of

---

[1] A good, relatively non-technical introduction is A. Dixit and B. Nalebuff, *The Art of Strategy* (W.W. Norton 2008, London).

Table 10.1 The prisoner's dilemma

	Confess	Don't confess	
Prisoner A	5, 5	0, 10	Confess
Prisoner B	10, 0	0, 0	Don't confess

Table 10.2 Profit and the prisoner's dilemma

	High Price	Low Price	
Company A	6, 6	2, 10	High Price
Company B	10, 2	2, 2	Low Price

uncertainty, the best move for either prisoner to make is to confess because that provides the least worst outcome, no matter what the other prisoner does. This idea can be adapted for an oligopolistic market with the outcomes being measured in profit, which would produce Table 10.2.

In this scenario, it is evident that it is worth charging the low price, if your competitor charges the high price, because you sell more and obtain a higher profit. If both companies charge a low price, they obtain low profits. If both charge high prices, they obtain the same level of profit, above that from both charging lower prices. In this situation, if a decision has to be made on a once-and-for-all basis, and the company has no information about its competitor's behaviour, the best move is to price low, again because this will produce the least worst outcome, no matter what the competitor does.

This helps to explain why one outcome of an oligopoly might be competitive pricing and an example of this might be competition amongst UK supermarkets, where there is a relatively small number of major players, but, according to the Competition Commission, competition is generally effective, with the exception of certain local areas and practices within the supply chain.[2] It should be clear that it is better for both companies to charge higher prices, rather than the lower ones. If certain assumptions behind this model are changed, then the outcomes change as well. So, if the choice is not a once-and-for-all choice and the participants in the game are able to observe each other's behaviour, then the optimal strategy is different and becomes what is known as 'tit-for-tat' strategy: in other words, a company cuts prices only if its competitor does the same. Indeed, the Competition Commission has pointed out that price increases might prove profitable because, if one company increases prices, its competitors can either follow or not follow. The former is likely to be the most profitable strategy as not following would lead to a reversal of the price rise and loss of the profitable opportunity.[3] So, in these sorts of circumstances, it would not be expected that competition would be fully effective. Note that the companies are able to accomplish this outcome without communicating with each other, which would be illegal, and without reaching an agreement. They have simply taken into account each other's likely behaviour and designed their company policy accordingly. This sort of behaviour is referred to as 'tacit collusion' or 'conscious parallelism' but these are misleading terms as there is no collusion in the normal sense of the word, nor is the parallelism conscious beyond a recognition of the

[2] Competition Commission, 'Groceries Market' (2008), p. 9 (para. 2).
[3] Competition Commission, *Merger Assessment Guidelines* (2003) at para. 3.35.

interdependencies of the companies. The OFT and the Competition Commission's preferred usage, in the context of mergers, is 'coordinated effects'.[4]

O'Donoghue and Padilla, an eminent lawyer and economist respectively, explain neatly that tacit collusion or coordinated effects are likely to occur when undertakings have the incentive to avoid competing and the ability to do so: that is, it is feasible to do so.[5] In order for this to be the case, there needs to be a common interest between the firms, there need to be low transaction costs in reaching an agreement, they must have the ability to effectively impose the coordinated effects on their customers and it must be difficult to defect from the tacit agreement.[6] What do these conditions entail?[7]

For there to be a common interest amongst the undertakings, it helps if the firms are similar, that is, have the same cost structures and similar market shares. It helps here if there are not any 'maverick' competitors, which are not inclined to follow the industry consensus. For there to be low transaction costs, this is easier the more concentrated the market is (because the more market participants, the more monitoring is needed). It helps if the market is stable and there are no great fluctuations in demand and it must be relatively easy to decide upon a price. In order to impose an agreement upon customers, it helps if demand elasticity is low (in other words, customers do not switch if prices rise), there are not sufficient actual or potential competitors to disrupt the equilibrium (that is, entry barriers are high), and customers do not have significant bargaining power. Finally, incentives to deviate should not be large. Incentives to deviate are high when demand elasticity is high, the market is characterised by rapid product innovation and the firms' capacities are different, so the firm with more capacity has an incentive to try and gain more market share. In order for there to be a credible threat of punishment for deviation, the market has to be sufficiently transparent so that behaviour can be observed, there has to be a credible mechanism for punishing those firms that deviate and it must be sufficiently strong.

Similar sorts of descriptions are given in the guidance by the competition authorities. The European Commission[8] says that it is easier to reach coordinated effects where the economic environment is relatively simple and stable and it cannot be undermined by outsiders, such as maverick firms. It also helps if the firms are relatively similar, especially in terms of cost structures, market shares, capacity levels and levels of vertical integration. It is easier to monitor deviations when the market is transparent,[9] which is often easier when the market is more concentrated, and, depending on how contracts are entered into, for example a public exchange is easier to monitor than confidential contracts. In addition, the deterrent mechanisms for preventing deviation must be credible and sufficiently severe.

The OFT takes the view that tacit coordination requires that undertakings are able to align their behaviour in the market. It also requires that:[10]

---

[4] OFT/CC, *Merger Assessment Guidelines* (2010) para. 5.5.1.

[5] R. O'Donoghue and J. Padilla, *The Law and Economics of Article 82 EC* (Hart Publishing, Oxford, 2006) at p. 139.

[6] Ibid.

[7] The next paragraph is based on ibid. at pp. 139–45.

[8] European Commission, *Guidelines on the assessment of horizontal mergers under the Council Regulation on the control of concentrations between undertakings*, OJ C31, 05.02.2004 (at paras 39–63).

[9] For an example of transparency in a market (groceries), see *http://www.mysupermarket.co.uk/Home.aspx* and *http://uk.shopping.com/xGS-supermarket%20prices~NS-1~linkin_id-8019935* (both price comparison sites) (accessed 06/08/12).

[10] OFT, *Assessment of Market Power* (2004), para. 2.16.

- each undertaking is able to monitor the compliance of the other undertakings with the common policy (i.e. transparency);

- the undertakings have incentives to maintain coordinated behaviour over time, so that coordination is sustainable (e.g. because deviations from the common policy are easy to detect and punish); and

- the foreseeable reactions of current and future competitors, as well as of customers, would not jeopardise the results expected from the common policy (e.g. new entrants, 'fringe' undertakings or powerful buyers could not successfully challenge the common policy).

A couple of examples from merger cases before the Competition Commission will help to indicate the type of markets where coordinated effects could be a concern. The first concerned a merger between Napier Brown Foods and James Budgett Sugar,[11] the first and second largest distributors of sugar that were not also producers. They competed with the two UK sugar producers, Tate & Lyle and British Sugar, and the four firms together had a market share of over 90% by volume. In addition, British Sugar and Tate & Lyle supplied the two merging firms with sugar, the producers did some deliveries to industrial customers of the merging firms direct, EU regulation of the sugar market provided significant information on producer costs, there was product homogeneity and price increase letters were circulated. One of the issues considered was whether the merger might lead to coordinated effects and the Competition Commission found evidence that there had been coordinated effects before the merger but that the merger was not likely to increase the problem. A second example is the case of Wienerberger Finance and Baggridge Bricks,[12] which involved the merger of the third and fourth largest brick manufacturers in Britain, thus reducing a four-firm market to a three-firm market, i.e. there were two other main competitors. In terms of coordinated effects, the Competition Commission considered whether the market was sufficiently transparent for there to be coordination over time and concluded that it was not because there were complex price and sales mechanisms, changes in plant capacity that were difficult to observe and the remaining firms did not have sufficient symmetry in relation to, among other things, operating costs.

The legal problem

Why is this situation a particular problem for competition law? First, it may be difficult to tell whether an oligopolistic market is competitive or not, simply on the basis of pricing policy. Similar prices for the same products may be either the outcome of intense competition or because of recognition of the strategic interdependencies between firms and a policy of not competing. Deciding what has happened, or is happening, can occur only after further analysis. Secondly, Articles 101 and 102 TFEU are both prohibitions, which imply that undertakings have done something wrong, either deliberately or negligently, to affect the competitive process. Indeed, the case law has consistently recognised, in the context of Article 101 TFEU, that undertakings have a right to adapt themselves intelligently to market conditions and, if they do this independently, there is no breach of Article 101 TFEU.[13] Therefore, in a situation where there has been no communication between undertakings, Article 101 TFEU

---

[11] Competition Commission, 'Napier Brown/James Budgett Sugars' (2005).

[12] Competition Commission, 'Wienerberger Finance/Baggridge Bricks' (2007).

[13] See, for example, Cases 40–8 etc. *Cooperatieve Vereniging 'Suiker Unie' v Commission* [1975] ECR 1663 at para. 174.

cannot be applied, at least insofar as it relates to agreements. This is not a problem which is peculiar to EU competition law. Under American law, s. 1 of the Sherman Act requires proof of an agreement, while s. 2 requires either proof of a monopoly or a dangerous probability that a company will become a monopolist. It is evident just from this description that s. 2 is not configured to catch oligopolistic markets and that s. 1 runs into the same problems in relation to agreements as EU law, without having the somewhat broader notion of a concerted practice.[14]

Using Article 101 TFEU

Can, however, the notion of concerted practices be stretched to cover these sorts of arrangements? The CJEU has said that the aim of the concept of a concerted practice:

> . . . is to bring within the prohibition of Article 85(1) [Article 101(1) TFEU] a form of coordination between undertakings which, without having reached the stage where an agreement properly so-called has been concluded, knowingly substitutes practical cooperation between them for the risks of competition. By its very nature, then, a concerted practice does not have all the elements of a contract but may inter alia arise out of coordination which becomes apparent from the behaviour of the participants. Although parallel behaviour may not by itself be identified with a concerted practice, it may however amount to strong evidence of such a practice if it leads to conditions of competition which do not correspond to the normal conditions of the market, having regard to the nature of the products, the size and number of the undertakings, and the volume of the said market.[15]

This quote suggests that Article 101 TFEU could be used to catch those situations where the undertakings have not entered into an agreement but the market is not sufficiently competitive[16] and evidence of this could be parallel behaviour. In terms of the quote, it depends on what 'practical cooperation' could mean and what might constitute conditions of competition which are not 'normal'. The first difficulty is that, in subsequent cases, there has been proof of contact between the undertakings concerned, although not necessarily proof that they have agreed to act in a particular way on the market. The CJEU has said that the concept of a concerted practice therefore:

> Does however strictly preclude any direct or indirect contact between such operators, the object or effect whereof is either to influence the conduct on the market of an actual or potential competitor or to disclose to such a competitor the course of conduct which they themselves have decided to adopt or contemplate adopting on the market.[17]

Another way it has been put is that the point of having the concept of concerted practices is to ensure that the Commission is able to catch all instances of collusion, even those falling short of an agreement. The problem is that, for the oligopoly situation we are concerned with, in theory there need be no contact between the parties. In the *Wood Pulp* case[18] (discussed in Chapter 2) the Commission tried to argue that parallel behaviour on its own could constitute

[14] On the difficulties of American law in dealing with oligopoly, see H. Hovenkamp, *Federal Antitrust Policy* (4th edn, West Publishing, St Paul, Minnesota, 2011) Sections 4.2–4.4.
[15] Cases 48/69 etc. *ICI v Commission* [1972] ECR 619 at paras 64–6.
[16] Whether a market is sufficiently competitive is a judgement and is the problem here!
[17] Cases 40–8 etc. *Cooperatieve Vereniging 'Suiker Unie' v Commission* [1975] ECR 1663 at para. 174.
[18] Cases C-89 etc. *Ahlström Oy v Commission (Wood Pulp II)* [1993] ECR I-1307.

evidence of collusion. In this case the Commission had levied fines on 43 wood pulp producers for breach of Article 101(1) TFEU. Although the Commission had, allegedly, some documentary evidence of contacts and exchange of information, this was excluded by the CJEU, forcing the case to rest entirely on the accusation of parallel behaviour in respect of pricing.[19] Very unusually, the CJEU commissioned economic experts to advise it on, among other things, the characteristics of the market and what form of price structure would exist on this type of market. The CJEU concluded that the explanation for the behaviour was not collusion or coordination between the undertakings concerned, but came down to the particular circumstances of the market. In terms of the legal principle, the CJEU said that:

> it must be noted that parallel conduct cannot be regarded as furnishing proof of concertation unless concertation constitutes the only plausible explanation for such conduct. It is necessary to bear in mind that, although Article 85 of the Treaty [Article 101 TFEU] prohibits any form of collusion which distorts competition, it does not deprive economic operators of the right to adapt themselves intelligently to the existing and anticipated conduct of their competitors.[20]

This not only puts the burden of proof on the Commission in cases of parallel behaviour, but it also recognises that there may indeed be market structures where competition is limited and that, so long as undertakings make their decisions independently, that is not an offence under Article 101 TFEU.

Using Article 102 TFEU

The alternative is to use Article 102 TFEU to catch oligopolies. Article 102 TFEU applies to an abuse of a dominant position by 'one or more undertakings', which suggests that it might cover oligopolies. The first problem is that often, in an oligopolistic industry, the largest undertaking will not fall within the definition of dominance. For example, at the end of 2007, in the UK groceries market the largest undertaking was Tesco, which has been reported as having a market share of sale of just over 27%, with Asda and Sainsburys being the largest competitors, with roughly just over 14% and just under 14% of the market respectively.[21] The notion of single firm dominance cannot, in these circumstances, be stretched to encompass Tesco, if we remember that the threshold is effectively 40% (as discussed in Chapter 3). In any event, this would not solve the problem, as the issue is not the behaviour only of the leading undertaking, but the strategic interrelationship between the participants on an oligopolistic market.

The initial problem was that the CJEU initially interpreted the phrase 'one or more undertakings' narrowly, as meaning a group and its subsidiaries.[22] Nevertheless, the Commission continued to try and develop this concept and it was eventually accepted by the GC in the *Italian Flat Glass* case.[23] This was a combined Article 101 and 102 TFEU case where the Commission accused three Italian flat glass producers of restricting competition through charging identical prices and exchanging glass between them. The Commission decided that the three undertakings were operating a cartel, that is, there were agreements between them, and held a collective dominant position and that their conduct constituted an abuse. The GC annulled the decision under Article 101(1) TFEU, on the grounds that the Commission had

---

[19] Ibid., paras 68–9.
[20] Ibid. at para. 71.
[21] Competition Commission, 'Groceries Market' (2008), Appendix 3.1.
[22] See Case 85/76 *Hoffmann-La Roche* v *Commission* [1979] ECR 461 at para. 39.
[23] Joined Cases T-68, 77 and 78/89 *Società Italiana Vetro (Italian Flat Glass)* [1992] ECR II-1403.

not established the facts of the infringement and also the decision under Article 102 TFEU, as the Commission attempted to just recycle the same factual assessment. However, as regards the questions of a collective dominant position, the GC said: 'There is nothing, in principle, to prevent two or more independent economic entities from being, on a specific market, united by such economic links that, by virtue of that fact, together they hold a dominant position vis à vis the other operators on the same market.'[24]

This was the first time that the GC had recognised the concept of collective dominance and it was confirmed by the CJEU in the *Almelo* case relating to the Dutch electricity supply market, where the Court said: 'However, in order for such a collective dominant position to exist, the undertakings in the group must be linked in such a way that they adopt the same conduct on the market . . .'[25] This approach left a number of issues uncertain. Was the reference to links a requirement or an example? If required, what does this mean? Did it mean that there needed to be some contractual links or contact between the undertakings concerned? If this was the case, how did the concept go beyond Article 101 TFEU?

Using the Merger Control Regulation

Attention in the case law then shifted to cases under the Merger Control Regulation (MCR). It should be stressed that, prior to 2004, the test within the MCR was whether the concentration would create or strengthen a dominant position which would impede effective competition within the common market. The text of the MCR said nothing about a collective dominant position but there was an important question about whether this could be used in merger control. The Commission took the view that the MCR did apply to a collective dominant position.[26]

The case which was determinative here was the *Kali und Salz* case,[27] which involved a merger between Kali und Salz (K+S), a firm located in western Germany which produced potash and fertilisers, and Mitteldeutsch (MKD), an undertaking located in eastern Germany which would have ceased trading were it not for the merger. On the German market this would have led to a *de facto* monopoly, and, on the wider European market, this would have led to the merged entity and a French undertaking, SCPA, having a dominant position. K+S had certain commercial links with SCPA and offered to withdraw from these links in order to obtain approval of the merger, and the Commission approved the merger, subject to these conditions. The French government challenged this decision arguing, among other points, that the text of the MCR did not allow for the use of collective dominance, that there was nothing in the legislative history that supported this interpretation and that use of the concept of collective dominance meant that decisions could affect undertakings that were not party to the merger and did not have the same procedural rights. The CJEU rejected the textual arguments and said that the MCR had to be interpreted by reference to its purpose and general structure. If that was the case, to interpret it in such a way as to exclude the possibility of it covering parties not concerned in the merger, but which strengthened their dominant position, would be to frustrate the purposes of the MCR. Hence, this concept could be used in proceedings under the MCR. As regards the concept itself, the CJEU said:

[24] Ibid., para. 358.
[25] Case C-393/92 *Almelo* v *NV Energiebedriijf Ijsselmij* [1994] ECR I-1477 at para. 42.
[26] See *Nestlé/Perrier* [1992] OJ L356/1.
[27] Cases C-68/94 and 30/95 *France* v *Commission* [1998] ECR I-1375.

In the case of an alleged collective dominant position, the Commission is therefore obliged to assess, using a prospective analysis of the reference market, whether the concentration which has been referred to it leads to a situation in which effective competition in the relevant market is significantly impeded by the undertakings involved in the concentration and one or more undertakings which together, in particular because of factors giving rise to a connection between them,[28] are able to adopt a common policy on the market and act to a considerable degree independently of their competitors, their customers and also of consumers.[29]

Interestingly, the CJEU also commented that a combined market share of just over 60%, divided 23% and 37%, did not point conclusively to the existence of a collective dominant position.[30] This is a different approach taken in this context from cases of single firm dominance where there is a presumption of dominance once market shares are above 50%. Although this case established that the concept could be used in the context of merger control, it still did not clarify whether there had to be some formal or express linkage between the undertakings concerned because, in all the cases up to this point, the undertakings had had some legal relationship. There was also a question as to whether the concept could be used in the same way in Article 102 TFEU cases as under the MCR.

Clarity was brought about in another MCR case, which involved a merger between two South African platinum firms, as a result of which the market would have consisted of two main undertakings after the merger (the merged entity and one other), which would have had a combined market share of about 70%. The Commission prohibited the merger on the grounds that it would have created a collective dominant position. This was challenged in the GC, which said that the concept of collective dominance was the same under Article 102 TFEU and the MCR and said, most importantly, that structural links were just an example and were not necessary for the finding of collective dominance (see Box 10.1).

KEY CASE EXTRACT   **Box 10.1**

Conditions for collective dominance

Source: Case T-102/96 *Gencor v Commission* [1999] 4 CMLR 971, para. 276:

[T]here is no reason whatsoever in legal or economic terms to exclude from the notion of economic links the relationship of interdependence existing between the parties to a tight oligopoly within which, in a market with the appropriate characteristics, in particular in terms of market concentration, transparency and product homogeneity, those parties are in a position to anticipate one another's behaviour and are therefore strongly encouraged to align their conduct on the market, in particular in such a way as to maximise their joint profits by restricting production with a view to increasing prices. In such a context, each trader is aware that highly competitive action on its part designed to increase its market share (for example a price cut) would provoke identical action by the others, so that it would derive no benefit from its initiative. All the traders would thus be affected by the reduction in price levels . . .

Question: What sort of markets would fit this description?

---

[28] ECR translation. Alternatively, 'correlative factors which exist between them'.
[29] Ibid., para. 221.
[30] Ibid., para. 226.

That this was the correct approach has been confirmed by the CJEU in the *Compagnie Maritime Belge* case,[31] which involved a liner conference, that is a group of shipping companies, with one competitor, which reacted to its presence by adopting a policy of 'fighting ships', that is, sailing at more or less the same time as the competitor and charging lower prices. One of the key issues was whether the members of the liner conference could be seen as collectively dominant. The CJEU held that it could and made the following comments (see Box 10.2).

KEY CASE EXTRACT   Box 10.2

Conditions for collective dominance

Source: Joined Cases C-395 & 396/96P *Compagnie Maritime Belge Transports (CMBT)* [2000] ECR I-1365 at paras 36 and 45:

> It follows that the expression 'one or more undertakings' in Article 86 of the Treaty [Article 102 TFEU] implies that a dominant position may be held by two or more economic entities legally independent of each other, provided that from an economic point of view they present themselves or act together on a particular market as a collective entity. That is how the expression 'collective dominant position', as used in the remainder of this judgment, should be understood . . . The existence of a collective dominant position may therefore flow from the nature and terms of an agreement . . . Nevertheless, the existence of an agreement or of other links in law is not indispensable to a finding of a collective dominant position; such a finding may be based on other connecting factors and would depend on an economic assessment and, in particular, on an assessment of the structure of the market in question.[32]

Question: Is this different from the test put forward in *Gencor v Commission*?

The combination of these two cases makes it clear that, in principle, the concept of collective dominance can be applied to an oligopoly depending on the economic assessment of the connecting factors and the structure of the market in question.

What the characteristics of the market were required to be became the central issue in another merger case, the *Airtours* decision (discussed in Chapter 13).[33] This involved a proposed merger between what was then Airtours and FirstChoice, two companies that offered short-haul package holidays. The combined entity would have had a market share of 32%, while its two biggest competitors would have had market shares of 27% and 20% respectively. The Commission prohibited the merger on the grounds that it would have led to a collective dominant position and this was appealed by Airtours to the GC, which overturned the Commission's decision. The GC laid down three conditions for the existence of collective dominance: the members of the oligopoly must be able to monitor each other's behaviour; the situation must be sustainable over a period of time, that is, it must be stable; and parties outside the oligopoly must not be able to disrupt it. In detail, the GC said:

1   Each member of the dominant oligopoly must have the ability to know how the other members are behaving in order to monitor whether or not they are adopting the common

---

[31] Joined Cases C-395 & 396/96P *Compagnie Maritime Belge Transports (CMBT)* [2000] 4 CMLR 1076.
[32] Ibid., paras 36 and 45.
[33] Case T-342/99 *Airtours* v *Commission* [2002] ECR II-2585.

policy . . . it is not enough for each member of the dominant oligopoly to be aware that interdependent market conduct is profitable for all of them but each member must also have a means of knowing whether the other operators are adopting the same strategy and whether they are maintaining it. There must, therefore, be sufficient market transparency for all members of the dominant oligopoly to be aware, sufficiently precisely and quickly, of the way in which the other members' market conduct is evolving;

2   The situation of tacit coordination must be sustainable over time, that is to say, there must be an incentive not to depart from the common policy on the market . . . it is only if all the members of the dominant oligopoly maintain the parallel conduct that all can benefit. The notion of retaliation in respect of conduct deviating from the common policy is thus inherent in this condition. In this instance, the parties concur that, for a situation of collective dominance to be viable, there must be adequate deterrents to ensure that there is a long-term incentive in not departing from the common policy, which means that each member of the dominant oligopoly must be aware that highly competitive action on its part designed to increase its market share would provoke identical action by the others, so that it would derive no benefit from its initiative . . . ;

3   To prove the existence of a collective dominant position to the requisite legal standard, the Commission must also establish that the foreseeable reaction of current and future competitors, as well as of consumers, would not jeopardise the results expected from the common policy.[34]

This has been further developed in the recent *Impala* case[35] (discussed in Chapter 13). This involved a proposed merger between Sony and the Bertelsmann Group, music companies, which the European Commission initially was minded to prohibit, on the grounds of the creation of a collective dominant position, but then changed its mind and allowed it to proceed. This decision was challenged by a group of independent music companies, Impala, which were successful before the GC. Sony and Bertelsmann appealed the decision to the CJEU, but, in the meantime, the European Commission had revisited the case and allowed the merger. One of the questions for the CJEU was whether the GC had applied the correct test for collective dominance in its judgment. The CJEU said that in the case of an alleged creation or strengthening of a collective dominant position, the European Commission is obliged to start with a prospective analysis of the reference market. The Commission must ask whether the concentration which has been referred to it will lead to a situation in which effective competition in the relevant market is significantly impeded by the undertakings which are parties to the concentration and one or more other undertakings which together, in particular because of correlative factors which exist between them, are able to adopt a common policy on the market in order to profit from a situation of collective economic strength, without actual or potential competitors, let alone customers or consumers, being able to react effectively.[36] What are these correlative factors? The CJEU said that they included the relationship of interdependence of parties to a tight oligopoly, which could come about in the appropriate market conditions:

● market concentration,

● transparency, and

● product homogeneity.

---

[34] Ibid., para. 62.
[35] Case C413/06P *Bertelsmann and Sony* v *Impala and Commission* [2008] ECR I-4951.
[36] Ibid., para. 120.

In these conditions, the participants are aware that any competitive action on their part would engender a response from the other market participants, thus rendering it not worthwhile. According to the CJEU, as the participants became aware of their common interests, they would consider it possible, economically rational, and hence preferable, to adopt on a lasting basis a common policy on the market with the aim of selling at above competitive prices, without having to enter into an agreement or resort to a concerted practice within the meaning of Article 101 TFEU and without any actual or potential competitors, let alone customers or consumers, being able to react effectively.[37] However, the CJEU pointed out that such coordination had to be sustainable, which meant that the market had to be sufficiently transparent, there had to be some form of credible deterrent mechanism and outsiders, such as fringe competitors or new entrants, should not be able to jeopardise the existing relationships.[38] The CJEU criticised the GC on this point for not carrying out a proper investigation of the postulated monitoring mechanism in the case;[39] and for this, and other errors of law, it overturned the GC decision.

To summarise, in order to establish a collective dominant position, the competition authority must show the following:

- there must be sufficient market transparency for all members of the dominant oligopoly to be aware, sufficiently precisely and quickly, of the way in which the other members' market conduct is evolving; and

- the situation of tacit coordination must be sustainable over time, there must be an incentive not to depart from the common policy on the market; and

- it must be established that the foreseeable reaction of current and future competitors, as well as of consumers, would not jeopardise the results expected from the common policy.

Even though it has been established that Article 102 TFEU covers a collective dominant position, merely establishing that does not complete the inquiry. For this concept to be effective it must be possible to show that the members of a collective dominant position have committed an abuse. The case law establishes that undertakings occupying a collective dominant position may engage in joint or individual abusive conduct and, as regards the latter, this can be penalised (see Box 10.3), although in the particular case the relationship was vertical, not horizontal.[40]

KEY CASE EXTRACT   Box 10.3

Abuse and collective dominance

Source: Case T-228/97 *Irish Sugar plc v EC Commission* [1999] 5 CMLR 1300, para. 66:

Whilst the existence of a joint dominant position may be deduced from the position which the economic entities concerned together hold on the market in question, the abuse does not necessarily have to be the action of all the undertakings in question. It only has to be

[37] Ibid., para. 122.
[38] Ibid., para. 123.
[39] Ibid., paras 130–4.
[40] See also European Commission Decision Case COMP/39.388, *German Electricity Wholesale Market* and Case COMP/39.389, *German Electricity Balancing Market* at para. 27.

> capable of being identified as one of the manifestations of such a joint dominant position being held. Therefore, undertakings occupying a joint dominant position may engage in joint or individual abusive conduct. It is enough for that abusive conduct to relate to the exploitation of the joint dominant position which the undertakings hold in the market.
>
> **Questions**: What sort of abuses might be carried out by the undertakings collectively? Is the ability to penalise a single undertaking a sufficient deterrent?

When it comes to possibility of the undertakings jointly committing an abuse, this is more problematic. If we consider tacit coordination of prices, the consensus in the academic literature seems to be that this does not constitute an abuse as it is the independent adaption to market conditions, which is usually allowed under EU competition law.[41] By contrast, charging excessively high prices could be an abuse, but the Commission has been reluctant to intervene in such cases (as discussed in Chapter 3). Anti-competitive abuses which involve trying to exclude other competitors from the market can be condemned, as was the issue in the liner conference cases, but there will be certain abuses, such as loyalty rebates and discriminatory pricing, where it may well be difficult to tell, as Jones and Sufrin point out,[42] whether they are anti-competitive or signs that competition is breaking out in the oligopoly. As O'Donoghue and Padilla point out, it will also be important to maintain a distinction between collusive conduct that falls under Article 101 TFEU and conduct which falls under Article 102 TFEU.[43] It is also far from clear that the common remedies of fines or requiring undertakings to bring the abuse to an end are effective means of dealing with the problems thrown up by oligopolies. This implies that structural remedies, such as breaking up an undertaking, should be used but this is a radical option and has only been available to the European Commission since 2004, after the coming into force of Regulation 1/2003, and has not yet been used in an Article 102 TFEU context.

Conclusions on collective dominance

What we can see from this discussion is that the prohibition contained in Article 102 TFEU, even with its range expanded by collective dominance, and the concept of concerted practices in Article 101 TFEU, is not suitable for addressing oligopolistic markets where competition is not working effectively. Although collective dominance had a role to play in the MCR prior to its reform in 2004, its usage in Article 102 TFEU cases remains problematic. In practice, outside the MCR, it has only been deployed in European cases where the undertakings concerned were united by some legal relationship, as in the liner conference cases,[44] and it has not been deployed where the problem is simply one of the market structure and its conditions. In the UK, the OFT has never brought a case based on collective dominance.[45] Although

---

[41] See G. Monti, 'The scope of collective dominance under Article 82 EC' (2001) 38 *Common Market Law Review* 131; R. Whish, 'Collective Dominance' in D. O'Keeffe and M. Andenas (eds) *Liber Amicorum for Lord Slynn* (Kluwer, Amsterdam, 2000).

[42] A. Jones and B. Sufrin, *EU Competition Law* (4th edn, Oxford University Press, 2011) at p. 848.

[43] O'Donoghue and Padilla (n. 5) at p. 163.

[44] Joined Cases C-395 and 396/96P *Compagnie Maritime Belge Transports (CMBT)* [2000] 4 CMLR 1076; Cases T-191 and 214/98 *Atlantic Container Line v Commission* [2003] ECR II-3275.

[45] The CC has suggested that coordinated conduct is only an Article 101 TFEU issue: CC, 'Review of Market Investigation Guidelines' (2012) para. 227.

some of the uncertainty surrounding the legal concept has been dispelled, there is still great uncertainty as to what could constitute abuse in these circumstances. So, if Article 102 TFEU cannot deal with oligopolistic markets where there is not effective competition, and this is not true of all oligopolies, are there any alternatives? Within the UK, the alternative is a market investigation by the Competition Commission and at EU level there is the possibility of a sectoral investigation, and we now turn to these.

Alternative devices to investigate oligopolistic markets

Background

There is a long history in the UK of official investigations into particular industries or sectors in order to assess their competitiveness. In the early 1950s, for example, the predecessor of the Competition Commission, the Monopolies and Restrictive Practices Commission, undertook investigations into dental goods, electric lamps, insulin and imported timber, among other products.[46] From 1973 the Fair Trading Act (FTA) gave responsibility for monopoly investigations to the Monopolies and Mergers Commission (MMC), the predecessor of the Competition Commission. In the period from 1988 to 1998, when reform of the UK system of competition law was being considered, one of the issues was whether this system of monopoly[47] investigations should be retained or whether it would be sufficient to rely on the domestic equivalent of Article 102 TFEU, that is, the Chapter II prohibition. The conclusion, after some debate, was to retain monopoly investigations but the opportunity was taken to rename and reform them under the Enterprise Act 2002 and since then they have been called 'market investigations'.

Market investigations

The FTA definition was criticised for being cumbersome and difficult to operate, as well as confusing jurisdictional with substantive tests.[48] The Enterprise Act 2002 introduced a new test which allows the OFT or sector regulators to make a reference to the Competition Commission where it has reasonable grounds for suspecting that any feature or combination of features of a market for goods or services prevents, restricts or distorts competition in the supply of goods or services.[49] A feature of the market is defined as meaning any structural characteristics of the market, any conduct by one or more persons in relation to the goods or services in the market or any conduct by the customers of suppliers of goods or services.[50] This redefinition removes the problem under the old system whereby a finding of a complex monopoly, necessary for jurisdictional purposes, would be interpreted by the press as effectively a finding of guilt on the companies concerned.

---

[46] See *http://www.competition-commission.org.uk/rep_pub/reports/1950_1959/index.htm* (accessed 01/09/12) for a list.

[47] A misleading name, as investigations could cover industries where there was no monopoly. See R. Brent, 'The Meaning of Complex Monopoly' (1993) 56 *Modern Law Review* 812.

[48] Ibid.

[49] Enterprise Act 2002, s. 131(1).

[50] Enterprise Act 2002, s. 131(2).

Although the OFT has the power to make references, Ministers also have powers to make a reference. Section 132 simply says that a Minister may make a reference to the Competition Commission if he or she is not satisfied with the OFT's decision not to refer the matter to the Competition Commission and if the Minister has reasonable grounds for suspecting that any feature or combination of features of a market for goods or services prevents, restricts or distorts competition in the supply of goods or services; in other words, the same test that the OFT must apply. This power has not, so far, been used by Ministers.

When an issue is referred to the Competition Commission, it is required to decide whether any feature, or combination of features, of each relevant market prevents, restricts or distorts competition in connection with the supply or acquisition of any goods or services in the United Kingdom or a part of the United Kingdom.[51] This is referred to as an adverse effect on competition (AEC). If, after investigation, the Competition Commission decides that there is an AEC, then it is under a duty to decide:

(a) whether action should be taken by it under section 138 for the purpose of remedying, mitigating or preventing the adverse effect on competition concerned or any detrimental effect on customers so far as it has resulted from, or may be expected to result from, the adverse effect on competition;

(b) whether it should recommend the taking of action by others for the purpose of remedying, mitigating or preventing the adverse effect on competition concerned or any detrimental effect on customers so far as it has resulted from, or may be expected to result from, the adverse effect on competition; and

(c) in either case, if action should be taken, what action should be taken and what is to be remedied, mitigated or prevented.[52]

Procedures in market investigations[53]

Market investigations are carried out by a group of CC members, who are part-time appointees, supported by CC staff. Groups are typically composed of between four and six members and they are the decision makers in any one case. Typically decisions in market investigations are unanimous, although the legislation does make provision for decisions by a two-thirds majority of the group.[54] Because market investigations are unique cases procedures can vary somewhat depending on the context, but the CC identifies a number of common stages.[55] The first phase of the inquiry is the information gathering one which starts with the CC requesting information from the parties that is readily available and progresses to the CC asking more detailed questions on the conditions in the market and financial information about the parties. Early on the CC will publish an initial issues statement which will set out what the CC sees as the competitive issues in the case, as well as carrying out site visits. The parties will be free to make submissions to the CC in relation to the issues statement and to make further submissions as they see fit. The CC will then compose what they call working papers which will address a variety of issues which they regard as relevant to the case, such as

---

[51] Enterprise Act 2002, s. 134(1).
[52] Enterprise Act 2002, s. 134(2).
[53] Generally, see Competition Commission, *Market Investigation References* (2003) although note that these were written before the CC carried out any market investigations and they are in the process of revision.
[54] Enterprise Act 2002, Schedule 11, para. 11.
[55] Generally, see CC, 'Review of Market Investigation Guidelines' (2012) paras 38–72.

barriers to entry and expansion and these will usually be published on the CC's website. There will then be a series of private oral hearings with the parties and the CC group. Towards the end of the first year of the market investigation, the CC aims to publish provisional findings and a notice of possible remedies (if this is relevant). The next six months of a standard case is then spent considering responses to the provisional findings before reaching a final decision on the issues and relevant remedies.

There are a number of points to notice about this process. First, there is a significant opportunity for the parties in a market investigation to put their points to the group deciding the case orally. Secondly, information gathering and analysis by the CC is a process that continues throughout the investigation and should not be seen as distinct processes. Thirdly, the process is relatively open: CC working papers and evidence[56] presented to the CC are published on the CC website, in addition to the issues statement, provisional findings and the remedies notice. The parties in an investigation may make submissions to the CC on any of these matters. Finally, the process of a market investigation is time consuming, especially when there are a large number of parties who may be affected by the findings. Although the CC intends that a standard market investigation will take eighteen months, in practice almost all of them have taken two years (see Table 10.3) to which must be added the time taken for an initial investigation by the OFT and the time taken after a final report by the Competition Commission to decide on the detail of any remedies, in the case where it has found an AEC.

In deciding whether an AEC has arisen, the CC says that it will look at three basic issues, although it cautions that this is not a chronological process:[57]

1 the main characteristics of the market and the outcomes of the competitive process;

2 the boundaries of the relevant market within which competition may be harmed (*market definition*); and

3 the features which may harm competition in the relevant market (the *competitive assessment* – which the CC frames within 'theories of harm'), considering also possible countervailing factors, such as efficiencies, which remove *or* mitigate the competitive harm of the features.

The main characteristics of the market include the structure of the market (market shares and concentration), the nature of the products or services referred, the nature of the customer base, the legal and regulatory framework, industry practices and the history of the market.[58] In terms of market outcomes, the CC looks at prices and profits and quality, innovation and other price indicators. Perhaps most controversially, as well as looking at price patterns and price–cost margins, the CC will also examine indicators that prices are too high. Although the CC does not dismiss an approach that compares the prices in the reference market with prices for similar products in other markets, it says that in general it is hard to draw meaningful conclusions unless it can be shown the costs are comparable.[59] The CC will instead look at the profitability of a firm or firms representing a significant part of the market. The basic idea is that the CC is interested in persistently high profits, which it takes to be profits which exceed the cost of capital.[60]

---

[56] With confidential material removed.

[57] CC, 'Review of Market Investigation Guidelines' (2012) para. 96. Emphasis in original.

[58] Ibid. para. 104.

[59] Ibid. para. 116.

[60] Ibid. para. 122.

The point of doing a market definition is that it enables the CC to identify the market participants and products that might be central to the identification of features which have an AEC.[61] Interestingly, the CC comments that it has found it hard to apply the hypothetical monopolist test rigorously in market investigations. It says that although this test helps to identify constraints that would prevent a hypothetical monopolist from exercising market power, it is less helpful in identifying market features that may be harming competition.[62] Therefore the CC applies pragmatic methods and the degree of precision it judges is best suited to each investigation. Otherwise it takes a conventional approach, looking at the product and geographical markets as well as other issues, such as customer groups and temporal dimensions.[63]

In terms of competitive assessment, the CC says that it generally bases its assessment around five types of theories of harm:[64]

1 Weak rivalry within the market.

2 Restrictions on entry and expansion.

3 Coordinated conduct.

4 Vertical relationships.

5 Weak customer response.

In looking at these theories, the CC will also consider whether there are any countervailing factors such as efficiencies, countervailing entry and countervailing buyer power.[65] The CC goes on to look at each of the theories of harm in more detail in its consultation paper.[66]

Remedies in market investigations

Thus decisions about what actions should be taken are the responsibility of the Competition Commission and it has a duty to remedy the adverse effects that it has discovered.[67] In order to do this it has powers to accept legally binding undertakings from any persons that it considers appropriate, normally those who have been party to the investigation.[68] So, for example, a company might agree ('undertake') to sell off a business or a factory to remedy the problems that the merger created. If undertakings cannot be agreed, or are considered not to be appropriate, the Competition Commission has power to make final orders, effectively the equivalent of delegated legislation.[69] The potential content of any order is set out in Schedule 8 to the Enterprise Act 2002. The Schedule gives wide powers to prohibit certain types of conduct, such as withholding supply or price discrimination, power to regulate prices, a power to order the divestiture and break-up of a company and power to require companies

---

[61] Ibid. para. 131.
[62] Ibid. para. 137.
[63] Ibid. paras 139–52.
[64] Ibid. para. 161.
[65] Ibid. para. 163.
[66] Ibid. paras 165–309.
[67] Enterprise Act 2002, s. 138.
[68] Enterprise Act 2002, s. 159.
[69] Enterprise Act 2002, s. 161.

to provide information.[70] For example, at the end of the inquiry into personal banking in Northern Ireland, the CC made an order which required banks to ensure that certain information was given to customers, that certain communications were easy to understand and that banks told customers that they could switch their personal current accounts to another bank.[71] Although these are extensive powers, they are narrower than the power to accept final undertakings, which is in practice limited only by the willingness of parties to agree to accept and be bound by undertakings. Monitoring and enforcement of orders and undertakings is typically the responsibility of the OFT, although persons damaged by the breach of an order or undertaking may also take action through the courts.[72]

It is important to understand that market investigations are entirely separate from the enforcement of Articles 101 and 102 TFEU and their domestic equivalents. Indeed, the Competition Commission is not a competition authority for the purposes of Regulation 1/2003 and so cannot enforce Articles 101 and 102 TFEU, which is a matter exclusively for the OFT and the sector regulators. Thus, decisions after market investigations are forward looking; they cannot penalise companies for acting in breach of Articles 101 and 102 TFEU.

Market investigations in practice

Since the Enterprise Act came into force in 2003, there have been fourteen market investigations (see Table 10.3). This seems to be rather less than was anticipated at the beginning of the process and there seems to be no pattern to the references so far. Northern Ireland Personal Banking, Home Credit and Payment Protection Insurance began originally as super-complaints to the OFT, while Store Cards was referred by the OFT subsequent to an encounter with the House of Commons Treasury Select Committee, which had been very critical of the store cards industry and the OFT's performance.[73] The OFT's market study of statutory audit services, and subsequent reference to the CC came in the wake of a recommendation by a House of Lords Committee, although the OFT said that it had been monitoring these services since 2002.[74] The reference on Railway Rolling Stock started with a complaint by the Department of Transport to the Office of Rail Regulation, which conducted a market study and concluded that a reference was appropriate. Movies on pay TV was a reference from the Office of Communications. The highest profile of the inquiries so far, that of Groceries, started with an OFT review of the supermarkets' Code of Practice which had been put in place following a monopoly investigation by the MMC in 2000. The OFT concluded that the Code

---

[70] The Competition Commission recommended that the British Airports Authority (BAA) sell off three of its airports: 'BAA Airports' (2009). BAA was unsuccessful in challenging the decision on procedural grounds: *BAA v Competition Commission* [2009] CAT 35 reversed by *Competition Commission v BAA* [2010] EWCA Civ 1097 (CA). It sold two of the airports to Global Infrastructure Partners (*http://global-infra.com/investments/transportation*) and was unsuccessful in challenging the sale of the third airport: *BAA v Competition Commission* [2012] CAT 3 and *BAA v Competition Commission* judgment of Court of Appeal, 26 July 2012 (unreported).

[71] See CC, 'The Northern Ireland PCA Banking Market Investigation Order 2008'.

[72] Enterprise Act 2002, ss. 92 and 94.

[73] Treasury Select Committee, 'Transparency of Credit Card charges', HC 125 (2003–04), Vol. I, paras 110–28 and Vol. II, Minutes of evidence, 9 September 2003.

[74] House of Lords Select Committee on Economic Affairs, 'Auditors: Market concentration and their role' (HL 119-I, 2010–12 at paras 27 and 190. For the OFT's position see: *http://www.oft.gov.uk/OFTwork/markets-work/references/statutory-audit/* (accessed 02/09/12).

Table 10.3 Market investigations

	Date started	Date finished (final report)	Size of market	Outcome
Store cards	18/03/04	07/03/06	£670 m	AEC
Bulk domestic liquid petroleum gas	05/07/04	29/06/06	~£120 m	AEC
Home credit	20/12/04	30/11/06	~£700 m	AEC
Classified directories	05/04/05	21/12/06	~£825 m	AEC
Northern Ireland personal banking	26/05/05	15/05/07	£167 m	AEC
Groceries market	09/05/06	30/04/08	£123,500 m	AEC
Payment protection insurance	07/02/07	29/01/09	~£5,350 m	AEC
BAA	29/03/07	19/03/09	~£2,500 m	AEC
Railway rolling stock	26/04/07	07/04/09	~£1,000 m	AEC
Local bus services	07/01/10	20/12/11	~£4,092 m	AEC
Movies on pay TV	04/08/10			AEC
Statutory audit services	21/10/11			
Private health care services	04/04/12			
Aggregates, cement and ready-mixed concrete	18/01/12			

Source: Using data from *http://www.competition-commission.org.uk/inquiries/index.htm* (accessed 19/06/12).

was working effectively and that there was no case for a market investigation reference. This was challenged by the Association of Convenience Stores in the CAT, which quashed the original decision and called on the OFT to undertake a fresh inquiry, which it did, concluding that a market investigation was appropriate.[75] What is noticeable about this history is that most of the market investigations seem to have been sparked by complaints, rather than being part of a clear plan of investigation by the OFT, with the possible exception of the BAA reference.

As can be seen from Table 10.3, in all the cases which have been completed, the Competition Commission has found that there was an adverse effect on competition (AEC) and that therefore remedies have been needed. A variety of remedies have been introduced, ranging from a price cap in the Classified Advertising case to recommending improvements to switching procedures in the Northern Ireland Personal Banks and domestic Liquefied Petroleum Gas cases to information remedies in almost all the cases. One of the most controversial remedies came in the inquiry into the groceries market. Although the Competition Commission found that, in general, competition in this market was working well at a national level, it found causes for concern in two respects.[76] First, at a local level, it found that several grocery retailers had strong positions in local markets. Secondly, it found the transfer of excessive risk and unexpected costs by the grocery retailers to their suppliers through various supply chain practices. In relation to the first problem, it proposed remedies to deal with the problem of the strong existing positions[77] and it also proposed, for the future, that a competition assessment should be implemented within the planning system which would be intended to prevent grocery retailers from obtaining too strong a position within local areas. In relation to the supply chain issues it recommended a new, strengthened Groceries Supply Code of Practice which would have an Ombudsman to enforce its provisions. It was, however,

[75] *Association of Convenience Stores* v *OFT* [2005] CAT 36; and OFT, 'Grocery market: Proposed decision to make a market reference' (2006).

[76] Competition Commission, 'Groceries Market' (2008), paras 2 and 3.

[77] Relating to the release of restrictive covenants and exclusivity deals for land.

unable to obtain the agreement of all the major supermarkets to this proposal and has made a formal recommendation to the Department for Business, Innovation and Skills that it should establish such a scheme which is being introduced in the Groceries Code Adjudicator Bill.[78] Tesco successfully challenged the recommendation for a competition assessment in the Competition Appeal Tribunal under s. 179 of the Enterprise Act and the Competition Commission was asked to re-examine the economic costs of the text and its proportionality and effectiveness. After re-examining the text, the Competition Commission reaffirmed its recommendation.[79] The other very controversial remedy was the recommendation that BAA sell off three of its airports which was a significant change to the structure of the market.[80]

Whether the market investigation system is an effective one is a good question. Since it has only effectively been in operation since 2004, with the first final reports arriving in 2006, it is still too early to make an assessment, especially given the limited number of cases. It should be noted, however, that there seems to be an increasing willingness on the part of parties to a market investigation to challenge the conclusions of the Competition Commission in front of the Competition Appeal Tribunal.[81] It is also too early to judge whether this will have a detrimental effect on the ability of the Competition Commission to decide on appropriate remedies.

Reform of the market investigation regime

One of the objectives of the government's reform of competition policy has been to improve the working of the market investigation regime. The two main concerns have been with the speed of market investigations, when all the phases are taken into account, and the relative lack of use of this provision. In terms of lack of use, it would seem that it is hoped that, by merging the OFT and the CC and creating a single Competition and Markets Authority, this will end any institutional tension. As regards time limits, the Enterprise and Regulatory Reform Bill proposes that the CMA will have an initial six months to decide whether to make a reference, then an additional six months to publish the market study and make a final decision. The investigation period is then reduced from twenty-four months to eighteen, although it can be extended to twenty-four months in special circumstances. Remedies are meant to be decided upon within six months, again with a possible extension for four months.[82]

The Bill makes two further significant changes to the markets regime. First, it provides for cross-market references.[83] Secondly, the Bill provides for public interest interventions in market investigations. The mechanism for this latter change is complicated. The power arises only after the CMA has published a market study report. After the publication of that report, the Secretary of State may issue a public interest intervention notice which will say that the

[78] Competition Commission, Press Release, 4 August 2009. HC Bill 113 2012–13.

[79] *Tesco v Competition Commission* [2009] CAT 6. See *http://www.competition-commission.org.uk/inquiries/ref2009/ groceries_remittal/index.htm* (accessed 06/08/12). Barclays successfully challenged the proposed remedies in relation to Payment Protection Insurance: *Barclays v Competition Commission* [2009] CAT 27. The CC reaffirmed its original decision: *http://www.competition-commission.org.uk/our-work/directory-of-all-inquiries/ppi-market-investigation-and-remittal* (accessed 06/08/12).

[80] See above, note 70 for details.

[81] *Tesco v Competition Commission* [2009] CAT 6; *Barclays v Competition Commission* [2009] CAT 27; *BAA v Competition Commission* [2009] CAT 35 and *BAA v Competition Commission* [2012] CAT 3.

[82] Enterprise and Regulatory Reform Bill, Schedule 12.

[83] Enterprise and Regulatory Reform HC Bill, cl. 25.

Secretary of State believes that it is or may be the case that one or more public interest considerations are relevant to the case.[84] Having done this, the Secretary of State then has to decide if the public interest matters are relevant. If the Secretary of State decides that they are not relevant, the Secretary of State shall make a reference for an ordinary market investigation if the CMA had decided that this is what they were going to do.[85] If the Secretary of State thinks that the public interest considerations are relevant then again it is mandatory to make a reference but there are two possible routes: a full public interest reference or a restricted one. When a full public interest reference is made,[86] the CMA is required to decide on whether any feature or features of the relevant market or markets prevents, restricts or distorts competition ('the competition test'), in other words, no change from its current responsibilities. If it thinks that there is an adverse effect on competition it shall also decide whether, taking into account only the adverse effect on competition and the public interest consideration(s), the feature or features which gave rise to the adverse effect on competition operate or may be expected to operate against the public interest. If the CMA thinks that there is a public interest issue or an adverse effect on competition, then it is required to make recommendations on remedies to the Secretary of State as regards the public interest matter and whether it should take action in relation to the adverse effect on competition. In addition, on these full public interest references, the Secretary of State may appoint an expert or experts to advise the CMA on the public interest questions and the CMA is obliged to have regard to the views of the expert.

If the CMA thinks that there are adverse effects against the public interest, the ultimate decision is given to the Secretary of State.[87] The Secretary of State is bound by the CMA's finding on the competition issues but not on the public interest matters and may, or may not, decide to make an adverse public interest finding. If the Secretary of State makes an adverse public interest finding, the Secretary of State is then given the power to take remedial action. There is provision for reversion to the CMA if the Secretary of State decides not to make a finding or fails to make a decision within the relevant period. By contrast, on a restricted public interest investigation, the CMA is limited to making a report on whether there are any adverse effects on competition. The Secretary of State may then make a decision on the public interest matters and take the appropriate remedial action.[88]

For the purposes of this provision, a public interest consideration has to be either a consideration specified in s. 153 of the Enterprise Act 2002 or a provision which the Secretary of State thinks ought to be so specified.[89] At the moment, all that is specified in s. 153 is national security.[90] If the Secretary of State thinks that other matters ought to be so specified in the section, then s. 139 requires the Secretary of State to, in effect, amend s. 153 to include the relevant public interest consideration.

This is all quite puzzling. In its response to the consultation, the government says, in three consecutive paragraphs,[91] of these proposals that:

---

[84] Ibid. cl 27(3).
[85] Ibid. cl 27(8).
[86] Ibid. cl 27(9).
[87] Ibid. Schedule 10, para. 14.
[88] Ibid. Schedule 10, paras 7, 13 and 15.
[89] Enterprise Act 2002 s. 139(4).
[90] By contrast, Enterprise Act 2002 s. 58 (mergers) covers national security, media plurality and the stability of the financial system.
[91] BIS, *Government Response to Consultation* (2012) at paras 4.11 to 4.13.

1 [The reforms will] put the competition regime at the heart of market inquiries currently undertaken by ad hoc commissions,

2 This will bring the public interest markets regime in line with the public interest mergers regime, and

3 The scope of public interest issues that may be considered in a markets case is not being widened by this reform.

These three statements are simply inconsistent. Number 3 is currently true, but this means that numbers 1 and 2 are untrue. If statement number 1 is taken as an aspiration then, in the longer term, statement number 3 will not remain true and the same is unlikely to be the case for statement 2. In any event, the thinking which apparently underlines statement 2 is problematic. It is not obvious that the same public interest considerations which might arise in merger cases will arise in market investigations. It is also not obvious that the model for public interest investigations derived from mergers is a good one to follow, given the experience so far, notably in relation to the Lloyds/HBOS merger and the NewsCorp/BSkyB proposal.[92]

Sector inquiries

The European Commission has had power to carry out inquiries into sectors of the European economy since the first procedural Regulation in 1962. It only carried out one such inquiry before the new Regulation 1/2003 and that was in 1999 in relation to certain aspects of the telecommunications industry, which led to the threat of enforcement action and ultimately a Council Regulation which dealt with some of the issues raised in the inquiry. Article 17 of Regulation 1/2003 gives the Commission power to conduct an inquiry into a particular sector of the economy where the trend of trade between Member States, the rigidity of prices or other circumstances suggest that competition may be restricted or distorted. In carrying out such inquiries, the Commission has power to request information from undertakings, to carry out inspections of business premises, to take statements and to request national competition authorities to carry out inspections for it. After investigating, it is required to publish a report but there is no power, however, to take decisions in relation to particular firms based upon this report, although there is a power to fine undertakings that do not cooperate with the investigation.

Since the entry into force of this Regulation in 2004, the Commission has undertaken four sector inquiries into: energy, retail banking, business insurance, and pharmaceuticals. The energy sector inquiry is perhaps the most interesting, because this is a sector where there has long been a policy of liberalising energy markets, something which has been controversial, particularly in France and Germany where there are strong incumbent companies. The energy sector inquiry was launched in 2005, according to the Commission, in order to tackle concerns voiced by consumers and new entrants in the energy sector about the development of wholesale gas and electricity markets and the limited competition that had developed for consumers. A final report was published in January 2007 and identified the following shortcomings:

---

[92] See A. Stephan, 'Did Lloyds/HBOS mark the failure of an enduring economics based system of merger regulation?' (2011) 62 *Northern Ireland Legal Quarterly* 539; S. Smith, 'Newscorp and BSkyB: Media plurality and fitness for purpose' (2011) 22 *Entertainment Law Review* 224. The issue is discussed in: Evidence to the Public Bill Committee, Enterprise and Regulatory Reform Bill, 21 June 2012 at Qs 249–252.

- too much market concentration in most national markets;

- a lack of liquidity, preventing successful new entry;

- too little integration between Member States' markets;

- an absence of transparently available market information, leading to distrust in the pricing mechanisms;

- an inadequate current level of unbundling between network and supply interests, which has negative repercussions on market functioning and investment incentives;

- customers being tied to suppliers through long-term downstream contracts;

- current balancing markets and small balancing zones which favour incumbents.

Subsequent to the report, the Commission has done two things. First, it has undertaken legislative action to try and improve the regulatory framework for the sector by presenting a new legislative package which was adopted in 2009 and due to come into force in 2011.[93] Secondly, it has pursued individual cases, most notably against the German companies E.ON and RWE and the French companies, EDF and GDF.[94] Table 10.4 gives a list of the cases and the outcomes. With the exception of the E.ON/GDF collusion case, in none of them did the European Commission reach a formal decision. Instead, the undertakings concerned entered into legally binding commitments to meet the competition concerns. The commitments are significant: in a number of cases the undertakings have agreed to divest themselves of certain operations, which is a structural change in the market and something it would be difficult for the European Commission to accomplish by means of a formal decision under Regulation 1/2003. Most of the cases have been taken under Article 102 TFEU, with the exception of the E.ON/GDF collusion case, where the undertakings agreed not to compete against each other and the Commission found that they were guilty of market sharing, fining them €553 million.[95] The cases are discussed in more detail later in the text (see Chapter 15).

The European Commission has also followed up its sector inquiry into pharmaceuticals by opening proceedings against undertakings which it suspects of delaying the entry of generic medicines on to the market.[96]

Conclusions on market investigations and sector inquiries

There are significant differences between market investigations and sector inquiries. The Competition Commission has a power to impose remedies, ultimately, at the end of market

---

[93] See *http://ec.europa.eu/energy/gas_electricity/legislation/legislation_en.htm* (accessed 06/08/12).

[94] Case COMP/B-1/37966, *Distrigaz* (2007), Case COMP/39.388, *German Electricity Wholesale Market* and Case COMP/39.389, *German Electricity Balancing Market* (E.ON) (26.11.2008), Case COMP/39.316, *Gaz de France* (GdF Suez) (3.12.2009), Case COMP/39.402 RWE, *Gas Foreclosure* (18.3.2009), Case COMP/39.317, *E.ON Gas* (4.5.2010), Case COMP/39.315, *ENI* (29.9.2010), Case COMP/39.386, *Long-term electricity contracts in France* (EDF) (17.3.2010), Case COMP/39.401, *E.ON/GDF Collusion* (16.10.2009); Case COMP/39.351, *Swedish Interconnectors* (14.4.2010); Case COMP/39.727, *CEZ* and confirmed unannounced inspections for suspected anti-competitive behaviour in several Central and Eastern European Member States on 27 September 2011; see Press Release MEMO/11/641.

[95] COMP/39.401 *E.On – GdF collusion*. See Press Release 8 July 2009. Fine reduced to €320 million on appeal in Case T-360/09 *E.ON Ruhrgas AG v Commission* judgment of 29 June 2012 (GC).

[96] See Commission Press Releases, IP/11/511 28 April 2011, IP/11/1228 21 October 2011, IP/12/835 30 July 2012 and IP/12/834 25 July 2012 and MEMO 12/593 25 July 2012.

Table 10.4 Energy cases after the sector inquiry

Name	Date started	Type of decision	Outcome
Distrigaz	2007	Commitments decision	Reduction of gas tied into long-term contracts
German electricity wholesale market (E.ON)	2006	Commitments decision	Divestiture of generation capacity and transmission system business
German electricity balancing market (E.ON)	2006	Commitments decision	As above (same case)
GDF Suez Gaz de France	2008	Commitments decision	Release of long-term reservations of gas imports, reduction of share of reservations
RWE gas foreclosure	2007	Commitments decision	Divestiture of gas transmission network
E.ON gas	2009	Commitments decision	Release of gas volumes at entry points
E.ON/GDF collusion	2007	Fine	Market sharing
ENI	2007	Commitments decision	Divestiture of shareholdings
Long-term contracts in France	2007	Commitments decision	Return of large customers to market
Swedish interconnectors	2009	Commitments decision	Swedish transmission system divided into two zones; no limit on trading capacity on interconnectors
CEZ	2009	Potential commitments decision	Divesting coal-fired generation capacity

investigations and these remedies may be quite far-reaching. By contrast, the European Commission can only issue a report. However, having said that, after a sectoral inquiry the evidence is that the European Commission can take coordinated action on the basis of its findings: either through bringing individual cases or through proposing new legislation. The Competition Commission cannot bring cases under Articles 101 or 102 TFEU, nor the national equivalents, nor can it bring forward legislative proposals. It can, if necessary, make recommendations to government or other agencies about the action that they ought to take to remedy a competition problem, but it is up to government and those agencies to act. Even when it accepts or imposes remedies, the initial monitoring and report on the effectiveness of the remedies is done by the OFT, and splitting the responsibility in this way could lead to difficulties.

In addition, market investigations suffer because of the fragmented institutional structure of competition and regulatory policy in the UK. So, for example, the banking industry as a whole was reviewed by the non-statutory Cruickshank Report for the Treasury in 2000.[97] This led to a monopoly investigation by the Competition Commission into the supply of banking services to small and medium-sized businesses which reported in 2002 and recommended, among other things, a price control on current account charges and improvements to switching.[98] The OFT established a Payments System Task Force in 2004 to identify, consider and seek to resolve competition, efficiency and incentive issues relating to payment systems over four years, particularly looking at network effects of the existing payment mechanisms, which was also a partial response to the Cruickshank Report.[99] A super-complaint led to the market

[97] HM Treasury, *Competition in UK Banking* (2000).
[98] Competition Commission, 'The supply of banking services by clearing banks to small and medium-sized enterprises' (2002).
[99] See OFT, *Final Report of the Payment Systems Task Force* (2007).

investigation into personal current accounts in Northern Ireland, which recommended a variety of informational remedies as well as improvements to the switching process. In 2007, after a review by the OFT, the Competition Commission lifted the price cap on small business accounts.[100] Outside the competition arena, the OFT launched a test case on unauthorised overdraft charges for bank accounts based on the Unfair Terms in Consumer Contracts Regulations which led to significant litigation.[101] In 2008, after a market study, the OFT concluded that the market for personal current accounts is not working well for consumers because of their complexity and lack of transparency.[102] It has now launched a review of this work as part of a wider investigation into retail banking in the UK, which is in part a response to a recommendation from the Independent Banking Commission.[103] Following the financial crisis, the government has undertaken a variety of measures in relation to the banking industry, including allowing the merger of HBOS and Lloyds TSB, despite the OFT's assessment that this raised competition issues worthy of assessment by the Competition Commission (discussed in Chapter 13). Most importantly, the government set up an Independent Banking Commission to consider the structure of the UK banking sector which is likely to lead to significant changes.[104] So, rather than attempting to review the banking industry as a whole, different aspects have been investigated at different times through different legal procedures, although they all seem to have concluded that there was a variety of, different, problems in the sector. This matters because banks are a complicated and integrated business, like many financial institutions, and intervention in only a part of their business risks being ineffective. So, to take a simple example, if banks can no longer raise so much income from unauthorised overdraft charges, they could compensate for this by introducing an annual account fee, since switching of personal bank current accounts is rare. By contrast, in energy the European Commission can be seen to be at least attempting a unified approach, although this will be subject to Council decisions on the legislative package and review by the courts of decisions in individual cases.

Conclusions

Competition law has large difficulties in dealing with oligopolistic markets. It is, first, difficult to identify if there is a competition problem on any particular oligopolistic market. Secondly, even if it is possible to identify problematic markets, the legal techniques available to the competition authorities for dealing with them under Articles 101 and 102 TFEU are not suitable. Alternative techniques, such as market investigations and sector inquiries, seem to offer a more promising way forward but have yet to be properly assessed. Overall, what might be concluded is that although the problems have been recognised, there is still some way to go before competition law addresses them effectively.

---

[100] Competition Commission, 'Notice of decision to release undertakings in relation to SME banking' (2007).

[101] See http://www.oft.gov.uk/OFTwork/consumer-enforcement/consumer-enforcement-completed/UTCCRs/ (accessed 01/09/12).

[102] See http://www.oft.gov.uk/news/press/2008/84-08 (accessed 17/08/09).

[103] See http://www.oft.gov.uk/OFTwork/financial-and-professional/retail-banking/ (accessed 01/09/12).

[104] See http://bankingcommission.independent.gov.uk/ for the report and http://www.hm-trEnterprise Actsury.gov.uk/ fin_stability_regreform_icb.htm for the government response (accessed 06/08/12).

Summary

➤ In certain types of oligopolistic market structures, there may be an incentive for undertakings not to compete vigorously against each other.

➤ It is difficult to take action against these market structures under Article 101 TFEU, because the concept of concerted practices gives undertakings the right to adapt themselves intelligently to market conditions. Parallel behaviour, on its own, is only evidence of a concerted practice when there is no other explanation for the behaviour.

➤ Two or more undertakings can be considered as collectively dominant provided that from an economic point of view they present themselves or act together on a particular market as a collective entity. There are problems in establishing abuse of a collective dominant position.

➤ In the UK, markets which seem to raise competition problems may be investigated by the Competition Commission which, if it finds an adverse effect on competition, may make recommendations for remedies for the future.

➤ The European Commission has undertaken a number of sectoral inquiries in markets where it has concerns over competition.

Further reading

Albors-Lorens, A., 'Horizontal Agreements and Concerted Practices in EC Competition Law' (2006) 51 *Antitrust Bulletin* 837. *Comprehensive examination of the case law in this area.*

Monti, G., 'The scope of collective dominance under Article 82 EC' (2001) 38 *Common Market Law Review* 131. *Excellent critical overview of the area.*

Root, N., 'The UK Market Investigations Regime: A review' (2009) 8 *Competition Law Journal* 312.

Van Gerven, G. and Varona, E., 'The Wood Pulp Case and the Future of Concerted Practices' (1994) 31 *Common Market Law Review* 575. *Excellent discussion of the case and the notion of concerted practices.*

Whish, R., 'Collective Dominance' in D. O'Keeffe and M. Andenas (eds) *Liber Amicorum for Lord Slynn* (Kluwer, Amsterdam, 2000). *Insightful overview of collective dominance.*

11 Distribution agreements

Introduction

This chapter examines distribution agreements, that is, agreements between manufacturers and those undertakings that distribute their products, either through selling them directly to consumers (retailers) or through serving as an intermediary between the manufacturer and the retailer (wholesalers). If we think about the typical UK high street, it is apparent that the most common arrangement is that a manufacturer's products are sold through a separate retailer such as Debenhams, Tesco, PC World, Waterstones etc. It is very uncommon for a manufacturer to have decided to become vertically integrated and engage in its own distribution and, although it is common to find a retailer selling its own label products, such as Tesco's Finest, usually this is done under contract with a manufacturer.[1] In addition, there are many examples

---

[1] An example is the niche product, fantasy wargaming, produced by Games Workshop, a company which both manufactures and retails its products.

where a brand or a service is provided locally through franchises, with well-known examples being McDonald's, Burger King, Pizza Hut or Subway.[2] Here, the central organisation provides the brand, know-how, training and other things, while the delivery of the service is provided by a local contractor, acting within the rules set down by the central organisation. In competition terms, franchise agreements raise similar issues to distribution agreements more generally, so they are treated together in this chapter.

Economic issues in relation to vertical agreements

So distribution agreements are commercially very common and they are also vertical agreements, that is, agreements between two undertakings operating at different levels of the production chain which are not in competition with each other. Why then, should this be of any concern to competition lawyers, as it is not immediately obvious that such agreements will have any effect on the competitive process? Historically, two polar opposite answers have been given to this question. Originally in the US, and indeed in the EU system, the answer was that insofar as the agreement imposed restraints on the freedom of action of the distributor, then this was a restriction on their commercial freedom and thus should be examined critically by competition law. In response to this proposition, members of the Chicago school in the US argued that any restraints put on a distributor by a manufacturer were justified by the manufacturer's commercial interests, had no effect on competition, and should be considered as legal.[3] How, then, do we decide between these two views, or is there some mid-point between them?

To do this, we need to consider the evidence from economic theory about vertical agreements and the reasons why particular restraints are put in such contracts (Box 11.1 lists some common examples). The generic problem faced by the manufacturer and the distributor or retailer in their relationship is that they do not necessarily have the same incentives. So, for example, a manufacturer may want the product advertised widely and sold by trained staff. A retailer may see the advertising and staff training simply as extra costs, which will not bring sufficient benefit in extra sales and therefore will not engage in such activities, leading to lower sales for the manufacturer. A distributor may, on the other hand, want exclusive rights to a product, whereas a manufacturer might prefer a wider distribution network, with the distributors being in competition with each other, thus leading to greater sales for the manufacturer but less profit for the distributors (assuming that the manufacturer always charges the same wholesale price). The solution to the first problem could be, for example, selective distribution combined with service requirements. The solution for the second could be a level of exclusive distribution for the retailer covering, for example, a particular geographical area, with other retailers restricted to their own areas.

---

[2] For some idea of the range of franchising, see: *http://www.theukfranchisedirectory.net/* (accessed 08/01/13) or just google 'franchise'.

[3] R. Bork, *The Antitrust Paradox* (2nd edn, Free Press, New York, 1993) is the classic statement.

KEY DEFINITIONS Box 11.1

Types of vertical agreements (which include restraints)

Exclusive distribution: distributors assigned exclusivity over a particular area or class of customer. For example, new car dealers are typically given a particular area, and distributors of certain building products will only sell to 'trade'.

Exclusive dealing: retailer is prohibited from stocking competing products. For example, petrol stations.

Selective distribution: only a limited number of retailers are selected on the basis of some criteria. For example, fine perfumes, upmarket designer clothes, expensive hi-fi equipment.

Franchising: a franchise is an agreement or licence between two parties which gives a person or group of people (the franchisee) the rights to market a product or service using the trademark of another business (the franchisor).[4] For example: Pizza Hut, Popstar Academy, Subway, McDonald's, etc.

Single branding: agreements which have as their main element that the buyer is induced to concentrate their orders for a particular type of product with one supplier. Exclusive distribution is an example, but this can also include quantity forcing and tying, discussed in this box. This is a concept used by the European Commission.[5]

Vertical restraints within agreements
Resale price maintenance (RPM): a retail price fixed by the producer. This can be either a maximum or a minimum price and the retailer is not allowed to deviate.

Non-linear pricing: two-part tariff with a franchise fee plus a constant per unit charge. For example, payment of £X to obtain the franchise, and a payment of £Y per unit sold.

Quantity forcing: a specified minimum quantity that the retailer is required to distribute.

Service requirements: a specified level of pre- and post-sales service or promotional effort.

Tying: distributors contractually required to take other products, or even an entire product range: the latter is referred to as full-line forcing.

Source: Adapted from P. Dobson and M. Waterson, *Vertical Restraints and Competition Policy* (OFT, London, 1996).

Questions: What is the commercial incentive for parties to enter into such arrangements? To what extent do they have similar effects?

---

[4] From *http://www.whichfranchise.com/resources.cfm* (accessed 29/07/12).
[5] See European Commission, *Guidelines on Vertical Restraints*, OJ C130/01, 19.05.2010.

Double monopolisation and free riding

The differing incentives of the manufacturer and retailer lead to two problems which have been identified in the economic literature, which vertical restraints are designed to solve: double monopolisation (marginalisation) and free riding.[6] Taking double monopolisation first, let us assume that the manufacturer has a monopoly in their market. The manufacturer will set a wholesale price at a monopoly level to the retailer. The retailer, in turn will take that monopoly price as its cost and then set a monopoly price on top of that. The result is obviously damaging to societal welfare, but it is also damaging to the interests of the manufacturer because the retailer's price will result in less of the manufacturer's goods being sold than if the retailer had put its price at a competitive level, even assuming that it has to factor in the monopoly wholesale price. The problem can be solved by vertical integration, resale price maintenance (setting a maximum price) or by quantity forcing (because if the retailer must take a certain quantity, then it will set the price to sell that quantity). This example is useful because it shows that the vertical restraint may be beneficial (greater output at a lower price) but also that different vertical restraints can be used to reach the same end. Here there is a choice between resale price maintenance (RPM) and quantity forcing, or indeed vertical integration. The first lesson to draw from this is that competition policy rules should ideally treat vertical restraints in a similar way to the extent that they can be used as substitutes for each other. A subsidiary point, for the purposes of this chapter, is that if the rules make vertical restraints too costly, then firms will resort to vertical integration through mergers if that is easier under competition law.

The problem of free riding is also a useful example. Here we assume a manufacturer produces a product which is sold to a number of retailers. In order to boost sales, the manufacturer would like the retailers to engage in advertising, provide trained staff and a good after-sales service. All of these are costs, which have to be added on to the wholesale price. If consumers are able to switch between retailers, it is in the interests of an individual retailer not to engage in advertising, staff training and after-sales service because, as long as one retailer does this, the individual costs are lower and the non-participating retailers will have greater sales because they are able to undercut the participating retailers due to their lower costs. The manufacturer sells fewer products than would be the case if all the retailers were engaged in the level of advertising and service that was optimal. From the manufacturer's point of view, this problem can be dealt with either through selective distribution, or through exclusive distribution within a particular geographical area or through RPM, this time through setting a minimum price.

Free riding and the double monopolisation problem are two of the most commonly cited problems that vertical restraints are designed to overcome, but there are a number of other commercial reasons why vertical restraints might be imposed.[7] When a manufacturer has launched an innovative product, or their product is launched for the first time in a new area, the distributor may well want some protection against the risk of failure or some compensation which acknowledges the risk that they have taken. One way of dealing with this is to give the distributor exclusive rights to market the product, as was the case with the launch of the i-Phone in the UK, which was only available on the O2 network. Another example might be

---

[6] See M. Motta, *Competition Policy* (Cambridge University Press, 2004), pp. 306–33; R. Van den Bergh and P. Camesasca, *European Competition Law and Economics* (2nd edn, Sweet & Maxwell, London, 2006) at pp. 217–19.

[7] Generally, see European Commission, *Guidelines on Vertical Restraints* (n. 5), paras 106–109.

where either the manufacturer or the distributor must make specific investments in order to carry out the arrangement. So the manufacturer may have to invest in specific equipment to produce the product or the distributor may have to train its staff to handle the product or, in the case of franchising, may have to invest in training and materials which are specific to that franchise. If the investment is made by the manufacturer, responses could include quantity forcing or exclusive purchasing. From the distributor's point of view, the issue could be addressed by exclusive distribution or exclusive supply.

Resale price maintenance

So far in our discussion, there has been no clear-cut example of a vertical restraint which has anti-competitive effects. Historically, much of the suspicion of vertical restraints originates in worries about minimum RPM. In the original US case which led to a *per se* rule against RPM, the court viewed this practice as akin to horizontal price-fixing, even though it was a manufacturer fixing prices for its distributor.[8] Two justifications have been presented for this position. First, it has been argued that, if there is an oligopolistic industry and the manufacturers all engage in RPM, then this makes it easier to engage in horizontal price-fixing, either explicitly through agreement or through tacit collusion.[9] Secondly, the practice can be looked at from the distributors' perspective. If the distributors can obtain the agreement of the manufacturer to engage in RPM, then they may have the equivalent of a horizontal cartel, albeit one that is brought about through vertical agreements. Although these have been presented as justifications, there are very few cases, certainly in European Union law, where these types of arrangements have been discovered. However, in the UK, two of the earliest high-profile cases involved arrangements which had this effect: replica football shirts and Littlewoods/Argos (both of which have been discussed in Chapter 8).[10] In the latter case, the concern was with the prices of toys and games sold by Littlewoods and Argos, major catalogue stores, and the manufacturer, Hasbro, was responsible for ensuring that they did not compete on price by engaging in RPM.

It has also been argued that resale price maintenance may be pro-competitive.[11] If a manufacturer wants a certain level of service to be provided for its products, this will create a free-riding problem in relation to its retailers as some, who do not wish to provide the services, will free ride on those who do, and charge lower prices. The result will be that no retailers will provide the manufacturer's desired level of service. By imposing minimum retail prices, the manufacturer eliminates price competition and forces the retailers to concentrate on non-price competition and thus obtains the desired level of service. It has also been argued that this restriction of competition within the brand helps to increase consumer choice because it allows, for example, the development of competing brands with different price/quality mixtures. It has also been argued that resale price maintenance can encourage the entry of new brands and products into the market. When a new product enters the market and a retailer stocks it, the retailer does not know whether the entire amount of the product will be sold. There is thus a risk of being left with unsold products which cannot, in this

---

[8] *Dr Miles Medical Co v John D Park*, 220 US 373 (1911).

[9] Van den Bergh and Camesasca (n. 6) at pp. 208–9.

[10] See OFT, *Price-fixing of replica football shirts* (2003) and *Hasbro/Argos/Littlewoods* (2003). Upheld ultimately in *Argos and Littlewoods v OFT* [2006] EWCA Civ 1318 (CA).

[11] Van den Bergh and Camesasca (n. 6) at pp. 210–13.

example, be returned to the manufacturer. There is the potential for higher losses if the retailers engage in discounting to dispose of stock and RPM protects them to an extent against the losses by preventing such discounting.

For present purposes the point to note here is that the economic theories about the effects of RPM are mixed: some point to anti-competitive effects, while others point to pro-competitive effects. As we shall see below, both UK and EU law have been very hostile to RPM as was historically the case in the United States where there was a *per se* rule against minimum vertical RPM. This position has now changed as the Supreme Court has overruled the *per se* rule and instead held that these cases should be subject to rule of reason analysis.[12] This was a controversial 5–4 decision which has generated a huge amount of comment[13] but it should be borne in mind when it comes to assessing the European and UK rules on RPM.

Foreclosure of markets to new entrants and damage to inter-brand competition

Two other main problems have been identified in the economic literature which may arise from vertical restraints. The first is that they may foreclose markets to new entrants and the second is that they may dampen inter-brand (or indeed intra-brand) competition to the detriment of the competitive process. To move further with the discussion, it is necessary to draw a distinction between intra-brand competition and inter-brand competition. The former occurs where there is competition within the market for the same brand or product, such as when supermarkets offer different prices for Heinz tomato ketchup. The latter refers to competition in the market between brands, such as the competition between Pepsi and Coke. When vertical restraints are aimed at affecting the intra-brand competitive process it is less likely that they will be of concern to the competition authorities, as the activities will be constrained by inter-brand competition. So, for example, if an automobile manufacturer only allowed its cars to be sold by dealers who offered full service facilities this would prevent its cars being sold, at lower prices, by dealers who had not invested in service facilities. However, given that the market for new cars is competitive, the price would be constrained by other manufacturers' decisions. A third problem which has been identified in the context of European Union law is that vertical restraints might damage market integration, although whether this creates a problem from the point of view of economic analysis is a separate question.[14] The clearest example here would be where a manufacturer agrees with a distributor that that distributor will have the sole and exclusive rights to the product in one particular country and the manufacturer will prevent its other distributors from selling into that country. This is a clear example of dividing up a common market into different national markets.

How might vertical agreements foreclose market entry? Start by assuming that there are a limited number of distributors available for a product and that entry into distribution is not possible, for example, because of planning restrictions. The manufacturer then imposes exclusive dealing obligations upon the distributors, which would have the result of making it more difficult for a new, more efficient, entrant, for example from a different geographical

[12] *Leegin Creative Leather Products, Inc.* v *PSKS, Inc.* 127 S Ct 2705 (2007).
[13] For example, L. McMillan, 'The Proper Role of Courts: The mistakes of the Supreme Court in Leegin' [2008] *Wisconsin Law Review* 405; R. Brunell, 'Overruling Dr. Miles: The Supreme Trade Commission in Action' (2007) 52 *Antitrust Bulletin* 475.
[14] European Commission, *Guidelines on Vertical Restraints* (n. 5) at para. 100(d).

region, from entering this market because it would have no way of distributing the product. The opportunity for entry would come on the renewal of the exclusive dealing contracts and economic theory suggests that the manufacturer, even though making a monopoly profit, will not be able to offer enough to the distributor that will make it worth the distributor's while not to enter into a contract with the new entrant. This is true in any event, because the price the manufacturer will have to pay the distributors must compensate them for losing the opportunity to stock other, competing, products. There are, however, some circumstances where it might be possible for the manufacturer to foreclose the market. First, if there is a related market on which the manufacturer operates and, by excluding the entrant from that related market, it is able to increase profits. In these circumstances, the manufacturer might be able to make an offer which is high enough to induce the distributor to accept the exclusive deal.[15] Alternatively, if there are many distributors in the market, which cannot coordinate their actions, and an entrant needs to secure a certain number of them in order to enter the market, then it is possible for exclusive dealing to exclude the new entrant. Broadly speaking, as long as the manufacturer can tie up sufficient distributors, there is no incentive on the remaining ones to move to the new entrant, as there is insufficient distribution for the new entrant to enter the market. In terms of societal welfare, this is not a desirable arrangement because the prices are kept higher and output lower than would be the case in a more competitive environment.

As far as inter- and intra-brand competition is concerned, where vertical restraints are used which ensure that the distributor takes all or most of its orders from one manufacturer, then the Commission has argued that this can reduce inter-brand competition because it can lead to a situation where only one brand is sold in a retail outlet and thus there is no in-store inter-brand competition.[16] Alternatively, if the manufacturer sells to only one or a limited number of buyers, through selective distribution or allocating particular territories, this can limit intra-brand competition because of the lack of choice of distributors.[17] What would happen here, according to Motta,[18] is that with the distributor acting as a brand monopolist, this will result in higher prices for that brand and also push rivals' prices higher. Motta goes on to make the point that the result does depend on the type of competition in the market. It may be that the rivals will not raise their prices, but will instead see it as more profitable to reduce prices and increase output and in this case the original manufacturer will have to design a contract to make its distributors more aggressive, lower prices and the result will be lower prices in the market and increased consumer welfare.

Conclusions on the economic issues

A couple of important general points can be taken from this discussion. First, it should be evident from all the examples given that, in order to affect the competitive process, either the manufacturer or the distributor must have some level of market power. If they do not have market power, then any vertical restraints are likely to be benign and entered into simply for commercial, efficiency enhancing reasons. Secondly, even if there is some market power at work, the welfare effects of vertical restraints are not always obvious. Some vertical restraints

[15] See Motta (n. 6) at p. 364.
[16] European Commission, *Guidelines on Vertical Restraints* (n. 5) at para. 130.
[17] Ibid. at para. 151.
[18] Motta (n. 6) at p. 350.

may end up improving consumer welfare. In other cases, there may well be a trade-off between the improvements in efficiency and the anti-competitive effects of the vertical restraints, such that the restraints actually improve consumer welfare.

These points lead to certain conclusions in relation to what would be a desirable policy for vertical restraints. First, intervention is only necessary when there is some level of market power on either side of the equation; manufacturer or distributor. What level of market power, and how that should be assessed, is a good question, as indeed is the question, at what point does this become an Article 102 TFEU question? Secondly, intervention needs to be based on the effects of the practice, not on how the practice is categorised. This is particularly important because a variety of contractual techniques can be used as substitutes to reach particular ends and if policy treats one set more harshly than the others, then it is likely to encourage resort to those others, which can distort commercial transactions.[19] Thirdly, given the prevalence of distribution agreements, there need to be clear rules so that undertakings are able to assess whether their arrangements fall foul of the competition rules. There is a tension between this idea and that of looking at the effects of a practice and economic theory suggests that the presumption should be that vertical agreements are benign or welfare enhancing and it is only in certain particular circumstances that the competition authorities should intervene.

The approach to vertical agreements under Article 101(1) TFEU

To appreciate the current approach in the law to vertical restraints, it is helpful to go through, briefly, some of the history behind its development. Before doing that, some introductory remarks are necessary. First, the main tool for dealing with vertical agreements has been Article 101 TFEU, although when an undertaking has a dominant position then Article 102 TFEU can be invoked against certain commercial practices. So, in principle, certain vertical restraints could be attacked under either Article 101 or 102 TFEU but, in this chapter, we will concentrate on Article 101 TFEU. Secondly, in order for a vertical agreement to cause a competition problem it must fall within Article 101(1) TFEU. In order to do this, there are four hurdles that any agreement must meet:

1 There must be an agreement between undertakings.

2 The agreement must have an appreciable effect on inter-state trade.

3 There must be an appreciable effect on competition.

4 The agreement must have the object or effect of restricting competition.

If these criteria are met, and the fourth is addressed in more detail later in this chapter, then the agreement is void unless it can benefit from an exemption, individual or block, under Article 101(3) TFEU. The key question today is whether a vertical agreement meets the criteria for exemption set out in the block exemption for vertical agreements, which will be discussed in detail later in this chapter. The point to notice is that any policy on vertical agreements depends, in the first instance, on the interpretation of Article 101(1) TFEU.

---

[19] See G. Zanarone, 'Vertical Restraints and the Law: Evidence from automobile franchising' (2009) 52 *Journal of Law and Economics* 691.

This point becomes clear if we consider the well-known case of *Consten and Grundig*,[20] which involved a vertical agreement between the German manufacturer Grundig and the French retailer Consten, giving the latter exclusive rights to distribute Grundig products, such as radios and televisions, in France and providing Consten with absolute territorial protection, as other Grundig distributors were not allowed to enter the French market. It was argued on behalf of the applicants that Article 101 TFEU only applied to horizontal agreements and, had it been successful, this argument would have taken vertical agreements entirely out of the scope of EU competition law. The CJEU, however, rejected this argument, holding that Article 101 TFEU refers in a general way to all agreements which distort competition within the common market and does not lay down any distinction between those agreements based on whether they are made between competitors operating at the same level in the economic process or between non-competing persons operating at different levels.[21] The effect of this decision was that *all* vertical agreements which met the four criteria listed above would be in breach of Article 101(1) TFEU. Under the system which existed at that point, the early 1960s, this meant that it was in undertakings' interest to notify their agreements to the Commission in order to obtain an exemption under Article 101(3) TFEU and apparently there were around 35,000 such notifications by the end of 1966.

Of these four criteria, it was the fourth that proved to be the most controversial, even though we have seen a wide interpretation of the notion of an agreement taken by the Commission, as well as a broad interpretation of the effects on inter-state trade by the Commission and the European Courts. The most controversial aspect of this was the Commission's approach to whether an agreement had the 'object or effect' of distorting competition. The Commission took what has been called the economic freedom or the freedom of action approach,[22] by which any restriction on the freedom of action of the contracting parties which adversely affected the position of a third party on the market constituted a restriction on competition. This approach reflected a Freiburg or Ordo-liberal approach to competition law (discussed in Chapter 1), which is not one that accords with what modern economists are thinking or, indeed, with decisions of the EU Courts on this issue. The effect of this approach was to shift analysis from Article 101(1) TFEU to Article 101(3) TFEU because almost all agreements were seen as having a restrictive effect on competition and therefore the question became whether the benefits outweighed the detriments to competition. This wide interpretation, when combined with *Consten and Grundig*, allowed the Commission to take what Deacon, a Commission official, referred to as a regulatory approach of laying down the types of agreements and detailed clauses that would be permitted or not permitted in order to gain an exemption.[23]

Given that this wide interpretation generated such a large amount of notifications, the Commission was unable to process them effectively on an individual basis by making formal decisions. Instead it made informal decisions, the so-called 'comfort letters' and, more importantly for our purposes, developed a series of block exemptions for individual types of agreements. These exemptions all took the same general form: they listed clauses which would not be allowed (black clauses) and clauses which would be allowed (white clauses). There was

---

[20] Cases 56 and 58/64 *Consten and Grundig v Commission* [1966] ECR 299.

[21] Ibid. at 339.

[22] See B. Hawk, 'System Failure: Vertical restraints and EC Competition Law' (1995) 32 *Common Market Law Review* 973; and D. Deacon, 'Vertical Restraints under EU Competition Law: New Directions' (1995) *Fordham Corporate Law Institute* 307.

[23] Deacon (n. 22) at p. 308.

no scope within these rules for analysis of the agreement's effect upon the market; all that mattered were the clauses contained in the agreement. Although these block exemptions were initially welcomed, by the early to mid 1990s substantial criticism was being levelled at the block exemptions for being too formalistic, constraining commercial developments because the incentive was to use clauses that had been approved, and having inadequate coverage (there was no block exemption for selective distribution). The criticisms were not confined to the block exemptions but extended to the Commission's interpretation of Article 101(1) TFEU and the entire notification system, although at the centre of this was the issue of the treatment of vertical agreements. The Commission responded to these criticisms with a set of proposals for reforming the treatment of vertical agreements, which were first outlined in a Green Paper, then a White Paper and culminated ultimately in a new Council Regulation in 1999, which came into force in 2000.[24] The idea behind this reform was that a more economic approach would be taken to the assessment of vertical agreements, which would be evident in the drafting of the block exemption and the Commission's treatment of such agreements under Article 101(1) TFEU. The Regulation became, in fact, the first step in the modernisation of EU competition law which has been followed by the new procedural regulation, Regulation 1/2003, reform of merger control and proposals relating to the reform of Article 102 TFEU. It expired in May 2010 and has been replaced by a new version with revised guidelines.[25]

Article 101(1) TFEU and vertical agreements

As we have seen, logically the structure of Article 101 TFEU suggests that the first question is whether an agreement falls within Article 101(1) TFEU and, if it does, then the second question is whether the agreement is eligible for an exemption. This is the structure that will be followed here but, in practice, it is easier and more sensible to ask the question whether the agreement will benefit from the block exemption *if* it is caught by Article 101(1) TFEU. As we shall see, although the Regulation provides some clear rules about what sorts of agreements are eligible, the case law on Article 101(1) TFEU is much less clear. We start by recalling that Article 101(1) TFEU draws a distinction between agreements which have as their *object* the restriction of competition and those which have the *effect* of restricting competition. The difference between the two categories is that if an agreement is found to have the object of restricting competition, no inquiry is needed into the agreement's effects. On the other hand, if the effects of an agreement are in issue, a more in-depth analysis of the agreement in its economic context is needed, as will be seen in the discussion below. The other point to make is that clauses in the agreement are being assessed, not the agreement as a whole, and it is clauses that will be declared void under Article 101(2) TFEU.[26] This may have the effect of making the entire agreement unworkable but the effect that it will have depends on the national rules as to what clauses can be removed from an agreement while still retaining its core (referred to as 'severance').

[24] European Commission Regulation (EC) No. 2790/1999 on the application of Article 81(3) of the Treaty to categories of vertical agreements and concerted practices, OJ L336, 29.12.1999.

[25] European Commission Regulation (EC) No. 330/2010 on the application of Article 101(3) TFEU to categories of vertical agreements and concerted practices, L102/1, 23.04.2010. European Commission, *Guidelines on Vertical Restraints.*

[26] See Case 56/65 *Société La Technique Minière* v *Maschinbeau Ulm* [1966] ECR 234.

> ## Vertical agreements with the object of restricting competition: absolute territorial protection and export bans

It has been clear since *Consten and Grundig* that the CJEU has taken the view that clauses within a contract which impose absolute territorial protection have the object of restricting competition and are in breach of Article 101(1) TFEU. It should be remembered that the clauses in the contract in question prevented Consten from exporting Grundig products outside France and also prevented other Grundig distributors, located outside France, from importing Grundig products into France. The justification for this policy is not an economic one, as we have seen that territorial protection is not necessarily anti-competitive. Would, for example, Consten have taken the commercial risk of distributing Grundig products in France without some form of protection against imports? The justification for such a policy goes back to the overriding objective of the European Union to create one single market throughout Europe and thus to prevent private undertakings from partitioning national markets from one another. The following extract in Box 11.2 from *Consten and Grundig* makes this point clear. The CJEU has also been very strict in relation to export bans, holding 'that, by its very nature, a clause prohibiting exports constitutes a restriction on competition, whether it is adopted at the instigation of the supplier or of the customer since the agreed purpose of the contracting parties is the endeavour to isolate a part of the market'.[27] In other words, the justification underlying this approach to export bans is the same as that which underlies the approach to absolute territorial protection.

KEY CASE EXTRACT   Box 11.2

Rationale for the treatment of absolute territorial protection

Source: Cases 56 and 58/64 *Consten and Grundig* v *Commission* [1966] ECR 299 at 471:

> An agreement between producer and distributor which might tend to restore the national divisions in trade between member states might be such as to frustrate the most fundamental objectives of the Community [Union]. The Treaty, whose preamble and content aim at abolishing the barriers between states, and which in several provisions gives evidence of a stern attitude with regard to their reappearance, could not allow undertakings to reconstruct such barriers. Article 85(1) [Article 101(1) TFEU] is designed to pursue this aim, even in the case of agreements between undertakings placed at different levels in the economic process.

Question: Does this leave any room for the analysis of the economic effects of such an agreement?

Both the Commission and the Courts have taken a very strong line on this, holding that agreements fall foul of this principle even when they are not explicitly phrased in these terms. So, for example, breaches of Article 101(1) TFEU have been found where export was permitted but only with the consent of the producer,[28] where goods are supplied to distributors but the invoice for supply bears the words 'export prohibited',[29] where guarantees are limited

---

[27] Case 19/77 *Miller* v *Commission* [1978] ECR 131 at para. 7.
[28] Case T-77/92 *Parker Pen* v *Commission* [1994] ECR II-549.
[29] Case C-227/87 *Sandoz* v *Commission* [1990] ECR I-45.

to the state where the products were purchased,[30] or where financial support is contingent on products supplied to distributors only being used within a distributor's allotted territory.[31] For example, the Commission sent a statement of objections to major record companies and Apple because the agreement between them relating to iTunes only allowed customers to purchase music from the store within their country of residence and this was seen as a breach of Article 101(1) TFEU. The issue was solved by Apple agreeing to equalise prices across the European Union.[32] This list is not exhaustive but serves to show that the Commission and the Courts have been alert to prevent the principle from being eroded, and undertakings which have been in breach of the principle can expect high fines. So, for example, in *Nintendo* the Commission imposed a fine of €167.8 million on Nintendo and seven of its European distributors for colluding through agreements and/or concerted practices to prevent exports from low price to high price countries.[33]

The GC took a different approach in a case relating to the resale of drugs from the Spanish market to the UK market.[34] Here the manufacturer, GlaxoSmithKline (GSK), operated a dual pricing system whereby it charged lower prices to distributors for those drugs which were destined for use in Spain and higher prices for those which could potentially be exported to the UK. Complaints about this pricing system were made to the Commission, which decided that GSK had committed a breach of Article 101(1) TFEU because the agreement had, first, the object of restricting competition and, secondly, the effect of restricting competition. GSK argued that the agreement did not have the object or effect of restricting competition because the national authorities, Spanish and UK, fixed the prices of medicines and therefore there was no properly competitive market. The GC took the view that the objective of Article 101(1) TFEU was to prevent undertakings from reducing the welfare of the final consumer by restricting competition.[35] If the clauses of the agreement did not, themselves, reveal an alteration of competition, then the analysis would have to be supplemented by taking into account the legal and economic context. The GC examined the context and concluded that, as the prices of the medicines concerned are to a large extent shielded from the free play of supply and demand owing to the applicable regulations and are set or controlled by the public authorities, it cannot be taken for granted at the outset that parallel trade tends to reduce those prices and thus to increase the welfare of final consumers.[36] Since this was considered to be a largely unprecedented situation, it was necessary to examine the *effects* of the agreement and here the GC held that the Commission had to show that there was an effect on competition, which it had done. This decision was difficult to reconcile with the other case law in the area and the Commission appealed the part of the decision relating to the interpretation of the object of the agreement.[37] The Advocate General, in her opinion, took the view that the GC's approach was legally incorrect in part because the wording of Article 101(1) TFEU did not mention this and also because the assessment of consumer benefit

---

[30] Commission Decision, 'Zanussi' [1978] OJ L322/26.

[31] Commission Decision, 'JCB' [2002] OJ L69/1.

[32] See Press Releases: Memo/07/126, 3 April 2007; and IP/08/22, 9 January 2008.

[33] Commission Decision, *Nintendo distribution* [2003] OJ L255/33. Nintendo was partially successful in an appeal regarding the amount of the fine: Case T-13/03 *Nintendo v Commission* [2009] ECR II-943.

[34] Case T-168/01 *GlaxoSmithKline v Commission* [2006] ECR II-2969.

[35] Ibid. at para. 118.

[36] Ibid. at para. 147.

[37] Cases C-501, 513, 515 and 519/06 [2009] ECR I-9291 [2009] 4 CMLR 2.

should be done under Article 101(3) TFEU.[38] The CJEU reiterated a point it has made consistently that Article 101(1) TFEU) aims to protect not only the interests of competitors or of consumers, but also the structure of the market and, in so doing, competition as such. Consequently, for a finding that an agreement has an anti-competitive object, it is not necessary that final consumers be deprived of the advantages of effective competition in terms of supply or price. The CJEU went on to agree with the AG that by requiring proof that the agreement entails disadvantages for final consumers as a prerequisite for a finding of anti-competitive object and by not finding that that agreement had such an object, the General Court committed an error of law.[39] As discussed earlier (see Chapter 2), this case was one of a number of 'object' cases before the CJEU where it affirmed the orthodox understanding of the case law, in contrast to the GC's decision here.

Resale price maintenance

Despite the economic arguments to the contrary, the Commission takes the view that the imposition of minimum resale prices on distributors has the object of restricting competition and is thus unlawful.[40] This position is clearly supported by judgments of the courts, primarily in cases involving the assessment of franchising and selective distribution systems, but they indicate that resale price maintenance is a restriction of competition in itself. Thus, it was said in the *Binon* and *Metro* cases that 'clauses fixing the prices to be adhered to in contracts with third parties themselves restrict competition within the meaning of Article 85(1) [Article 101(1) TFEU]' and that 'price competition is so important that it can never be eliminated'.[41] As we shall see, the Commission makes a distinction between minimum and maximum resale price maintenance, which is not reflected in the case law. Leaving this point aside for the moment, it is clear that in European and UK terms, clauses imposing minimum resale price maintenance are clearly seen as being clauses which have the object of restricting competition and therefore no analysis of their effects is needed. Whether there will be some reconsideration of this position in the light of the change in law in the United States from a *per se* prohibition to a rule of reason approach is an open question. It would, among other things, seem to go against the text of Article 101(1) TFEU, which gives as an example of agreements restricting competition directly or indirectly fixing purchasing or selling prices and this makes such a change much more difficult. Also, as mentioned above, two of the earliest and most high-profile UK cases under the Competition Act 1998 concerned RPM, namely in relation to replica football shirts and toys and games produced by Hasbro (including, ironically, Monopoly).

The categories of vertical agreements or clauses within them which may have the object of restricting competition are not closed. Pierre Fabre Dermo-Cosmétique is a good illustration of this.[42] Here a French cosmetics company operated a selective distribution agreement, one of the terms of which was that the cosmetics had to be sold in a physical space where a

---

[38] See paras 102–18 of the opinion for the full discussion.

[39] Ibid. at paras 63–64.

[40] Although a more nuanced appreciation of the issues is shown at the end of the *Guidelines on Vertical Restraints* (n. 5): see paras 223–29.

[41] Respectively Case 234/83 *SA Binon v SA Agence et Messageries de la Presse* [1985] ECR 2015 at para. 44; Case 26/76 *Metro-SB-Grossmärkte v Commission (No. 1)* [1977] ECR 1875 at para. 21; and see also Case 161/84 *Pronuptia de Paris v Pronuptia de Paris Irmgard Schillgallis* [1986] ECR 353 at para. 25.

[42] Case C-439/09 *Pierre Fabre Dermo-Cosmétique SAS v Président de l'Authorité de la Concurrence* [2011] 5 CMLR 31.

qualified pharmacist was present. The effect of such a clause was to prevent the distributor selling the cosmetics over the Internet. The CJEU held that, in the context of a selective distribution system, this amounted to a restriction of competition by object where, following an individual and specific examination of the content and objective of that contractual clause and the legal and economic context of which it forms a part, it is apparent that, having regard to the properties of the products at issue, that clause is not objectively justified. This last point relates to the case being a preliminary reference under Articl 267 TFEU from the French courts, which meant that the CJEU could not make a definitive ruling.

Agreements which have the effect of restricting competition

If an agreement does not have the object of restricting competition, it may have the effect of restricting competition. In order to determine this, the agreement has to be assessed in its economic and legal context. According to the Commission's Guidelines on the application of Article 101(3) TFEU, 'for an agreement to be restrictive by effect it must affect actual or potential competition to such an extent that on the relevant market negative effects on prices, output, innovation or the variety or quality of goods and services can be expected with a reasonable degree of probability'.[43] The Commission goes on to say in this context that negative effects on competition are likely to occur when the parties have market power which may be created or strengthened by the agreement in question. The relevant level of market power which is needed is less than that needed for a finding of dominance under Article 102 TFEU, according to the Commission. This approach by the Commission is different from the one that it historically adopted prior to the Verticals Regulation and the modernisation of competition law after Regulation 1/2003. The factors which the Commission will take into account in assessing whether an agreement appreciably restricts competition are set out in Box 11.3 and it can be seen that the focus is on the issue of market power. So, for example, market position relates, 'first and foremost', to the market share of the supplier, competitor or buyer. The Commission will also look at the cost advantages of suppliers and other factors in relation to buyers, such as a wide geographic spread of outlets. Entry barriers are measured by the extent to which they allow incumbents to increase prices above the competitive level, again an indication of market power. Although this is a sensible approach, as we shall see, it is not entirely reflected in the case law. To present the case law in an understandable way, it is necessary to look at categories of agreements, which is what we do now.

KEY LEGAL PROVISION **Box 11.3**

Factors which determine whether an agreement brings about an appreciable restriction of competition

Nature of the agreement

Market position of the parties

Market position of competitors

---

[43] European Commission, *Guidelines on the application of Article 81(3) of the Treaty*, OJ C101, 27.04.2004 (at para. 24).

Market position of the buyer of the contract products

Entry barriers

Maturity of the market

Level of trade

Nature of the product

Other factors

Source: European Commission, *Guidelines on Vertical Restraints* (n. 5) at para. 111.

Questions: What information is needed to answer these questions? How easy is it to come to a definitive conclusion?

Single branding agreements

Single branding, sometimes referred to as exclusive dealing, is where, according to the Commission, a buyer is under an obligation or there is an incentive scheme which ensures that the buyer purchases practically all of its requirements on a particular market from one supplier.[44] As we have seen earlier (see Chapter 4), a seller in a dominant position that enters into such exclusive distribution arrangements is likely to be found to have committed an abuse and this suspicion of such arrangements is found also in the analysis under Article 101(1) TFEU because it can create problems of market foreclosure, facilitation of collusion between suppliers and, where the buyer is a retailer, a lack of in-store inter-brand competition.[45] Perhaps the most well known of these types of arrangements are in relation to pubs and bars where the outlet is not owned by a brewery but, in return for certain benefits, such as cheap loans, the pub or bar will agree to stock one brewer's set of products exclusively. Less well known are those arrangements where only particular types of refreshment are available at leisure events: for example, at Wembley Stadium, Walkers is the only supplier of snacks and savoury crisps, Carlsberg of beer and Coke is the official supplier of soft drinks.[46]

The *Delimitis* principles

How do we decide whether arrangements like these have the effect of restricting competition? The most important guidance for this came in the *Delimitis* case, which involved obligations placed on a café proprietor to purchase most of his beer from one supplier.[47] The CJEU in this case took the view that such agreements did not have the *object* of restricting competition but, in order to determine whether they had the *effect* of restricting competition, it was necessary to examine them in context, in particular looking at what the collective effect of such agreements would be on the market. To do so, the CJEU suggested that there were four steps needed in the analysis (see Box 11.4) which would allow the deter-mination of whether the market was foreclosed to competitors (sometimes known as the first *Delimitis* test).

---

[44] European Commission, *Guidelines on Vertical Restraints* (n. 5) at para. 138.
[45] Ibid.
[46] See *http://wembleystadium.com/Organisation/Sponsors* (accessed 29/07/12).
[47] Case C-234/89 *Delimitis v Henniger Brau* [1991] ECR I-935.

The *Delimitis* approach to determining the effect of an agreement

Source: Case C-234/89 *Delimitis* v *Henniger Brau* [1991] ECR I-935:

Determine relevant product market

Determine relevant geographic market

Consider possibilities of entry into the market

Assess the operation of competitive forces

Questions: What information is needed to answer these questions? How easy is it to come to a definitive conclusion?

If the answer to this question was affirmative, then a second question had to be asked, which was whether the agreements in question appreciably contributed to the foreclosure effect (referred to as the second *Delimitis* test).

A good example of how this approach has been applied can be found in *Van den Bergh Foods* v *Commission*.[48] Here Van den Bergh Foods (known as HB), a subsidiary of Unilever, produced ice cream for sale and immediate consumption (called impulse ice cream) in shops in Ireland. As part of its marketing strategy it supplied ice cream retailers with freezer cabinets at a nominal charge, provided that they were used exclusively for HB ice creams, and maintained the cabinets. Such agreements were terminable at two months' notice. Masterfoods, a subsidiary of the US company Mars, entered the Irish ice cream market and HB took action in the Irish courts to ensure that its freezer cabinets were used to stock only its products and not those of its competitor, Mars. Mars complained to the Commission which, after some negotiation with HB, made a decision that the distribution agreements were incompatible with Article 101 TFEU and, indeed, Article 102 TFEU, although we will only deal with the Article 101 TFEU issues here. The Commission, after defining the market as impulse ice creams,[49] took the view that the HB agreements restricted the ability of retailers to sell competing brands in circumstances where the only freezer cabinet or cabinets for the storage of impulse ice cream in place in retail outlets would have been provided by HB, where the HB freezer cabinet (or cabinets) was unlikely to be replaced by a cabinet owned by the retailer and/or supplied by a competitor, and where it was not economically viable to allocate space to the installation of an additional cabinet. It considered that the effect of this restriction was that the competing suppliers were precluded from selling their products to those outlets, thereby restricting competition between suppliers in the relevant market. The problem was that retailers only had space for one freezer cabinet[50] and that, in Ireland at the time, only 17% of the freezer cabinets in retailers were not subject to an exclusivity clause. This meant that in some 40% of outlets in Ireland at the time, HB provided the only freezer, which meant that the retailers were effectively tied to HB, and other ice cream manufacturers were foreclosed from

---

[48] Case T-65/98 [2003] ECR II-4653.
[49] As opposed to ice cream bought in packages, tubs or cartons from supermarkets.
[50] Ask your local newsagent whether they could fit in a second freezer cabinet.

access to those outlets. The agreements were thus a breach of Article 101(1) TFEU and did not qualify for an exemption under Article 101(3) TFEU, as well as being an abuse of a dominant position. HB was ordered to cease its infringement, that is, no longer insist on exclusivity.

This truncated description indicates that the Commission followed the *Delimitis* analysis by defining the market, impulse ice cream in Ireland, and considered the possibility of entry into the market (poor because of the 40% exclusivity) and the operation of competitive forces (limited for retailers with HB cabinets). For its part, the GC thought[51] that it was appropriate to consider whether all the similar agreements entered into in the relevant market, and the other features of the economic and legal context of the agreements at issue, showed that those agreements cumulatively had the effect of denying access to that market to new competitors (the first *Delimitis* condition). If, on examination, that was found not to be the case, the individual agreements making up the bundle of agreements could not impair competition within the meaning of Article 101(1) TFEU. If, on the other hand, such examination revealed that it was difficult to gain access to the market, it was then necessary to assess the extent to which the agreements at issue contributed to the cumulative effect produced, on the basis that only those agreements which made a significant contribution to any partitioning of the market were prohibited (the second *Delimitis* condition). So the specific economic context of the operation of the agreements had to be examined. The GC took the view that the agreements operated as a *de facto* tie on those retailers which had only HB freezer cabinets.[52] It was not impressed by the argument that the agreements could be terminated after two months, because factually they were terminated after eight years.[53] The GC also found that there was no objective link between the supply of freezer cabinets subject to a condition of exclusivity and the sale of ice creams.[54] Since retailers were not inclined to buy their own cabinet, because all the major manufacturers offered a freezer under similar terms and selling ice cream was only a marginal part of their business, this meant that smaller suppliers, with a more limited range, would find it very difficult to enter this market. After this examination, the GC held that the Commission had been right to conclude that HB's agreements had an appreciable effect on competition and contributed significantly to the foreclosure of the market.

On economic grounds, this is a controversial decision. In the UK, as opposed to Ireland, the Competition Commission has investigated the sale of impulse ice creams and the issue of freezer exclusivity twice and arrived at differing conclusions, seeing no problem in the earlier investigation, but finding problems in the later one.[55] Critical commentary on these decisions has been divided, with some commentators arguing that freezer exclusivity does lead to market foreclosure, while others have argued that it does not.[56] This makes the point that it is important not to jump to conclusions in relation to single branding agreements. As Jones and Sufrin point out,[57] after *Delimitis*, the Commission has found single branding

---

[51] *Van den Bergh Foods* v *Commission* (n. 48) at para. 83.
[52] Ibid. at para. 98.
[53] Ibid. at para. 105.
[54] Ibid. at para. 113.
[55] Competition Commission, 'Ice cream' (1994) and 'The supply of impulse ice cream' (2000).
[56] Compare A. Robertson and M. Williams, 'An ice cream war: The law and economics of freezer exclusivity: Part 1' (1995) 16 *European Competition Law Review* 70 with D. Ridyard, 'With the benefit of hindsight – the 2000 UK impulse ice cream investigation' (2005) 26 *European Competition Law Review* 533.
[57] A. Jones and B. Sufrin, *EC Competition Law* (4th edn, Oxford University Press, 2011) at pp. 665–6.

agreements which do not infringe Article 101(1) TFEU,[58] agreements which do infringe Article 101(1) TFEU but meet the Article 101(3) TFEU criteria[59] and agreements which do infringe Article 101(1) TFEU but do not meet the Article 101(3) TFEU criteria (of which *Masterfoods* is an example).

Commission guidance on single branding agreements

The Commission has given detailed guidance on how it will approach single branding agreements in the context of Article 101(1) TFEU in the guidelines on vertical restraints. It takes the view that one needs to assess the market position of the supplier and the duration of any non-compete, that is, single branding, obligation. The higher the market share and the longer the non-compete obligation, the more significant the foreclosure is likely to be. The Commission says that single branding obligations are more likely to result in anti-competitive foreclosure.[60] For non-dominant companies, non-compete obligations of less than a year are not problematic, those longer than five years are not in general acceptable, while those between one and five years require a balancing of the pro- and anti-competitive effects.[61] The Commission goes on to say that in cases where the market share of the largest supplier is below 30% and the market share of the five largest suppliers is below 50% there is unlikely to be an anti-competitive effect.[62] The Commission also thinks that the 'level of trade' is important. What it means is that, in its view, it matters whether the agreement deals with intermediate or final products and distribution at a wholesale or retail level. For intermediate products, foreclosure is less likely, as long as less than 50% of the market is tied.[63] For final products where the agreement relates to the wholesale level (for example, a publisher's agreement with Amazon), it depends on the type of wholesaling and the entry barriers at that level. As regards retail products, the Commission takes the view that significant anti-competitive effects may start to arise if a non-dominant supplier ties 30% or more of the relevant market.[64] If all the companies have market shares below 30% then a cumulative foreclosure effect is unlikely if the total tied market share is less than 40%.[65]

The lesson that can be drawn from the case law and the Commission's guidelines is, first, that it is difficult for dominant companies to engage in single branding agreements (and see Chapter 4 as well). Secondly, once a company has above a 30% market share, even if it is not dominant, it seems likely that if it has single branding agreements which are mirrored by other industry participants, this will be considered a breach of Article 101(1) TFEU and it may be difficult to obtain an exemption under Article 101(3) TFEU. Finally, if the company has a market share below 30%, this should not typically be a problem, unless the tied market share is above 50% (intermediate products) or above 40% (retail products). If the company's market share is below 30% it can obtain the benefit of the block exemption Regulation for

---

[58] Commission Decision IP/98/67, *Roberts/Greene King*, upheld on appeal Case T-25/99 *Roberts* v *Commission* [2001] ECR II-1881.

[59] Commission Decision, *Bass* [1999] OJ L186/1 and *Whitbread* [1999] OJ L88/26.

[60] European Commission, *Guidelines on Vertical Restraints* (n. 5) at para. 133. (Compare with the discussion in Chapter 4.)

[61] Ibid.

[62] Ibid. at para. 135.

[63] Ibid. at para. 138.

[64] Ibid. at para. 140.

[65] Ibid. at para. 141.

vertical agreements which allows non-compete obligations with duration of up to five years, subject to there being no hard-core restraints, discussed below. As we shall see, it is much easier, if the market share is below 30%, to determine whether the agreement contains any clauses which are prohibited by the block exemption Regulation on vertical agreements, than to engage in the *Delimitis* analysis to determine if the agreement is caught by Article 101(1) TFEU.

Exclusive distribution agreements

An exclusive distribution agreement is defined by the Commission as one where a supplier agrees to sell his or her products only to one distributor for resale in a particular territory.[66] The distributor is usually limited in the active selling (see Box 11.5 for the definition) that they may do into other exclusive allocated territories.

KEY LEGAL PROVISION   **Box 11.5**

Definition of active and passive sales

'Active' sales mean actively approaching individual customers by, for instance, direct mail, including the sending of unsolicited emails, or visits; or actively approaching a specific customer group or customers in a specific territory through advertisement in media, on the Internet or other promotions specifically targeted at that customer group or targeted at customers in that territory. Advertisement or promotion that is only attractive for the buyer, if it (also) reaches a specific group of customers in a specific territory, is considered active selling to that customer group or customers in that territory.

'Passive' sales mean responding to unsolicited requests from individual customers including delivery of goods or services to such customers. General advertising or promotion that reaches customers in other distributors' (exclusive) territories or customer groups but which is a reasonable way to reach customers outside those territories or customer groups, for instance to reach customers in one's own territory, are considered passive sales. General advertising or promotion is considered a reasonable way to reach such customers if it would be attractive for the buyer to undertake those investments also if they would not reach customers in other distributors' (exclusive) territories or customer groups.

Source: European Commission, *Guidelines on Vertical Restraints* (n. 5) at para. 51.

Question: How useful is this distinction in the age of Internet selling?

On their own, these agreements differ from single branding because the distributor may be allowed to stock competing products or provide competing services. The amount of protection that can be given for the territories can vary from the manufacturer agreeing not to sell the product itself within the allocated territory, but not restricting exclusive distributors in other territories from selling into an allocated territory, to limiting distributors to selling

[66] Ibid. at para. 151.

within their own territory, but allowing them to respond to orders from outside their territory, or preventing distributors from making any sales outside their territory at all. It is quite clear from *Consten and Grundig* that this latter, absolute territorial protection is in breach of Article 101(1) TFEU because it has as its object the restriction of competition. The CJEU has, however, recognised that there may be positive benefits arising from exclusive distribution agreements, particularly when they are necessary to allow the manufacturer to penetrate a new market.[67]

The Commission's approach to exclusive distribution on a territorial basis[68] is that, on its own, this is only a problem if inter-brand competition is limited, so that the market position of the supplier and its competitors is of major importance. Below a 30% market share, the block exemption Regulation provides an exemption for exclusive distribution agreements even if combined with other non-hard-core vertical restraints, such as non-compete obligations no longer than five years, quantity forcing or exclusive purchasing.[69] Above a 30% market share threshold there may be a risk of a significant reduction in intra-brand competition and therefore in order to fulfil the conditions of Article 101(3) TFEU, the loss of intra-brand competition may need to be balanced with real efficiencies.[70] One of the problems here is that although strong competitors may mean that any reduction in intra-brand competition is outweighed by inter-brand competition, this can also play the other way. If all the manufacturers have similar market shares and operate similar distribution systems, the Commission takes the view that the risks of collusion may increase, particularly where there are multiple exclusive dealerships, that is, where different suppliers share the same distributor.[71] The Commission is not particularly concerned with the exclusion of other distributors, so long as the supplier appoints a high number of exclusive distributors and does not prevent them supplying other non-appointed distributors.[72] At a retail level, the main problem with a loss in intra-brand competition arises if exclusive distribution is combined with large territories, because final consumers may have little choice between high price/high service retailers and low price/low service ones.[73]

Exclusive distribution is more of a problem for the Commission when it is combined with single branding or exclusive purchasing. If exclusive distribution and single branding leads to a problem, then the analysis discussed above needs to be applied. If there is not significant foreclosure, the Commission accepts that this combination may be pro-competitive by increasing the incentive on the exclusive distributor to promote a particular brand.[74] Exclusive distribution combined with exclusive purchasing may lead to a problem because it prevents the exclusive distributors from purchasing from each other, because they must purchase from the supplier, which makes it possible for the supplier to price discriminate between the distributors and, according to the Commission, allows the supplier to limit intra-brand competition.[75]

---

[67] Case 56/65 *STM* v *Maschinbeau* [1966] ECR 234 at p. 249.
[68] Similar principles apply to exclusive customer allocation: see European Commission, *Guidelines on Vertical Restraints* (n. 5) at paras 168–173.
[69] Ibid. at para. 152.
[70] Ibid. at para. 153.
[71] Ibid. at para. 154.
[72] Ibid. at para. 156.
[73] Ibid. at para. 159.
[74] Ibid. at para. 161.
[75] Ibid. at para. 162.

⬤ Selective distribution agreements

Selective distribution systems are where the supplier appoints a limited number of distributors and puts some restrictions on resale. Unlike exclusive distribution, where distributors are selected in relation to geographic territories or customer groups, in selective distribution the selection is, in theory, made on the basis of criteria related to the product. For example, the supplier may require the outlet to present the product in a particular way or for the staff to be trained in a certain way. The resale restrictions are typically aimed at stopping sale to other, unauthorised distributors; in other words, to prevent free riding. Typically the retailers carry some competing brands, which helps to distinguish selective distribution from franchising. Franchising tends also to be used in the service area and typically involves the transfer of intellectual property rights and know-how to the franchisee, which will allow them to run the business, which again distinguishes it from selective distribution. Selective distribution tends to be used in relation to products and services where the image presented to the consumer of the supplier's product is important or where the product is a complex one and the final consumer may need some guidance. A standard example of selective distribution agreements is that of fine perfumes which are sold within retailers from dedicated sections of the store, although selective distribution is also pervasive in the selling of new motorcars.[76]

Two interesting aspects need to be noted about selective distribution agreements. First, the agreement involves a limitation on the number of distributors or retailers. The entire point for the supplier is to limit the number of persons with whom the supplier has to deal and to ensure that, by limiting distribution, those that distribute the product have sufficient incentive to promote it. In other words, the limitation is not done on a territorial basis. Secondly, common definitions suggest that there is an element of RPM in this arrangement,[77] something which is clearly a restriction of competition by object, if it is spelled out in the agreement. Since selective distribution is often used for luxury or branded products, one of the ideas behind it is to prevent, or discourage, price discounting as this is seen as incompatible with a luxury image.

The starting point for understanding the legal treatment of this method of distribution is the first of the two *Metro* cases.[78] Here a manufacturer of electrical equipment (televisions, radios and tape recorders), SABA, ran a selective distribution network in Germany. Metro was a cash and carry wholesaler whose main business was to sell to retailers that resold the product but there was also an element of selling to 'institutional' consumers, such as schools and hospitals. Metro applied to be a member of SABA's selective distribution network but SABA refused to agree to this, unless Metro stopped selling to retailers, presumably because this could undermine the selective distribution network. Metro complained to the Commission, which held that certain aspects of the system were outside Article 101(1) TFEU and others were within it, but granted an exemption for those under Article 101(3) TFEU. Metro then appealed to the CJEU, which found that such a distribution network did not breach Article 101(1) TFEU (see Box 11.6). In order not to breach Article 101(1) TFEU, however, there are four cumulative conditions which have to be met:

---

[76] There is a specific block exemption for this area: European Commission Regulation (EC) 461/2010 of 27 May 2010 on the application of Article 101(3) TFEU to categories of vertical agreements and concerted practices in the motor vehicle sector, OJ L129/52, 28.05.2010.

[77] See *http://www.answers.com/topic/selective-distribution?cat=biz-fin* (accessed 29/07/12), although admittedly an American website.

[78] Case 26/76 *Metro-SB-Grossmärkte v Commission (No. 1)* [1977] ECR 1875.

KEY CASE EXTRACT Box 11.6

The CJEU's view of selective distribution agreements

Source: Case 26/76 *Metro-SB-Grossmärkte v Commission (No. 1)* [1977] ECR 1875 paras 20–1:

In the sector covering the production of high quality and technically advanced consumer durables, where a relatively small number of large- and medium-scale producers offer a varied range of items which, or so consumers may consider, are readily interchangeable, the structure of the market does not preclude the existence of a variety of channels of distribution adapted to the peculiar characteristics of the various producers and to the requirements of the various categories of consumers.

On this view the Commission was justified in recognizing that selective distribution systems constituted, together with others, an aspect of competition which accords with Article 85(1) [Article 101(1) TFEU], provided that resellers are chosen on the basis of objective criteria of a qualitative nature relating to the technical qualifications of the reseller and his staff and the suitability of his trading premises and that such conditions are laid down uniformly for all potential resellers and are not applied in a discriminatory fashion.

It is true that in such systems of distribution price competition is not generally emphasized either as an exclusive or indeed as a principal factor. This is particularly so when, as in the present case, access to the distribution network is subject to conditions exceeding the requirements of an appropriate distribution of the products. However, although price competition is so important that it can never be eliminated it does not constitute the only effective form of competition or that to which absolute priority must in all circumstances be accorded.

For specialist wholesalers and retailers the desire to maintain a certain price level, which corresponds to the desire to preserve, in the interests of consumers, the possibility of the continued existence of this channel of distribution in conjunction with new methods of distribution based on a different type of competition policy forms one of the objectives which may be pursued without necessarily falling under the prohibition contained in Article 85(1) [Article 101(1) TFEU], and, if it does fall thereunder, either wholly or in part, coming within the framework of Article 85(3) [Article 101(3) TFEU].

Questions: Is price competition really not important in relation to high quality and technically advanced consumer durables? Consider the case of laptops. How can this approach be reconciled with other case law and the views of the Commission?

---

1   the characteristics or nature of the product in question necessitate a selective distribution system; and[79]

2   the distributors are chosen by reference to objective criteria of a qualitative nature which are set out uniformly and are not used arbitrarily to discriminate against a certain retailer; and

3   the criteria do not go beyond what is necessary for the product in question; and

4   the market must not be foreclosed to competitors by a network of similar agreements to which the agreement in question contributes appreciably.[80]

---

[79] This results from the interpretation of the notion of objectivity mentioned in *Metro (No. 1)* above. See: *NV L'Oréal and SA L'Oréal v PVBA De Nieuwe AMCK* [1980] ECR 3775 at para. 16 and *Groupement d'Achat Edouard Leclerc v Commission* [1994] ECR II-441 at para. 112.

[80] This is the *Delimitis* criteria as applied in this context: see *NV L'Oréal and SA L'Oréal v PVBA De Nieuwe AMCK* [1980] ECR 3775 at para. 19; and *Société d'Hygiène Dermatologique de Vichy v Commission* [1992] ECR II-415 at paras 58 and 59.

The first three of these are criteria do not contain any element of economic analysis; they simply consider the nature of the product and the criteria applied. By contrast, the fourth condition does require economic analysis of the agreement in its context and what competition would be like if the agreement had not been entered into. We need to examine these criteria in more depth.

The nature of the product

The first *Metro* judgment suggests that selective distribution is justified in relation to high quality and technically advanced consumer goods or, to put it another way, luxury products and technically complex ones. In practice, in the past, the Commission has accepted that a wide range of goods justify a selective distribution system ranging from perfumes, motor cars (the selective distribution systems for which have their own block exemption), televisions, hi-fis, cameras and luxury watches (although not all watches).[81] Some doubt was cast on the need for selective distribution in relation to plumbing fittings, at least at the wholesale level, in the context of a system which tried to ensure that the plumbing equipment was only sold to professional plumbing contractors.[82] This has led one commentator to conclude, contrary to what seems to be implied in *Metro (No. 1)* and the Commission's view,[83] that almost any product may validly be the subject of some kind of selective distribution system.[84] Although this does seem too wide, it is clear that it is important that the distribution system is applied consistently; in other words, that similar distributors are appointed in different states and that the supplier does not operate an Internet site for selling the product while the physical retailers have to be members of a selective distribution system.[85] Past case law may also not necessarily be a guide for the future because, although in 1977 when *Metro (No. 1)* was decided, televisions and radios may have been considered technically complex, this is probably not the case today, certainly with radios. It is, in any event, not immediately obvious why the treatment of a product should depend on its classification by a competition authority or a court. In the absence of market power, the choice of a selective distribution system, or not, should be left up to the manufacturer or supplier and its success or failure will be the result of market conditions.

Qualitative not quantitative criteria

As well as the products having to be of the appropriate nature, selection of the distributors must be done on the basis of quality criteria, not quantitative ones. The idea here is to prevent suppliers from picking a limited number of distributors for their products in a particular area, thus limiting intra-brand competition. One of the problems is that the distinction between a qualitative and a quantitative restraint can be difficult to make because the restriction is broader than just a numerical limit included in the contract. So, for example, in the Vichy cosmetics case, admission to the selective distribution network depended on the retailer being qualified as a dispensing chemist which, on its face, looks like a qualitative

---

[81] *ETA Fabriques d'Ebauches v DK Investments* [1985] ECR 3933 at para. 16.

[82] *Grohe* [1985] OJ L19/17.

[83] See European Commission, *Guidelines on Vertical Restraints* (n. 5) at para. 175.

[84] J. Goyder, *EU Distribution Law* (4th edn, Hart Publishing, Oxford, 2005) at p. 115.

[85] In *Société d'Hygiène Dermatoligique de Vichy v Commission* [1992] ECR II-415 at para. 71 the Vichy group fell foul of this, arguing that its cosmetic products had to be sold through qualified dispensing chemists but then selling some of its products through beauticians.

criteria. However, in the Member States concerned there was a ceiling on the number of dispensing chemists which meant that this was effectively a quantitative restraint, even though the number of potential sales outlets was quite high.[86] It seems clear that criteria relating to the technical qualifications of the retailer and his or her staff, the suitability of trading premises and the provision of after-sales service are all restrictions which are considered to be qualitative.

Discriminatory application of the criteria

There are two stages to the assessment here. First, if the criteria are capable of being used in an arbitrary and discriminatory manner, then this means that they fall foul of Article 101(1) TFEU. Thus, for example, when there was a dispute over Yves St Laurent's distribution system for its perfumes, one of the clauses within it which set the criteria for acceptance related to the scale of other activities carried on in the outlet, with the carrying on of other activities beyond 40% of the activity in the outlet receiving a negative mark. The CJEU remarked that this was discriminatory as it tended to favour specialist perfumeries over multi-product shops with areas laid out for the sale of perfumes.[87] Secondly, the same case makes it clear that it was for national courts to ensure that the criteria, for example on professional qualifications, the sale of other goods and shop windows, were not applied in a discriminatory manner.

Criteria must not go beyond what is necessary

This is neatly illustrated by the Vichy case, where it was a requirement of the selective distribution system for cosmetic products that the member should be a dispensing chemist. The CJEU said that such a requirement was simply not necessary for the distribution of such products and that Vichy's concern to offer its customers the same advice as that prescribed for the use of medicinal preparations could not be regarded as a necessity deriving from the characteristics of the products in question but must be seen as a marketing strategy intended to create and maintain a brand image benefiting from the reputation of the pharmaceutical profession.[88] Similarly in *Pierre Fabre Dermo-Cosmétique*[89] the question was whether a clause, which required the sale of cosmetics in the physical presence of a pharmacist, thus preventing Internet selling, was necessary for the sale of such products.

Networks of agreements

This final condition comes from the *Metro (No. 2)* case.[90] It will be remembered that SABA received an exemption under Article 101(3) TFEU for its distribution agreement, but this exemption was time limited. When it expired, SABA applied for it to be renewed, but Metro objected, arguing that the conditions in the market had changed and that many other electronics companies operated selective distribution systems and therefore it had become much more difficult for wholesalers like Metro to obtain supplies. The CJEU responded as follows (see Box 11.7).

---

[86] Ibid. at paras 67–8.
[87] *Groupement d'Achat Edouard Leclerc v Commission* [1994] ECR II-441 at paras 152 and 153.
[88] *Société d'Hygiène Dermatoligique de Vichy v Commission* [1992] ECR II-415 at paras 69 and 71.
[89] Case C-439/09 *Pierre Fabre Dermo-Cosmétique SAS v Président de l'Authorité de la Concurrence* [2011] 5 CMLR 31.
[90] Case 75/84 *Metro-SB-Grossmärkte v Commission (No. 2)* [1986] ECR 3021.

KEY CASE EXTRACT   **Box 11.7**

Effect of networks on selective distribution agreements

Source: Case 75/84 *Metro-SB-Grossmärkte* v *Commission (No. 2)* [1986] ECR 3021, paras 40–1:

It must be borne in mind that, although the Court has held in previous decisions that 'simple' selective distribution systems are capable of constituting an aspect of competition compatible with Article 85(1) [Article 101(1) TFEU] of the Treaty, there may nevertheless be a restriction or elimination of competition where the existence of a certain number of such systems does not leave any room for other forms of distribution based on a different type of competition policy or results in a rigidity in price structure which is not counter-balanced by other aspects of competition between products of the same brand and by the existence of effective competition between different brands.

Consequently, the existence of a large number of selective distribution systems for a particular product does not in itself permit the conclusion that competition is restricted or distorted. Nor is the existence of such systems decisive as regards the granting or refusal of an exemption under Article 85(3) [Article 101(3) TFEU], since the only factor to be taken into consideration in that regard is the effect which such systems actually have on the competitive situation.

Questions: In a competitive market, would you expect a wide variety of distribution systems, with different costs and arrangements? What does the CJEU mean by rigidity in price structure?

The CJEU rejected Metro's arguments, saying that it had not produced any evidence that the growth in number of selective distribution systems had had an effect on the process of competition. In other words, what was required was the sort of economic analysis envisaged by the CJEU in *Delimitis*.

In summary, the case law suggests that only relatively simple selective distribution systems will fall outside Article 101(1) TFEU. Assessment of the compatibility of a selective distribution system with Article 101(1) TFEU depends on four criteria, which are difficult and somewhat uncertain to operate in practical terms. By contrast, the block exemption Regulation (BER) exempts selective distribution regardless of the nature of the products concerned[91] and restrictions are allowed, so long as they do not constitute hard-core restrictions. For those agreements which do not fall within the BER, of particular importance to the Commission is the coverage of a market by networks of selective distribution agreements.[92] Its Guidelines suggest that there is unlikely to be a problem where the share of the market covered by such agreements is below 50%, nor where the overall coverage is above 50% but the aggregate market share of the five largest suppliers is below 50%. Where the market coverage is above 50% and the aggregate share of the five largest suppliers is also above 50%, then it depends on whether the largest suppliers all apply selective distribution. If this is the case, competition concerns are considered to arise if the agreements apply quantitative criteria which limit the amount of authorised dealers. Combinations of qualitative restrictions with a requirement to make a minimum amount of annual purchases are less likely, in the Commission's view, to have negative effects, if the amount does not represent a significant proportion of the

---

[91] European Commission, *Guidelines on Vertical Restraints* (n. 5) at para. 176.
[92] Ibid. at para. 179.

dealer's turnover and does not go beyond what is necessary for the supplier to recover the relationship-specific investment and/or realise economies of scale in distribution. If the market share of a supplier is below 5%, the Commission in general considers that this does not contribute significantly to a cumulative effect.[93] The other situation that the Commission is particularly concerned about is the combination of selective distribution with single branding, in which case the approach taken to single branding applies.[94]

Franchising

Franchises are agreements where one party (the franchisor) agrees to license to another party (the franchisee) certain intellectual property rights and know-how which will allow the franchisee to carry on the business of selling products or services in accordance with an approach laid down by the franchisor. Typical examples are Subway, Burger King and Pizza Hut. In return, the franchisee will typically make a single payment to the franchisor (franchise fee) and will also make periodic payments to the franchisor based on the performance of the franchise.[95] To enable a franchise to function properly, there tend to be a number of other clauses. Thus, there is some selection concerning those who apply to run a franchise, similar to selective distribution agreements, and typically there is some limitation on the number of franchises that will be appointed in a particular area. Franchises sell only the products or services provided by the franchisor, so in that sense they are similar to single branding agreements. In addition, there is typically some control of pricing as the goods or services will be sold at uniform prices in the same markets. To put it another way, each McDonald's charges the same price for its food as every other McDonald's.

There has only ever been one judgment by the CJEU on a franchising system, the *Pronuptia* case, which arose out of a dispute between a franchisor and a franchisee over the payment of fees.[96] The franchisee claimed that the franchise contract was in breach of Article 101(1) TFEU and a German court referred a number of questions over the legality of the franchise contract to the CJEU. The CJEU pointed out that it was concerned here with what it called a 'distribution franchise'; that is, where the franchisee simply sells certain products in a shop which bears the franchisor's business name or symbol, in contrast to service and production franchises.[97] The compatibility of such arrangements could not be assessed in the abstract but depended on the type of clauses included within them. In the CJEU's view, there were two vital conditions that had to be met for a franchise to work effectively:[98]

1 the franchisor must be able to communicate his know-how to the franchisees and provide them with the necessary assistance in order to enable them to apply his methods, without running the risk that that know-how and assistance might benefit competitors, even indirectly; and

2 the franchisor must be able to take the measures necessary for maintaining the identity and reputation of the network bearing his business name or symbol.

---

[93] Ibid.
[94] Ibid. at para. 183.
[95] Ibid. at para. 189 for the Commission's definition.
[96] Case 161/84 *Pronuptia de Paris* v *Pronuptia de Paris Irmgard Schillgallis* [1986] ECR 353.
[97] Ibid., para. 13.
[98] Ibid., paras 16–17.

The first condition meant that the franchisor could impose restrictions on the franchisee, preventing them from opening a shop of a similar nature, but outside the franchise, during the period of the contract and for a reasonable period thereafter and from selling the shop without the franchisor's consent. The second condition meant that there could be clauses requiring the franchisee to do the following:[99]

- apply the business methods and know-how developed by the franchisor;
- sell the goods only in premises laid out in accordance with the franchisor's instructions;
- obtain the franchisor's approval for the location of the shop;
- only assign his or her rights and duties under the contract with the franchisor's approval;
- obtain approval of all advertising from the franchisee;
- sell only products supplied by the franchisor in the shop.[100]

On the other hand, the CJEU was not prepared to accept provisions relating to territorial restrictions, such as a clause which prevents the franchisee from opening a second, franchised, shop in a different territory. This was seen as a partitioning of markets, similar to *Consten and Grundig* and therefore unacceptable under Article 101(1) TFEU although, since a franchisee would not have entered into such an agreement without the hope of some sort of protection, this would need to be examined under Article 101(3) TFEU. Also, provisions which restricted the franchisee's ability to determine prices were also restrictive of competition, although this was not the case where price guidelines were all that was provided.[101]

The Commission's Guidelines devote relatively little space to franchising agreements, treating them to an extent as a subset of selective distribution, non-compete agreements or exclusive distribution. The Guidelines also indicate that most of the obligations contained in franchise agreements can be assessed as being necessary to protect intellectual property rights or maintain the common identity and reputation of the franchised network and will thus fall outside Article 101(1) TFEU.[102]

The block exemption on vertical agreements[103]

As can be seen from the discussion above, the rules as to when particular agreements are caught by Article 101(1) TFEU are not straightforward. Therefore, in practice, the easiest thing for undertakings to do when concerned about their agreements possibly being in breach of Article 101(1) TFEU is to consider whether they will be entitled to obtain the benefit of the block exemption Regulation (BER). The BER, which first came into force in 1999, represents the first phase in the modernisation of EU competition law and so is supposed to take a more economic approach to the issue of whether vertical agreements have an anti-competitive effect on competition. In practice, as we shall see, the more economic side of the analysis is

---

[99] Ibid., paras 16–22.
[100] Although the franchisee must not be prevented from obtaining those goods from other franchisees.
[101] Ibid., paras 23–5.
[102] European Commission, *Guidelines on Vertical Restraints* (n. 5) at para. 191.
[103] European Commission Regulation (EC) No. 330/2010 on the application of Article 101(3) TFEU to categories of vertical agreements and concerted practices, L102/1, 23.04.2010 (hereafter BER).

focused on the market share threshold. The basic analysis that should be followed under the BER is as follows:

1 Is this a vertical agreement concerned with purchase and distribution of goods or services?

2 Is it a vertical agreement which falls within Article 101(1) TFEU?

3 Is the market share of the supplier and the buyer, generally, below 30%?

4 Does the agreement contain any hard-core restrictions?

5 Does the agreement contain any non-compete obligations?

In order to gain the benefit of the BER, the answer has to be yes to the first three questions and no to the fourth. If the answer to the fifth question is yes, then the issue is whether those obligations can be severed from the agreement. If they can, then the agreement can benefit from the BER. If not, it cannot. There are, however, fallback provisions which allow the Commission, or a national competition authority, to withdraw the benefit of the block exemption from an individual agreement and which allow the Commission to decide that the Regulation does not apply in particular circumstances. The BER itself is relatively short but the Commission has provided extensive advice in the form of Guidelines on the Commission's approach on a number of issues. We now need to look at this basic outline in more detail.

Definition of a vertical agreement

Vertical agreements are defined in Article 1(a) of the BER as follows (Box 11.8).

KEY LEGAL PROVISION   **Box 11.8**

Definition of vertical agreements

. . . agreements or concerted practices entered into between two or more undertakings each of which operates, for the purposes of the agreement, at a different level of the production or distribution chain, and relating to the conditions under which the parties may purchase, sell or resell certain goods or services.

Source: BER, Article 1(a).

Question: Think of examples of these types of agreement.

The Commission goes on to say in its Guidelines that there are four elements in this definition.[104] First, the BER applies to agreements and concerted practices, not unilateral conduct of undertakings, which leads to a discussion of when the Commission feels that acquiescence with a unilateral policy can be established. Secondly, the agreement must be between undertakings, that is, the BER does not cover agreements between undertakings and final consumers. Thirdly, the undertakings that are parties to the agreement must be operating, for the purposes of the agreement, at different levels of production: for example, a manufacturer and a distributor. Fourthly, the agreements relate to the conditions under which the parties agree to

---

[104] European Commission, *Guidelines on Vertical Restraints* (n. 5) at para. 25.

purchase, sell or resell goods and services. The BER is meant to apply to purchase and distribution agreements but this raises issues about the distinction between such agreements and, for example, agreements relating to the licensing of intellectual property, which will be discussed shortly.

Vertical agreements between competing undertakings are excluded from the benefit of the BER, and competing undertakings are defined as actual or potential suppliers in the same market.[105] There are two exceptions, which relate to non-reciprocal vertical agreements. First, if the supplier is a manufacturer and a distributor of goods, while the buyer is a distributor and not a competing undertaking at the manufacturing level; or, secondly, if the supplier is a provider of services at several levels of trade, while the buyer provides its goods or services at the retail level and is not a competing undertaking at the level of trade where it purchases the contract services.[106] According to the Commission, these exceptions cover dual distribution of either goods or services, and in these situations it is considered that in general any potential impact on the competitive relationship between the manufacturer and retailer at the retail level is of less importance than the potential impact of the vertical supply agreement on competition in general at the manufacturing or retail level.[107]

As regards the relationship with intellectual property rights, the BER applies to vertical agreements containing IPR provisions (see Box 11.9) so long as this is not the primary purpose of the agreement. If the transfer of IPR is the primary purpose of the agreement, it falls to be considered under the Technology Transfer Block Exemption Regulation, discussed in detail later (see Chapter 12).

KEY LEGAL PROVISION   **Box 11.9**

Intellectual property rights in vertical agreements

The exemption provided for in paragraph 1 shall apply to vertical agreements containing provisions which relate to the assignment to the buyer or use by the buyer of intellectual property rights, provided that those provisions do not constitute the primary object of such agreements and are directly related to the use, sale or resale of goods or services by the buyer or its customers. The exemption applies on condition that, in relation to the contract goods or services, those provisions do not contain restrictions of competition having the same object or effect as vertical restraints which are not exempted under this Regulation.

Source: BER, Article 2(3).

Question: What types of intellectual property rights might it be necessary to cover in a vertical agreement? For example, think about franchising agreements.

According to the Commission's Guidelines, this means that five conditions must be fulfilled to fall within the BER:[108]

1 The IPR provision must be part of a vertical agreement.

2 The IPRs must be assigned to, or for use by, the buyer.

---

[105] BER Article 1(c).
[106] BER Article 2(4).
[107] European Commission, *Guidelines on Vertical Restraints* (n. 5) at para. 28.
[108] Ibid. at para. 31. Licensing issues in relation to intellectual property rights are dealt with later (see Chapter 12).

3 The IPR provisions must not constitute the primary purpose of the agreement.

4 The IPR provisions must be directly related to the use, sale or resale of goods or services by the buyer or his customers.

5 The IPR provisions, in relation to the contract goods or services, must not contain restrictions of competition having the same object or effect as vertical restraints which are not exempted under the BER: that is, they are not hard-core restrictions nor non-compete restrictions.

Does the vertical agreement fall within Article 101(1) TFEU?

We have seen from the discussion above that certain vertical agreements do not fall within Article 101(1) TFEU, such as simple selective distribution agreements and certain types of franchising agreements. If this is clearly the case, then there is no need to consider whether the BER applies. In addition, agreements which do not have an appreciable effect on competition and agreements between small and medium-sized enterprises are not considered by the Commission to fall within Article 101(1) TFEU. In essence, vertical agreements between undertakings whose market share does not exceed 15% are generally considered not to fall within Article 101(1) TFEU, unless those agreements contain hard-core restrictions.

Also excluded from the scope of Article 101(1) TFEU are agency agreements between undertakings. An agency agreement is defined by the Commission as where a legal or physical person (the agent) is given the power to conclude contracts on behalf of another person (the principal) either in the agent's or the principal's own name for the purchase or sale of goods and/or services by the principal.[109] An arrangement such as this does not fall within Article 101(1) TFEU because the agent is acting on behalf of the principal; in other words, it is equivalent to the agent being part of the principal and therefore the agreement has no effect on competition. The problem is that such arrangements do not necessarily take such a simple form and, in the Commission's view, the determining factor is the financial or commercial risk borne by the agent in relation to the activities for which he has been appointed an agent. Financial or commercial risks may relate to contractually specific risks, market specific risks, such as investments required for the type of activity envisaged, or risks relating to other activities undertaken by the agent at its own risk.[110]

Working out whether an arrangement is a true agency arrangement, and thus falls outside Article 101 TFEU, is not a straightforward matter. The Commission takes the view that the agreements have to be looked at on a case-by-case basis. Having said this, the Commission's view is that Article 101(1) TFEU will not generally be applicable where property in the contract goods does not vest in the agent or the agent does not supply the contract services and where the agent does not do a variety of things, including not maintaining at his own costs or risk stocks of the product, or does not create or operate an after-sales service, or does not make market specific investments in equipment, premises, etc.[111]

---

[109] European Commission, *Guidelines on Vertical Restraints* (n. 5) at paras 12–21.
[110] Ibid., at paras 13–14.
[111] Ibid., at para. 16. There are seven conditions listed.

The case law examples also suggest that it can be difficult to determine in practice whether an agency agreement falls outside Article 101(1) TFEU. In *DaimlerChrysler*,[112] the Commission decided that Mercedes Benz agents were independent and that therefore there was a breach of Article 101(1) TFEU as they were subject to export bans. The GC reviewed the arrangements between Mercedes Benz and its agents closely and came to the conclusion that the Commission had misunderstood the nature of the relationship. The sales price of the cars was determined by Mercedes Benz, which took on the principal risk. Other obligations which were imposed on the agents, such as arranging the transportation of cars, did not, in the GC's view, demonstrate a passing of risk in contrast to the arrangements for dealers. In *Confederación Española de Empresarios de Estaciones de Servicio* v *Compañía Española de Petróleos SA*,[113] the question, on an Article 267 TFEU reference, was whether operators of service stations in Spain were agents or independent dealers. Although the CJEU did not decide this issue, it set out some guidelines for determining whether the relationship was one of agency or not. In particular, it said that the relationship must be analysed 'on the basis of criteria such as ownership of the goods, the contribution to the costs linked to their distribution, their safe-keeping, liability for any damage caused to the goods or by the goods to third parties, and the making of investments specific to the sale of those goods'[114] and that the risk must be more than negligible.

Market share

One of the key provisions of the BER is that it only applies where the market share of the supplier and the buyer is 30% or below.[115] We should note that 30% as a limit is some way short of the presumption of dominance – 50% – and therefore it is possible to fall outside the BER even if an undertaking is not dominant. The 30% market share limit is a proxy for market power, the assumption being that below this limit there is no, or insufficient, market power and that above it there is a question to answer. Of course, in order to calculate the market share of an undertaking, it will be necessary to define both the product and geographic markets, something which is not, as we have seen (in Chapters 1 and 3), an entirely straightforward exercise. In addition, an undertaking's market share will have to be monitored because if it goes above 30%, then the benefit of the block exemption will be lost. The BER does provide some transitional protection here, stating that if the market share was originally below 30% and then rises above it, but below 35%, then the exemption will continue to apply for two calendar years. If the market share rises to above 35%, the exemption only applies for one calendar year and the two provisions cannot be combined.[116]

Hard-core restrictions

The benefit of the BER will be lost if the agreement contains any hard-core restrictions and these are listed in Box 11.10.

---

[112] Case T-325/01 *DaimlerChrysler* v *Commission* [2005] ECR II-3319.
[113] Case C-217/05 [2006] ECR I-11997.
[114] Ibid., para. 60.
[115] Guidance on how to do this is found in Article 7 of the BER and Section V of the Commission Guidelines.
[116] BER Article 7(d) and (e).

KEY LEGAL PROVISION   **Box 11.10**

Hard-core restrictions

(a) the restriction of the buyer's ability to determine its sale price, without prejudice to the possibility of the supplier's imposing a maximum sale price or recommending a sale price, provided that they do not amount to a fixed or minimum sale price as a result of pressure from, or incentives offered by, any of the parties;

(b) the restriction of the territory into which, or of the customers to whom, the buyer may sell the contract goods or services, except:

   – the restriction of active sales into the exclusive territory or to an exclusive customer group reserved to the supplier or allocated by the supplier to another buyer, where such a restriction does not limit sales by the customers of the buyer,

   – the restriction of sales to end-users by a buyer operating at the wholesale level of trade,

   – the restriction of sales to unauthorised distributors by the members of a selective distribution system, and

   – the restriction of the buyer's ability to sell components, supplied for the purposes of incorporation, to customers who would use them to manufacture the same type of goods as those produced by the supplier;

(c) the restriction of active or passive sales to end users by members of a selective distribution system operating at the retail level of trade, without prejudice to the possibility of prohibiting a member of the system from operating out of an unauthorised place of establishment;

(d) the restriction of cross-supplies between distributors within a selective distribution system, including between distributors operating at different levels of trade;

(e) the restriction agreed between a supplier of components and a buyer who incorporates those components, which limits the supplier to selling the components as spare parts to end-users or to repairers or other service providers not entrusted by the buyer with the repair or servicing of its goods.

Source: BER, Article 4.

Questions: What are the sources for these hard-core restrictions? To what extent do they address practices which are damaging to competition?

It should be noted that there is no element of economic analysis of the effect of these restrictions: if they are contained in the agreement, then it automatically falls outside the BER and the issue becomes whether an individual exemption will be available. Insofar as hardcore restrictions are concerned, the Commission has indicated that it is unlikely that an individual exemption will be available, although undertakings may attempt to demonstrate that there are pro-competitive effects in an individual case.[117] It is therefore important to understand the limits of these restrictions precisely as the inclusion of such a provision is very likely to mean that the agreement is in breach of Article 101(1) TFEU and will not qualify for

[117] European Commission, *Guidelines on Vertical Restraints* (n. 5) at para. 47.

any exemption, thus rendering the agreement void and the parties to the agreement liable to civil actions by other parties that are damaged by the agreement.

Restriction of price

This part of the BER concerns resale price maintenance and is easy to apply if the contractual provisions explicitly stipulate minimum prices. In the Commission's view, this definition goes further because it is possible to engage in RPM by what they call indirect means.[118] It gives a number of examples of this, such as: fixing the maximum level of discount that a distributor can grant from a fixed price level, linking the prescribed prices to those charged by competitors, threats, warnings, penalties or delays in delivery all due to a failure to observe a given price level. It makes the point that these measures are more effective when combined with means of identifying price-cutting behaviour, such as a price monitoring system or asking retailers to provide examples of when other retailers have not observed the recommended price. Simply setting a recommended retail price or, indeed, a maximum price, does not lead to RPM. It is, however, clear that one cannot assess whether RPM is taking place simply by looking at the contractual terms in isolation; it is necessary to examine the surrounding circumstances to see whether RPM is being carried out by indirect means.

Territorial or customer restrictions

This restriction relates to contracts that restrict the territory into which the buyer can sell the contract goods or services and contracts that restrict the type of customers to which the buyer can sell. As an example of the latter, think of builders' merchants that will sell only to the trade,[119] rather than individual consumers, or a wholesale distributor of a particular line of goods, which will not sell to consumers. This is one of the more complex restrictions because it is expressed as a general rule, with four exceptions, outlined in Box 11.10 above. Its origins are the market integration objectives of the Union, but the problem is that, in terms of economic analysis, in the absence of market power, such restrictions are not considered to be a problem. So the BER tries to provide some exceptions to this general prohibition which cover common commercial practices but the result is a very complex provision.

In the same way as RPM, the Commission points out that territorial or customer restrictions may be direct or indirect.[120] Examples that it gives of indirect restrictions are where bonuses or discounts are refused or lowered because of a breach of the restrictive provisions, a refusal to supply, a reduction of supply such as limiting supplies to the demand within the allocated territory or group.[121] Another example is where the supplier refuses to provide a Union-wide guarantee service but makes arrangements to provide guarantees only where goods are bought within the specified territories of the distributors.[122] Again, such practices are more likely to be viewed as hard-core restrictions when they are combined with systems for monitoring the destination of the contract goods. It is not, however, a hard-core restriction to prevent resale to certain end-users if there are objective justifications for doing so, such as health and safety reasons.

---

[118] Ibid., para. 48.

[119] Given that builders' merchants sell a variety of products, this is normally a commercial decision, not one imposed by their suppliers.

[120] European Commission, *Guidelines on Vertical Restraints* (n. 5) at para. 50.

[121] Remember, in this context, the practices carried out in the *Bayer* case, Cases C-2 and 3/OIP [2004] ECR I-23.

[122] *ETA Fabriques d'Ebauches v DK Investments* [1985] ECR 3933.

The first exception to this hard-core restriction allows suppliers to prevent the 'active' sale by a distributor into an exclusive territory or customer group allotted by the supplier to another distributor, or reserved for the supplier. These two provisions may be combined, so a supplier may allocate an exclusive distributor for a particular customer group in a particular territory. Although the contract may prohibit 'active' sales, it must allow 'passive' ones, so a critical question is what exactly these two terms mean? The Commission defines the terms as in Box 11.5.

So, for example, an active sale would cover direct mailing of specific customer groups or specific territories outside that allotted to you as a distributor. A passive sale is where the customer simply walks into the store, or contacts the distributor in order to buy the product or service but the distributor has made no effort to solicit that custom. This distinction is difficult with the use of the Internet for sales and distribution because it is quite common for a supplier, which advertises on the Internet, to ship their goods to any country, not just the country that they are physically based in. According to the Commission, the use of the Internet is not in general considered to be a form of active selling, since it is a reasonable way to reach every customer and it does not matter what language is used on the website or in the communications.[123] The Commission regards certain arrangements as hard-core restrictions of passive selling.[124] These are, first, an agreement that the (exclusive) distributor shall prevent customers located in another (exclusive) territory from viewing its website or automatically re-routing its customers to the manufacturer's or other (exclusive) distributors' websites. Secondly, an agreement that an (exclusive) distributor will terminate customers' transactions over the Internet once it is revealed that their address is not within the distributor's (exclusive) territory. Thirdly, an agreement that the distributor shall limit its proportion of overall sales made over the Internet. Finally, an agreement that the distributor shall pay a higher price for products intended to be resold by the distributor online than for products intended to be resold offline. A website is only considered active selling if it is in some sense targeted to customers within other distributors' exclusive territory or customer groups. So, for example, if there was another website that was so limited, such as the internal site for a university, and a link was placed on that website to the distributor's site then that would constitute active selling. Unsolicited emails are considered by the Commission to be active selling.

The other three exceptions are somewhat more straightforward and allow for the restriction of both active and passive sales. The second exception is a restriction on sales to end-users by a buyer operating at the wholesale level of trade. This is fairly common and the idea is that it allows the supplier to protect their distribution system because, if end-users could approach wholesalers direct, this would undermine the position of the retailers. The third exception allows for the restriction of sales to unauthorised distributors by members of a selective distribution system. The rationale for this is again to protect the distribution system, because the distributors have been selected on some quality criteria and it would undermine the system if authorised distributors could sell to the unauthorised ones. So, for example, it is quite difficult to buy certain premium perfumes, such as Guerlain, Givenchy and Chanel, outside authorised channels.[125] The fourth exception allows for a restriction on a buyer's ability to sell components, supplied for the purposes of incorporation, thus preventing the buyer from

---

[123] European Commission, *Guidelines on Vertical Restraints* (n. 5) at para. 52.
[124] Ibid.
[125] Although not impossible. Consider also how designer labels end up in TK Maxx.

reselling them to competitors of the supplier that would use them to manufacture goods in competition with the supplier. The rationale here is more directly to protect the business of the supplier.

Restricting sales to end-users by members of a selective distribution system

This provision means that members of a selective distribution system, operating at the retail level, cannot be restricted to the users to whom they can sell and this covers both active and passive sales. A member of such a system can, however, be prevented from operating out of an unauthorised place of business, because it is usually the case that selective distribution systems have some quality requirements in terms of the shop. In the Commission's view, this also means that the distributor can be prevented from operating out of a new location if this is not approved by the supplier. In addition, the Commission takes the view that a member of a selective distribution system should be free to advertise and sell with the help of the Internet.[126] This provision is really the counterpart of Article 4(b) which prohibits limitations on customer allocation but makes it clear that retailers in a selective distribution system must be allowed to sell to all end-users, that is, consumers. It is also aimed at preventing selective distribution systems from including territorial allocations by including clauses which prevent the distributors from selling to consumers from outside their allocated territory.

Restriction of cross-supplies between distributors in a selective distribution system

The basic idea here is that, within an authorised distribution system, the supplier cannot prevent its distributors from engaging in active or passive sales between themselves. The effect of this is to hinder the supplier from charging different prices in different territories or to different customer groups through charging different prices to its distributors. If the supplier charges high prices to one group of distributors and low prices to another, those being charged the high prices have the opportunity to obtain the goods from other distributors that are being charged lower prices. This will thus allow those distributors that were being charged the higher price to bring their prices closer[127] to the lower level. This restriction only applies to selective distribution systems. If something similar happened in an exclusive distribution system, this is covered by Article 4(b), which allows the prohibition of active sales, but not the prohibition of passive sales.

Restrictions on components

The final hard-core restriction is aimed at preventing limitation on access to components. So, if a supplier provides components to a buyer that incorporates those parts into their own equipment, the agreement must not limit the supplier from selling those components to end-users, independent repairers or service providers, even if they are not approved to service the equipment by the buyer that makes the equipment. So, for example, if a manufacturer of mufflers for car exhausts sells those mufflers to an automobile manufacturer, the muffler manufacturer cannot be prevented from selling those mufflers to consumers that want to put them on their cars directly or garages engaged in servicing cars. The automobile manufacturer cannot restrict access to those parts to their own approved service network.

---

[126] European Commission, *Guidelines on Vertical Restraints* (n. 5) at para. 56. See also: Case C-439/09 *Pierre Fabre Dermo-Cosmétique SAS* v *Président de l'Authorité de la Concurrence* [2011] 5 CMLR 31.

[127] Closer because there will be some mark-up on purchases from those distributors that have bought at the lower price.

Non-compete obligations

If the agreement contains any hard-core restrictions, then the agreement as a whole cannot qualify under the BER. As regards non-compete obligations, it is only the obligations themselves that the BER does not apply to. In other words, if the agreement can be operated without such obligations, then it may continue and qualify for exemption under the BER. So, what are non-compete obligations? These are defined in Box 11.11.

KEY LEGAL PROVISION   **Box 11.11**

Definition of non-compete obligation

'Non-compete obligation' means any direct or indirect obligation causing the buyer not to manufacture, purchase, sell or resell goods or services which compete with the contract goods or services, or any direct or indirect obligation on the buyer to purchase from the supplier or from another undertaking designated by the supplier more than 80% of the buyer's total purchases of the contract goods or services and their substitutes on the relevant market, calculated on the basis of the value of its purchases in the preceding calendar year.

Source: BER, Article 1(d).

Question: What is the purpose of inserting these provisions into an agreement?

A non-compete obligation is, as its name suggests, aimed at ensuring that the distributor does not sell, or sells only at a minimal level, goods or services which compete with those supplied by the supplier. This is a fairly common commercial provision, particularly in relation to franchising, as branches of McDonald's do not sell Burger King beefburgers, for example. In recognition of this, the BER does not ban such clauses outright, but simply seeks to prevent them being excessive: in particular, it seeks to prevent them from lasting for too long or indefinitely. The idea is that, at the end of any such contract, the buyer may re-tender the contract, which thus opens up the buyer to competing products. An indirect obligation would be an obligation which encourages the buyer to obtain all their supplies from that one supplier. A good example would be a discount or rebate which was available only if all, or above 80%, of the buyer's needs were obtained from the seller. The limits on non-compete obligations are spelled out in Box 11.12.

KEY LEGAL PROVISION   **Box 11.12**

Limits to non-compete obligations

(a) any direct or indirect non-compete obligation, the duration of which is indefinite or exceeds five years. The time limitation of five years shall not apply where the contract goods or services are sold by the buyer from premises and land owned by the supplier or leased by the supplier from third parties not connected with the buyer, provided that the duration of the non-compete obligation does not exceed the period of occupancy of the premises and land by the buyer;

➡

(b) any direct or indirect obligation causing the buyer, after termination of the agreement, not to manufacture, purchase, sell or resell goods or services, unless such obligation:

- relates to goods or services which compete with the contract goods or services, and
- is limited to the premises and land from which the buyer has operated during the contract period,
- is indispensable to protect know-how transferred by the supplier to the buyer, and provided that the duration of such non-compete obligation is limited to a period of one year after termination of the agreement; without prejudice to the possibility of imposing a restriction which is unlimited in time on the use and disclosure of know-how which has not entered the public domain;

(c) any direct or indirect obligation causing the members of a selective distribution system not to sell the brands of particular competing suppliers.

Source: BER, Article 5 (text has been re-arranged).

Questions: What are the justifications for these limits? For example, why five years as opposed to four or six?

The first point is that the maximum allowed duration is five years; indefinite non-compete obligations are not allowed. Nor are non-compete obligations allowed when they can be tacitly renewed, for example, when, if nothing is done, the agreement is simply rolled forward. The Commission takes the view that the obligations will be allowed when the renewal requires explicit consent and there are no obstacles in the agreement that prevent the buyer from terminating the contract at the end of the five-year period.[128] An example given by the Commission of something which might hinder termination is if the buyer has a loan from the supplier for a term longer than five years.[129] Five years is a bit of an arbitrary figure and probably at the outer boundaries of acceptability. It should be remembered that, in an exclusive purchasing contract, the supplier may well make certain investments in order to supply the buyer and will need a period of time to make a profit on those investments. If, for example, a supermarket bought all its carrots from one supplier, that supplier might well have to invest in packaging and quality control technology to meet the level of demand and, as a result, in the early years of the contract, not make a profit. The contract would only become profitable in the later years, although how much later is an empirical question. There are some contracts that become profitable quite quickly, others might need the entire five-year period to be worthwhile and, in principle, there may be some that need more than five years: for example, the Eurostar service between London and Paris.[130]

The five-year time limit does not apply when the goods and services are sold from premises and land owned by the supplier or leased by the supplier from parties not connected to the buyer. So, for example, if the buyer was a pub landlord operating from premises owned by a brewery, here the non-compete obligation may be of the same duration as the occupancy.

---

[128] European Commission, *Guidelines on Vertical Restraints* (n. 5) at para. 66.
[129] Ibid.
[130] See *http://news.bbc.co.uk/1/hi/business/4010527.stm* in relation to the first ten years (accessed 21/07/12).

The Commission explains that the reason for this exception is that it is normally unreasonable to expect a supplier to allow competing products to be sold from premises and land owned by the supplier without its permission.[131]

Secondly, obligations which, after the termination of the contract, cause the buyer not to manufacture, purchase, sell or resell goods or services are also covered by Article 5 in order to prevent suppliers from limiting the commercial freedom of buyers after the conclusion of the contract. There is, however, an exception to this provision. The obligation must relate to competing goods or services and must be limited to premises and land from which the buyer has operated during the contract period and must be indispensable to protect the know-how transferred from the supplier to the buyer. There is a time limit of one year on such obligations, although the restriction may be indefinite in order to protect know-how which is not in the public domain. Know-how is defined in the BER as being non-patented practical information which is secret, substantial and identified.[132] Secret means not generally known or easily accessible. So, for example, it is doubtful that the business model for Southwest Airlines, one of the original low-cost airlines in the United States, would fit into this category because it has been widely publicised and apparently studied by Ryanair.[133] Substantial means that the know-how includes information which is indispensable to the buyer for the use, sale or resale of the contract goods or services. An example of the sort of thing that would be allowed under this are provisions in a franchise agreement which would prevent the franchisee from setting up a competing business after the expiration of the franchise agreement on the same site, using certain knowledge obtained from running the franchise. So, having run a Pizza Hut franchise, when that expires, another pizza business cannot be run on the same site using similar techniques to the Pizza Hut franchise.

Finally, obligations which cause the members of a selective distribution system not to sell the brands of particular competing suppliers will not benefit from the BER. As the Commission explains, it is possible under the BER to combine selective distribution with non-compete obligations, so long as the non-compete obligations apply to competing brands in general. What a seller cannot do, however, is to prevent a buyer in a selective distribution system from stocking the products of a particular competitor. As the Commission has said, 'the objective of the exclusion of this obligation is to avoid a situation whereby a number of suppliers using the same selective distribution outlets prevent one specific competitor or certain specific competitors from using these outlets to distribute their products (foreclosure of a competing supplier which would be a form of collective boycott).'[134]

Conclusions on hard-core restrictions and non-compete obligations

A preliminary point to remember is that the BER applies only when the supplier's market share is below 30% and, as the Commission says in its Guidelines on Article 81(3) [Article 101(3) TFEU], negative effects on competition are likely to occur when parties have some degree of market power and the agreement contributes to the creation, maintenance or strengthening of that market power.[135] In the non-horizontal merger Guidelines, the point is

---

[131] European Commission, *Guidelines on Vertical Restraints* (n. 5) at para. 67.
[132] Article 1(g) BER.
[133] See, e.g., J.H. Gittell, *The Southwest Airlines Way* (McGraw-Hill, New York, 2002).
[134] European Commission, *Guidelines on Vertical Restraints* (n. 5) at para. 69.
[135] European Commission, *Guidelines on the application of Article 81(3) of the Treaty* (n. 41) at para. 25.

made that there are unlikely to be competition concerns if, post-merger, the market share of the merged entity is below 30% and the post-merger HHI is below 2000.[136] So it would seem unlikely, in the Commission's view, that parties which can benefit from the BER have significant market power; if that is the case, why do we need these provisions on hard-core restrictions and non-compete obligations? After all, if the parties to an agreement do not have any, or much, market power, then they cannot damage the competitive process by their agreement.

One answer to this is that the case law, starting with *Consten and Grundig* and based on the market integration objective of the EU, means that the Commission has had no alternative but to include provisions to this effect, which in particular explains Article 4(b)–(d). The case law discussed above also clearly states that RPM is an abuse by object, so this has also had to be included in Article 4(a). What the Commission seems to have done, in particular as regards the exceptions to Article 4(b), is to recognise that a number of commercial practices are not harmful to competition and make allowance for them. The analysis is still formalistic because it focuses on the terms of the agreement, rather than the effect on competition, but that helps with certainty and the need for self-assessment by undertakings that now exists. The BER is also an improvement because it lists what it prohibits: if parties to an agreement design a new clause, which is not prohibited by the BER, they are perfectly free to include it, and that represents important progress in relation to the previous block exemptions.

Withdrawal of the benefit of the block exemption

In part because in 1999 this approach was new, and also as a good general policy, the first version of the BER provided that the benefit of the exemption can be withdrawn in certain circumstances from individual agreements or categories of agreements as well as disapplied in certain circumstances. The benefit of the BER can be withdrawn from individual agreements, even though they fall within the BER, in two circumstances:

- The Commission decides that the agreement has effects which are incompatible with the conditions laid down in Article 101(3) TFEU, and in particular where access to the relevant market or competition therein is significantly restricted by the cumulative effect of parallel networks of similar vertical restraints implemented by competing suppliers or buyers.[137]

- The national competition authority decides that the agreement has effects incompatible with the conditions laid down in Article 101(3) TFEU in the territory of that Member State, or in a part thereof, which has all the characteristics of a distinct geographic market.[138]

Alternatively, the Commission has power to declare, by Regulation, where parallel networks of similar vertical restraints cover more than 50% of a relevant market, that the BER shall not apply to vertical agreements containing specific restraints, those restraints to be specified in the Regulation made by the Commission.[139] The Commission refers to this as the 'disapplication procedure'.

The Commission has explained that, when using the withdrawal procedure, the burden of proof is on it to show an agreement is within Article 101(1) TFEU and does not meet the

---

[136] European Commission, *Guidelines on the assessment of non-horizontal mergers under the Council Regulation on the control of concentrations between undertakings*, OJ C265, 18.10.2008 (at para. 25).

[137] European Commission, *Guidelines on Vertical Restraints* (n. 5) at paras. 74–78.

[138] Recital 14 BER and Article 29(2) Regulation 1/2003.

[139] Article 6 BER.

criteria within Article 101(3) TFEU.[140] If this procedure is used, it implies that the Commission will take a decision establishing an infringement of Article 101(1) TFEU.[141] The concern is with the cumulative effect of parallel networks of agreements, such as the agreements between pubcos and pub landlords, where it could be considered that there is a network of agreements. The assessment must consider the anti-competitive effects caused by each individual network of agreements and it may be appropriate to withdraw the benefit of the BER from only one type of restriction. As regards withdrawal of the benefit of the block exemption by national competition authorities, the Commission takes the view that it has a concurrent jurisdiction to withdraw the benefit of the block exemption but that such cases lend themselves to decentralised enforcement.[142] The withdrawal procedure has never been used, at either national or Union level.

The disapplication procedure, which also has never been used, has different consequences. In particular, the Commission has said that it does not imply that there will be a decision establishing an infringement, merely that it will restore the full application of Articles 101(1) and (3) TFEU.[143] Where appropriate, the Commission will take a decision in an individual case. The mere fact that the 50% threshold has been breached does not place an obligation on the Commission to act. It is only likely to act where access to the market is appreciably restricted: for example, if selective distribution networks covering more than 50% of a market use selection criteria not required by the nature of the relevant goods or discriminate against certain forms of distribution.[144] It will also consider whether it would be more appropriate to use the withdrawal procedure, which may depend on the number of competing undertakings contributing to a cumulative effect or the number of geographical markets involved;[145] in other words, to what extent this is a general problem in the market.

If a Regulation is adopted, it will define the relevant product and geographical market and identify the type of vertical restraint in respect of which the BER will no longer apply. According to the Commission, the scope of the Regulation will be modulated (which seems to mean targeted) to cover the competition concerns which it wants to address.[146] In other words, it may not cover, for example, all non-compete obligations, but only such obligations exceeding a certain duration.

Treatment of vertical agreements under UK law

Vertical agreements which affect trade between Member States, and remember that this is interpreted broadly, are dealt with under the rules discussed above in relation to Article 101 TFEU and the BER. Agreements which do not affect trade will be dealt with under the Chapter I prohibition; however, until 30 April 2005, all vertical agreements in the UK were excluded from the Chapter I prohibition.[147] With the coming into force of Regulation 1/2003, it made

---

[140] European Commission, *Guidelines on Vertical Restraints* (n. 5) at para. 77.
[141] Ibid. at para. 80.
[142] Ibid. at para. 78.
[143] Ibid. at para. 80.
[144] Ibid. at para. 81.
[145] Ibid. at para. 82.
[146] Ibid. at para. 83.
[147] Competition Act 1998 (Land and Vertical Agreements Exclusion) Order 2000, SI 2000/310.

sense to align UK and EU law on vertical agreements. So after that date the Chapter I prohibition is applied to vertical agreements and it is to be interpreted consistently with EU law according to s. 60 of the Competition Act 1998 and in accordance with the BER by virtue of s. 10 of the Competition Act, which provides for a system of parallel exemptions; that is, if an agreement would be exempt under the BER it should be treated as exempt under UK law. The OFT has published guidance on its interpretation of the rules in this area.[148]

As a result of the exclusion until 2005, there have been only a few cases where the OFT has taken decisions on vertical agreements.[149] Interestingly, in a number of cases the OFT has found that vertical agreements have breached the Chapter I prohibition because they imposed minimum resale price maintenance. The most high-profile of these decisions was in relation to the price-fixing of replica football kits where the OFT imposed fines totalling £18.6 million for a variety of price-fixing practices. Some of the findings of infringement were annulled by the Competition Appeal Tribunal, which also reduced some of the fines, although the decision was ultimately upheld by the Court of Appeal.[150] The Hasbro/Argos/Littlewoods case is discussed below in 'Competition law in practice'.

COMPETITION LAW IN PRACTICE

Hasbro/Argos/Littlewoods[151]

Background

Hasbro is one of the largest toy and games suppliers in the UK, producing well-known items such as 'Action Man' and 'Monopoly'. Argos and Littlewoods are both major high street retailers which run a catalogue business. Instead of the customer being able to see the merchandise on the shelves, items are chosen from a catalogue and then delivered at a service point. The main idea behind this model is that it can save on costs but it also produces some inflexibility in pricing because it is difficult to alter prices once they are in the catalogues, which are typically produced twice a year, for Spring/Summer and Autumn/Winter. Argos was the largest supplier of traditional toys and games, as opposed to electronic ones, with a market share of around 17%, while Littlewoods was the fifth biggest, with a market share of around 4%. Littlewoods is the main catalogue competitor to Argos.

OFT investigation and decision

In 2001 the Director General of Fair Trading (the predecessor of the OFT) started an investigation and came to an initial decision in February 2003. Margins for retailers on toys and games are quite low and, from 1998, Hasbro became aware that retailers were dissatisfied with the margins that they were obtaining and began a number of initiatives

---

[148] OFT, *Vertical Agreements* (2004).

[149] OFT, 'DSG Retail' (2004) and 'Lucite International' (2002) were about whether the exclusion could be withdrawn.

[150] OFT, *Football kit price fixing* (2003); *JJB v Office of Fair Trading* [2004] CAT 17; *Umbro v Office of Fair Trading* [2005] CAT 22; *Argos & Littlewoods v Office of Fair Trading* [2006] EWCA Civ 1318.

[151] OFT, *Hasbro/Argos/Littlewoods* (2003).

aimed at ensuring retailers kept to the recommended retail price (RRP) and did not undercut this. This initiative started working in 1999 and ran through to 2001. In order to make this scheme work, Hasbro needed the cooperation of both Argos and Littlewoods because each was worried that they would be undercut by the other. The OFT found that there were effectively three agreements and/or concerted practices:

1 an overall agreement between Hasbro, Argos and Littlewoods to stick to RRPs;

2 an agreement between Hasbro and Argos to stick to RRPs;

3 an agreement between Hasbro and Littlewoods to stick to RRPs.

The latter two agreements were interlinked and each retailer entered into an agreement on the understanding that the other one would as well. This was important because, as catalogue retailers, they had to commit themselves to price in advance of a season and without knowing what the other one was doing; this would only become apparent once the catalogues were published, at which point it would be too late to do anything about undercutting. The OFT found that the object of these agreements was to fix prices and that there was therefore no need to show any restrictive effects. There was no case for an individual exemption. Argos and Littlewoods were required to pay combined penalties of around £22.5 million; Hasbro was assessed as being liable for around £15.5 million but it applied for leniency and was granted a 100% reduction in return for its cooperation.

Competition Appeal Tribunal decision and aftermath

The decision of February 2003 was appealed to the Competition Appeal Tribunal (CAT),[152] which decided initially to remit the case to the OFT so that it could put three witness statements to the retailers. The OFT took a new decision in December 2003, which was also appealed to the CAT. The CAT upheld the decisions on liability,[153] but reduced the penalties to just under £20 million.[154] The retailers then appealed to the Court of Appeal, which dismissed the appeals both on liability and the penalty.[155]

Analysis

This case is interesting from a number of perspectives. First, it is a combination of horizontal and vertical agreements and therefore a warning that concepts which may be analysed separately for presentational purposes are often combined in the real world. Although there was no evidence of contact between Argos and Littlewoods, it was clear that the vertical agreements between Hasbro and the retailers were underpinned by an understanding that both retailers would stick to the RRP. There was also evidence that Hasbro passed information regarding each retailer's pricing intentions to the other. So this is an excellent example of vertical agreements on resale price maintenance being used to underpin what was effectively horizontal price-fixing between these two retailers. Indeed, the price

➡

---

[152] *Argos* v *OFT* [2003] CAT 16.
[153] *Argos* v *OFT* [2004] CAT 24.
[154] *Argos* v *OFT* [2005] CAT 13.
[155] *Argos* v *OFT* [2006] EWCA Civ 1316.

offerings of other retailers were monitored and representations were made to Hasbro to prevent other retailers undercutting the RRP. Secondly, the Competition Act 1998 only came into force in 2000 and the penalties only relate to the period after the Act came into force. Thirdly, this is a case where it is helpful that the OFT is able to describe the arrangements as an agreement and/or a concerted practice, without having to engage in a precise classification. There was never any evidence of a formal written agreement. As an internal email put it, 'never ever put anything in writing, it's highly illegal and it could bite you right in the arse!!!'[156] There was clearly an understanding and the Court of Appeal saw the arrangements as definitely falling within the ambit of a concerted practice. Finally, the entire process from first investigation to Court of Appeal judgment took around five years, undoubtedly using up substantial OFT resources, as well as those of the parties. Although in theory consumers might have had a remedy for the price-fixing, no such actions were taken.

Conclusions

The introduction of the BER and the associated guidelines in 1999 represented a major change in the European Commission's approach to vertical agreements and was a move that was much more in keeping with the insights of economic analysis. There was an element of caution and compromise in this development because, in part, the Commission was constrained by previous case law of the Courts, as well as having to take into account its own decisional practice. The Commission's review of the working of this regime described the experience as 'positive'.[157] Given the lack of controversy the arrangements seem to have generated, for example, in terms of journal articles, this seems a fair assessment, although contrary views have been expressed.[158] The new Regulation does not encompass any radical changes, so there is still, for example, the long list of hard-core restrictions in Article 4. It is certainly possible to argue that, even though an improvement on previous practice, the current regime could be even more liberal.

---

[156] OFT, *Hasbro/Argos/Littlewoods* (2003) at para. 73.

[157] European Commission, 'Draft Commission Regulation on the application of Article 81(3) of the Treaty to categories of vertical agreements and concerted practices', recital 2. Available at *http://ec.europa.eu/competition/consultations/2009_vertical_agreements/index.html* (accessed 29/07/12).

[158] See F. Dethmers and P.P. de Boer, 'Ten Years On: Vertical agreements under Article 81' (2009) 30 *European Competition Law Review* 424.

Summary

➤ In order to affect the competitive process either the manufacturer or the distributor must have some level of market power.

➤ If they do not have market power, then any vertical restraints are likely to be benign and entered into simply for commercial, efficiency enhancing reasons. Even if there is some market power at work, the welfare effects of vertical restraints are not always obvious.

➤ Vertical agreements with the object of restricting competition are in breach of Article 101(1) TFEU. This is clearly the case for those agreements which provide for absolute territorial protection and RPM.

➤ Vertical agreements which may have the effect of restricting competition must be looked at in their economic context and the Commission will look at the following factors:

- market position of the supplier,
- market position of competitors,
- market position of the buyer,
- entry barriers,
- maturity of the market,
- level of trade,
- nature of the product,
- other factors.

➤ For single branding agreements, in order to determine whether they have the effect of restricting competition the first stage is to:

- determine relevant product market,
- determine relevant geographic market,
- consider possibilities of entry into the market,
- assess the operation of competitive forces.

If there is a restriction of competition in the market as a whole, the question must be asked if the agreement at issue appreciably contributes to the restriction.

➤ Selective distribution agreements are not in breach of Article 101(1) TFEU if:

- the characteristics or nature of the product in question necessitate a selective distribution system; and
- the distributors are chosen by reference to objective criteria of a qualitative nature which are set out uniformly and are not used arbitrarily to discriminate against a certain retailer; and
- the criteria do not go beyond what is necessary for the product in question; and
- the market must not be foreclosed to competitors by a network of similar agreements to which the agreement in question contributes appreciably.

➤ Franchise agreements may not breach Article 101(1) TFEU, so long as the clauses are limited to two objectives:

- the franchisor must be able to communicate his know-how to the franchisees and provide them with the necessary assistance in order to enable them to apply his methods, without running the risk that that know-how and assistance might benefit competitors, even indirectly; and

- the franchisor must be able to take the measures necessary for maintaining the identity and reputation of the network bearing his business name or symbol.

➤ Vertical agreements may obtain the benefit of the block exemption if neither the supplier nor the buyer's market share is greater than 30% and they contain no hard-core restrictions.

➤ Hard-core restrictions are:

- resale price maintenance;
- restrictions on the territory into which, or of the customers to whom, the buyer may sell the contract goods or services (subject to certain exceptions);
- restricting active or passive sales to end-users by members of a selective distribution system operating at the retail level of trade;
- restricting cross-supplies between distributors within a selective distribution system, including between distributors operating at different level of trade;
- restrictions agreed between a supplier of components and a buyer who incorporates those components, which limits the supplier to selling the components as spare parts to end-users or to repairers or other service providers not entrusted by the buyer with the repair or servicing of its goods.

➤ Certain non-compete restrictions are allowed. Others are not, but the agreement may still benefit from the BER if they are severable.

➤ The benefit of the block exemption may be withdrawn from particular agreements by the Commission or a national competition authority. The Commission may decide that the BER does not apply to certain categories of vertical agreements.

Further reading

Official publications

European Commission Regulation (EC) No. 330/2010 on the application of Article 101(3) TFEU to categories of vertical agreements and concerted practices, L102/1, 23.04.2010. *The core rules on how vertical agreements are to be treated.*

European Commission, *Guidelines on Vertical Restraints*, OJ C130/01, 19.05.2010. *Exposition of Commission's approach to vertical agreements in general, as well as its interpretation of the BER.*

Other

Dethmers, F. and de Boer, P.P., 'Ten Years On: Vertical agreements under Article 81' (2009) 30 *European Competition Law Review* 424. *Critical assessment of the Guidelines and the BER, pointing out what the authors see as certain problems that need a solution.*

Dobson, P. and Waterson, M., *Vertical Restraints and Competition Policy* (OFT, London, 1996). *Although dated, excellent and accessible introduction to the economic issues involved.*

Goyder, J., *EU Distribution Law* (6th edn, Hart Publishing, 2011). *Comprehensive discussion of the law.*

Hawk, B., 'System Failure: Vertical restraints and EC Competition Law' (1995) 32 *Common Market Law Review* 973. *The classic criticism of the Commission's previous approach to vertical agreements.*

Trade and Industry Select Committee, *Pub Companies* (2004) HC 128-I. *Official investigation of a controversial area dominated by vertical agreements. Chapters 6–9 in particular.*

12 Intellectual property and competition law

Introduction

Intellectual property rights (IPRs) are an important underpinning of a modern economy. This book, for example, has been written on a computer using word processing software which is not a physical product but a collection of commands for the hardware to execute; in other words, the software is an intellectual product, rather than a tangible piece of property. This is true for all computer software and is also true for other parts of the economy, notably the entertainment industry. If we think about films and music, what is important in them is what they are expressing and how interesting or attractive we find it. We can consume films or music in a variety of ways: in a cinema, over the television, listening to radio, through an MP3 player, on a computer, on a mobile phone, etc. This points to an important difference between intellectual property and physical property. If you manufacture a product, say an item of clothing, it is relatively easy to control its sale and distribution. You agree a contract with the buyer, deliver the product and receive payment. You do not have to worry too much about the buyer reproducing the product, because this would involve replicating your manufacturing process, although this can happen, particularly in the world of fashion. By contrast, once a band releases a song, it is very easy for a buyer to copy that song and distribute it to others, even if some form of protection has been incorporated. Indeed, probably most of the people reading this book have, at some time or another, listened to or watched music and films that have been copied from their original format. Since intellectual property is very easy to copy or to appropriate, this creates an incentive problem, namely, why should someone put time and effort into production of an intellectual good which others will find easy to copy or appropriate?

The answer, at least in western societies, has been to create a system of IPRs, which, broadly, give the holder of such rights the exclusive right to exploit them and prevent anyone else from using them without the permission of the right holder. These exclusive rights are typically granted by legislation and are also typically time limited: for example 20 years for patents, depending on the type of right granted. The idea, therefore, is to solve the incentive problem: the holder of the IPR has an exclusive right for a period of time to exploit their intellectual property, thus repaying them for their investment in creating it. After its expiration, others can use it and, hopefully, improve upon it, thus restarting the cycle of innovation.

At this point, we can see the beginnings of why there might be a clash or tension between competition law and IPRs. The aim of competition law is to ensure that markets remain competitive and we instinctively associate this with a large number of competitors producing similar goods. IPRs, on the other hand, allow their owners exclusive rights to produce something which looks like they are in receipt of a monopoly granted by the state. This is indeed how the relationship between antitrust and intellectual property law was viewed in the United States up until roughly the latter end of the twentieth century.[1] If, however, we think about the issues more deeply, the so-called clash or tension begins to dissolve and become more manageable. Why is this?

First, it is commonplace today to say that competition law and intellectual property law both have the same ultimate aims: to increase consumer welfare and promote the efficient allocation of resources (see Box 12.1). They do this through different mechanisms, namely protecting competitive markets and providing protection to innovators, allowing them to exploit their products, but the ultimate aim is the same. Secondly, the grant of an exclusive right in a product is not generally equivalent to a monopoly. You may have an exclusive right to a song, or a particular design for a product, be it a mobile phone or a mousetrap, but this does not stop other people from producing songs, mobile phones or mousetraps – it stops them from reproducing *your* product, not theirs. Thirdly, as will be explained in more detail later, IPRs are not only limited in terms of time, but also in terms of their scope. Thus, for example, copyright protects the expression of an idea, not the idea itself, so it is possible for two people to have the same idea, for example, for a story or a film, expressed in different ways, and both may be protected by copyright. Finally, and more generally, it could be said that in order for a competitive market to operate properly, there must be a system of property rights underpinning it and those rights must extend to intellectual, as well as physical property.

[1] See E. Gellhorn *et al.*, *Antitrust Law and Economics* (5th edn, Thomson West, St Paul, Minnesota, 2004), pp. 477–8. This was best exemplified by the Department of Justices's statement of the 'Nine no-nos' – patent related practices it condemned as unlawful automatically in the 1970s. Discussed in W.K. Tom and J.A. Newberg, 'Antitrust and Intellectual Property: From Separate Spheres to Unified Field' (1998) 66 *Antitrust Law Journal* 167 at 178–84. See now *Illinois Tool Works Inc* v *Independent Ink, Inc.*, 547 US 28 (2006).

KEY LEGAL PROVISIONS   Box 12.1

The relationship between IP and competition law

Indeed, both bodies of law share the same basic objective of promoting consumer welfare and an efficient allocation of resources. Innovation constitutes an essential and dynamic component of an open and competitive market economy. Intellectual property rights promote dynamic competition by encouraging undertakings to invest in developing new or improved products and processes. So does competition by putting pressure on undertakings to innovate. Therefore, both intellectual property rights and competition are necessary to promote innovation and ensure a competitive exploitation thereof.

Source: European Commission, *Guidelines on the application of Article 81 of the EC Treaty to Technology Transfer Agreements*, OJ C101, 27.04.2004 (at para. 7).

. . . antitrust and intellectual property are properly perceived as complementary bodies of law that work together to bring innovation to consumers: antitrust laws protect robust competition in the marketplace, while intellectual property laws protect the ability to earn a return on the investments necessary to innovate. Both spur competition among rivals to be the first to enter the marketplace with a desirable technology, product, or service.

Source: US Department of Justice/Federal Trade Commission, *Antitrust Enforcement and Intellectual Property Rights* (2007) at p. 2.

Question: How convincing do you find these arguments?

Although we can conclude that, in general, there is no clash between intellectual property and competition law, there are still particular circumstances where competition lawyers may want to scrutinise the use of IPRs. For example, in some markets what happens is competition *for* the market, rather than competition *in* the market. In these cases it is possible that the market can reach a tipping point, after which one technology or product becomes the market standard or, to put it another way, has a monopoly position. Examples of this are the QWERTY layout of a standard English keyboard (originally there were alternative layouts) and the competition between Blu-ray and HD-DVD, which was won by the former.[2] In these circumstances, which are said to characterise new, high-technology industries, competition authorities will often keep a close eye on the activities of the winner, as in the various Microsoft cases in the United States and Europe (discussed in Chapter 4). This is a version of the general problems of Article 102 TFEU, namely is an undertaking in a dominant position and has it abused it? In this context, there is a special twist, because part of the essence of IPRs is the ability of the rights holder to control their exercise and exclude others from access to them. Should there be circumstances where competition law intervenes in regard to these rights and requires, for example, the holder of an IPR to license its use to a third party, possibly competing with the right holder?

The second area where competition authorities have been active has been in the case of agreements involving IPRs, notably agreements licensing the use of IPRs. This is a particularly important issue in high-technology sectors of the economy where innovation often depends on using or combining a number of products which are protected by intellectual property

---

[2] See *http://en.wikipedia.org/wiki/High_definition_optical_disc_format_war* (accessed 13/08/12).

rights.[3] The general issue is thus to try to distinguish between agreements that are neutral or pro-competitive and those that are anti-competitive, which raises a number of the same issues as we find in other sectors. Are the agreements horizontal, between competitors, or are they vertical – for example, the owner of an IPR licensing another undertaking to produce goods using the IPR? If the former, we should be more cautious in allowing them than in the latter case, where there is not an obvious negative effect on competition – indeed the agreement may be pro-competitive, although there may still be issues of foreclosure and market exclusion in certain circumstances (as discussed in Chapter 11). As we shall see, the European Commission has attempted to move towards a more economics-based approach in its assessment of these agreements, as part of a more general move away from the earlier formalism of its approach to agreements under Article 101(1) TFEU, which left economic analysis to the Article 101(3) TFEU stage.

The plan of the chapter is therefore as follows. First there is discussion of what are IPRs, how do you obtain them, what do they cover and what are their limits? There is a discussion of the general approach to IPRs in EU law, given that IPRs are dealt with, for the most part, on a national rather than a Union basis. The second main part of the chapter focuses on issues surrounding the use of Article 101 TFEU in this context, which leads into a detailed discussion of the block exemption regulation for technology transfer agreements (TTBER as it is commonly known) and its accompanying guidelines (these are agreements which, roughly, involve the owner of the IPR licensing another party to use that IPR). This section ends by looking at agreements which fall outside the TTBER, notably trade mark and copyright licences, both types of IPR. The final part of the chapter looks at Article 102 TFEU and IPRs, in particular the controversial issue of compulsory licensing or a duty to deal with those who want access to information protected by IPRs, which was a central issue in the European Microsoft case.

As can be seen, the focus of this chapter is on EU law and there will be no explicit discussion of UK law. This is because, even though the Chapter I and II prohibitions of the Competition Act 1998 will apply to IPRs, there is no specific UK approach to these issues.[4] Instead, we would expect them to be applied in a manner which is consistent with EU law, following s. 60 of the Competition Act 1998. More specifically, the Competition Act provides for a system of parallel exemptions, under s. 10, so that any agreement which would receive the benefit of the TTBER would be exempt from the Chapter I prohibition. So in this area it can be assumed, subject to any reservations about market integration considerations, that the UK authorities will follow EU law and procedure.

What are IPRs?

For our purposes, there are the following types of IPR:

- patents
- copyright

---

[3] C. Shapiro, 'Navigating the Patent Thicket: Cross Licenses, Patent Pools and Standard Setting', in A. Jaffe *et al.* (eds) *Innovation Policy and the Economy Vol. 1* (National Bureau for Economic Research, Cambridge, Mass., 2001) is good at describing the issues.

[4] The institutional exception is that these issues may arise in market investigations.

- trade marks
- designs
- know-how and trade secrets.

Specific protection has been created for other forms of IPR, such as computer software and plant breeders' rights,[5] but this section just deals with the characteristics of the most important categories.

Patents[6]

A patent gives the inventor a monopoly, granted by the state, to work the invention to the exclusion of others for a fixed period of time. In return, the patent holder must disclose details concerning the invention.[7] A patent is given for an invention which is novel and the novelty of it is judged by a patent office or agency, that is, a state or public agency, through a procedure which is open to challenge. Within the UK, the invention must be new, involve an inventive step (something not obvious to those who know the area) and be capable of industrial application, and is stated not to apply to certain literary or creative activities.[8] The patent application will describe the invention in some detail, to the point of allowing a person to be able to construct the invention on the basis of the description, and is made publicly available. On receipt of the patent, the holder is granted an exclusive right, typically for 20 years, to make, use or sell the novel invention.[9] On the expiration of the 20-year period, the invention enters into the public domain and anyone can produce it, using the information contained in the patent application.

It is worth noting a number of points here. First, the exclusive right deriving from a patent is clearly a reward for innovation by the inventor. Secondly, as a condition of the grant of the exclusive right, the patent holder must put substantial information about the patent into the public domain and the idea behind this is that the release of information will allow others to develop the technology contained in the patent. Thirdly, there are exceptions to the exclusive rights of the patent holder. For example, under UK law, it is not an infringement of the patent if the act is done privately, rather than commercially, or if it is done for experimental purposes.[10] Fourthly, there are typically provisions in patent legislation which allow for the possibility of compulsory licensing in certain circumstances and, in particular, if the patent holder has not exploited the patent, even though these provisions are rarely used.[11] To summarise, although the patent gives its holder the exclusive right for 20 years to exploit the invention, this is subject to a number of conditions, which ensure that the information is in the public domain and that the holder of the patent exploits it and does not use it as a means of suppressing innovation and, thereby, arguably competition.

---

[5] See Council Directive 91/250 on the protection of computer programs [1991] OJ L122/42; Council Regulation 2100/94 on plant variety rights [1994] OJ L227/1.

[6] Generally, see D. Bainbridge, *Intellectual Property* (9th edn, Pearson Longman, Harlow, 2012), Part 4; W. Cornish and D. Llewelyn, *Intellectual Property* (7th edn, Sweet & Maxwell, London, 2010), chs 4–7.

[7] See Bainbridge (n. 6) at p. 363.

[8] Patents Act 1977, s. 1.

[9] Note how often ownership of a patent becomes an issue on *Dragons' Den*!

[10] Patents Act 1977, s. 60(5)(a) and (b).

[11] For example, see Patents Act 1977, ss. 48, 48A and 48B. On use, see S. Anderman, 'The competition law/IP interface: An introductory note', in S. Anderman (ed.) *Intellectual Property Rights and Competition Policy* (Cambridge University Press, 2007) at p. 14.

The licensing of patents may raise Article 101 TFEU issues and their use, or non-use, may raise Article 102 TFEU issues if the patent holder has a dominant position. The case law on IPRs and Article 102 TFEU is discussed later in this chapter. In addition, as mentioned above, the patent system involves applications to a public agency by those who wish to obtain a patent. Within the United States there has been substantial litigation and debate over the use of the patent system to protect or obtain a monopoly in a way that is contrary to antitrust law, specifically s. 2 of the Sherman Act, which deals with attempts to monopolise markets. In these cases, the claim has been that the person filing, or in possession of the patent, knew that it was unenforceable but represented the facts otherwise.[12] A similar issue has now arisen in EU law after the European Commission fined AstraZeneca €60 million in 2005 for misusing the national patent systems in order to obtain an extension to patent protection for its anti-ulcer medicine Losec, which delayed the introduction of generic competitors into the market.[13] This case is discussed in more detail at the end of this chapter but, more generally, the EU Commission's investigation into the pharmaceutical sector highlighted the importance of the use of the patent system in the business activities of the drug companies.[14]

Copyright[15]

A copyright gives the creator of original work exclusive rights to it, usually for the period of the life of the author plus 70 years. Unlike a patent, there is no process for registration before a public agency but it arises automatically when the work is set down or recorded in some form. The owner of the copyright can prevent others from copying it without permission and typically has the right to be recognised as the author of the piece. The protection, however, extends only to the expression of the idea(s) in that particular form, not to the underlying ideas themselves. Thus it is possible for two people to have the same idea, a story for example, and exploit it in different ways without either of them breaching the other's copyright. In addition, most copyright law, according to Anderman, contains doctrines of 'fair use' or 'fair dealing', which allows some copying for purposes of review, criticism, reporting or educational and research purposes.[16]

For the purposes of EU competition law, it is worth noting that there is substantial variation between Member States in their approach to copyright law. In particular, within the UK, copyright can be obtained for works developed simply through the effort of the author, whereas in continental European systems more emphasis is put on the originality that went into the work. It has been argued that this was a significant factor in the one compulsory licensing case, *Magill*, concerning the licensing of information relating to television broadcasts, discussed in more detail below.[17]

---

[12] See H. Hovenkamp, *The Antitrust Enterprise* (Harvard University Press, Cambridge, Mass., 2005) at pp. 267–8 and H. Hovenkamp, *Federal Antitrust Policy* (4th edn, West Publishing, St Paul, Minnesota, 2011) s. 7.11.

[13] Commission Decision of 15 June 2005, *AstraZeneca*; Case T-321/05 *AstraZeneca v Commission* [2010] ECR II-2805. On appeal Case C-457/10P. For discussion, see M. Negrinotti, 'Abuse of regulatory procedures in the intellectual property context: The AstraZeneca case' (2008) 29 *European Competition Law Review* 446; S. Gallasch, 'Astrazeneca v the Walker process – a real EU–US divergence or just an attempt to compare apples to oranges?' (2011) 7 *European Competition Journal* 505.

[14] European Commission, 'Pharmaceutical Sector Inquiry Preliminary Report' (2008).

[15] Generally, see Bainbridge (n. 6), Part 2; Cornish and Llewelyn (n. 6), chs 11–14.

[16] Anderman (n. 11), p. 16.

[17] Cases C-241–242P *RTE v Commission* [1995] ECR I-743.

Copyright protection is critical in what might be called the 'creative' industries, such as film, music, theatre, broadcasting, writing, etc. It has become a particularly controversial topic because of the ease of copying items which are available in a digital form and the inadequacies of the protection systems which are incorporated in these works. In terms of what have been called creative works above, such copying does not raise competition law issues, although copyright licensing has raised some, limited, competition law issues, discussed below.

Trade marks[18]

A trade mark is a mark used in relation to certain goods or services by a trader which is distinctive in some way.[19] In UK law the definition is a sign which is capable of being represented graphically and capable of distinguishing the goods or services of one undertaking from those of another, such as the Longman ship on the cover of its books.[20] Trade marks may be established either through use or through registration with the appropriate office and can constitute, among other things, words, designs or logos. The establishment of a trade mark prevents other persons from using that mark, but not from offering competing goods and services under other marks. Trade marks may be renewed and can be continued indefinitely. As can be seen from this brief description, they protect less than patents and copyrights and so typically raise less of an issue for competition law, although there is one particular issue discussed below. It is, however, worth noting that the assignment of a trade mark in *Consten and Grundig*,[21] which allowed Consten to enforce territorial exclusivity against third parties, played a central role in this case.

Design rights[22]

Design rights are available to protect the original, non-commonplace aspects of products and may be registered or unregistered. An unregistered right arises automatically on the creation of the product and grants protection for a non-renewable term of 15 years from the time it was first recorded in a design document and it provides protection against copying.[23] There is, however, an automatic licence of right during the last five years allowing any person to copy the design, subject to payment. The right only applies to the three-dimensional features of the design; two-dimensional features, such as patterns of wallpaper, have to be protected via copyright. Design features which enable products to be functionally fitted or aesthetically matched get no protection, in order to allow for competing designs for spare parts. A registered design right initially gives up to five years' protection, but it may be renewed for a maximum of 25 years and is available for designs which are new and have an individual character.[24] Design in this context means the appearance of the whole or a part of a product resulting from the features of, in particular, the lines, contours, colours, shape, texture or

---

[18] Generally, see Bainbridge (n. 6), Part 6; Cornish and Llewelyn (n. 6), ch. 18.
[19] See Bainbridge (n. 6) at p. 626.
[20] Trade Marks Act 1994, s. 1.
[21] Cases 56, 58/64 [1966] ECR 299.
[22] Generally, see Bainbridge (n. 6), Part 5; Cornish and Llewelyn (n. 6), ch.15.
[23] Generally, see Copyright, Designs and Patent Act 1988, ss. 213–245.
[24] Generally, see Registered Designs Act 1949, as amended.

materials of the product or its ornamentation. This is different from a patent, which is concerned with the function, operation or manufacture of a particular item. Registration gives the owner of the right the exclusive right to use the design. These have rarely been the subject of competition law issues.

Trade secrets and know-how[25]

This category covers information which is kept secret or confidential within a commercial organisation which distinguishes its products or processes from those of its competitors. Typically this information is protected through contractual provisions, that is, terms in the contracts of the employees, or through an implied obligation of confidence. A definition of this concept is given below in Box 12.2. The category has been important in the context of the licensing of IPRs, and at one point there was even a specific block exemption for know-how licensing;[26] it is now treated within the TTBER.

KEY LEGAL PROVISION   **Box 12.2**

Definition of know-how

'know-how' means a package of non-patented practical information, resulting from experience and testing, which is:

(i)   secret, that is to say, not generally known or easily accessible,

(ii) substantial, that is to say, significant and useful for the production of the contract products, and

(iii) identified, that is to say, described in a sufficiently comprehensive manner so as to make it possible to verify that it fulfils the criteria of secrecy and substantiality;

Source: TTBER, Article 1(i).

Question: Can you think of examples of information which might fit this definition?

IPRs in summary

Looking at Table 12.1 below, which summarises IPRs, it should be clear that IPRs are both time and subject limited. Whether in any particular case the limits are too generous, or not generous enough, is a separate argument but for the purposes of competition law the point is that a decision has been made, by a legislature, about the balance between exclusive rights and the incentive to innovate.[27] Competition law should not destabilise this balance on a case-by-case basis. A further point to notice is that because IPRs are granted by public authorities, and that such grants may be challenged in the courts, this opens up the possibility of strategic use of the IPR system or litigation to maintain or reinforce market power. This is

---

[25] Generally, see Cornish and Llewelyn (n. 6), ch. 8.

[26] Regulation 556/89 [1989] OJ L257/15.

[27] The point is discussed in G. Ghidini, *Intellectual Property and Competition Law* (Edward Elgar, Cheltenham, 2006).

Table 12.1 Summary of IPRs

Type of IPR	Scope of protection	Length of protection
Patent	Covers making or use of the product or process or providing means or information to make use of the product or process	20 years
Copyright	Copying the work, communicating the work to the public in general, and adapting the work	Lifetime of author and 70 years (50 years for sound recordings and broadcasts)
Trade mark	Prevents use of identical or similar signs without consent	10 years, but may be renewed; potentially indefinite
Design	Registered: prevents unauthorised use and copying Unregistered: prevents copying	25 years (registered)
Know-how and trade secrets	Prevents disclosure to third parties	15 years (unregistered)

behaviour which has not been uncommon in the United States and has now started to emerge as a competition law issue in the European Union.

One area where it looks like the intersection of competition law and IPR is going to be controversial is that of pharmaceuticals. In their inquiry into the sector, the Commission divided companies into originators, those who developed new drugs, and generics, those who produced generic versions of drugs originally developed by other companies.[28] Originator companies sought to protect the income from their original drugs through a variety of strategies including filing many patents for an original drug (patent clusters), engaging in patent disputes with generic companies, concluding settlement agreements in these disputes and switching patents from first to second generation products, that is, from older to newer products. Although the inquiry did not express any opinion on the legality of these practices, the Commission has taken action against AstraZeneca, a pharmaceutical company, for abuse of the patent system, discussed below, and this sector inquiry has been followed by individual actions against pharmaceutical companies, as was the case after the energy sector inquiry, discussed later in the text (see Chapter 15).[29]

IPRs and European Union law

Although there have been attempts to harmonise IPR protection across the European Union, these have been unsuccessful and IPR protection depends, generally, on the provisions of national law, although there are certain areas where specific provision has been made within EU law.[30] There are therefore differing national approaches as to IPRs, most notably in the field of copyright, where it is much easier to obtain copyright protection in common law than in civil law systems. So, for example, it is easier to obtain copyright protection in the UK and Ireland, as opposed to France. Generally the European Courts have been concerned to ensure that national IPRs are not used in a way to prevent free movement of goods

---

[28] European Commission, 'Pharmaceutical Sector Inquiry Preliminary Report' (2008).

[29] See European Commission Press Notice, 'Commission enforcement action in pharmaceutical sector following sector inquiry' MEMO/12/593 25 July 2012.

[30] Notably in relation to trade marks, design and specific copyright areas. See Bainbridge (n. 6), ch. 24.

throughout the internal market. At the same time, the Courts have had to recognise the legitimacy of the IPRs granted by national systems which include certain abilities to control them. In order to manage this tension, a distinction has developed within the case law between the 'existence' of the IPRs and their 'exercise'.[31] So while EU law cannot challenge or question the existence of an IPR, limitations can be placed on its exercise by competition law and this, as we shall see, has become critical in relation to abuse of dominance and IPRs.

The distinction between the 'existence' and the 'exercise' of an IPR has been criticised by a number of commentators[32] and it is not straightforward. However, as Faull and Nikpay, a European Commission and an OFT official respectively, point out, although not quite in these terms, if IPRs are not to be effectively exempt from the free movement and competition provisions of the EU, then there needs to be some mechanism for reviewing the way they have been exercised by a proprietor, while at the same time recognising that a legitimate right has been granted and this is the aim of the distinction.[33]

EU law also contains a doctrine of the 'exhaustion' of IPRs,[34] which applies once the property owner has received the benefit of the specific subject matter of the right. This doctrine also operates to control the exercise of IPRs by their holders through preventing them, once they have put a product into circulation in one Member State, from stopping it being exported into another Member State through claiming a breach of their IPRs. It can be seen that the concern here is to stop holders of IPRs from discouraging parallel trade in their products and to prevent markets being partitioned on national lines.

The Technology Transfer Block Exemption Regulation[35]

One of the most important and controversial areas has been that of the licensing of intellectual property. Typically the owner of intellectual property will license the use of it to another party, who will use that intellectual property to manufacture goods or provide services incorporating it. Typical clauses in such agreements are described in Table 12.2 below.

Such agreements look, on the face of them, to be pro-competitive, as they are a means of ensuring the introduction of new ideas on to the market. This is recognised in Recital 5 of the Regulation, which states: 'Such agreements will usually improve economic efficiency and be pro-competitive as they can reduce duplication of research and development, strengthen the incentive for the initial research and development, spur incremental innovation, facilitate diffusion and generate product market competition.'

This is a relatively new attitude towards these sorts of agreements within EU competition law. Perhaps surprisingly, in its first encounter with patent licensing agreements in the early 1960s the Commission had taken a liberal approach and viewed many restrictions in patent

---

[31] Cases 56 and 58/64 *Consten and Grundig* [1966] ECR 299; Case 24/67 *Parker, Davis v Probert* [1968] ECR 55.

[32] For example, I. Govaere, *The Use and Abuse of Intellectual Property Rights in EC Law* (Sweet & Maxwell, London, 1996) at para. 3.41.

[33] J. Faull and A. Nikpay, *The EC Law of Competition* (2nd edn, Oxford University Press, 2007) at para. 10.20.

[34] Case 78/70 *Deutsche Grammophon v Metro* [1971] ECR 487.

[35] Commission Regulation (EC) No. 772/2004 of 27 April 2004 on the application of Article 81(3) of the Treaty to categories of technology transfer agreements, OJ L123, 27.04.2004, pp. 11–17. See also European Commission, *Guidelines on the application of Article 81 of the EC Treaty to technology transfer agreements*, OJ C101, 27.04.2004, pp. 2–42 (hereafter 'TTBER Guidelines').

Table 12.2 Typical clauses in IP licences

Type of clause	Description	Rationale
Royalty	Payment for use of the IPR	Reward to licensor, may be structured in a way to incentivise licensee to exploit the IPR
Territorial exclusivity	Protects licensee from intra-technology competition in a geographical area in relation to either production or sales	Gives licensee's investment protection from competition and time to recover the investment. May create market division problems
Exclusive licence	Where only the licensee is allowed to exploit the IPR	Gives licensee incentive to develop the technology
Sole licence	Where the licensee and the licensor may both exploit the IPR	Allows both licensee and licensor to develop the technology
Field of use	Licensee limited to producing for particular purposes	Protects licensor's position. Potential to divide markets
Non-competition clause	Licensee not allowed to use competing technology to produce competing goods	Encourages exploitation of licence but may lead to foreclosure problems
No challenge clause	Licensee agrees not to challenge validity of IPR	Licensee often has best view of challengeability – licence might not be granted if possibility of challenge
Improvements	Licensee required to give licensor access to any improvements	Improves licensor's position, but may deprive third parties of access to improvements
Tying and bundling	Requirement to take another technology or product	May be quality control or efficiency reasons for this. May raise foreclosure problems

licences as falling outside Article 101(1) TFEU so long as they did not go beyond the scope of the patent rights of the licensor.[36] Subsequent to the decision in *Consten and Grundig*, which held that Article 101 TFEU applied to both horizontal and vertical agreements, the Commission's position changed to the view that almost all patent licensing agreements fell within Article 101(1) TFEU and needed a decision from the Commission that they met the requirements for an exemption under Article 101(3) TFEU. As experience was gained with these sorts of agreements, block exemptions were developed for patent licensing and technology transfer agreements, but they were criticised for being too narrow, unduly formalistic and unduly constraining: for example, as well as listing hard-core restraints that were forbidden, they also listed clauses that were allowed (white listed), which meant that there was an incentive to use such clauses in agreements, for safety's sake. The Commission undertook a review of the block exemptions in 2001, which broadly endorsed these criticisms and presented proposals for a new Regulation. The idea was that the new Regulation would follow the approach taken in the block exemption for vertical agreements, that is, concentrate on the economic effects of agreements, which would also enable it to be consistent with the new enforcement Regulation 1/2003, which was also on the horizon at that point. These proposals were controversial – in particular the proposals that below a particular market

---

[36] A discussion of the history can be found in S. Anderman and H Schmidt, *EU Competition Law and Intellectual Property Rights* (2nd edn, Oxford University Press, 2011), ch. 14; and I. Maher, 'Competition Law and Intellectual Property Rights', in P. Craig and G. de Búrca, *The Evolution of European Union Law* (Oxford University Press, 1999).

share, and subject to certain conditions, the agreement would automatically meet the conditions for exemption – and generated substantial debate, some of which the Commission took on board.[37]

The general scheme of the TTBER is similar to that of the verticals block exemption Regulation. After defining which agreements are covered by the Regulation, it then provides an exemption for those agreements that fall beneath a market share threshold, which varies depending on whether the agreement is between competitors and non-competitors, provided that the agreement does not contain any hard-core restrictions. There is also a set of excluded restrictions, that is clauses within contracts, to which the exemption will not apply, as well as provisions allowing for the Commission to withdraw the benefit of the Regulation in individual cases and in more general situations, typically where the market is foreclosed by networks of similar agreements. In the same way as the verticals Regulation, the TTBER is also accompanied by substantial guidance from the Commission on the application of Article 101 TFEU to technology transfer agreements; in other words, the scope of the guidance goes beyond simply explaining how the TTBER will be applied. The central thrust of the approach is neatly set out by Anderman and Kallaugher, respectively an eminent academic and a senior practitioner:

> The central theme of the Guidelines is the need to identify competitive harm and to identify economic benefits that might outweigh those competitive harms in order to determine whether a licence agreement raised Article 81 [Article 101 TFEU] issues. The system of assessment created by the Guidelines entails a fundamental change in the way that practitioners must address competition law issues in the intellectual property context. In place of a purely legalistic evaluation of the content of licensing agreements, the new system demands a new type of legal and economic assessment of individual agreements . . . Since the TTBER has practically no value other than as a reference for identifying hard core restraints effective counselling . . . requires lawyers to accept the need to combine legal and economic analysis in vetting licensing agreements under Article 81 [Article 101 TFEU].[38]

A point which comes out less clearly in European discussions is that much of the activity in this area is undertaken by large global corporations and they are concerned to ensure that the competition rules that they are subject to are consistent across jurisdictions. The US authorities produced Guidelines in 1995 on the licensing of IPRs and antitrust issues and it is evident that the TTBER and its associated Guidelines were designed to be consistent with the approach of the American authorities.[39] To take one example, the TTBER says that agreements between competitors where they have a combined market share of no more than 20% and do not contain certain clauses, will meet the criteria for exemption under Article 101(3) TFEU, which is consistent with the approach taken by the American authorities in their guidance.[40]

The TTBER expires in 2014 and the European Commission is currently reviewing its operation, in part through a consultation process, in preparation for producing a new version.[41]

---

[37] See S. Anderman and J. Kallaugher, *Technology Transfer and the New EU Competition Rules: Intellectual Property Licensing After Modernisation* (Oxford University Press, 2006), ch. 2.

[38] Ibid., paras 1.19–1.20 and 1.23.

[39] See S. Anderman, 'Substantial Convergence: The US influence on the development of the regulatory framework for IP licensing in the EC', in P. Marsden (ed.) *Handbook of Research in Trans-Atlantic Anti-trust* (Edward Elgar, Cheltenham, 2006).

[40] See US Department of Justice and Federal Trade Commission, *Antitrust Guidelines for the Licensing of Intellectual Property* (1995) at para. 4.3.

[41] See *http://ec.europa.eu/competition/consultations/2012_technology_transfer/index_en.html* (accessed 14/08/12).

The responses to the consultation suggest that, overall, the TTBER has worked well and provides reasonable guidance. Notably, no cases appear to have been litigated under it. Concerns were raised over the complexity of the TTBER and the difficulties of applying the market share tests in the context of rapidly changing technology markets.

Definitions

The exemption applies in relation to technology transfer agreements between *two* undertakings[42] permitting the production of contract products, that is, products which incorporate or are produced with the technology licensed under the agreement.[43] In other words, it is aimed at agreements where the owner of technology (the licensor) licenses the technology to another party (the licensee) in order so that they may produce a product either through using the technology in the process of production or incorporating the technology within the product as opposed to the purchase of goods and services or the licensing of other types of intellectual property. It also covers sublicensing, where the licensee sublicenses the technology to third parties, provided that the production of contract products is the primary purpose of the arrangement, and subcontracting, where the licensee produces the products for the licensor.[44] In addition, the TTBER covers agreements where the licensee must carry out development work before obtaining a product or process that is ready for commercial exploitation, provided that a contract product is identified at the outset as opposed to carrying out further research and development.[45] The TTBER provides a list of technology transfer agreements:

- a patent licensing agreement,
- a know-how licensing agreement,
- a software copyright licensing agreement,
- a mixed patent, know-how or software copyright licensing agreement, or
- assignments of patents, know-how, software copyright or a combination thereof where part of the risk associated with the exploitation of the technology remains with the licensor.

Other types of intellectual property, such as trademarks and copyright, are covered only to the extent that they are directly related to the exploitation of the licensed technology and do not constitute the primary aim of the agreement.[46] The Commission takes the view that the licensing of copyright for the production and distribution of work is similar to technology transfer, so will be treated in the same way, but that the licensing of rights in performance and other rights related to copyright cannot be treated in a similar manner.[47] This is because the value in the work is not created by reproduction or sale but by each individual performance and the individual circumstances of the work and the performance(s) must be taken into account. Trade mark licensing is also considered to fall outside technology transfer and is

---

[42] So it does not cover multi-party agreements, although the Commission says that it will apply by analogy the principles set out in the TTBER to multi-party agreements: Guidelines (n. 35), para. 40.

[43] TTBER, Art. 2.

[44] TTBER Guidelines (n. 35) at paras 42 and 44. Subcontracting is also covered by a specific Commission Notice: see P. Roth (ed.) *Bellamy and Child: European Community Law of Competition* (6th edn, Oxford University Press, 2008) at paras 6.189–6.195 for discussion.

[45] TTBER Guidelines (n. 35) at para. 45.

[46] Ibid. at para. 50.

[47] Ibid. at paras 51 and 52.

considered more akin to distribution agreements. If it is directly related to the use, sale or resale of goods and services and does not constitute the primary purpose of the agreement, then the Commission takes the view that this should be dealt with under the verticals block exemption.[48]

The benefit of the block exemption is available so long as the parties meet the relevant market share thresholds (see Box 12.3).

KEY LEGAL PROVISION   Box 12.3

Market share thresholds for the TTBER

1 Where the undertakings party to the agreement are competing undertakings, the exemption . . . shall apply on condition that the combined market share of the parties does not exceed 20% on the affected relevant technology and product market.

2 Where the undertakings party to the agreement are not competing undertakings, the exemption . . . shall apply on condition that the market share of each of the parties does not exceed 30% on the affected relevant technology and product market.

Source: TTBER, Article 3.

Question: How easy is it to determine an undertaking's share of the market?

Competing and non-competing undertakings

The first point to notice is that the Regulation distinguishes between competing and non-competing undertakings and this needs further explanation, although it seems intuitive. The Commission makes a distinction between the product market and the technology market. As it explains, technology is an input which can be integrated into either the product or the production process. When technology is licensed it can affect competition on either market. Thus, for example, imagine two undertakings, A and B, which make non-competing products, using different technology, which could be adapted to produce either product. If B licenses A's technology in order to produce its original product then the market that is affected is not the product market, but the technology market. If B licenses A's technology in order to produce a product that competes with A's original product, then both the technology and the product market are affected. This situation is illustrated in Figure 12.1.

In order to determine whether the undertakings are actual or potential competitors, the Commission looks at what the position would have been in the absence of the agreement.[49] The parties are actual competitors if they are active on the same product and technology markets. They are potential competitors if either they would have undertaken the necessary investment to enter the relevant market or if they own substitutable technologies. The Commission goes on to point out that there may be cases where the undertakings produce competing products but they can be considered non-competitors because the new licensed

---

[48] Ibid. at para. 53.
[49] This paragraph summarises paras 27–33 of the TTBER Guidelines (n. 35).

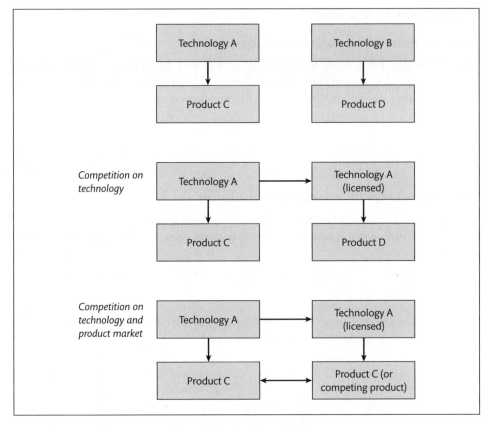

Figure 12.1 Non-competing technology and product markets

technology represents such a drastic innovation that the older technology has become obsolete or, in other words, a new market has been created. The example given is the replacement of LPs by CDs and the Commission points out that it was not obvious at the beginning that this was the case, so one would start by considering the parties as competitors, at the time of the agreement. This is a controversial point, because it is often argued that technology markets may be so fast moving that conventional means of measuring market shares, or indeed defining markets, cannot be applied.[50] Although there is some recognition of the point by the Commission, arguably it does not go far enough.

Market share of technology is measured by the presence of the technology on the product market, rather than relating this to licensing income. The licensor's market share will be the combined share of the product market of the licensor and its licensees and this is based on sales of the products incorporating the technology.[51]

---

[50] For example, see D. Teece and C. Pleatsikas, 'The Analysis of Market Definition and Market Power in the Context of Rapid Innovation' (2001) 19 *International Journal of Industrial Organisation* 665.
[51] TTBER, Art. 3(3).

Hard-core restrictions[52]

Hard-core restrictions between competitors

The 'safe harbour' provided by the TTBER does not exist if the arrangements contain hard-core restrictions and, as in market shares, a distinction is drawn between what is acceptable between competitors and what is acceptable between non-competitors (see Box 12.4).

KEY LEGAL PROVISION   Box 12.4

Hard-core restrictions between competitors

The exemption provided shall not apply to agreements which, directly or indirectly, in isolation or in combination with other factors under the control of the parties, have as their object:

(a) the restriction of a party's ability to determine its prices when selling products to third parties;

(b) the limitation of output, except limitations on the output of contract products imposed on the licensee in a non-reciprocal agreement or imposed on only one of the licensees in a reciprocal agreement;

(c) the allocation of markets or customers except:

    (i) the obligation on the licensee(s) to produce with the licensed technology only within one or more technical fields of use or one or more product markets,

    (ii) the obligation on the licensor and/or the licensee, in a non-reciprocal agreement, not to produce with the licensed technology within one or more technical fields of use or one or more product markets or one or more exclusive territories reserved for the other party,

    (iii) the obligation on the licensor not to license the technology to another licensee in a particular territory,

    (iv) the restriction, in a non-reciprocal agreement, of active and/or passive sales by the licensee and/or the licensor into the exclusive territory or to the exclusive customer group reserved for the other party,

    (v) the restriction, in a non-reciprocal agreement, of active sales by the licensee into the exclusive territory or to the exclusive customer group allocated by the licensor to another licensee provided the latter was not a competing undertaking of the licensor at the time of the conclusion of its own licence,

    (vi) the obligation on the licensee to produce the contract products only for its own use provided that the licensee is not restricted in selling the contract products actively and passively as spare parts for its own products,

---

[52] Generally, see S. Enchelmaier, 'Hardcore restrictions in Technology Transfer Agreements under Regulation (EC) No 772/2004', in S. Anderman and A. Ezrachi (eds) *Intellectual Property and Competition Law: New Frontiers* (Oxford University Press, 2011).

> (vii) the obligation on the licensee, in a non-reciprocal agreement, to produce the contract products only for a particular customer, where the licence was granted in order to create an alternative source of supply for that customer;
>
> (d) the restriction of the licensee's ability to exploit its own technology or the restriction of the ability of any of the parties to the agreement to carry out research and development, unless such latter restriction is indispensable to prevent the disclosure of the licensed know-how to third parties.
>
> *Source*: TTBER, Article 4(1).
>
> **Question**: To what extent do you think that each of these clauses is clearly restrictive of competition?

As regards agreements between competitors, the basic hard-core restrictions are:

- restrictions on the ability to fix prices;
- limiting output;
- allocating markets or customers; and
- preventing the licensee or any of the parties to the agreement from carrying out further research and development, unless that restriction is indispensable to prevent the disclosure of the information to third parties.

The point of the last hard-core restriction is to prevent clauses in agreements which limit the further development of technology, whereas the first three of these restrictions are what might be seen as classic cartel restrictions, although there are some important twists to them in this context and, as regards customer or market allocation, seven exceptions, discussed below. To understand these twists and exceptions, it is important to appreciate that the Regulation draws a distinction between reciprocal and non-reciprocal agreements. A reciprocal agreement is, broadly, where undertakings grant each other a licence for technology which is either competing or can be used to produce competing technologies. A non-reciprocal agreement is where one undertaking grants the other a licence or where two undertakings grant each other a licence but these licences do not concern competing technologies.[53] So, output limitations can be imposed on a licensee in a non-reciprocal agreement and on one of the parties in a reciprocal agreement. As the Commission points out in its Guidelines, reciprocal restrictions on output in an agreement look like having the object and effect to reduce output in a market, whereas non-reciprocal restrictions can represent either integration of technology or the higher valuation placed on the technology by one of the parties.[54] So, for example, if firm A, which produces product C, licenses firm B to use its technology to produce product C and they both agree to limit their output of product C, this looks like one element of a price-fixing agreement because a limitation of supply would typically drive prices up. If, however, firm B alone agrees to the output restriction this does not restrict supply, because firm A can provide more output. Firm B might agree to this proposal because, for example, it was the only way

---

[53] TTBER, Art. 1(c) and (d).
[54] TTBER Guidelines (n. 35), paras 82–3.

it could enter the market for product C. As a result of this, in general a more relaxed approach is taken to non-reciprocal agreements, and there are a number of exceptions to the basic definition of a hard-core restriction.

Exceptions to hard-core restrictions

Once this distinction is grasped, the exceptions begin to make more sense. The first two allow for clauses in the agreement that will restrict the use of the technology to certain areas. The first exception allows for clauses which will restrict the licensee to using the technology only in specific areas, known as 'field of use'. To put it simply, if the licence is granted to produce product A, the licensee cannot use it to produce product B, and this restriction is allowed. This type of arrangement will allow the technology to spread to other fields, which might well not happen if the licensor was concerned about the possibility of competition in its own field. The second exception, which applies to non-reciprocal agreements, allows for the agreement to specify certain uses to which the technology cannot be put, either by the licensor or the licensee. To give a simple example, the licence may allow the production of products A, B and D, but the licensee is prevented from producing product C. This also, however, extends to restrictions on the products produced or the territories within which they may be produced. So, for example, the licensor can agree to license the technology for use in a particular geographical area or for a particular product *and can* agree not to produce that product or to produce products in that geographical area. The Commission makes the point that the object of this agreement may be to give the licensee the incentive to invest and develop the technology.[55] A similar justification may be seen to underlie the third exception, whereby the licensor may agree not to license competing technology in the same territory, although this extends to reciprocal, as well as non-reciprocal agreements. The fourth exception is clearly seen by the Commission as being justified by the incentive argument, as it allows clauses in a non-reciprocal agreement that prevent the parties to the agreement selling into the exclusive territory or customer group allocated to the other party.[56]

The fifth exception allows restrictions in a non-reciprocal agreement that prevent the licensee from engaging in active selling into a geographical area or customer group allocated by the licensor to another licensee. An important condition here is that the other licensee was not a competitor of the licensor at the time of the agreement of its own licence. The Commission's explanation is that, 'By allowing the licensor to grant a licensee, who was not already on the market, protection against active sales by licensees which are competitors of the licensor and which for that reason are already established on the market, such restrictions are likely to induce the licensee to exploit the licensed technology more efficiently.'[57] By contrast, if there is an agreement not to do this between licensees, this does not involve a transfer of technology, thus falling outside the TTBER and, in the Commission's view, amounts to a cartel.[58]

The sixth exception allows for the licensee to be restricted to producing the contract products for its own use, provided it can sell the contract products actively or passively as spare parts. The final exception excludes from the hard-core list an obligation on the licensee in a

---

[55] Ibid. at para. 86.
[56] Ibid. at para. 87.
[57] Ibid. at para. 89.
[58] Ibid.

non-reciprocal agreement to produce the contract products only for a particular customer with a view to creating an alternative source of supply for that customer.

Hard-core restrictions in agreements between non-competitors

As regards agreements between non-competitors, there are three basic hard-core restrictions:

1 minimum resale price maintenance;

2 territorial and/or customer restrictions; and

3 the restriction of active or passive sales[59] to end-users by members of a selective distribution system, although there may be a restriction on them operating out of an unauthorised place of establishment (the full list is in Box 12.5).

These are similar to the list of hard-core restrictions found in Article 4 of the block exemption for vertical agreements (discussed in Chapter 11), to which reference can be made. It is important to note that here, the territorial and/or customer restrictions referred to cover only *passive* selling. In other words, it is legitimate in technology transfer agreements between non-competitors to include restrictions on active selling into particular territories or to particular customer groups, provided that the market share thresholds are met.

KEY LEGAL PROVISION   **Box 12.5**

Hard-core restrictions for agreements between non-competitors

The exemption shall not apply to agreements which, directly or indirectly, in isolation or in combination with other factors under the control of the parties, have as their object:

(a) the restriction of a party's ability to determine its prices when selling products to third parties, without prejudice to the possibility of imposing a maximum sale price or recommending a sale price, provided that it does not amount to a fixed or minimum sale price as a result of pressure from, or incentives offered by, any of the parties;

(b) the restriction of the territory into which, or of the customers to whom, the licensee may passively sell the contract products, except:

  (i) the restriction of passive sales into an exclusive territory or to an exclusive customer group reserved for the licensor,

  (ii) the restriction of passive sales into an exclusive territory or to an exclusive customer group allocated by the licensor to another licensee during the first two years that this other licensee is selling the contract products in that territory or to that customer group,

  (iii) the obligation to produce the contract products only for its own use provided that the licensee is not restricted in selling the contract products actively and passively as spare parts for its own products,

---

[59] Passive sales being, roughly, where the customer comes to the undertaking, active sales being where the undertaking seeks out the customer's business. (See Chapter 11 for the Commission's definition.)

> (iv) the obligation to produce the contract products only for a particular customer, where the licence was granted in order to create an alternative source of supply for that customer,
>
> (v) the restriction of sales to end-users by a licensee operating at the wholesale level of trade,
>
> (vi) the restriction of sales to unauthorised distributors by the members of a selective distribution system;
>
> (c) the restriction of active or passive sales to end-users by a licensee which is a member of a selective distribution system and which operates at the retail level, without prejudice to the possibility of prohibiting a member of the system from operating out of an unauthorised place of establishment.
>
> *Source*: TTBER, Article 4(2).
>
> **Question**: To what extent do you think that each of these clauses is clearly restrictive of competition?

The first exception allows for a restriction on passive sales into an exclusive territory or customer group reserved for the licensor. The justification for this, according to the Commission, is that, 'It is presumed that up to the market share threshold such restraints, where restrictive of competition, promote pro-competitive dissemination of technology and integration of such technology into the production assets of the licensee.'[60] The licensor does not have to be engaged in selling within that territory or to that group; they may be reserved for future exploitation. The second exception allows for restrictions on passive sales into an exclusive territory or customer group allocated to another licensee for the first two years that that licensee is selling in that territory or to that group. The Commission points out that new entrants into a market may have to make substantial investments in developing technology and promoting products, which they would be unlikely to get back if they exited the market. Therefore, they will require some protection of their investment for the initial period.[61]

The third and fourth exceptions are the same as the sixth and seventh exceptions in relation to agreements between competitors, namely restrictions on producing the contract products for the licensee's own use and restrictions where the licensee is only supposed to produce the contract products for a particular customer and the licence was granted to provide an alternative source of supply to that customer.

The fifth exception allows the licensor to impose an obligation on a licensee not to sell to end-users, but only to retailers. The Commission takes the view that this allows the licensor to assign the wholesale distribution function to the licensee and that this is normally outside Article 101(1) TFEU.[62] The final exception allows restrictions on the licensee not to sell to unauthorised distributors. This exception allows the licensor to impose on the licensees an obligation to form part of a selective distribution system, although they cannot be prevented from selling to end-users, that is, final consumers.

---

[60] TTBER Guidelines (n. 35) at para. 100.
[61] Ibid. at para. 101.
[62] Ibid. at para. 104.

Excluded restrictions

In addition to a prohibition on hard-core restrictions, the TTBER also provides for limitations on what the Commission calls excluded restrictions. These are provisions, listed in Article 5, which are not covered by the block exemption but require individual assessment of their pro- and anti-competitive effects. If they are included in an agreement and considered to be anti-competitive, the rest of the agreement may still gain the benefit of the block exemption, provided it meets the conditions, so long as the agreement can still be operated without these restrictions. This is referred to by the Commission as being severable. The list of restrictions is contained in Box 12.6.

The first two excluded restrictions concern exclusive grant backs or assignments to the licensor or a designated third party of severable improvements to the technology. This is where the licensee is required to disclose and transfer all improvements made (including related know-how acquired) in the licensed technology during the licensing period *only* to the licensor or the person that has been designated. An improvement is severable if it can be exploited without infringing on the licensed technology, that is, it can be exploited separately from the licensed technology. Such obligations are, according to the Commission, likely to reduce the licensee's incentive to develop the technology since they will make it more difficult for the licensee to exploit the improved technology.[63] Non-exclusive grant backs are allowed, even if the agreement is non-reciprocal because they may promote innovation and dissemination of technology through giving the licensor the ability to pass on the new technology to other licensees. A non-severable improvement is one which cannot be exploited by the licensee without the licensor's permission because it infringes the licensor's technology and thus these do not fall under this provision.[64]

KEY LEGAL PROVISION   **Box 12.6**

Excluded restrictions

(a) any direct or indirect obligation on the licensee to grant an exclusive licence to the licensor or to a third party designated by the licensor in respect of its own severable improvements to or its own new applications of the licensed technology;

(b) any direct or indirect obligation on the licensee to assign, in whole or in part, to the licensor or to a third party designated by the licensor, rights to its own severable improvements to or its own new applications of the licensed technology;

(c) any direct or indirect obligation on the licensee not to challenge the validity of intellectual property rights which the licensor holds in the common [internal] market, without prejudice to the possibility of providing for termination of the technology

---

[63] Ibid. at para. 109.

[64] Compare Department of Justice/Federal Trade Commission, 'Antitrust Guidelines for the Licensing of Intellectual Property' (1995) at s. 5.6. Available at: *http://www.justice.gov/atr/public/guidelines/0558.htm#t56* (accessed 14/08/12).

transfer agreement in the event that the licensee challenges the validity of one or more of the licensed intellectual property rights;

(d) any direct or indirect obligation limiting the licensee's ability to exploit its own technology or limiting the ability of any of the parties to the agreement to carry out research and development, unless such latter restriction is indispensable to prevent the disclosure of the licensed know-how to third parties.

Source: TTBER, Article 5.

Question: What is the justification for limiting the use of such clauses?

The third excluded restriction covers what are known as 'non-challenge' clauses. The Commission's explanation for this is that licensees are normally in the best position to determine whether an intellectual property right is invalid.[65] It is in the interests of undistorted competition and the principles underlying IPRs, according to the Commission, that invalid IPRs should be challenged because invalid rights stifle innovation rather than promote it.[66] This does, however, allow for the possibility that the licence will be terminated if a challenge is made, which means that the risk of continuing to use the technology will remain with the licensee.

Finally, excluded from the scope of the block exemption, in the case of agreements between non-competitors, are any direct or indirect obligations limiting the licensee's ability to exploit their own technology or limiting the ability of the parties to the agreement to carry out research and development, unless such latter restriction is indispensable to prevent the disclosure of licensed know-how to third parties. The content of this condition is the same as that of the hard-core list concerning agreements between competitors. The difference is, according to the Commission, that there may be cases where the parties are non-competitors but the licensee owns competing technology, but does not exploit it and the licensor is not an actual or potential supplier on the product market. In those cases, it is restrictive of competition to prevent the licensee from exploiting and developing their own technology because it represents a competitive constraint on the market. Such restrictions are normally considered by the Commission to be a breach of the prohibition in Article 101(1) TFEU and as not satisfying the conditions of Article 101(3) TFEU.[67] In other words, this looks very much like a hard-core, rather than an excluded restriction. Where the licensee does not own competing technology, different considerations apply. The Commission takes the view that there is likely to be a restriction of competition only where a few technologies are available. Here the parties may be an important source of new innovation and in such a case the conditions for an individual exemption are unlikely to be met. In other cases, where there are several technologies available and the parties do not possess special skills (for example, in research), such a restraint is likely to fall outside the prohibition for lack of an appreciable effect or to satisfy the conditions for an individual exemption. The Commission's view is that the restraint may promote the dissemination of new technology by assuring the licensor that

[65] Ibid. at para. 112.
[66] Ibid.
[67] Ibid. at para. 115.

the licence does not create a new competitor and by inducing the licensee to focus on the exploitation and development of the licensed technology.[68]

Withdrawal and non-application of the TTBER

The TTBER also provides for its withdrawal in individual cases and non-application in more general cases. In relation to individual agreements, the benefit may be withdrawn by the Commission[69] if:

- access of third parties' technologies to the market is restricted, for instance by the cumulative effect of parallel networks of similar restrictive agreements prohibiting licensees from using third parties' technologies;

- access of potential licensees to the market is restricted, for instance by the cumulative effect of parallel networks of similar restrictive agreements prohibiting licensors from licensing to other licensees;

- without any objectively valid reason, the parties do not exploit the licensed technology.[70]

In relation to non-application, the Commission may declare the TTBER non-applicable to agreements containing specific restraints where parallel networks of similar technology transfer agreements cover more than 50% of a relevant market.[71] Neither of these provisions appear to have been used.

Agreements outside the TTBER

As was mentioned at the beginning of the discussion of the TTBER, it applies to only certain types of arrangements. Agreements which fall outside the TTBER will have to be assessed under Article 101 TFEU. In addition, agreements involving undertakings whose market share is in excess of limits in the TTBER will also have to be assessed under Article 101 TFEU. In this section, therefore, we look at the Commission's approach in general to such agreements and also at certain types of agreements which have raised particular problems or are worth a short discussion.

The starting point for the Commission is that there is no presumption of illegality just because an agreement falls outside the TTBER; it is necessary to undertake an individual assessment of the agreement. The Commission goes on to say that outside hard-core restrictions there is unlikely to be an infringement of Article 101 TFEU where there are four or more independently controlled technologies, in addition to the technologies controlled by the parties to the agreement, that may be substitutable for the licensed technology at a comparable cost to the user.[72] Whether the technologies are sufficiently substitutable

---

[68] Ibid. at para. 116.

[69] Or the national competition authority if the effects relate to the territory of a Member State or part of that territory which is a distinct geographical market.

[70] TTBER, Art. 6(1).

[71] Ibid., Art. 7.

[72] TTBER Guidelines (n. 35) at para. 131. Again, this is consistent with the approach of the American authorities: see US Department of Justice and Federal Trade Commission, *Antitrust Guidelines for the Licensing of Intellectual Property* (1995), para. 4.3.

will depend on their commercial strength and that, in its turn, depends on things like network effects and an assessment on whether there is a real competitive constraint. It should be noted that this is a reasonably stiff test: four competing technologies may well constitute a large number.[73] Outside this so-called safe harbour, it will be necessary to examine the working of competition on the market in question and the Commission lists the following relevant factors:[74]

(a) the nature of the agreement;

(b) the market position of the parties;

(c) the market position of competitors;

(d) the market position of buyers of the licensed products;

(e) entry barriers;

(f) maturity of the market; and

(g) other factors.

These will be familiar from previous chapters, but it is worth noting a couple of points made in the subsequent analysis. First, although the Commission states that high market share is usually a good indicator of market power, this may not be the case where entry barriers are low. Secondly, there is a need to look at the competitive relationship between the licensor and the licensee, particularly in the case where the licensee owns a competing technology which it is not currently exploiting.[75] Thirdly, buyer power needs to be taken into account, although the Commission distinguishes between cases where buyer power prevents the exercise of market power and those cases where strong buyers just extract more favourable terms or simply pass on the above competitive prices to their consumers. Finally, entry barriers are said to be low when effective entry can occur within one or two years and the Commission takes the view that entry barriers can arise from a wide variety of factors, such as government regulation, essential facilities or sunk costs (those costs which, once committed, cannot be recovered).

▇ Assessment of particular clauses in technology agreements

After this general discussion, the Commission goes on to explain its general approach in relation to particular clauses that are often found in technology agreements, even though those agreements may be outside the scope of the TTBER. The Commission regards certain obligations as not in general restrictive of competition (see Box 12.7).

---

[73] This is similar to the US rule: see Department of Justice/Federal Trade Commission, 'Guidelines' (n. 40) at para. 4.3.

[74] TTBER Guidelines (n. 35) at para. 132.

[75] Ibid. at para. 135.

KEY LEGAL PROVISION   Box 12.7

Obligations not generally restrictive of competition

- Confidentiality obligations
- Obligations on licensees not to sub-license
- Obligations not to use the licensed technology after the expiration of the agreement, provided that the IPR protection remains valid and in force
- Obligations to assist the licensor in enforcing the licensed IPRs
- Obligations to pay minimum royalties or to produce a minimum quantity of products incorporating the licensed technology
- Obligations to use the licensor's trade mark or indicate the name of the licensor on the product.

Source: TTBER Guidelines, para. 153.

Question: Is there any way of using such obligations to restrict competition?

Outside these obligations, the Commission starts by distinguishing between clauses which limit production to a single territory (exclusive or sole licences) and those which limit the sale of products incorporating the technology into a particular territory (sales restrictions), although the two ideas may be combined.

Exclusive or sole licences

An exclusive licence gives the licensee the exclusive right to make the product using the technology in a territory, whereas a sole licence gives the licensee protection against the licensor licensing other third parties in a particular territory, but not protection against the licensor in that territory. The Commission's treatment of such clauses depends importantly on whether the agreement is between competitors or between non-competitors. Reciprocal exclusive licensing between competitors is a hard-core restriction, as discussed above, while reciprocal sole licensing will gain the benefit of the block exemption up to the 20% market share threshold. Non-reciprocal exclusive licensing will gain the benefit of the block exemption up to the 20% threshold, but once that threshold is breached, there is a need to assess the possible anti-competitive effects, since an exclusive licence implies that the licensor no longer supplies products to that territory. The question, so far as the Commission is concerned, is the competitive significance of the licensor and it points out that if the licensor has a limited market position or lacks the capacity to exploit the technology, there is unlikely to be a breach of Article 101(1) TFEU. By contrast, the Commission takes the view that exclusive licensing between non-competitors is likely to fulfil the conditions of Article 101(3) TFEU. Its main area for concern is where a dominant licensee obtains a licence to one or more competing technologies because, in circumstances where entry into the technology market is difficult, this may foreclose other third party licensees of the technology and thus protect market power. The Commission is also concerned with arrangements whereby two or more parties cross-license each other and undertake not to license third parties because the package of technologies resulting from the cross-licences may create, effectively, an industry standard to which third parties must have access in order to compete effectively on the market. These cases will be assessed on a similar basis to technology pools, which are discussed in more detail below.

Sales restrictions

As regards sales restrictions,[76] such restrictions in a reciprocal agreement between competitors are considered either hard-core restrictions or in breach of Article 101(1) TFEU and unlikely to qualify for an exemption under Article 101(3) TFEU as they are equivalent to market sharing. In the case of non-reciprocal agreements, the block exemption provides protection for certain restrictions up to the market share threshold of 20%. Above that level, such agreements may be caught if one of the parties has a significant degree of market power. However, the Commission indicates that if it thinks that the restraint may be indispensable for the dissemination of valuable technologies or the penetration of a new market, particularly where the licensee is in a weak market position, then the conditions for an individual exemption under Article 101(3) TFEU will be made out. Note that restrictions on passive sales by a licensee into a territory or customer group allocated to another licensee are considered a hard-core restriction. As regards sales restrictions between non-competitors, these are block exempted up to a 30% market threshold. Above this, restrictions on active or passive sales by the licensee into territories or customer groups reserved for the licensor may fall outside Article 101(1) TFEU (that is, they would not be unlawful) if it is concluded that the licensing would not take place without this restriction. As the Commission says, a licensor cannot normally be expected to create competition with itself on the basis of its own technology. Outside this situation, such arrangement may be caught by Article 101(1) TFEU where the licensor has a significant degree of market power or there is a network of such arrangements by licensors. Conversely, sales restrictions on the licensor, if they are caught by Article 101(1) TFEU, are, according to the Commission, likely to meet the criteria in Article 101(3) TFEU in order to induce the licensee to invest in the production, marketing and sale of the products, which it would be less likely to do if faced with competition from the licensor. As regards restrictions on active sales between licensees, above the market share threshold, these may be caught by Article 101(1) TFEU where the licensee has sufficient market power but they may meet the conditions of Article 101(3) TFEU if they are needed to prevent free riding and to induce the licensee to exploit their technology efficiently. Restrictions on passive sales are, again, considered a hard-core restriction.

Field of use restrictions

Another common clause in technology agreements is what is known as a 'field of use' restriction, which aims to limit the use of the licensed technology by the licensee.[77] The Commission recognises that these clauses may have pro-competitive effects because they can encourage the licensor to license the use of the technology for areas outside their main business. Insofar as field of use restrictions are combined with sole and exclusive licensing, they are treated in a similar way to that discussed above. As regards field of use restrictions on licensees in agreements between competitors the Commission's main concern is what it calls 'asymmetrical'

---

[76] This paragraph summarises TTBER Guidelines (n. 35) at paras 168–74.
[77] This paragraph summarises TTBER Guidelines (n. 35) at paras 179–85.

field of use restrictions. This is where the one party is restricted to the use of the technology to produce one product, or operate one process, and the other party is restricted to using the technology to produce a different product or different process. What the Commission is worried about here is where the licensee could compete with the licensor but it ceases to do so because of the field of use restriction, which causes it to concentrate its efforts on the area for which it has obtained the licence. If this leads to a reduction of output outside the field of use, the Commission states that this will be caught by Article 101(1) TFEU. By contrast, according to the Commission, symmetrical field of use restrictions – agreements whereby the parties are licensed to use each other's technologies within the same field(s) of use – are unlikely to be caught by Article 101(1) TFEU. Such agreements are unlikely to restrict competition that existed in the absence of the agreement. Field of use restrictions in agreements between non-competitors are seen as either neutral or efficiency enhancing.

Captive use restrictions

The Guidelines also consider captive use restrictions,[78] which is where a licensee is limited to producing the quantities required for his or her own use and the maintenance and repair of their own products. So, for example, if an automobile manufacturer has a licence to use a particular process to produce parts for their cars, a captive use restriction would limit them to producing the quantities they needed for production and repairing their models. They would not be allowed to produce the product for other automobile manufacturers that might have to license the process from the licensor. In relation to competitors, this potentially stops a competitor being an alternative supplier to third parties, although this depends on whether the licensee was engaged in that activity before the agreement. If it was not, then there is no competition problem. If it was, then this may result in a competition problem if, by agreeing to the licence and its terms, the licensee ceases to be a supplier of components to third parties. In relation to such licences between non-competitors, the Commission recognises that there may be competition issues because of, first, the restriction of intra-technology competition on the market for the supply of inputs because the licensee will be limited to producing for their own needs. Secondly, the captive use restriction will prevent the creation of a market for the product between the licensees, thus enhancing the possibility for imposing discriminatory royalties on licensees because they will not be able to obtain the input from a licensee who has lower costs (this is referred to as the prevention of arbitrage). On the other hand, there may be pro-competitive benefits for encouraging the dissemination of technology, whilst not at the same time encouraging the creation of a competitor to the licensor.

Tying and bundling

There is also a discussion of tying and bundling,[79] where the Commission makes the point that for this practice to be likely to have anti-competitive consequences, it is necessary that the licensor must have a significant degree of market power in the tying product, so as to restrict competition in the tied product. The Commission also recognises that tying may give rise to efficiency gains where, for instance, the tied product is necessary for a technically satisfactory

---

[78] This paragraph summarises TTBER Guidelines (n. 35), paras 186–90.

[79] Tying in this context is where the licensing for one technology is conditional on taking another technology or product. Bundling is where two technologies are only sold together. See TTBER Guidelines (n. 35) at paras 191–205. Compare Department of Justice/Federal Trade Commission, 'Guidelines' (n. 40) at s. 5.3.

exploitation of the licensed technology or for ensuring that production under the licence conforms to quality standards respected by the licensor and other licensees. This is normally not restrictive of competition or is covered by Article 101(3) TFEU.

Non-compete obligations

Guidance is also given on non-compete obligations, that is, an obligation placed on a licensee not to use technology which competes with the licensed technology.[80] Such obligations are exempted in the TTBER up to the market share thresholds for agreements between competitors and non-competitors; that is, up to 20% joint market share for competitors and 30% joint market share for non-competitors. The Commission recognises that non-compete obligations may have pro-competitive effects, through preventing the risk of misuse of licensed technology, through providing an appropriate incentive on the licensee to exploit the licensed technology properly and, possibly, as an encouragement to the licensor to make client specific investments in, for example, training. The main risk, from the Commission's point of view is that non-compete obligations could foreclose access to the market by competing third party technologies, as well as facilitating collusion between licensors where there is cumulative use. The Commission explains that foreclosure may arise where a substantial part of the potential licensees are tied to one or more sources of technology which can result from a series of agreements with one licensor with market power or the cumulative effect of a number of agreements. In the latter case, the Commission's view is that there is unlikely to be a problem as long as less than 50% of the market is so tied up. Above this threshold significant foreclosure is likely to occur if the barriers to entry are high. Where it is a case of a series of agreements with one licensor, there is a greater risk of foreclosure the higher the market share that that licensor has. From the Commission's point of view, the non-compete obligations do not have to cover a significant part of the market if those non-compete obligations are targeted at undertakings which are most likely to use competing technologies. The risk is said to be highest where there is only a limited number of licensees using the technology for their own purposes.

Settlements[81]

An issue which has become increasingly important has been the question of settling litigation around patents. This came up as a particular issue in relation to the pharmaceutical industry and was first highlighted in the European Commission's sector inquiry into pharmaceuticals.[82] The basic issue is quite simple: until the patent to an original branded drug expires or is found to be invalid or limited in scope, then it is not possible for a generic drug manufacturer to enter the market with an alternative. The generic drug manufacturer may bring a court action against the originator drug company claiming either that the patent is unlawful or that it does not restrict its production of the generic drug. Rather than going to court, the parties may prefer to settle the case for a number of reasons, for example to avoid the high costs of litigation. What has concerned the European Commission, however, has been settlements where the originator pharmaceutical company pays a sum of money to the generic company,

---

[80] This paragraph summarises TTBER Guidelines (n. 35) at paras 196–203.

[81] Generally see P. Treacy and S. Lawrance 'Intellectual Property Rights and Out of Court Settlements' in S. Anderman and A. Ezrachi (eds) *Intellectual Property and Competition Law: New Frontiers* (Oxford University Press, 2011).

[82] See European Commission, 'Executive summary of the Pharmaceutical Sector Inquiry Report' (2009) at paras 3.2.4 and 3.3.4.

on the condition that the generic company does not pursue market entry for a particular period of time, so-called 'pay for delay' settlements. The Commission's concern is that these settlements delay the onset of effective competition, to the detriment of consumers. Although the TTBER Guidelines contain some discussion of settlements, they do not cover explicitly these sorts of arrangements.[83] The Commission has been undertaking a monitoring programme in relation to settlement agreements and has begun action over agreements which have prevented the entry of generic drugs on to the market.[84]

The issue of pay for delay settlements has been particularly controversial in the United States and the Federal Trade Commission has seen it as one of its top priorities to try to oppose such agreements.[85] Although the issue seems to arise partly because of the specific legislative rules adopted in the United States (commonly referred to as the Hatch-Waxman Act), the way it has been dealt with by the US courts may be a useful comparison for the European context. The issue was dealt with by US Court of Appeals for the Third Circuit in the K-Dur[86] case, which reviewed the previous case law on other circuits. There was a difference of opinion between those circuits which applied strict antitrust scrutiny and others which took the view that such agreements were permissible, provided that they did not exceed the potential exclusionary scope of the patent. The Court took the former view, directing that there should be a quick look rule of reason inquiry and that, 'any payment from a patent holder to a generic patent challenger who agrees to delay entry into the market [should be treated] as *prima facie* evidence of an unreasonable restraint of trade, which could be rebutted by showing that the payment (1) was for a purpose other than delayed entry or (2) offers some pro-competitive benefit.'[87] This is a strong approach but it remains to be seen whether it will be adopted by other US courts and, indeed, whether such an approach will be adopted in a European context.

Technology pools[88]

A specific issue worth some discussion is that of technology pools; that is, where a group of owners of certain technology pool its various aspects and then license out the combined technology to themselves and third parties. Such pools can allow for the development of new products or the creation of common standards which allow the development of new products or industries.[89] At the same time, such technology pools may also raise competition concerns as the development of common standards might prevent the development of new, alternative technology or the cooperation between the parties to a pool may work as the equivalent to a

---

[83] See TTBER Guidelines (n. 35), paras 204–209.

[84] For the monitoring reports see: *http://ec.europa.eu/competition/sectors/pharmaceuticals/inquiry/index.html* (accessed 14/08/12). For the Commission's actions, see Press Releases IP/12/834 25 July 2012 and IP/12/835 30 July 2012. A similar issue arose in relation to Johnson and Johnson and Novartis: Commission Press Release IP/11/1228, 21 October 2011.

[85] See *http://www.ftc.gov/opa/reporter/competition/payfordelay.shtml* (accessed 14/08/12).

[86] *In Re K-Dur Antitrust Litigation*, decision of 16 July 2012. Available at: *http://www.ca3.uscourts.gov/opinarch/102077p.pdf* (accessed 14/08/12).

[87] Ibid. at 33.

[88] Generally, see Anderman and Kallaugher, *Technology Transfer and the New EU Competition Rules* (n. 37) at paras 9.31–9.50.

[89] Such pools have a relatively long history: see R.J. Gilbert, 'Antitrust for Patent Pools: A Century of Policy Evolution', *Stanford Technology Law Review* (April 2004), available at *http://stlr.stanford.edu/2004/04/antitrust-for-patent-pools/* (accessed 14/08/12).

price-fixing cartel. Given their potential importance, the Commission's approach to technology pools is addressed in the Guidelines, but the pools themselves fall outside the TTBER, largely because they are agreements between more than two parties.

In assessing these arrangements, the Commission starts by making what it calls two basic distinctions between: technological complements and technological substitutes; and essential and non-essential technologies. Technologies, according to the Commission, are complements when they are both required to produce the product or carry out the process to which the technologies relate. Conversely, two technologies are substitutes when either technology allows the holder to produce the product or carry out the process to which the technologies relate.[90] A technology is essential if there are no substitutes for it either inside or outside the pool and it constitutes a necessary part of the package of technologies either for manufacturing the product or for carrying out the process using the pooled technologies. It will be appreciated that it is easier to state this distinction in theory than to apply it in practice.

The Commission takes the view that the inclusion in the pool of substitute technologies restricts inter-technology competition and comprises collective bundling. Furthermore, if the pool is mainly composed of substitute technologies, this is seen as amounting to collective price-fixing and the Commission views such arrangements as a breach of Article 101(1) TFEU, and it is unlikely that the conditions of Article 101(3) TFEU will be fulfilled.[91] By contrast, where the pool consists of technologies which are essential and are complementary, the Commission's view is that the creation of such arrangements falls outside Article 101(1) TFEU, although the conditions under which the pool's products are licensed might be caught.[92]

The Commission is also concerned with the position where non-essential but complementary technology is included in the pool, as it sees this as raising a risk of foreclosure of technology. This is because, where it is essential to license certain technology, but this licence requires the inclusion of certain other non-essential technology, there is less, or no, incentive on the licensee to look for a competing technology for the non-essential part of the package. This may also involve the licensee in paying for technology that it does not need and amounts to collective bundling. Where the pool has a significant position on the market, it is likely to be caught by Article 101(1) TFEU.[93] In assessing whether the inclusion of such non-essential technologies will lead to the foreclosure of other technologies, the Commission says that it will look at four factors, among others:[94]

1 whether there are pro-competitive reasons for including the non-essential technologies in the pool;

2 whether the licensors remain free to license their technologies independently;

3 whether, in cases where the pooled technologies have different applications, some of which do not require use of all of the pooled technologies, the pool offers the technologies only as a single package, or whether it offers separate packages for distinct applications; and

4 whether the pooled technologies are available only as a single package or whether licensees have the possibility of obtaining a licence for only part of the package with a corresponding reduction of royalties.

[90] TTBER Guidelines (n. 35) at para. 216.
[91] Ibid. at para. 219.
[92] Ibid. at para. 220.
[93] Ibid. at para. 221.
[94] Ibid. para. 222.

The Commission's view is, broadly, that there is less likely to be a competition problem if the non-essential technology is capable of being separated from the essential technology, that is, that there is no bundling.

When looking at the operation of such a pool,[95] the Commission takes the view that licensing terms should be fair and non-discriminatory and that licences should be non-exclusive. This does not, however, preclude the charging of different royalties for different uses, provided that those different uses are within different product markets, in other words, that there should be no discrimination within product markets. Licensors and licensees must also be free to develop competing products and must be free to grant and obtain licences outside the pool. Obligations to grant back improvements to the technology to the licensor should be non-exclusive and be limited to developments that are essential or important to the use of the pooled technology. Finally, in order to prevent the creation of a pool from shielding invalid patents against challenge, the right to terminate a licence in case of a challenge must be limited to the licensor of that particular technology and not extended to all technology within the pool.

As regards the organisational structure of the pool,[96] the Commission prefers pools which are open to all interested parties and where different interests are represented because it feels that the technologies selected will be done on the basis of their price and quality and that the licensing terms are more likely to be open and non-discriminatory. In addition, the extent to which independent experts are involved in the creation and operation of the pool is also important, because often these technology issues depend on matters of expert judgement. The Commission says that it will take into account how these experts are selected and what functions they are expected to undertake. The Commission will also look carefully at arrangements for exchanging sensitive information between the parties, such as pricing and output data. Finally, it is best if any dispute resolution mechanism is entrusted to persons or bodies independent of the pool mechanism.

Trade mark licences

Trade mark licences fall outside the TTBER and thus are dealt with under Article 101 TFEU. There is fairly limited discussion of such licences in the case law of the Courts and the Commission, but it does seem to be clear that Article 101(1) TFEU applies if a trade mark licence gives rise to a system of absolute territorial protection.[97] In the *Moosehead/Whitbread* case, which was decided in 1990, Moosehead, a Canadian brewer, had licensed its trade mark to Whitbread so that Whitbread could sell that beer in the United Kingdom. The Commission decided that the exclusive character of the trade mark licence was an appreciable restriction of competition because it excluded other parties, mainly the five other large brewers, from using that trade mark as licensees. However, the conditions for an individual exemption in Article 101(3) TFEU were met as the agreement would contribute to the improvement of the production and distribution of the product in the UK, as the Canadian brewer did not have sufficient turnover in the UK to warrant building its own UK breweries, and the agreement with Whitbread gave it access to substantial means of distribution. Consumers would benefit

---

[95] This paragraph summarises TTBER Guidelines (n. 35) at paras 225–9.
[96] This paragraph summarises TTBER Guidelines (n. 35) at paras 230–5.
[97] Case 28/77 *Tepea* v *Commission* [1978] ECR 1391.

because of the new product and there was no possibility of eliminating competition on the UK beer market.[98]

Copyright licences

Copyright licensing in general falls outside the TTBER, but the Commission makes a distinction between copyright licensing for the purposes of the reproduction and distribution of the work and licensing in relation to performance. In the former case, because the agreements relate to the production and sale of products on the basis of IPRs, the Commission considers them to be of a similar nature to technology transfer agreements and raising comparable issues.[99] It will thus as a general rule apply the principles in the TTBER and Guidelines. The licensing of performance rights is considered a different matter and the Commission takes the view that what is important is the specificities of the work and the way in which it is exploited.[100] There has been very little case law in this area, both in terms of court and Commission decisions. In a case known as *Coditel II*,[101] the CJEU decided that an exclusive licence to show a film in a particular country, which prevented the showing of the film in that country by others, was not enough in itself to show a breach of Article 101(1) TFEU, given the nature of cinema broadcasting. The Court did, however, recognise that there might be economic or legal circumstances in which the exercise of those exclusive rights had the effect of restricting film competition to an appreciable degree or distorting competition in the market. This could happen through, for example, creating artificial barriers to the distribution of films, charging too high fees for their exhibition or having exclusivity which was for too long a period of time. An indication of how this might be applied by the Commission came in relation to a decision on film purchases by German television stations.[102] This involved an exclusive broadcasting licence for MGM/UA films in Germany for a period of 15 years. The agreement was held to be within Article 101(1) TFEU because of the number of films covered,[103] and their importance, and because its duration was described as disproportionate. The agreement was ultimately exempted after provision was made for third-party broadcasters to apply to show the films at times not shown by the licensees. The Commission also objected to 'most favoured nation' clauses in agreements between Hollywood studios and European pay-TV broadcasters, where the clause gave the studio the right to enjoy the most favourable terms agreed between a pay-TV company and any one of the studios. The Commission took the view that this led to price alignment between the studios but withdrew its objections when most of the studios withdrew the clauses or indicated that they would not enforce them.[104]

Conclusions on Article 101 TFEU and the TTBER

The combination of the TTBER and its accompanying Guidelines provides a framework for analysing IPR agreements which is consistent with the new, 'modernised' and more economic

---

[98] *Moosehead/Whitbread* [1990] OJ L100/32. To similar effect, see *Campari* [1978] OJ L70/69.

[99] TTBER Guidelines (n. 35) at para. 51.

[100] Ibid. at para. 52.

[101] Case 262/81 *Coditel v SA Ciné Vog Films* [1982] ECR 3381.

[102] *Film Purchases by German Television Stations* [1989] OJ L284/36.

[103] The agreements covered around 1,300 old films, access to at least 150 new films a year, 14 James Bond films, plus cartoons and television material.

[104] See Press Release IP/04/1314.

approach to agreements under Article 101 TFEU and also consistent with US approaches, thus making global licensing easier. The consensus view[105] seems to be that this represents an improvement over previous approaches although, as has been pointed out, the extent of the safe harbour created by the TTBER is extremely limited because it only extends to, at best, a market share of 30%.[106] Outside of this area, the Guidelines provide advice on how to assess agreements. This advice will, however, not only have to include legal analysis of the particular clauses in the agreement but also an assessment of the economic effect of the agreement on the particular market concerned. The market context may change, therefore such agreements will have to be reviewed regularly.

Intellectual property and Article 102 TFEU

Article 102 TFEU applies to conduct which is an abuse of a dominant position. Holding an IPR may, in the appropriate circumstances constitute a dominant position, a point recognised in early case law from the CJEU.[107] The issue is whether the IPR gives its holder the appropriate level of market power, which can only be answered by defining the market and conducting an economic analysis. Thus, for example, when Xerox invented the first photocopier, which it will have patented, and assuming the patent prevented other photocopiers from being developed for a time, the IPRs would have given Xerox market power, because at the time there would have been no substitute for a Xerox photocopier. If a holder of an IPR has been found to be in a dominant position, the question arises as to whether their conduct has constituted an abuse. The most controversial cases have arisen in the context of a refusal to license an exercise of the IPR by the right holder and these will be discussed first. There are other possibilities of abuse in relation to IPRs, notably as regards patents, and these will be discussed later.

Compulsory licensing

All of these cases involve two markets: an upstream and a downstream market. It is useful to distinguish three situations, the first being where the undertaking with the IPR (the upstream market) (for example, a patent) uses it to produce goods or services on the downstream market. Secondly, as well as producing the goods or services, it may, or may not, also license its IPR to other competitors on the downstream market. The third situation is where the holder of the IPR does *not* use it to produce a good or service on the downstream market. Figure 12.2 illustrates this situation.

The reason for the distinction is that, arguably, the first and the third situations are similar and should be treated differently from the second because in them the IPR owner has made a decision about (not) exploiting their rights by themselves, whereas in the second situation the IPR owner has agreed to license the rights to a downstream competitor. So, arguably, it is less intrusive in the second situation to impose additional licensing on the IPR owner and

---

[105] Critical views can be found in R. Lind and P. Muysert, 'The European Commission's draft technology transfer block exemption Regulation and guidelines: A significant departure from accepted competition policy principles' (2004) 25 *European Competition Law Review* 181.

[106] See Anderman and Kallaugher (n. 37) at para. 5.67.

[107] Case 24/67 *Parke, Davis* v *Probel* [1968] ECR 55.

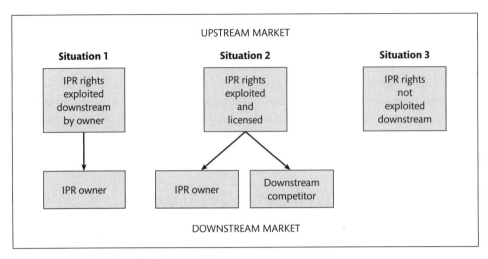

Figure 12.2 Exploitation of IPRs

there would be fewer objections to intervening on competition law grounds here. Preventing the IPR owner from terminating the arrangement with a downstream competitor is, perhaps, another matter as it involves an attempt to move from the second situation to the first one. It is worth noting that the position in US law is that the holder of a patent has no antitrust duty to license that patent to others and that this approach has been extended to copyright.[108] We will, however, see that the European cases have taken a different approach although they do not, for the most part, involve patents. The European Commission deals with compulsory licensing as a branch of refusal to supply and says that it will consider the matter an enforcement priority if three conditions are met:[109]

1 the refusal relates to a product or service that is objectively necessary to be able to compete effectively on a downstream market,

2 the refusal is likely to lead to the elimination of effective competition on the downstream market, and

3 the refusal is likely to lead to consumer harm.

Early case law

The issue is discussed in a series of cases, starting with *Volvo v Veng*,[110] which was one of two cases where Volvo wished to prevent Veng from importing body panels used to repair Volvos into the UK, which were manufactured outside the UK without permission from Volvo. In other words, they were spare parts for Volvo cars produced by another manufacturer outside the UK for sale within the UK. An action was brought in the High Court, which asked the CJEU, by way of preliminary reference, whether it was an abuse of a dominant position to

---

[108] See H. Hovenkamp, *Federal Antitrust Policy* (4th edn, West Publishing, St Paul, Minnesota, 2011) at s. 7.11d.

[109] European Commission, *Guidance on the Commission's enforcement priorities in applying Article 82 of the EC Treaty to abusive exclusionary conduct by dominant undertakings*, COM (2009) 864 final (9 February 2009) at para. 81.

[110] Case 238/87 *Volvo v Erik Veng* [1988] ECR 6211.

refuse to license others to produce the spare parts? The CJEU responded that the refusal of a proprietor to grant such a licence, even for a reasonable royalty, was not an abuse in itself because to impose such an obligation would be to remove the very essence of the right enjoyed by its holder, which was to control the ability of others to reproduce the protected parts. The CJEU did, however, say that the exercise of that right could be an abuse if it involved certain abusive conduct such as the arbitrary refusal to supply spare parts to independent repairers, the fixing of prices for spare parts at an unfair level or a decision no longer to produce spare parts for a particular model even though many cars of that model are still in circulation.[111] This can be seen as a conventional decision, which depends on the distinction between the existence and exercise of IPRs and interpreting the situation as one equivalent to the first one outlined in Figure 12.2.

The *Magill* case

Much more controversial was a later case, generally referred to as *Magill*.[112] Here television broadcasters in the Republic of Ireland and Northern Ireland produced listings of television programmes for their own output but allowed only limited access to this information for other parties. As a result, there was at the time no comprehensive weekly programme guide available for television broadcasting in this area, although the broadcasters produced their own magazines giving details of their programmes. Advance information about television programmes was protected under copyright law in Ireland and the UK which, apparently, would not have been the case in other Member States of the EU. Magill wished to produce a comprehensive weekly television guide and complained to the Commission about the failure to give it access to the relevant information. The Commission's response was a decision requiring the broadcasters to give access to this information on a non-discriminatory basis and, if they licensed it, to do this on the basis of reasonable royalties. The broadcasters challenged this decision in the General Court and, on appeal, in the CJEU, with both of the Courts upholding the Commission's decision. The CJEU referred to *Volvo* v *Veng* but pointed out that the exercise of an IPR could constitute an abuse in exceptional circumstances. The CJEU took the view that the behaviour of the broadcasters had been an abuse of a dominant position because there was no actual or potential substitute for this information and the refusal to supply it prevented the development of a new product which they did not offer and for which there was a potential consumer demand. There was no justification for that refusal based on their activities as either broadcasters or producers of television magazines. Finally, the effect of this behaviour was to reserve for themselves the secondary market of comprehensive listings magazines and eliminate all competition on this market.

This judgment was very controversial because it raised the possibility that IPR holders could be required to grant compulsory licences in certain circumstances even if the IPR holder had not been exploiting the right: that is, the third situation identified in Figure 12.2. In other words, this looked like a judgment that ignored the distinction between the existence and exercise of IPRs because at the heart of copyright protection is the ability to prevent the unauthorised reproduction of the information. Less radically, it can be seen as an example of the first situation in Figure 12.2, like *Volvo* v *Veng*, but with exceptional circumstances.

---

[111] Ibid. at para. 9.

[112] Case T-69/89 *RTE* v *Commission* [1991] ECR II-485 (GC); Cases C 241–242P *RTE to ITP & Commission* [1995] ECR I-743 (CJEU).

However, it was very unclear what would constitute exceptional circumstances. One explanation which is regularly given for this decision is that the CJEU took the view that, although the information was protected by copyright, this was a weak protection because it was information which would not have been so protected outside the UK and Ireland. In other words, the information was not deserving of protection as an IPR. The problem with this as an explanation is that there is no reference to it in the decisions of either the CJEU or the GC.

Developments after *Magill*

Arguments about IPRs and compulsory licensing became entwined with the case law on access to essential facilities and refusal to supply indispensable inputs (discussed in Chapter 4) and it became evident after *Magill* that the GC and CJEU were seeking to place some limitations on the extent of the doctrine enunciated in *Magill*. This became evident in the *Ladbroke* case brought before the GC in 1997.[113] Here Ladbroke, which operated betting shops in Belgium, wanted to obtain a feed of sound and pictures from French racecourses, but the organisation which owned these rights, and was also responsible for off-course betting in France, refused to grant a licence to Ladbroke, even though it had granted a licence to a German organisation. Ladbroke complained to the Commission that this was a breach of Article 102 TFEU, which, after some delay, decided that it was not. Ladbroke appealed this decision to the GC, which upheld the Commission's decision on the Article 102 TFEU point. The GC took the view that the betting markets were national, that the French organisation did not operate on the Belgian market and did not license anyone else in Belgium. Since the betting markets were national, the French organisation could not be found to have engaged in market partitioning and, since it did not operate on the Belgian market or sell its broadcasts to anyone else in Belgium, it could not be accused of discriminating against Ladbroke (in other words, the equivalent of situation three, above). Licensing the German market was not abuse because there was no competition, by definition, between the German and Belgian markets. In any event, the GC went on to say, *Magill* was not in point because, unlike the situation there, Ladbroke was present on the Belgian betting market (it had the largest market share), while the French organisation was not and was not directly or indirectly exploiting its asset on the Belgian market. Even if the presence of the French organisation on the Belgian market was not crucial, the requirements of *Magill* were not fulfilled because televising of horseracing was not indispensable for the activity of taking bets, since it took place after bets had already been laid, and indeed Ladbroke did take bets on French races in the Belgian market.

The limits to *Magill* were put at their clearest in the *Oscar Bronner* case,[114] which did not involve intellectual property rights, but access to a newspaper distribution system; the CJEU laid down three conditions for the *Magill* approach to be applied:

1 the refusal of the service must be likely to eliminate all competition on the part of the person requesting the service;

2 such refusal must be incapable of being objectively justified; and

3 the service in itself must be indispensable to carrying on that person's business, inasmuch as there is no actual or potential substitute.[115]

---

[113] Case T-504/93 *Tiercé Ladbroke v Commission* [1997] ECR II-923.
[114] Case C-7/97 *Oscar Bronner v Mediaprint* [1998] ECR I-7791.
[115] Ibid., para. 41.

These criteria have, however, been further developed in the context of IPRs by the cases discussed below.

The *IMS Health* case

Welcome clarification of the approach came in the *IMS Health* case, which was decided by the CJEU in 2004.[116] What happened here is that IMS Health collected information on the sale of pharmaceuticals by German pharmacies and sold this information to drug companies. As a result of strict German privacy laws, this information could only be collected on a basis that aggregated the data on drug sales of individual pharmacies, so that no individual pharmacy could be identified. IMS, working with the industry, had developed a system which divided up Germany into certain geographical areas, referred to as the 1860 brick system, which was copyrighted, and information was returned on this basis. A potential competitor, NDC Health, also wanted to market information on sales of drugs by German pharmacies but it was unable to develop an alternative system and IMS Health refused to give it access to the 1860 brick system. NDC Health challenged this refusal in the German courts and by complaining to the Commission, which led to a complicated procedural history for this affair.[117] For our purposes, the important decision is that of the CJEU in response to a preliminary reference from the German courts on the question of whether the refusal to license the 1860 brick structure was an abuse of a dominant position. The Court took the view that in general the refusal of a copyright owner to grant a licence could not be an abuse of a dominant position. However, it could be an abuse in exceptional circumstances and, in order for a refusal by a copyright owner of access to a product or service which was *indispensable* for the carrying on of a business to be abusive, three cumulative conditions had to be met:

1 that the refusal must prevent the emergence of a new product for which there is a potential consumer demand;

2 that it is unjustified; and

3 that it is such as to exclude any competition on a secondary market.[118]

As regards this third question, the CJEU made it clear that it was necessary to identify two different, interconnected, stages of production for this criteria to be met: that is, there must be an upstream and a downstream market and the output from the upstream market must be indispensable for carrying on the downstream activity. In addition, it was not necessary for the downstream market to be an actual existing market; it was sufficient if it was a potential or even a hypothetical market (fairly clearly, there was a market for the information on drug sales by German pharmacies). Whether these conditions were met in the case was something that the CJEU left up to the German court, as it did the question of whether the refusal to supply had prevented the emergence of a new product.

The *IMS Health* case clarified the previous case law by making it clear that two markets were necessary and that, in order for there to be an abuse, it was necessary for the refusal to license the IPR to prevent the creation of a new product. The idea that the secondary market

---

[116] Case C-418/01 *IMS Health* v *NDC Health* [2004] ECR I-5039.

[117] The Commission made a decision imposing interim measures on IMS Health. IMS appealed both the decision and the requested suspension of the interim measures, which was granted: Case T-184/01R *IMS Health* v *Commission* [2001] ECR II-3193 and Case C-481/01P (R) *IMS Health* v *Commission* [2002] ECR I-3401. As a result of developments in Germany, the Commission decided not to proceed to a final decision.

[118] Case C-418/01 *IMS Health* v *NDC Health* [2004] ECR I-5039 at para. 38.

could be hypothetical looks more difficult, but this is to some extent controlled by the related notion that there needs to be a new product for which there is a consumer demand; in other words, this new secondary market is unlikely to be too hypothetical, as there presumably has to be some evidence of demand for the product. This requirement of there having to be a new product is in part what distinguishes this line of case law, relating to IPRs, from other case law relating to the refusal to supply physical goods or allow access to physical facilities. It also provides a justification for interfering with the exercise of the IPR in the first and third situations because the failure of the IPR holder to allow access to the IPR is preventing the development of something new that will meet a consumer demand.

The *Microsoft* case

This was confirmed most recently in the *Microsoft* case,[119] which, for our current purposes, revolved around the refusal of Microsoft to give information allowing interoperability between its Windows programs for PCs and operating systems for servers to potential competitors that requested it. It had, however, provided such information in the past, so this looks like an attempt to move from situation two to situation one. For the purposes of this point, the Commission assumed that such information about the Windows program was protected by IPRs and the GC proceeded on the basis that this was correct; in other words, it adopted the most favourable position for Microsoft's arguments. Following the case law described above, the GC summarised this as a four-part test:

1 the refusal must relate to a product or service indispensable to the exercise of a particular activity on a neighbouring market;

2 it must be of such a kind as to exclude any effective competition on that neighbouring market;

3 it must prevent the appearance of a new product for which there is potential consumer demand;

4 it must not be objectively justified.[120]

There was extensive argument around all four of these criteria, with the GC finding for the Commission on each point. It is noticeable in this case, as Whish and Bailey have pointed out,[121] that the GC took a relatively relaxed view as to the requirement that the refusal to supply the information prevented the development of a new product. It did not require the Commission to come to a finding that the refusal had prevented the creation of a specific new product; rather it was enough that there could be a restriction of technical development and the Commission was entitled to base its decision on this.[122] The refusal to supply the information, in the GC's view, meant that consumers were increasingly locked into Microsoft platforms at the level of servers for work groups (basically networked PCs) and competitors were prevented from developing operating systems distinguishable from the Windows systems already on the market. This view of the GC judgment is shared by John Vickers, an eminent economist and past head of the OFT, who is worried that the GC decision in

---

[119] Case T-201/04 *Microsoft* v *Commission* [2007] ECR II-3601.
[120] Ibid., paras 332–3.
[121] R. Whish and D. Bailey, *Competition Law* (7th edn, Oxford University Press, 2012) at p. 801.
[122] *Microsoft*, para. 665.

Microsoft suggests that the criteria set out in *IMS Health* can be met in circumstances which are not exceptional and this will make it too easy for complainants before the Commission and, potentially, in national courts.[123] The result being that, in the future, there will be less incentive to develop these types of products if persons/companies are then forced to provide the information to competitors. In this context, it is worth noting that there have been further complaints about Microsoft and interoperability and the Commission has opened another investigation on this issue.[124]

Misuse of patents and the patent system

One of the characteristics of a number of IPRs is that they are granted by public authorities after an application by the person who has, allegedly, developed the right. Such systems also provide a mechanism for challenging the grant of such rights. The existence of such systems also allows for the possibility of abusing them in order to forestall the development of competition. This arose for the first time in the EU context with the Commission's decision in relation to *AstraZeneca*.[125] Here AstraZeneca held a patent for the drug Losec. Typically, what happens with branded drugs when patent protection runs out is that additional manufacturers enter into the market providing a non-branded, generic alternative. Here the Commission found that AstraZeneca had committed an abuse through persuading various national authorities to grant it supplementary protection certificates for Losec, which extended the period of patent protection, on the basis of misleading information as part of what the Commission described as a proactive exclusionary strategy. Secondly, AstraZeneca had a market authorisation allowing it to sell the drug in capsule form. It withdrew the capsules from the market, which had the consequence that the generic drug manufacturers could no longer market the drug in capsule form. This decision was challenged in an appeal to the GC which upheld the Commission's decision.[126] The decision was a novel interpretation of Article 102 TFEU and indicates the Commission's view, supported by *Continental Can*, which involved applying Article 102 TFEU to a merger, that the categories of abuse listed in Article 102 TFEU are not exhaustive, although it might be argued to the contrary that this conduct is an example of Article 102(b) TFEU, limiting production, markets or technical development to the prejudice of consumers. The GC took the view that an abuse of a dominant position did not necessarily have to consist in the use of the economic power conferred by that dominant position.[127] It went on to say that submitting misleading information to public authorities which led to the grant of exclusive rights to which the undertaking was not entitled, or was not entitled for that period, was a practice which did not constitute competition on the merits and was of such a type that it may be particularly restrictive of competition.[128]

---

[123] J. Vickers, 'A Tale of Two EC Cases: *IBM* and *Microsoft*' (2008) 4 *Competition Policy International* 3.

[124] See Press Notice MEMO/08/19, 14 January 2008.

[125] Decision of 15 June 2005. A similar case was opened against a German company, Boehringer, for abuse of the patent system but settled when commitments were given to meet the Commission's competition concerns. See Commission Case COMP/39.246 and Press Release IP/11/842, 6 July 2011.

[126] Case T-321/05 *AstraZeneca v Commission* [2010] ECR II-2805. On appeal Case C-457/10P.

[127] Ibid. para. 354.

[128] Ibid. para. 355.

Although not strictly a patent case, it is worth mentioning the OFT's decision in *Reckitt Benckiser* in this context.[129] This case involved an antacids drug, Gaviscon Original Liquid (GL), which came out of patent and the undertaking had developed a new version, Gaviscon Advance (GA), which would remain under patent until 2016. Under the prescribing system operating in the NHS, doctors are encouraged to substitute generic medicines for branded ones and the prescribing software that is used allows them to search for a branded drug but then replace it with a generic one. This will only work effectively if the branded drug is available and there is a generic name for its replacement. What Reckitt Benckiser did in this case was to withdraw GL from the NHS prescribing channel before a generic name for it had been assigned, in the hope that this would shift sales into GA, for which there was no generic equivalent. The OFT decided that the withdrawal was motivated by a desire to hinder generic competition and was commercially irrational had it not been for the benefits of hindering generic competition. This was not therefore normal competition.[130] Since the withdrawal tended to restrict competition or could have that effect, it was an abuse of a dominant position. It is interesting to see the OFT's reliance on the GC's decision in *AstraZeneca* and that the essence of the abuse was exclusionary actions which were not commercially rational.

The European Commission has also taken action against Rambus, a manufacturer of a particular type of computer chip, alleging that it was claiming unreasonable royalties for them subsequent to a type of behaviour known as a 'patent ambush'. What this means is that there was a procedure, in which a number of manufacturers participated, for setting the standards for this type of chip, in which Rambus participated but without, the Commission alleged, disclosing the existence of patents which were relevant to the standard setting exercise. As a result, Rambus was able to charge unreasonable royalties for the use of those chips.[131] The same issue has arisen as regards Rambus in the US, with the Federal Trade Commission (FTC) taking action against the company after it sued manufacturers for the infringement of the patents which it had not disclosed that it was in possession of during the procedure. This decision by the FTC was overturned by the District Circuit Court on appeal and the Supreme Court declined to review this decision.[132] Unlike the proceedings in the US, the Commission was able to obtain commitments from Rambus in relation to the licensing of its chips regarding the level of royalty payments.[133] The issue of disclosure of patents has become an important area of work for the Commission and it has opened proceedings against Motorola and Samsung to try and ensure that their standard-essential patents are made available in fair, reasonable and non-discriminatory terms.[134]

---

[129] OFT, 'Reckitt Benckiser' (2011).

[130] Ibid para. 6.1.

[131] See Press Release of 23 August 2007, MEMO/07/330, Press Release of 29 November 2009. Rambus entered into commitments which, among other things, capped the royalty payments: see Press Release of 9 December 2009.

[132] *Rambus Inc.* v *Federal Trade Commission* 522 F 3d 456, 2008 WL 1795594, CADC (22 April 2008).

[133] European Commission Decision Case COMP/38.636 *Rambus*, 9 December 2009.

[134] See J. Almunia, 'Antitrust enforcement: Challenges old and new', speech given to 19th International Competition Law Forum, St. Gallen, 8 June 2012. Available at: *http://europa.eu/rapid/pressReleasesAction. do?reference=SPEECH/12/428* (accessed 14/08/12). European Commission Cases COMP/39.985 and 39.986 *Motorola – Enforcement of ETSI standard essential patents* and Case COMP/39.939 *Samsung – Enforcement of ETSI standard essential patents*. See also 'Huawei seeks EU action against InterDigital patent fees', available at: *http://www.reuters.com/article/2012/05/24/us-huawei-interdigital-eu-idUSBRE84N0KD20120524* (accessed 14/08/12).

Conclusions on Article 102 TFEU

Although the main focus of attention here has been on the issue of compulsory licensing of IPR rights, recent cases indicate that Article 102 TFEU can be applied in a variety of contexts where IPRs are involved. There does seem to be some indication from recent cases started by the Commission that it is interested in investigating these issues in the high technology areas of the economy and it has followed its investigation into the pharmaceutical sector with specific competition law cases. It is evident, as regards compulsory licensing, that although the general rule is that a refusal to licence is not a breach of Article 102 TFEU in itself, there may be exceptional circumstances where such a duty is imposed. The scope of these exceptional circumstances is unclear which means, arguably, that the EU rules could be having a chilling effect on innovation.

COMPETITION LAW IN PRACTICE

AstraZeneca[135]

Background
AstraZeneca (AZ) is one of the leading pharmaceutical companies in the world and in 2005 the European Commission fined the AZ group a total of €60 million for two separate infringements of Article 102 TFEU relating to a drug called Losec. Creating new drugs is a very expensive and time-consuming business and a crucial part in the development of a new drug is in obtaining patent protection for it so that the company has an exclusive right to exploit it and, hopefully, earn a good return on its investment. Losec slows or prevents the production of acid within the stomach and it was a major product for AZ. It is used, among other things, to treat conditions where reduction in acid secretion is required for proper healing, including stomach and intestinal ulcers (gastric and duodenal ulcers). The active substance in Losec is called omeprazole. AstraZeneca obtained patent protection for this ingredient through the European Patent Convention and, for states which were not signatories to this Convention, by national patents. The patents were filed in 1979 and were due to expire in 1999.

Generic drug manufacturers produce non-branded, generic, versions of drugs. These are typically cheaper than the branded version but can only be produced with the consent of the patent holder or at the expiration of the patent. Therefore, the longer that a company like AZ can maintain patent protection, the more profitable its operations will be.

Factual background
In 1993 and 1994 AZ submitted applications to a number of national patent offices to obtain supplementary protection certificates (SPC) which, in effect, would extend the life of the original patent. One of the reasons for this system is that there may be a delay between the time when the basic patent is granted and the grant of an authorisation for a medicine based on the basic patent, which would mean that the owner of the patent would have less than 20 years to exploit it. The SPC is granted to cover the period between the submission of the basic patent and the *first* authorisation to market the

➡

---

[135] Commission Decision, Case COMP/A.37.507/F3 *AstraZeneca*, 15 June 2005.

product as a medicine. To complicate matters further, because AZ's patent had been registered before the SPC regime came into force, it fell under a transitional regime, which meant that the first authorisation had to have been obtained after 1 January 1985. In its various applications for SPCs, AZ claimed that the first date of authorisation in the EU had been in March 1988. The Commission argued that the first date of authorisation had been before January 1988, which meant it would not have been eligible for an SPC and that AZ's submissions to the relevant patent offices had been misleading.

AZ was also accused of having committed a second abuse, namely the withdrawal from the market of Losec capsules and the surrender of their marketing authorisation and their replacement by tablets. The idea behind this was to delay the introduction of competing generic drugs, as they could only be introduced if the original drug was still being marketed.

The Commission's decision

The Commission's case was that AZ had made misleading representations with the intent to exclude its generic competitors from the market in its applications for SPCs, something which AZ denied. The Commission said:

> The use of public procedures and regulation, including administrative and judicial processes, may also, in specific circumstances, constitute an abuse, as the concept of abuse is not limited to behaviour in the market only and misuse of public procedures and regulations may result in serious anticompetitive effects on the market. The fact that in such cases the effects in the market may be dependent on further action by public authorities is not decisive to exclude the existence of an abuse. Even when the behaviour is implemented in the market, the effect of exclusionary practices is often dependent on the subsequent reaction of other operators in the market (such as purchasers).[136]

Although the conduct did not always succeed – SPC applications were rejected in Denmark and the UK, for example – this did not, in the Commission's opinion, mean that an abuse had not been committed. As for the second alleged abuse, the Commission found that there was exclusionary intent and that there was no objective justification for AZ's behaviour.

AZ's challenge before the GC

AZ challenged the Commission's decision,[137] arguing that its definition of the market was incorrect, which affected the finding of dominance. In addition, it argued, regarding the alleged misrepresentations with respect to patents, that such misleading representations made in the course of applications for intellectual property rights cannot in law amount to an abuse unless and until the dishonestly obtained rights are enforced or are capable of being enforced. It also challenged the factual basis of the Commission's decision.

The GC rejected all the grounds of challenge. In particular, the GC took the view that an abuse of a dominant position did not necessarily have to consist in the use of the economic power conferred by that dominant position.[138] It went on to say that submitting

---

[136] Ibid. at paras 328 and 743.
[137] Case T-321/05 *AstraZeneca* v *Commission* [2010] ECR II-2805. On appeal Case C-457/10P.
[138] Ibid. para. 354.

misleading information to public authorities which led to the grant of exclusive rights to which the undertaking was not entitled, or was not entitled for that period was a practice which did not constitute competition on the merits and was of such a type that it may be particularly restrictive of competition.[139] As regards the argument about enforcement, the court rejected this argument because, when granted by a public authority, IPRs are normally assumed to be valid. The mere possession of such a right normally results in keeping competitors away.[140]

Analysis

The argument that misusing patent procedures constitutes an abuse under Article 102 TFEU is a novel one in the EU, although similar cases have been heard in the United States. If this is accepted by the European Courts, it is significant because it indicates that the categories of potential abuse are not closed and that the examples given in Article 102 TFEU are indeed just that, examples. This can be seen, perhaps, as another example of teleological interpretation but it is certainly a broad interpretation of abuse.

Secondly, much of the Commission's case rested on what it has perceived as the exclusionary intent of AZ, based on the written documentation that it obtained. This raises difficult issues as it requires drawing some line between what is acceptable behaviour for a company and what is not. The Commission's view was clearly that AZ knew that its submissions to the patent offices were misleading, whereas AZ argued that the situation was less clear. The GC was clear that AZ's behaviour was not competition on the merits.

Summary

➤ In principle, IPRs and competition law have the same aims: the encouragement of innovation.

➤ IPRs are, in general, decided upon on a national basis and are limited in time and scope.

➤ EU law does not challenge the existence of IPRs, but may regulate their exercise.

➤ The TTBER applies to bilateral agreements involving the transfer of technology for the production of products stipulated in the contract. It covers:

- a patent licensing agreement,
- a know-how licensing agreement,
- a software copyright licensing agreement,
- a mixed patent, know-how or software copyright licensing agreement, or
- assignments of patents, know-how, software copyright or a combination thereof where part of the risk associated with the exploitation of the technology remains with the licensor.

[139] Ibid, para. 355.
[140] Ibid. para. 362.

➤ The market share cap in the TTBER is 20% for competing undertakings and 30% for non-competing undertakings.

➤ To qualify for an exemption under the TTBER, the agreement must not contain any hard-core restrictions which are listed in Article 4.

➤ Article 5 contains a list of excluded restrictions but the agreement may still have the benefit of the TTBER if these are severable.

➤ Agreements outside the TTBER must be assessed on the basis of Article 101 TFEU but there is no presumption that they are unlawful. Guidance on how to carry out this assessment is contained in the Guidelines.

➤ Compulsory licensing under Article 102 TFEU will occur only when the following test is met:
  (i)   the refusal must relate to a product or service indispensable to the exercise of a particular activity on a neighbouring market;
  (ii) it must be of such a kind as to exclude any effective competition on that neighbouring market;
  (iii) it must prevent the appearance of a new product for which there is potential consumer demand;
  (iv) it must not be objectively justified.

Further reading

Anderman, S. and Ezrachi, A. (eds) *Intellectual Property and Competition Law: New Frontiers* (Oxford University Press, 2011). *A useful collection of essays on a variety of issues relating to the competition law/IP interface.*

Anderman, S. and Kallaugher, J., *Technology Transfer and the New EU Competition Rules: Intellectural Property Licensing After Modernisation* (Oxford University Press, 2006). *Eminent academic and senior solicitor combine to provide exhaustive investigation of intellectual property licensing. Good combination of legal and economic analysis.*

Geradin, D. and Rato, M., 'Can standard-setting lead to exploitative abuse? A dissonant view on patent hold-up, royalty stacking and the meaning of FRAND' (2007) 3 *European Competition Journal* 101. *Long article discussing standard setting and potential anti-trust problems.*

Ritter, C., 'The New Technology Transfer Block Exemption Regulation under EC Competition Law' (2004) 31 *Legal Issues of Economic Integration* 161. *Ex-Commission official gives an introduction and general overview to the TTBER.*

Shapiro, C. and Varian, H., *Information Rules: A Strategic Guide to the Network Economy* (Harvard Business School Press, 1999). *Non-legal, accessible introduction to many of the commercial and economic issues in this chapter, as well as more broadly. A classic of its time.*

Ullrich, H., 'Patent Pools: Approaching a Patent Law Problem via Competition Policy', in Ehlermann, C.-D. and Atanasiu, I., *European Competition Law Annual 2005: The Interface between Competition Law and Intellectual Property Law* (Hart Publishing, Oxford, 2006). *Detailed discussion of issues surrounding patent pools.*

US Department of Justice/Federal Trade Commission, *Antitrust Enforcement and Intellectual Property Rights* (2007). *Overview report by American competition law enforcement agencies. Although inevitably based on US law, contains excellent discussion of principles at stake in a variety of contexts.*

13 Merger control in the EU

Introduction

The place of merger control in competition law

A merger occurs where two previously independent undertakings become one. This can happen by agreement or through a hostile takeover but how it happens is not something that concerns competition law.[1] Mergers are of concern for competition law for two broad reasons. First, mergers result in changes to market structures and competition law would be incomplete as a system if it controlled only the activities of undertakings within existing markets but had no mechanism for preventing the creation of market structures which were not effectively competitive. Secondly, from the point of view of the undertaking, a merger could be simply a strategy for controlling the market.[2] So, for example, if there was a wide prohibition on restrictive agreements, but no merger control, it would make sense for an undertaking that wished to control the market to merge with its competitors, rather than try to reach an agreement with them.

Mergers policy is therefore the third major part of what might be considered the 'core' competition policy provisions, the other two being control of restrictive agreements and abuse of a dominant position (discussed in Chapters 2 to 4). Merger control is, however,

---

[1] For takeovers, see J. Lowry and A. Reisberg, *Pettet's Company Law: Company and Capital Markets Law* (4th edn, Longman, Harlow, 2012), ch. 20.

[2] M. Williams, 'The Effectiveness of Competition Policy in the United Kingdom' (1993) 9 *Oxford Review of Economic Policy* 94.

different in a number of respects to these provisions. First, where the provisions on restrictive agreements and abuse of dominant position prohibit behaviour and the competition authorities punish undertakings for past misdemeanours, merger control involves the authorities trying to predict what the effect in the future will be of a merger and whether to allow it to proceed. In other words, there is no element of imposing a sanction for past misbehaviour. Secondly, there are different legal provisions for the control of mergers at national and European level, which have different procedures and different substantive tests, unlike control of restrictive agreements and abuse of dominant position, where the substantive law is the same between the UK and the EU. Because of this, UK merger control is treated separately (see Chapter 14). A third element which is different is that of time: investigations of anti-competitive agreements and abuse of dominant position may take some time – generally it takes at least a year before the agency makes a decision. For example, it took the OFT three years to make its first decisions on price-fixing for replica football kits and collusive tendering for flat-roofs in the West Midlands. This sort of timescale is of no use to undertakings that wish to merge; they need a quick decision on whether the transaction will be allowed. Consequently, merger control in the EU and UK runs to very strict timetables, which are relatively speedy because even in the most complicated cases the competition authorities only have around four months, at a maximum, to take a decision. Finally, there is an international dimension to mergers because a merger of two undertakings in, for example, the United States, may require the approval of both the American and the European Union authorities and the businesses concerned would like the same rules to be applied in both jurisdictions.

The format of this chapter is that after a discussion of the different types of mergers and their possible competition problems, this is followed by a discussion of merger control by the European Commission, looking at: jurisdiction, procedure, assessment, remedies and the role of the courts. When discussing the types of mergers and their effects on competition, material is used from the UK authorities as well as the European Commission, because some of the ideas are explained more clearly in the UK material.

Types of merger and the potential problems they cause for competition law

Horizontal mergers

A horizontal merger is a merger between two undertakings that operate at the same level of production – for example, two manufacturers or two distributors – and so automatically results in a reduction in the number of competitors on a market. From the point of view of the merging undertakings, two reasons can broadly be distinguished for engaging in such a merger, which may be interrelated. On the positive side, the merger may create efficiencies: for example, the merged undertakings' configuration of factories might enable it to produce more products at lower cost than the two entities operating separately. A simple example would be where there is spare capacity and a less efficient factory can be closed, while maintaining the same output levels. On the negative side, the merger could increase the market power of the combined undertaking, as compared with the two separately, thus giving it greater scope to raise prices and reduce output. The potential harmful effects of such a merger, indeed of all mergers, are usually put under one of two headings: unilateral and coordinated effects. In relation to unilateral effects, the concern for competition authorities is that the merger of two competitors will create a new entity which will have market power that the existing companies did not have on their own and thus will have scope to raise prices and reduce output and will not be constrained in its behaviour by competitive forces. The extreme example of this would be a merger to monopoly.

The notion of coordinated effects is a more subtle one, and is again recognition of the oligopoly problem mentioned earlier (Chapter 2 and discussed in detail in Chapter 10). As the UK Competition Commission explained,[3] when markets are sufficiently concentrated, the actions of individual undertakings affect their competitors and vice versa. If this situation persists, it is not only possible, if the conditions are right, that all the undertakings in a market will not cut prices but that they may also raise prices to non-competitive levels as the undertakings recognise that they have a mutual interest in not competing against each other, without the need to enter into an agreement or a concerted practice. The Competition Commission and the OFT take the view that there are three conditions which are necessary for such behaviour:

1 Firms need to be able to reach and monitor the terms of coordination.

2 Coordination needs to be *internally* sustainable among the coordinating group – firms have to find it in their individual interests to adhere to the coordinated outcome.

3 Coordination needs to be *externally* sustainable, in that there is little likelihood of coordination being undermined by competition from outside the coordinating group.[4]

The CC and the OFT point out two factors which will help identify the likelihood of coordinated effects. The first is whether there is evidence of pre-existing coordination and, secondly, the role of concentration and symmetry. Generally, in a market where there was coordination, a merger will be likely to make coordination more sustainable or effective. The second point is that coordination is easier in more concentrated industries (it is easier for there to be coordination between two undertakings than six) and if the undertakings are similar in terms of market share or other more general similarities, such as using the same production methods.[5] An example of the type of merger that would raise such concerns was the merger between D.S. Smith and Linpac, both undertakings which produced corrugated sheets and cases made out of those sheets. The merger reduced the number of major suppliers from six to five, which increased the amount of awareness of competitor behaviour and increased the similarity of the business models of the main manufacturers. However, although this raised issues in relation to the first two criteria above, the CC found that the merger would not have had an effect on the third one, competitive constraints.[6]

The European Commission takes the view that in some markets the structure may be such that firms would consider it possible, economically rational, and preferable to adopt on a sustainable basis a course of action on the market aimed at selling at increased prices.[7] This is more likely to arise in markets where it is relatively simple to reach a common understanding

---

[3] Competition Commission, *Merger References: Competition Commission Guidelines* (2003), paras 3.32–3.36.
[4] CC/OFT, *Merger Assessment Guidelines* (2010), para. 5.5.9.
[5] Ibid., paras 5.5.5–5.5.8 and 5.5.11.
[6] Competition Commission, 'D.S. Smith/Linpac' (2004).
[7] European Commission, *Guidelines on the assessment of horizontal mergers under the Council Regulation on the control of concentrations between undertakings*, OJ C31, 05.02.2004, pp. 5–18 at para. 39.

on the terms of coordination. In addition, three conditions are necessary for coordination to be sustainable: first, it must be possible for firms to monitor whether the terms of coordination are being complied with; secondly, there must be some form of credible deterrent mechanism, such as the existence of spare capacity which can be utilised if a firm deviates from prevailing practices and, thirdly, that the reactions of outsiders should not be able to jeopardise the results expected from the coordination.[8] We can see from this that the authorities are focusing on the same problem, although the terminology is slightly different.[9] As we shall see later, the European Commission has had some difficulty in dealing with cases where the concern has been with coordinated effects. This is not surprising because, as the UK Competition Commission has observed,[10] identifying coordinated effects is difficult because while intense competition results in similar or identical prices, so too do coordinated effects. Indicators which might help distinguish the two situations would be levels of profitability, something that the European Commission tends not to look at for reasons discussed earlier (see Chapter 3), or variations in prices.

Vertical mergers

A vertical merger involves a merger between two undertakings at different levels of the production chain: for example, the merger of a manufacturer and a distributor or the merger of a supplier of raw materials with a manufacturer. Unlike a horizontal merger, vertical mergers do not automatically reduce the number of competitors on a market and so there is a presumption that they are much less likely to cause competitive problems unless the undertakings concerned have large market power.[11] Indeed, it is generally accepted that one of the main commercial reasons for vertical mergers is to try to improve the efficiency of the merging undertakings. Thus, for example, a manufacturer's merger with a distributor might lead to a more integrated supply chain and generally reduce the cost of the products. If the consumer market was competitive, it would be expected that these efficiency gains would be passed to the consumers. So, as the competition authorities put it (in Box 13.1):

KEY OFFICIAL GUIDELINES   **Box 13.1**

Approach to vertical mergers

Non-horizontal mergers are generally less likely to significantly impeded effective competition than horizontal mergers. First, unlike horizontal mergers, vertical or conglomerate mergers do not entail the loss of direct competition between the merging firms in the same relevant market . . . Second, vertical and conglomerate mergers provide substantial scope

---

[8] Ibid. at para. 41 and European Commission, *Guidelines on the assessment of non-horizontal mergers under the Council Regulation on the control of concentrations between undertakings*, OJ C265, 18.10.2008, at para. 81.

[9] The US agencies take a similar view: see Department of Justice/Federal Trade Commission, 'Horizontal Merger Guidelines' (2010) at s. 7.2.

[10] Competition Commission (n. 3) at para. 3.43.

[11] M. Motta, *Competition Policy* (Cambridge University Press, 2004) at pp. 377–8.

for efficiencies . . . However, there are circumstances in which non-horizontal mergers may significantly impede effective competition, in particular as a result of the creation or strengthening of a dominant position. This is essentially because a non-horizontal merger may change the ability and incentive to compete on the part of the merging companies and their competitors in ways that cause harm to consumers.

Source: European Commission, *Guidelines on the assessment of non-horizontal mergers under the Council Regulation on the control of concentrations between undertakings*, OJ C265, 18.10.2008, at paras 12–15.

Non-horizontal mergers can lead to efficiencies . . . and this may result in the merged firm having increased incentives to compete to take business from rivals. This greater incentive to compete can result in an increase in rivalry. However, under certain conditions, non-horizontal mergers can weaken rivalry. The theories of harm raised by such mergers typically involve the merged firm harming the ability of its rivals to compete post-merger, for example by raising effective prices to its rivals, or by refusing to supply them completely. Such actions may harm the ability of the merged firm's rivals to provide a competitive constraint into the future.

Source: CC/OFT, *Merger Assessment Guidelines* (2010) at paras 5.6.4 and 5.6.5.

Question: When might vertical mergers raise competition problems?

For both the European Commission and the UK authorities, competition concerns arise when the vertical merger results in 'foreclosure', which is defined in Box 13.2.[12]

KEY OFFICIAL STATEMENT   **Box 13.2**

Definition of foreclosure

. . . any instance where actual or potential rivals' access to supplies or markets is hampered or eliminated as a result of the merger, thereby reducing these companies' ability and/or incentive to compete. As a result of such foreclosure, the merging companies – and, possibly, some of its competitors as well – may be able to profitably increase the price charged to consumers. These instances give rise to a significant impediment to effective competition.

Source: European Commission, *Guidelines on the assessment of non-horizontal mergers under the Council Regulation on the control of concentrations between undertakings*, at para. 18.

The theories of harm raised by such mergers typically involve the merged firm harming the ability of its rivals to compete post-merger, for example by raising effective prices to its rivals, or by refusing to supply them completely. Such actions may harm the ability of the merged firm's rivals to provide a competitive constraint into the future

Source: CC/OFT, *Merger Assessment Guidelines* (2010), para. 5.6.5

Question: What conditions have to be met for foreclosure?

---

[12] European Commission, *Guidelines on the assessment of non-horizontal mergers under the Council Regulation on the control of concentrations between undertakings*, OJ C265, 18.10.2008, pp. 6–25 (at para. 18).

In terms of non-coordinated effects, it is possible that vertical mergers can result in a firm trying to use its market power in one market to create or strengthen its market power in the vertically related market through, for example, not supplying a downstream rival (called 'input foreclosure'). Alternatively, the merging firm can try to use its power to restrict its upstream rivals' access to a sufficient customer base (called 'customer foreclosure').[13] Note that foreclosure does not mean that rivals must exit the market; the concept includes raising rivals' costs and leading rivals to compete less effectively.[14] It is also possible that a vertical merger would make it easier for the firms within a market to engage in coordinated effects through, for example, reducing the number of competitors on the market, increasing the degree of symmetry between the firms active in the market and increasing the level of market.[15]

Conglomerate mergers

Conglomerate mergers involve firms that are not in the same market and are also not vertically related: for example, a merger between a car and an airplane manufacturer. They may, however, produce related complementary products. In the GE/Honeywell merger, discussed in detail below, GE produced aircraft engines and Honeywell guidance systems for aircraft. Although different products, both are needed in an aircraft. In general,[16] the view has been that these mergers will not raise competition issues, although there may be a small number of cases where this becomes a concern. The European Commission's main concern is that the combination of products in related markets may confer on the merged entity the ability and incentive to leverage a strong market position from one market to another by means of tying and bundling or other exclusionary practices.[17] The UK authorities recognise that conglomerate mergers can raise concerns that the merged firm might increase the selling price of one of its products when sold on a stand-alone basis, but might not do so if customers buy both the merged firm's products; this would give customers an incentive to buy the second product from the merged firm as well, putting rivals in the second product market at a disadvantage.[18] To take the GE/Honeywell example above, one concern that the European Commission had was that the merged entity might make the purchase of, for example, GE aircraft engines conditional on the purchase of Honeywell guidance systems. The approach of the UK authorities is similar to that of the European Commission's approach to conglomerate mergers,[19] although the European Commission's guidance focuses more on tying and bundling.[20]

---

[13] Ibid. paras 29–78.
[14] Ibid. para. 29.
[15] Ibid. paras 83–86.
[16] Ibid. at para. 92: 'in the majority of circumstances'.
[17] Ibid. at para. 93.
[18] CC/OFT, *Merger Assessment Guidelines* (2010), para. 5.6.13.
[19] One CC staff member has said, 'borrowed from': see *http://webarchive.nationalarchives.gov.uk/20110907151741/ http://www.competition-commission.org.uk/our_role/ms_and_fm/seminar_010609.htm*, 'Transcript of seminar' at page 68 (acessed 23/08/12).
[20] European Commission (n. 8) at paras 91–121.

The control of mergers by the European Commission

Introduction

The Treaty of Rome contained no provisions for merger control, even though this had been part of the European Coal and Steel Treaty. The reasons for this are not entirely clear, but it would seem that the Member States saw control of mergers as an important part of their economic policy, which they were not willing to cede to the control of a supranational body. At the time, 1957, there were few cross-border mergers in Europe. The lack of a system of merger control was first drawn attention to by the European Commission in 1966 and proposals for merger control were made by the Commission in 1972. It was not, however, until 1989 that agreement was reached between the Member States and the first merger control Regulation (MCR) was promulgated, coming into force in 1990. The original MCR was amended in 1997, which was followed by subsequent amendments in 2004.[21]

The MCR explicitly states two objectives: to protect the common market against lasting damages to competition from mergers; and that mergers with an impact beyond the national borders of one Member State should, as a general rule, be reviewed exclusively at Union level, in accordance with what is called the 'one-stop shop' system, that is, that businesses should need to go to only one competition authority in order to obtain a decision on their proposed merger. In procedural terms, the first ten years or so of the operation of the MCR were successful. It was very clear which transactions fell within the MCR, despite some uncertainty over joint ventures, the European Commission was able in all cases to stick to the time limits laid down in the MCR, a major concern of business, and there were no successful challenges to merger decisions in the European Courts. Given this successful background, and after one round of minor amendments, the European Commission launched a consultation on reform of the MCR in 2001 which, among other things, proposed extending its jurisdiction and served also as a catalyst for discussion about the scope of the MCR and the appropriate substantive test. The landscape changed dramatically late in 2002 when, for the first time, the European Commission lost, in quick succession, three cases before the GC where it had prohibited mergers.[22] Not only did it lose the cases, but the GC was very critical of the European Commission's reasoning in each of them and its use of evidence. It also became clear that the standard of review that the GC and CJEU would apply was stricter than had first been thought. The European Commission responded in part by a series of internal changes which were meant to bolster their economic expertise, for example, through the appointment of a Chief Economist, and which were meant to meet some of the procedural objections.[23] At the same time, there was a major reorientation of EU competition law through Regulation 1/2003, which gave more responsibility to Member States for its enforcement. This is reflected in the amendments to the MCR, where a more pragmatic attitude to case allocation

---

[21] Council Regulation (EC) No. 139/2004 of 20 January 2004 on the control of concentrations between undertakings (the EC Merger Regulation), OJ L24, 29.01.2004, pp. 1–22, Art. 3(4). (Hereafter 'MCR'.)

[22] Case T-342/99 *Airtours v Commission* [2002] ECR II-2585; Case T-310/01 *Schneider Electric v Commission* [2002] ECR II-4071; Case T-5/02 *Tetra Laval v Commission* [2002] ECR II-4381, affirmed in Case C-12/03P *Commission v Tetra Laval* [2005] ECR I-987.

[23] See M. Monti, 'Merger Control in the European Union: A radical reform', speech given on 7 November 2002, Brussels, for details of the proposed changes. Available at: *http://ec.europa.eu/competition/speeches/index_2002.html* (accessed 23/08/12).

is now taken, as will be discussed later in this chapter. As regards substantive assessment, the European Commission has had less success in defending merger cases in front of the GC than Article 101 and Article 102 cases[24] and it has seemingly become very reluctant to prohibit mergers outright, having prohibited only four mergers outright since 2001, whereas it had prohibited sixteen between 1995 and the end of 2001. So, in recent years, the focus has switched from prohibition to remedying competitive problems with mergers through accepting commitments from the parties, and this process of discussion is conducted in the shadow of the GC and its powers of review.

Jurisdiction[25]

The MCR applies to 'concentrations' which have a Community [Union] dimension. A concentration arises when there is a change of control on a lasting basis, which arises either through a merger or through the acquisition of control of one undertaking by another undertaking or persons who control that other undertaking. The idea of a merger is straightforward: it is where two or more independent undertakings form a new undertaking and cease to exist as legal entities.[26] 'Control' is a more difficult concept because there are various ways of gaining control of a company short of owning a majority of the shares in it. The question is whether there is the ability to have 'decisive influence' on an undertaking[27] and this may occur in a number of ways. In particular, it is not necessary to have a majority shareholding to exercise control. For example in RTL/M6,[28] RTL had a 48% shareholding in M6, but only 34% of the voting rights. The Commission decided that this was sufficient to constitute control as the remaining 51% of the shares and votes were distributed amongst small shareholders, who were unlikely to act together.[29] The limitations to this became apparent in the Ryanair case. Here Ryanair had obtained a stake of just under 30% of the shares of Aer Lingus, the Irish national airline. It then announced a bid for the entire share capital of Aer Lingus. This bid was investigated by the European Commission and the acquisition was prohibited.[30] The question then arose as to whether the Commission should have required Ryanair to sell off its minority stake in Aer Lingus. The Commission took the view that it had no power to do so, and this position was upheld by the GC because the shareholding of just under 30% did not confer control and therefore was outside the jurisdiction of the MCR.[31] By contrast, it is possible under UK law to investigate this shareholding, as the UK uses the broader concept of 'material influence' and this limitation has been referred to as an

---

[24] D. Neven, 'Competition economics and antitrust in Europe' (2006) 21 *Economic Policy* 741 estimates that the Commission has a 60% success rate in merger cases, as opposed to 75% and 98% for Article 101 and 102 cases. See also D. Geradin and N. Petit, 'Judicial Review in European Union Competition Law: A Quantitative and Qualitative Assessment', TILE (Discussion Paper DP 2011-008 (2010)).

[25] Generally, see European Commission, 'Consolidated Jurisdictional Notice under Council Regulation (EC) No. 139/2004 on the control of concentrations between undertakings', OJ C95, 16.04.2008.

[26] Ibid. para. 9.

[27] MCR, Art. 3(2).

[28] Case M.3330, 12.03.2004.

[29] See also Case IV.M/258 CCIE/GTE 25.09.1992; Case IV/M.906 *Mannesamnn/Vallourrec* 03.06.1997 and M.4994 *Electrabel/Compagnie Nationale du Rhone* 10.06.2009.

[30] See M.4439 *Ryanair/Aer Lingus* 27.06.2007. Ryanair subsequently launched another bid for Aer Lingus – this will be case M.6663.

[31] Case T-411/07 *Aer Lingus v Commission* [2010] ECR II-3691 at paras 64 and 78.

enforcement gap by the Commissioner in charge of competition who has asked his staff to examine whether it is significant.[32]

In many cases, it is fairly straightforward to see that what has taken place falls within the definition of a concentration but more difficulty is raised when undertakings engage in joint ventures. A joint venture can be described broadly as where two undertakings agree to conduct some operations on a market together. This may take any number of forms, ranging from a cooperation agreement to a merger between the subsidiaries of the two companies. Depending on the form taken, the competition implications may be assessed under Article 101 TFEU or the MCR and, as far as businesses are concerned, it is preferable to have it assessed under the MCR as there are strict time limits and the European Commission has to give a definitive ruling. According to the MCR, the creation of a joint venture performing on a lasting basis all the functions of an autonomous entity is taken to constitute a concentration.[33] According to the European Commission, this means that the joint venture must have sufficient resources to operate independently on the market (which means, among other things, not simply selling and purchasing from and to its parents), carry out more than one specific function for the parent companies and be operated on a permanent basis.[34]

The main rule for whether a concentration has a Community [Union] dimension is given in Box 13.3. This is the original jurisdictional limit that was put in place in 1989 and although the European Commission has argued for it to be increased, so that more concentrations fall within its remit, this has been resisted by the Member States. The only change has been the inclusion of Article 1(3), which provides a very complicated test for concentrations which affect at least three Member States but do not quite reach the threshold set in Article 1(2). No further change has been made to the jurisdiction of the European Commission but there have been procedural changes, discussed below, which address this issue to some extent.[35]

KEY LEGAL PROVISION Box 13.3

Community [Union] dimension

2 A concentration has a Community [Union] dimension where:

(a) the combined aggregate worldwide turnover of all the undertakings concerned is more than €5,000 million; and

(b) the aggregate Community-wide [Union-wide] turnover of each of at least two of the undertakings concerned is more than €250 million,

unless each of the undertakings concerned achieves more than two-thirds of its aggregate Community-wide [Union-wide] turnover within one and the same Member State.

3 A concentration that does not meet the thresholds laid down in paragraph 2 has a Community [Union] dimension where:

➡

---

[32] OFT, 'Ryanair' (2011), Joaquin Almunia speech of 10 March 2011 available at: *http://europa.eu/rapid/pressReleases Action.do?reference=SPEECH/11/166* (accessed 23.08.12).

[33] MCR, Art. 3(4).

[34] European Commission, 'Consolidated Jurisdictional Notice under Council Regulation (EC) No. 139/2004 on the control of concentrations between undertakings' (n. 25) at paras 91–109.

[35] For a review, see European Commission, *Report on the functioning of Regulation 139/2004*, COM (2009) 281 final.

(a) the combined aggregate worldwide turnover of all the undertakings concerned is more than €2,500 million;

(b) in each of at least three Member States, the combined aggregate turnover of all the undertakings concerned is more than €100 million;

(c) in each of at least three Member States included for the purpose of point (b), the aggregate turnover of each of at least two of the undertakings concerned is more than €25 million; and

(d) the aggregate Community-wide [Union-wide] turnover of each of at least two of the undertakings concerned is more than €100 million,

unless each of the undertakings concerned achieves more than two-thirds of its aggregate Community-wide [Union-wide] turnover within one and the same Member State.

Source: MCR, Article 1(2) and (3).

Questions: How easy is it for transactions between non-European companies, for example American and Japanese companies, to fall within this test? What effect will inflation have on this test?

It is important to understand that, unlike the test for Articles 101 and 102 TFEU of affecting trade between Member States, the test under the MCR is designed to provide a clear rule about where any particular transaction should be considered, as this is important from the point of view of the businesses subject to it.

The test does not require the undertakings to be based or have their headquarters within the European Union; what is important is that they do significant business within the EU to bring them within the MCR's jurisdiction. Thus the European Commission has ruled on proposed mergers between American companies, South African companies and Asian companies because they have met the Article 1(2) criteria. Nor does this test depend on whether the proposed concentration raises competition concerns; it simply makes the size of the transaction the governing factor. As a result, many concentrations are obliged to be notified which do not raise competitive concerns.

Procedure

The first point is that concentrations which fall within the MCR must be notified to the European Commission prior to their implementation. This notification may take place prior to the agreement between the undertakings, the announcement of a public bid or the acquisition of a controlling interest. Notification may also take place earlier, if the parties can show a good faith intention to make an agreement or have publicly announced their intention to make a bid.[36] A failure to notify lays the parties open to the imposition of penalties of up to 10% of the aggregate turnover of the undertaking concerned.[37] The date that the parties notify the European Commission of the concentration is the date from which the time limits for action by the European Commission are calculated.

---

[36] MCR, Art. 4(1).

[37] MCR, Art. 14(2) and see Commission Press Release IP/98/166 of 18 February 1998 for an example of a fine imposed on Samsung for a failure to notify a concentration.

Notification is by no means a simple or straightforward process. Parties are required to make their notifications on the basis of Form CO,[38] which is not so much a form, but a series of very detailed questions about the concentration, the markets affected and the competitive conditions in those markets. The form itself describes the information requested as 'substantial'. Not surprisingly, in practice there are discussions between the European Commission and the parties to a merger before the formal notification, something that the European Commission describes as an important part of the process and helpful even in straightforward cases.[39]

Case allocation

One important issue which may arise prior to notification is if the parties to the concentration inform the European Commission that the concentration may significantly affect competition in a market within a Member State which presents the characteristics of a distinct market and so should be examined by the competition authorities of that state. The Commission refers that request to the Member State and, unless the Member State disagrees, may refer the whole or part of the case to the competition authorities of that state if it considers that such a distinct market exists and that competition in that market may be significantly affected by the concern. Such a decision has to be made within 25 working days of the parties' submission.[40]

On a similar theme, if a concentration does not have a Community [Union] dimension, but is capable of being reviewed under the competition laws of three Member States, before notification the parties may suggest to the European Commission that it is the competent body to examine the concentration. Again, the European Commission is required to consult Member States and the reference to the European Commission can only be made if none of the Member States disagree with it.[41] These two procedures represent a breach of the one-stop shop principle, and have been used in a significant number of cases, although much more commonly to make references to the European Commission for concentrations which fall within three Member State jurisdictions. They can be viewed as a corrective mechanism to deal with cases which would be allocated incorrectly if the strict rules were followed or as part of a wider trend in European Union competition law, where the idea is to allocate cases to the appropriate authority.

After notification, there are a number of processes which can result in the reallocation of a case. The first is Article 9, which allows Member States to request a concentration be referred to its own authorities, on the ground that it threatens significantly to affect competition in a market within a Member State, which is a distinct market or is not a substantial part of the common market.[42] The European Commission is given a wide discretion to decide whether to refer such a case back to the national authorities.[43] Initially, there were very few requests to the European Commission, which also appeared reluctant to make referrals back, but, since about 1996, there has been a small but steady stream of referrals made by the European Commission to the Member States.

---

[38] Available at: *http://ec.europa.eu/competition/mergers/legislation/regulations.html#impl_reg* (accessed 23/08/12).
[39] DG Competition, 'Best Practices on the conduct of EC merger control proceedings', at para. 5. Available at: *http://ec.europa.eu/competition/mergers/legislation/legislation.html* (accessed 23/08/12).
[40] MCR, Art. 4(4).
[41] MCR, Art. 4(5).
[42] Sometimes known as the 'German' clause, because it was apparently inserted at the behest of Germany.
[43] See Case T-119/02 *Royal Phillips Electronics* v *Commission* [2003] ECR II-1433.

The converse of Article 9 is Article 22, which provides a mechanism whereby one or more Member States can refer a concentration to the European Commission, even though it does not have a Community [Union] dimension under Article 1 if it affects inter-state trade and significantly affects competition within the Member State concerned. The original version of this Article was put into the MCR to help those Member States that did not have merger control systems in place. This is no longer the case (only Luxembourg does not have a merger control system), but there is still a place for this provision, which is used about three or four times a year. An example of this provision in operation was the planned acquisition of the Dutch stores of Toys R Us by a competing Dutch retail operator, Blokker, at a time when there was no merger control in the Netherlands. A reference was made at the request of the Dutch authorities to the European Commission, which concluded that the acquisition would strengthen a dominant position in the Netherlands and lead to a significant impediment to effective competition.[44] About two cases a year are referred to the Commission under this provision but this pattern has received some criticism in the literature for blurring the jurisdictional boundaries.[45]

In addition to these provisions which deal with the allocation of cases, there is also a provision which allows Member States to, in effect, withdraw cases from the Commission if they think important, non-competition interests are at stake. This is Article 21(4) (see Box 13.4 for the text), which allows Member States to take measures to protect legitimate interests which would not be taken into account under the MCR process. Three are identified within the Article: public security, plurality of media and prudential rules, i.e. rules in particular relating to the stability of the banking system. If a Member State seeks to rely on other public interest grounds, it must communicate them to the European Commission, which will make an assessment of their compatibility with the general principles of Union law. A straightforward example of this process at work happened in *Lyonnaise des Eaux/Northumbrian Water group*,[46] where the European Commission accepted that the principles of comparative competition underlying the UK's regulatory system for the water industry constituted a legitimate interest and therefore allowed the merger to be dealt with by the UK authorities, which could balance competition and regulatory concerns.

KEY LEGAL PROVISION   Box 13.4

MCR, Article 21(4)

. . . Member States may take appropriate measures to protect legitimate interests other than those taken into consideration by this Regulation and compatible with the general principles and other provisions of Community [Union] law.

Public security, plurality of the media and prudential rules shall be regarded as legitimate interests within the meaning of the first subparagraph.

---

[44] European Commission Case No. IV/M.890, 'Blokker/Toys R Us', 26 June 1997. Other examples are; Case COMP/M.5675 'Syngenta/Monsanto's Sunflower Seed Business' 17 November 2010 and Comp M.4980 'ABF/ GB Business' 23 September 2008.

[45] See G. Drauz, S. Mavroghenis and S. Ashall, 'Recent Developments in EU Merger Control' (2012) 3 *Journal of European Competition Law and Practice* 52.

[46] Case IV/M.567, [1996] 4 CMLR 614. See Competition Commission, 'Lyonnaise des Eaux/Northumbrian Water Group' (1995), where it was recommended that the merger be approved, subject to price cuts.

> Any other public interest must be communicated to the Commission by the Member State concerned and shall be recognised by the Commission after an assessment of its compatibility with the general principles and other provisions of Community [Union] law before the measures referred to above may be taken.
>
> **Questions**: What measures might a Member State take? What other public interest concerns might a Member State raise?

This Article has been invoked rarely, but there have been some recent high-profile cases which have raised the question about whether Member States are becoming more protectionist.[47] The best example is the bid in 2006 by E.ON (a German energy company) for Endesa (the main Spanish electricity operator), which was cleared by the European Commission under the MCR. Spain's major gas company, Gas Natural, wanted to obtain control of Endesa as well, before the E.ON bid, and this transaction fell outside the Commission's jurisdiction.[48] Shortly after the announcement of E.ON's bid, a decree was passed in Spain allowing the national energy regulator to review acquisitions in the energy sector. The regulator approved the E.ON bid, but subject to some important conditions. The Commission took the view that these conditions were contrary to European Union law, even after modification, and that there had been a breach of Article 21.[49] Faced with the inaction of the Spanish state, the Commission brought a case before the CJEU, which ruled that Spain was in breach of its obligations under the EU Treaties.[50] E.ON then withdrew its initial bid and reached an agreement with ENEL (the major Italian energy company) and Acciona (a Spanish utility company) whereby they would bid for Endesa but share the assets. Again, the Spanish energy regulator imposed certain conditions on the bid and, again, the European Commission decided that there had been a breach of Article 21.[51] Ultimately, the bid from ENEL and Acciona was successful. As we can see from this example, although cases under Article 21 are relatively rare, they are important, but it appears difficult for the Commission to intervene effectively and it may be that, in times of economic stress, Member States use this provision more often.

Outside the MCR, Article 346 TFEU provides that Member States can act as necessary in the interests of their security as regards the production or trade in arms, munitions and war material. This provision is not affected by the MCR and allows Member States to direct undertakings not to notify the military aspects of a concentration. This has been utilised very rarely.

Decisions and outcomes

Once a concentration has been notified to the European Commission, the Commission has 25 working days to make a decision under Article 6, sometimes referred to as Phase I.[52] If the

---

[47] A comprehensive discussion is contained in D. Gerard, 'Protectionist threats against cross-border mergers: Unexplored avenues to strengthen the effectiveness of Article 21 ECMR' (2008) 45 *Common Market Law Review* 587.

[48] Because more than two-thirds of their turnover was in one Member State: MCR, Art. 1.

[49] Case COMP/M.4197, *E.ON/Endesa*, 20 December 2006.

[50] Case C-196/07 *Commission v Spain* [2008] ECR I-41.

[51] Case COMP/M.4685, 'ENEL/Acciona/Endesa', 5 December 2007.

[52] This may be extended to 35 days if a Member State makes a request under Article 9 or if the undertakings offer commitments to make the concentration compatible with the common market: Art. 10(1).

decision is not taken within the time limit, then the concentration is deemed to have been declared compatible with the common market.[53] Under Article 6, there are three possible decisions:

1 the concentration does not fall within the MCR's jurisdiction;

2 the concentration does not raise serious doubts as to its compatibility with the common market; or

3 the concentration does raise serious doubts as to its compatibility with the common market and proceedings should be initiated – the so-called Phase II proceedings.

The vast majority of decisions, about 90% over the life of the MCR, are taken under Article 6(1)(b), simply ruling that the concentration is compatible with the common market (see Table 13.1 for statistics). Around 4% of the cases are dealt with by the use of Article 6(2), which allows the European Commission to attach conditions and obligations to its decision to ensure that the parties will comply with the commitments that they have given with a view to ensuring that the concentration is compatible with the common market. In other words, the parties have agreed to modify the concentration to meet any competition concerns and the issue of how effective such commitments are will be dealt with later.

In the first phase, the procedure seems dominated by European Commission requests for information and the submission of written documentation by the notifying parties and other interested parties and market participants. There is no requirement for any meetings before the adoption of a decision under Article 6(1), although, as a matter of best practice, the European Commission will normally offer what it calls a 'state of play meeting' to the parties where it appears that there are 'serious doubts' which may lead to an Article 6(1)(c) decision.[54]

In about 3% of cases, the European Commission will open proceedings with the aim of making a decision under Article 8 and these decisions have to be made within 90 working days, or 105 days if the parties offer commitments to ensure that the concentration is compatible with the common market. If a decision is not made within these time limits, the concentration

Table 13.1 European Union merger control statistics

	2001	2002	2003	2004	2005	2006	2007	2008	2009	2010	2011
Notifications	335	277	211	247	313	356	402	347	259	274	309
Article 4 full referral to Member State				2	11	13	5	9	6	7	10
Article 4(5) referral to Commission		2	1	16	24	39	50	22	25	24	17
Article 22 referral		2	1	1	3	3	2	3	1	2	2
Article 9 referral	1	4	8	2	3	1	1	2	1	4	2
Phase 1 compatible	299	238	203	220	276	323	368	307	225	253	299
Phase 1 compatible w/commitments	11	10	11	12	15	13	18	19	13	14	5
Phase 2 proceedings	21	7	9	8	10	13	15	10	5	4	8
Phase 2 compatible	5	2	2	2	2	4	5	9	0	1	4
Phase 2 compatible w/commitments	9	5	6	4	3	6	4	5	3	2	1
Phase 2 prohibition	5	0	0	1	0	0	1	0	0	0	1

[53] MCR, Art. 10(6).
[54] DG Competition, 'Best Practices on the conduct of EC merger control proceedings' at para. 33. Available at: *http://ec.europa.eu/competition/mergers/legislation/legislation.html* (accessed 23/08/12). MCR, Art. 4(4).

will be deemed to be compatible with the common market.[55] If the European Commission intends to take any decision other than one declaring the concentration compatible with the common market, it is required to hear the parties before such a decision, which means that it will issue what is known as a Statement of Objections (SO), setting out the concerns that the Commission has with the concentration.[56] The SO must contain all the objections against the concentration which the Commission intends to rely upon in its final decision.[57] If the parties request it, an oral hearing must be given to them, which may also be available to other parties that are involved.[58] The oral hearing is conducted by an official of the European Commission known as the Hearing Officer, who operates independently of the case team.[59] After the hearing, but before making a decision, the European Commission has to consult the Advisory Committee on Concentrations, composed of representatives of the Member States, and the Committee's decision is published.[60] In some controversial cases, it has been evident that there were disagreements between the Advisory Committee and the European Commission.[61] Again, there are three possible outcomes to this procedure:

1 the concentration can be deemed compatible with the common market;

2 the undertakings may make modifications to the concentration, which means that it is deemed compatible with the common market; or

3 it can be deemed incompatible with the common market, that is, the proposed concentration will be prohibited from going ahead.

The most common outcome is that the concentration is declared compatible with the common market after modifications by the undertakings concerned, which takes place in around 40% of the cases, and about 30% of the cases are declared compatible with the internal market. Up until December 2011, there had been only 22 prohibition decisions made by the European Commission; and only three had been made since 2002, with the most recent ones being the prohibition of Ryanair's attempted takeover of Aer Lingus and Olympic Air/Aegean Air.[62] What the simple statistics suggest is that, for concentrations which raise competition concerns, the process of offering commitments and having them accepted by the European Commission is the most important part of the process.

Substantive assessment of mergers by the European Commission

Introduction

The MCR sets down that concentrations are to be assessed under the following criteria (see Box 13.5). The European Commission has also issued guidelines setting out its interpretation

---

[55] MCR, Art. 10(3) and (6). There is provision for suspension of the time limit if the European Commission has to request information by decision or order an inspection: Art. 10(4).

[56] Commission Regulation (EC) No. 802/2004 of 7 April 2004 implementing Council Regulation (EC) No. 139/2004 on the control of concentrations between undertakings, Article 14: OJ L133, 30.04.2004, pp. 1–39.

[57] MCR, Art. 18(3).

[58] Ibid., Art. 15.

[59] Ibid., Art. 16.

[60] Ibid., Art. 19(3)–(7).

[61] See Case M 53, *Aerospatiale/Alenia/de Havilland*, 15 May 1991.

[62] Case COMP/M.4439 *Ryanair/Aer Lingus*, 27 June 2007. Upheld on appeal, Case T-342/07 *Ryanair v Commission* [2010] ECR II-3457; Case No. COMP/M.5839 *Olympic Air/Aegean Air* 26 January 2011, on appeal Case T-202/11 *Aeroporia Aigaiou Aeroporiki and Marfin Investment Group Symmetochon v Commission*, not yet decided.

of these criteria and explaining its approach.[63] The basic test is whether the concentration would significantly impede effective competition in the common market or a substantial part of it, in particular as the result of the creation or strengthening of a dominant position. This was a change from the previous test which had linked competition problems to the creation or strengthening of a dominant position, which meant that no action could be taken unless dominance was established. Arguably this created a problem for certain mergers in oligopolistic markets which could not be solved by employing the concept of collective dominance and the European Commission got in some difficulties through trying to expand the idea of collective dominance, most notably in the *Airtours* case.[64] The new text represents a compromise between those that wanted to retain the dominance test and those that wanted it replaced with a substantial lessening of competition (SLC) test, which is used in a number of other jurisdictions, notably the USA and the UK.[65] Although the wording of the test has changed, the European Commission takes the view that the creation or strengthening of a dominant position is a primary form of competitive harm and it expects that most cases of incompatibility will continue to be based upon a finding of dominance.[66]

KEY LEGAL PROVISION   **Box 13.5**

Criteria for substantive assessment: MCR, Article 2

1 Concentrations within the scope of this Regulation shall be appraised in accordance with the objectives of this Regulation . . . with a view to establishing whether they are compatible with the common market.

In making this appraisal, the Commission shall take into account:

(a) the need to maintain and develop effective competition within the common market in view of, among other things, the structure of all the markets concerned and the actual or potential competition from undertakings located either within or outwith the Community [Union];

(b) the market position of the undertakings concerned and their economic and financial power, the alternatives available to suppliers and users, their access to supplies or markets, any legal or other barriers to entry, supply and demand trends for the relevant goods and services, the interests of the intermediate and ultimate consumers, and the development of technical and economic progress provided that it is to consumers' advantage and does not form an obstacle to competition.

---

[63] European Commission, *Guidelines on the assessment of horizontal mergers under the Council Regulation on the control of concentrations between undertakings*, OJ C31, 05.02.2004, pp. 5–18 (hereafter *Horizontal Guidelines*); and see also European Commission, *Guidelines on the assessment of non-horizontal mergers under the Council Regulation on the control of concentrations between undertakings*, OJ C265, 18.10.2008 (hereafter *Non-horizontal Guidelines*).

[64] Case T-342/99 *Airtours v Commission* [2002] ECR II-2585.

[65] Originally the Commission had envisaged no change in the substantive test: see European Commission, 'Green paper on the review of Council Regulation (EEC) No. 4064/89', COM (2001) 745/6 final. For the arguments on the other side, see Z. Biro and D. Parker, 'A New EC Merger Test? Dominance versus Substantial Lessening of Competition' (2002) 1 *Competition Law Journal* 157.

[66] *Horizontal Guidelines* (n. 63), paras 2 and 4.

2 A concentration which would not significantly impede effective competition in the common market or in a substantial part of it, in particular as a result of the creation or strengthening of a dominant position, shall be declared compatible with the common market.

3 A concentration which would significantly impede effective competition, in the common market or in a substantial part of it, in particular as a result of the creation or strengthening of a dominant position, shall be declared incompatible with the common market.

In order to assess the competitive effects of a concentration, the European Commission compares the results that would emerge from the notified concentration with the results that would have taken place without the merger, this latter situation sometimes being referred to as the 'counter-factual'.[67] This will require a definition of the relevant product and geographic markets and a competitive assessment of the merger. In its guidelines, the European Commission takes the view that non-horizontal mergers are less likely to create competition concerns than horizontal ones.[68] The process by which market definition is carried out is not, in principle, different from the inquiry undertaken in other competition cases and the earlier discussion (see Chapter 1) should be referred to, while Box 13.6 serves as a reminder.

KEY CASE EXTRACT   **Box 13.6**

Market definition

Product market

- Demand-side substitutability
- Supply-side substitutability

   . . . the relevant product or service market includes products or services which are substitutable or sufficiently interchangeable with the product or service in question, not only in terms of their objective characteristics, by virtue of which they are particularly suitable for satisfying the constant needs of consumers, but also in terms of the conditions of competition and/or the structure of supply and demand on the market in question.

Source: Case T-504/93 *Tiercé Ladbroke* v *Commission* [1997] ECR II-923 at para. 81.

Geographic market

   . . . the territory in which all traders operate in the same or sufficiently homogeneous conditions of competition in so far as concerns specifically the relevant products or services, without it being necessary for those conditions to be perfectly homogeneous.

Source: Case T-219/99 *British Airways* v *Commission* [2004] 4 CMLR 1008 at para. 108.

---

[67] Ibid., para. 9.
[68] *Non-horizontal Guidelines* (n. 63), para. 11.

Having established the relevant markets, the European Commission's first step is to assess the significance of the merger and it does this through examining market shares and concentration levels to give a first indication of whether the case is of concern. In order to assess concentration levels the European Commission often applies the Herfindahl-Hirschman Index (HHI), a technique which was developed in an American context. The HHI is calculated by summing the squares of the individual market shares of all the firms in the market and a worked illustration is set out in Box 13.7.

EXAMPLE **Box 13.7**

HHI calculations

A market with ten undertakings, each with a market share of 10%, will have an HHI of 1,000 because $10^2 \times 10 = 1,000$. In other words, since each individual market share is 10%, that is squared and the results are summed. If two of those firms merge, there will be eight undertakings with a market share of 10% and one with a market share of 20%, leading to an HHI calculation of $(10^2 \times 8) + (20^2 \times 1) = 1,200$, so the delta here would be 200.

A market with five undertakings, each with a market share of 20% will have an HHI of 2,000. If two of those undertakings were to merge, there would be three undertakings with a market share of 20% each and one with a market share of 40%, leading to an HHI calculation of $(20^2 \times 3) + (40^2 \times 1) = 2,800$, so the delta here would be 800.

Question: Create your own examples to illustrate different levels of concentration in markets.

The absolute level of the HHI gives an indication of the level of competitive pressure in the market but it is the change between the pre- and post-merger situations (referred to technically as the delta) which serves as a proxy for the change in concentration brought about by the merger. In a horizontal merger, if the combined market share of the merging parties is under 25%, then there is a presumption that this is compatible with the common market.[69] The European Commission takes the view that there are unlikely to be competition concerns in a horizontal merger with a post-merger HHI of below 1,000.[70] The Commission is also unlikely to find competition concerns in horizontal markets with a post-merger HHI between 1,000 and 2,000 and a delta below 250 or a post-merger HHI above 2,000 and a delta below 150 except where there are special circumstances such as:

- merger with a potential or new entrant,
- one of the merging parties is an important innovator,
- there are significant cross-shareholdings among the market participants,
- one of the merging firms is a maverick with a high likelihood of disrupting coordinated conduct,
- there are indications of coordinated practices, and
- one of the merging parties has a pre-merger market share of 50% or more.[71]

[69] *Horizontal Guidelines* (n. 63), para. 18.
[70] Ibid., para. 19.
[71] Ibid., para. 20.

The Commission is unlikely to find competition concerns in non-horizontal mergers, if the post-merger market share of the new entity is below 30%, in each of the markets concerned, and the post-merger HHI is below 2,000 unless there are exceptional circumstances such as:[72]

- the merger involves a company that is likely to expand significantly in the near future;
- there are significant cross-shareholdings or cross-directorships among the market participants;
- one of the merging firms is a firm with a high likelihood of disrupting coordinated conduct;
- indications of past or ongoing coordination are present.

A number of responses to the consultation regarded this approach as conservative in the context of non-horizontal mergers given that the guidance says that non-horizontal mergers are less likely to significantly impede effective competition.[73]

By contrast, the US agencies have a more relaxed approach. They divide markets into three categories:[74]

1 Unconcentrated markets: HHI below 1,500
2 Moderately concentrated markets: HHI between 1,500 and 2,500
3 Highly concentrated markets: HHI above 2,500.

Any HHI increase of less than 100 points or which results in an unconcentrated market is considered unlikely to have adverse competitive effects. In moderately concentrated markets an increase of above 100 points is considered to raise potentially significant concerns and will require further analysis. In highly concentrated markets, an increase of between 100 and 200 points is considered to raise potentially significant concerns and will require further analysis. An increase of more than 200 points will be presumed to be likely to enhance market power (and therefore subject to challenge). Although this guidance is given in the context of horizontal mergers, the US authorities will also challenge non-horizontal mergers.[75]

Horizontal mergers: unilateral effects

Having used concentration levels as a first filter, the European Commission then goes on to examine whether the merger would have anti-competitive effects in the relevant markets, in the absence of any countervailing factors. As regards horizontal mergers and non-coordinated effects, the Commission looks at the following:

- whether the firms have a large market share,
- were the merging firms close competitors?
- what possibilities do customers have of switching supplier?
- will competitors increase output if the merged entity raises prices?

[72] *Non-horizontal Guidelines* (n. 63), paras 25–6.
[73] E.g. ABA, RBB, Freshfields available at: *http://ec.europa.eu/comm/competition/mergers/legislation/non_horizontal_ consultation.html#comments* (accessed 23/08/12); *Non-horizontal Guidelines* (n. 63), para. 11.
[74] DOJ/FTC, 'Horizontal Merger Guidelines' (2010) s. 5.3.
[75] See Department of Justice, 'Antitrust Division Policy Guide to Merger Remedies' (2011) at p. 5 and, *US v Google and ITA Software*, documentation available at: *http://www.justice.gov/atr/cases/google.html* (accessed 23/08/12).

- could the merged entity hinder expansion by competitors? and
- would the merger eliminate an important competitive force?[76]

The countervailing factors are, broadly, whether or not there is buyer power which may counter the merger and whether new entry would be likely to deter or defeat any potential anti-competitive effects of the merger. As the Commission explains, one source of countervailing buyer power is the credible threat to resort to alternative sources of supply, either through switching, vertical integration into the upstream market or sponsoring upstream expansion or entry.[77] It is felt more likely that large and sophisticated customers will possess this sort of power (Tesco, John Lewis and Marks & Spencer would be examples). It is not sufficient, in the Commission's view, if the countervailing buyer power only protects a particular segment of buyers with particular bargaining strength. As for entry, this has to be shown to be likely, timely and sufficient to deter or defeat any potential anti-competitive effects.[78] For entry to be likely it has to be sufficiently profitable and this will be affected by the barriers to entry. Low barriers to entry suggest a greater likelihood of constraint on the merging parties. In this context, the Commission describes as barriers to entry legal advantages (for example, licensing), technical advantages and the established position of the incumbent firm. Technical advantages include preferential access to essential facilities, natural resources, innovation and R&D or intellectual property rights. They may also include economies of scale and scope, distribution and sales networks and access to important technologies. As for the incumbent's position, this includes loyalty to a brand, the importance of advertising, customer relationships and other reputational advantages. It can be seen from this discussion that the Commission operates with a wide definition of what might constitute barriers to entry, although this is consistent with the UK authorities.[79]

A good, but controversial, illustration of this approach came in the proposed merger between Ryanair and Aer Lingus. Ryanair is a budget airline which has a major base of operations in Ireland, particularly from Dublin, while Aer Lingus was the former Irish national carrier, whose main base is also Dublin. The Commission concluded that the merged entity would have had a market share of around 80%, that Ryanair and Aer Lingus were the main competitive constraints on each other, that the merger would have reduced consumer choice on a number of routes, that other competitors were unlikely to enter into direct competition because Ryanair had a reputation for retaliating aggressively against new entrants and the merged entity would have a greater ability to protect its competitive position. As a result, the merger was prohibited, although the decision was unsuccessfully challenged in the GC.[80]

The approach can also be illustrated by the prohibition decision in Olympic Air/Aegean Airlines.[81] The main issue in this case was that the merger between Olympic Air, which provided a variety of domestic flights in Greece, and Aegean Air, which also provided domestic flights in Greece, would have resulted in an entity which would have had 90–100% of all

---

[76] *Horizontal Guidelines* (n. 63), paras 24–38.

[77] Ibid. paras 64–67.

[78] Ibid. paras 68–75.

[79] CC/OFT, *Merger Assessment Guidelines* (2010) para. 5.8.5. See also Department of Justice/Federal Trade Commission, 'Horizontal merger Guidelines' (2010) s. 9.

[80] Case COMP/M.4439 *Ryanair/Aer Lingus*, 27 June 2007. Upheld on appeal, Case T-342/07 *Ryanair v Commission* [2010] ECR II-3457.

[81] Case COMP/M.5830 *Olympic/Aegean Airline* 26 January 2011.

passengers out of Athens Airport on domestic routes and that the parties were close competitors, having similar services, similar networks and strong brands.[82] There were a number of barriers to entry on this market, as a new entrant would require a base at Athens Airport, a strong brand, there would be high sunk costs and a new entrant would need access to domestic distribution channels.[83] The Commission went through a detailed analysis of the particular routes on which the parties' services overlapped and came to the conclusion that it would lead to the elimination of competition on nine domestic routes, and a dominant position as regards time-sensitive passengers on all routes. For non-time-sensitive passengers, the merger would create a significant impediment to effective competition because of the closeness of competition between the merging parties.[84] The parties have appealed the decision.[85]

Horizontal mergers: coordinated effects

The issue of coordinated effects has been one that has caused a number of difficulties for the European Commission. The pre-2004 version of Article 2 of the MCR said that a concentration that creates or strengthens a dominant position as a result of which effective competition would be significantly impeded in the common market or in a substantial part of it shall be declared incompatible with the common market. A problem arises because there may be a concentration between two undertakings which does not, in itself, create a dominant position but creates the conditions whereby there might be coordinated effects between the merged entity and other undertakings remaining on the market. So, for example, if there were four manufacturers with market shares of 35%, 35%, 15% and 15% respectively and the two smallest merged to create an entity with a 30% market share, it would be unlikely that the merged entity could be said to be dominant, but such a merger could create the incentives for the remaining three companies not to compete very hard against each other (although this would not in itself be a breach of competition law). On the pre-2004 wording, it looked as if the European Commission could not intervene in these circumstances, as no dominant position had been created or strengthened unless it could be said that the relationship between the remaining three entities constituted a collective dominant position.

Fairly early on, the European Commission took an expansive view of the MCR and applied it to situations of collective dominance.[86] This approach was challenged in a case involving a concentration between Kali und Salz (K&S) and Mitteldeutsch (MDK), which were two German manufacturers of potash in, respectively, what had been West Germany and what had been East Germany. The merged entity would have had a *de facto* monopoly on the German market and, as regards the European market, this would have created a collective dominant position with a French undertaking, SCPA; and the French and the German undertakings together would have had, post-merger, a market share of around 60%. In addition there were contractual links between the undertakings as they jointly participated in an export cartel and SCPA handled the distribution of K&S's products in France. The European Commission permitted the concentration subject to certain commitments by the German parties which would reduce their links with SCPA. The issue of the German market was dealt

---

[82] Ibid. para. 511 and paras 5.21–5.41.

[83] Ibid. paras 553–664.

[84] Ibid. paras 1692–93.

[85] On appeal Case T-202/11 *Aeroporia Aigaiou Aeroporiki and Marfin Investment Group Symmetochon v Commission*, not yet decided.

[86] Commission Decision M.190, *Nestlé/Perrier* [1992] OJ L356/1.

with via the 'failing firm' defence, which is discussed later in this chapter. The decision was challenged by France, which argued that the wording of the MCR did not cover collective dominance, that the legal basis of the Regulation did not justify importing the concept from Article 102 TFEU and there was nothing in the legislative history to support it.[87] The CJEU rejected these textual arguments, basing itself on its view as to the purpose and general structure of the MCR. The CJEU took the view that if the Regulation applied to only the parties to a concentration which created or strengthened a dominant position it would be deprived of a not insignificant part of its effectiveness, and therefore concluded that collective dominant positions fell within the MCR.[88]

The next question then became what constituted a collective dominant position. In this decision, the European Commission had based itself on the degree of concentration on the market, structural factors relating to the nature of the market and the product, and the contractual links between the undertakings. The CJEU decided, however, that, on the evidence, the European Commission had not proven that there was a collective dominant position and, in particular, that the links between the two undertakings were not as tight as had been alleged. The problem is that, if the key component of collective dominance is formal links between the undertakings, this would cover only a limited category of coordinated effects. That the notion of collective dominance was wider became apparent in the *Gencor* case,[89] which involved a merger between two South African mining companies that produced, among other things, platinum. The result would have been the creation of a collective dominant position between the merged entity and the other main South African producer, both with market shares of around 35%, although there were no formal links between them. (Box 13.8 sets out a statement made by the GC.)

KEY CASE EXTRACT　　　　　　　　　　　　　　　　　　　　　**Box 13.8**

Conditions for collective dominance

Source: Case T-102/96 *Gencor* v *Commission* [1999] ECR II-753 at paras 276–7:

> [T]here is no reason whatsoever in legal or economic terms to exclude from the notion of economic links the relationship of interdependence existing between the parties to a tight oligopoly within which, in a market with the appropriate characteristics, in particular in terms of market concentration, transparency and product homogeneity, those parties are in a position to anticipate one another's behaviour and are therefore strongly encouraged to align their conduct in the market, in particular in such a way as to maximise their joint profits by restricting production with a view to increasing prices. In such a context, each trader is aware that highly competitive action on its part designed to increase its market share (for example a price cut) would provoke identical action by the others, so that it would derive no benefit from its initiative. All the traders would thus be affected by the reduction in price levels.

Question: Try to think of examples of these types of market.

---

[87] Cases 68/94 and C-30/95 *France* v *Commission* [1998] ECR I-1375 at paras 152–4.
[88] Ibid. at para. 171.
[89] Case T-102/96 *Gencor* v *Commission* [1999] ECR II-753.

The importance of this case was that it established that collective dominance could be applied in a situation where there were no legal links between the undertakings in an industry but where the economic conditions and market structure was such it might lead to coordinated effects, even though single party dominance could not be identified. The European Commission tried to move this on further in the Airtours case, which involved the merger of two UK package holiday companies, Airtours and First Choice. The relevant market was the market for short-haul package holidays and, on that market, the merged entity would have had a market share of 32%, facing two other main competitors – Thomson and Thomas Cook with market shares of 27% and 20% respectively – with the rest of the market held by other operators. The European Commission prohibited the merger,[90] on the grounds that it would create a collective dominant position, in that the three major operators would no longer have an incentive to compete against each other and this would occur in relation to output or capacity on the market, rather than price. More controversially, the European Commission took the view that it was not necessary to show that the parties would adopt a common position on the market, nor that it was necessary to show that retaliatory mechanisms existed to prevent cheating.[91] The GC annulled the decision. In order to prove collective dominance, the GC said that there were three conditions:

1   each member of the dominant oligopoly must have the ability to know how the other members are behaving in order to monitor whether they are adopting the common policy;

2   the situation of tacit coordination must be sustainable over time, that is to say, there must be an incentive not to depart from the common policy on the market (in other words, there must be retaliatory mechanisms available to prevent cheating); and

3   the foreseeable reaction of current and future competitors, as well as of consumers, would not jeopardise the results expected from the common policy, and these conditions have now been incorporated into the Commission's guidance.[92]

There are still difficulties with these sorts of mergers, as became apparent with the merger between Sony and Bertelsmann: both undertakings' main activities, in this context, were music recording and publishing. This was a proposal which the Commission saw as raising serious issues, so it was subjected to a second phase examination. In its statement of objections to the merger, the main argument was that this merger would create a collective dominant position between the merged entity and the other music publishers and was therefore incompatible with the common market. Following a meeting with the undertakings, the Commission appeared to change its mind and decided to approve the merger and this decision was challenged by a group of independent music publishers.[93] The GC annulled the decision, broadly speaking on the ground that the evidence presented by the European Commission in its decision did not support the conclusion; if anything, it pointed towards the creation of a collective dominant position. Since this was an annulment of a decision to allow a merger, the case returned to the Commission, in order to allow it to be reconsidered and, after reconsidering it, the merger was again allowed.[94]

---

[90] Case IV/M.1524 *Airtours/First Choice* [2000] OJ L93/1.
[91] Ibid. at paras 51–6.
[92] Case T-342/99 *Airtours v Commission* [2002] ECR I-2585 at para. 62.
[93] Case T-464/04 *Independent Music Publishers and Labels Association (Impala) v Commission* [2006] ECR II-2289.
[94] See Press Release IP/07/1437, 3 October 2007.

The GC's decision was appealed to the CJEU, which set aside the decision and referred it back to the GC primarily on the grounds that the GC had misconstrued its role in reviewing such decisions. It did, however, make a clear statement in relation to the conditions for and definition of collective dominance (Box 13.9).

KEY CASE EXTRACT   **Box 13.9**

Collective dominance

Source: Case C-413/06P *Bertelsmann and Sony v Commission* [2008] ECR I-4951, paras 122–3:

A collective dominant position significantly impeding effective competition in the common market or a substantial part of it may thus arise as the result of a concentration where, in view of the actual characteristics of the relevant market and of the alteration to those characteristics that the concentration would entail, the latter would make each member of the oligopoly in question, as it becomes aware of common interests, consider it possible, economically rational, and hence preferable, to adopt on a lasting basis a common policy on the market with the aim of selling at above competitive prices, without having to enter into an agreement or resort to a concerted practice within the meaning of Article 81 EC [Article 101 TFEU] and without any actual or potential competitors, let alone customers or consumers, being able to react effectively.

Such tacit coordination is more likely to emerge if competitors can easily arrive at a common perception as to how the coordination should work, and, in particular, of the parameters that lend themselves to being a focal point of the proposed coordination . . . Moreover, having regard to the temptation which may exist for each participant in a tacit coordination to depart from it in order to increase its short-term profit, it is necessary to determine whether such coordination is sustainable. In that regard, the coordinating undertakings must be able to monitor to a sufficient degree whether the terms of the coordination are being adhered to. There must therefore be sufficient market transparency for each undertaking concerned to be aware, sufficiently precisely and quickly, of the way in which the market conduct of each of the other participants in the coordination is evolving. Furthermore, discipline requires that there be some form of credible deterrent mechanism that can come into play if deviation is detected. In addition, the reactions of outsiders, such as current or future competitors, and also the reactions of customers, should not be such as to jeopardise the results expected from the coordination.

Questions: What are deterrent mechanisms? What is meant by the reactions of outsiders?

With the revision of the MCR in 2004 it is no longer crucial in these circumstances to show a collective dominant position, as the issue is whether the concentration significantly impedes effective competition, *in particular*, as a result of the strengthening or creation of a dominant position. The issue now is whether the proposed merger will lead to coordinated effects which create a significant impediment to effective competition. The case is still relevant because it sets the parameters for the test. As the Commission puts it, there are three conditions for coordination to be sustainable:[95]

---

[95] *Horizontal Guidelines* (n. 63), para. 41.

1 the coordinating firms must be able to monitor to a sufficient degree whether the terms of coordination are being adhered to,

2 there must be some form of credible deterrent mechanism that can be activated if deviation is detected, and

3 the actions of outsiders (current and future competitors, customers) should not be able to jeopardise the results expected from the coordination.

As regards the first condition, this is more likely in a less complex and stable economic environment, with homogeneous products and stable demand and supply conditions.[96] This is less likely in markets with frequent entry or which are characterised by innovation. It is also helpful if customers have simple characteristics that allow allocation either by customer type or geographical location and if the firms are relatively similar. As regards the second condition, it is important that there is a sufficient degree of transparency in market transactions, in order that coordinating firms can monitor their rivals' behavior and see whether they are cheating.[97] This depends partly on the number of players in the market and how transactions take place. For example, individually negotiated transactions are much more difficult to monitor. The deterrence mechanism has to be timely and there must be sufficient incentive, and ability, to use it. Typically this would involve increasing output and lowering prices, which implies some level of spare capacity.

A good example of the application of these tests came in the ABF/GBI merger case which involved the acquisition by Associated British Foods (ABF) of certain yeast businesses run by GBI and the effects of this transaction on the Portuguese and Spanish markets.[98] The basic issue was that on the Portuguese and Spanish markets there were only three competitors: the two merging firms and a French company, Lesaffre. The Commission found that there was significant transparency on prices, sales and capacity levels of the producers. There were historical relationships between producers, distributors and customers and relatively stable demand, reflected in stable market shares. In addition, distributors were given exclusive territories, which helped encourage tacit coordination.[99] There were credible deterrence mechanisms, as all three players in the market had excess capacity sufficient to initiate a price war in the case of deviation.[100] There were also high barriers to entry, which would prevent outsiders undermining the tacit coordination, mainly through the need to develop a recognised brand and an effective distribution network.[101] In order to meet the Commission's objections, ABF agreed to divest certain of GBI's businesses in Portugal and Spain.

Vertical mergers

As regards vertical mergers, the European Commission distinguishes between raising the costs of downstream rivals by restricting access to important inputs (input foreclosure) such as raw materials and raising the costs of upstream rivals by restricting their access to a sufficient customer base (customer foreclosure).[102] Foreclosure is defined as 'any instance where

[96] Ibid. paras 44–48.
[97] Ibid. paras 52–55.
[98] COMP/M.4980 *ABF/GB Business* 23.09.08. See also the discussion by A. Almelio *et al.*, 'ABF/GBI Business: Coordinated effects baked again' [2009] *Competition Policy Newsletter*, No. 1, 91.
[99] Ibid. para. 221.
[100] Ibid. para. 242.
[101] Ibid. paras 159–66.
[102] *Non-horizontal Guidelines* (n. 63), para. 30.

actual or potential rivals' access to supplies or markets is hampered or eliminated as a result of the merger, thereby reducing these companies' ability and/or incentive to compete'.[103] It has been commented[104] that this is ambiguous, depending on whether the emphasis is placed on the first part of the sentence ('any instance' to 'merger') or the second ('thereby' to 'compete'). The former suggests a stronger presumption against vertical or conglomerate mergers, while the latter seems to focus on the anti-competitive effects. The Commission proposes to focus its analysis on foreclosure issues and suggests that in general the question is whether, post-merger, the new entity has the ability to foreclose access to inputs, the incentive to do so and whether it would have a significant detrimental effect on competition in the downstream market.[105] Foreclosure does not simply mean that the rivals are forced to exit the market; it is sufficient that they are led to compete less effectively. As in horizontal mergers, a distinction is drawn between non-coordinated and coordinated effects and the analysis of coordinated effects is similar to the discussion in relation to horizontal mergers.[106]

For either input or customer foreclosure to be a concern, the European Commission recognises that the merged entity must have significant market power in the upstream market (for input foreclosure) or the downstream market (for customer foreclosure)[107] (see Figures 13.1 and 13.2).[108] Input foreclosure may vary from a simple refusal to deal to a restriction of supplies and/or raising price and/or making the conditions of supply less favourable. It is only important when the downstream input is important, for example if it is a significant cost factor or is a critical component. Input foreclosure is only possible if the downstream customers cannot turn to alternative suppliers, for whatever reason. Whether there is the incentive to foreclose depends on whether this would be profitable. When a firm stops selling to its downstream customers, it no longer has this revenue stream. The question is whether or

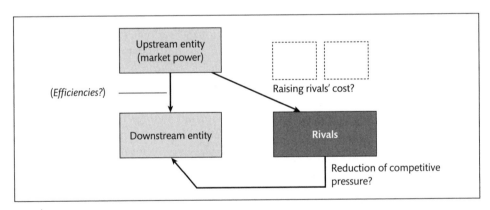

Figure 13.1 Input foreclosure

Source: Adapted from 'Guidelines on the assessment of non-horizontal mergers under the Council Regulation on the control of concentrations between undertakings', *Official Journal of the European Union* (2008/C 265/07), p. 10 (Figure 1): see original at *http://eur-lex.europa.eu/LexUriServ.do?uri=OJ:C:2008:265:0006:0025:EN:PDF*.

[103] Ibid. para. 18.

[104] RBB Economics, *Response to Draft Non-Horizontal Merger Guidelines*, p. 8, available at: *http://ec.europa.eu/comm/ competition/mergers/legislation/non_horizontal_consultation.html#comments* (accessed 26/07/09).

[105] *Non-horizontal Guidelines* (n. 63), paras 32 and 59.

[106] Ibid. paras 79–90.

[107] Ibid. paras 35 and 61.

[108] Both diagrams from *Non-horizontal Guidelines* (n. 63), paras 31 and 58.

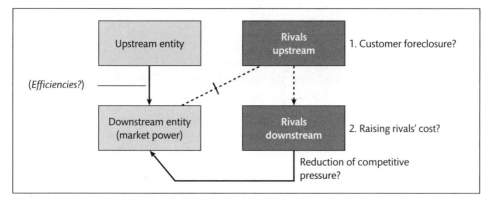

Figure 13.2 Customer foredosure

Source: Adapted from 'Guidelines on the assessment of non-horizontal mergers under the Council Regulation on the control of concentrations between undertakings', *Official Journal of the European Union* (2008/C 265/07), p. 16 (Figure 2): see original at *http://eur-lex.europa.eu/LexUriServ.do?uri=OJ:C:2008:265:0006:0025:EN:PDF*.

not this can be compensated for by the increased downstream sales or prices. This will depend on the upstream and downstream margins and the effect on the downstream business of the input foreclosure – will it obtain more customers, will it be able to raise prices? The two types of anti-competitive foreclosure that the Commission highlights are where the vertical merger allows the merging parties to increase the costs of downstream rivals in the market thereby leading to an upward pressure on their sales prices. Secondly, effective competition may be significantly impeded by raising barriers to entry to potential competitors.[109] It also acknowledges that the effects on competition have to be judged against any efficiencies substantiated by the merging parties.[110]

Customer foreclosure occurs when a supplier integrates with an important customer in a downstream market. This may create a problem for non-integrated competitors because they may no longer have access to that customer. For this to be a concern, not only must the customer have a sufficient degree of market power, but there must also be economies of scale or scope.[111] In other words, without access to this customer, competing suppliers cannot benefit from such economies. This may also render potential entry less attractive because there will not be a sufficient customer base to enter on the necessary scale. The incentive issue here is whether the costs of no longer obtaining products from upstream rivals are offset by any possible gains, for example from raising prices in the upstream or downstream markets.[112] The Commission takes the view that the negative impact on consumers may take some time to work through, when the question is that of customer foreclosure.[113] A sufficiently large fraction of upstream output must be affected and it may also raise barriers to entry by potential competitors.[114] The effect on competition must be assessed in the light of countervailing factors, such as buyer power.

[109] Ibid. paras 48–9.
[110] Ibid. paras 52–7.
[111] Ibid. paras 60–7.
[112] Ibid. paras 68–71.
[113] Ibid. para. 73.
[114] Ibid. paras 74–5.

An example is the European Commission's in-depth investigations into the proposed acquisition by Tom Tom, which makes satellite navigation systems, of Tele Atlas, which produces navigable digital maps, in the Netherlands. The concern here was a vertical one, because Tele Atlas is one of two current map suppliers for all of Europe and the question was whether the acquisition would limit the access of other producers of satellite navigation systems to these maps. After a phase 2 investigation, the Commission concluded that the merged entity would not have the incentive to stop supplying maps to its downstream competitors and so cleared the concentration.[115]

Conglomerate mergers

As regards conglomerate mergers, the foreclosure concerns are somewhat different, as here the major concern is the leveraging of a strong market position from one market to another by the use of tying and bundling of products together. In order for this to be a concern, the merged entity must have a significant degree of market power, which does not necessarily amount to dominance in one of the markets concerned.[116] Generally, the European Commission takes the view that 'the foreclosure effects of bundling and tying are likely to be more pronounced in industries where there are economies of scale and the demand pattern at any given point in time has dynamic implications for the conditions of supply in the market in the future'.[117] What this means is that if a product (Product A) is tied with a complementary product (Product B) and the effect of this is to reduce the scope for those competitors who sell only Product B to expand their business or if that tie makes it more difficult for potential competitors who only wish to offer Product B to enter the market, then this may raise potential competition problems. To give an example, this was the sort of argument that the European Commission used in relation to tying Windows Media Player (Product B) with the Windows Operating System in the Article 102 TFEU case brought against Microsoft (discussed in the previous chapter). Again, the incentive to undertake such a strategy depends on its profitability and the effects of the strategy have to be assessed, in particular the effects on potential entry, as well as the potential efficiencies of the transaction.

An example of the Commission's approach is the merger between the chip maker Intel and the provider of software security products McAfee.[118] Although the Commission recognised that there were no vertical or horizontal relationships between the parties, it saw the products as closely linked.[119] Intel has a very high market share in its products. McAfee, by contrast, had a much smaller market share in its products; at its greatest it has a 10–20% market share in endpoint security.[120] The Commission concluded that the merged entity would have the ability and incentive to hinder interoperability between its chipsets and security solutions, favouring McAfee over competitors, and that this would have significant negative effects on the relevant market.[121] The Commission also concluded that the merged entity would have the ability and incentive to technically tie its chipsets with the security products and that this

---

[115] European Commission, Case COMP/M4854, *TomTom/Teleatlas*, 14 May 2008. For another example see: Case COMP/M.5675 *Syngenta/Monsanto's Sunflower Seed Business*, 17 November 2010.
[116] Non-horizontal guidelines (n. 63), para. 99.
[117] Ibid. para. 101.
[118] Case COMP/M.5984 *Intel/McAfee* 26 January 2011.
[119] Ibid. at para. 120.
[120] Paras 63–8.
[121] Paras 173–4.

would have a negative effect on the market.[122] By contrast, although the Commission thought that there was the ability to engage in a bundling strategy, there were limited incentives to do so and likely to be limited effects on the market.[123] The Commission did, however, think that a combination of strategies could cause a competition problem.[124] The Commission's objections were met by Intel giving commitments which in essence aimed at ensuring that rivals to McAfee would have all the necessary technical information for their products, that they would ensure that rival products would not work less well on their chipsets and that McAfee products would work sufficiently well on competitors' chipsets. These remedies will be monitored by a trustee.

Overall, this brief examination of the *Non-horizontal Guidelines* suggests that the European Commission has been concerned with the competitive effects of vertical and conglomerate mergers. This has certainly been reflected in past practice where the European Commission has either prohibited or intervened in such mergers in a variety of industries, such as broadcasting, energy, aircraft engines and avionics, and packaging and bottling.[125] Having said this, the majority of activity where the European Commission intervenes in proposed mergers relates to concerns over horizontal mergers – it has been its attempts to intervene in vertical, and especially conglomerate, mergers which have been particularly controversial.

Efficiencies and the failing firm defence

One of the general arguments for mergers is that they will create efficiencies for the merging parties, even though the empirical evidence in support of this is ambiguous.[126] In its original incarnation, there was some doubt that efficiencies could be taken into account by the European Commission in their assessment of a merger. Recital 29 of the current Regulation says that it is appropriate to take into account substantiated and likely efficiencies which are put forward by the parties and this has been developed by the European Commission in its Guidelines. In brief, for the parties to show that the efficiencies outweigh the anti-competitive effects of the proposed merger there are three cumulative conditions to be met: they must benefit consumers, be merger specific and be verifiable.[127] Efficiency arguments will also be evaluated in the context of non-horizontal mergers on the basis of the same principles as expressed in the horizontal mergers Notice,[128] whilst recognising that there may be specific efficiencies in these types of case, although one of the responses to the Draft Notice was that insufficient attention was being paid to these efficiencies.[129] Although efficiencies have been considered in a number of cases, there is as yet no example where a merger has been cleared simply because the efficiencies that it would create outweigh the anti-competitive effects.[130]

---

[122] Paras 219–21.

[123] Paras 289–91.

[124] Paras 292–96.

[125] See also P. Lahbabi and S. Moonen, 'A closer look at vertical mergers' (2007) *Competition Policy Newsletter* 2, 11–17 for other examples.

[126] See L.-H. Röller and M. de la Mano, 'The Impact of the New Substantive Test in European Merger Control' (2006) 2 *European Competition Journal* 9 at 17.

[127] *Horizontal Guidelines* (n. 63) para. 78.

[128] *Non-horizontal Guidelines* (n. 63), para. 21.

[129] See, e.g., RBB Economics, American Bar Association at p. 6, available at: *http://ec.europa.eu/comm/competition/mergers/legislation/non_horizontal_consultation.html#comments* (accessed 24/08/12).

[130] See C. Boeshertz and S. Moonen, 'Inco/Falconbridge: A nickel mine of applications in efficiencies and remedies' (2006) *Competition Policy Newsletter*, No. 3, pp. 41–9.

Another argument that is often made is what is known as the 'failing firm' argument. Essentially, the point here is that the merger does not cause the deterioration in the competitive structure of the market because one of the parties to the merger is failing and therefore would have exited the market in the future anyway and its assets or market share would have gone to the other firm. The European Commission has set down three criteria for this to be met:

1 the allegedly failing firm would in the near future be forced out of the market because of financial difficulties if not taken over by another undertaking;

2 there should be no less anti-competitive alternative; and

3 in the absence of a merger, the assets of the failing firm would inevitably exit the market.[131]

The earliest example of this is *France v Commission*,[132] where a potash manufacturer in what had been West Germany agreed to take over another manufacturer in what was previously East Germany, which would have led to a monopoly for the merged entity on the German market in potash. The Commission accepted that the concentration did not cause the deterioration in competition because the acquired entity would have been forced out of the market in any event and the acquiring undertaking was the only other relevant participant, and this decision was upheld by the CJEU.[133]

Remedies

The MCR makes it clear that when undertakings notify a concentration, they should be able to modify it by making commitments which will meet the concerns about competition expressed by the European Commission.[134] The European Commission has power, under both Article 6 and Article 8, to attach conditions and obligations to its decisions which, in effect, make the commitments given by the undertakings legally enforceable. It is, however, up to the undertakings concerned to offer commitments, not for the European Commission to suggest appropriate ones, although the European Commission's views on the competition problems may have an influence on the commitments offered by the undertakings.[135] Because of the importance of this process, the European Commission has issued Guidelines on the remedies that are acceptable in merger cases. Before discussing the guidelines, a preliminary distinction needs to be made between two broad types of remedies: structural and behavioural. A structural remedy is a remedy which has an effect on the structure of the market, such as where some of the operations such as a factory or a business are divested, whereas a behavioural remedy is one that relates to the behaviour in the future of the parties to the merger. An example would be a promise to offer access to a facility or raw materials to competitors on reasonable terms. This distinction is somewhat crude because, as the UK Competition Commission has pointed out, some remedies may have features of structural or behavioural remedies depending on their formulation.[136]

---

[131] *Horizontal Guidelines* (n. 63), para. 90.

[132] Cases 68/94 and C-30/95 *France v Commission* [1998] ECR I-1375.

[133] For other applications, see Case IV/M.2314 *BASF/Pantochim/Eurodial* and Case IV/M.2876 *Newscorp/Telepiù*.

[134] MCR, recital 30.

[135] See Case T-282/02 *Cementbouw v Commission* [2006] ECR at paras 311 and 314.

[136] Competition Commission, 'Merger Remedies' (2008) para. 2.2.

The starting point is the *Gencor* case, where the GC observed that the basic aim of commitments was to ensure a competitive market structure.[137] Therefore, commitments which were structural in nature were preferable because they solved the competition problem and did not require monitoring in the future. Behavioural commitments could not automatically be ruled out as being ineffective in dealing with competition concerns and this needed to be determined on a case-by-case basis. This illustrates a preference for structural remedies, which is reflected in the European Commission's guidelines. Whatever sort of commitment is offered, the European Commission can only accept commitments if they make the concentration compatible with the common market and it is sufficiently certain that this will be their effect.[138]

The most common remedy is the structural one of divestiture, that is where the merging parties divest a business or assets in order to create a new competitive entity or to strengthen existing competitors.[139] So, for example, if the merging parties have four plants making their products in total, they might offer to divest one of them to deal with the competition issues either to a completely new purchaser or to an existing competitor. It is in the parties' interests in this situation not to create an effective new competitor, and the Guidelines lay down some basic principles that have to be met so that divestiture is effective.[140] First, the divested activities must be a viable business, which is typically an existing one which can operate on a stand-alone basis. This may include activities which are related to markets where the European Commission did not have competition concerns in order to create a viable entity. Secondly, there has to be a suitable purchaser for the business. The purchaser is normally expected to be a viable existing or potential competitor, unconnected to the parties, possessing the financial resources, expertise and with the incentive to develop the business as an active competitive force. Of course, the purchaser must not raise its own competition problems.[141] The sort of behavioural remedies which are considered appropriate, without being exclusive, are the termination of existing exclusive agreements and agreeing to allow access to necessary infrastructure or to key technology.[142] The commitments entered into in the Intel/McAfee case, discussed above are a good example of behavioural commitments.[143]

The European Commission conducted a major in-house review of the effectiveness of its remedies practice, which was published in 2005 and raised a number of issues of concern.[144] Only half of the phase 2 remedies in the study were considered to be fully effective. As regards divestitures, there were particular issues in relation to the scope of the businesses which were divested, with the study suggesting that often the scope had not been wide enough. There were problems with the divestiture process, in particular as regards whether the purchasers

---

[137] Case T-102/96 *Gencor v Commission* [1999] ECR II-753 at para. 319. See also Case T-87/05 *EDP v Commission* [2005] ECR II-3745 at para. 100.

[138] Case T-210/01 *General Electric v Commission* [2005] ECR at para. 555.

[139] See W. Wang and M. Rudenko, 'EU Merger Remedies and Competition Concerns: An Empirical Assessment' (2012) 18 *European Law Journal* 555 which covers the period up to 2008.

[140] European Commission, 'Notice on remedies acceptable under Council Regulation (EC) No. 139/2004 and under Commission Regulation (EC) No. 802/2004' [2008] OJ C267/01, paras 22–57.

[141] Ibid., para. 48.

[142] Ibid., paras 61–70.

[143] Other examples are COMP/M.5650 *Orange/T-Mobile* 01 March 2010 and COMP/M.5756 *DFDS/Norfolk* 17 June 2010.

[144] Available at: *http://ec.europa.eu/competition/mergers/legislation/notices_on_substance.html#remedies* (accessed 24/08/12).

were suitable because of an inadequate review of their business plans or a failure to take account of the seller's incentives to sell to weak or non-competing purchasers. The few access remedies which were examined proved to be much less effective than the divestiture remedies. The current remedies notice has been amended to take on board these points.

Review by the Courts

Review by the GC or the CJEU is based on Article 263 TFEU, with the exception of reviewing fines and periodic penalty payments, which is provided for in the Regulation (Article 16) and provides unlimited jurisdiction for the Courts. By contrast, Article 263 TFEU is limited to certain specific grounds:

- lack of competence,
- infringement of an essential procedural requirement,
- infringement of the Treaties or of any rule of law relating to their application, or
- misuse of powers.

What this means is that, under Article 263 TFEU, the role of the European Courts is to determine the legality of decisions, not to substitute their own judgment of the merits of the case for that of the European Commission. In the context of mergers, the two main grounds that are relevant are infringement of an essential procedural requirement or infringement of the Treaties or of any rule of law relating to their application. This latter ground is very wide (as can be seen from Chapter 5) but it includes the ground of a 'manifest error of appraisal' by the European Commission as a ground for intervention. The idea behind this is that the Court will intervene when a particularly serious mistake has been made in a decision.

Given that merger control, and indeed competition law in general, requires complicated appraisal of economic theories and contested factual scenarios, and in merger control it is future predictions which are critical, it has tended to be thought that intervention by the Courts on judicial review grounds was ultimately 'limited'.[145] This was seemingly supported by a general statement in relation to review:

> Examination by the Community [Union] judicature of the complex economic assessments made by the Commission must necessarily be confined to verifying whether the rules on procedure and the statement of reasons have been complied with, whether the facts have been accurately stated and whether there has been any manifest error of appraisal or misuse of powers.[146]

This seemingly deferential standard of review, combined with the practical issues in relation to bringing a challenge, suggests that there would be few challenges to decisions by the European Commission under the MCR. Although this seems to have been the case up until 2002, since then the landscape has altered and there has been a steady stream of challenges to European Commission decisions both from the parties involved in the merger and competitors who feel that they will be affected by the merger. Decisions of the GC have overturned decisions of the European Commission that have prohibited mergers, as well as one that approved mergers, and have done so on procedural grounds and also on the grounds of a manifest error of assessment.

[145] A. Jones and B. Sufrin, *EC Competition Law* (2nd edn, OUP, 2004) at p. 1153. In the 4th edition they say that it now comes down to what the Union judicature considers to be a 'manifest error of appraisal' and that practice has not been consistent. In the merger context, review has been particularly rigorous: at p. 1140.

[146] Cases C-204, 205, 211, 217 and 219/00P *Aalborg Portland v Commission* [2004] ECR I-123 at para. 279.

What happened in 2002 was that, in the space of three months, the GC overturned three prohibition decisions by the European Commission and it was very critical (in all of these) of the European Commission's approach to the evidence and on the analysis relied upon.[147] In the *Airtours* case, as well as being very critical of the European Commission's approach to the evidence, the GC also rejected an attempt to expand the concept of collective dominance. In the *Schneider* case, this turned again on a poor approach to the evidence and an egregious procedural error, the consequences of which are discussed below. Both of these could be seen as cases which fit within the conventional standard of review, but in the *Tetra Laval* case the European Commission took the view that the GC had exceeded its role and substituted its view for that of the European Commission.[148]

The *Tetra Laval* case involved the acquisition of Sidel by Tetra Laval. Tetra's primary business was in the making of aseptic (sterile) cartons and carton packaging machines, with approximately an 80% market share, which were used for packaging a variety of drinks: liquid dairy products, fruit juices, fruit-flavoured still drinks, beer and tea/coffee. Sidel made stretch blow moulding machines which made transparent plastic bottles (PET) which could also be used for packaging some but not all of the liquids mentioned above. It had a leading position in this market but was not dominant. Although there were a number of horizontal and vertical overlaps between the businesses, the most controversial part of the European Commission's decision was its view that competition problems would be caused by Tetra exploiting its dominant position on the carton markets by leveraging into the market for PET packaging. The argument for this was that the carton market and PET markets were closely related, in that liquids could be packaged in either, with a common pool of customers and because the use of PET was growing, Tetra could lever its carton dominance into PET through price discrimination. The GC annulled the decision, finding that there was 'not convincing evidence' of the factual background claimed by the European Commission, particularly as regards the growth in the use of PET. The decision was appealed to the CJEU, which upheld almost all of the GC's decision and produced a general statement of the standard of judicial review (see Box 13.10).

KEY CASE EXTRACT   **Box 13.10**

Standard of review

Source: Case C-12/03P *Commission* v *Tetra Laval* [2005] ECR I-987 at paras 38–9:

[T]he basic provisions of the Regulation, in particular Article 2, confer on the Commission a certain discretion, especially with respect to assessments of an economic nature, and that, consequently, review by the Community [Union] Courts of the exercise of that discretion, which is essential for defining the rules on concentrations, must take account of the margin of discretion implicit in the provisions of an economic nature which form part of the rules on concentrations. Whilst the Court recognises that the Commission has a margin of discretion with regard to economic matters, that does not mean that the Community [Union] Courts must refrain from reviewing the Commission's interpretation of information of an economic nature. Not only must the Community [Union] Courts, inter alia,

➡

---

[147] Case T-342/99 *Airtours* v *Commission* [2002] ECR II-2585; Case T-310/01 *Schneider Electric* v *Commission* [2002] ECR II-4071; Case T-5/02 *Tetra Laval* v *Commission* [2002] ECR II-4381, affirmed in Case C-12/03P *Commission* v *Tetra Laval* [2005] ECR I-987.
[148] Press Release IP/02/1952.

> establish whether the evidence relied on is factually accurate, reliable and consistent but also whether that evidence contains all the information which must be taken into account in order to assess a complex situation and whether it is capable of substantiating the conclusions drawn from it.
>
> **Question**: How much discretion is left to the Commission under this test?

This is an important development in the law, and it indicates that the European Courts will exercise a close scrutiny of decisions by the Commission. The level of scrutiny will vary depending on the issue which is being examined.[149] As regards issues of law, the Courts are the final decision makers and do not have to defer to the European Commission's view. Control of factual matters is also regarded as intensive, as well as the inferences to be drawn from them. As regards the assessment of the facts, this is seen as a more restrained level of control although it has also been said that the scope of the margin of assessment will vary depending on the novelty or level of controversy surrounding the theory of harm in the case. This comes from both *Airtours* and *Tetra Laval*, where the Court referred to a 'close examination', 'convincing evidence' or a 'particularly plausible' analysis in the context of cases involving difficult issues of collective dominance and conglomerate effects. This suggests that although, in principle, the Court accepts that there may be problems in these sorts of cases, it will be more difficult for the European Commission to establish this than, for example, where horizontal issues are concerned and the issues are more straightforward.

Potentially of major significance are the GC and CJEU's recent decisions in *Schneider Electric*.[150] This arose out of the European Commission's prohibition of a merger between Schneider and LeGrand, which both produced electrical panel board components and various electrical equipment used in outfitting houses and offices. The Commission investigated the transaction and issued a prohibition decision. Unusually, the sale of LeGrand to Schneider had been contractually agreed in advance of the decision, so Schneider was required by the European Commission to divest LeGrand. The prohibition decision was challenged in front of the GC, which annulled it, finding, among other things, that there had been a breach of Schneider's rights of defence in that the European Commission had stated for the first time in its decision an objection to the merger that was not contained in the Statement of Objections, and the decision was therefore unlawful.[151] The case was remitted to the Commission for reconsideration and it again felt that the concentration raised competition problems. Schneider offered various commitments which the Commission felt would not solve the problems, so, before a decision was finally taken, Schneider sold LeGrand to another undertaking. Schneider then sued the European Commission under Article 340 TFEU which provides that in the case of non-contractual liability, the Union shall, in accordance with the general principles common to the laws of the Member States, make good any damage caused by its institutions or by its servants in the performance of their duties. Schneider

---

[149] For this argument, see B. Vesterdorp, 'Standard of Proof in Merger Cases' (2005) 1 *European Competition Journal* 3–33, from which the next three sentences are drawn, as well as the opinion of AG Tizzano in Case C-12/03P *Commission v Tetra Laval* [2005] ECR I-987.

[150] Case T-351/03 *Schneider Electric v Commission* [2007] ECR II-2237 [2008] 4 CMLR 22; Case C-440/07P *Commission v Schneider Electric* [2009] 5 CMLR 16.

[151] Case T-310/01 *Schneider Electric v Commission* [2002] ECR II-4071.

claimed damages of over €1.6 billion! Previous case law on this provision suggests that claimants have a heavy evidential burden to prove such a case as they must show a 'grave and manifest' disregard of the limits of the institution's discretion and that the losses flowed directly from the erroneous conduct. Here the GC found that the breach lay in the disregard of the rights of the defence of Schneider, not the errors that were committed in relation to the economic analysis. However, the GC awarded only limited damages to Schneider, which would have covered some of the fees it would have had to pay due to the re-examination of the case and partial compensation for having to sell LeGrand at a lower price than would have been usual. The GC's decision was appealed to the CJEU by the Commission but the CJEU upheld the GC's finding that there had been a sufficiently serious breach of a rule of law intended to confer rights on individuals. It did, however, set aside the decision of the GC to award compensation for the reduction in the sale price of LeGrand, holding that this was due to Schneider's own decision.[152] The decision does mark a significant step in the control operated by the European Courts over the decision making process in merger cases but the GC was not willing to see the errors of analysis in the *Airtours* case as being sufficiently serious to give rise to non-contractual liability.[153]

A number of themes come out of this case law. First, there has been substantial criticism of the factual basis of European Commission decisions and the analysis which was allegedly based on these factual foundations. This is expressed most clearly in *Airtours* and *Tetra Laval*, although it remains a worry even in the recent *Impala* case. Secondly, there are a number of procedural problems with the way the cases are run, most obviously in relation to *Schneider*, but also in the *Impala* case, where the implication was that the European Commission took too much notice of the views of the merging parties without giving third parties an appropriate opportunity to comment. Thirdly, the most controversial elements of these decisions relate to vertical effects, conglomerate effects and collective dominance. As regards non-horizontal effects, the Courts suggest that the European Commission needs a much better evidential base before acting on these theories of harm, although they accept that there may be anti-competitive effects in such situations.

Conclusions

There is no doubt that in procedural terms the MCR has been a success. It is generally clear which cases fall within the Commission's jurisdiction and there are various devices within the Regulation for ensuring that cases are dealt with at the appropriate level regardless of whether they meet the formal criteria in Article 1. It is more difficult to assess the overall performance of the Commission in terms of its substantive assessment. It is clear from the statistics given in Table 13.1 above that prohibition of mergers has been off the Commission's agenda since 2001, except in the very clearest cases. This has been noted and discussed in academic literature, although there is no consensus on why this might be so.[154] It may be a

---

[152] Case C-440/07P *Commission* v *Schneider Electric* [2009] 5 CMLR 16.

[153] Case T-212/03 *MyTravel Group* v *Commission* [2008] ECR II-1967.

[154] See F. Maier-Rigaud and K. Parplies, 'EU Merger Control five years after the introduction of the SIEC test: What explains the drop in enforcement activity?' [2009] 30 *European Competition Law Review* 565; O. Budzinski, 'An Institutional Analysis of the Enforcement Problems in Merger Control' (2010) 6 *European Competition Journal* 445.

reaction to the more searching review of Commission decisions by the GC and the court's reluctance to approve relatively novel or controversial approaches to mergers. It may also be that parties are just not bringing mergers which would be likely to be prohibited. Whatever the explanation, the practice of the Commission means that it is the design and selection of remedies to deal with identified anti-competitive problems that now takes centre stage.

COMPETITION LAW IN PRACTICE

The General Electric/Honeywell Merger

Background

In 2000, General Electric (GE) agreed to merge with Honeywell, in an arrangement which would make Honeywell a subsidiary of GE and which has been described as possibly the biggest industrial merger ever contemplated at the time; and it fell within the jurisdiction of both the European and US authorities. The proposal was notified to the European Commission in 2001, which ultimately decided to prohibit the merger, unlike the US authorities, which decided not to challenge it, after the parties had agreed to make certain minor modifications to the transaction. This makes a very good case study as it involves arguments over market definition, horizontal, vertical and conglomerate concerns, different approaches between the European Commission and the American authorities, as well as the role of the GC in reviewing such decisions.[155]

GE is one of the largest corporations in the world, with operations in a number of sectors, but in this context its key activity was the manufacture of jet aircraft engines. As well as manufacturing jet engines, GE leased aircraft to airlines through a subsidiary (GECAS), which bought new airplanes but only with GE engines, and arranged financing for various deals in the aerospace industry through another subsidiary, GE Capital. Honeywell is a technology and manufacturing company which, among other things, produces aerospace products and services of which the most important were jet engines, avionics and non-avionics products and engine controls. Avionics systems are equipment used for controlling the aircraft, while non-avionics systems relate to various sub-systems on an aircraft such as power, landing gear and environmental systems. Such systems can either be bought by the airlines or be supplied by the manufacturers of the aircraft.

The problems identified by the commission

The European Commission took the view that GE had a dominant position on the market for large commercial jet engines, basing this analysis on its market share as well as its operations in leasing aircraft to operators through GECAS and the financial strength provided by GE Capital. Honeywell it regarded as having a leading position on the avionics and non-avionics markets, but did not find that it was dominant.[156]

---

[155] There is a substantial literature on this case: see, for examples, J. Grant and D. Neven, 'The Attempted Merger Between General Electric and Honeywell: A Case Study of Transatlantic Conflict' (2005) 1 *Journal of Competition Law and Economics* 595; B. Nalebuff, 'Bundling, Tying and Portfolio Effects: Part 2 – Case Studies' (2003) DTI Economics Paper No. 1 (DTI, London), Sections 4 and 5; C. Caffarra and M. Pflanz, 'The economics of GE/Honeywell' (2002) 23 *European Competition Law Review* 115.

[156] European Commission, Case No. COMP/M. 2220, *General Electric/Honeywell* at para. 330.

According to the European Commission, competition problems arose in a number of areas. First, the European Commission took the view that the main effect of the proposed transaction on the markets for avionics and non-avionics products would be the combination of Honeywell's activities with GE's financial strength and vertical integration into financial services, aircraft purchasing and leasing, as well as into aftermarket services.[157] This would work through GE using its power in relation to aircraft leasing through GECAS or through arranging favourable financing through GE Capital, with such deals being conditional on the use of Honeywell products. In addition, the merged entity would also offer package deals, tying together the various products and possibilities of financing. The result would be that existing competitors would find it increasingly difficult, if not impossible, to compete with the merged entity and this was likely to lead them to exit the market.[158]

Secondly, Honeywell also manufactured engine controls, notably starters, which had the potential of creating a vertical relationship with GE's engine manufacturing business. Honeywell was the only independent supplier of engine starters as its main competitor supplied one of the other jet engine manufacturers exclusively. This would help to strengthen GE's position as a manufacturer of aircraft engines since the merged entity would have the incentive to delay or disrupt the supply of starters to GE's competitors as well as raise the prices.[159]

Thirdly, GE and Honeywell both produced jet engines for large regional jets and for medium corporate-sized jets – in other words, there were horizontal overlaps in their market activities. In the context of large regional jet engines, the result would be that the merged entity would have a market share of around 100%. For corporate jets, the market share would be around 60% of the installed base, rising to 90% for medium-sized jets. The result would be the withdrawal of any competitors from these markets.[160]

This was a highly controversial decision, especially as the US authorities had cleared the transaction. The US authorities took that view that GE was not dominant in the large jet engine market, that the financial strength of GE Capital was not a concern, more a reflection of its efficiency, that GECAS would not be able to tip the engine market through its policy of only buying GE engines, and that rivals were unlikely to leave the market. The US view was seemingly that the merger would simply create a more efficient company, which would make life more difficult for its competitors but this raised no competition problems.[161]

The GC's decision

GE and Honeywell challenged the decision before the GC, which upheld the prohibition, but only in relation to the finding of dominant position on the large jet engine

[157] Ibid. at para. 342.
[158] Ibid. at paras 347, 348, 354 and 398–400.
[159] Ibid. at para. 420.
[160] Ibid. at paras 434 and 444.
[161] See W. Kolasky, 'Conglomerate Mergers and Range Effects: It's A Long Way From Chicago To Brussels', available at *http://www.usdoj.gov/atr/public/speeches/9536.htm#P52_8017*; and D. Platt Majoras, 'GE-Honeywell: The US Decision', available at *http://www.usdoj.gov/atr/public/speeches/9893.htm* (both accessed 04/09/12).

market and the horizontal overlaps.[162] As regards perhaps the centrepiece of the European Commission's analysis, the idea that the merged entity would engage in bundling of its products and thus drive out competitors from the market, the GC found that the European Commission had no evidence of any past practice of bundling engines and avionic and non-avionic products, it did not have a credible economic analysis which would predict that bundling would take place and there was no evidence that this was going to be the future strategy of the merged entity.[163] As regards the vertical integration in relation to engine starters, the GC thought that it was obvious in this situation that the interests of the merged undertaking would be in favour of it disrupting its competitor's business.[164] However, such disruption would almost certainly be unlawful under Article 102 TFEU and it was incumbent on the European Commission to investigate whether this would be a sufficient deterrent on the merged entity to prevent it undertaking such conduct. As it had not undertaken such an analysis, this part of the decision could not stand.[165] In contrast, the GC found that the European Commission's analysis that the merger would create or strengthen a dominant position in the market for regional and corporate jet engines, despite an argument that the market had not been defined correctly, was defensible and that the merger could be prohibited on these grounds.[166]

Analysis

The case demonstrates a number of important issues. First, it shows just how controversial market definition and the assessment of the competitive constraints may be. Throughout the case, GE offered alternative bases for deciding upon its market share. For example, a significant proportion of its market share in commercial jet aircraft came from GE's engines being used exclusively on Boeing 737s, the most popular commercial jet aircraft in the world. If this was excluded, then GE's market share was reduced from around 65% to 44%. Secondly, the case shows how important it is to base worries about the conglomerate and vertical effects of mergers either on clear factual evidence or on convincing economic theories which can be validated in the particular context. As the GC points out, this is particularly important in the context of conglomerate mergers, where the behaviour may cover a period of time stretching far into the future and the 'chains of cause and effect following a merger may be dimly discernible, uncertain and difficult to establish'.[167] The European Commission fell down on both of these points, in particular through not having a credible economic theory to support its views on bundling.[168] Finally, it demonstrates the importance in EU merger control of review by the GC and just how carefully it will scrutinise decisions of the European Commission.

---

[162] Case T-210/01 *General Electric* v *Commission* [2005] ECR II-5575.

[163] Ibid., paras 438–73.

[164] Ibid., para. 297.

[165] Ibid., paras 286–314.

[166] Ibid., paras 474–584. There was also a horizontal overlap on small marine gas turbines (paras 585–620) which was also held to be incompatible with the common market.

[167] Ibid., para. 66.

[168] At one point it seemed to adopt one theoretical approach to bundling, only to resile from this in the final decision – see para. 352 of Case No. COMP/M.2220 *General Electric/Honeywell*.

Summary

➤ Mergers occur when two previously independent undertakings become one. They can be classified into horizontal, vertical and conglomerate mergers.

➤ When assessing mergers, a distinction is made between non-coordinated and coordinated effects. The former relate to the effects caused by the merged entity on its own, the latter to effects that the merger may have on the strategic behaviour of the remaining participants in the market.

➤ The European Merger Control Regulation applies to 'concentrations' which have a 'Community [Union] dimension'. This latter test is based on the amount of worldwide turnover and the turnover of the undertakings in Europe. This catches certain joint ventures and mergers which take place between undertakings which are not primarily based in Europe.

➤ Notification of a concentration is compulsory and the European Commission has 25 days to make a decision in phase 1 as to whether it has serious doubts about the compatibility of the concentration with the common market. If it does, it then has up to 105 days to make its decision in phase 2.

➤ When assessing a merger, the Commission asks if the concentration would significantly impede effective competition, in the common market or in a substantial part of it, in particular as a result of the creation or strengthening of a dominant position. If it does, then it must be declared incompatible with the common market.

➤ Parties to a merger may claim that the efficiencies in a merger outweigh the anti-competitive effects or that one of them was a 'failing firm'.

➤ Remedies in merger control can be divided into structural and behavioural remedies. A structural remedy is a remedy which has an effect on the structure of the market whereas a behavioural remedy is one that relates to the behaviour in the future of the parties to the merger. The European Commission's preference is for structural remedies.

➤ Merger decisions are reviewed by the GC under Article 263 TFEU.

Further reading

Reference works

Rosenthal, M. and Thomas, S., *European Merger Control* (Hart Publishing, Oxford, 2010). *Joint authored reference work.*

Official publications

European Commission, *Guidelines on the assessment of horizontal mergers under the Council Regulation on the control of concentrations between undertakings*, OJ C31, 05.02.2004, pp. 5–18.

European Commission, *Guidelines on the assessment of non-horizontal mergers under the Council Regulation on the control of concentrations between undertakings*, OJ C265, 18.10.2008.

Articles

Aigner, G., Budzinski, A. and Christiansen, A., 'The Analysis of Coordinated Effects in EU Merger Control: Where do we stand after *Sony/BMG* and *Impala?*' (2006) 2 *European Competition Journal* 311.

Biro, Z. and Parker, D., 'A New EC Merger test? Dominance versus Substantial Lessening of Competition' (2002) 1 *Competition Law Journal* 157. *General discussion of arguments for and against SLC test as opposed to dominance.*

Dethmers, F., Dodoo, A. and Morfey, A., 'Conglomerate Mergers under EC Merger Control: An Overview' (2005) 1 *European Competition Journal* 265.

Ezrachi, A., 'Behavioural Remedies in EC Merger Control – Scope and Limitations' (2006) 29 *World Competition* 459–80.

Kokkoris, I., 'The Development of the Concept of Collective Dominance in the ECMR: From its Inception to its Current Status' (2007) 30 *World Competition* 419–48.

Röller, L.-H. and de la Mano, M., 'The Impact of the New Substantive Test in European Merger Control' (2006) 2 *European Competition Journal* 9–28. *Chief Economist of the European Commission and colleague discuss what difference, if any, the new substantive test has made.*

Rose, V., 'Margins of Appreciation: Changing Contours in Community and Domestic Case Law' (2009) 5 *Competition Policy International* 3. *One of the CAT Chairmen gives her view on the extent of review by the European Courts and the CAT.*

Vesterdorf, B., 'Standard of Proof in Merger Cases: Reflections in the Light of Recent Case Law of the Community Courts' (2005) 1 *European Competition Journal* 3. *President of the GC reflects on the appropriate role for the Court in reviewing merger decisions.*

14 Merger control in the UK[1]

Chapter outline

This chapter discusses:

➤ What sorts of merger are controlled in the UK

➤ How does the OFT decide whether a merger should be referred to the Competition Commission?

➤ How does the Competition Commission decide whether a merger may be expected to result in a substantial lessening of competition (SLC)?

➤ The way public interest mergers are controlled

➤ The role of the Competition Appeal Tribunal in controlling decisions of the OFT and the Competition Commission.

Introduction

UK merger control was substantially reformed by the Enterprise Act 2002, which was the culmination of a lengthy process involving major changes to the entire regime of competition law in the UK. As regards merger control, the previous regime, based on the Fair Trading Act 1973, had been subject to severe criticism on three, interrelated grounds: the level of political interference in decisions; the lack of transparency in decision making; and the wide and nebulous public interest criteria applied to mergers. The aim of the 2002 Act was to address this criticism and it has been substantially successful in so doing. The economic issues facing the UK competition authorities in regard to mergers are the same as those facing the European Commission, and were discussed in the previous chapter, but the institutional structure and the legal tests to be applied for considering those issues are different. Initially, in this part of the chapter, we will examine the general rules for merger control, but there are specific provisions for public interest mergers and mergers in the media and water industries, which will be dealt with separately.

---

[1] For more detailed discussions, see J. Parker, A. Majumdar and S. Pritchard, *UK Merger Control* (Hart Publishing, Oxford, 2011).

The basic structure of UK merger control is that the OFT investigates mergers and, if the OFT feels that they raise a sufficiently serious competition problem, it is under a duty to refer them to the Competition Commission (CC), which will decide whether they are likely to lead to a substantial lessening of competition (SLC) and, if so, what to do about it. A major difference between the EU and the UK system is that it is not compulsory for merging firms to notify proposed mergers to the OFT; they may, if they so wish, complete the merger and take the risk that the authorities will decide it raised competition problems and has to be reversed. Thus the Enterprise Act 2002 has different provisions for completed and anticipated mergers. As we shall see, it is by no means uncommon for mergers to have been completed before they come to the notice of the OFT.

Although the Enterprise Act 2002 improved the working of merger control in the UK, there were still a number of problems with the existing system, notably the speed of decision making over the entire, two-phase system, and problems created by having a system of voluntary notification. These issues combined with the election of a coalition government in 2010 which wanted to review the role of public agencies led to a wide-ranging review of competition law and policy. The main result of this has been a decision to merge the OFT and the CC to create a new Competition and Markets Authority (CMA), while at the same time retaining the two-phase procedure for merger control. In addition, there are a number of more detailed changes which are planned, which will be referred to in the course of this chapter. The changes are contained in the Enterprise and Regulatory Reform Bill and are planned to come into effect in 2014.

In terms of activity, the OFT reports that since 2009 it has had between 70 and 100 cases each year which it has looked at, although not all of them have qualified for examination under the Enterprise Act 2002. In a small number of cases, around four to six each year, the OFT accepts undertakings in lieu of a reference to the CC. Only between seven and nine cases each year have been referred to the CC, which is on average 11–14% of qualifying cases.[2] Of those cases that are referred, a number each year are abandoned by the parties, presumably because they do not wish to go through the intensive CC procedure, which meant that between 2009 and mid-2012 the CC had completed on average around six merger cases per year.[3] It can be seen from this that mergers that raise competition concerns are a relatively small sub-set of all merger activity.[4]

Jurisdiction

A relevant merger situation arises under the Enterprise Act 2002 if two conditions are met (see Box 14.1). Like the MCR, the idea is that this test should provide clear rules as to when a merger is subject to review by the competition authorities, without having any implications as to whether the merger is likely to lead to an SLC. The OFT has estimated that around 80% of the cases that it looks at in one year will not raise any serious competition problems.[5]

---

[2] OFT, *Annual Report 2011–12* Annex D.

[3] Data in this paragraph is drawn from CC Annual Reports.

[4] The Office for National Statistics publishes information on merger and acquisition activity available at: *http://www.ons.gov.uk/ons/index.html* (accessed 15/08/12).

[5] OFT, *Mergers Procedural Guidance* (2003) at para. 5.16.

Qualifying mergers

- two or more enterprises cease to be distinct or there must be arrangements in progress or in contemplation which, if carried into effect, will lead to the enterprises ceasing to be distinct; *and*

- the value of the turnover in the UK of the enterprise being taken over exceeds £70 million; *or*

- in relation to the supply of goods or services of any description, at least one-quarter of all the goods or services of that description which are supplied in the UK, or a substantial part of it, are supplied by or to one and the same person (referred to as the 'share of supply test').

Source: Adapted from Enterprise Act 2002, s. 23.

Questions: What is the effect of inflation on these rules? Is share of supply the same as an economic market?

An enterprise for the purpose of the Act is simply the activities, or part of the activities, of a business,[6] so it is possible that the disposal of some of the assets of a firm to another may constitute a merger; it does not require the transfer of a legal entity. Enterprises will cease to be distinct when they are brought under common ownership or control. The Act makes allowance for three levels of control: a controlling interest (*de jure* or legal control), ability to control the policy of an enterprise (*de facto* control), and ability materially to influence the policy of an enterprise, all of which would bring a transaction within the scope of merger control. A controlling interest is taken by the OFT in general as meaning having a shareholding of above 50%, whereas the other two situations have to be assessed on a case-by-case basis.[7] The OFT presumes that a shareholding of 25% is enough to provide material influence (as it allows the shareholder to block special resolutions), and it will look at shareholdings of between 15% and 25%, although an important factor is whether the acquiring firm has, or is able to have, representation on the board.[8] The joint guidance suggests that the key question is whether the acquiring party is able, in practice, to exert influence.[9]

The other two limbs of the jurisdictional test point in slightly different directions. The turnover test of £70 million is designed to ensure that only transactions of sufficient importance are caught by the legislation.[10] The share of supply test, which is peculiar to UK merger

---

[6] Enterprise Act 2002, s. 129(1).

[7] OFT, *Mergers: Jurisdictional and procedural guidance* (2009) at para. 3.32; CC/OFT, *Merger Assessment Guidelines* (2010) at paras 3.2.5–3.2.19.

[8] OFT, *Mergers: Jurisdictional and procedural guidance* (2009) at paras 3.15–3.28.

[9] CC/OFT, *Merger Assessment Guidelines* (2010) at para. 3.2.10. For an example, see *British Sky Broadcasting Group plc v the CC and the Secretary of State* [2008] CAT 25.

[10] There was some controversy over the appropriate limit during the passage of the Enterprise Act. The government at one point was suggesting a £40 million threshold; the House of Lords raised this to £100 million, which was altered to the final figure of £70 million.

control, catches transactions which fall beneath the turnover test but look like they may have an important effect on the supply of goods and services in the UK. This latter test is not equivalent to a market definition exercise, as the OFT and the CC make clear in their guidelines, which also say that they will have regard to any reasonable description of a set of goods and services to determine whether this test is met.[11] The result is that quite small transactions in local markets may fall within merger control, particularly as there is no statutory definition of what constitutes a substantial part of the United Kingdom and the leading case simply says that the area or areas considered must be of such size, character and importance as to make it worth consideration for the purposes of merger control.[12] A recent, perhaps extreme, example would be the acquisition by Vue Entertainment of A3 and its sole operating subsidiary, Ster. Vue operated some 48 cinemas in the UK, while Ster operated just six. The OFT decided that the share of supply test had been met solely in relation to Edinburgh, while the CC noted that it was also met in Basingstoke, Norwich and Romford, which meant effects on a combined population of around 1.17 million or just under 2% of the population at the time. The conclusion was that the merger was likely to lead to a substantial lessening of competition in relation to cinema exhibition in Basingstoke and the remedy was for Vue to divest one of its two cinemas in that town.[13] Given the public costs of a merger reference to the CC, in excess of £400,000 in general, and Ster's profit before tax in 2004 was only £2.1 million, there is an issue as to whether the UK system catches mergers where the benefits of the process are outweighed by its costs. As will be seen, the OFT has some discretion in relation to small mergers, which is discussed below.

The role of the OFT in controlling mergers in the UK

OFT procedure

There are two main procedures that may be used for notifying the OFT of a merger (it looks as if the broad outline of this process will not change once the OFT is transformed into the CMA). The first is a voluntary statutory pre-notification procedure under s. 96 of the Enterprise Act 2002. This procedure is available only for anticipated mergers which have been publicly announced and the required information must be submitted on a prescribed form, along with the requisite fee. Once the form is submitted, the OFT has 20 working days to decide whether to make a referral to the CC. If it has not made a decision within this period, the merger is automatically cleared. The OFT's view is that this procedure is really only suitable for mergers where there is no material anti-competitive concern and the parties need clearance within a fixed time period.[14] The second main procedure is what is known as an informal submission and this is available for all types of mergers, both anticipated and completed. Unlike the

---

[11] CC/OFT, *Merger Assessment Guidelines* (2010) at para. 3.3.5; and OFT, *Mergers: Jurisdictional and procedural guidance* (2009) at para. 3.35.

[12] *R v Monopolies and Mergers Commission, ex parte South Yorkshire Transport* [1993] 1 WLR 23.

[13] Competition Commission, 'Vue Entertainment Holdings (UK) Ltd and A3 Cinema Ltd' (2006). Note also OFT, 'Arriva/Stagecoach' (2007) which involved the acquisition of assets relating to bus services in Darlington, Durham, Stockton and Hartlepool.

[14] OFT, *Mergers: Jurisdictional and procedural guidance* (2009) at para. 4.54.

statutory procedure, there is no strict timetable, but the OFT tries to ensure that a decision is taken within 40 working days of notification, assuming that all the relevant information is provided.[15]

As there is no duty on the parties to notify a merger, the beginning of the process is more difficult to follow than in the European context. The easiest place to start is with anticipated mergers which the parties are going to notify to the OFT. Notification is not a simple process and a great deal of information is required by the OFT, as under the MCR. It is therefore sensible to make contact with the OFT to discuss exactly what sort of information will be required, especially as most parties use the informal submission route where there is no pre-scribed form to complete. In addition to this meeting, the OFT offers two means of obtaining pre-notification information: informal advice and pre-notification discussions. Informal advice is given for confidential transactions where there is a good faith intention to proceed and evidence of ability to do so and a genuine issue in relation to the duty to refer. Advisers are expected to articulate the theory of harm that might be considered in the case.[16] The informal advice given by the civil servants involved is explicitly stated not to be binding on the OFT, which is sensible, given that the advice will be based solely on the parties' evidence. Pre-notification discussions take place when parties have decided to notify the merger and want to discuss the notification with the OFT. The discussion will cover a variety of areas, such as the information that needs to be provided, an explanation of the transaction, a discussion of how certain issues might be approached and whether it might be possible to avoid a reference by offering undertakings.[17]

Given that there is no duty to notify a merger before it takes place, the competition authorities in the UK may have to assess completed mergers. The Enterprise Act 2002 provides that the OFT must make a decision on them within four months after it has been given notice of the material facts. Notice, in this context, includes the transaction being made public, which means that it is generally known or readily ascertainable – in other words, there is no obligation to tell the OFT about the merger.[18] When the OFT discovers a completed, but non-notified, merger, it may request the parties to make an informal submission or it may exercise its powers to request information from the parties.[19] A failure to comply with the statutory request means that the clock stops running. In addition, in relation to completed mergers, the OFT has powers which it can use to try to stop the integration of the two enterprises continuing.[20] As the OFT points out, completing a merger without notifying the OFT runs a number of risks, of which the most serious is that, after a reference to the CC, the CC could order the merger to be undone.[21]

Once a merger has been notified to the OFT there is a reasonably clear process that takes place before a decision is made on whether to refer a merger to the Competition Commission.[22] The OFT will typically consult third parties such as competitors or customers,

---

[15] Ibid. at para. 4.65. The Enterprise and Regulatory Reform Bill will introduce a statutory time limit of 40 working days for the first phase.

[16] Ibid. at para. 4.32.

[17] Ibid. at paras 4.42–4.48.

[18] Enterprise Act 2002, s. 24.

[19] Enterprise Act 2002, s. 31.

[20] Enterprise Act 2002, ss. 71–72.

[21] OFT, *Mergers: Jurisdictional and procedural guidance* (2009) at paras 4.21–4.24.

[22] Ibid. at s. 6.

either through a general invitation to submit comments or, in some cases, approaching specific third parties. The majority of cases, around 80% the OFT estimates, do not raise competition issues and are dealt with within the mergers group by means of a decision paper which is looked at by an internal OFT review group. If the merger raises more difficult issues, an 'issues' letter, setting out the case for a reference to the CC, is sent to the parties by the case officer and they are invited to an issues meeting with the mergers group. The parties may respond in writing, orally or via both methods. Following this meeting, an outline decision will be drafted which is subject to scrutiny by an internal case review meeting where, typically, one person will act as a 'devil's advocate' against the outline decision. After the case review meeting there will then be a decision meeting at which the decision to refer the merger to the CC, or not, will be taken.

Substantive assessment: the decision to refer

The statutory rules that the OFT operates under in deciding whether to make a reference are set out in Box 14.2. It should be noted that the OFT is under a duty to make a reference if it believes that it is or may be the case that a relevant merger may be expected to result in a substantial lessening of competition.

KEY LEGAL PROVISION   **Box 14.2**

The OFT's duty to make a reference

The OFT shall make a reference to the CC if the OFT believes that it is or may be the case that either:

- a relevant merger situation has been created, or that

- arrangements are in progress or in contemplation which, if carried into effect, will result in the creation of a relevant merger situation; and

- the creation of that situation may be expected to result in a substantial lessening of competition within any market or markets in the United Kingdom for goods or services.

Source: Enterprise Act 2002, ss. 22 and 33 (the box combines the two provisions with some excisions).

The precise approach that the OFT should take to this test has been the subject of some controversy and formed the subject matter of the first appeal to the CAT under the Enterprise Act in *IBA Health* v *OFT*.[23] This involved the acquisition by iSOFT of Torex, both companies supplying IT systems to the NHS. Although the OFT found that the post-market merger shares of the parties would be substantial, either 39% or 44% depending on how measured, no reference was made, largely because a new procurement system for IT in health care was being launched and therefore it felt that past market shares were not a good guide to market power

---

[23] [2003] CAT 28; [2004] EWCA Civ 142 (CA).

in the future. This decision was challenged by a competitor and the OFT's initial decision was quashed by the CAT and the CAT's decision was upheld by the Court of Appeal, although there was disagreement over the appropriate approach to take. The CAT favoured a two-part test, which meant that the OFT must be satisfied that: (i) as far as the OFT is concerned there is no significant prospect of a substantial lessening of competition; and (ii) there is no significant prospect of an alternative view being taken in the context of a fuller investigation by the CC.[24] The Court of Appeal rejected this approach as running against the words of the Enterprise Act 2002 and having the consequence that it would make other provisions unworkable. By contrast, the Court of Appeal took the view that the OFT had to have a belief, which was reasonable and objectively justified by the facts, that it is or may be the case that the relevant merger situation may be expected to result in an SLC. What this meant is that a greater than 50% chance of an SLC was certainly encompassed by these words, but it was also possible that, if the OFT thought that the possibility of an SLC was more than merely fanciful, but less than 50%, it could also make a reference.[25] This approach has been reflected in the joint CC/OFT Guidelines (see Box 14.4). The *IBA* case was remitted to the OFT for it to decide again: although it was decided that a reference should be made, there was no need to do so as iSOFT offered to divest itself of the entire business of Torex, thus removing the potential competition problems.[26]

The OFT's approach to the substantive question, what constitutes an SLC, is similar to that of the CC, as represented by their joint guidelines although there are some differences because the OFT is undertaking a first phase inquiry within a more limited time frame than the CC. Discussion of the approach and the issues is dealt with in more detail below. Here we concentrate on those matters which impinge on the first phase in particular. The OFT's approach is to consider two related issues: the first is the definition of the market; and the second is the competitive effects of the merger on the market.[27] Market definition has been discussed earlier (see Chapter 1). Given its role, the OFT will usually make an initial estimate of the relevant market, but may not reach a definitive conclusion, as this is not always necessary at the first phase.[28] Having defined the market, the OFT may use market shares and concentration measures, although when it does this, it will do so on the basis of narrowest defined market.[29] Although there are no clear safe harbours, the Guidelines suggest that the OFT is less likely to identify competition concerns in cases with certain thresholds. In horizontal mergers of firms with undifferentiated products, the OFT is unlikely to be concerned if the combined market shares are less than 40%. For non-horizontal mergers, it does not have sufficient experience but will take into account the European Commission's guidance, and is unlikely to be concerned if the market share of the merged firm is less than 30%. Given that vertical mergers are later said generally to be efficiency enhancing, this tougher treatment is inconsistent. In relation to mergers involving retailers, the OFT has not usually been concerned about mergers that reduce the number of competitors from five to four (or above). To put it another way, a 3-to-2 merger would raise concerns. As regards the HHI, the

---

[24] Ibid. at para. 197.
[25] Ibid. at paras 43–9.
[26] OFT, 'iSOFT/Torex' (2004).
[27] CC/OFT, *Merger Assessment Guidelines* (2010) at para. 5.1.1.
[28] Ibid. at para. 5.2.4.
[29] Ibid. para. 5.3.5.

view is that any market with a post-merger HHI of 1,000 or over is concentrated, while a post-merger HHI of 2,000 or over is highly concentrated. In a concentrated market a delta[30] of 250 or less is unlikely to cause concern, while in a highly concentrated market a delta of 150 or less is unlikely to cause concern. Some examples to illustrate this point are given below (Box 14.3).

HHI EXAMPLES   Box 14.3

Market A: 10 firms, each with a market share of 10%. This produces an HHI of 1,000 (concentrated). If two firms merge, then there are 8 firms with a market share of 10% and 1 firm with a market share of 20%. The HHI is 1,200 ($[10^2 \times 8] + [20^2 \times 1]$) which means that the delta is 200.

Market B: 6 firms, 3 with market shares of 20%, one with a market share of 30% and two with market shares of 5%. This gives an HHI 2,150 (highly concentrated): ($[20^2 \times 3] + [30^2 \times 1] + [5^2 \times 2]$) If the firm with 30% market share merges with one of the firms with 5% market share this gives an HHI of 2,450: ($[20^2 \times 3] + [35^2 \times 1] + [5^2 \times 1]$). The delta here is 300. Interestingly, this would be a 6-to-5 merger, which the Guidelines suggest, in a retail context, is not a problem.

Question: In 2011, it was estimated that market shares for supermarkets in the UK were as follows:

	Market share	Market share squared
Aldi	3.6	13
Co-Op	6.9	48
Lidl	2.6	7
Sainsbury	16.1	259
Waitrose	4.3	18
Asda	17.1	292
Iceland	1.9	4
Morrisons	11.7	137
Tesco	30.5	930
Others	5.3	18
Total	100	1,726

On the basis of the guidance, this is a concentrated market. On the basis of the HHI guidance, which mergers, if any, would require further thought by the competition authorities?

By comparison, the US Department of Justice/Federal Trade Commission Guidelines on mergers have a slightly more relaxed approach. Unconcentrated markets have an HHI below 1,500, moderately concentrated markets have an HHI between 1,500 and 2,500 and highly concentrated markets have and HHI above 2,500. Any increase in the HHI of less than 100 is not considered a problem. In moderately concentrated markets, any increase of an HHI above 100 is likely to raise significant competition concerns. In a highly concentrated market, increases in the HHI between 100 and 200 raise significant competitive concerns while an increase of more than 200 points will be presumed to increase market power.[31]

[30] This is neatly explained in Department of Justice/Federal Trade Commission, 'Horizontal Merger Guidelines' (2010) at s. 5.3: 'The increase in the HHI is equal to twice the product of the market shares of the merging firms. For example, the merger of firms with shares of five percent and ten percent of the market would increase the HHI by 100 ($5 \times 10 \times 2 = 100$).'

[31] Ibid. at s. 5.3.

KEY LEGAL PROVISION   **Box 14.4**

When is a reference made to the CC?

In considering whether to refer a merger to the CC, the OFT must form a reasonable belief, objectively justified by relevant facts, as to whether or not it is or may be the case that the merger has resulted, or may be expected to result, in an SLC. The OFT must make a reference to the CC when it believes that the merger is more likely than not to result in an SLC. The Act also contemplates reference at lower ranges of probability. If the OFT believes that the relevant likelihood is greater than fanciful, but below 50 per cent, it has a wide margin of appreciation in exercising its judgement. In such cases, it has a duty to refer when it believes there to be a realistic prospect that the merger will result in an SLC.

Source: CC/OFT, *Merger Assessment Guidelines* (2010) at paras 2.5–2.6.

There are, however, certain exceptions to this duty. No reference shall be made:

- if the merger raises 'public interest' considerations (strictly defined, see below),
- if the OFT is deciding whether to accept undertakings in lieu of a reference,
- where undertakings have been accepted in lieu of a reference,
- where the Secretary of State has accepted undertakings in a public interest case,
- if the statutory pre-notification procedure has been used and the time period has elapsed,
- if a request has been made under Article 22 of the MCR for the European Commission to look at a merger, or
- if a reasoned submission under Article 4(5) has been made requesting that the European Commission deal with that decision.[32]

There are also three situations where the OFT has discretion ('may') not to make a reference even though it thinks that there may be competition concerns:

- where the arrangements are not sufficiently far enough advanced to make a reference worthwhile,
- where the customer benefits outweigh the SLC and its adverse effects, and
- if the market is not of sufficient importance.

These latter two are worth an explanation, as is the OFT's practice in relation to undertakings in lieu of a reference.

The exception of markets of insufficient importance is primarily designed, as the OFT explains, to avoid references where the costs would be disproportionate to the size of the markets involved and, at the time of writing, the OFT explained that the average public cost of a CC reference was in the order of £400,000.[33] This discretion seems to be exercised around half a dozen times a year. The OFT guidance makes it clear that markets are of sufficient importance if their total value is above £10 million. Where the annual turnover in the

---

[32] Enterprise Act 2002, ss. 22(3) and 33(3).

[33] OFT, *Mergers: Exceptions to the duty to refer and undertakings in lieu of reference guidance* (2010), paras 2.3, 2.7 and 2.11.

markets is less than £3 million, and there are no clear-cut undertakings which may be made in lieu of a reference, the OFT would not expect generally to make a reference in such a case.[34] In the range between £3 million and £10 million the basic test is whether it feels that the benefits of the reference to the CC, in terms of remedying customer harm, will outweigh the costs of the reference. The OFT looks at three broad issues: in principle, are undertakings in lieu of a reference available, whether the customer harm resulting from the reference is likely to exceed the costs of the reference and would the reference be proportionate, taking into account the wider implications of any decision.[35] As regards undertakings, the OFT takes a conservative, in principle, approach. In other words, the undertakings have to clearly solve the competition problem that has been identified – most usually when they involve divestiture of part of the transaction to an independent third party. When considering the issue of consumer harm, the OFT will look at the interaction of four variables:[36]

1 the size of the market

2 the strength of the OFT's concern that harm will occur

3 the magnitude of the competition lost as a result of the merger, and

4 the durability of the merger's impact.

When considering the size of the market, the OFT is only concerned with markets where there is a realistic prospect of an SLC because not all aspects of a merger will raise competition concerns. For example, in the Atlas Copco/Penlon merger, the parties' activities overlapped in manufacture of plant supply and equipment, and manifolds and valves, as well as in installation and maintenance services. The OFT did not see a realistic prospect of an SLC in any of these activities but did see one in the provision of terminal units, because the combined share of supply was around 90%. But because the size of the market was so small, the OFT exercised its discretion not to refer.[37] The OFT will also consider the future prospects for the market and, if turnover in the market is 'lumpy' (e.g., when the market consists of contracts which are periodically re-tendered), it will consider the value over a number of years. In terms of the magnitude of competition, the OFT generally thinks that 2-to-1 (that is, merging the only two significant competitors) and 3-to-2 mergers would typically be expected to lead to large price increases and/or quality and innovation cutbacks.[38] A good example of this was the proposed merger between Dods and Dehavilland, which both provided political intelligence services, on a market the OFT estimated as worth between £3 and £8 million. On the OFT's interpretation of the market, they saw this as a merger between the two largest rivals in the market that would not face other constraints. The loss of such a rivalry could, the OFT felt, lead to a substantial deterioration in the competitive conditions on the market. The OFT therefore did not treat this as a *de minimis* case and referred the merger to the CC and the transaction was abandoned.[39] The OFT will also consider whether a substantial proportion of any likely detriment will be felt by vulnerable customers.

---

[34] For example, OFT, 'Rentokil Initial/Connaught' (2011).

[35] OFT, *Mergers: Exceptions to the duty to refer and undertakings in lieu of reference guidance* (2010) para. 2.16.

[36] Ibid. at para. 2.28.

[37] OFT, 'Atlas Copco/Penlon' (2011).

[38] OFT, *Mergers: Exceptions to the duty to refer and undertakings in lieu of reference guidance* (2010) para. 2.36.

[39] OFT, 'Dods/DeHavilland' (2012). Contrast OFT, 'Sports Universal/Prozone' (2011), a 2-to-1 merger but with mitigating factors such as potential entry and technological change.

The issue of the wider impact of small mergers is neatly illustrated by looking at the bus industry. In its report on local bus services, the CC recommended that the OFT take a cautious approach to the exercise of its *de minimis* discretion in these cases because small operators (on a national scale) could have a significant impact on local markets and the cumulative effect of anti-competitive conduct and/or a number of individually small mergers can be substantial, both within individual bus markets and sometimes more widely.[40] An illustration would be the acquisition of by Midland General of Felix Bus Services commercial services, which involved services between Ilkeston and Derby. Although the size of the market was small, around £1 million, it involved a 2-to-1 merger, so the OFT considered the exercise of its discretion carefully. It decided to exercise the discretion not to refer, because Felix was likely to exit, it was not a particularly strong competitor and the transaction was very small and therefore not replicable (six buses were involved).[41] The case is also a good example of the OFT using this discretion to cut down the costs of the first phase inquiry as Midland General was willing to waive its procedural rights to the extent that the OFT would exercise its discretion not to refer.

As for the exception on relevant customer benefits, these are defined in the Enterprise Act 2002 as improvements in price, quality or choice in goods or services or greater innovation in relation to them. The benefit must have accrued as a result of the relevant merger situation, be likely to take effect within a reasonable period and to have been unlikely to have been created without the merger.[42] The OFT says that these will be rare cases and that the claimed customer benefits must be clear and that the evidence must be compelling, that is, there must be detailed and verifiable evidence provided by the parties to substantiate their claims. There must be incentives for the parties to pass on the benefits to their customers and will outweigh the consequences of the SLC. It is in principle possible that the benefits can occur in a separate market from the one where the SLC has arisen and outweigh the effects of the SLC.[43]

Undertakings in lieu of a reference

As regards undertakings in lieu of a reference, these may occur only where the OFT has decided that it is going to make a reference to the CC. The Enterprise Act 2002 provides that the OFT may accept such undertakings, in order to prevent an SLC or any adverse effects arising from it. In accepting such an undertaking, the OFT is required to have regard to achieving as comprehensive a solution as possible and to have regard to relevant customer benefits.[44] The OFT takes the view that undertakings in lieu of a reference are therefore appropriate only where the competition concerns raised by the merger and the remedies proposed to address them are clear-cut, and those remedies are capable of ready implementation; this involves about half a dozen cases a year. Undertakings are offered by the parties to the merger, the OFT has no power to impose them, it can only choose from amongst the options which are offered. The OFT takes the view that it must be confident that all the potential competition concerns that have been identified in its investigation would be resolved by means of the undertakings

---

[40] CC, 'Local bus services' (2009), paras 15.344 and 15.357.

[41] OFT, 'Midland General/Felix Bus Services' (2012).

[42] Enterprise Act 2002, s. 30.

[43] OFT, *Mergers: Exceptions to the duty to refer and undertakings in lieu of reference guidance* (2010), paras 4.1–4.13. For an example see: OFT, 'Ordnance Survey/Local Government Improvement and Development' (2011) at paras 94–101.

[44] Enterprise Act 2002, s. 73.

in lieu without the need for further investigation because once it accepts the undertakings, it is no longer able to make a reference to the CC. For that reason it says:

> Undertakings in lieu of reference are therefore appropriate only where the remedies proposed to address any competition concerns raised by the merger are clear cut. Furthermore, those remedies must be capable of ready implementation.[45]

This means that there must be no material doubt about the effectiveness of the remedy and that monitoring the implementation of it would not require unworkable resources. The starting point would be to return competition to the levels existing before the merger and to remedy or prevent competition concerns, rather than just mitigate them. This leads, typically, to a preference for structural remedies, since a merger is a change to the structure of the market, which means, normally, the sale of one of the overlapping businesses. The OFT's starting point is to require the divestment of the business that has been acquired, although it will consider other alternatives. As part of such a remedy, the OFT will require that it should be able to approve the purchaser in order to ensure that the purchaser meets its standard criteria, which are:[46]

- acquisition by the proposed purchaser remedies, mitigates or prevents the SLC concerned or any adverse effect which has or may have resulted from it, or may be expected to result from it;
- the proposed purchaser is independent of and unconnected to the merging parties;
- the proposed purchaser has the financial resources, expertise (including the managerial, operational and technical capability), incentive and intention to maintain and operate the relevant business in competition with the merged party and other competitors in the relevant market;
- the proposed purchaser is reasonably to be expected to obtain all necessary approvals, licences and consents from any regulatory or other authority; and
- the acquisition by the proposed purchaser does not itself create a realistic prospect of a substantial lessening of competition within any market or markets in the UK.

The divestment typically has to be done within a certain period. If the divestment is not accomplished, or does not look like being accomplished, then there is normally provision for the appointment of a divestment trustee who may sell the assets at no minimum price if the sale has not been accomplished in the period.[47] The trustee and the mandate under which they will work will need the approval of the OFT. In certain circumstance the OFT will seek an upfront buyer before agreeing to the undertakings in lieu. This may be the case where there are doubts about the viability of the package to be divested or where there are only a small number of possible purchasers.[48]

The OFT is generally sceptical about whether behavioural remedies will provide a clear-cut solution to the competition problems identified.[49] Behavioural remedies bring their own

---

[45] OFT, *Mergers: Exceptions to the duty to refer and undertakings in lieu of reference guidance* (2010), para. 5.7.
[46] Ibid. at para. 5.26.
[47] Ibid. at para. 5.33.
[48] Ibid. For an interesting example of where a proposed divestiture failed because of a lack of a purchase see: OFT, 'General Healthcare Group' (2011).
[49] Ibid. at paras 5.38–5.43.

risks; for example, some of them can increase price transparency and make it easier for competitors to collude or coordinate. They also reduce the incentives for innovation. They are difficult to design in a way that leaves no loopholes and breaches of them may go undetected. The costs of monitoring compliance may also be significant. Finally, it is more difficult to design such remedies within the first phase of a merger assessment, where time is limited.[50]

It is for this reason that undertakings in lieu have typically been used in merger cases in the past where a substantial lessening of competition arises from an overlap that is relatively small in the context of the merger (e.g. a few local markets affected by a national merger).[51] So, for example, in the *Pendragon/Reg Vardy* merger,[52] Pendragon, which was involved in the sale and servicing of new cars, among other things, acquired Reg Vardy, which had some 96 car dealerships throughout the UK. The OFT decided that there would be an SLC in four local areas and that it had a duty to refer the merger to the CC. Pendragon undertook to divest those four dealerships and the OFT took the view that this met the competition concerns and therefore did not make the reference. There have, however, been instances where behavioural undertakings have been accepted in lieu of a reference. In *Tetra Laval/Carlisle*, granting of exclusive irrevocable intellectual property rights to a named purchaser was seen as a solution to an SLC in relation to particular cheese-making equipment, while in *FlyBe/BA Connect*, where the problem was loss of competition on air routes between Southampton and Manchester, the problem was solved by FlyBe undertaking to, among other things, vacate a parking slot at Southampton, which would allow new entry.[53]

The role of the Competition Commission in controlling mergers in the UK

Procedure before the Competition Commission

On receipt of a reference from the OFT, the CC begins a new investigation, although it receives the OFT papers, with a time limit of around six months. Once a reference has been made to the CC, the chairman will appoint a group for that specific reference, usually consisting of five members, one of whom will chair the inquiry.[54] The CC gathers a substantial amount of information in written form from the parties and invites submissions from anyone else who may be interested in the merger. After this fact-finding stage, which may include hearings with the parties or with other interested parties, the CC will then produce what is known as an 'Issues Letter', which is its first effort at identifying the issues at stake in the merger. This will typically be followed by a main hearing with the parties to the merger, as well as continuing with other hearings and obtaining other evidence as necessary. This process ultimately culminates in the CC issuing a provisional decision as to whether the merger will lead to an SLC. If the answer is yes, at the same time the CC will issue a remedies notice, which sets out its initial thoughts on what would be the appropriate remedies for the

---

[50] For an example where behavioural remedies were offered but rejected see: OFT, 'McGill's Bus Services/Arriva Scotland' (2012), a merger which was cleared by the CC.

[51] OFT, *Mergers: Substantive Assessment Guidance* (2003), para. 8.3.

[52] OFT, 'Pendragon/Reg Vardy' (2006).

[53] OFT, 'Tetra Laval/Carlisle' (2006); OFT, 'FlyBe/BA Connect' (2007).

[54] Often this will be the chairman or one of the deputy chairmen of the CC.

case in hand. After the issue of provisional findings there is a period of consultation, primarily aimed at the main parties, so that they can put forward any reasons as to why the CC should alter its provisional findings. In general, the CC confirms its provisional findings but there have been cases where the view changed from a finding of an SLC to one of no SLC between the provisional findings and the final report because new evidence was submitted. In one case, the CC had assumed in its provisional findings that the target company would have remained in business and therefore its acquisition would have led to an SLC, but received evidence after the provisional findings that in fact the company would have exited the market and therefore the acquisition did not lead to an SLC.[55]

A couple of aspects of this process are worth noting. Unusually for a competition authority, the CC makes extensive use of oral hearings with interested parties. Generally these are private meetings between the group in charge of the inquiry and the parties concerned, at which the group seeks to understand the evidence and arguments underlying the parties' positions. Hearings are a formal affair, with a written transcript being taken, and the main parties will usually arrive with their legal representatives and their economic advisers, although the idea is that most of the questions are answered by the parties rather than their advisers.

Although the detailed discussions between the CC and the parties remain confidential, the process as a whole is very transparent. The main CC documents are always published on the website and supporting information and analysis may also be published, such as surveys. Main parties will typically provide a version of their evidence that can also be published on the CC website and submissions from third parties, or summaries of them, will also usually be published. Although confidential information is excised from these publications, it is certainly relatively easy to see the main lines of argument used in most inquiries.

It is worth remembering that the decision of the CC is the decision of the particular inquiry group, typically five members, and that the system allows for majority judgments. So, for example, in *Francisco Partners*, the merger was allowed to proceed, but only on a 3–2 vote of the group members.[56]

With the creation of the CMA a number of aspects of this process will change. Instead of having two separate institutions, the phase 1 and phase 2 processes will be conducted within the same institution. For phase 2 inquiries, the CMA will maintain a panel of members available to form inquiry groups as required. The inquiry group will be constituted as required by the chair of the CMA and they will be supported by CMA staff.[57]

Substantive assessment by the Competition Commission

The statutory questions that the CC has to answer in an inquiry are set out in Box 14.5. If the CC decides that a merger is likely to result in an SLC, then it must go on to ask if it should take action to remedy the SLC or any adverse effects resulting from it or recommend the taking of action by others to remedy the SLC.[58] In deciding what to do, the CC is required to find as comprehensive a solution as possible and to take into account relevant customer benefits.[59]

---

[55] CC, 'British Salt' (2005).
[56] CC, 'Francisco Partners/G International' (2005).
[57] Generally see Enterprise and Regulatory Reform Bill, Schedule 4. Bill 61 2012–13.
[58] Enterprise Act 2002, ss. 35(3) and 36(2).
[59] Enterprise Act 2002, ss. 35(4)–(5) and 36(3)–(4).

KEY LEGAL PROVISION   **Box 14.5**

Questions for the CC

The Commission shall decide the following questions:

- whether a relevant merger situation has been created, or
- whether arrangements are in progress or in contemplation which, if carried into effect, will result in the creation of a relevant merger situation, and
- if so, whether the creation of that situation may be expected to result in a substantial lessening of competition within any market or markets in the United Kingdom for goods or services.

Source: Enterprise Act 2002, ss. 35 and 36 (the box is a combination of the provisions).

The merger assessment guidelines make it clear that in order for it to reach a conclusion that an SLC is expected, it will have to consider that this outcome is more likely than not, which means a greater than 50% chance.[60] When assessing the merger, the CC will draw up what are called 'theories of harm'. These provide the framework for assessing the effects of a merger and whether it could lead to an SLC. They describe possible changes arising from the merger, any impact on rivalry and expected harm to customers as compared with the situation likely to arise without the merger.[61] The CC is not restricted to the theories of harm identified by the OFT in the first phase.[62] In applying the statutory test, the CC says that it will evaluate the competitive constraints on firms with the merger as compared to what would have been the case without the merger (the counter-factual). Typically, this would be in the absence of the merger under consideration, although this need not always be the case. The three examples given in the Guidelines of where a different counter-factual would be used are:[63]

- the exiting firm scenario;
- the loss of potential entrant scenario; and
- where there are competing bids and parallel transactions.

The questions on the exiting firm scenario are whether the firm would have exited and, if so, would there have been an alternative purchaser for the firm, other than the acquirer and what would have happened to the assets of the firm in event of the exit. For example, in the proposed Stagecoach/Preston Bus merger, Stagecoach argued that Preston Bus was a failing firm which would have gone out of business and could not have been successfully restructured by another company. Therefore, without the merger, Stagecoach would have ended up as the dominant bus supplier in Preston and there was not, therefore, an SLC. The CC did not accept

---

[60] See CC/OFT, *Merger Assessment Guidelines* (2010) at para. 2.12 and *IBA Health Ltd* v *OFT* [2004] EWCA Civ 142 at para. 46.

[61] Ibid. at para. 4.2.1.

[62] Ibid. at para. 4.2.6.

[63] Ibid. at para. 4.3.7.

this analysis, arguing that Stagecoach had, prior to the merger proposal, engaged in abnormal competition with the aim of removing Preston Bus from the market or making it unattractive for a purchaser.[64] Regardless of who is correct, and Stagecoach unsuccessfully challenged the CC's report before the CAT,[65] this is a good illustration of how the selection of the counter-factual may determine the outcome of a case.

In relation to the loss of a potential entrant, the CC will consider whether the counter-factual situation should include the entry by one of the merger firms into the market of the other firm or, if already within the market, whether the firm would have expanded had the merger not taken place.[66] When it comes to competing bids and parallel transactions, for the CC it depends on the circumstances of the case.[67] When one transaction is referred to the CC, the counter-factual will be either the pre-merger competitive situation or the sale of the company to an alternative bidder. If all the potential bids are referred to the CC, the counter-factual is usually the pre-merger situation, although the CC may consider the possibility of a sale to a party that does not raise competition concerns. If two or more bids are referred to the CC, but other bids are not, then the counter-factual is likely to be the sale to a purchaser that does not raise competition concerns or the pre-existing situation.

KEY LEGAL PROVISION   Box 14.6

Substantive merger analysis by the OFT and CC

(a) market definition;

(b) measures of concentration;

(c) horizontal mergers – unilateral effects (including any vertical effects of horizontal mergers);

(d) horizontal mergers – coordinated effects;

(e) non-horizontal mergers – unilateral and coordinated effects;

(f) efficiencies;

(g) entry and expansion; and

(h) countervailing buyer power.

Source: CC/OFT, *Merger Assessment Guidelines* (2010) at para. 5.1.2.

Unlike the European Commission, almost all of the CC's merger investigations under the Enterprise Act 2002 have been concerned with horizontal mergers, for which there is a well-understood methodology for determining whether there is an SLC, even though there may be great controversy about its application to particular facts. A summary of the approach taken to substantive assessment by *both* the OFT and the CC is provided in Box 14.6 The CC's approach is to consider two related issues: the first is the definition of the market; and the

---

[64] CC, 'Stagecoach/Preston Bus' (2009) at paras 6.1–6.6.
[65] *Stagecoach* v *Competition Commission* [2010] CAT 14.
[66] See CC/OFT, *Merger Assessment Guidelines* (2010) at para. 4.3.19.
[67] Ibid. at paras 4.3.20–4.3.29.

second is the competitive effects of the merger on the market.[68] According the joint guidance, a merger gives rise to an SLC when it has a significant effect on rivalry over time, and therefore on the competitive pressure on firms to improve their offer to customers or become more efficient or innovative.[69] There are said to be three main reasons why a merger may give rise to an SLC:[70]

1 unilateral effects

2 coordinated effects

3 vertical or conglomerate effects.

Unilateral effects arise in horizontal mergers, where the merger involves two competing firms and removes the rivalry between them, allowing the merged firm to profitably raise prices. The loss of competition may be either for an existing or a potential competitor. The Guidelines distinguish between markets with undifferentiated and differentiated products (e.g. cement versus cars). As regards undifferentiated products they say:[71]

> unilateral effects are more likely where: the market is concentrated; there are few firms in the affected market post-merger; the merger results in a firm with a large market share . . . ; and there is no strong competitive fringe of firms. Unilateral effects resulting from the merger are more likely where the merger eliminates a significant competitive force in the market.

On the basis of what is said earlier in the Guidelines, a concentrated market is one where the post-merger HHI exceeds 1,000, a large market share is where the market share of the post-merger firm is above 40% and few firms means that the number of firms in the market has been reduced from four to three.[72]

For differentiated products, the question is whether those products compete closely.[73] Typically what stops a firm raising prices is that it will lose profit because customers will go to other firms; either the other firm involved in the merger or other competitors. If the products are close substitutes, unilateral effects are more likely because, if the merged firm raises prices, it will recapture a significant share of the sales lost because of the price rise because customers will switch to the other firm involved in the merger. Also, if customers are not price sensitive, then unilateral effects are more likely, since the loss of profits from a price rise will be less. Finally, if variable profit margins (sales revenue minus the direct cost of sales) are high, again unilateral effects are more likely. The CC will also want to look at the possible responses of other suppliers and whether they would respond to a price rise by raising their own prices and whether they have the capacity to meet demand from customers who would like to switch.

As for potential competition, there are said to be two possibilities.[74] The first is where the merger removes actual potential competition, that is, a firm likely to enter in the absence of the merger which would increase competition. The second is where the merger removes perceived potential competition, that is, a firm that is not in the market but there is a threat that it would enter if prices were increased.

---

[68] Ibid. at para. 5.1.1.
[69] Ibid. at para. 4.1.3.
[70] Ibid. at para. 4.1.5.
[71] Ibid. at paras 5.4.4–5.4.5.
[72] Ibid. at para. 5.3.4.
[73] Ibid. at paras 5.4.6–5.4.12.
[74] Ibid. at paras 5.4.13–5.14.18.

According to the guidance, 'Coordinated effects may arise when firms operating in the same market recognise that they are mutually interdependent and that they can reach a more profitable outcome if they coordinate to limit their rivalry.'[75] Coordinated effects may also occur in the context of horizontal and non-horizontal mergers. Coordination can involve keeping prices higher but it may also involve other aspects of competition such as the amount produced, the allocation of markets and territories, etc. It can also be explicit or tacit. In looking at this issue, the question is whether the conditions in the market are conducive to coordination. An initial question is whether there was coordination prior to the proposed merger and, if so, whether the merger will make that more or less difficult. Typically a merger in a market where there are already coordinated outcomes would be likely to lead to an SLC. Outside this, for coordination to be possible, there are three conditions:[76]

(a) Firms need to be able to reach and monitor the terms of coordination.

(b) Coordination needs to be internally sustainable among the coordinating group – i.e. firms have to find it in their individual interests to adhere to the coordinated outcome.

(c) Coordination needs to be externally sustainable, in that there is little likelihood of coordination being undermined by competition from outside the coordinating group.

On the first point, relevant questions are the number of firms in the market, the complexity of the environment and the transparency of the actions of the firms.[77] Coordination is more likely in a market with few firms, homogeneous products and transparent transactions. Internal sustainability depends on whether there is sufficient profit from coordination and whether there are sufficient devices for punishing those who deviate from the coordination.[78] On external sustainability, the question is whether someone from outside the coordinating group can change things. This will involve consideration of the effectiveness of any competitive fringe, whether entry barriers are high or low, customer buying power and if there are any maverick firms.[79]

As regards vertical or conglomerate effects, the Guidelines start with the observation that 'it is a well-established principle that most [non-horizontal mergers] are benign and do not raise competition concerns.'[80] There are three questions which are asked in these cases:[81]

(a) *Ability*: Would the merged firm have the ability to harm rivals, for example through raising prices or refusing to supply them?

(b) *Incentive*: Would it find it profitable to do so?

(c) *Effect*: Would the effect of any action by the merged firm be sufficient to reduce competition in the affected market to the extent that, in the context of the market in question, it gives rise to an SLC?

To reach an SLC finding, all of these questions need to be answered in the affirmative. It is also clear that the questions may overlap and do not necessarily divide neatly. The Guidelines go on to discuss various possible theories of harm which might occur in this situation. The

[75] Ibid. at para. 5.5.1.
[76] Ibid. at para. 5.5.9.
[77] Ibid. at paras 5.5.10–5.5.14.
[78] Ibid. at paras 5.5.15–5.5.16.
[79] Ibid. at paras 5.5.17–5.5.18.
[80] Ibid. at para. 5.6.1.
[81] Ibid. at para. 5.6.6.

most detailed discussion relates to partial input foreclosure, that is, where an upstream firm which supplies an input downstream merges with a downstream customer and then raises the price of its supply to other downstream customers that are not competitors with it.[82] There are a number of questions here: how important is the input in the price of the final product, are there alternative sources of supply, could the increased prices be passed on to customers? In addition, increasing the price may mean a loss of profit on this market as the downstream firms switch to other suppliers, this might be compensated for by a general rise in prices on the downstream market which means customers switch to the merged firm's products but this will depend on their quality and the price sensitivity of customers. It also depends on the relative profitability of the upstream and downstream markets. The other possibilities are total input foreclosure, where the merged firm will not supply downstream at all, and customer foreclosure.[83] This is where in mergers involving a manufacturer and a distributor, the distributor either raises the prices of rivals' good or stops stocking them altogether. With conglomerate mergers, the potential concern is with the tying and bundling of related products in a way that would put rivals at a disadvantage if they were unable to offer the bundle.

Efficiencies

Unlike the MCR, the UK system provides explicitly for the consideration of efficiencies in relation to mergers. In order to make out an efficiency case:[84]

(a) the efficiencies must be timely, likely and sufficient to prevent an SLC from arising (having regard to the effect on rivalry that would otherwise result from the merger); and

(b) the efficiencies must be merger specific, i.e. a direct consequence of the merger, judged relative to what would happen without it.

The Guidelines go on to consider various examples of the types of efficiencies that can be claimed, dividing them into two categories: supply side (cost savings) and demand side (product improvements).[85] Supply side efficiencies may include cost reductions through economies of scale, better production processes and better coordination of production and distribution. The competition authorities are more interested in reductions in marginal costs as these tend to stimulate competition and be passed on to consumers, rather than reductions in fixed costs, which they say tend to be taken as profit by the firms concerned. Vertical mergers may also allow the new firm to remove any pre-existing double mark-ups. For example, if there is a manufacturer and a distributor, both will set prices independently and charge a mark-up. Because of the separate incentives on the firms, this maybe result in prices which are too high and this could be removed by the merger. A merged firm may also have greater incentives to invest and it may also result in product repositioning, although the effects of this are more difficult to judge. On the demand side, examples of efficiencies given are network effects, pricing effects and one-stop shopping. Network effects arise where the combined platform is more attractive to the customers. Pricing effects may happen where the products are complements and reducing the price of one product increases the demand for it and other, related products.

[82] Ibid. at paras 5.6.9–5.6.12.
[83] Ibid. at para. 5.6.13.
[84] Ibid. at para. 5.7.4.
[85] Ibid. paras 5.7.1–5.7.18.

Barriers to entry and expansion

The final point of analysis for the CC will be the reaction of other firms to the merger. It is possible that new entry into the market, or expansion by existing firms in the market, may prevent an SLC from arising. The CC also recognises that simply the threat of new entry may be sufficient, although this is felt to be rare.[86] It requires entry to be so quick and costless that an entrant could profitably come into the market to exploit an opportunity afforded by high prices even if the merged firm quickly responded to the entry by lowering its prices.[87] For the entry or expansion to prevent an SLC it must be: timely, likely and sufficient.[88] In assessing the likelihood of entry, one of the key questions is what barriers to entry exist and the guidance points to four broad categories:[89]

1 Absolute advantages, e.g., government regulations limiting the number of market participants.

2 Intrinsic or structural advantages, e.g., arising from technology, production methods or other factors necessary to establish an effective presence in the market. This will be more of an issue if a significant proportion of the costs are sunk.

3 Economies of scale: this tends to prevent small scale entry and large scale will be successful only if it expands the market or replaces one of the existing firms.

4 Strategic advantages, e.g. through experience or reputation or customer loyalty.

As well as looking at the scale of barriers to entry, the CC will look at the likelihood of entry and whether firms have the ability or incentive to enter. As an example, the Guidelines point out that a market may have low barriers to entry, but firms will be discouraged from entry by its small size. The entry also has to be of sufficient scope and it must be timely, that is, within two years. In assessing this issue, there are a number of factors that are looked at, including the history of past entry and expansion, evidence of planned entry and expansion, the costs involved and the period of time over which such costs can be recovered, to mention some of them.[90]

Finally, there is the question of whether there is any countervailing buyer power which will help to prevent an SLC.[91] This can arise either through the ability to switch to other suppliers, to sponsor new entry into the market or to enter the market by itself via vertical integration. Even if the buyers have no or limited choice they may still be able to impose costs on the supplier, for example through not buying other products from the supplier. The questions for the CC is whether, if any group of buyers have countervailing buyer power, this will protect the entire group of buyers.

Remedies

Under the Fair Trading Act 1973, remedies were a matter for the Secretary of State, who made the final decision, based on recommendations from the CC and the OFT, although the Secretary of State was not bound by these recommendations and departed from them in a

---

[86] Ibid. at para. 5.8.2.
[87] Ibid. at para. 5.8.14.
[88] Ibid. at para. 5.8.3.
[89] Ibid. at paras 5.8.5–5.8.7.
[90] The complete list is at ibid. para. 5.8.12.
[91] Ibid. at paras 5.9.1–5.9.8.

significant number of cases. Under the new arrangements, the decision on remedies in cases where an SLC is found is a matter primarily for the CC and the CC has published specific guidance on its approach to remedies.[92]

Under the Enterprise Act 2002, the CC considers first whether it should take action to remedy the SLC and also whether it should recommend that others (e.g. government departments or regulatory agencies) should take action. The CC is required to have regard to achieving as comprehensive a solution as is reasonable and practicable for the SLC and any adverse effects resulting from it.[93] When deciding on the remedies to be imposed, the CC may have regard to effects on any relevant customer benefits, which are defined as lower prices, higher quality, greater choice or greater innovation.[94] The benefit must have occurred because of the relevant merger and have been unlikely to occur without the merger and the relevant lessening of competition and the burden is on the parties to provide evidence of this.[95] Having said this, the CC's view is that it is not normally to be expected that a merger leading to an SLC would provide benefits for customers.[96]

When deciding on the implementation of remedies, the CC has a choice of accepting undertakings from the parties or, if that is not possible, imposing an Order on the parties. The CC's preference is for the former path because, in part imposing an order is subject to the limitations on the order-making power in Schedule 8 to the Enterprise Act 2002.[97] Like the European Commission and the OFT, the CC has a preference for structural over behavioural remedies, because structural remedies are likely to deal with an SLC and its resulting adverse effects directly and comprehensively at source by restoring rivalry; behavioural remedies may not have an effective impact on the SLC and its resulting adverse effects, and may create significant costly distortions in market outcomes; and structural remedies do not normally require monitoring and enforcement once implemented.[98]

Table 14.1 gives some crude figures for the number of cases decided, the amount of SLCs found and the remedies decided upon, split between those decisions where the merger was prohibited and other remedies. There have been a limited number of prohibitions by the CC but what the table does not show is that the most common form of remedy is to require a partial divestment in those markets where the CC has found that there is an SLC. A good example of this is when Somerfield acquired 115 mid-range stores (that is, not convenience stores or one-stop shop (large) supermarkets) from Morrisons. Competition in relation to these types of supermarket is something that takes place at a local level and the CC analysed the level of competition in relation to each of the stores and concluded that, in 12 cases, acquisition of the stores would lead to an SLC and in 103 cases there was no competition problem. Somerfield was required to sell the 12 stores to a purchaser that would maintain the stores as an active and viable competitor.[99] By contrast, the CC has only used behavioural undertakings in four cases,[100] and in one of those, LSE, the transaction did not go ahead.

---

[92] CC, *Merger Remedies* (2008).

[93] Enterprise Act 2002, ss. 35(4) and 36(3).

[94] Enterprise Act 2002, s. 30.

[95] Enterprise Act 2002, s. 30(2)–(3).

[96] CC, *Merger References* para. 4.35.

[97] The Enterprise and Regulatory Reform Bill amends Schedule 8 to deal with some of the limitations.

[98] CC, *Merger Remedies* (2008) at para. 2.14.

[99] CC, 'Somerfield Plc and Wm Morrison' (2005).

[100] CC, 'Drager/Air Shields' (2004); 'Firstgroup/Scotrail' (2004); 'London Stock Exchange' (2005); 'Macquarie UK/National Grid' (2008).

Table 14.1

Year[101]	References decided	No SLC	SLC	Prohibition	Other remedy
2004	10	6	4	2	2
2005	12	8	4	2	2
2006	7	6	1	0	1
2007	13	4	9	3	6
2008	2	1 (3–2)	1	–	1
2009	6	4	2	–	2
2010	2	2	–	–	–
2011	7	6	1	–	1
	59	37	22	7	15

Completed mergers

Remedies issues also arise at an earlier stage in the process. Given that there is no requirement to notify the competition authorities in advance of a merger, the parties may decide to complete the merger before receiving approval or, indeed, before the competition authorities are aware of the merger. When these completed mergers come to the attention of the competition authorities, it becomes necessary to put some provisions in place to ensure that the businesses remain sufficiently separate whilst the investigation is being conducted so that no remedies, typically a divestiture, will be compromised. There is some evidence that the number of completed mergers dealt with by the OFT and CC has risen, possibly, because the parties believe it is possible that the OFT will not investigate their merger. This has led to a number of cases where the CC has ended up unscrambling the transaction to a greater or lesser extent when it has found that there has been an SLC.[102] This was an issue which concerned the government when it was considering the reform of competition policy. The radical option that was considered was to move from a voluntary to a compulsory notification regime, similar to the EU one, but this proved to be very unpopular and was rejected. Instead, the Enterprise and Regulatory Reform Bill provides new powers for the CMA to make an order preventing the parties to a merger from taking pre-emptive action before a merger has been properly considered. The Bill also provides that financial penalties may also be imposed on parties that do not comply with these orders.[103]

Public interest, media and water mergers

For a limited category of mergers, there are special arrangements. Although political influence has largely been removed from the merger process, the Secretary of State still has a role to play in public interest and media cases through having the power to make a reference to the CC, and to be the ultimate decision maker. The power to make references exists in 'public interest' cases, which is defined as those matters specified in s. 58 of the Act or, if they are not so specified, which ought, in the opinion of the Secretary of State, to be so specified.[104]

---

[101] Source: using data from *http://www.competition-commission.org.uk/inquiries/completed/index.htm* (accessed 04/09/12).

[102] See S. Pritchard, 'Caveat emptor . . . or, getting the deal stuck – contemporary issues in UK merger control', 10 September 2007, available at: *http://www.oft.gov.uk/news/speeches/2007/0307* (accessed 17/08/12).

[103] Business Enterprise and Regulatory Reform Bill, Clauses 22 and 23. Bill 61 2012-13.

[104] Enterprise Act 2002, s. 42(3).

Section 58 specifies national security, stability of the financial system and the accurate presentation of news, free expression of opinion and the need for a plurality of news in newspapers, as well as the need for plurality of media ownership, a wide range of broadcasting and a genuine commitment by those in control of media enterprises to the attainment of standards set out in the Communications Act 2003. The mechanism by which this procedure works is that the Secretary of State issues an intervention notice to the OFT, specifying the public interest considerations which are regarded as relevant to the merger situation. The OFT[105] then reports back to the Secretary of State and the report will include, *inter alia*, decisions on whether there has been a substantial lessening of competition, and advice and recommendations on the public interest considerations. The Secretary of State is then empowered to make a reference to the CC either on the basis of the substantial lessening of competition and the public interest concerns or, even if there is no substantial lessening of competition, only on the basis of the public interest concerns.[106] The Secretary of State is obliged to accept the CC's findings on the competition issues, but may make a decision on the public interest question and, in so doing, has the remedial powers of the CC.

The second circumstance where the Secretary of State may make a reference is under s. 59,[107] which relates to mergers involving government defence contractors, newspapers supplying more than one-quarter of that type of newspaper, and broadcasting involving at least one-quarter of that type of broadcasting in the United Kingdom, or a substantial part of it; these are referred to as 'special public interest cases'. A similar mechanism of report by the OFT, and Ofcom[108] in the relevant cases, and power to refer to the CC is created here with the ultimate decision on the public interest issues resting with the Secretary of State. One significant difference is that it is assumed that there are no competition issues in these cases and the CC is only obliged to report on the public interest issues.

There have been three high-profile cases using these procedures. The first involved BSkyB's acquisition of a 17.9% shareholding in ITV. Here the Secretary of State issued an intervention notice on the grounds that the transaction raised concerns about there being sufficient plurality of persons with control of media enterprises for the audience. As this was a media merger, both the OFT and the Office of Communications (Ofcom) compiled reports, with the former focusing on the competition issues and the latter on the issues of media plurality. The OFT came to the conclusion that there was a risk of an SLC, broadly because BSkyB's shareholding could influence ITV's corporate strategy and dilute competition by free to air digital offerings and BSkyB's paid for offering, while Ofcom had concerns over media plurality. As a result, the Secretary of State referred the transaction to the CC on both issues. The CC concluded that there was likely to be an SLC on the all TV market, although not in relation to advertising or news, but that there were no plurality concerns in relation to news. The Secretary of State accepted the conclusions of the CC and accepted the CC's recommendations on remedies which combined a reduction of the stake to 7.5% and related behavioural undertakings from BSkyB. The report of the CC and the subsequent decision of the Secretary of State were challenged in the CAT by BSkyB, which challenged the finding that there was a relevant merger situation and the SLC finding, and Virgin Media, which challenged the conclusion

---

[105] Ofcom will also make a report in media cases.
[106] Enterprise Act 2002, s. 45.
[107] As amended by the Communications Act 2003, s. 378.
[108] The Office of Communications, responsible for the regulation of communications markets.

that there was no public interest problem.[109] The CAT dismissed BSkyB's challenges but found in favour of Virgin, on the grounds that the CC had misconstrued s. 58A(5) of the Enterprise Act 2002 when assessing the plurality issue. The CAT's decision was challenged in the Court of Appeal, which upheld the findings on a relevant merger situation and the SLC, but reversed the CAT's view on media plurality.

The second major case came about as a result of the banking crisis in late 2008 and involved the takeover of HBOS by Lloyds TSB. Here the merger was agreed between the two companies in September 2008 and the government agreed that it would provide financial support to the combined group, conditional on the merger going ahead;[110] the merger was referred to the OFT in early October. By the end of October, the Enterprise Act 2002 had been amended to include the stability of the financial system as a relevant public interest matter within s. 58 so that this merger could be dealt with under this procedure. The OFT report to the Secretary of State concluded that the merger was likely to lead to an SLC in relation to personal current accounts and that there was a realistic prospect of an SLC as regards the mortgage market. The OFT therefore recommended that the merger should be referred to the CC for further investigation.[111] The Secretary of State declined to make such a reference, giving as his reason that the interests of financial stability of the UK banking system outweighed the competition issues.[112] A further twist came when a body called the Merger Action Group challenged the Secretary of State's decision before the CAT but this challenge was rejected by the CAT.[113]

As regards the Lloyds TSB/HBOS merger it has been argued quite strongly that the government's decision to allow the merger was mistaken, not least because of the problems for competition policy that it might create for the future.[114] As discussed earlier (see Chapter 7), the European Commission has required Lloyds to divest itself of a significant number of branches as part of the price for receiving state aid, which suggests that the OFT's analysis was correct. Leaving that point aside, the procedure by which the decision was made was markedly more open than would have been the case prior to the Enterprise Act 2002. Not only was the OFT's report published prior to the decision but the Secretary of State was required to give reasons for his decision not to refer the merger to the CC and for the decision to amend the Enterprise Act to allow this process to take place. From that perspective, it can be argued that the process was a success.

The most high-profile public interest merger has been the proposal by NewsCorp, a media company controlled by its then Chairman and Chief Executive Rupert Murdoch and his family, who at the time owned *The Sun*, *News of the World* and *The Times*, as well as around 39% of the shares in BSkyB, to purchase the remaining 60% of the outstanding share capital of BSky B. The proposed merger qualified as a concentration with a Community [Union] dimension

---

[109] *British Sky Broadcasting Group* v *Competition Commission* [2008] CAT 25, *British Sky Broadcasting* v *Competition Commission* [2010] EWCA Civ 2.

[110] It has never been clear to what extent the government encouraged the merger.

[111] OFT, 'Anticipated acquisition by Lloyds TSB plc of HBOS plc' (2008).

[112] 'Decision by the Secretary of State not to refer to the Competition Commission the merger between Lloyds TSB Group and HBOS', available at *http://www.berr.gov.uk/whatwedo/businesslaw/competition/mergers/public-interest/financial-stability/index.html* (accessed 26/07/09).

[113] *Merger Action Group* v *Secretary of State* [2008] CAT 36.

[114] J. Vickers, 'The Financial Crisis and Competition Policy: Some Economics' (2008) *Global Competition Policy*, December, 2.

and was examined by the European Commission, which decided that the proposed merger would not significantly affect competition within the EU.[115] At that point the Secretary of State for Business, Innovation and Skills (BIS)[116] issued what is called a European intervention notice[117] and asked the OFT to investigate whether there was a merger as defined by the Enterprise Act and Ofcom to investigate the issues of media plurality and whether a reference ought to be made to the CC. The issue was that the acquisition would bring together one of the three main providers of TV news with the largest provider of newspapers. The effect of the merger would have been that the merged group was the second largest provider of news in the UK, behind the BBC.[118] Ofcom recommended that the issue should be referred to the Competition Commission for fuller investigation. Before a decision could be made by the Secretary of State for BIS, extracts from a conversation between himself and two journalists, posing as his constituents, were published in *The Daily Telegraph* under the headline, 'I have declared war on Rupert Murdoch'.[119] This statement obviously disqualified him from making an impartial decision on the proposed merger and so responsibility for the decision making was transferred to the Secretary of State for Culture, Media and Sport.[120] The Secretary of State for the DCMS was minded to refer the matter to the Competition Commission but, before doing so, he gave NewsCorp and BSkyB the chance to offer undertakings which would meet the concerns over plurality.[121] After some discussion between the agencies and the parties, undertakings were offered which dealt with the plurality concerns. There was further consultation on the content of the undertakings and a further revised set of undertakings were published on 30 June 2011 for consultation with the intention that they would be accepted and no reference to the Competition Commission would be made. The week after that, the phone hacking scandal at the *News of the Word* entered the public domain and gave rise to, among other things, the Leveson inquiry into the ethics of the press.[122] NewsCorp withdrew its offer of undertakings at that point. As a result of these events, the Secretary of State for the DCMS decided to refer the matter to the Competition Commission. NewsCorp then abandoned its bid for BSkyB.

The case is interesting for a number of reasons. It highlights the difficulty of involving politicians as the ultimate decision makers in mergers, especially media mergers. In the same way that Dr Vince Cable was not considered impartial, allegations have also been made that Jeremy Hunt was not impartial in relation to the merger and that there was substantial informal contact between Jeremy Hunt and advisers to NewsCorp. Although in the process of negotiating undertakings, Jeremy Hunt took the advice of Ofcom and the OFT, such allegations do undermine the credibility of the process, particularly in the context of a process

---

[115] Case COMP/M.5932.

[116] Who at the time was Dr Vince Cable.

[117] This is a mechanism provided in the Enterprise Act 2002, ss. 67–8 in order for the UK to invoke the protection of legitimate interests exception under Article 21 (4) MCR.

[118] For discussion, see Ofcom, 'Report on public interest test on the proposed acquisition of British/Sky Broadcasting Group plc by News Corporation' (2010); paras 1.16–1.48 give a summary of Ofcom's view.

[119] See *http://www.telegraph.co.uk/news/politics/liberaldemocrats/8217253/Vince-Cable-I-have-declared-war-on-Rupert-Murdoch.html* (accessed 22/08/12).

[120] HC Debs 18 January 2011 col. 35WS. The relevant minister was Jeremy Hunt.

[121] The relevant documentation can be found at: *http://www.culture.gov.uk/what_we_do/media_mergers/7880.aspx* (accessed 22/08/12).

[122] *http://www.levesoninquiry.org.uk/* (accessed 22/08/12).

where there are close personal relationships between various actors.[123] These sort of allegations have been made in past about mergers, but it is interesting to see how much more information about the process now comes into the public domain, partly because of the arrangements put in place by the Enterprise Act 2002. It also highlights how decisions based on public interest criteria, such as media plurality, may be more intractable than the economic considerations about the effect of a merger on competition where there is a reasonably agreed framework to ask specific questions.

Mergers between water companies are treated differently, because water companies are local monopolies, which are regulated by the Office of Water Services (Ofwat) on the basis of a regulatory technique which fundamentally depends on the ability of Ofwat to compare the performance of the water companies against each other. A reduction in the number of water companies, through merger, thus makes it more difficult for Ofwat to use this regulatory technique. The Water Industry Act 1991 provides that the OFT has a duty to refer mergers between water companies, without having to consider whether the merger will lead to an SLC. There is an exception for small mergers, defined as being where the value of the enterprise being taken over is not greater than £10 million.[124] The question for the CC is not whether an SLC has been created, but whether the merger may be expected to prejudice the ability of Ofwat, in carrying out its functions, to make comparisons between companies.[125] An example of a water merger has been the merger of Mid Kent Water and South East Water, where the CC decided that the merger would prejudice the ability of Ofwat to make comparisons, but that this would be a limited prejudice. The CC allowed the merger, but insisted on a one-off price reduction to mitigate the adverse effects of the merger, as well as trying to ensure that the benefits of the merger were passed on through the regulatory process.[126] There has been concern that these provisions are too rigid and the government is proposing to alter them by giving the OFT a power not to make a reference if it feels that the merger will not prejudice the ability of Ofwat to carry out its regulatory functions or, even if it does prejudice its ability, the prejudice is outweighed by the relevant customer benefits arising from the merger. The OFT is also being given the power to accept undertakings in lieu of a reference. In both types of cases, before making a decision, the OFT must seek the opinion of Ofwat on the effect of the merger on its ability to carry out its functions.[127]

Review of OFT and CC decisions by the Competition Appeal Tribunal

Section 120 of the Enterprise Act 2002 provides that any person who is aggrieved by a decision of the OFT or the CC may apply to the CAT for a review of that decision and, in deciding that application, the CAT will apply judicial review principles.[128] This is an important safeguard

---

[123] There is voluminous documentation available on the Leveson inquiry website. See in particular the evidence for 24 April 2012 and HC Debs 25 April 2012 col. 955 which is Jeremy Hunt's response to the allegations.

[124] Water Industry Act 1991, ss. 32–3.

[125] Enterprise Act 2002, s. 36(1), as modified by reg. 11 of the Water Mergers Regulations.

[126] See CC, 'Mid-Kent Water/South-East Water' (2007).

[127] Draft Water Bill, Clauses 12 and 13.

[128] Decisions of Ofcom and the Secretary of State under this legislation may also be reviewed.

but it is a more limited jurisdiction for the CAT than it has in relation to decisions under the Competition Act 1998 for breaches of Articles 101 and 102 TFEU and the equivalent domestic provisions. In those cases, there is an appeal which may go to the merits of the decision, whereas, in the context of mergers, the CAT is only allowed to look at the legality of the decision. Under the previous legislation, the Fair Trading Act 1973, challenges to decisions of the competition authorities through judicial review had been rare and were almost always unsuccessful. Under the new arrangements, challenges have occurred regularly and with greater success, even though the grounds of review have not changed.

The starting point was the *IBA Health* case, which involved a challenge to the decision of the OFT not to refer a merger to the CC. Although the central issue was about the interpretation of the OFT's duty to refer, the CAT also considered the general issue of its approach to judicial review. Here the CAT observed that judicial review principles varied according to the context of the case and that it was created as a specialised tribunal, possibly implying that it might take a more interventionist approach than a non-specialised tribunal.[129] In the Court of Appeal, Carnwath LJ took the view that the ordinary principles of judicial review were flexible enough to be adapted to the particular context and, although the existence of a specialised tribunal would aid consistency and speed of decision making, there was no difference in the substantive principles to be applied.[130] The argument that a more interventionist approach should be taken by the CAT because it is a specialised tribunal has been consistently rejected since this case.[131]

The second case involving a challenge to an OFT decision not to refer a proposed merger was *Unichem v Office of Fair Trading*.[132] This case involved a proposed merger between Phoenix Healthcare, which engaged in wholesale distribution of pharmaceutical products across the UK, as well as running retail pharmacies, and East Anglian Pharmaceuticals, which was a wholesaler of pharmaceuticals in East Anglia. In terms of the wholesale supply of pharmaceuticals in East Anglia, which was the relevant geographic market, this meant a reduction in suppliers from four to three. After giving confidential guidance and assessing the merger proposal, the OFT decided not to refer the merger to the CC, primarily on the grounds that the remaining two wholesalers, one of which was Unichem, would be well placed to offer a competitive constraint to the merged entity. Unichem challenged this decision on a number of grounds, the main ones being that the OFT had relied on the merging parties' assessment of whether Unichem could compete with them, as opposed to checking these factual contentions with Unichem. The CAT took the view that the Tribunal has jurisdiction, acting in a supervisory rather than appellate capacity, to determine whether the OFT's conclusions are adequately supported by evidence, that the facts have been properly found, that all material factual considerations have been taken into account, and that material facts have not been omitted; and, in addition, whether a fair procedure has been followed must also be taken into account.[133] Although the CAT thought that the decision was finely balanced, it came to the conclusion that the OFT did not have a sufficient factual basis for key elements of its decision and that the failure to seek Unichem's comments on certain issues was a key

[129] *IBA Health Ltd* v *OFT* [2003] CAT 28, [2004] EWCA Civ 142 (CA) at paras 218–20.
[130] Ibid. at para. 100.
[131] See *Stagecoach Group* v *Competition Commission* [2010] CAT 14 at para. 41.
[132] [2005] CAT 8.
[133] Ibid. at para. 174.

procedural failing, which led the CAT to quash the decision and remit it to the OFT for a new decision, whereupon the OFT took into account Unichem's evidence and came to the same conclusion.[134]

In terms of the intensity of review, this case has set the standard for the approach taken by the CAT and the only other subsequent challenge to a decision of the OFT not to refer was unsuccessful.[135] The intensity of review can be illustrated by looking at the *Stagecoach* case.[136] This was a merger between Stagecoach and Preston Bus. The key issue in this case was what the relevant counter-factual should be and at what point it should have been considered to exist. Stagecoach has argued that Preston Bus was a failing firm which would have left the market. The CC rejected this argument, saying that the failure had been brought about through the non-commercial activities of Stagecoach and that the appropriate counter-factual was to look at how the market would have developed in the absence of Stagecoach acting in a way that was non-commercial. Stagecoach argued that this decision was irrational on *Wednesbury* grounds, as there was no evidence that its activities were non-commercial. The CAT reviewed the evidence and the CC's reasoning carefully and came to the conclusion this was not a finding that was open to the CC on the evidence before it. This did not affect the main conclusion that the merger had given rise to an SLC. Attempts to challenge CC decisions in relation to remedies in merger cases, as opposed to an SLC finding, have been unsuccessful; although Virgin was successful in the *BSkyB* case, this was on a matter of interpretation of the statutory provisions.[137]

What should be evident from this brief discussion is that the role of the CAT in reviewing decisions of the OFT and the CC in the context of merger inquiries has become a real constraint. It is not only that applicants have had some success in the context of OFT decisions, but it is also evident in the unsuccessful cases that the CAT scrutinises the decision making process very carefully as well as the factual basis underlying the decision.

Conclusions on the UK

At the time of writing, major changes to the institutional structure of UK merger control will be taking place by merging the OFT and the CC to form a new CMA. No substantive change to the basic rules is envisaged, although the Enterprise and Regulatory Reform Bill does make changes which are intended to speed up the process and to deal with some of the issues arising out of the problem of completed mergers. The area of merger control which has been most problematic has been that of public interest mergers but no change is contemplated here.

---

[134] OFT, 'Phoenix Healthcare/East Anglian Pharmaceuticals' (2005).
[135] *Celesio* v *OFT* [2006] CAT 9.
[136] *Stagecoach Group* v *Competition Commission* [2010] CAT 14.
[137] *Somerfield* v *Competition Commission* [2006] CAT 4; *Stericycle International* v *Competition Commission* [2006] CAT 21; *SRCL Ltd* v *Competition Commission* [2012] CAT 14.

Summary

➤ The basic structure of UK merger control is that the OFT investigates mergers and, if the OFT feels that they raise a serious competition problem, is under a duty to refer them to the Competition Commission (CC), which will decide whether they are likely to lead to a substantial lessening of competition (SLC) and, if so, what to do about it.

➤ There is no obligation to notify mergers to the OFT. The Enterprise Act 2002 makes provision for anticipated and completed mergers.

➤ The test for reference to the CC will be met if the OFT has a reasonable belief, objectively justified by relevant facts, that there is a realistic prospect that the merger will lessen competition substantially. By the term 'realistic prospect', the OFT means not only a prospect that has more than a 50% chance of occurring, but also a prospect that is not fanciful but has less than a 50% chance of occurring.

➤ The question for the CC is whether the merger may be expected to result in a substantial lessening of competition within any market or markets in the United Kingdom for goods or services.

➤ If the CC finds that the merger would lead to an SLC, it considers first whether it should take action to remedy the SLC and also whether it should recommend that others (e.g. government departments or regulatory agencies) should take action. The CC is required to have regard to achieving as comprehensive a solution as is reasonable and practicable for the SLC and any adverse effects resulting from it. When deciding on the remedies to be imposed, the CC may have regard to effects on any relevant customer benefits, which are defined as lower prices, higher quality, greater choice or greater innovation. The benefit must have occurred because of the relevant merger and have been unlikely to occur without the merger and the relevant lessening of competition, and the burden is on the parties to provide evidence of this.

➤ Decisions of the OFT and CC are reviewable by the CAT, acting under judicial review principles.

Further reading

Competition Commission, *Merger Remedies* (2008).

Competition Commission/Office of Fair Trading, *Merger Assessment Guidelines* (2010).

Offical publications
Office of Fair Trading, *Mergers: Jurisdictional and procedural guidance (2009).*

Office of Fair Trading, *Mergers: Exceptions to the duty to refer and undertakings in lieu of reference guidance* (2010).

Reference works
Parker, J., Majumdar, A. and Pritchard, S., *UK Merger Control* (Hart Publishing, Oxford, 2011). *Multi-authored reference work.*

Articles

Hoehn, T. and Rab, S., 'UK merger remedies: Convergence or conflict with Europe? A comparative assessment of remedies in UK mergers' (2009) 30 *European Competition Law Review* 74. *Excellent overview of the practice in relation to remedies by the competition authorities.*

Holmes, S., 'Policy Issues in Change of Control' (2005) 1 *European Competition Journal* 67–70. *Explains why the definition of 'control' is important.*

Lever, J., '"Control" for the purposes of Section 26 of the Enterprise Act 2002' (2005) 1 *European Competition Journal* 51–66. *Detailed examination of a vexed issue by an eminent QC.*

Rose, V., 'Margins of Appreciation: Changing Contours in Community and Domestic Case Law' (2009) 5 *Competition Policy International* 3. *One of the CAT chairmen gives her view on the extent of review by the European Courts and the CAT.*

15 Competition law and energy and telecommunications

Introduction

This chapter looks at the approach taken by competition law and policy to the energy[1] and telecommunications industries. The reason for focusing on these industries is, first, that they all depend on the existence of some form of network, as in electricity transmission or the telecommunications network and that the existence of this network has certain consequences in terms of economic theory. Secondly, these are industries that have undergone significant changes in the last 25 years or so in the UK, to a large extent stemming from their privatisation and the subsequent liberalisation of these markets. The policy of liberalising these markets has been adopted at European Union level, so they are interesting examples of moving a market from a monopoly to some form of competition. Thirdly, there are also non-economic goals or objectives that states have in relation to these industries. These can differ between countries and over time but include such matters as the need to provide universal service (that is, access to the services provided over the networks), concern over the environmental impacts of the industries (notably in energy) and a concern to ensure security of supply in energy, to mention just some issues. They thus serve as interesting examples of the interrelationship between competition law and other policies, as well as examples of what might be

---

[1] By which is meant electricity and gas.

seen as the limits, or limited reach, of competition law for dealing with certain sorts of issues. In both industries, it was considered necessary in the UK to set up a regulator to deal with a number of these issues: in other words, competition law on its own was felt not to be adequate. This raises the problem of the interrelationship between what might be called regulatory law and competition law, something which has been, as we shall see, a particular issue in telecommunications.

Economic policy issues

The concept of a natural monopoly

We start, then, with an important economic characteristic that these industries share, along with some other industries: important parts of them are a 'natural monopoly' (defined in Box 15.1).

KEY DEFINITION   **Box 15.1**

Natural monopoly

A natural monopoly exists in a particular market if a single firm can serve that market at lower cost than any combination of two or more firms. Natural monopoly arises out of the properties of productive technology, often in association with market demand, and not from the activities of governments or rivals. Generally speaking, natural monopolies are characterized by steeply declining long-run average and marginal-cost curves such that there is room for only one firm to fully exploit available economies of scale and supply the market.

Source: OECD, 'Glossary of statistical terms' available at *http://stats.oecd.org/glossary/detail.asp?ID=3267* (accessed 05/09/12).

Question: Think of examples of natural monopolies. What incentives exist for a natural monopolist to behave efficiently?

In the industries that this chapter is concerned with, examples of natural monopolies are the electricity transmission and distribution networks, the gas pipelines and the main fixed line telecommunications network. There are other examples of natural monopolies, of which the most obvious is the system of pipes used to deliver water and to take away sewage,[2] but the reason for concentrating on the industries mentioned is that they have undergone substantial transformation in the sense of introducing competition into key areas in a way that has not been the case with water supply, which is still characterised by regional monopolies, although there have been attempts to introduce more competition into this industry.[3] The transformation of

---

[2] Railways raise similar issues, although they are in competition with other modes of transport.

[3] See M. Cave, *Independent Review of Competition and Innovation in Water Markets* (DEFRA, 2009), available at *http://archive.defra.gov.uk/environment/quality/water/industry/cavereview/index.htm* (accessed 08/08/12); Defra, *Water For Life* (2011, CM 8230); Defra, 'Draft Water Bill' (2012, Cm 8375).

energy and telecommunications is also not merely a UK phenomenon, as we will see; the issue of what the market structure of these industries should be has also engaged policy makers at a European Union level.

Problems raised by natural monopolies

Natural monopolies raise a difficult problem for economic policy. The definition of natural monopoly states that for certain industries it is more efficient to have only one producer, rather than several producers. Intuitively, this makes sense because it would seem obviously inefficient to have competing electricity transmission lines or competing water pipes going to the same destination. The problem, however, is that a monopoly is still a monopoly and that there are limited incentives on it to act efficiently. If you control the only pipeline to a certain place then, in principle, you have a substantial amount of freedom in terms of your pricing decisions and on the price/quality mix that you can offer because there is no competition to constrain your decisions. There are some limits on your decision making power because at certain price levels insufficient people will use your facilities to make the operation profitable. To put it more technically (as discussed in Chapter 1), in a perfectly competitive market, where price discrimination is not possible, price will equal marginal cost. If monopoly is in place instead of competition, then price will equal marginal revenue and the result will be higher prices and less output. This does seem to bring the argument in a circle: monopoly leads to higher prices and less output but a natural monopoly will be more productively efficient than a competitive market and, the theory implies, it will be impossible to maintain more than one firm operating in this market in any event. What this suggests, therefore, is that in order to reap the benefits of a natural monopoly, productive efficiency, there will have to be some form of intervention which restrains the power over price. This will probably require action outside competition law because competition authorities find dealing with allegations of excessive pricing difficult and controversial (see Chapter 3).

Potential resolution to the natural monopoly problem

There are a number of possible responses to this problem, which do not necessarily involve competition law, strictly speaking.[4] One answer would be for governments to organise a periodic franchising process for the natural monopoly and thus replace competition in the market with competition for the market. This has been done in a variety of contexts (e.g. rail passenger services in the UK), but may suffer from a number of problems, notably that of the incumbent's advantage over new bidders. A second alternative would be for government to set up a regulatory agency which would have legal powers to control the prices charged and quality of service provided by the natural monopoly. This has been done widely in the United States and, as we shall see, subsequent to the privatisation of certain industries in the UK. This also has disadvantages because the regulators have less information than the industry on its workings and there is a danger that, for this and other reasons, the regulator will make decisions which are too favourable to the natural monopoly. A third alternative is to bring the natural monopoly into public ownership, which would seem

---

[4] Generally, see R. Baldwin, M. Cave and M. Lodge, *Understanding Regulation* (2nd edn, Oxford University Press, 2012).

particularly attractive where the facilities are built wholly or in part using public funds. The idea here is that decision on pricing and quality of service can be made on public interest grounds and that, since the monopoly is no longer in private hands, there is no requirement to provide a return to investors, which gives the incentive to exploit monopoly power. This approach was used widely in the UK in the twentieth century, especially post World War II, and in continental Europe.[5] This potentially has some of the same disadvantages of regulation, as well as opening up the possibility of decisions being made on short-term political grounds. Nor does it liberate the industry from financing concerns as decisions still have to be made over prices and investment.

The impact of privatisation

None of these responses is without difficulties and all were tried, with greater or less success, in Europe and the United States throughout the twentieth century. However, in the late twentieth century, a significant policy innovation came about from the UK through the creation of a programme of privatisation of state-owned enterprises, some of which, although not all, were natural monopolies.[6] Although the political headlines at the time were all about the transformation of state enterprises in telecommunications and energy into private companies, from our point of view the significant development was a rethinking of the idea of natural monopoly in the industries concerned and the place that could be played by competition. This can be illustrated by looking at the electricity industry, which can crudely be described as having four major activities: generation, transmission, distribution and supply. Prior to privatisation this was done by one entity, the Central Electricity Generating Board, which was vertically integrated: in other words, it generated the electricity, which it then transmitted, distributed and supplied throughout the entire UK, and the industry as a whole was thought of as a natural monopoly. On closer examination, it becomes clear that not all these activities are natural monopolies. It is evident that, for example, the activities of generating and supplying electricity could be competitive. It is possible to envisage that there could be numerous companies engaged in generating electricity and selling it to other companies that are supplying it to consumers. The only part that looks like a natural monopoly is the activity of transmitting the electricity, at a high voltage, and then distributing it locally, at a lower voltage: that is, the wires look like a natural monopoly. This brief description ignores one of the most important aspects of electricity, namely that it cannot be stored and that supply and demand across an electricity system needs to be balanced and that this requires a sophisticated coordination system which tends to encourage some level of integration between the various activities. Nevertheless, there is an important point here, which is that there are parts of these industries which can be made competitive.

In broad outline, what happened in the UK was that the telecommunications and energy industries were moved from public ownership into private ownership through legislation in, respectively, 1984 and 1989. At the same time regulatory agencies were created for these industries and a policy decision was taken to liberalise the operation of the industries, which meant, in the context of electricity, a restructuring of the industry, while in the context of telecommunications it meant allowing competitors access to the main fixed line tele-

[5] See T. Prosser, *Nationalised Industries and Public Control* (Clarendon Press, Oxford, 1986) for the UK.
[6] The official history of privatisation is D. Parker, *The Official History of Privatisation* (Routledge, London, 2008), Vol. 1 and Vol. 2 (2012).

communications network, although this was done very cautiously. From our point of view, the interesting part of this development was the idea that competitive markets could be introduced into aspects of what had previously been seen as a natural monopoly. To put it another way, the creation of regulatory agencies was combined with a restructuring of the industries and a liberalisation of entry into the industry.

Non-economic policy issues

There is, however, a further level of complexity which needs to be considered in this context. For all these industries there are a number of non-economic issues.[7] For example, it is generally considered in the UK that everyone should have access to energy supply and some access to the communications network and these ideas are, to a greater or lesser extent, enshrined in the legislation surrounding these industries. These are social or distributional concerns but there are other policy issues relevant to the industries. As far as energy is concerned, for example, government is concerned with its impact on the environment and also with ensuring that there is a sufficient supply of energy to meet the country's needs in the future. These are all non-economic concerns and competition law does not have any answers to such questions. Nor can they be solved simply by the introduction of competitive markets (this is most obvious in relation to distributional issues). Governments have undertaken a variety of interventions into the industries in order to accomplish what they regard as appropriate policy goals which cannot be met by competitive markets – the important point for present purposes is that the market within which these industries work has been constructed by governments, through a process of liberalisation, but this has been done in a way that attempts to take into account these non-economic concerns. In other words, it is misleading to think of these markets as simple free markets to which the ordinary tools of competition law can be applied; there is often another layer of policy concerns which explains particular decisions or compromises. Although these concerns do not often feature in competition law decisions,[8] they are often a background against which governments do, or do not, take decisions in relation to competition matters.

In order to discuss these issues, each industry is dealt with in turn in this chapter. The format of each section is similar: for each industry, there is a short discussion of the relevant characteristics of the industry, followed by a discussion of how policy has developed and concluding with a description of the regulatory arrangements and a discussion of selected competition law issues and cases. In the confines of this text, this is a very broad-brush approach requiring selective description; at the end, further reading is given for those who are interested.

The energy industries

Background to the UK system[9]

In the UK, energy covers two industries, gas and electricity, which overlap in relation to space heating but have very different characteristics. Natural gas is the simpler of the two industries,

---

[7] See, for illustration, HM Treasury/DECC, 'Energy Market Assessment' (2010).
[8] Although remember Case C-320/91 *Corbeau* [1993] ECR I-2533.
[9] The focus here is on Great Britain, that is, not Northern Ireland.

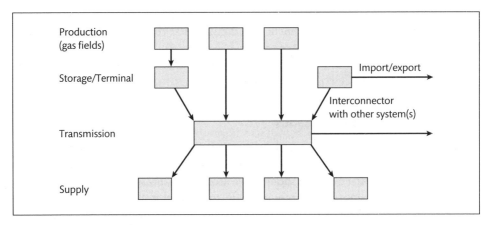

Figure 15.1 Gas network

being a liquid which is extracted from the earth and refined for use. It can be stored and is transported in pipelines, and in container ships, from the point of origin to the final consumer. Within the UK there are actually two forms of pipelines: a high pressure National Transmission System (NTS) and a lower pressure distribution system which takes the gas from the NTS to the consumer. Historically, the UK produced most of its gas from fields in the North Sea and there are only two pipelines that connect the UK system to Europe: one from Belgium to Norfolk and another from Norway to Scotland. The significance of this is that the UK is gradually becoming more dependent on the importation of gas, rather than relying on production in the North Sea.[10] A significant proportion of electricity generation is now done through gas-fired generating stations, so the two sectors are related. In terms of competition law, it should be clear from this description that the pipelines are a natural monopoly but the production and supply of gas are potentially competitive. However, the key issue will be the terms of access to the pipeline (Figure 15.1 gives a schematic illustration of the industry).

By contrast, electricity is more complicated. As mentioned above, it can be divided into four segments: generation, transmission, distribution and supply (see Figure 15.2), and one critical characteristic is that it cannot be stored, unlike gas. As a result of this, and because power stations cannot be turned on and off immediately, it is critical to ensure that supply and demand is always matched, which means that there is an important element of cooperation within the electricity industry without which it cannot function. Bearing this in mind, it can be seen that the transmission and distribution systems are natural monopolies, whereas the generation and supply are potentially competitive.

The energy industries in the UK have been dramatically transformed since the mid 1980s when their privatisation was followed by liberalisation and the opening up of the markets. Originally the gas industry was privatised as a single entity, that is, as a monopoly business under the Gas Act 1986. This was perceived as a mistake so that when the electricity industry was privatised, under the Electricity Act 1989, the idea was that generation, transmission and supply of electricity would all be separate activities (with distribution remaining with the supply companies). The key idea behind this arrangement was that electricity companies

[10] This partially explains the interest in encouraging renewable energy and nuclear generation.

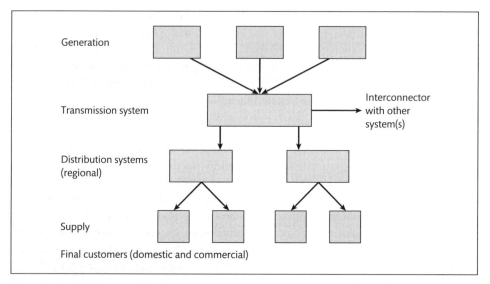

Figure 15.2 Electricity system

would no longer be vertically integrated; in particular, would not engage in supply and generation. So two major, non-nuclear generating companies were created and fourteen Regional Electricity Companies (RECs), responsible for supply and distribution, and a transmission company. Although the government put some short-term protective measures into the constitution of the electricity companies, on their expiration there were a number of takeover bids and the issues were judged using the pre-Enterprise Act 2002 merger control system, where the crucial decisions were taken by ministers. A brief description of what happened gives some insight into the rationale for removing ministers' powers from the merger control process (discussed in Chapter 14), as well as helping to explain how the industry reached its present position.

Government intervention in the structure of the electricity markets

From 1995, the RECs became subject to a large number of takeover bids, from a variety of companies; some from America, two water companies, one bid from Scottish Power and, most importantly, two bids from the generating companies: National Power and PowerGen. In broad terms, these bids could be said to raise three issues: should the RECs be controlled by overseas companies, what would be the effect on the regulatory system of the creation of multi-utility companies, and what would be the effect on the competitive market in the electricity supply industry which was premised on keeping the generators separate from the distribution and supply companies? Although these issues would all seem suitable for investigation by the CC, and this was recommended in separate instances by the Director General of Fair Trading and the Director General of Electricity Supply (the predecessor of Ofgem), the government refused to make any references to the CC, with the exception of the bids by the generating companies. Instead, certain undertakings were negotiated between the acquiring companies and the Director General of Electricity Supply. As regards the bids by the generating companies, the CC recommended, by a majority, that the bids should be allowed to go ahead, subject to certain undertakings, but the Conservative government rejected the CC's recommendation and blocked the bids.[11] However, with the change of government in 1997, a more active reference policy was initially followed when the Trade and Industry Secretary referred the bid by the US company Pacificorp for the Energy Group (essentially Eastern Electricity) to the CC against the advice of the Director General of Fair Trading. The CC found that there was no problem for the public interest which could not be solved by the giving of similar undertakings as in the other cases.[12] In the event, Pacificorp was beaten to this target by an American rival, Texas Utilities.

The next major event was when PowerGen made a bid for East Midlands Electricity and National Power made a bid for Midlands Electricity. In the two cases, both the Director General of Fair Trading and the Director General of Electricity Supply recommended that a reference should be made to the CC but this advice was rejected by the Secretary of State, who sought undertakings from the companies concerned that they would divest themselves of four gigawatt's worth of power stations. Suitable undertakings were obtained from PowerGen and a bid for these stations was made by Edison Mission Energy.[13] The interesting point about allowing this takeover was that it represented a major shift away from a policy of preventing vertical integration.

The record of governments on electricity takeovers from 1995 is quite extraordinary. With the lapse of the protection against takeover, there was a spate of takeover bids, none of which were referred to the CC, despite initial regulatory views, until the bids by the generating companies for the RECs. Despite the CC recommending approval, subject to conditions, the bid was blocked. With the change of government in 1997, a bid with no obvious competition implications was referred to the CC, which recommended approval. Then, when further bids were made by the generating companies for RECs, instead of following the Director General of Fair Trading's advice to refer these bids to the CC, the government sought suitable undertakings in lieu of a reference. What is notable from these events is that there was a complete lack of consistency and clarity over what the government's approach to takeovers in the electricity industry should be, regardless of the change in the political complexion of the government. Subsequently, the English electricity companies were bought by German and French energy companies, and these transactions fell within the scope of the European Community [Union] merger control regulation and so were cleared by the European Commission.

Government intervention in the structure of the gas industry

A similar issue in relation to government intervention can be seen as regards the gas industry, which was privatised as a monopoly. There were a number of issues relating to the performance of British Gas which culminated in a reference to the Competition Commission. The CC recommended that British Gas should be broken up, separating the transportation business

---

[11] For the reports: Competition Commission, 'National Power and Southern Electric' and 'Powergen and Midlands Electricity' (both 1996). The government decision was announced in DTI Press Notice P/96/313, 24 April 1996.

[12] Competition Commission, 'Pacificorp and the Energy Group' (1997).

[13] See DTI Press Notice P/98/719, 24 September 1998; Press Notice P/98/837, 29 October 1998; Press Notice P/98/938, 25 November 1998; Press Notice P/99/308, 9 April 1999; and Offer/Ofgas Press Notice R24/99, 12 May 1999.

from the pipeline business and that competition in domestic supply should be introduced cautiously.[14] The government rejected the separation option,[15] in a short press release, but instead decided to move quickly to a fully competitive domestic gas market, a policy decision which culminated in the Gas Act 1995 and the introduction of competition throughout Britain by the end of 1998. Again, we can see the unpredictable nature of government intervention under the legal structures existing before the Enterprise Act 2002.

Today, the supply of electricity and gas is competitive and there are six major companies that offer such supplies (and supply around 99% of the domestic households), and they are also engaged in the distribution of electricity.[16] The transmission system is a separate company from the other electricity companies. There are around 30 major power-producing companies, some of which are part of the six major suppliers of electricity: in other words, there is an element of vertical integration.[17] In a sentence, the UK energy industry can be characterised, roughly, as an oligopolistic industry where the main players are vertically integrated. For example, E.ON, the successor to PowerGen, describes itself as an integrated power and gas company with a retail business supplying electricity and gas to around 5 million accounts (domestic and commercial) and with a generation business involved in every link of the energy chain.[18]

UK competition law as applied to the energy industry

The transformation of the energy industry has also been accompanied by a transformation in the legal structure under which the industry operates. Put very simply, carrying out activities in the energy industry requires a company to obtain a licence, which sets out the terms and conditions under which it will operate. Those licences are granted, and their terms are enforced, by an independent regulatory authority, known familiarly as Ofgem.[19] As well as having specific powers to enforce what might be called the regulatory rules, Ofgem also has powers under the Competition Act 1998, as well as under Articles 101 and 102 TFEU, which it operates concurrently with the OFT, and it is these concurrent Competition Act powers that will be the focus of discussion.[20] Ofgem also has powers to make market investigation references to the Competition Commission, but this power has not, as yet, been exercised; although Ofgem has undertaken a major investigation of the supply of energy in the UK, in the light of price increases in 2008. The approach that will be taken by Ofgem is set out in guidance published by the OFT, but which was drafted in conjunction with Ofgem.[21] The

[14] Competition Commission, 'Gas' (1993).

[15] Ultimately, the distribution side of British Gas was separated from the supply side and sold to National Grid, the company that runs the electricity transmission networks.

[16] British Gas, E.ON, EDF Energy, nPower, Scottish and Southern Energy and Scottish Power.

[17] This was always the case in Scotland, where the two major companies were privatised as vertically integrated entities, that is, they had interests in generation, distribution and supply.

[18] See *http://eon-uk.com/about/businesses.aspx* (accessed 08/08/12).

[19] Its formal name is the Gas and Electricity Markets Authority (GEMA) but the older name is more commonly used, for example, on its website.

[20] See Competition Act 1998, s. 54. See also OFT, *Concurrent application to regulated industries* (2004). Prior to the Competition Act, there was no statutory equivalent to these powers although there was a fair trading condition in telecommunications licences.

[21] OFT, *Application in the energy sector* (2005) (Guidance 428). See also Ofgem, 'Enforcement Guidelines on complaints and investigations' (2012).

Guidelines make the point that a number of issues peculiar to the energy industries will have to be taken into account by Ofgem when operating its competition law powers. The starting point is the recognition that there are incumbents in these industries, such as British Gas, which may have certain advantages over new entrants. The guidelines state that Ofgem will be particularly vigilant in seeking to ensure that the conduct of undertakings does not restrict the opportunities of others to compete in the energy markets.[22] The Guidelines go on to set out what Ofgem views as the most important characteristics of the energy markets that will affect its application of the competition rules:[23]

- the existence of monopoly providers of gas transportation, and electricity transmission and distribution networks, which are unlikely to be replicated due to the cost conditions faced by any undertaking seeking to duplicate such networks (including the high sunk costs associated with construction and other costs arising from planning and environmental constraints);
- the importance in the transition from monopoly to competition across a range of activities of ensuring effective separation of the network services from the potentially competitive parts of the supply chain;
- the extent of market power of incumbent undertakings in parts of the gas and electricity industries, including supply, metering, connections and storage markets;
- the existence of price controls for gas transportation and electricity transmission and distribution, where market power is particularly strong;
- the low elasticity of supply and demand for electricity and gas, particularly over short periods and in specific locations. In part this results from the limited storability of electricity, and to a lesser extent gas, which limits the substitution opportunities between time periods on either the supply side or the demand side;
- the relative complexity of and the mandatory adherence by market participants to the various rules, codes and agreements in the gas and electricity markets. These include codes that aim to keep the gas and electricity networks operating within safe and efficient operational limits, and which govern customer transfers as well as the connection to and the use of electricity and gas systems; and
- the economic linkages between different parts of gas and electricity supply chains, including: horizontal and vertical linkages, between spot and forward markets,[24] and between electricity and gas wholesale markets.

Ofgem decisions under the Competition Act 1998

Although Ofgem has had competition law powers since 2000, they have had little use. Between 2000 and 2004, there were 44 complaints to Ofgem of breaches of the Competition Act 1998 and none of them were upheld. The majority of complaints were about discrimination, either price or non-price based. Ofgem commented that the main reason a significant number of complaints had been closed was the poor quality of information provided, which

---

[22] Ibid. at para. 3.3.
[23] Ibid. at para. 3.5.
[24] A spot market is where the product purchased is delivered immediately. A forward market is where the product purchased is delivered at some point in the future.

meant that it was not possible to decide whether there had been an infringement.[25] Since 2004, there appear to have been only two complaints which were formally investigated and neither were upheld.[26] This lack of use of the Competition Act powers is not peculiar to Ofgem, which made one of the two decisions by regulators under the Competition Act, and was a particular concern to the government when it came to reform the competition regime.[27] The Enterprise and Regulatory Reform Bill makes a number of changes to the legal framework, largely in Schedule 14, to try to encourage greater usage of these powers.

The first, and so far only, formal decision of an infringement of the Competition Act from Ofgem came after an investigation into National Grid's practice in relation to domestic metering arrangements for gas supply. Ofgem found that National Grid had abused its dominant position, contrary to UK and EU law, through entering into long-term contracts which set out the terms under which gas supply operators could replace the gas meters provided by National Grid with those from other meter suppliers and imposed a financial penalty of £41.6 million. The background to this is that National Grid had been the sole supplier of gas meters, of which there are two types – credit and pre-payment – for a number of years. Gas customers are obliged, under statute, to take their gas supply through a meter. The market for metering was liberalised and competing meter operators (CMOs) were allowed to enter the market and offer to rent their meters to gas suppliers. Typically domestic meters have to be read by a meter reader, but there have been technological developments leading to meters that can, among other things, be read remotely. National Grid entered into two long-term contracts with gas suppliers, of eighteen and seven years, which provided, among other things, that the suppliers would have to pay financial penalties to National Grid if they replaced the National Grid meters with other meters above an agreed rate.[28] In addition, the provision of meters was bundled in the contract with their maintenance, so that only National Grid could maintain its meters. The competition problem, as identified by Ofgem, was that these arrangements made it more difficult for CMOs to enter the market because the allowance for replacement meters was typically taken up by having to replace faulty or inaccurate meters or at a customer's request. In essence, the agreements imposed significant switching costs on those suppliers that wanted to change more meters than were allowed for under their agreement with National Grid.

The decision was appealed to the CAT broadly under the grounds that National Grid was not dominant in the relevant market, that the contracts were pro- not anti-competitive, that the penalty was excessive and that the directions given by Ofgem were unclear and unlawful, and that National Grid could not identify what it needed to do to comply with these directions. The judgment of the CAT substantially upheld Ofgem's decision, although it reduced the fine to £30 million and restricted the effect of the decision to one of the two contracts.[29] The judgment is interesting in that, as regards the question of a dominant position, it recognises that in the years immediately after the opening up of a statutory monopoly, market shares need to be approached with caution because although the incumbent may have a high market share, the possibility of market entry may mean that the incumbent has little market power

[25] Ofgem, *Complaints considered by Ofgem under the Competition Act 1998* (2004).

[26] See *http://www.ofgem.gov.uk/About%20us/enforcement/Investigations/Pages/Invstigtions.aspx* (accessed 08/08/12).

[27] BIS, 'A Competition Regime for Growth: A consultation on options for reform' (2011) at Ch. 7.

[28] Given that National Grid had a significant investment in meters, one of the objects of these contracts was to try to protect this investment.

[29] *National Grid Plc v Gas and Electricity Markets Authority* [2009] CAT 14.

and will lose market share rapidly.[30] The CAT also made the point that the issue of counter-vailing buyer power is a matter of degree and it could not be assumed that regulatory constraints necessarily restricted market power. As regards the question of abuse, the CAT upheld Ofgem's finding that one of the contracts had had an actual effect on competition in the market after comparing it in principle with the fidelity rebates used in *Michelin I*.[31] National Grid appealed to the Court of Appeal which upheld the CAT's findings on the law, but reduced the fine to £15 million on the grounds that Ofgem had been involved in discussions about the contracts and the relative novelty of the issue.[32] Two follow-on actions have been instituted by meter suppliers in the CAT.[33]

The energy supply probe and the retail market review

The other recent major investigation by Ofgem has been the energy supply probe, as it is known.[34] This was an investigation undertaken using Enterprise Act powers, as a preliminary to deciding whether to make a market reference to the Competition Commission, which looked at the domestic energy market. The background was a dramatic rise in world prices for energy which fed through into increases in the prices charged to domestic customers in the UK. One of the questions that this investigation sought to answer was whether the market was sufficiently competitive because, among other things, there had been accusations that the largest energy supply companies were running a cartel – remembering in this context that there are six major energy companies. Ofgem came to the conclusion that, in general, the market was working well and was competitive, but there were a number of areas where further action was needed. It recommended a programme that would, among other things, promote more active customer engagement with the market and provide more information to customers, thus hoping to increase switching rates and competitive pressure among suppliers. In addition, it also proposed action to address what were seen as unfair price differentials and to do this by imposing a licence condition on suppliers that the terms for different types of payments for electricity should be cost-reflective and that there would be a new licence condition which would prohibit undue price discrimination. Although, in strict terms, the legal mechanism for imposing these new obligations is not competition law (that is, it is not done under the competition legislation), the aim of these obligations is to help create more competitive markets. It is thus an illustration of the interrelationship between the regulatory and the competition law regimes which pervades all these industries. The proposals have been highly controversial. One member of the board of Ofgem resigned in protest at the policy and there have been serious criticisms from academic economists as well.[35] Their argument, in broad terms, is that price discrimination is not necessarily anti-competitive (see the previous discussion in Chapter 4), and that to impose provisions

[30] Ibid. at para. 51.

[31] Ibid. at para. 97.

[32] *National Grid v Gas and Electricity Markets Authority* [2010] EWCA Civ 114.

[33] Case 1199/5/7/12 *Capital Meters Ltd v National Grid* and Case 1198/5/7/12 *Siemens v National Grid*.

[34] See Ofgem, 'Energy supply probe – Initial Findings Report' (2008) and the material available at: *http://www.ofgem.gov.uk/Markets/RetMkts/ensuppro/Pages/Energysupplyprobe.aspx* (accessed 08/08/12).

[35] See *Utility Week*, 29 May 2009, Response of Professor Catherine Waddams to Ofgem consultation, available at *http://www.ofgem.gov.uk/Pages/MoreInformation.aspx?docid=49&refer=Markets/RetMkts/ensuppro* (accessed 08/08/12); and see also *http://www.ofgem.gov.uk/Pages/MoreInformation.aspx?docid=95&refer=Markets/RetMkts/ensuppro* (accessed 08/08/09) for Sir John Vickers' view.

preventing price discrimination will actually lessen competition in the markets and harm consumer welfare. The issue has remained controversial and was addressed again in Ofgem's Retail Market Review which looked at the effectiveness of energy markets and, among other things, whether the licence condition on non-discrimination should be retained.[36] It was again subject to criticism from economists, who argued that it was likely that the provision had not benefited consumers.[37]

◼ The enforcement of competition law at the EU level[38]

The treatment of the energy industries at a European level has been an issue fraught with controversy because the European Commission has, since around the mid 1980s, been advocating the liberalisation of energy markets, somewhat on the UK lines, whereas this has been resisted by a number of Member States that have dominant incumbents. The general policy that was agreed between Member States was to liberalise the energy industries and the rules surrounding this was embodied in two Directives, for electricity and gas.[39] Progress towards this goal has been slow and in 2005 the European Commission began a sector inquiry into energy markets, the results of which were published in 2007.[40] The report identified four main fundamental deficiencies in the electricity and gas markets in Europe:

- structural conflicts of interest: a systemic conflict of interest caused by insufficient unbundling of networks from the competitive parts of the sector;
- gaps in the regulatory environment: a persistent regulatory gap, particularly for cross-border issues. The regulatory systems in place have loose ends, which do not meet;
- a chronic lack of liquidity, both in electricity and gas wholesale markets: the lifeblood for our markets is lacking and the market power of pre-liberalisation monopolies persists;
- a general lack of transparency in market operations in the sector.[41]

A progress report in 2008[42] found a mixed picture in terms of developments. In particular, a major concern was the incomplete implementation of the European legislation. To try to improve the situation, the European Commission adopted a two-pronged strategy: on the one hand, it has pursued individual competition law cases against energy companies, as well as using its powers in relation to merger control and state aids; while, on the other hand, it presented new proposals to improve the legislation, which were adopted in 2009 and came into force in 2011, although a European Commission staff working paper in 2011 described

---

[36] Ofgem, 'Retail Market Review' (2011).

[37] For the responses see: *http://www.ofgem.gov.uk/Pages/MoreInformation.aspx?docid=95&refer=Markets/RetMkts/ ensuppro* (accessed 08/08/12).

[38] Generally, see P. Cameron, *Competition in Energy Markets: Law and Regulation in the European Union* (2nd edn, Oxford University Press, 2007).

[39] Directive 2003/54/EC of the European Parliament and of the Council concerning common rules for the internal market in electricity, OJ L136/37, 15.07.2003 (hereafter 'Electricity Directive') and Directive 2003/55/EC of the European Parliament and of the Council concerning common rules for the internal market in natural gas, OJ L176, 15.07.2003 (hereafter 'Gas Directive').

[40] DG Competition, 'Report on energy sector inquiry', SEC (2006) 1724 (10 January 2007).

[41] European Commission, 'Communication from the Commission Inquiry pursuant to Article 17 of Regulation (EC) No. 1/2003 into the European gas and electricity sectors', COM (2006) 851 final (at para. 52).

[42] European Commission, 'Report on progress in creating the internal gas and electricity market', SEC (2009) 287.

the progress towards transposition as not reassuring.[43] Given our space constraints, we will not look at the issue of state aids and energy in this chapter.[44]

The new Directives, often referred to as the 'Third package',[45] recognise and allow Member States to impose public service obligations on undertakings of general economic interest so long as they are clearly defined, transparent, non-discriminatory and verifiable, and guarantee equality of access for EU electricity companies to national consumers.[46] The Electricity Directive provides, furthermore, that there shall be an authorisation and open tendering procedure for the construction of new capacity. Transmission system and distribution operators are to be designated, unbundled from any vertical integration and to operate on a non-discriminatory basis. There is also to be a system of third-party access to the transmission and distribution systems, thus allowing competition, and Member States are to allow access to their own electricity markets. The system in each Member State is to be overseen by national regulatory authorities acting independently from the electricity industry. The Gas Directive envisages a similar structure, albeit with some variations to take into account the different characteristics of the industry. The vision, therefore, is for something that might look a bit like the UK energy market, albeit on a European level, with effective competition at the generation and supply levels. Notably there is no provision for a European level regulatory agency, although an EU agency for the cooperation of energy regulators has been established and they also discuss issues of common concern through the Council of European Energy Regulators.[47]

Energy and competition law in the EU – introduction

Before discussing the substantive issues relating to Articles 101 and 102 TFEU, it is worth-while discussing one of the most important cases in this area, namely *Almelo*.[48] This was a case brought by a local authority in the Netherlands against a regional electricity distributor in relation to their agreement, which provided that it should purchase all its electricity from the regional electricity distributor and it was not allowed to import electricity from competing providers. In this particular case, it challenged the provision as being contrary to Article 101(1) TFEU, among other provisions of the EU Treaties. The CJEU held, not surprisingly, that such clauses led to the compartmentalisation of the common market and that the clause had a restrictive effect on competition. It was, however, argued on behalf of the regional distributor that such a clause was necessary in order for it to carry out its public service obligations. The

---

[43] European Commission Staff working document, '2009–2010 Report on progress in creating the internal gas and electricity market' (2011), available at: *http://ec.europa.eu/energy/gas_electricity/legislation/benchmarking_reports_en.htm* (accessed 08.08/12).

[44] Cameron (n. 38), ch. 15 gives an introduction to this.

[45] Directive 2009/72/EC of the European Parliament and of the Council of 13 July 2009 concerning common rules for the internal market in electricity, OJ L 211/55, 14.08.2009 (the Electricity Directive) and Directive 2009/73/EC of the European Parliament and of the Council of 13 July 2009 concerning common rules for the internal market in natural gas, OJ L 211/94, 14.08.2009 (the Gas Directive).

[46] Electricity Directive, Art. 3.

[47] See Regulation (EC) No. 713/2009 of the European Parliament and of the Council of 13 July 2009 establishing an Agency for the Cooperation of Energy Regulators OJ L 211/1, 14.08.2009 and *http://acernet.acer.europa.eu/portal/page/portal/ACER_HOME*. For the Council, see: *http://www.energy-regulators.eu/portal/page/portal/EER_HOME* (both accessed 08/08/12).

[48] Case 393/92 *Gemeente Almelo v Energiebedrijf Ijsselmij* [1994] ECR I-1447.

CJEU accepted that this argument could be made out, in principle, but said that this was a matter for the national court to determine. The importance of this case is twofold. First, it is confirmation that the competition rules apply to the electricity sector, which was raised in one of the foundational cases of EU law.[49] Secondly, it is a good example of where non-competition issues, in this case security of supply, can be used, at least in principle, to argue for a derogation from the full rigour of the competition rules.

Article 101 TFEU issues[50]

There have been a number of competition concerns in relation to both electricity and gas over contractual arrangements. As will be apparent from Figures 15.1 and 15.2 outlining the structure of the energy industries, if the various stages are operated by different organisations or companies, this will normally be done on the basis of a contract between them. In the energy sector, for the most part, these will be considered to be vertical contracts, because they would involve entities at different stages of the production process. It is worth remembering certain basic points about the regulation of vertical agreements under Article 101 TFEU. First, the Commission is not interested in vertical agreements if the market share of the parties is under 15%. If the market share is above this, but below 30%, then the agreement may benefit from the block exemption for vertical agreements provided that there are no hard-core restraints or that non-compete obligations are severable. The important hard-core restrictions for our purposes here are resale price maintenance and controls over the territory into which the buyer may sell the goods purchased. For agreements where one of the parties has a market share above 30%, there will have to be individual assessment of the agreement. Issues which the Commission has flagged up as of particular concern to it are exclusive purchasing contracts[51] and long-term purchasing contracts, in both cases because these might restrict access to the markets by potential competitors. The benefit of the Regulation may be withdrawn in cases where access to the market is restricted by networks of parallel agreements. Having outlined some potential concerns, we can now look at how some of these contractual arrangements have developed in practice.

Article 101 TFEU and the gas industry

Beginning with the gas industry, it is relatively easy to appreciate that exploration for gas and its subsequent production is an expensive and time-consuming business, which requires large capital investment and where there are significant sunk costs. The producers will have an incentive, therefore, to seek contractual arrangements guaranteeing the sale of as much of their production as possible for as long a period of time as possible. In a system which has not been liberalised, as has been the case in most European countries prior to the Directives, there would be a monopolist supplier which would want to ensure that it could meet demand and also have arrangements that would prevent the growth of competition. These incentives manifested themselves in a number of contractual arrangements, in the context of vertical agreements, which have been challenged by the Commission over the years, although most of these cases did not result in formal decisions, but were settled.

[49] Case 6/64 *Costa* v *ENEL* [1964] ECR 585.
[50] Generally, see J. Faull and A. Nikpay (eds) *The EC Law of Competition* (2nd edn, Oxford University Press, 2007) at paras 12.174–12.368.
[51] European Commission, *Guidelines on Vertical Restraints*, OJ C291/01 13.10.2000 (at paras 202–14).

A particular concern for the Commission in gas contracts between suppliers and buyers was the practice of inserting territorial restrictions in the contracts, thus preventing the buyer from selling the gas outside a particular territory. This is a clear example of market partitioning, something which has always been seen as a breach of Article 101(1) TFEU and very unlikely to meet the criteria for exemption in Article 101(3) TFEU. Perhaps the most high-profile example was in relation to Gazprom, the Russian gas producer, which had arrangements in a number of countries, notably in Italy with ENI, the Italian gas supplier, where the contracts included provisions in essence preventing the gas from being sold on outside the territory to which it was supplied. The Commission objected to these arrangements and, in the Italian case, ENI agreed to sell significant volumes of gas outside Italy, largely to Germany and Austria, and also to increase the capacity of its pipeline that transported Russian gas to Italy via Austria.[52]

The Commission has also been alert to deal with clauses which limit the uses to which the buyer can put the gas, which are seen as hard-core restrictions. A good example of this is the so-called DUC/DONG case.[53] Here the Danish Underground Consortium (DUC), comprised of three large gas companies, produced gas and sold it to the Danish incumbent, DONG. Most of the gas was consumed in Denmark, but certain amounts were exported to Sweden and Germany. The Commission was concerned about a number of clauses but there is one which is of particular interest here. In order to benefit from a certain price formula, DONG was required to report to DUC the volumes of gas that it sold to particular categories of customers. The Commission saw this as a use restriction, because DONG could not sell the gas to whichever customer it thought most profitable, as this would mean it would be at risk of losing the benefit of the price formula. The issue was dealt with by the parties agreeing to amend their contracts in such a way to give DONG freedom to sell its gas to whomsoever it chose.

Another common contractual arrangement in both gas and electricity has been exclusive supply clauses where, for example, a power plant agrees to sell all its output to one consumer, such as an incumbent distributor and supplier. In the past, these contracts have typically been entered into for a relatively long duration. From the parties' point of view, such long-term contracts economise on transaction costs and may help to reduce uncertainty. From a societal point of view, the contracts may facilitate entry and investment and, therefore, help contribute to security of supply through improving the fuel mix.[54] The competition problems that may be created are neatly summed up by Faull and Nikpay:[55]

> Long-term exclusive purchase obligations/non-compete obligations raise competition concerns as they can result in significant foreclosure effects. During the lifetime of the contract the buyer is prevented from switching to another supplier. Alternative suppliers lose a possible output for their products . . . The anti-competitive effects of this strategy are reinforced if key customers, who would justify a market entry in their own right, are obliged to procure their entire demand from a supplier or if there is a network of parallel contracts sealing off a large part of the consumption in the market concerned.

[52] See European Commission, Press Release IP/03/1345, 6 October 2003 and H. Nyssens, C. Cultrera and D. Schnichels, 'The territorial restrictions in the gas sector: A state of play' (2004) *Competition Policy Newsletter*, No. 1, pp. 48–51.

[53] See European Commission, Press Release IP/03/566, 24 April 2003.

[54] For these arguments, see J.-M. Glachant and A. de Hautelocque, 'Long-term Energy Supply Contracts in European Competition Policy: Fuzzy not Crazy', EUI Working Papers RSCAS 2009/06. Available at *http://ideas.repec.org/p/rsc/rsceui/2009-06.html* (accessed 05/09/12).

[55] Faull and Nikpay (n. 50) at para. 12.213.

In the gas industry, there are a number of examples of the Commission intervening in relation to these sorts of contracts. In a Spanish case, Endesa, an electricity generator, was required to purchase its entire gas requirements for new gas-fired power plants from Gas Natural for a period of more than 20 years. The Commission intervened and the parties agreed to modify the contract by, among other things, reducing the amount of gas Endesa was obliged to purchase and shortening the contract period to around 12 years.[56] Another good example of this type of arrangement was the contract between EDF-Trading, a French company, and Wingas, a German wholesaler, whereby EDF agreed to supply Wingas with around 20% of its annual requirements for a period of ten years, roughly 2% of the overall supply of gas in Germany, renewable for another five years. Here the Commission's concern was not to reduce the period of the contract, but to ensure that it was amended to ensure that EDF was able to sell to other wholesalers in the German market.[57]

The most recent high-profile case under Article 101 TFEU was the European Commission's decision that E.ON and Gaz de France (GDF) had agreed not to compete in each other's markets. In this case, E.ON and GDF had set up a joint venture in 1975 to construct a gas pipeline running from the Czech border, across southern Germany up to the French border and the pipeline was opened in 1980. The critical part of the agreement was that GDF and E.ON's capacity on the pipeline was to be booked on the basis it was for the provision of gas which would be consumed in their respective countries. In addition, GDF agreed not to supply any gas in connection with the agreement to any customer in Germany. These provisions were contained in what were referred to as 'side letters' to the agreement. Although there was some dispute, the agreement was considered by the Commission to have ended in 2005. The Commission fined each participant €553 million and described the agreement as 'one of the worst types of antitrust infringement'.[58] E.ON appealed this decision to the GC and two of its arguments are of interest.[59] First, it argued that the provisions in the side letters were ancillary restrictions necessary for the contract and proportionate to the objectives pursued. They argued that GDF needed property rights in the pipeline to ensure security of supply and that, without the non-compete provision in Germany, GDF could have competed and jeopardised E.ON's investment. The GC rejected this argument, partly because it was admitted that, without the side letters, E.ON would have constructed the pipeline on its own and offered GDF capacity on the pipeline. Since a joint undertaking was not necessary to construct the pipeline, it followed that the side letters were not necessary. Even if this were wrong, the court did not find any evidence that this would have made the main operation difficult to operate without the restriction in GDF's operation in Germany. E.ON also argued that the two undertakings were not potential competitors in Germany before the beginning of 2000 because the German market was effectively closed to competition from outside the country. Although there was no legal ban on new suppliers entering the market during this period, German law allowed an exemption from competition law which allowed the existing gas suppliers to protect their own territories and enter into exclusive agreements to provide gas distribution networks. As regards France, GDF had a legal monopoly at least until 2000, the due date for the transposition of one of the first EU Directives. The GC agreed with E.ON that there was no real possibility of competition on the German gas market until 1998. It did not agree with

---

[56] Press Release IP/00/297, 27 March 2000.
[57] Press Release IP/02/1293, 12 September 2002.
[58] European Commission, Press Release IP/09/1099, 8 July 2009.
[59] Case T-360/09 *E.ON Ruhrgas AG* v *Commission* judgment of 29 June 2012 (GC).

another argument which was, when the agreement was signed, that the effect on competition was neutral, given the economic context of the time (that is, two monopoly industries). The court took the view that liberalisation could not have been precluded in the long term and could reasonably have been envisaged. The aim of the side letters was to share the market in the event of changes in circumstances, particularly the coming of liberalisation. Finally, the GC reduced the fine to €320 million, largely because of disagreements with the Commission over the duration of the infringement.

Article 101 TFEU and the electricity industry

There are also a number of cases in the electricity industry and an influential trilogy, described by Cameron, demonstrates some of the same themes:[60]

- in each case a power purchase agreement had been concluded between a new electricity generator and the incumbent monopoly;
- the agreement notified to the Commission had a long duration;
- the duration was rejected by the Commission, partly because of the exclusivity of supply involved and the restriction on the generator from supplying consumers other than the incumbent monopoly; and
- Commission approval in each case was conditional on a reduction of the duration to 15 years.

Article 102 TFEU issues

Subsequent to the energy sector inquiry, where the Commission expressed concern about the effects of long-term contracts, in legal terms the focus of its activities has changed from Article 101 TFEU to bringing cases under Article 102 TFEU, largely because the focus has been on contracts between incumbent suppliers and their customers. It has so far opened ten cases subsequent to the sector inquiry and it is possible that more may follow as it has conducted inspections in a number of places in Central and Eastern Europe and opened proceedings against Gazprom.[61] Table 15.1 gives a list of these cases. In the *Distrigaz* case, the European Commission objected to the practices of a dominant supplier of gas to industrial customers in Belgium which tied its customers into long-term contracts for the supply of gas and, because of its dominance, ensured a large proportion of the supply in Belgium was committed. The case was settled after Distrigaz made a number of commitments, which were meant to have the effect of releasing more gas on to the market and not to conclude new contracts with industrial consumers of more than five years, amongst other commitments.[62] Following on from this case, the European Commission also opened proceedings against EDF and Electrabel, a Belgian electricity company, relating to their use of long-term contracts for industrial consumers in the electricity market and the possibility that this may have foreclosed the relevant markets to new competitors but subsequently closed the inquiry.[63]

---

[60] Cameron (n. 38) at para. 13.24, describing Commission Decisions *Electricidade de Portugal/Pego* [1993] OJ C265/3; *REN/Turbogas* [1996] OJ C118/7; *ISAB Energy* [1996] OJ C138/3.
[61] See European Commission Press Release MEMO/12/78, 07.02.2012. Commission Press Release IP/12/937, 04.09.12.
[62] See Commission Decision of 11 October 2007, Case COMP/B-1/37.966, *Distrigaz*.
[63] See Commission Case COMP/39.387, *Long term electricity contracts in Belgium*.

Table 15.1 Energy cases after the sector inquiry

Case name	Date proceedings opened	Outcome	Remedy	Commission concerns
Distrigaz	2007	Commitments decision	Reduction of gas tied into long-term contracts	Market foreclosure through long-term and large-volume contracts
German electricity wholesale market (E.ON)	2006	Commitments decision	Divestiture of generation capacity and transmission system business	Withdrawal of capacity to raise prices, deterring investment by third parties through long-term contracts and offering a share in E.ON plants
German electricity balancing market (E.ON)	2006	Commitments decision	As above (same case)	
GDF Suez Gaz de France	2008	Commitments decision	Release of long-term reservations of gas imports, reduction of share of reservations	Essential input, refusal to supply; strategic limitation of investment
RWE gas foreclosure	2007	Commitments decision	Divestiture of gas transmission network	Essential facility, refusal to supply, margin squeeze
E.ON gas	2009	Commitments decision	Release of gas volumes at entry points	Essential facility, refusal to supply
E.ON/GDF collusion	2007	Fine		Market sharing
ENI	2007	Commitments decision	Divestiture of shareholdings	Essential facilities, constructive refusal to supply, deliberately avoiding capacity expansion
Long-term contracts in France	2007	Commitments decision	Return of large customers to market	Exclusive contracts, long duration, restriction of resale of electricity
Swedish interconnectors	2009	Commitments decision	Swedish transmission system divided into two zones; no limit on trading capacity on interconnectors	Discrimination on national grounds (destination of electricity)
CEZ	2009	Potential commitments decision	Divesting coal-fired generation capacity	Hoarding transmission capacity

In the gas markets, the European Commission has taken action against operators in the French, German and Italian markets regarding allegations of foreclosure of these markets to competitors.[64] The French undertaking has offered commitments aimed at resolving the situation, through agreeing to reduce the amount of long-term import capacity that it had reserved to itself for the French market and the Commission has agreed that this was an acceptable solution.[65] The European Commission's case against RWE for foreclosure of the German gas market was resolved when RWE agreed, by way of legally binding commitments,

---

[64] COMP/39.316, *GdF foreclosure*; COMP/39.315, *ENI*; COMP/39.402, *RWE gas foreclosure*.
[65] See European Commission, Press Release MEMO/09/536, 3 December 2009.

to dispose of its West German high pressure gas transmission network.[66] The idea behind this remedy is that, without control of the transmission network, RWE will no longer be able to favour its own supply company. In the ENI case, the Commission was concerned that ENI undertook capacity hoarding on its pipelines, made it more difficult for third parties to purchase capacity and, most unusually, had engaged in a strategic limitation of investment into new capacity. Although ENI did not agree with this analysis, it agreed to divest itself of shareholdings in a number of transmission companies.

A very significant decision was taken in the Commission's proceedings against E.ON, and some other undertakings, in the German wholesale electricity and electricity balancing markets.[67] Although E.ON only had a 20–30% market share, it was seen as part of a collectively dominant arrangement with two other undertakings which, in total, had between two-thirds and three-quarters of the market share. In the wholesale market, the issue arose in part because electricity cannot be stored. It therefore has to be produced on demand, which fluctuates over a day, and the German market operated on the basis of a bidding system, that is, those power generators that wished to provide power would make a bid into the system. The price would fluctuate depending on how much power was being offered. The bids that were made by power producers reflected the costs of their plant, for example nuclear-generated electricity is cheaper than that provided from a gas-fired plant. If certain types of generating capacity are withdrawn from this bidding system, it can raise the price of electricity significantly because the more expensive plants come on line. Although the undertaking withdrawing the generating capacity does not get a return on that capacity, it then gets a higher return on other parts of its portfolio. The Commission was concerned that E.ON was in a position to raise the price in the short term and also that this behaviour would have long-term effects through E.ON's long-term electricity supply contracts and offering potential competitors a stake in E.ON's power plants.

The balancing market concerns the issue of keeping an appropriate supply of electricity on the transmission system to maintain the appropriate tension level in the network. E.ON was the owner of the transmission system operator, hence it was a monopoly buyer. The Commission was concerned that it would raise its own costs by favouring its, more expensive, affiliates and subsidiaries, and that it was preventing the import of balancing energy by power producers from outside Germany. In order to deal with these objections, E.ON offered a series of commitments, which involved it in selling off a number of power plants and, most significantly, its transmission system business. A similar remedy is proposed in relation to the Czech electricity incumbent, CEZ, where the Commission is concerned that the incumbent may have been hoarding transmission capacity.[68] Like E.ON, CEZ has agreed to divest itself of certain generating capacity.

There are a number of interesting points about the Commission's recent activity in this area. First, it is noticeable that, with the exception of the decision in relation to the E.ON/GDF collusion dealt with under Article 101 TFEU, none of the cases have progressed to a final decision but have been dealt with by the companies offering legally binding commitments.

---

[66] See Press Release IP/09/410, 18 March 2009.
[67] COMP/39.389, *German electricity balancing market* and COMP/30.388, *German electricity wholesale market*. See European Commission, Press Release IP/08/1774, 26 November 2008; and Commission Decision, 26 November 2008.
[68] Commission Case COMP/397/27 CEZ.

The Commission has been able in these cases to obtain remedies through this process, such as divestiture, which it has not been able to obtain through formal decision making. The Commission has also relied, in a number of the cases, on the ideas of essential facilities and refusal to supply to support its position. This seems to be a continuation of a long-standing Commission position. Prior to the first version of the Gas and Electricity Directives, a senior Commission official took the view that such a doctrine existed and could be applied in the energy sector:[69]

> The company which operates the network cannot refuse a third party access to this network at least whenever:
>
> (1) it is ready to give reasonable remuneration;
> (2) there are capacities available;
> (3) there are no technical obstacles which would make this access impossible;
> (4) the construction of a direct line would not be an economically viable alternative; and
> (5) the supply is done under a programme which permits proper planning on the part of the operator of the network.

The Commission implemented this approach in what has been called the *Marathon* case, which involved a complaint by Marathon, a gas producer based off Norway, about the refusal of access to gas pipelines in Germany, France and the Netherlands.[70] The Commission began its investigation in 1996, Marathon settled its own claims in 2000 and the last case was concluded, by a settlement with the Commission, in 2004. The basic idea behind the (detailed) settlements was to improve the arrangements for third party shippers' access to the relevant pipelines and the Commission obtained a number of improvements. The length of time this case took suggested that, in commercial terms, antitrust enforcement of access rights is going to have limited practical effectiveness.[71] This criticism could not, however, be levied at the cases taken by the Commission subsequent to the sector inquiry, although the commitments offered seem to be more straightforward to implement and monitor. Finally, there are some innovative ideas in the Commission's decisions. This is notable in the ENI case, where the Commission introduces the idea of a strategic limitation of investment as an abuse of Article 102 TFEU and that it is not necessarily justified to refuse access even if there is no existing capacity.

In theory, some of these problems might disappear with the adoption of the new Directives in the electricity and gas sector, the aim of which is to ensure effective unbundling of generation and supply from the operation of the network(s), thus reducing the incentive for vertically integrated companies to favour their own subsidiaries. There are a number of different models from which to choose, but the big question is whether the legislation will work in practice. If it is perceived not to, then it is likely that the Commission will continue to take antitrust cases in this sector.

---

[69] C. Ehlermann, 'The Role of the European Commission as regards National Energy Policies' (1994) 12 *Journal of Energy and Natural Resources Law* 342 at 349.

[70] For details, see Cameron (n. 38) at paras 13.101–13.137; and M. Fernandez Salas, R. Klotz, S. Moonen and D. Schichnels, 'Access to gas pipelines: Lessons learnt from the Marathon case' (2004) *Competition Policy Newsletter*, No. 2, pp. 41–3.

[71] See Cameron (n. 38) at para. 137.

Merger control[72]

In addition to bringing cases against energy companies for the breach of competition rules, the Commission has also used the merger control process to try to encourage mergers which are compatible with a liberalised energy market, as well as trying to stop Member States from putting unjustified restrictions in the way of mergers. Given the earlier discussion of mergers (see Chapter 14), most of the activity has taken place in terms of conditions being imposed on mergers between energy companies, although there has been one high-profile prohibition decision.

The prohibition decision

The prohibition decision involved the proposed merger between the vertically integrated incumbent Portuguese electricity company (EDP) and its equivalent in the gas sector (GDP) with the aim of forming one large energy company in Portugal. The state had significant shareholdings in both companies and the merger was being pursued as part of a policy which was being adopted towards the energy industry by the Portuguese state. The merger was notified to the Commission, which ultimately decided to prohibit the merger because of its effects on competition.[73] In particular, the Commission felt that the merger would have prevented the entry of the gas company on to the wholesale electricity market[74] and its subsequent entry on to the retail electricity market, and this lack of entry by a potential competitor would have strengthened the already existing position of the incumbent electricity supplier. In terms of the plausibility of this argument, we only need to look at the British market, where British Gas is a major supplier of gas and electricity at the retail level, as well as being engaged in electricity generation. Similarly, the merger would prevent EDP from entering into the retail gas market, in the same way that electricity companies in Britain have entered the market to compete with British Gas. In addition, the Commission felt that the merger would give EDP access to confidential information relating to its competitors, preferential access to natural gas resources, the merged entity would have had the ability and incentive to raise rivals' costs either through raising the price of gas or diluting the quality of supply. In response to these concerns, the parties put forward some proposed remedies which, broadly speaking, involved the divestiture of certain gas assets, as well as certain promises about how the merged entity would behave in the future. The Commission rejected these as inadequate and prohibited the merger. This decision was appealed by the parties to the GC.[75]

The companies argued, among other grounds, that the Commission had required commitments which went beyond the requirements of the Merger Regulation and were aimed at encouraging the liberalisation of the electricity and gas markets and that this was unlawful, as being a misuse of power. This was rejected swiftly by the GC.[76] The GC did, however, accept the applicants' argument that the Commission had not properly taken into account the effects on the gas market, in the context of Portugal's derogation from the Gas Directive.[77]

---

[72] See Cameron (n. 38), ch. 14.
[73] European Commission, Case COMP/M.3440, *ENI/EDP/GDP* at paras 362–4.
[74] Through the use of combined cycle gas turbines.
[75] Case T-87/05 *Energias de Portugal (EDP)* v *Commission* [2005] ECR II-3745.
[76] Ibid. at paras 86–98.
[77] Ibid. at paras 113–33.

What this meant was that, because of the derogation, GDP had a monopoly position on the gas market in Portugal which, by definition, cannot be strengthened! This was not, however, sufficient for the GC to declare the decision unlawful, as there were still the problems that the Commission had identified in relation to the electricity market which were not sufficiently remedied by the commitments offered. Cameron concludes that this was correct because the merger would have eliminated a significant competitor to EDP and that the case sent an important signal to other market participants as to the limits to the Commission's policy on mergers.[78]

This can be illustrated by a subsequent case, involving the merger of Gaz de France (GDF) with Suez, a French company but one that was active on the gas and electricity markets in Belgium, as well as France.[79] GDF provided gas at a wholesale level in Belgium as well as engaging in gas supply at a retail level. Within the Belgian gas markets the effect of this merger would have been to create a company with a near monopoly share in the various gas markets, as well as eliminating the main competitor to Suez, that is, GDF, in the context of a market where, the Commission felt, there were very substantial barriers to entry. Similarly, looking at the gas markets in France, the transaction would strengthen GDF's position by increasing its market share and eliminating an important competitor. On the electricity generating market in Belgium, the transaction would allow Suez, the dominant company, to strengthen its dominant position by eliminating its main competitor and would have had the same effect in a number of markets for electricity supply. In response to the Commission's objections the parties eventually proposed that the Belgian gas operations of Suez would be divested to a new company, GDF would sell off its shares in its Belgian electricity subsidiary and that gas storage and transmission in Belgium would be reorganised and become the responsibility of a company that was independent of the merged entity. The Commission took the view that these proposals would remedy the damage to competition caused by the proposed merger and approved the merger, subject to these conditions. Distrigaz was sold to an Italian energy company, ENI, while the GDF stake in the Belgian electricity subsidiary was sold to the French incumbent electricity company, EDF.

Some recent energy mergers continue this theme of the Commission approving the proposals subject to the divestiture of certain operations in order to deal with identified competition problems. So, for example, when RWE, a German electricity firm, acquired Essent, a Dutch company with, among other things, interests in the German wholesale electricity market through its controlling shareholding in Stadtwerke Bremen, the Commission found that the original form of the transaction would have strengthened RWE's collective dominant position on the German wholesale market by removing an actual competitor and giving RWE an incentive to withdraw generation capacity to raise prices. The Commission agreed to the merger on the condition that the controlling shareholding was divested to an appropriate party.[80] There do not, however, appear to be any such merger cases since the beginning of 2010.

---

[78] Cameron (n. 38) at para. 14.97.

[79] European Commission, Case COMP/M.4180, *Gaz de France/Suez*, 14 November 2006.

[80] See Press Release IP/09/987, 23 June 2009. Similarly, see the conditions imposed on the merger of Nuon Energy, a Dutch firm, with Vattenfall, a Swedish firm: Press Release IP/09/978, 22 June 2009; 'EDF/Segebel' Commission Decision M.5549, 23.09.2009 and *GDF Suez/International Power* Commission Decision M.5978, 26.01.2011.

COMPETITION LAW IN PRACTICE[81]

Gas, long-term contracts and remedies

Distrigaz,[82] which at the time of the decision was part of the French Suez group, was the dominant gas supplier on the Belgian gas market, having around 70–80% of the relevant market.

Distrigaz had entered into long-term contracts with its industrial customers, that is, those customers using high volumes of gas. Some of the contracts required the customers to buy all of their gas from Distrigaz. Others specified an annual minimum quantity that must be purchased and an annual maximum quantity. The contracts were generally of a year's duration, although a number of them had no specified date of termination and some were automatically renewable. On the basis of this, the Commission did a calculation of the proportion of the market tied to Distrigaz, which is illustrated below:

Period	Proportion of the market already tied to Distrigaz under the contracts in force on 1 January 2005
Six months ahead: 1 July 2005	50–60%[83]
One year ahead: 1 January 2006	35–45%
18 months ahead: 1 July 2006	30–40%
Two years ahead: 1 January 2007	20–30%
Three years ahead: 1 January 2008	20–30%

The Commission took the view that these arrangements significantly foreclosed the market in a way which could amount to an abuse of a dominant position because they made it difficult for alternative suppliers to enter the Belgian gas market. This was because long-term gas supply contracts would prevent customers from switching supplier and would thereby limit the scope for other gas suppliers to conclude contracts with customers and so foreclose their access to the market.

In order to solve this problem, Distrigaz proposed a range of commitments, that is, changes to its commercial practices. The Commission put these out to consultation, which resulted in some modification to the commitments. Distrigaz agreed, among other things, as follows:

- to ensure that on average at least 70% of the gas it supplied each year would return to the market, that is, the contract would be available for alternative suppliers to bid for;

- no new contracts for users or electricity producers would be over five years' duration;

- it would not include any use, resale or destination clauses or any tacit renewal clauses in future gas supply agreements and would remove (or not enforce) any such clauses from existing gas supply agreements.

---

[81] Commission Decision, Case COMP/B-1/37966, *Distrigaz*, 11 October 2007.

[82] Alternatively, Distrigas is used in the text of the Commission decision.

[83] As a result of commercial confidentiality, the Commission only gives a range estimate of market share.

Analysis

This case is interesting because it shows, first, how incumbents can maintain a strong market position even after liberalisation. The second reason why it is interesting is the approach to remedies and the wider context of the case. In terms of remedies, this has been one of the first cases where the European Commission, rather than proceeding to a formal decision imposing sanctions, has accepted commitments from the parties concerned to take action to remedy the problems which have been identified. It is worth noting that a similar decision was taken by the German competition authority, the Bundeskartellamt, in relation to E.ON Ruhrgas.[84] The wider context was the merger between the Suez group, of which Distrigaz was a member, and Gaz de France. One of the conditions for agreeing to this merger, laid down by the Commission, was that Distrigaz should be divested and it was eventually sold to ENI, an Italian energy company.

Telecommunications[85]

Background to the telecommunications industry

Telecommunications was the first of the major privatisations in the UK, with the legislation being passed in 1984, and it is an industry that has undergone major changes in the last 25 years, driven in particular by technological changes. The two major, related, changes have been the invention of mobile phones and their rapid take-up and the digitalisation of communications signals, that is, converting electronic communications into a series of binary signals which are converted into the appropriate format at the consumer's end. This has meant that a much greater variety of information may be carried over telecommunications networks, which are no longer restricted to voice messages. Thus all sorts of data, from pictures, videos, etc., are now carried over telecommunications networks and this data is accessed in a variety of ways: over phones, through computers, or even, although currently less common, through televisions. So, currently, telecommunications regulation is seen as part of communications regulation, although a very different legal regime applies to the activities of those engaged in broadcast television, with which we will not be concerned.

Telecommunications is a network industry in two respects. First, the key component of the industry is the network, which will link all users on that network. Creating the actual physical infrastructure is, however, very expensive and entails large fixed costs and so is very difficult to replicate, although not impossible, since some physical infrastructure has been created for mobile networks. So, like electricity transmission, the main fixed line network can be seen as a natural monopoly. Secondly, there are also what are more technically referred to as 'network effects', which means that the value of a network grows in relation to the number of users who are connected to it. This point is fundamental to telecommunications. This is

---

[84] See European Commission, Press Release MEMO/07/407, 11 October 2007 and *http://www.bundeskartellamt. de/wEnglisch/News/Archiv/ArchivNews2006/2006_01_17.php* (accessed 09/08/12).

[85] Generally, see I. Walden (ed.), *Telecommunications Law and Regulation* (3rd edn, Oxford University Press, 2009), especially ch. 9.

perhaps intuitively obvious: the whole point of a telecommunications network is that you will want to be able to communicate with anyone else who has a phone or communications device. Taken together, these two points mean that a key issue for any telecommunications provider is the ability to gain access to any other telecommunication provider's network. You could not, for example, offer a mobile phone network where your subscribers could contact only other subscribers on that network but not, for example, people who subscribed to BT.[86] So, at the centre of any telecommunications regulatory regime is the issue of access and interconnection. Although this issue is addressed in competition law by the doctrines relating to refusal to supply and essential facilities (discussed in Chapter 4), these issues have been dealt with in telecommunications by the creation, as we shall see, of specific regulatory regimes.

BT, or as it was then known, British Telecommunications, was privatised under the Telecommunications Act 1984, which also created a regulator, the Director General for Telecommunications (DGT). Unlike the arrangements in electricity, BT was privatised intact but provision was made for there to be one competitor, Mercury Communications, a subsidiary of Cable and Wireless, which had terms in its licence designed to give it an incentive to build its own infrastructure. This cautious policy towards competition continued until 1991 when, after a review, access to BT's network was allowed to telecommunications companies other than Mercury. There was still, however, a strong emphasis in encouraging the development of infrastructure within regulatory policy. This policy changed from about 1998 to a greater emphasis on service provider based competition partly because of the influence of EU Directives and partly because of the inability of providers to obtain funding for infrastructure projects.[87] There was a similarly cautious approach to competition in relation to the development of mobile communications, which started initially as a duopoly in the early 1980s but was opened up to two more competitors in 1993.[88]

More recently, the major influence on the development of telecommunications law in the UK has been the creation of an EU regime for electronic communications. This has partly been in recognition of the growing economic importance of telecommunications to the European Union and partly because of a desired policy to liberalise the provision of telecommunications services and thus obtain the benefits of competitive markets, as most of the provision of telecommunications services in the EU has historically been done by state-owned enterprises with monopoly powers. The rules are now contained in a series of Directives which set down a basic framework for the regulation of telecommunications services and which have been implemented in the UK through the Communications Act 2003; and these Directives are discussed below.

The Communications Act 2003 set up the Office of Communications (Ofcom), which has responsibility for regulating telecommunications and other forms of communication, that is television broadcasting and radio. Unlike the situation in energy, telecommunications providers do not have to be licensed by Ofcom; instead, they all have to abide by a set of general conditions which are prescribed in the legislation and include, among other things, an obligation to negotiate interconnection with other telecommunications providers. Providers considered by Ofcom to have 'Significant Market Power' (SMP – discussed below) are subject to certain special conditions. Ofcom has a variety of powers to ensure compliance with either

---

[86] Think about Skype in this context.

[87] Ofcom, 'Telecommunications Review' (2005), paras 4.19–4.20.

[88] See D. Geradin amd M. Kerf, *Controlling Market Power in Telecommunications* (Oxford University Press, 2003), ch. 6.

General or Special conditions and, in addition, it also has powers to enforce the Competition Act 1998 and Articles 101 and 102 TFEU concurrently with the OFT.

Enforcement of UK competition law

In the same way as in the energy sector, the OFT has published a set of guidelines explaining the application of the Competition Act rules to the telecommunications sector.[89] The guidance explains the relationship between UK and EU law, the relationship between the various pieces of UK legislation and sets out the OFT's approach to market definition and market power in this area. It is worth noting that the focus is on market power, which is defined as meaning where the undertaking is not effectively constrained by competition, giving it in practice the power to raise prices consistently and profitably above the competitive level.[90] There is also a brief description of the various abuses of market power that may be relevant, of which the most interesting part is the general approach which will be taken to pricing abuses. Here the OFT sets out the peculiarities of the telecommunications industry, which is characterised by economies of scale and scope. For example, long distance and local calls are carried, in part, over the same network. What this means is that most telecommunications companies are multi-product companies where a large proportion of the costs do not vary with the output and are common between products. Thus, the OFT takes the view that the appropriate cost base is, in general, long-run incremental cost, as opposed to say, average variable cost (see Chapter 3 and the discussion on predatory pricing for more).[91]

The enforcement of the Competition Act provisions is the responsibility of Ofcom. Although, in quantitative terms, most of Ofcom's enforcement activity relates to non-competition law issues, relating to regulation and consumer protection, it has taken up a number of competition cases, generally in response to complaints or information brought by companies to it.[92] Since 2003 it has decided at least 20 Competition Act cases and currently is investigating one case.[93] With one exception,[94] all the cases involve Article 102 TFEU issues and are primarily about access to a network, although there have been other complaints relating to discount schemes[95] and the placing of BT's directory inquiry number on the front of the phonebook. It is noticeable that Ofcom has not yet found an infringement of the Competition Act. Like Ofgem, it has taken more enforcement action in relation to its regulatory responsibilities.

The phonebook decision[96] is interesting because here, at the time when directory inquiry services were opened up to competition, a number of BT's competitors claimed that BT was

---

[89] OFT, 'Competition Act 1998: The application in the telecommunications sector' (OFT 417)', available at *http://www.oft.gov.uk/about-the-oft/legal-powers/legal/competition-act-1998/publications* (accessed 09/08/12). The guidance is somewhat dated, as it refers to the Director General of Telecommunications throughout.

[90] Ibid. at para. 6.2.

[91] Ibid. at paras 7.5–7.11.

[92] Ofcom, *Enforcement Report* (2009) at para. 4.9.

[93] See *http://stakeholders.ofcom.org.uk/enforcement/competition-bulletins/closed-cases/* (accessed 09/08/12) for the closed cases, described as the most important ones.

[94] Complaint about the joint selling of national radio broadcast rights to Football Association Challenge Cup ('FA Cup') matches by the Football Association to a single purchaser: CW/00790/09/04, closed October 2005.

[95] BT's volume discount scheme for IPStream and DataStream: CW/00657/07/03 (2004), closed when BT changed the scheme.

[96] Decision of the Director General of Telecommunications, BT publishing its 118500 directory inquiries number on the front of the BT phonebook: Case CW/604/03/03 (2003).

abusing its dominant position by advertising the number for its directory inquiry services on the phonebook. The Director General of Telecommunications (DGT), Ofcom's predecessor, investigated and, although he decided that BT had a dominant position in relation to phone-books and that it was possible in principle to leverage the dominance from phonebooks to directory inquiry services, he concluded, on the basis of statistical analysis, that the use by BT of its advertising advantage had not had a material adverse impact on competition. In other words, rather than relying on the likely effects of a practice, as has typically been the case in Article 102 TFEU cases, the DGT carried out an analysis of the actual effect.

Enforcement of EU competition law

The European Commission has had a long-standing interest in the development of tele-communications in the EU, seeing a thriving telecommunications industry as a key part of the European economy. Although it has produced guidance on the application of competition law in the telecommunications area,[97] most of its formal decisional activity has concentrated on dealing with strategic alliances and merger control, although there have been five important cases: one on predatory pricing, one on roaming agreements in Germany (discussed in Chapters 3 and 2 respectively),[98] one on refusal to supply[99] and two on margin squeeze (discussed below). The Commission has conducted sector inquiries in this area, one dealing with the local loop,[100] one on leased lines and one on mobile roaming. The leased line inquiry ended when it became apparent that there had been substantial price decreases, while the local loop issue was solved with the adopting of a Council Regulation.[101] Similarly, the investigation into mobile roaming charges has led to the adoption and amendment of a Regulation to deal with the issue.[102]

Regulation of telecommunications at European level

Liberalisation of European telecommunications has a relatively long and chequered history, which began with hotly contested unilateral moves by the Commission to liberalise certain aspects of telecommunications, using its legislative powers under Article 106(3) TFEU.[103] Having won this battle, the Commission shifted to developing general legislative rules to govern this sector, the most recent of which are contained in the so-called new regulatory

---

[97] European Commission, *Guidelines on the Application of EEC Competition rules in the telecommunications sector* [1991] OJ C233/2; 'Notice on the application of the competition rules to access agreements in the tele-communications sector' [1998] OJ C265/2.

[98] Case T-340/03 *France Télécom SA* v *Commission* [2007] ECR II-107; Case T-328/03 *O2* v *Commission* [2006] ECR II-1231.

[99] Commission Decision COMP/39.525, *Telekomunikacja Polska*, 22.06.2011.

[100] That is, the physical circuit which links the subscriber to the local switch and from there to the telecom-munications network.

[101] See European Commission Press Release IP/01/1852, 11 December 2002; and Regulation (2000/2887/EC) on unbundled access to the local loop, OJ L336, 30.12.2000.

[102] Regulation (EC) No. 717/2007 of the European Parliament and of the Council of 27 June 2007 on roaming on public mobile telephone networks within the Community and amending Directive 2002/21/EC, OJ L171/50, amended by Regulation (EC) No. 544/2009 of the European Parliament and of the Council of 18 June 2009.

[103] For the early history, see P. LaRouche, *Competition Law and Regulation in European Telecommunications* (Hart Publishing, Oxford, 2000), sections 1 and 2.

framework of 2002.[104] One of the difficulties for the Commission has been that Member States and incumbent operators have had different attitudes towards the liberalisation process, with a number of them being, at best, unenthusiastic about this development. This is reflected in the rules which give the Commission specific powers of intervention in order to ensure that the rules are applied appropriately, as we shall see.

National regulatory authorities

The starting point is the Directive that sets up a common regulatory framework for electronic communications, which means services provided wholly or mainly by the conveyance of signals on electronic communications networks,[105] so it covers providers other than just telecommunications providers. Member States are required to set up National Regulatory Authorities (NRAs), which are to be independent of the industry, although not necessarily from government, and which are to carry out the tasks set under the Directive.[106] A right of appeal, on the merits, is to be available against decisions of the NRA.[107] The job of the NRAs is, among other things, to promote competition in the provision of electronic communication services and ensure that there is no distortion or restriction of competition in this sector.[108] The NRAs have a number of non-competition objectives such as contributing to the development of the internal market and promoting the interests of European citizens through promoting a high level of consumer protection and ensuring access to universal service. In other words, there is likely to be some balancing of competition objectives against other objectives.

As mentioned above, a critical issue in the context of telecommunications is the ability of operators to have access to and interconnect with networks of their competitors and this is the subject of a specific Directive.[109] This Directive is meant to harmonise the way that Member States regulate access to and interconnection with electronic networks and ensure that there are no barriers to undertakings negotiating access and interconnection agreements between themselves. NRAs are required to encourage – and, where appropriate, ensure – adequate access and interconnection, and interoperability of services, exercising their responsibility in a way that promotes efficiency and sustainable competition, and gives the maximum benefit to end-users.[110] A major problem area revolves around incumbents, which may well feel that it is not in their commercial interest either to allow access and interconnection or to make it too easy for competitors. To cater for this, the Directive provides that NRAs must have the power to impose specific obligations on undertakings that they have decided have Significant Market Power (SMP) on specific markets.[111] These are obligations of transparency,

---

[104] The relevant Directives are: Directive (2002/21/EC) on a common regulatory framework, OJ L108/33, 24.04.2002; Directive (2002/19/EC) on access and interconnection, OJ L108/7, 24.04.2002; Directive (2002/20/EC) on the authorisation of electronic communications networks and services, OJ L108/21, 24.04.2002; Directive (2002/22/EC) on universal service and users' rights relating to electronic communications networks and services, OJ L108/51, 24.04.2002; Directive (2002/58/EC) on privacy and electronic communications, OJ L201/37, 31.07.2002; Directive (2002/77/EC) on competition in the markets for electronic communications networks and services, OJ L249/21, 17.09.2002; Regulation (2000/2887/EC) on unbundled access to the local loop, OJ L336, 30.12.2000.

[105] Directive (2002/21/EC) on a common regulatory framework, OJ L108, 24.04.2002, Art. 2(c).

[106] Ibid. at Art. 3.

[107] Ibid. at Art. 4.

[108] Ibid. at Art. 8.

[109] Directive (2002/19/EC) on access and interconnection, OJ L108, 24.04.2002.

[110] Ibid. at Art. 5.

[111] Ibid. at Art. 8.

non-discrimination, accounting separation, access to and use of specific network facilities, price control and cost accounting obligations.[112] The idea behind these obligations is to provide the NRA with sufficient legal tools to prevent an incumbent making access and interconnection to its network too difficult.

In addition to this area, when they have decided that certain markets are not effectively competitive, the NRAs may, having identified undertakings with SMP, impose regulatory controls on them in relation to their retail services, the minimum set of leased lines that they provide and carrier pre-selection.[113] As regards retail services, a given retail market must be identified and the obligations imposed may include requirements that the identified under-takings do not charge excessive prices, inhibit market entry or restrict competition by setting predatory prices, show undue preference to specific end-users or unreasonably bundle services.

It can be seen, therefore, that there are two crucial issues for the decision making of NRAs: market definition and the assessment of SMP. One of the aims of the new regulatory frame-work is to ensure consistency of practice across NRAs on both these issues and two mechanisms are provided for in the Framework Directive. First, the Commission is required to adopt a recommendation on product markets and services, as well as guidelines on market analysis and significant market power.[114] Secondly, if the NRA proposes to take certain decisions, these have to be communicated to the Commission in advance for comment. Decisions on market definition and market analysis, as well as the imposition of obligations under the Access and Interconnection Directive and the Universal Service Directive, are communicated to the Commission, which may comment on them, and the NRA is required to take the 'utmost account' of the Commission's comments.[115] However, when defining the relevant markets, if an NRA wishes to depart from the recommendations and the guidelines, or the NRA is considering whether to designate an undertaking as having SMP, not only must it inform the Commission but, ultimately, the Commission may take a decision requiring the NRA to withdraw the draft measure.[116] In other words, the Commission has the last word on certain issues.[117]

The relationship between the regulatory framework and EU competition law

A key question is the relationship between the so-called new regulatory framework and EU competition law because of the overlap of certain issues. In its guidance, the Commission makes the point that markets will be defined and significant market power identified using the same methodologies as are used in competition law.[118] One of the key issues in this area is market definition, partly because of the complexity of the telecommunications market and also because, for an NRA to impose special conditions on an operator, it must

---

[112] Ibid. at Arts 9–13.

[113] Directive (2002/22/EC) on universal service and users' rights relating to electronic communications networks and services, OJ L108, 24.04.2002, Arts 17–19.

[114] Directive (2002/21/EC) on a common regulatory framework, OJ L108, 24.04.2002, Art. 15.

[115] Ibid. at Art. 7.

[116] Ibid.

[117] And has vetoed certain decisions: see European Commission, Press Release MEMO/08/620, 15 October 2008 for a list. See *http://ec.europa.eu/information_society/policy/ecomm/implementation_enforcement/eu_consultation_procedures/index_en.htm* for current developments (accessed 09/08/12).

[118] European Commission, *Guidelines on market analysis and the assessment of significant market power under the Community regulatory framework for electronic communications networks and services*, OJ C165, 11.07.2002, pp. 6–31 (at para. 24).

find that it has significant market power (SMP). SMP is defined in the Framework Directive, Article 14:

> An undertaking shall be deemed to have significant market power if, either individually or jointly with others, it enjoys a position equivalent to dominance, that is to say a position of economic strength affording it the power to behave to an appreciable extent independently of competitors, customers and ultimately consumers.

The Commission's view is that SMP is 'aligned' with the concept of dominance and should therefore be assessed using the same approach with, however, one important difference. This is because, when assessing SMP, national regulatory authorities are making a decision for the future, so the assessment is forward looking. When deciding whether an undertaking has a dominant position, in order to determine whether there has been a breach of Article 102 TFEU, a competition authority is looking at the position in the past. The Commission goes on to point out that market shares are often used as a proxy for market power. In its view undertakings with a market share below 25% are unlikely to enjoy single dominance, while undertakings with very large market shares, above 50%, may be presumed to have SMP if that share has remained stable over time.[119] The Commission goes on to emphasise that the existence of a dominant position cannot be established on the sole basis of large market shares and that NRAs should undertake a thorough and overall analysis of the economic characteristics of the relevant market before coming to a conclusion as to the existence of SMP.[120] It gives a list of criteria to be considered, although it points out that a dominant position can derive from a combination of these criteria, which need not be determinative if taken separately:

- overall size of the undertaking,
- control of infrastructure not easily duplicated,
- technological advantages or superiority,
- absence of or low countervailing buying power,
- easy or privileged access to capital markets/financial resources,
- product/services diversification (e.g. bundled products or services),
- economies of scale,
- economies of scope,
- vertical integration,
- a highly developed distribution and sales network,
- absence of potential competition,
- barriers to expansion.

It goes on to say that a finding of dominance depends on ease of market entry and that there may be high barriers to entry in this sector because of legislative and regulatory requirements which limit the number of entrants and also because of the large investment needed to enter some of these markets. The Commission does, however, recognise the importance of innovation and the competitive threats that may arise from new innovation.

[119] Ibid. at para. 75.
[120] Ibid. at para. 78.

As the discussion above indicates, market definition in the area of telecommunications is by no means straightforward and part of the aim of the new framework is to allow the European Commission to exercise some level of control and ensure some consistency of approach by the national regulatory authorities. The issue of the relationship between decisions of national regulators and the application of EU competition law has become particularly controversial and it is to that we now turn.

Regulatory conflict and margin squeeze

The area where this has arisen revolves around the question of margin squeeze, which was discussed briefly earlier in the text (see Chapter 3). To remind ourselves, as O'Donoghue and Padilla explain,[121] this abuse may occur when there are two markets, an upstream and a downstream one, and the upstream product is a necessary component in the good or service provided on the downstream market. If there is a vertically integrated undertaking which has a dominant position in an upstream market, there may be allegations that either (1) it is charging too high a price for the upstream input which it is selling to its downstream competitors, or (2) it is charging too low a price for its downstream products. The essence of the allegation is that the difference between the upstream and the downstream prices (the margin) is such that a non-vertically integrated competitor on the downstream market cannot trade profitably. The result of such practices will be that the downstream rivals are driven out of the market or become marginal competitors. Figure 15.3 illustrates the factual situation that this entails.

This has become particularly important in relation to telecommunications and the first important case involved Deutsche Telekom (DT).[122] This case arose out of the decision to require DT to offer fully unbundled access to the local loop. Under the relevant German legislation, the wholesale access charges had to be approved by the German telecommunications regulatory

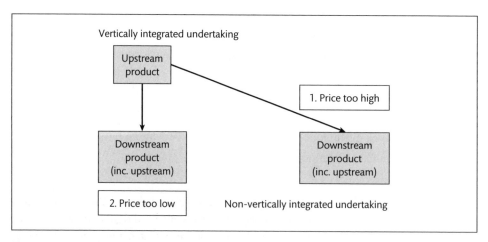

Figure 15.3 Margin squeeze

---

[121] R. O'Donoghue and J. Padilla, *The Law and Economics of Article 82 EC* (Hart Publishing, Oxford, 2006) at p. 304.

[122] Case T-271/03 *Deutsche Telekom v Commission* [2008] ECR II 477.

authority (RegTP) and those charges were required, by the relevant legislation, to be based on the 'costs of efficient service provision'. At the retail level, DT's charges for access to analogue and ISDN lines were regulated by a price cap system, whereas prices for access to ADSL were set at its own discretion, although they could be reviewed later by the regulator, as in fact happened in 2001. The Commission decided that DT had infringed Article 102 TFEU by operating a margin squeeze by charging its competitors prices for wholesale access that were higher than its charges for retail access to the local network. DT argued, in a general sense, that there could not be abusive pricing in the form of a margin squeeze, because the wholesale price was fixed by the regulatory authority as was, indeed, the retail price too during the relevant period. DT went on to point out that not only had the procedure been put in place to ensure through advance regulation that there was no abusive pricing, but that the German regulator had decided a number of times during the relevant period that no margin squeeze existed. The Commission's response to this argument was that DT had scope to increase the prices it charged for retail access within the existing regulatory system. The GC held that, on the facts, DT had scope to avoid the margin squeeze by increasing its retail charges.

DT also challenged the Commission's calculation of the margin squeeze, because this calculation was based on DT's charges and costs as a vertically integrated dominant undertaking, rather than the charges and costs of its competitors. In addition, DT criticised the Commission's decision because it only took into account revenues from the access services, excluding revenues from other services which might be supplied by the access network. The GC's response to the first argument was as follows:

> ... the abusive nature of a dominant undertaking's pricing practices is determined in principle on the basis of its own situation, and therefore on the basis of its own charges and costs, rather than on the basis of the situation of actual or potential competitors ... any other approach could be contrary to the general principle of legal certainty. If the lawfulness of the pricing practices of a dominant undertaking depended on the particular situation of competing undertakings, particularly their cost structure – information which is generally not known to the dominant undertaking – the latter would not be in a position to assess the lawfulness of its own activities.[123]

The case then went on appeal to the CJEU, which upheld the GC's decision. Importantly, the CJEU confirmed that margin squeeze was, in itself, an abuse of a dominant position and it was not necessary to establish that either the wholesale or the retail prices were abusive.[124] The CJEU was unsympathetic to the argument that Deutsche Telekom's wholesale prices were controlled by RegTP, pointing out that it was accepted that it had the scope to alter its retail prices to avoid a margin squeeze and that the Commission could not be bound by the decision of a national body.[125]

Subsequent to this case came a preliminary reference from Sweden, *TeliaSonera*, which again raised the question of margin squeeze.[126] Here the Swedish competition authority had taken action against TeliaSonera for a margin squeeze, in breach of Article 102 TFEU and the Swedish Court referred a series of questions about the doctrine to the CJEU. The court took a very expansive approach to margin squeeze, holding that it was an independent form of abuse

---

[123] Ibid. at paras 188 and 192.
[124] Case C-280/08 P *Deutsche Telekom AG v European Commission* [2010] ECR I-9555 at para. 183.
[125] Ibid. paras 77–96.
[126] Case C-52/09 *Konkurrensverket v Telia Sonera Sverige Ab* [2011] 4 CMLR 982.

distinct from that of refusal to supply and that it was irrelevant that there was no regulatory obligation to supply the appropriate input.[127] It was also irrelevant that the supply was to a new customer, nor would it be relevant if the new clients were not yet active on the market. In other words, there could be an abuse of dominant position both in relation to existing customers, new customers and potential customers. It was, however, made clear that the practice would only be considered a problem if it excluded operators that were as efficient as the incumbent ('equally efficient').

Similar issues have been raised in the *Telefónica* case, which was also appealed to the GC.[128] One of the interesting differences in this case is that the Spanish regulator had attempted to design a price control for wholesale access which was meant to avoid the problem of margin squeeze. The Commission's response to the argument that therefore there could not be an abuse under Article 102 TFEU was that the cost data used in an *ex ante* decision was inappropriate because it was not based on historical costs but on estimates and that those estimates were lower than the actual historical costs.[129] It was therefore not successful in avoiding the margin squeeze, as was demonstrated by the Commission's investigation which was based on actual costs. The Commission's decision was upheld by the GC, which followed the approach taken by the CJEU in *TeliaSonera*.

The margin squeeze cases have been very controversial. One criticism is that there is no need for this competition law doctrine as the problems that it purports to address can be dealt with by other doctrines, such as predatory and excessive pricing.[130] In support of this, the critics point out that American antitrust law has developed in a different direction to the point where margin squeeze is almost impossible to prove, absent other antitrust violations.[131] It has been argued that the idea of margin squeeze is much more of a regulatory doctrine because it is used to encourage entry into newly liberalised industries, even by competitors that are not as efficient as the incumbent. This has led to a broad approach to the doctrine of margin squeeze, which is said to be incompatible with the objectives of competition law.[132]

The second area of controversy is the relationship between Commission decisions and those of the NRAs. In doctrinal terms there is no question: insofar as there is a conflict between a national regulatory authority and the Commission, it is the Commission's view that prevails. To put it another way, competition law norms contained in the Treaties are superior to regulatory objectives contained in other legislation.[133] Although this approach has been criticised on the grounds that national regulators should be allowed to trade off allocative and dynamic efficiency and take non-economic considerations into account,[134] this does not seem to be an accurate description of what the national regulators were doing in either of these two cases. The general thesis about trade-offs is also, in its turn, controversial.

---

[127] Ibid. para. 56 and 59.
[128] Case COMP/38.784, *Wanadoo España vs. Telefónica*, 4 July 2007, appealed as Case T-398/07 *Spain v Commission* judgment of 29 March 2012 (GC).
[129] Ibid. at para. 494.
[130] G. Faella and R. Pardolesi, 'Squeezing price under EC antitrust law' (2010) 6 *European Competition Journal* 255 make this argument.
[131] Ibid. and see also N. Dunne, 'Margin squeeze: Theory, practice, policy' (2012) 33 *European Competition Law Review* 29 and 61.
[132] H. Auf'mkolk, 'The "Feedback Effect" of Applying EU Competition Law to Regulated Industries: Doctrinal Contamination in the Case of Margin Squeeze' (2012) 3 *Journal of European Competition Law & Practice* 149.
[133] See, for example, Case T-398/07 *Spain v Commission* judgment of 29 March 2012 (GC) at para. 56.
[134] See G. Monti, 'Managing the Intersection of Utilities Regulation and EC Competition Law', LSE Law, Society and Economy Working Papers 8/2008.

Conclusions

Perhaps the most interesting lesson from this chapter is that it points out the limitation of competition law as a policy. In both energy and telecommunications, policy decisions have been made to liberalise the industries and change their structures. This far-reaching change is something that has required the use of legislation and, in addition, the creation of specialised regulators. The role of competition law is to ensure that, once markets are created, they continue to function effectively. There is much room for argument about how much intervention that should entail.

The other point to notice is that the European Commission has been more active in applying competition law in the energy sector as opposed to telecommunications. This seems partly due to the fact that technological changes in telecommunications have made it a more competitive industry and that there has been greater willingness on the part of Member States to adopt a framework of rules reflecting these technological changes. This does not mean that the Commission does not have a role to play, as the discussion above indicates that it has a central role, but that this largely takes place outside what is conventionally considered competition law. It is also worth noting that many of the Commission's more recent cases in the energy sector seem to have begun after the sector inquiry, which seems to have given the Commission a deeper understanding of how the industry functions.

Summary

➤ Both the energy and telecommunications industries have elements of natural monopoly within them. In addition, there are policy objectives other than competition which are considered relevant in these areas.

➤ Both industries have been subject to privatisation, in the UK, as well as liberalisation at both the UK and EU level. Within the UK the regulation of these industries is overseen by a sector specific regulator that has powers to enforce competition law, as well as specific regulatory powers.

➤ There is a specific framework of EU rules for both industries.

➤ Although there have been a number of allegations of anti-competitive conduct in the energy and telecommunications industries, there has been only one case where a regulator has found a breach of competition law in the UK.

➤ In relation to energy, the European Commission has been active in pursuing cases against long-term and exclusive supply contracts under Article 101 TFEU.

➤ Under Article 102 TFEU, the Commission has been concerned with a variety of practices which it sees as foreclosing access to markets. It has dealt with many of these cases through settlements, rather than formal decisions.

➤ A new legislative package has been implemented in the energy sector to address a number of the problems that the Commission has identified.

➤ One of the most controversial aspects of Commission practice in the telecommunications sphere has been the cases on margin squeeze, where undertakings have tried to defend themselves by arguing that their rates were approved by national regulatory authorities. So far, this defence has been rejected by the GC and the CJEU.

Further reading

Cameron, P., *Competition in Energy Markets: Law and Regulation in the European Union* (2nd edn, Oxford University Press, 2007). *A comprehensive overview of the area. Very clearly written.*

Koenig, C., Bartosch, A., Braun, J.-D. and Romes, M. (eds) *EC Competition and Telecommunications Law* (2nd edn, Kluwer, Deventer, 2009). *Multi-authored comprehensive reference work.*

Nyssens, H. and Schnichels, D., 'Energy', in J. Faull and A. Nikpay (eds) *The EC Law of Competition* (2nd edn, Oxford University Press, 2007). *Two senior Commission officials give their exposition of the law in the area.*

Walden, I. (ed.) *Telecommunications Law and Regulation* (3rd edn, Oxford University Press, 2009). *Multi-authored volume which gives a comprehensive overview of telecommunications law, including a good section on competition law.*

Margin squeeze

Auf'mkolk, H., 'The "Feedback Effect" of Applying EU Competition Law to Regulated Industries: Doctrinal Contamination in the Case of Margin Squeeze' (2012) 3 *Journal of European Competition Law & Practice* 149. *Interesting argument contrasting 'regulatory' and 'competition law' approaches to margin squeeze.*

Dunne, N., 'Margin Squeeze: Theory, practice, policy' (2012) 33 *European Competition Law Review* 29 and 61. *Good discussion of EU and US case law, contrasting different approaches.*

Faella, G. and Pardolesi, R., 'Squeezing Price under EC Antitrust law' (2010) 6 *European Competition Journal* 255. *Balanced discussion of the economic issues surrounding margin squeeze cases and early case law.*

Chapter outline

This chapter discusses:

➤ Why there is an international aspect to competition law

➤ The general approach of public international law

➤ The American approach to anti-competitive agreements concluded outside the US

➤ The EU approach to activities which take place outside the EU

➤ The provisions of UK legislation

➤ Arrangements for bilateral cooperation between the EU and US authorities

➤ Forums for multilateral cooperation between competition authorities

➤ Conclusions.

Introduction

So far this book has discussed competition law in terms of the impact that it will have on commercial practices within the economy of the UK, whether brought about by UK or EU law. This does, however, neglect an important aspect of economies today, namely their international dimension. There are many companies that operate on a global dimension, such as Microsoft, Toyota and General Electric, and decisions taken outside the UK, and indeed the EU, can have important effects on the economy and consumers within the UK and EU. The economic and financial crisis which hit the UK from late 2008, for example, had some of its origins in the collapse of the American sub-prime mortgage market.[1] From the business perspective, multinational companies will have to deal with a number of competition agencies and one of their goals here will be to have consistent treatment across the various agencies in different countries. From a business point of view, it can be very frustrating and costly to be allowed to do something in one country but forbidden from doing it in another. For example, GE's proposal to merge with Honeywell (discussed in Chapter 13) was approved by the US authorities but blocked by the European Commission, which meant that the plan could

---

[1] Roughly, mortgage lending to high risk customers.

not go ahead. Generally we think of competition law enforcement as being a domestic matter that is confined to the territory of the country concerned, although the EU is a conspicuous exception to this, being an attempt to connect disparate economies and therefore needing a set of common rules and enforcement of them. With the increasing globalisation of economic affairs, it becomes necessary to think about competition law in a different manner and this chapter deals with two challenges for competition law brought about by globalisation. First, there is the question of the reach of competition law: in other words, to what extent can a system based in a particular geographical area deal with practices which take place wholly or partly outside that geographical area? The second challenge is to construct systems or means of international cooperation on competition matters so that there can be consistency of practice and so that anti-competitive practices do not fall into the gaps between national agencies. This leads on to a third, more theoretical, question because once cooperative systems of competition law enforcement are created, the question arises as to whether it would be sensible to go a step further and create an international competition authority to enforce a common set of rules. This third challenge is not something we will deal with here, although it has been the subject of substantial discussion;[2] primarily because, at the time of writing, there seems to be little prospect of such a development and the main focus has been on the second issue.

One of the major trading partners of the UK and EU, if not *the* major trading partner, is the United States so in practical terms an important issue is the relationship between these systems of competition law because many companies which operate in the EU have a US presence and vice versa; for example, car manufacturers and drug companies.[3] Given that the US authorities take the view that their competition, or antitrust, law is capable of being applied to activities outside the territory of the US, this needs discussion because it has been very controversial. One issue which will not be touched upon in depth is the extent to which EU and US systems differ in terms of their substantive rules. This is a topic which has also been widely discussed, but is not suitable for the focus of this book.[4]

The plan of this chapter is to start by discussing, briefly, the general rules of international law which deal with the ability of states to make laws affecting areas outside their geographical territory and their ability to enforce those laws. Having done this, we go on to look at the American approach to extraterritorial enforcement of antitrust law. This is followed by an examination of the position under EU and UK law. The second half of the chapter covers the development of international methods of cooperation, moving from bilateral agreements to multilateral ones, as well as discussing more informal means of cooperation and looking at potential future developments.

---

[2] The entire area has become a very hot topic: for in-depth discussions, see E. Elhauge and D. Geradin, *Global Antitrust Law and Economics* (2nd edn, Hart Publishing, Oxford 2011); M. Dabbah, *International and Comparative Competition Law* (Cambridge University Press, 2010); C. Noonan, *The Emerging Principles of International Competition Law* (Oxford University Press, 2008).

[3] Other important trading partners, such as China and Russia, do not have competition law systems which pursue activity outside their own jurisdiction.

[4] For a stimulating discussion, see W. Kovacic, 'Competition Policy in the European Union and the United States: Convergence or Divergence?', speech given at Bates White Fifth Annual Antitrust Conference, June 2008, available at *http://www.ftc.gov/speeches/kovacic.shtm* (accessed 03/02/12).

Public international law[5]

There are two issues which are relevant in international law and competition law relationships: first is the capacity of states to make laws and the second is their ability to enforce those laws. As a general rule, the approach of international law to the first issue is that states have the capacity to make laws which cover their own territorial jurisdiction, that is, within their own boundaries – sometimes called 'subject-matter' jurisdiction. This is intuitively obvious, but there is a more difficult case, namely, what happens if there is behaviour which takes place outside the state, but has effects within it? The classic example given is of someone who shoots a gun from one side of a state border, killing someone on the other side. Can the second state's laws cover the person who was acting outside its boundaries? International law does recognise this as possible, on the basis of a principle known as 'objective territoriality' which covers the shooting situation above because part of the offence would take place within the jurisdiction of the second state. The problem is that this principle really only covers physical conduct and is not seen as capable of being extended to the 'effects' of conduct which takes place outside a state. So, for example, if there was a cartel of Japanese companies which limited exports to the UK, there would be no conduct within the UK, but there would be effects on the UK market. To what extent should the UK be able to take action against such a cartel? This is a controversial issue within international law.

This is, however, only half the story because simply having a rule against conduct which originates outside the country does not mean that it is enforceable in an effective manner, sometimes called the 'enforcement' jurisdiction. If we take, for example, a hard-core cartel, which was contrary to the criminal law of the UK but the agreement was made outside the UK, even though its implementation took place within the UK. The activities would clearly be unlawful under UK law but there could be difficult problems of enforcement. How would the UK authorities obtain evidence of the agreement if all the documentation was held outside the UK? What if the particular individuals or companies involved remained outside the UK? How could any sanctions be imposed, given that the jurisdiction of the enforcement agencies is limited to the territory of the UK? The answer, in terms of international law, is that enforcement can only be done with the agreement of the state concerned, which can be obtained through either bilateral (treaties between two countries) or multilateral arrangements (treaties between three or more countries, such as NATO); and examples of bilateral arrangements in the competition law area will be discussed later in the chapter.

US antitrust law[6]

It is worth remembering at this point that the major statute in the US that deals with anti-competitive agreements is s. 1 of the Sherman Act, which says:

---

[5] Generally, see M. Shaw, *International Law* (6th edn, Cambridge University Press, 2008), ch. 12; and Noonan (n. 2), ch. 7.

[6] See Noonan (n. 2), pp. 223–72 for discussion and H. Hovenkamp, *Federal Antitrust Policy: The Law of Competition and its Practice* (4th edn, West Publishing, St Paul, Minnesota, 2011), section 21.2.

> Every contract, combination in the form of trust or otherwise, or conspiracy, in restraint of trade or commerce among several States, or with foreign nations, is hereby declared to be illegal. [Violators] . . . shall be deemed guilty of a felony . . .

In other words, it is a statute which imposes criminal, as well as civil, penalties. Public enforcement is done primarily by the Antitrust Division of the Department of Justice through cases brought in federal courts and secondarily, for our purposes, by the Federal Trade Commission. Private enforcement of American antitrust law is commonplace as well and, again, takes place through actions brought in the federal courts. The Sherman Act itself does not specify any jurisdictional limits, which have been developed through the case law.

The starting point in understanding the American approach is the famous *Alcoa* case.[7] Here the Department of Justice, the equivalent of the OFT in current arrangements, had taken action against a group of aluminium producers, with the organisation based in Switzerland, which had fixed prices and imposed quotas in relation to aluminium production in the US; and the question was whether the US legislation, the Sherman Act, applied to a Canadian company which had participated in the cartel. Judge Learned Hand stated that:[8]

> It is settled law . . . that any state may impose liabilities, even upon persons not within its allegiance, for conduct outside its borders which has consequences within its borders which the State reprehends; and these liabilities other states will ordinarily recognise.

This is a statement of what is known as the 'effects' doctrine, namely that a state may have jurisdiction, as to subject matter, in relation to conduct which has effects within its borders, even if the conduct originated outside its jurisdiction. Although the quote suggests that this doctrine was commonly accepted, this was not true and it has been very controversial.[9] Although later US court decisions seemed to suggest some softening of this view by developing a doctrine of comity (that is, respect for the legal decisions of other nations), which would allow the courts to take into account the non-American state's view of the conduct and balance that against the seriousness of the alleged breach, recent legislation and US Supreme Court decisions have not gone down this road. Section 6a of the Foreign Trade Antitrust Amendment Act 1982 (FTAAA) states that the Sherman Act shall not apply to conduct involving trade or commerce with foreign nations unless such conduct has a 'direct, substantial and foreseeable effect' on trade or commerce in the US and there is no mention of comity or taking into account the other state's view. The most recent US Supreme Court decision was *Hartford Fire*, a case where the practices of insurers at Lloyds of London, which were legal under UK law, were challenged on the grounds that they were in breach of the Sherman Act and produced anti-competitive effects within the US insurance market.[10] The majority opinion of the US Supreme Court took the point that the Sherman Act applied to conduct that was meant to produce and did in fact produce some substantial effect within the United States. In response to the defendants' argument that the application of US antitrust law conflicted with UK regulatory policy for the insurance market, the majority responded that there was no conflict, because the UK law did not compel the defendants to act in a manner contrary

---

[7] *United States* v *Aluminium Company of America (Alcoa)* 148 F 2d 416 (2nd Cir. 1945).
[8] Ibid. at 444.
[9] There have been UK statutes which have attempted to prevent the application of US antitrust law to the activities of UK companies: see Shaw (n. 5) at pp. 691–4.
[10] *Hartford Fire Insurance* v *California* 509 US 764 (1993).

to US antitrust law. Therefore, because they were not forced to act in this way, the court did not have to take into account the reasons behind the foreign state's policy and balance that against the US interest in enforcing its antitrust rules. In other words, matters of comity did not arise. This case was notable for a strong dissent from Justice Scalia who argued that this was not a case where the exercise of the extraterritorial jurisdiction was appropriate and that the majority decision would bring the Sherman Act into sharp and unnecessary conflict with the legitimate interests of other countries.

Despite the controversy surrounding the majority judgment, this broad approach to extra-territorial jurisdiction of US antitrust law does seem to represent the current state of US law. This is certainly the position of the US authorities (the Department of Justice and the Federal Trade Commission), which make it clear in their joint 1995 Guidelines that they will apply the approach under *Hartford Fire* and the FTAAA when faced with such questions. They also point out, however, that before deciding whether to assert extraterritorial jurisdiction, they will undertake a comity analysis which will involve looking at all relevant factors. They do not expect that this analysis will be second-guessed by the US courts.[11] These Guidelines only apply in cases brought by the public authorities and it should be remembered that most antitrust cases in the US are brought by private plaintiffs. The Sherman Act is a criminal, as well as a civil, statute, so this wide approach to jurisdiction means not only that civil sanctions can be imposed on companies in breach of the Sherman Act but also that criminal penalties may be imposed on individuals who are found to have breached US law.[12] This is particularly controversial in a European context because there are very few states in Europe where there is criminal liability for breach of competition law and, of course, there is no criminal liability for breach of EU competition law. It should be noted that other provisions of US antitrust law have an extraterritorial effect, not only the Sherman Act.

The criminal law side of the Sherman Act has proved particularly controversial as the US authorities have sought to extradite people to stand trial in the US for breaches of antitrust law. The most high-profile case in the UK has been *Norris*.[13] This arose from the carbon graph-ite cartel which operated in both the United States and Europe and involved, among other companies, Morgan Crucible, of which Norris had been the Chief Executive for a number of years. The US government sought to extradite Norris on the grounds that he had been involved in a price-fixing cartel between 1989 and 2000. Norris resisted the extradition on the grounds that such behaviour was not a criminal offence in the UK until after the passage of the Enterprise Act 2002 and therefore he could not be extradited to the US. It was argued on behalf of the US Government that price-fixing was a common law offence prior to the Enterprise Act and therefore the conditions for extradition had been met. Although this argu-ment succeeded in the Divisional Court, it failed in the UK Supreme Court, which ruled that price-fixing had never been an offence under the common law unless there were aggravating circumstances, such as fraud, violence or intimidation, and that therefore the conditions for extradition had not been met. Norris had also been charged with obstruction of justice and the UK Supreme Court held that it was possible to be extradited for this offence; and a District Court subsequently ruled that he could be so extradited and this decision was upheld by the

[11] Department of Justice/Federal Trade Commission, *Antitrust Enforcement Guidelines for International Operations* (1995), section 3.2. Available at: *http://www.justice.gov/atr/public/guidelines/* (accessed 03/02/12).

[12] *United States* v *Nippon Paper Industries* 109 F 3d (1st Cir. 1997).

[13] *Norris* v *United States* [2008] UKHL 16. Aggravating circumstances would be things such as fraud, misrepre-sentation, violence, intimidation or inducement of a breach of contract. See also *R* v *GG Plc* [2008] UKHL 17.

High Court.[14] After a trial in the United States he was sentenced to eighteen months' imprisonment, which was upheld on appeal.[15] This case relates to conduct which took place before the passage of the Enterprise Act 2002 and the creation of a criminal offence and therefore such conduct today would be extraditable.

The adoption of this broad doctrine relating to the extraterritorial effects of US antitrust law has led to another, perhaps surprising, development. If companies can be prosecuted in the US courts for breaches of US antitrust law for their activities outside the US, why shouldn't a non-American citizen bring a private action in the US courts claiming damages for activities committed outside the US? This would have a number of attractions for such plaintiffs, given that such actions are common in the US courts, treble damages can be obtained and the unsuccessful plaintiffs do not have to pay the costs of the defendants. The issue reached the US Supreme Court in the *Empagran* case,[16] which arose out of the vitamins cartel and concerned the purchasers of vitamins in Ukraine, Panama, Australia and Ecuador, who complained that they had been damaged by the actions of the defendants. For the purposes of the case, it was assumed that the foreign effects of the cartel were independent of the domestic effects, because otherwise the cause would have been actionable. In these circumstances, the US Supreme Court ruled that the foreign plaintiffs could not invoke US antitrust law because such an application of the law created a serious risk of substantial interference with a foreign state's ability to regulate its own commercial affairs and the justification for that interference was insubstantial, given that there were no effects in the US. As the US Supreme Court put it:

> Why should American law supplant, for example, Canada's or Great Britain's or Japan's own determination about how best to protect Canadian or British or Japanese customers from anti-competitive conduct engaged in significant part by Canadian or British or Japanese or other foreign companies?

This approach does, however, leave open the question of whether foreign plaintiffs can sue in the US courts when the injury that they have suffered cannot be separated from the domestic harm which has been caused. Subsequent to this decision, the US courts have consistently taken the line that the domestic effects of the anti-competitive action must be the direct and proximate cause of the plaintiff's injury and have tended to reject most such claims.[17] It has been noted by the Antitrust Modernization Commission that no court has foreclosed all alternative theories by which such a claim might be made, which led the Commission to recommend that, as a general principle, purchases made outside the US from a seller outside the US should not give rise to a claim under the Sherman Act.[18]

---

[14] See [2008] *European Competition Law Review* N203–4; *Norris v United States* [2009] EWHC 995.

[15] See *http://www.justice.gov/atr/public/press_releases/2010/265028.htm* and *http://www.justice.gov/atr/cases/norris0.htm* (both accessed 03/03/12).

[16] *F. Hoffmann-La Roche v Empagran SA* 542 US 155 (2004).

[17] *In re Monosodium Glutamate Antitrust Litigation* 477 F 3d 535 (2007). See Antitrust Modernization Commission, *Final Report*, p. 237, notes 128–30 for references. Available at *http://govinfo.library.unt.edu/amc/report_recommendation/toc.htm* (accessed 03/02/12).

[18] Antitrust Modernization Commission, *Final Report* (n. 17) at pp. 225–30.

Extraterritorial application of EU law[19]

Articles 101 and 102 TFEU

Article 101 TFEU prohibits agreements which have the object or effect of restricting competition *within the common market* and which affect trade between Member States. It is, however, possible that agreements relating to countries outside the EU may have an effect on competition within the common market. For example, the *Javico* case[20] involved an agreement to restrict the distribution of perfumes in Russia, Ukraine and Slovenia (before Slovenia entered the EU) to those countries, that is, not to allow perfumes exported to those countries to be reimported into the EU, between two EU-based undertakings. Here the CJEU held that such an agreement was prohibited by Article 101(1) TFEU if it restricted competition on the common market, which would be more likely if the market was oligopolistic or if there was a substantial price difference for the product within and outside the EU.

In terms of undertakings established outside the EU many of the potential problems have been circumvented by the adoption of the 'economic entity' doctrine. This can be illustrated by looking at the case where it was first adopted, *Dyestuffs*.[21] Here three non-EU undertakings, amongst others, had been convicted of illegal price-fixing by the Commission (discussed in Chapters 2 and 10). It was argued that the actions within the EU were taken by the subsidiary company, not the parent one, and therefore liability could not be imputed to the parent company as it was a separate legal entity from its subsidiary. The CJEU rejected this argument, holding that the subsidiary's conduct could be imputed to the parent company in situations where the subsidiary, although it had a separate legal personality, did not decide independently on its own conduct and did not have real autonomy of action. This argument has been used on numerous occasions by the Commission and, although it has been criticised for lack of legal certainty (see the discussion in Chapter 2), it does mean that many practical problems, such as who would bear the responsibility for the actions, in relation to the enforcement of EU competition law which might arise from the separate legal entity doctrine are thereby avoided.

What this doctrine does not do, of course, is deal with the situation where the undertaking concerned does not have a presence in the EU and agreements are made outside the EU, which nevertheless have an effect on markets within the EU. For this reason, historically the Commission has always argued that there is an effects doctrine in EU law similar to that in US law.[22] Most recently, it has said that Articles 101 and 102 TFEU apply irrespective of where the undertakings are located or where the agreement has been concluded, provided that the agreement or practice is either implemented inside the Union, or produces effects inside the Union.[23] As we shall see, this comment on the effects doctrine does not appear to represent the case law.

---

[19] See Noonan (n. 2), pp. 273–84.
[20] Case C-306/96 *Javico v Yves St Laurent* [1998] ECR I-1983.
[21] Cases 48/69 etc. *ICI v Commission* [1972] ECR 619.
[22] This has also been supported by certain Advocates General: see AG Mayras in Cases 48/69 etc. *ICI v Commission* [1972] ECR 619 and AG Darmon in Cases 114/85 etc. *Ahlström Oy v Commission (Wood Pulp I 1)* [1988] ECR 5193.
[23] European Commission, *Guidelines on the effect on trade concept contained in Articles 81 and 82 of the treaty*, OJ C101, 27.04.2004 (at para. 100).

The issue arose squarely in the *Wood Pulp* case, where the Commission decided that there was a concerted practice between a number of undertakings, all of which were based outside the EU. The Commission decided that Article 101 TFEU could be applied on the basis of the effects of the practice within the common market and the undertakings challenged this in front of the CJEU, arguing that as the decision was based solely on the effects of the practice, it was contrary to international law. As mentioned above, the Advocate General took the view that the effects doctrine did exist in EU law and could be applied in these circumstances. The CJEU dealt with the issue quite briefly,[24] pointing out that the conduct prohibited by Article 101(1) TFEU had two elements: the formation of the concerted practice (in this case) and the implementation of it. If the applicability of the prohibitions depended on the place where the agreements were made, or concerted practices entered into, then this would provide an easy means of evasion. The critical question was where the concerted practice was implemented and this was within the common market. It was not relevant in this respect whether the undertakings had used subsidiaries, agents or branches to make their contact with purchasers in the EU. The jurisdiction of the Union was thus founded on the territoriality principle recognised in international law, because the agreement was implemented on the EU's territory, and it could not be argued that the EU rules contradicted the rules of the other states involved, since the other states simply allowed, but did not require, the conduct at issue (a similar point to the Supreme Court in *Hartford Fire*). So what this case establishes is that what matters is whether the agreement, or conduct in an Article 102 TFEU case, is *implemented* within the EU.[25] What it does not cover is a situation where, for example, a cartel is formed and implemented outside the EU, but has effects on the common market. This problem will help take us into consideration of the situation in relation to merger control.

Merger control

A merger is an agreement between two companies to become one. So a merger between two non-EU based companies, but with operations within the EU, could be considered as an agreement implemented outside the EU but having effects within it. The Merger Control Regulation is drafted to catch these types of mergers. It applies to concentrations with a Community [Union] dimension and this is defined, in its simplest forms, as where the combined aggregate worldwide turnover of all the undertakings concerned is more than €5,000 million; and the aggregate Community-wide [Union-wide] turnover of each of at least two of the undertakings concerned is more than €250 million, unless each of the undertakings concerned achieves more than two-thirds of its aggregate Community-wide [Union-wide] turnover within one and the same Member State.[26] It is clear therefore (and has been discussed in Chapter 13) that the Regulation will catch transactions between undertakings which may conduct a substantial amount of their business outside the EU. This is not a particular problem because these are simply turnover thresholds and do not indicate that there is

---

[24] Cases 114/85 etc. *Ahlström Oy v Commission (Wood Pulp I)* [1988] ECR 5193, paras 15–22.

[25] The European Commission has opened proceedings against the Russian gas company, Gazprom, for conduct suspected of breaching Article 102 TFEU in certain EU member states: European Commission Press Release IP/12/937, 4 September 2012.

[26] Council Regulation (EC) No. 139/2004 of 20 January 2004 on the control of concentrations between undertakings (the EC Merger Regulation), OJ L24, 29.01.2004, Art. 1(2)(a).

any competition problem and some of these concentrations may benefit from a simplified procedural regime.[27]

This is not the case for all mergers and substantial controversy was caused in the *Gencor* case.[28] This involved a merger between two South African mining concerns, which had been approved by the South African authorities but was prohibited by the Commission on the grounds that it created a dominant duopoly in the platinum and rhodium[29] markets. Gencor appealed this decision to the GC on the grounds, among others, that the Commission did not have the jurisdiction to make this decision. The GC divided its examination of this objection into two parts: the territorial scope of the merger control Regulation; and its compatibility with public international law. On the first question, the GC found that the Merger Control Regulation clearly did cover this concentration, as was evident from the terms relating to a Community [Union] dimension mentioned above, and it was not prepared to construe the terms narrowly. As regards the international law issues, the Court said that the application of the Merger Control Regulation would be justified if the concentration at issue would have an immediate, substantial and foreseeable effect in this case. The Court then looked at the circumstances and decided that these criteria were met because the merger would have created a dominant duopoly in the European market and that this would have affected a substantial proportion of the sales in western Europe. The GC then went on to consider whether, in the exercise of this jurisdiction, any principle of non-interference or proportionality had been violated by action in this case (in other words, did comity require a different decision). Again, it decided that there was no issue here because, although the South African authorities had allowed the concentration, they had not required it to take place. This rather ignores the South African government's preference for the merger and that the merger would have a greater effect on the South African economy than the European one.[30] The outcome of this case is that if a merger meets the conditions for having a Community [Union] dimension as outlined above, then it is subject to the control of the European Commission, regardless of the fact that the companies concerned might be based outside the EU.

It is important to understand that what this case does *not* do is introduce an effects doctrine into EU law, despite the Commission's contention.[31] In form, this is a two-stage test. First, the GC applies the terms of the Merger Control Regulation, equating them effectively to the implementation test in *Wood Pulp*, and incidentally clarifying that sales alone will constitute implementation. Secondly, the GC goes on to consider whether there are reasons within international law *not* to apply the Merger Control Regulation. This would only become an issue in the unlikely event that the merger was required by another state.

The overall result seems to be that Articles 101 and 102 TFEU apply when an agreement or conduct is implemented within the internal market and the Merger Control Regulation applies when a concentration is within its terms. Assuming the *Gencor* analysis is applicable outside the Merger Control Regulation, there is then a second stage when the principles of

---

[27] See European Commission, 'Notice on a simplified procedure for treatment of certain concentrations under Council Regulation (EC) No. 139/2004', OJ C56, 05.03.2005.

[28] Case T-102/96 *Gencor* v *Commission* [1999] ECR II-753.

[29] A form of platinum.

[30] See E. Fox, 'The Merger Regulation and its Territorial Reach' (1999) 20 *European Competition Law Review* 334.

[31] European Commission, *Guidelines on the effect on trade concept contained in Articles 81 and 82 of the treaty*, OJ C101, 27.04.2004 (at para. 100).

international law, in particular the question of comity, are applied in order to see whether an exception should be made and EU law not be applied to the agreement or conduct at issue. This is, in the first instance, a question for the Commission to consider, although a court may have to consider these issues in the context of private litigation.

Enforcement of EU law

Having established jurisdiction over the subject matter is simply the first step in relation to extraterritorial jurisdiction because there is also the question of whether it is possible to enforce the law outside the EU. There is generally not much discussion of this, presumably because of, in part, the cooperation regimes reached between the EU and other regimes, discussed below, and the practical matter that many non-EU companies have subsidiaries within the EU which can be served with the relevant documents and demands.

When the Commission starts proceedings under Article 101 or 102 TFEU, the procedural rules require that the undertakings concerned must be informed. Although there is an argument that, as regards non-EU undertakings, this would be a breach of international law, since it involves enforcement without that country's consent, this has been rejected by the ECJ. In the case of *Geigy* v *Commission*,[32] a statement of objections was served on the undertaking at its head office in Switzerland (i.e. outside the EU) and the undertaking objected that this was invalid under Swiss law and therefore invalid under the rules of public international law. This argument was rejected by the ECJ: since there was no possibility of serving the statement of objections in a way that was valid under Swiss law, therefore international law could not be invoked to prevent the EU taking steps to make sure anti-competitive conduct could be controlled. Furthermore, since the main purpose of the notice was to allow the undertaking concerned to exercise the rights it possessed under the EU Treaties, it was not invalid simply because it had been served in a country outside the EU. The result is that it is sufficient notification for the Commission to send a registered letter to non-EU undertakings.

Having started proceedings, the question then arises of how the Commission is to obtain information. It can clearly simply ask for information under Article 18(2) of Regulation 1/2003, but there is no compulsion to comply with the request. It seems unlikely that it can demand that information under Article 18(3) because the demand would have no legal force outside the EU. The question of whether it can compel a subsidiary of a non-EU legal entity to provide documents of that non-EU legal entity remains an open one. It is certainly clear that the Commission cannot carry out an investigation outside the EU without the authority of the state concerned because its legal powers are only recognised, as a general matter, within the territory of the EU.

As regards final decisions about liability, the same approach is taken as giving notice of proceedings, in that the CJEU accepts that direct service on non-EU undertakings is valid if the decision reaches the undertaking and it is able to take notice of it.[33] As regards orders and fines made against non-EU undertakings, although the CJEU has no objection to these, they cannot be enforced outside the EU without the cooperation of the state concerned.

---

[32] Case 52/69 [1972] ECR 787.
[33] Case 6/72 *Europemballage and Continental Can* v *Commission* [1973] ECR 215 at para. 10.

Extraterritorial application of UK law

Chapter I and II prohibitions

The Chapter I prohibition is set out in s. 2 of the Competition Act 1998 and subs. (3) provides that the prohibition applies only if the agreement, decision or concerted practice is, or is intended to be, implemented in the UK. This provision is intended to give effect to the implementation doctrine set out above in *Wood Pulp I*, which is incidentally consistent with the UK's traditional hostility to the effects doctrine. As Whish and Bailey have pointed out,[34] an interesting problem could arise if the CJEU extended the effects doctrine into EU law as s. 60 of the Competition Act 1998 requires that there should be no inconsistency between EU and UK law. They go on to point out that s. 60 also provides that consistency must be achieved 'having regard to any relevant differences between the provisions concerned' and that this would presumably be a relevant difference.

Market investigations and merger control

The provisions of the Enterprise Act 2002 are designed to cover, in terms of jurisdiction, only the UK-wide activities, that is, they are not designed for extraterritorial jurisdiction. For both mergers and market investigations this comes about because the relevant provisions refer to a 'market in the United Kingdom', which may refer to a market wider than the UK (i.e. supranational) or a market in part of the United Kingdom (i.e. sub-national).[35] In relation to mergers, the relevant tests also refer to turnover within the UK or the share of supply for a market within the UK. As regards the enforcement provisions, the legislation is silent on the question of extraterritorial application but it seems unlikely that either the information-gathering powers or the remedial powers can be used outside the UK's territorial jurisdiction. There is the possibility of problems occurring when the UK authorities are considering remedies which clash with the legal obligations of the companies concerned in their home jurisdictions.

Bilateral relations between the EU and the US

After the *Wood Pulp* case and with the coming of the Merger Control Regulation in 1991 it became evident there needed to be more formal arrangements for cooperation between the EU and other jurisdictions in order to try to avoid enforcement clashes and, more positively, to try to promote cooperation of enforcement between antitrust authorities. The EU and the US entered into a bilateral cooperation agreement in 1991, which was updated in 1998 and the EU currently also has bilateral agreements on competition law with Canada and Japan. The EU also has specific arrangements with a number of other countries, ranging from agreements to forums for consultation.[36] In this section we look at the arrangements

[34] R. Whish and D. Bailey, *Competition Law* (7th edn, Oxford University Press, 2012) at p. 501.
[35] Enterprise Act 2002, ss. 22(1) and 33(1) (mergers) and 131(6) (market investigations).
[36] See *http://ec.europa.eu/competition/international/bilateral/*for a list (accessed 16/02/12).

between the US and the EU as this is one of the most developed sets of arrangements, as well as potentially one of the most important.[37]

The EU/US agreement

The EU/US agreement contains four elements: an agreement to notify the other party of relevant activities; an agreement to exchange certain information; what is known as the 'traditional comity' procedure where each party agrees to take into account the interests of the other when making decisions; and a so-called 'positive comity' procedure by which either party can invite the other to take action on the basis of its rules against anti-competitive behaviour which is having an effect on the other party's territory.

Article II of the 1991 agreement sets out that each party shall notify the other when it becomes aware that its enforcement activities may affect important interests of the other party. Although 'important interests' is not defined, there is a list of activities where notification will be appropriate, which covers five categories:

1 enforcement activities relevant to the enforcement activities of the other party;

2 enforcement in relation to anti-competitive activities which are being carried out in a significant part of the other party's territory;

3 if the activity affects a merger involving a company which is incorporated or organised in either party's jurisdiction;

4 if it involves conduct believed to have been encouraged or required or approved by either party;

5 if it involves remedies which would, in significant respects, require or prohibit conduct on the other party's territory.

In any of these cases, the authority taking action is required to notify the other authority, in sufficient time, and providing sufficient information, for them to make representations in the case concerned and have their views taken into account. In addition, the cooperation agreement also provides for notification when the competition authorities participate in regulatory or judicial proceedings which do not arise from their enforcement activity; for example, if an agency submitted an *amicus curiae* brief in a private enforcement action which had effects on the other party's interests.

In addition, this agreement provides for the authorities to share certain information, in order to facilitate their activities. The first part of this is very simple, organising meetings between appropriate officials at least twice a year to discuss enforcement activities and priorities, exchange information on economic sectors of current interest, to discuss policy changes that they are considering and to discuss other issues of mutual interest. The agreement goes further and provides that each party will provide to the other significant information that it believes may warrant enforcement action by the other, as well as allowing each

---

[37] The *Annual Reports on Competition Policy* between 2003 and 2005 give information about numbers of formal notifications under the cooperation agreements. For the EU/US agreements this was between 80 and 100 notifications a year, for both the EU/Canada and EU/Japan agreements, formal notifications never reached double figures and, in the case of Japan, did not reach five. This information is no longer given in the latest reports. See B. Zanettin, *Cooperation between Antitrust Agencies at the International Level* (Hart Publishing, Oxford, 2002) at p. 79 for figures up to 2000.

side to request information from the other side that it considers relevant to its enforcement activities. This latter provision is subject to the limitation that the information cannot be provided if to do so would be contrary to the law of either party or if providing the information would be incompatible with the important interests of the party in possession of the information. So, for example, this does not allow for the European Commission to pass confidential business information to the US antitrust authorities.

The 1991 agreement does, however, go further than just sharing information and informing each other of relevant activities. Under Article IV, it is agreed that each side will render assistance to the other in its enforcement activities, subject to resources, its laws and its own important interests. An example of this might be the coordination of investigations, in the different European and American time zones, in the marine hose case, discussed below in 'Competition law in practice'. In addition, if they have a mutual interest in pursuing enforcement activities, they may agree to coordinate those activities. The details of how this coordination will work are not spelled out but it seems to involve, among other things, sharing information if that is possible and presumably coordinating the obtaining of information. Furthermore, Article V provides for what is known as 'positive comity', that is, the taking of action by one authority against anti-competitive activity within its territory which has an effect within the territory of the other authority. This is to be done by notification from one party to the other of the issue concerned. Article VI provides that the parties will endeavour to avoid conflicts over enforcement activities. What this means is that the parties will take into account, at the various stages of the enforcement action, the important interests of other parties, as reflected in laws, decisions or statements of policy by the competent authorities. Article VI also provides a set of factors that are to be taken into account when potential conflicts of interest arise; for example, the relative significance of the anti-competitive activities involved.

It is difficult to work out just how this agreement functions in practice and how well the US and the EU authorities cooperate, although the marine hoses cartel, described below, is an example of excellent cooperation. The European Commission's Annual Reports on competition policy contain a brief description of the international activities undertaken during the year, but this contains little detail. The Annual Reports generally say that there is frequent contact between officials at the European Commission and those at the Department of Justice and the Federal Trade Commission, both as regards individual cases and also over more general policy matters. Occasionally particular cases are highlighted as good examples of cooperation but it can be difficult to find evidence of what exactly took place. For example, in the 2010 Annual Report talks about close cooperation in the mergers between Cisco/Tandberg and Novartis/Alcon.[38] When the text of the EU decisions is examined, however, there is no mention of cooperation with the US authorities, although it should be remembered that the point of the decision text is to explain why the decision was made by the European Commission, not necessarily to consider wider issues.

Mergers

In terms of mergers, the general framework within which cooperation under the agreement takes place is governed by an EU/US Agreement on Best Practices on Cooperation in Merger

---

[38] European Commission, Staff Working paper accompanying *Annual Report on Competition Policy* (2010) COM(2011) 328 final at para. 420.

Investigations.[39] The document makes the point that good cooperation depends not only on the agencies, but also on the willingness of the parties to the merger to facilitate cooperation by, for example, waiving rights to confidentiality of information. Much of the document is concerned with ensuring coordination of the timing of decisions by the Commission and the US agencies and ensuring that consultation takes place, at an appropriate level, before certain key decisions are made. So, for example, it suggests that there should be consultation before the Commission opens a phase II inquiry in a merger case or decides to close a merger case without initiating a phase II inquiry. A significant amount of emphasis is also place on coordination between the agencies when remedies for a merger are discussed. What can be seen from this brief description is that the document is confined to setting up a procedural framework within which cooperation on merger cases can take place. It does not dictate the substance of the exchanges, merely tries to provide a framework within which communication may take place in a timely manner.

In terms of merger control, it does seem that in recent years a good degree of cooperation has been shown to exist between the EU and the US, and a reasonably common approach seems to be applied to most mergers in substance. The very controversial merger decisions were Boeing/McDonnell Douglas and the GE/Honeywell merger (both discussed in Chapter 13) and these were made in 1997 and 2001 respectively and, since then, there have been no cases which have raised an equivalent level of controversy. In terms of policing international cartels, the EU and the US appear to have very similar policies. The main area of difference relates to Article 102 TFEU and can be seen in some of the responses to the Microsoft case in Europe (discussed in Chapter 4). This difference is discussed in the conclusion to this chapter in a bit more detail, but it is arguable that the differences are not that great and may relate to different enforcement priorities between the Department of Justice and the European Commission, some of which, in relation to the Department of Justice, may have been because of the enforcement priorities of the Bush administration, which seem to have changed under the Obama administration.[40]

Multilateral cooperation

Having looked at bilateral arrangements between the EU and the US, it is also worth looking briefly at what has happened as regards multilateral cooperation over competition policy. As we shall see, currently the prospects for developing a multilateral framework are very poor but there has been substantial discussion between competition agencies over how they undertake their roles and this has led to some progress in cooperation between them, outside the framework discussed above.

World Trade Organization (WTO)[41]

The World Trade Organization is an international organisation[42] which deals with the rules of trade between nations at global or near global level, according to its official description.

---

[39] Available at *http://ec.europa.eu/competition/mergers/legislation/international_cooperation.html* (accessed 03/02/12).
[40] See US Department of Justice Press Release, 11 May 2009 available at *http://www.usdoj.gov/opa/pr/2009/May/09-at-459.html* (accessed 03/02/12).
[41] Noonan (n. 2), ch. 11.
[42] It has a membership of 153 countries as of February 2012.

The rules started with those contained in the General Agreement on Tariffs and Trade (GATT), which were originally written after World War II and agreed to in 1948 by some 23 countries. They were revised in 1995, which saw the founding of the WTO as an organisation to operate the rules, settle disputes and provide a forum where its members could negotiate agreements on trade amongst themselves. Broadly speaking, the aim of the WTO is to liberalise trade between countries, which is largely done through trying to liberalise tariffs and to prevent discrimination between states on the grounds of nationality. The WTO describes the system as, above all, 'a system of rules dedicated to open, fair and undistorted competition'.[43] This sounds very similar to the basic objectives of certainly the EU system of competition law and, given this connection, there has been substantial interest in developing rules of competition law for the WTO. This was recognised at the inception of the GATT when there were plans to incorporate international rules on competition policy but this never developed into any general rules. There are some specific, general rules for telecommunications and obligations not to encourage or compel anti-competitive conduct contained within the relevant Treaties but this is not the equivalent of an international system of competition law.[44]

The interaction between competition law and trade law[45] is a complex matter and one that was felt worthy of further study in the WTO and, subsequent to a meeting in Singapore in 1996, two working groups on the issue were formed.[46] At the Doha ministerial conference in 2001, the main meeting of the WTO, it was decided to take the issue further and to explore certain areas, such as hard-core cartels, and examine the possibility of developing the WTO Treaties further to encompass competition issues. Negotiations on the Doha Round broke down, for a variety of reasons not related to competition policy, and in July 2004 it was decided that the issue of competition policy was not to form part of the work programme for the WTO and so active work by the WTO in this area has ceased. It is, however, worth noting that, although progress at this level has stalled, regional trade agreements, either bilateral or multilateral, often include provisions covering competition law issues.[47]

United Nations conference on trade and development (UNCTAD)[48]

UNCTAD was founded in 1964 with the aim of promoting the development-friendly integration of developing countries into the world economy. Working under the aegis of the UN, but based in Switzerland, it serves as a forum for intergovernmental cooperation, undertakes research and policy analysis and provides technical assistance. Part of its work focuses on competition policy and it hosts an annual intergovernmental group of experts on competition law and policy to discuss matters of common concern. It also operates a voluntary Peer Review Mechanism for competition law systems of countries that choose to submit to it, as

---

[43] WTO, *Understanding the WTO* (WTO, Geneva, 2007) at p. 12.

[44] See Noonan (n. 2) for details.

[45] The issue is discussed in M. Taylor, *International Competition Law: A New Dimension for the WTO?* (Cambridge University Press, 2006).

[46] For a discussion of the issue, see World Trade Organization, *Synthesis Paper on the Relationship of Trade and Competition Policy to Development and Economic Growth* (1998). Available at *http://www.wto.org/english/tratop_e/comp_e/wgtcp_docs_e.htm* (accessed 03/02/12). A. Papadopoulos, *The International Dimension of EU Competition Policy* (Cambridge University Press, 2010) ch. 6 discusses the negotiations and the EU's role.

[47] See O. Solano and A. Sennekamp, 'Competition provisions in regional trade agreements', OECD Trade Policy Working Paper No. 31 (2006), available at *http://www.oecd.org/trade* (accessed 03/02/12). See also Papadopoulos (note 46) chs. 4–5.

[48] See *http://www.unctad.org/Templates/StartPage.asp?intItemID=2239&lang=1* (accessed 16/02/12).

well as offering other sorts of technical assistance. From 2004 to 2007, its capacity building and technical assistance activities focused on developing countries in Africa, Asia, Latin America and the Caribbean. In summary, UNCTAD is an arena for the discussion of common problems and issues, with a bias towards issues relevant to developing countries.

Organisation for Economic Cooperation and Development (OECD)

The OECD is an international organisation of 34 countries described as committed to democracy and the market economy. The membership is primarily North American and western European but it includes Japan and Korea. It has had an interest in competition law issues for some time and operates a Competition Committee, supported by staff, which provides policy advice to governments as well as organising conferences, writing analytical papers and providing best practice recommendations. The OECD originally produced recommendations on cooperation between member countries on anti-competitive practices in 1967, which have been an influential template for designing such agreements.[49] Of particular interest is a substantial paper it published in 2005 which was a, not uncritical, peer review of the European Union competition law and policy.[50] It has done substantial work on hard-core cartels, looking at their definition and methods for enforcing the law against them.[51] The OECD is, however, limited to doing studies and making recommendations. It does not have the potential, or ambition, to become an international competition authority.

International Competition Network

The International Competition Network arose out of an American initiative in the late 1970s, the International Competition Policy Advisory Committee, which recommended in its final report that the US authorities should explore the creation of a global venue where governmental officials, private organisations and non-government organisations could explore issues of common interest in competition policy. The International Competition Network was subsequently launched in 2001 by officials from 14 states: Australia, Canada, European Union, France, Germany, Israel, Italy, Japan, Korea, Mexico, South Africa, United Kingdom, United States, and Zambia. It has since grown to become an organisation that encompasses almost all the competition authorities in the world. According to its website,[52] its mission statement is to:

> . . . advocate the adoption of superior standards and procedures in competition policy around the world, formulate proposals for procedural and substantive convergence, and seek to facilitate effective international cooperation to the benefit of member agencies, consumers and economies worldwide.

It holds an annual conference, as well as workshops on particular issues, such as mergers and cartels, and the members work together to produce documents and exchange ideas on areas of common interest. It has produced recommended practices on a number of topics, again with a major focus on merger control, as well as reports on unilateral conduct and competition

---

[49] The latest version is *Revised recommendation of the Council Concerning Cooperation between Member Countries on Anticompetitive Practices affecting International Trade* (1995).
[50] OECD, *Competition Law and Policy in the European Union* (2005).
[51] OECD, *Hard Core Cartels: Recent Progress and Challenges Ahead* (2003).
[52] *http://www.internationalcompetitionnetwork.org/* (accessed 05/09/12).

policy in an economic downturn. It should be evident from this brief discussion that it serves as an arena for the discussion of areas of common interest between officials responsible for implementing competition policy. Its influence should not be underestimated and its activities have grown but it does not take decisions on individual cases, nor can it make decisions which are binding on national competition authorities.

Conclusions

We can see from the discussion above that, although the issue of some form of international competition law and international competition authority is very interesting, and possibly appealing, there has been little progress in this direction and it seems unlikely, in the current economic climate, that there will be further developments, given the temptation to nation states to move away from international trade and adopt protectionist policies. There has, however, been widespread adoption of competition laws by countries across the world and this has led to an increasing interest in developing links, discussing best practice and trying to ensure, at least in an informal manner, coordination of activities. The best witness to this is the growth and development of the International Competition Network from its founding in 2001 by 14 members to its present position where it has members from every continent in the world. It will be very interesting to see how this body develops in the future.

In terms of US–EU relations, although the US asserts a very wide jurisdiction for its anti-trust law, in practical terms this seems to have become less of an issue because, it seems, the scope of US antitrust law is narrower than EU competition law and so something which is an offence under US law would equally be an offence under EU law. If a multinational company is participating in a cartel, this is likely to be a worldwide cartel; the evidence is that the European Commission would be as enthusiastic about sanctioning such an activity as the US authorities, so, as a matter of discretion, the US authorities can concentrate on the American side and the European Commission can concentrate on the European side. The questions will remain controversial if they are raised through private enforcement, which is much the more dominant approach in the US.

This position is reinforced, as far as the public authorities are concerned, by what appears to be very good relationships between the American and the European agencies. Although there have been a couple of well publicised divergences of approach and opinion, such as *Boeing/McDonnell Douglas* and *GE/Honeywell*, by and large routines of cooperation seem to be well established and there seems to be a general commonality of approach, especially over mergers and cartels. As regards Article 102 TFEU in Europe and monopolisation cases in the US, the substantive law is different and this difference has been exacerbated by the Department of Justice, during the Bush presidency, being largely unwilling to take mono-polisation cases.[53] It may be that this particular policy stance will alter under the Obama

---

[53] It is, however, not clear that the Obama Justice Department has been any more active in monopolisation cases. See D. Crane, 'Has the Obama Justice Department Reinvigorated Antitrust Enforcement?', available at: *http://www.stanfordlawreview.org/online/obama-antitrust-enforcement*. The issue of the difference between the two administrations is controversial; see: J. Baker and C. Shapiro, 'Evaluating Merger Enforcement during the Obama Administration', available at: *http://www.stanfordlawreview.org/online/obama-antitrust-enforcement* (both accessed 05/09/12). The dispute between them is, however, over merger enforcement, not monopoly enforcement.

administration and it may also be that the interpretation of Article 102 TFEU will gradually change as well, towards one that is more consistent with a US approach. These cases are, however, exceptional. The bread and butter issues of international cooperation are cartels and mergers, and here the evidence suggests that the European and American authorities have a good record in terms of cooperation.

COMPETITION LAW IN PRACTICE

The marine hose cartel

Background
The marine hose market is a specialised market for the production and supply of hoses used to transfer oil and petroleum products into and out of tankers. The business is worldwide and it is entirely possible for a company to supply its products on a world-wide basis. There seem to have been six main manufacturers in this industry: two based in Japan, one in the UK, one in France and two in Italy. A cartel existed between these participants from around 1986 to 2007 which had the aim of, broadly, price-fixing. The participants met regularly to allocate market share, fix prices, agree not to compete for each other's customers, exchange information and engage in bid-rigging.

Operation of the cartel
The operation of the cartel was described in a British court thus:[54]

> The cartel was run as it had to be with meticulous attention to detail. Code names were used, clandestine meetings were organised and held, agreements were reached, both in relation to the market share and for the bogus contract bids. All of this was illustrated and monitored by monthly reports. There was a formally agreed decision-making process by which the successful company would be nominated as the champion for that contract. There were rules for compliance. The parties communicated through the use of code names when they or their companies became more concerned about compliance; and they disguised their contact with one another and with you through the use of email accounts that, of course, had no connection with the companies they represented. Then, all of the bid documentation had to be prepared. I have seen an illustration of this and can well believe that this was indeed a labour intensive exercise, time consuming and highly sophisticated.

In order to do this a coordinator was required and one of the executives of the British company was designated as a coordinator and, indeed, paid $50,000 per year for carrying out this role.

Investigation and prosecution
In May 2007, the US Department of Justice, the European Commission and the OFT carried out surprise investigations at the business premises of the members of the cartel, as well as interrupting a cartel meeting. The European Commission, for the first time, also conducted an investigation of a private home.[55] As a result, the European Commission

---

[54] Judge Rivlin, QC, available at *http://www.oft.gov.uk/shared_oft/prosecutions/remarks.pdf* (accessed 05/09/12).
[55] See Press Release IP/09/137, 28 January 2009.

fined the participants in the cartel a total of €131 million, although one of the Japanese companies received a 100% reduction by complying with the terms of the leniency notice and one of the Italian companies received a 30% reduction.

In the United States, the British manufacturer pleaded guilty to criminal charges and agreed to pay a fine of $4.5 million. The same Italian company that received a reduction in the fine under EU law agreed to pay a fine of $2 million in the US. The French company involved agreed to pay fines of £3.5 million in the US.

In addition, within the US, criminal charges were pursued against a number of individuals who the Department of Justice considered were responsible for the actions of their companies. These resulted in a number of fines being imposed on the individuals concerned up to £100,000, as well as prison sentences of up to two years.[56]

In the UK, the executives of the British company were charged with the cartel offence under the Enterprise Act 2002, the first people to be so charged, and were duly convicted and sentenced to between two and a half and three years' imprisonment, as well as being disqualified for a period from being company directors. In this case the prosecution argued that the result of the cartel in the UK was an increase in prices of around 15%, which the judge accepted equated to around £2.5 million extra profit for the company. The periods of imprisonment and disqualification were reduced by around six months on appeal.

Private enforcement

In addition to public enforcement, there have also been private actions for damages. A worldwide settlement has been negotiated with one of the Italian companies, which, according to the lawyers who negotiated the agreement: 'allows any purchaser of marine hose from Parker anywhere in the world, other than direct purchasers of marine hose in US commerce, to claim compensation in respect of losses arising from the cartel, irrespective of where they reside or where the marine hose was purchased from.'[57] The same lawyers are also advising a Libyan company which is bringing an action against the UK company that was a member of the cartel.

Recent developments

The Australian Competition and Consumer Commission took action against some of the participants in the cartel, which resulted in them being fined over $8 million.[58] Action has apparently also been taken by Japan's Fair Trade Commission against the participants in the cartel,[59] as well as the South Korean Trade Commission which also imposed a fine of around US $500,000 on the participants.

---

[56] See US Department of Justice Press Release, 1 December 2008, available at *http://www.usdoj.gov/opa/pr/2008/December/08-at-1055.html* (accessed 03/02/12).

[57] See *http://www.hausfeldllp.com/pages/current_investigations/167/marine-hose-* (accessed 03/02/12).

[58] See Press Release, 14 April 2010, available at: *http://www.accc.gov.au/content/index.phtml/itemId/923519/fromItemId/142* (accessed 05/09/12).

[59] *Japan Times*, 23 February 2008, available at *http://search.japantimes.co.jp/cgi-bin/nb20080223a7.html* (accessed 03/02/12).

Analysis

This is a good example of a well-organised cartel operating in a niche, and relatively small, market: the UK sentencing judge estimated that in 2005 it was of the value of in excess of £60 million worldwide. It is also an excellent example of cooperation between competition law agencies because carrying out simultaneous investigations in different jurisdictions and time zones is a very tricky task. In addition, there was information sharing between the authorities and coordination of enforcement in relation to criminal charges between the UK and the US.[60] Being a worldwide cartel, public enforcement has not been restricted to Europe and the US but we have also seen the Asian authorities taking actions against this cartel. So it is a good illustration of the potential effectiveness of international cartel enforcement. In addition, given that the customers will have been relatively large companies, there is also scope for private action against the members of the cartel.

Summary

➤ Conduct outside the US which causes direct, substantial and reasonably foreseeable effects on US commerce falls within the Sherman Act.

➤ Enforcement of the Sherman Act may be either criminal or civil.

➤ Foreign plaintiffs may only sue in the US courts if their injuries have been directly and proximately caused by the domestic effects of the anti-competitive action.

➤ Articles 101 and 102 TFEU apply when an agreement or conduct is implemented within the common market.

➤ The Merger Control Regulation is applicable to all transactions that have a Community [Union] dimension as defined in Article 1.

➤ Application of EU law may be inappropriate if the matter in hand does not have immediate, substantial and foreseeable effects or if a principle of non-interference is violated.

➤ The provisions of UK competition law only apply to agreements and conduct within, or implemented in, the UK.

➤ The US and the EU have entered into an agreement which allows them to share information about their enforcement actions and to coordinate their efforts where appropriate.

➤ There are no multilateral arrangements for competition law enforcement but the competition authorities meet and communicate regularly under the International Competition Network.

---

[60] See the OFT presentation at *http://www.internationalcompetitionnetwork.org/uploads/library/doc352.pdf* (accessed 05/09/12).

Further reading

Dabbah, M., *The Internationalisation of Antitrust Policy* (Cambridge University Press, 2003). *Although dated, a good starting point which reviews all the issues.*

Fox, E., 'World Competition Law – Conflicts, Convergence, Cooperation', in V. Dhall (ed.) *Competition Law Today* (Oxford University Press India, 2007). *Good general overview of the issues with a particular emphasis on the needs of developing nations.*

Noonan, C., *The Emerging Principles of International Competition Law* (Oxford University Press, 2008). *Comprehensive monograph by a New Zealand academic. Primary emphasis on US law and practice, although some discussion of the EU.*

Papadopoulos, A., *The International Dimension of EU Competition Law and Policy* (Cambridge University Press, 2010). *Examines the EU's position in relation to bilateral cooperation agreements, bilateral and multilateral regional agreements which include competition provisions, and the EU's role in relation to the WTO.*

Sweeney, B., *The Internationalisation of Competition Rules* (Routledge, London, 2009). *Monograph by Australian academic looking at whether there is a justification for global competition rules.*

Zanettin, B., *Cooperation between Antitrust Agencies at the International Level* (Hart Publishing, Oxford, 2002). *Although now somewhat dated, still an excellent discussion of the issues surrounding cooperation between antitrust agencies.*

Websites

International Competition Network: *http://www.internationalcompetitionnetwork.org*

OECD: *http://www.oecd.org/about/0,3347,en_2649_37463_1_1_1_1_37463,00.html*

WTO: *http://www.wto.org/english/tratop_e/comp_e/comp_e.htm*

UNCTAD: *http://www.unctad.org/Templates/StartPage.asp?intItemID=2239&lang=1*

Appendix: Competition law on the Web

Competition law is a fast-moving subject. Helpfully, the competition authorities all have very useful websites which provide access to all their decisions and to the rules on which those decisions are based. The main ones for the UK and EU are listed below.

European Commission, Competition Directorate
http://ec.europa.eu/competition/index_en.html
Everything that you need to know, including a link to CJEU and GC judgments, although not the Attorney Generals' opinions.

Court of Justice of the European Union
http://curia.europa.eu/jcms/jcms/Jo2_6999/
All cases decided by the CJEU and the GC from 17 June 1997, plus Attorney Generals' opinions. Also provides access to appeals filed, but not decided, the diary of the Courts and activity reports.

Office of Fair Trading
http://www.oft.gov.uk/
All the decisions of the OFT, as well as those of the sectoral regulators using competition powers, plus its guidance documents and consultations.

Competition Commission
http://www.competition-commission.org.uk/
CC inquiry reports, and those of its predecessor bodies, back to the 1950s as well as all the documentation in the public domain for recent inquiries. Also access to CC rules and guidance.

Competition Appeal Tribunal
http://www.catribunal.org.uk/
Access to all CAT judgments, as well as cases lodged and transcripts of hearings.

British and Irish Legal Information Institute (BAILII)
http://www.bailii.org/
British and Irish case law and legislation, European Union case law, Law Commission reports, and other law-related British and Irish material.

Office of Public Sector Information (OPSI)
http://opsi.gov.uk/legislation/revised
UK legislation, revised and amended.

Glossary of economic terms

Note: Glossary terms followed by '**(OECD)**' are taken or adapted from the OECD website at *http://stats.oecd.org/glossary/index.htm* and are from the original source publication *Glossary of Industrial Organisation Economics and Competition Law*, compiled by R.S. Khemani and D.M. Shapiro, commissioned by the Directorate for Financial, Fiscal and Enterprise Affairs, OECD, 1993. Copyright OECD. Glossary terms followed by '**(CC)**' are taken or adapted from *Merger references: Competition Commission Guidelines*, June 2003. Copyright Competition Commission 2003.

Allocative efficiency This state occurs when resources are so allocated that it is not possible to make anyone better off without making someone else worse off. (OECD)

Anti-competitive agreements Agreement refers to an explicit or implicit arrangement between firms normally in competition with each other to their mutual benefit. Agreements to restrict competition may cover such matters as prices, production, markets and customers. (OECD)

Antitrust Antitrust refers to a field of economic policy and laws dealing with monopoly and monopolistic practices. Antitrust law or antitrust policy are terms primarily used in the United States, while in many other countries the terms competition law or policy are used. Some countries have utilised the phrases fair trading or antimonopoly law. In Europe, including the UK, antitrust and competition law are often used interchangeably. (OECD)

Average total cost (ATC) The total costs involved in the production of one unit of output, i.e. total cost divided by the number of units produced.

Average variable cost (AVC) The variable costs (q.v.) involved in the production of one unit, i.e. variable costs added up and divided by the number of units produced.

Avoidable costs The costs that will not be incurred if an undertaking ceases a particular operation.

Bilateral agreement Agreement between two parties.

Block exemption A set of general rules laid down in a Regulation, which, if complied with, will allow an agreement to escape the prohibition in Article 101(1) TFEU.

Cartel A cartel is a formal agreement among firms in an oligopolistic industry. Cartel members may agree on such matters as prices, total industry output, market shares, allocation of customers, allocation of territories, bid-rigging, establishment of common sales agencies, and the division of profits or combination of these. (OECD)

Cellophane fallacy Problem in applying SSNIP test (q.v.) when the existing price is above the competitive level: for example, where the market is to some extent monopolised. In some cases, prices will have already been raised to the level at which a further price rise would lead a significant number of purchasers to stop buying, or switch to alternatives that would not otherwise have been regarded as reasonable substitutes. The application of the SSNIP test might, therefore, erroneously suggest that other products should be included in the resulting product market even though they would not have been seen as substitutes had the competitive price level been used as the starting point for the test. (CC 2.9) Named after the US case in which the product concerned was cellophane and the problem was not noticed: *US v E I du Pont de Nemours* 351 US 377 (1956).

Chain of substitution In the process of defining a market, two products that are not direct substitutes can at times be included in the same market. This happens when product B, for example, is a direct substitute to products A and C, but C is not a direct substitute to A and vice versa. There is then a 'chain of substitution' running from A to B to C. Despite not being direct substitutes, A and C may, in some instances, be considered to be in the same market if they are constrained by their common relationship with B. (CC 2.30)

Collective dominance Sometimes referred to as joint dominance. Term of EU competition law referring to a situation where two or more undertakings, when taken together, are considered to have a dominant position (q.v.) between themselves.

Collusive tendering The practice among companies making tenders for a job of sharing inside information between themselves, with the objective of fixing the end result.

Conglomerate mergers A merger between firms in unrelated business, for example, between an automobile manufacturer and a food processing firm. (OECD)

Coordinated effects Refers to the position in oligopolistic markets (q.v.) where companies recognise that the actions of individual companies can have identifiable effects on their competitors. If this position is maintained, the recognition of this interdependence can have a significant effect on business decisions. In particular it can become rational to refrain from initiating price cuts which would be unavoidable in more competitive circumstances. Although there may be coordination in such situations, it does not mean that the companies have been in contact with each other.

Distribution agreements A vertical agreement whereby a manufacturer makes arrangements for the distribution of its goods, either directly to consumers or to distributors or wholesalers which then sell the goods to retailers.

Divestiture Refers to firms selling part of their current operations, divisions or subsidiaries.

Dominant position Legal term in EU competition law. Indicates an undertaking which has a level of market power that means its behaviour should be subject to competition law.

Dynamic efficiency Refers to balancing short- and long-run concerns and the ability to improve efficiency, typically productive, over time.

Economies of scale Refers to the phenomenon where the average costs per unit of output decrease with the increase in the scale or magnitude of the output being produced by a firm. (OECD)

Economies of scope Exist when it is cheaper to produce two products together (joint production) than to produce them separately. (OECD)

Fixed costs Those which do not change with output over a given time period.

Franchise A form of business organisation in which a firm that already has a successful product or service (the franchisor) enters into a continuing contractual relationship with other businesses (franchisees) operating under the franchisor's trade name and usually with the franchisor's guidance, in exchange for a fee.

Hard-core restraints Term used in EU competition law[1] to identify a variety of provisions in a contract that are considered particularly damaging to competition. Lists of such provisions can be found in the block exemption Regulations (q.v.). Whether or not all such provisions are damaging to competition is a matter of controversy.

Herfindahl-Hirschman Index (HHI) A measure of industry concentration. The value of the index is the sum of the squares of the market shares of all firms in an industry. Higher values indicate greater concentration. One of several ways to measure concentration.
(Source of definition: IMF, 2004, Compilation Guide on Financial Soundness Indicators, IMF, Washington DC, Appendix VII, Glossary.)

Horizontal agreement An agreement between two firms or companies at the same level of production. For example, an agreement between two car manufacturers.

Horizontal merger A merger between two firms operating at the same level of production.

Hypothetical monopolist test See SSNIP test. Alternative term for this test.

Inter-state trade Strictly, trade between two states or nations. In EU competition law, refers to agreements or conduct which have an effect on trade between Member States of the EU. The concept has been interpreted broadly to include agreements or conduct within one Member State (because they may affect the ability of other producers to enter this market) and to cover potential, as well as actual, effects.

Long-run incremental cost (LRIC) The total long-run costs of supplying a specified additional unit of output, taking into account both capital and operating costs.

Marginal cost The increase in total costs of a firm caused by increasing its output by one extra unit.

Marginal revenue The increment in total revenue resulting from the sale of an additional unit. (OECD)

Market integration Central policy objective of the EU. The idea is to break down barriers in markets which exist between Member States so that, ideally, there is one European-wide market for products.

Market power The ability of a firm (or group of firms) to raise and maintain price above the level that would prevail under competition is referred to as market or monopoly power. The exercise of market power leads to reduced output and loss of economic welfare. (OECD) Since markets are never perfectly competitive, all firms have some level of market power.

---

[1] Don't go anywhere else!

Market share threshold Shorthand used in competition law to describe situation where, once an undertaking goes above a certain market share, it will be treated less favourably within competition law. For example, block exemptions (q.v.) specify a market share below which the undertakings can obtain the benefit of the block exemption. Above that level they cannot use the block exemption, although this does not necessarily imply that their action is anti-competitive.

Merger When two companies become one, 'the merged firm'. Usually done by agreement between the two companies, although not always the case.

Monopoly A situation where there is a single seller in the market. (OECD)

Monopsony A market with a single buyer. (OECD)

Multilateral agreement Agreement between three or more parties.

Non-coordinated effects Sometimes called unilateral effects, occurs when a merger (q.v.) enhances the ability of the merged firm to exercise market power independently, without the need to second-guess the strategies of other firms in the market. (CC 3.28)

Oligopolistic industry/markets An oligopoly is a market characterised by a small number of firms which realise they are interdependent in their pricing and output policies. The number of firms is small enough to give each firm some market power. (OECD)

Oligopoly problem The problem that oligopolistic industries/markets create for competition authorities. The problem is that oligopolies may or may not be highly competitive and it may be difficult to distinguish the two situations. In addition, independent behaviour which recognises interdependence is not an offence under EU and UK competition law.

Ordo-liberalism A German political philosophy relating to, among other things, the regulation of competitive markets.

Price-fixing agreements An agreement between two companies or firms to fix prices.

Productive efficiency When the production of a product is achieved at the lowest cost possible.

Resale price maintenance The practice whereby a manufacturer and its distributors agree that the latter will sell the former's product at certain prices. These prices may be either a minimum or a maximum.

Selective distribution Arrangement between a manufacturer and a distributor or retailer where the manufacturer selects the distributor on the basis of some criteria. Criteria often relate to the quality of service offered by the distributor or retailer to customers.

Severance/severability Contract law doctrine which refers to the ability of certain clauses in a contract to be deleted or ignored but will allow the substance of the contract to be carried out.

Short-run marginal cost (SRMC) The marginal cost based on a firm's existing plant and output, not on that which would be the most efficient.

Social market economy Economic model usually associated with Germany and Ordo-liberalism (q.v.). An attempt to find a middle way between unbridled capitalism and socialism/communism.

SSNIP test (Small but Significant Non-Transitory Increase in Price) In competition law, before deciding whether companies have significant market power which would justify government intervention, the test of Small but Significant and Non-transitory Increase in Price is often used to define the relevant market in a consistent way.

Stand-alone costs The costs which are involved in producing a product without taking into account that some of these costs are shared with the production of other products.

Sunk costs Costs which, once committed, cannot be recovered. Sunk costs arise because some activities require specialised assets that cannot readily be diverted to other uses. Second-hand markets for such assets are therefore limited. (OECD)

Supply-side substitutability Where producers react to an increase in the price of a product either by increasing their production or switching their production facilities to produce the product whose price has increased.

Total cost The total costs of production.

Unilateral action Action taken by one undertaking.

Unilateral agreements A contradiction. Refers to those cases in EU competition law where the question has been whether or not two undertakings have entered into an agreement or, instead, one of them has imposed its will on the other.

Upstream/Downstream market Some products are not sold directly to the final customer. They are first sold to an intermediary, who then either sells on directly to another customer (wholesaler) or transforms the products for sale to customers. Markets for products at an earlier stage of production are generally designated as upstream markets; and those at a later stage, typically to the final customer, downstream markets.

Variable costs Those costs which do change with output.

Vertical agreement An agreement between two firms or companies at different levels of production. For example, an agreement between a manufacturer and a retailer or distributor.

Vertically integrated undertaking The ownership or control by a firm of different stages of the production process: for example, petroleum refining firms owning 'downstream' the terminal storage and retail gasoline distribution facilities and 'upstream' the crude oil field wells and transportation pipelines. (OECD)

Vertical merger A merger between two firms operating at different levels of production. For example, the merger of a distributor and retailer.

Index